ALSO BY DORIAN LYNSKEY

33 Revolutions Per Minute: A History of Protest Songs

The Ministry of Truth: A Biography of George Orwell's 1984

EVERYTHING MUST GO

EVERYTHING MUST GO

The Stories We Tell About the End of the World

DORIAN LYNSKEY

Pantheon Books, New York

 Published in the United States by Pantheon Books, a division of Penguin Random House LLC, New York, and distributed in Canada by Penguin Random House Canada Limited, Toronto. Originally published in hardcover in Great Britain in 2024 by Picador, an imprint of Pan Macmillan.

Pantheon Books and colophon are registered trademarks of Penguin Random House LLC.

Library of Congress Cataloging-in-Publication Data
Names: Lynskey, Dorian author
Title: Everything must go : the stories we tell about the end of the world / Dorian Lynskey.
Description: First American edition | New York : Pantheon Books, 2025.
Identifiers: LCCN 2024028627 | ISBN 9780593317105 ebook | ISBN 9780593468647 trade paperback | ISBN 9780593317099 hardcover
Subjects: LCSH: End of the world | Apocalypse in motion pictures | Apocalypse in literature | End of the world in literature | Apocalypse—Social aspects | End of the world—Social aspects
Classification: LCCBT877 L96 2025 | DDC 236.9—dc23/eng/20240822
LC record available at https://lccn.loc.gov/2024028627

www.pantheonbooks.com

Jacket image based on *Comet of 1811*, an illustration from *Flowers of the Sky* by Richard A. Proctor. Courtesy of the Library of Congress, Washington, D.C.
Jacket design by Eli Mock

Printed in the United States of America
First American Edition

2 4 6 8 9 7 5 3 1

For Dom Phillips (1964–2022)

'Anticipating the end of the world is humanity's oldest pastime . . . The End is what we want, so I'm afraid the End is what we're damn well going to get.'

— David Mitchell, *Cloud Atlas* (2004)

'Despite everything, the world had not ended yet. What was the reflex that made it catch itself? What was the balance it regained?'

— Patricia Lockwood, *No One Is Talking About This* (2021)

Contents

PART FOUR: MACHINES

PART FIVE: COLLAPSE

PART SIX: PANDEMIC

PART SEVEN: CLIMATE

ANNIVERSARY
TEST TUBE
DAISY DIES
Mallorca
F.A. Cup Cancelled

INTRODUCTION
APOCALYPSE ALL THE TIME

> Theories that involve the end of the world
> are not amenable to experimental verification
> – or, at least, not more than once.
>
> Carl Sagan (1983)

It is a sunny afternoon in Taormina, Sicily, and two wealthy couples on holiday are drinking Aperol Spritz on a balcony overlooking the sea. Harper, who runs on anxiety and guilt, says that she has trouble sleeping because of 'everything that's going on in the world'. Daphne, who runs on pleasure and denial, asks what she means. 'Oh, I don't know,' says Harper. 'Just, like, the end of the world.' Daphne laughs. 'Oh no, Harper! The world's not ending, it's not that bad.' She doesn't follow the news any more. 'And even if it was as bad as they say it is, I mean what can you really do, you know?' Harper and Daphne are sitting on the same beautiful hotel balcony, drinking the same expensive drinks, but only one of them is tormented by the sense that we are all doomed. 'It's like we're all entertaining each other while the world burns,' says Harper.

This is a scene from season two of the HBO series *The White Lotus*, starring Aubrey Plaza as Harper and Meghann Fahy as Daphne. The show leaves open the question of whether Harper's position is a morally responsible reaction to vast and dangerous problems or a yelp of impotent despair. 'Such convictions in the mouths of safe, comfortable people playing at crisis, alienation, apocalypse and desperation, make me sick,' complains the protagonist of Saul Bellow's 1964 novel *Herzog*. 'We must get it out of our heads that this is a doomed time, that we are waiting for the end, and the rest of it . . . Things are grim enough without these shivery games . . . We love apocalypses too much.' What would Herzog say now? Conservatives and progressives offer competing narratives of decline and doom. Many climate activists speak of irreparable breakdown and even human extinction. There are new terms such as *doomer*, *polycrisis* and *Generation Dread*. A peer-reviewed 2021 survey of people aged between sixteen and twenty-five around the world found that 56 per cent agreed with the statement, 'Humanity is doomed.' In a 2020 YouGov poll, nearly one in three Americans said that they expected an apocalyptic event in their lifetimes, with the Christian Judgement Day relegated to fourth place by a pandemic, climate change and nuclear war; zombies and aliens brought up the rear. While promoting his doomsday satire *Don't Look Up* in 2021, director Adam McKay awkwardly tried to define this era: 'the Great Awfulization . . . or the Gilded Rage . . . You can just really call it collapse culture . . . There's such a list of things to keep your eye on.'

This is not the religious end of time, or *eschaton*, that has fascinated humanity for thousands of years (we'll get to that) but the end of the world as a pervasive mood – a vibe. 'It's pretty clear the world is ending,' Marc Maron says in his comedy special *End Times Fun*. 'I don't want to shock anybody. Seems to be happening though.' Everybody laughs. Nobody responds as if this were a preposterous claim, just as no reviewer of Sally Rooney's *Beautiful World, Where Are You* seemed taken aback by one character's insistence that there is 'no chance for the planet, and no chance for us' and 'we are standing in the last lighted room before the darkness, bearing witness to something.' Sheila Heti compares life in 2022 to 'being in a plane that was slowly twirling to the ground' in her quietly apocalyptic novel *Pure Colour*. 'Hey, what can you say?' sings the comedian Bo Burnham in his satirical ballad 'That Funny Feeling'. 'We were overdue / But it'll be over soon, you wait.' An entirely routine way to express dissatisfaction with the world is to say that it is ending.

In her 2021 novel *Fake Accounts*, Lauren Oyler pokes fun at what she sees as a propensity to wallow in self-loathing and impotence: 'the popular turn to fatalism could be attributed to self-aggrandizement and an ignorance of history, history being characterized by the population's quickness to declare apocalypse finally imminent despite its permanently delayed arrival.' This is a fallacy known as presentism, or chronocentrism: the delusion that one's own generation is experiencing what has never been experienced before and will never be experienced again. Such temporal egotism has been baked into apocalyptic thought since John of Patmos promised 'The time is at hand' in the Book of Revelation. As Frank Kermode argued in his classic 1967 book *The Sense of an Ending*, we resist the idea that we live in the middle of history, unable to know how it all ends or to be a part of the climactic drama. To make sense of life, Kermode wrote, 'we need fictions of beginnings and fictions of ends, fictions which unite beginning and end and endow the interval between them with meaning.'

Therefore, even if we are not religious, we like to think that our own time is a unique and crucial turning point. The word *crisis* comes from a medical Latin term for the point in an illness that decides whether the patient will recover or die. We seem to be built to imagine that we live, if not at the end of the world, then at least at the end of an era. We love to talk about the death of this and the fall of that, and to boast that we are there to witness it. We do like to feel special. 'We always want a "conclusion", an *end*, we always want to come, in our mental processes, to a decision, a finality, a full-stop,' D. H. Lawrence wrote not long before his death in 1930. 'This gives us a sense of satisfaction. All our mental consciousness is a movement onwards, a movement in stages, like our sentences, and every full-stop is a mile-stone that marks our "progress" and our arrival somewhere.' The fact that this is an illusion, Lawrence thought, does not make it any less powerful. In this way we attempt to take the mess and mystery of the future, which has always been frightening because it is the ultimate unknown, and tidy it into a story.

It is hard to deny that we live in perilous times. As of January 2023, the hands of the Doomsday Clock, the symbolic timepiece maintained by the *Bulletin of the Atomic Scientists* since 1947, point for the first time to ninety seconds to midnight on account of the climate crisis, Covid-19, disruptive technologies, rising authoritarianism and the revenant menace of nuclear war arising from Russia's invasion of Ukraine. Martin Rees, the UK's Astronomer Royal, believes that the twenty-first century could be the one 'where we as humans destroy ourselves'. But it should not diminish the importance of the problems that we face now to say that the anxieties of earlier generations felt no less profound. We are not inclined to appreciate the bad things that have not happened to us – the conflicts and famines avoided, the diseases prevented, the lives saved – nor to measure our anxieties against the ordeals of the past.

There have always been doomers. In 1974, the year I was born, the French president Valery Giscard D'Estaing declared, 'The world is unhappy. It is unhappy because it does not know where it is going and because it senses that if it knew, it would discover that it was heading for disaster.' One week in September 1965, the most popular song in America was Barry McGuire's warning that we were on 'the eve of destruction'. In 1945, H. G. Wells wrote in his final book, 'this world is at the end of its tether. The end of everything we call life is close at hand and cannot be evaded.' In 1919, the Dutch historian Johan Huizinga wrote that it was 'bad form to praise the world and life openly. It was fashionable to see only its suffering and misery, to discover everywhere signs of decadence and of the near end – in short, to condemn the times or to despise them.' He was ostensibly describing the late Middle Ages. In AD 250, Cyprian of Carthage asked, 'Who cannot see that the world is already in its decline, and no longer has the strength and vigor of former times? There is no need to invoke Scripture authority to prove it. The world tells its own tale and in its general decadence bears adequate witness that it is approaching its end.' You get the picture.

What is notable now is that apocalyptic angst has become a constant: all flow and no ebb. One might have assumed from the millions of words devoted to the end of the world during the 1990s that the noise about it would reach a millennial crescendo, but instead it has grown and grown. In 1989, Susan Sontag suggested that the title of Francis Ford Coppola's movie *Apocalypse Now* was wishful thinking and what we are living with instead is 'Apocalypse From Now On'. This must come to some degree from the fact that we absorb more news, which is to say bad news, than at any time in history. Speaking during the Second World War, long before twenty-four-hour news or the internet, the poet Wallace Stevens argued that the 'pressure of reality' overwhelms our sense of perspective:

'It is not possible to look backward and to see that the same thing was true in the past. It is a question of pressure, and pressure is incalculable and eludes the historian.'

One can feel the pressure of reality in the frenzied overload of R.E.M.'s 1987 hit 'It's the End of the World as We Know It (And I Feel Fine)' or the work of Don DeLillo. In DeLillo's 1991 novel *Mao II*, the author Bill contends that the novel has been displaced as a source of truth and meaning by the news, which 'provides an unremitting mood of catastrophe. This is where we find emotional experience not available elsewhere. We don't need the novel . . . We don't even need catastrophes, necessarily. We only need the reports and predictions and warnings.' When Daphne's fatuous husband Cameron (Theo James) damns the news as 'an apocalyptic soap opera' in *The White Lotus*, he has a point. In the online era, we have a baleful new word for this experience: *doomscrolling*. Social media gives the impression that things are worse than they are while at the same time making things worse than they need to be. More than ever, the surest way to be praised for speaking to the times is to say that the times are awful. It can seem almost unserious to believe that things are not getting irreversibly worse.

While writing my previous book, *The Ministry of Truth: A Biography of George Orwell's* 1984, I investigated the expression of fear of the future in political dystopias. I came to feel that existential dread might be an equally useful way to explore the interaction between fiction, politics, science and the public mood. I wondered whether total immersion in visions of the end might also clarify my own thoughts about the world to come and force me to confront facts and emotions that I had been successfully avoiding. I figured that it might make me feel better in a funny way, gorging on unrealized nightmares, and that I would be in good company.

It is a resonant little phrase, *the end of the world*, which retains its dreadful power no matter how profligately it is used. In a secular sense, it denotes three varieties of very bad news: the total demolition of the planet itself, the extinction of the human race, and the collapse of civilization, which is to say the end of the world as we know it. Most stories are about the last of these – the post-apocalyptic

– because, as the novelist Stephen King put it, 'No survivors, no story, am I right?' The Christian apocalypse, as outlined in the Book of Revelation, occupies a fourth category. Its process of destruction, judgement and renewal means the end of history but not the end of the human experience; transcendence rather than annihilation; something for the righteous to look forward to.*

Let us be clear: the world *will* end. Between five and eight billion years from now, the Sun will run out of hydrogen, expand into a red giant two hundred times its present size and swallow the nearest planets, ours most likely included. Much sooner than that, perhaps a mere billion years into the future, the Sun will generate so much heat that the oceans will evaporate, the land will burn and Earth will become unsurvivably hot. In the meantime, there are existential threats that, while extremely improbable in the near term, have contributed to the five major mass extinctions that we know about. We could be struck by a large comet or asteroid, like the object that very probably eradicated 75 per cent of species, including all non-avian dinosaurs, 66 million years ago. Earth could be blasted with ozone-destroying rays by a nearby supernova, have its orbit disrupted by the close passage of another star, or even have a chance encounter with a black hole. The greatest terrestrial catastrophe would be the eruption of one or more climate-wrecking supervolcanoes, like the ones that may have caused the end-Triassic extinction event 201 million years ago. Then there are the potential catastrophes whose existence we are not yet aware of. In 1893, the French astronomer Camille Flammarion compared humanity to a man walking down a street lined with snipers: 'our planet will be at a loss to choose among so many modes of death.'

Since Flammarion's time, calculating the probability of these competing modes has spawned a lively industry of books about existential risk, at least four of which are called *The End of the World*. The most readable of these is a prize-winning 1930 book by Geoffrey

*The meaning of *apocalypse* has sprawled so far that it is fruitless to be a stickler but I have tried to use it in the context of transformation rather than termination. The adjective *apocalyptic* is more flexible, denoting a violent, visionary tone. *Moby-Dick* or *King Lear* are apocalyptic without being about the end of the world, while Nevil Shute's 1957 novel *On the Beach* is about the end of the world without being apocalyptic.

Dennis, a former official for the League of Nations, from which I have borrowed the structure of seven distinct but overlapping parts. Around that time, the novelist Olaf Stapledon, the scientist J. B. S. Haldane and the philosopher C. E. M. Joad all swam in the same dark waters, but the striking thing about secular speculations about the end of the world before 1945 is that there was no significant chance of it happening in the writer's lifetime. Dennis's seven possibilities – comet, fire, water, drought, cold, crash and God – were either very unlikely or very distant, and none of them necessitated human agency. He did not consider a deadly virus, despite having lived through the Spanish flu pandemic. Nor the atomic bomb, which did not yet exist, although Stapledon, Joad and H. G. Wells all saw it coming. He didn't mention another world war, although he had fought in one and worked to avert another. He foresaw no menace from technology, although he might have been aware of *R.U.R.*, the Czech writer Karel Čapek's 1920 play about an intelligent automaton called the robot. More understandably, Dennis did not register the consequences of carbon emissions from the burning of fossil fuels. Almost nobody in 1930 was thinking about that. For these writers, the end was most likely millions or billions of years away, and would be nobody's fault.

This cheering timeframe collapsed into months, weeks, days on the morning of 16 July 1945, when J. Robert Oppenheimer's team at Los Alamos National Laboratory detonated the world's first atomic bomb in the New Mexico desert, and human ingenuity developed the capacity for auto-destruction. Never again could we imagine ourselves as blameless victims of the outrageous movements of the heavens. Geoffrey Dennis thought that the imminence promised in the Book of Revelation was our ancestors' logical response to the precarity of life: 'Man dreaded the end; therefore he believed it near, as he believed all his enemies near, and as usually they were: want and plague and tribal foes, none of them lurking far away.' With the advent of the Bomb, the twentieth century suddenly re-encountered imminence on a global scale. As Susan Sontag wrote in her 1965 essay 'The Imagination of Disaster', 'from now on to the end of human history, every person would spend his individual life under the threat not only of individual death, which is certain, but of something almost insupportable psychologically – collective incineration and extinction which could come at any time, virtually without warning.' It was inevitable that the Bomb would require the longest section in this book by a considerable margin. For more than forty years, it was the world-changer, the mind-filler, the paramount fact. Not until the early twenty-first century, when climate change became first the climate crisis and then the climate emergency, did another single menace achieve such imperial primacy over the catastrophic imagination. The American psychiatrist Robert Jay Lifton has described these two phenomena as 'apocalyptic twins'.

Modern thinking on existential risk began in 1996 with yet another book called *The End of the World*, this one by the Canadian philosopher John Leslie. To the post-war menu of natural, cosmic and anthropogenic risks mentioned above, Leslie added new technological hazards such as genetic engineering, nanotechnology, massive computer failure and uncontrollable artificial intelligence (AI). 'I myself give our species up to a 70 per cent probability of surviving the next five centuries,' Leslie wrote. 'If it did, then it could stand quite a good chance of colonizing its entire galaxy.' The Swedish philosopher Nick Bostrom, founder of Oxford's Future of Humanity Institute, and the Serbian astronomer Milan M. Ćirković invited experts to put meat on the bones with their 2008 essay collection *Global Catastrophic Risks*. They defined a catastrophic risk as one that 'might have the potential to inflict serious damage to human well-being on a global scale' and an existential risk as 'one that threatens to cause the extinction of Earth-originating intelligent life or to reduce its quality of life . . . permanently and drastically'. Like H. G. Wells a century earlier, Bostrom believes that it is possible to study the future as carefully as the past. 'Traditionally, this topic domain has been occupied by cranks,' he complained in 2015. 'By popular media, by science fiction – or maybe by a retired physicist no longer able to do serious work . . . academics don't want to be conflated with flaky, crackpot type of things.' Nonetheless, the field is growing fast. In his 2020 book *The Precipice: Existential Risk and the Future of Humanity*, Toby Ord, an Australian philosopher who has worked with Bostrom at the Future of Humanity Institute, estimated the natural risk of an existential catastrophe within the next one hundred years (from impacts, supervolcanoes or stellar explosions) as one in ten thousand and the anthropogenic risk (from 'nuclear war, climate change, other environmental damage, engineered pandemics and unaligned AI') as one in six.*

Ord cited Leslie and Bostrom as forerunners of longtermism, a school of thought which he christened in 2017 along with another Oxford-based philosopher, William MacAskill. In his 2022 book *What We Owe the Future*, MacAskill describes longtermism as both common sense and a moral revolution: 'Distance in time is like distance in space. People matter even if they live thousands of miles away. Likewise, they matter even if they live thousands of years hence.' He calculates that if humanity were to survive for one million years at its current population size, then eighty trillion more people would be born. Introduce the prospect of transhumanism (tech-enabled evolution into a new species) and the settlement of other worlds and the number becomes so mind-bendingly large that the entirety of human history so far is merely the opening of an eyelid.

Longtermists are therefore obsessed with averting extinction, which is not just the extermination of everybody who is alive at the time but the cancellation of the legacy of everybody who has ever lived and the infinite potential of everybody not yet born. If the cause were to be anthropogenic then it would be the ultimate crime, omnicide, violating our collective obligation to preserve the past and future of the species. The end of history, of memory, of possibility, of any consciousness that could apprehend what those concepts meant, would be an eternal defeat. 'To me, the only real immorality is that which endangers the species; and the only absolute evil, that which threatens its annihilation,' said the film director Stanley Kubrick in 1968. Longtermists, whose ranks include Elon Musk and Martin Rees, argue that when the stakes are that high, minimizing even an extremely unlikely existential risk is of paramount importance, although they point out that projects such as pandemic preparedness will also serve us well in the near term. When there are so many things to worry about, however, nobody can agree what to prioritize. While no hazard seems to vanish entirely from the horizon of the world's imagination, they do rise and fall.

*If AI is not aligned with human values, then it is considered 'unaligned' or 'unfriendly'.

It takes effort to consider all of them simultaneously and place each one in context.

This book is not about existential risk but how we think about it and the stories we tell. Nor is it a history of religious eschatology, although that is the cultural backcloth, especially in countries with a tradition of Christianity. The more I read about competing fears of the end of the world, the more I understood the deathless appeal of Revelation's single, God-given plot. In the literature of last things, fiction and non-fiction alike, there are simply too many options. In Robert Silverberg's witty 1972 short story 'When We Went to See the End of the World', time tourists are able to witness the earth's last gasp, but each one sees something different. 'How come everybody gets to visit a different kind of end of the world?' protests one character. 'You'd think there'd be only one kind of end of the world. I mean, it ends, and this is how it ends, and there can't be more than one way.'

'From the deluge in the Babylonian zodiac myth of Gilgamesh to contemporary fantasies of twentieth-century super-science, there has clearly been no limit to our need to devise new means of destroying the world we inhabit,' argued the novelist J. G. Ballard. 'I would guess that from man's first inkling of this planet as a single entity existing independently of himself came the determination to bring about its destruction.' Secular eschatology, however, is relatively young. It is generally agreed to have begun in 1816, when Lord Byron killed the whole world in his poem 'Darkness', and then expanded into novels ten years later, when his friend Mary Shelley retained the planet but erased almost all of the human race in *The Last Man.* The genre has certainly made up for lost time. The corpus of end-of-the-world stories is immense and ever-growing. In the past decade or so, we have seen dramas (*Melancholia*), horrors (*It Comes at Night*), war movies (*World War Z*), comedies (*This is the End*) and satires (*Don't Look Up*); sitcoms (*The Last Man on Earth*), animations (*The Mitchells vs. the Machines*) and songs (Phoebe Bridgers's 'I Know the End'); TV shows based on comic books (*The Walking Dead*), computer games (*The Last of Us*) and bestselling novels (*Station Eleven*). These stories are increasingly pessimistic: the comet hits, the zombies reign, the planet burns. Anyone who attempted to represent them all, let alone the work of scientists, philosophers and theologians, would end up with a catalogue rather than a book. I have chosen to focus on examples that reveal something important about the enterprise, and about the times in which they were created. There is simply no end of ends.

Most obviously, these stories turn fear into entertainment. Through movies which make the unthinkable enjoyable, wrote Susan Sontag in her 1965 essay, 'one can participate in the fantasy of living through one's own death and more, the death of cities and the destruction of humanity itself.' Contemplating annihilation can certainly be a valuable means of reckoning with death, loss, abandonment and a capricious universe, but one can also detect the rumbling of a bad conscience – a dark suspicion that the end might be richly deserved. Usually, a writer will pass some kind of judgement on the world that is in peril. It is rarely hard to tell the optimists from the pessimists, the activists from the nihilists and the humanists from the misanthropes. Sometimes there is an explicit craving for the end, because the world is exhausting and insoluble. In the character of Justine in Lars von Trier's movie *Melancholia*, or the novels of Kurt Vonnegut, or Morrissey crying, 'Come, Armageddon!' on 'Everyday is Like Sunday', we find a vivid desire for it all to be over. Multiple impulses can coexist in the same story because, when the subject is humanity itself, it is reasonable to be ambivalent. These are the questions that make the genre fizz: Do we expect the end of the world? Do we deserve it? Do we secretly long for it? What would we miss and what would we love to banish to oblivion?

End-of-the-world stories create a feedback loop between fiction and reality. In thinking about such fresh horrors as 9/11, Hurricane Katrina, AIDS or Covid-19, people have frequently turned to books and movies to show them that what seems unimaginable has in fact been imagined in some form. Real-life catastrophes trigger our collective memory bank of plots and images and cry out for new ones. In turn, characters cite those real events to make sense of their fictional tribulations. Often, we find that people in these stories know the same stories as we do. 'Rose had read books, Rose had seen movies, Rose knew how this story would end,' writes Rumaan Alam in his 2020 novel *Leave the World Behind.* Stories can influence the thinking of politicians and scientists, too. H. G. Wells conceived the atomic bomb three decades before the Manhattan Project built one, Arthur C. Clarke's novels inspired asteroid detection programmes, and the imaginary AIs HAL (in *2001: A Space Odyssey*) and Skynet (in the *Terminator* series) have informed conversations about the jeopardy of real AI. Movies even played a role in Ronald Reagan's nuclear diplomacy.

Writers of fictional doomsdays all reveal what they love or hate about the world as it is, and what they fear. Such stories are like ice-core data for dating the life cycle of existential concerns. On one level, then, this is a history of fear: the trauma following awful things that have happened and the dread of terminally awful things that could have happened but haven't yet. As Stephen King has observed, 'It may be that nothing in the world is so hard to comprehend as a terror whose time has come and gone.'

Activists are storytellers, too, and their strategic deployment of catastrophic narratives invariably meets resistance. *My* fears are valid and urgent; *your* fears are hysterical delusions. The anti-apocalypticists claim that fears of nuclear war, Y2K meltdown, multiple 9/11s, a swine flu pandemic and a shredded ozone layer did not materialize, and that those fears were wasted energy. They refer to Chicken Little and crying wolf. The apocalypticists counter that the wolf is often at the door – fear inspired the actions that averted those catastrophes, and will be needed again if we are to stave off others. But fear itself can be dangerous. It can galvanize but it can also paralyse or derange. Secular eschatology is the history of deciding what to worry about, and what to do about it.

Many friends asked me if submerging myself in this subject for two years was depressing. On the contrary, I found that it relieved the 'pressure of reality' and the narcissism of the present. The signal fact about the end of the world is that it has not happened yet, despite numerous predictions. In Emily St John Mandel's 2014 pandemic novel *Station Eleven*, an actress who has been studying art history remarks that 'you see catastrophe after catastrophe, terrible things, all these moments when everyone must have thought the world was ending, but all those moments, they were all temporary. It always passes.' Of course, in that novel it *doesn't* pass and almost everybody dies. The world is too full of nasty surprises for us to be complacent.

But still, the unrealized fears of the past can be a comfort because the conviction that one is living in the worst of times is evergreen. For Kurt Vonnegut, one of literature's most dedicated pessimists, the only way to manage dread of the future was to remember that the past was no picnic. 'Yes, this planet is a terrible mess,' he wrote. 'But it has always been a mess. There have never been any "Good Old Days," there have just been days.'

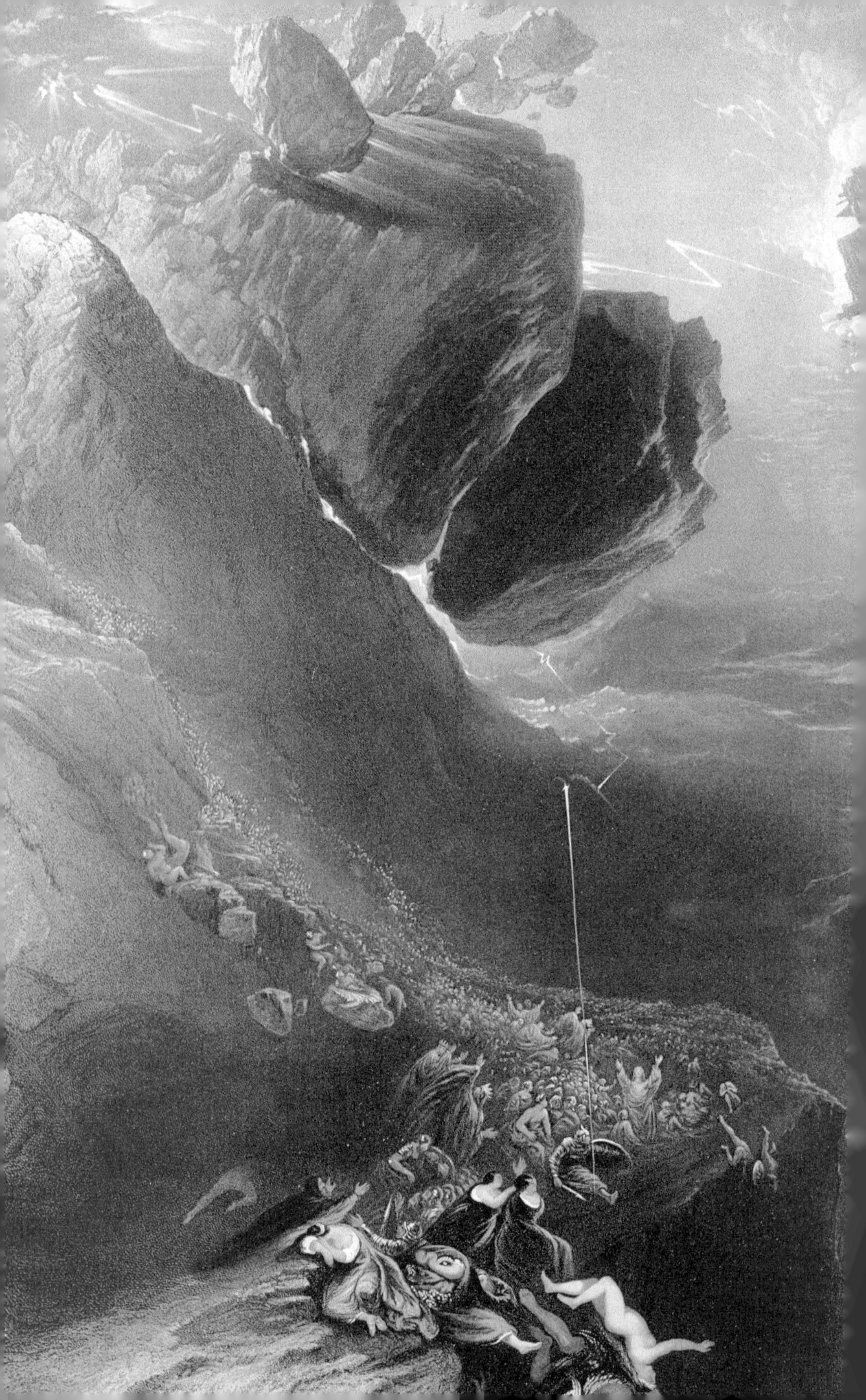

PROLOGUE
GOD

HURRY UP PLEASE IT'S TIME

T. S. Eliot, *The Waste Land* (1922)

The end of the world, as an idea, seems to have begun in Persia. Most ancient religions believed that the history of the world was a cycle, moving from creation to corruption to destruction to rebirth: the 'Great Year'. The ancients' shared experience of natural disasters inspired parallel myths of flood and fire while their shared unhappiness with the state of things led them to believe that they were living in the worst phase, which would precede the best: the Age of Iron in Greek mythology, or the Kali Yuga in Hinduism. The Zoroastrians of ancient Persia, however, taught that time moved like an arrow, not a wheel. They told a linear story with a beginning, a middle and an end, segmented into four phases of three thousand years, leading to a final conflict in which good would vanquish evil, renovate the universe, reunite the righteous with the deity and render the world smooth and perfect for ever. One might call the *Frashokereti*, or 'making wonderful', the original end of history. The origins of this myth are unknown, as is the process by which it influenced end-times myths in other cultures, but Judaism also came to embrace a linear view of history in a way that Norman Cohn, the great scholar of eschatology, has argued could not have been coincidental. Cohn described it as 'a totally new perception of time and of the prospects for mankind'.

Like the Zoroastrians, the Bible claims that the world was once perfect and that it will be perfect again but that, in the meantime, everything is broken. The whole of human history is a problem that needs fixing. Only six chapters into Genesis, a mere ten generations into life on earth, God has a change of heart about his corrupt and violent creation and commits mass murder in a version of the Mesopotamian flood myth: the Deluge.* 'Every thing that is in the earth shall die,' God declares, except for Noah and the population of his ark. When the waters have subsided, God promises never to do it again, or at least not in the same way: 'The waters shall no more become a flood to destroy all flesh.' Although the Deluge is not strictly an apocalypse, it has been referenced over and over again in apocalyptic fiction as a myth of violent purging and renewal – what the poet Frederick Turner diagnosed as our 'nightmare lust for cleanliness'. The word *cataclysm* derives from the Greek for deluge, *kataklusmos*. It is worth noting that, on its own terms, the Deluge was a failed experiment: humanity was not fixed.

Before it became a synonym for the end of the world in the nineteenth century, *apocalypse* described a genre rather than an event; it was a form of storytelling. From *apokalypsis*, the Greek word for revelation or disclosure, an apocalypse is a book in which a supernatural intermediary gives a pseudonymous prophet secret knowledge of the end times. Monsters, angels and occult phenomena abound. Proto-apocalyptic passages appeared in the writings of Jewish prophets around the time of the Babylonian exile in the sixth century BC, including the Books of Ezekiel, Isaiah, Jeremiah and Zechariah, designed to offer reassurance in a time of suffering and defeat, but the full-blown apocalypse was a renegade, underground genre which rarely won the approval of religious authorities. Of more than a dozen Jewish apocalypses, only the Book of Daniel made it into the Biblical canon. The rabbis may have regretted giving even Daniel the green light because it radically rewrote Jewish notions of prophecy and the afterlife, providing a gateway to Revelation.

Although the unknown authors of Daniel located their prophecies during the period of the Babylonian exile, the book was actually written around 164 BC, during the reign of the Syrio-Greek

*Scholars agree that the Mesopotamian myth was a fictional representation of a real, localized flood, although there is no consensus on its nature, date or location.

Seleucid emperor known as Antiochus Epiphanes (Antiochus, God Manifest) – or, to his detractors, Antiochus Epimanes (Antiochus the Madman). Antiochus made Jewish rites and traditions, from circumcision to possession of the Torah, capital offences and erected a statue of Zeus in the Temple in Jerusalem. Motivated by apprehension about a rebellion, these insults guaranteed one. Jewish fighters led by Judas Maccabeus recaptured the city, rededicated the Temple and declared an independent Jewish state, a victory commemorated in the festival of Hanukkah. Conceived as rousing propaganda, Daniel was a series of unusually entertaining and dramatic visions. Most of Daniel's 'prophecies' are allegorical retellings of historical events leading up to the reign of Antiochus before moving on to describe the 'latter days' when, after the time of tribulation and the final conflict, all the dead will be resurrected for the Last Judgement. Daniel made Babylon coterminous with decadence and downfall.

D. H. Lawrence observed in his posthumously published 1931 book *Apocalypse* that in order to tell a story of final, irreversible victory to an audience that craved solace, the Jewish revelators 'needed to know the end as well as the beginning'. And it had to be imminent. But when exactly? Daniel himself is twice told by an angel that the end will come after 'a time, two times, and half a time'. This was interpreted as three-and-a-half years, meaning forty-two months, which works out as 1,260 years, according to the Biblical tradition of reading days as years. But other numbers are also significant, and all of them had to be reconciled with the belief that the world would last for six thousand years, represented by the six days of creation. The flexibility about which number you use, and which date you start counting from, has inspired more than two thousand years of attempts to draw up a timetable for the end of the world.

Apocalypses flourished under the Roman occupation of Judea after 63 BC. Jesus emerged during a period when the province teemed with mystics, preachers, radicals, would-be messiahs and apocalyptic sects, of which Christianity was to prove the most successful. Jesus cites Daniel in the so-called 'Little Apocalypse' of the Gospels, when he tells his disciples that wars, earthquakes and famines shall herald the 'tribulation', followed by the return of the 'Son of Man' for the 'day of judgement', and that 'this generation shall not pass, till all these things be done.' This combination of violence and imminence is the scaffolding John of Patmos built upon in the Book of Revelation.

By far the most important text about the end of the world is either the authentic word of God, a masterpiece of propaganda or, as the Founding Father Thomas Jefferson put it, 'merely the ravings of a maniac'. For our purposes, it is a story. There is simply no escaping Revelation's inexhaustible stockpile of scenarios, characters, images, phrases and ciphers: the battle of Armageddon, the four horsemen, the seven seals, Alpha and Omega, the Whore of Babylon, Antichrist, the number 666 and the reinvention of Satan as the supreme villain. Revelation has given us such works as Hieronymus Bosch's *The Last Judgement*, William Blake's 'Jerusalem', Julia Ward Howe's 'The Battle Hymn of the Republic', Ingmar Bergman's *The Seventh Seal*, Ralph Vaughan Williams's *Sancta Civitas*, and, less enduringly, the Arnold Schwarzenegger movie *End of Days*.

Revelation supplies the Bible with a narrative arc and gives humanity's story a theatrical finale. The historian Perry Miller has described John's vision as 'not only the last, but also the finest show on earth, because it would be the perfect combination of aesthetic and moral spectacle'. Even more than the pageantry of violence or the dualism of good and evil, this is the fundamental appeal of eschatology to this day: it rescues believers from the endless mess of history by weaving past, present and future into a coherent, satisfying whole with an author, a message and an ending. In eschatology, everything that happens, whether good or bad, acquires significance because the reader belongs to the lucky generation that will finally experience closure.

Revelation owes its place in the canon to the assumption that John of Patmos was John the Apostle but the style, content and timing of the book suggest that he was someone else entirely. He was most likely a Jewish convert who grew up in Judea, speaking Aramaic, and became an itinerant prophet wandering from town to town in Asia Minor during the reign of the emperor Domitian, crowd-testing the material that would be written down towards the end of the first century AD. While it is true that apocalypses were often a compensatory fantasy for the persecuted, Domitian was a relatively tolerant ruler; mainstream Christians were able to prosper under Roman rule. The angry, alienated John of Patmos was not one of them. His burning hatred for Rome was matched by his contempt for 'lukewarm' Christians who made accommodations with the regime, especially merchants, not to mention rival prophets, women and sexual activity of any kind. John craved conflict and martyrdom but had to settle for a histrionic fantasy of power and revenge in which the elect get eternal paradise and everyone else gets what's coming to them. While the Christ of the Gospels talked of forgiveness, humility and loving one's enemies, John's Christ is a ruthless warrior-king with eyes of fire and a robe dipped in blood.

D. H. Lawrence perceived Revelation as 'the hidden side of Christianity' which excites the 'pseudo-humble' with bloody apparitions of vengeance and vindication. He believed that John's hatred of Babylon was a righteous mask for envy: he wanted to destroy what he could not have. 'The second half of the Apocalypse is flamboyant hate and a simple lust, lust is the only word, for the end of the world.' It is telling that mystical combat takes up twenty chapters while eternal bliss requires only two and the glorious Millennium is skipped over all together. Revelation has imprinted the horror and disaster genres because it *is* horror and disaster, paving the road to eternity with blood, fire, plagues and monsters. The impression one gets from Revelation is that John didn't really like human beings at all.

As St Augustine admitted in *The City of God*, Revelation is a very confusing book: 'No doubt, though this book is called the Apocalypse, there are in it many obscure passages to exercise the mind of the reader, and there are few passages so plain as to assist us in the interpretation of the others, even though we take pains; and this difficulty is increased by the repetition of the same things, in forms so different, that the things referred to seem to be different, although in fact they are only differently stated.' The Irish writer George Bernard Shaw described it, more pungently, as 'a curious record of the visions of a drug addict'. John's visions are so hallucinatory and cryptic that any detailed account of the plot inevitably dissolves into incoherence. Its story of persecution, revenge and salvation is reiterative rather than sequential; almost musical in its patterning of rhymes and motifs. When somebody misremembers the title as Revelation*s*, they are inadvertently indicating the multiplicity of the text itself, and the numerous translations, interpretations and embellishments that make it what it is today. Still, it is worth summarizing the raw material.

After some throat-clearing chapters in which John addresses the seven churches of Asia Minor, the Lamb opens the seven seals on God's book and commences the seven-year Tribulation. The first four seals unleash the horsemen (conquest, war, famine and death), the fifth resurrects the martyrs, and the sixth initiates the 'great day of his wrath': 'Lo, there was a great earthquake; and the sun became black as sackcloth of hair, and the moon became as blood; And the stars of heaven fell unto the earth.' The seventh seal summons forth seven angels with trumpets, who introduce a further torrent of mayhem which destroys one-third of the world. At this point, a seven-headed beast rises out of the sea, joined by a second, two-horned beast better known as Antichrist: the first beast's 'false prophet' and propagandist. These are not to be confused with their commander, Satan, a red dragon who is forced down to earth after a war in heaven. Christ returns (the Second Coming, or *Parousia*) to do battle with Satan at Armageddon. Along the way, we meet the 'woman clothed with the sun', the 144,000 white-robed virgins, the sickles that reap the grapes of wrath, the Whore of Babylon, the falling star Wormwood and 'locusts' with the bodies of horses, the faces of men, the teeth of lions and the tails of scorpions. There's a lot going on.

Although the battle of Armageddon is often equated with the end of the world, in Revelation these are two distinct events separated by one thousand years. After the battle, the two beasts are thrown into the lake of fire and Satan is chained in the bottomless pit (*abyss* comes from *abussos*, the Greek for bottomless) while Christ and his saints reign on earth for one thousand years: the Millennium. But Satan is not finished. The Millennium abruptly concludes when he returns with his thuggish new allies Gog and Magog for one last doomed battle. Off to the lake of fire he goes, along with Death and Hell. With evil banished for ever, everyone who has ever lived is resurrected and judged on their deeds: *doom* comes from the Old English for *judgement*. Those sinners whose names do not appear in the 'book of life' are cast into the lake of fire while the righteous enter 'a new heaven and a new earth', where the streets are paved with gold, and history comes to an end. The ambiguity as to whether this means the actual abolition of Earth or just its transformation has kept believers busy ever since, but either way the story concludes: 'There should be time no longer.'

Revelation is manic with numerology – not just 1,260 and three-and-a-half from the Book of Daniel but 666 and sevens, sevens, sevens. From a strictly historical perspective, at least, much of John's code is not hard to crack: Babylon is Rome, the seven heads of the Beast are Rome's seven hills, the mark of the Beast is Roman coinage, and the Beast itself is probably the emperor Nero. Writing about his own time, not the distant future, John did not expect that the world would be around long enough to attract generations of readers who would identify Antichrist as Muhammad, or George III, or Napoleon, or Mussolini, or Reagan, or no end of popes, and perceive 666 in barcodes and credit-card numbers. Nor would he have appreciated these improvisations. 'If any man shall add unto these things,' he warns, 'God shall add unto him the plagues that are written in this book.' Had he been able to foresee his enduring influence, he might well have considered it evidence of devastating failure: the world had neglected to end.

If John of Patmos had not been mistaken for John the Apostle, then his bloodthirsty, psychedelic visions might have been excluded from the canon along with the lurid Apocalypses of Peter, Paul and Thomas. In the West during the second century AD, Revelation was cited more often than any other book in the Bible, making John's militarized Christ more popular than the humble peacemaker of the Gospels, although the bishops of the eastern churches resisted it for centuries.

Characters and motifs from Revelation began to blaze through European art towards the end of the fourth century, when Christianity became the Roman Empire's official religion, but the victorious church realized that it might inspire dissent against Rome's new rulers. In the early fifth century, Augustine proposed a way to take the heat out of it. At one time a believer in the 'carnal' truth of

Revelation, he had come around to a spiritual interpretation: the story was an allegory from beginning to end and all prophecies of the last day could be disregarded as the 'ridiculous fantasies' of those who were 'called by the spiritual Chiliasts, which we may literally reproduce by the name Millenarians', words which derive respectively from the Greek and Latin words for *thousand.* Augustine opposed reading natural phenomena as signs of the times, uncoupled the Beast from Rome and claimed that the Millennium was in fact the current reign of the church. The world would indeed be 'burned and renewed' someday, he agreed, but nobody could claim to know when. As Jesus says in Mark 13, 'But of that day and that hour knoweth no man, no, not the angels, which are in heaven, neither the Son, but the Father.' Augustine drolly advised Christians to 'relax your fingers, and give them a little rest'.

Adopted by the church at the Council of Ephesus in 431, Augustine's sober wait-and-see reading could not entirely extinguish the flame of chiliasm but it did diminish it for several centuries. Although nineteenth-century writers such as Camille Flammarion and H. G. Wells routinely referred to the apocalyptic terror that preceded the year 1000, there is scant evidence that this actually occurred. The Biblical Millennium is not pegged to the historical millennium and Augustine's interpretation still held sway. What's more, even in Europe most people didn't use the Christian calendar, so they didn't even know it *was* the year 1000. While there are scattered accounts of millenarian activity around 1000 and 1033, the thousandth anniversary of the crucifixion and resurrection, it was far from being a widespread frenzy.

Expectations of Christ's physical return lay dormant until the late twelfth century, when the Italian monk Joachim of Fiore used innovative numerology to snatch Revelation back into the here and now: the end would begin 'in your own days, few and evil'. Dividing history into three ages based on the Trinity, he predicted that the third, the utopian Age of the Holy Spirit, would dawn around 1260 after the brief reign of Antichrist. The critic Frank Kermode credited Joachim as 'the man responsible for converting the original insights into schemes capable of directing the imagination of the future'. Some of the most powerful people in Europe, including England's King Richard I, sought Joachim's advice. In Italy, 1260 saw the kind of genuine millenarian delirium that 1000 had not, giving rise to a violent doomsday cult named the Apostolic Brethren. 'Antichrist' became a standard term of abuse in medieval politics, hurled back and forth between popes and kings. Joachim was a reformer rather than a revolutionary but he opened the floodgates for more subversive readings of Revelation. Not content with poring over every line, some prophets embroidered John's story with exciting new concepts and characters. The oracles of the Tiburtine Sibyl, for example, introduced the Last World Emperor who would reign over the last days, inspiring speculation across Europe as to his identity. The Germans thought he would be a descendant of Frederick II; the French looked forward to a second Charlemagne.

Gutenberg's invention of the printing press in the 1440s enabled the proliferation of not just apocalyptic pamphlets but picture-book versions of John's prophecies. Artists such as Hieronymus Bosch, Albrecht Dürer and Matthias Gerung dipped their pens in the foaming ink of Revelation. Most millenarians were quietists who withdrew from society to wait peacefully for the great day, but political unrest inspired what Norman Cohn described, in his pioneering 1957 study *The Pursuit of the Millennium*, as 'revolutionary millenarianism', from the Flagellants who massacred Jewish communities across Europe during the Black Death to the Taborites, whose attempt to build a utopian community in 1420s Bohemia descended into bloody schisms and purges. In the 1490s, the Dominican friar Girolamo Savonarola declared war against the modern world in thrilling sermons which promised that Florence would become Christ's own city, provided it was purged of vice. Under his de facto command, Florence became a millenarian compound for three years before he was arrested, hanged and burned in 1498.

Leading Protestant reformers were chary of Revelation. John Calvin omitted it from his commentaries on the New Testament while Martin Luther held the book in 'small esteem' because 'Christ is neither taught in it nor recognised', although he came to appreciate its political utility as anti-papal propaganda. Revolutionary millenarian movements, however, believed in using violence to bring about the complete overthrow of the existing order and the birth of a new and perfect society. They attracted the alienated and powerless in times of upheaval with charismatic leaders who claimed privileged access to esoteric knowledge. One such man was Thomas Müntzer, the mesmerizing lunatic who led the Peasants' Revolt in Thuringia in 1525. 'The time of the harvest has come!' he wrote. 'That is why he himself has hired me for his harvest. I have sharpened my sickle . . .' Müntzer was sympathetic to a radical new group of Protestant reformers called the Anabaptists. Their swelling ranks produced a demagogic playwright and tailor who presided over the most notorious chiliastic uprising of them all: Jan Bockelson, or John of Leiden.

In February 1534, Anabaptists led by a gaunt Dutch baker-turned-prophet named Jan Matthys seized control of the Westphalian town of Münster and transformed it into a fanatical theocracy, expelling thousands of Catholics and Lutherans and consigning every book except the Bible to bonfires in the town square. The Anabaptists claimed that all the world was doomed except for Münster, the New Zion. When the expelled bishop, Franz von Waldeck, organized an army to lay siege to the town, killing Matthys, Bockelson became a messianic dictator whose reign of terror extended the death sentence to infractions such as avarice, lying, insubordination and idle conversation. Come the autumn, he was proclaimed the new David, king of the world. Although the Anabaptists abolished private property, King Jan himself enjoyed fine robes and jewellery, as did his inner circle and his sixteen teenage wives. He installed a throne, draped with gold cloth, in the town square, where he personally beheaded followers who had defied or displeased him. Many more of his nine thousand citizens, most of them women and children, starved to death during the siege, having been reduced to eating moss, chalk and corpses, before Münster finally fell to von Waldeck's forces in June 1535. In January 1536, the man that Luther dismissively called 'the Tailor-King' was tortured to death with red-hot irons and his body hung in an iron cage from a church steeple as a warning to would-be prophets.

Never before or since Münster has Revelation directly inspired such a murderous nightmare, but Hitler, Stalin, Mao and Robespierre staged their own gigantic equivalents in their pursuit of a secular Millennium. In 1936, four hundred years after Bockelson met his unprophesied end, the German author Friedrich Reck-Malleczewen was reading accounts of Münster as research for *Bockelson: History of a Mass Delusion*, a historical novel which functioned as an anti-Nazi allegory. 'I am shaken,' he wrote in his diary. 'In every respect, down to the most ridiculous details, that was a forerunner of what we are now enduring . . . Hitler and his sycophants face the same inevitable end as Bockelson.' Norman Cohn later traced his own interest in millenarianism to his work in the Intelligence Corps in post-war Europe, where he interrogated former officers of the so-called Thousand-Year Reich or Third Reich (phrases with Joachimite roots) and encountered refugees from Stalinism. Cohn argued that 'the tradition of apocalyptic fanaticism . . . – secularised and revivified – was inherited by Lenin and by Hitler.'

Each regime constructed a grand, pseudo-religious chronology of destruction and renovation and attempted to force reality to conform to it at gunpoint. Totalitarianism demanded apocalyptic myths of a golden past, an accursed present and a glorious future. Whenever the violence of the elect is purported to purify the world and give birth to a new society, the mythic logic of Revelation is at play and the alleged incarnations of evil, be they the Jews or the bourgeoisie, must be annihilated as surely as the non-believers of Münster.

In March 1647, a Puritan preacher named William Sedgwick made the ruinous mistake of prophesying the final day a mere fortnight in advance. For the rest of his life, he was mockingly known as Doomsday Sedgwick. Never mind that Jesus explicitly forbade date-setting; a more pressing deterrent was the fact that if somebody chose a date within their own lifetime and the end didn't arrive, then they looked rather foolish. But there is so much irresistible numerology in the Bible that the practice persists to this day. Individual dates can be disconfirmed without the whole story being discredited. The most widely accepted calculation for almost two hundred years was published by James Ussher, the Anglican archbishop of Ireland, in 1650. Accepting that the conventional date for Jesus's birth was an error because Herod was now believed to have died in 4 BC, Ussher counted back four thousand years from there and determined that time began at nightfall on Saturday, 22 October 4004 BC, the Deluge began on Sunday, 7 December 2349 BC, and the Millennium would occur on 23 October 1996. While intrepidly precise, this was at the time a safe distance away.

Doomsday prophecies had been gathering momentum in Reformation England for decades. Among those who identified the pope with Antichrist were the poets John Milton, John Donne and Edmund Spenser, the influential millenarian scholar Joseph Mede, the mathematician John Napier, and King James I. The pope complained that James 'called him Antichrist at every word' when they dined together. By 1640, the Puritans had turned their fire on the English clergy and the monarchy. Among numerous competing prophecies, the years 1656 (the number of years before the Deluge) and 1666 (the number of the Beast, kind of) exerted the strongest magnetic pull. Millenarianism did not cause the English Civil Wars but it certainly animated many Puritans. 'It is difficult to exaggerate the extent and strength of millenarian expectations among ordinary people,' wrote the historian Christopher Hill.

After Charles I's defeat by Oliver Cromwell, England swarmed with would-be messiahs and prophetic texts. The Ranter prophet John Robins proclaimed himself a divine being and announced a plan to recruit 144,000 saints to liberate the Holy Land. A group of fanatics called the Fifth Monarchy Men (a reference to the kingdom of God in the Book of Daniel) even attained influence in parliament, provoking concerns about an English Münster, before Cromwell stamped them down. 'You fix the name of antichristian upon anything,' he scolded their leader, John Rogers. The Fifth Monarchists believed that the execution of Charles I would initiate the Kingdom of the Saints and lead to the Second Coming in 1666, although by the time that year arrived their leaders had been executed. Cromwell, too, was dead, King Charles II had reclaimed his throne and millenarianism had been discredited. 'Take heed of computation,' the Puritan theologian John Owen advised in 1680. 'How woefully and wretchedly have we been mistaken by this!'

Even as millennial prophecy was waning in England, tarred with extremism, regicide and failure, it was waxing in the New World. America and apocalypse had been intertwined since the first Europeans landed there. 'God made me the messenger of the new heaven and the new earth of which he spoke in the Apocalypse of St. John . . . and he showed me the spot where to find it,' wrote the Revelation-obsessed Christopher Columbus in 1500. America was to the Pilgrim settlers what Florence had been to Savonarola: God's chosen place. In 1662, a clergyman named Michael Wigglesworth published the colonies' first ever bestseller, an epic poem called *The Day of Doom: or, A Poetical Description of the Great and Last Judgment.* 'For a century it was read in every household in New England,' according to the historian Perry Miller.

Cotton Mather, the leading Puritan who delivered Wigglesworth's eulogy, declared that Christ would build the New Jerusalem in America after the cleansing fire, but America's creation myth electrified even Enlightenment rationalists. 'We have it in our power to begin the world over again,' Thomas Paine wrote in *Common Sense.* 'A situation, similar to the present, hath not happened since the days of Noah until now. The birthday of a new world is at hand . . .' The apocalypse has always been the rocket fuel of religious revivalism in America. Jonathan Edwards, the Massachusetts preacher who ignited the First Great Awakening in the 1730s, wrote an exegesis called *Notes on the Apocalypse*, arguing that Antichrist's rule would end in 1866. Revelation was also the cornerstone of the Second Great Awakening, the revival that swept through New England seventy years later and produced the most famous humiliation in the history of date-setting.

In 1832, a farmer and Baptist lay preacher from New York State named William Miller published his calculation that the Second Coming would occur in 'about 1843'. Miller applied the standard year–day transposition to the 2,300 days prophesied in Daniel 8:14 and set the clock running in 457 BC, with the Persian king's decree to rebuild Jerusalem. 'Finding all the signs of the times and the present condition of the world, to compare harmoniously with the prophetic descriptions of the last days, I was compelled to believe that this world had about reached the limits of the period allotted for its continuance,' he wrote. Readers were intrigued. Miller preached throughout New England, accumulating a healthy following, before settling in the area of western New York that came to be known as the 'Burned-over District' due to its susceptibility to the fire of religious enthusiasm. The popular philosopher Ralph Waldo Emerson marvelled at New England's array of 'madmen, madwomen, men with beards, Dunkers, Muggletonians, Come-Outers, Groaners, Agrarians, Seventh-Day Baptists, Quakers, Abolitionists, Calvinists, Unitarians and Philosophers'. After newspapers such as *Signs of the*

Times and *The Midnight Cry* began spreading the word, the ranks of Millerites swelled to around fifty thousand. Nor was this merely an eccentric fringe. The depression that followed the Panic of 1837 made Americans unusually pessimistic. According to the historian Whitney R. Cross, 'the whole of American Protestantism came so very close to the same beliefs . . . All Protestants expected some grand event about 1843, and no critic from the orthodox side took any serious issue on basic principles with Miller's calculations.'

Under pressure from his growing fanbase to be more precise, Miller said that he was using the Jewish rather than the Christian calendar, so the date would be somewhere between 21 March 1843 and 21 March 1844. The appearance of the Great Comet of 1843 in February appeared promising but the Second Coming did not come. One of Miller's followers, Samuel S. Snow, ran the numbers again and came up with 22 October 1844; Miller went along with it. 'If [Christ] does not come within 20 or 25 days,' Miller said when the fateful month arrived, 'I shall feel twice the disappointment I did this spring.' More than a century later, this refusal to admit defeat partially inspired the social psychologist Leon Festinger to originate the concept of cognitive dissonance. Many Millerites quit their jobs, abandoned their businesses and sold all their worldly possessions. One put up a sign: 'This shop is closed in honor of the King of Kings who will appear about the 20th of October. Get ready, friends, to crown him Lord of all.' On the day that became known as the Great Disappointment, recalled one broken Millerite, 'Our fondest hopes and expectations were blasted, and such a spirit of weeping came over us as I never experienced before. It seemed that the loss of all earthly friends could have been no comparison. We wept and wept till the day dawn.'

Widely reported and ridiculed, the Great Disappointment discouraged date-setting for decades to come and made Miller a byword for folly: the American Doomsday Sedgwick. But one newspaper correctly predicted that 'the follies of 1843 . . . will continue to be so long as professing Christians retain in their faith all the elements of this fatal delusion . . . The *gullibility* of the people remains, though the predictions and computations of Miller have all failed.' Many Christians believed that John of Patmos's story held up; it just needed more astute readers. A teenage Millerite called Ellen

Harmon went on to found the Seventh-Day Adventists in 1863. End-time prophecies were also central to the Church of Jesus Christ of Latter-Day Saints (the Mormons) and the Jehovah's Witnesses, whose founder, Charles Taze Russell, claimed that the Second Coming had begun, invisibly, in 1874 and that the kingdom of God would commence on 1 October 1914. But the person who did the most to reinvent apocalyptic Christianity in America was not even American.

Beginning in 1859, the Anglo-Irish preacher John Nelson Darby toured the US several times to promote dispensationalism, a new creed which popularized (though did not invent) two concepts that could be found nowhere in Revelation. One was the Rapture. In John of Patmos's account, the righteous and unrighteous alike will suffer the Tribulation before they are separated. Drawing on a single line from I Thessalonians 4:17, Darby offered Christians the far more appealing prospect of being whisked up to heaven just before the Tribulation and viewing the carnage from a safe distance. 'We Christians are sheltered from the approaching storm,' he promised. His second innovative claim was that the Second Coming could not occur until the Jewish people had returned to the Holy Land. This cemented the strange phenomenon of Christian Zionism, in which anti-Semitism can go hand in hand with staunch support for the state of Israel, the future site of Armageddon.

Thanks to the endorsement of the influential Bible publishers Dwight L. Moody and Cyrus R. Scofield, Darby's innovations became integral to the apocalyptic narrative of fundamentalism after the American Civil War, inspiring hundreds of prophecy books. Millennialism was not confined to white people. Nat Turner's doomed slave uprising in 1831 was spurred by Turner's experience of an apocalyptic vision during a solar eclipse. A Native American variant developed in 1889 when an influential Northern Paiute spiritual leader named Wovoka claimed to have experienced a vision in which God told him that a ritual five-day dance would abolish evil in the western United States and bring about a golden age of peace and prosperity. When his prophecy was adopted by the Lakota people, the ritual became known as the Ghost Dance. Across the world, as indigenous peoples were forcibly exposed to Christian teachings, some groups improvised their own eschatological belief systems: among them the Pai Mārire of New Zealand, the followers of the Xhosa prophet Makana in southern Africa, the Rastafarians in Jamaica and the Taiping Heavenly Kingdom in China, which commanded at its peak nearly thirty million people.

During the nineteenth century, American Christianity bifurcated in regard to the Millennium. Literal-minded premillennialists, like William Miller, believed that they were already living in the end times and that things needed to get worse so that Christ could return, defeat Antichrist and commence the Millennium. Allegorically minded postmillennialists, like the Social Gospel movement, thought that Jesus wouldn't return until Christians had established the reign of the saints on earth, and therefore dedicated themselves to improving the world. (Amillennialists, in the tradition of St Augustine, believed that the Millennium had already begun. There weren't so many of them.) The schism was essentially a disagreement about whether earthly progress was possible. While many postmillennialists joined the movement to abolish slavery (imagery from Revelation courses through both Harriet Beecher Stowe's *Uncle Tom's Cabin* and 'The Battle Hymn of the Republic'), Cyrus Scofield argued that the Millennium would not be achieved via 'blessedness and peace, but in sudden and awful ruin'. Over time, optimistic reformers tended to lose interest in the Millennium altogether while pessimistic revolutionaries became the vanguard of American Christianity, raining fire on such improving schemes as the New Deal and the League of Nations. One British convert, the former suffragette Christabel Pankhurst, dismissed her celebrated feminist activism as 'the childish, nay foolish dreams of a human-made Utopia'. Pankhurst went looking for 'signs of the times', but there is always enough misery and mayhem in the world to support a claim that it is the end of days, if that is what you wish to see. Quoting Christ's prophecy that 'there shall be famines, and pestilences, and earthquakes, in divers places,' the seismologist Charles Francis Richter once quipped, 'Assuredly, no safer forecast was ever made.'

As the historian Richard Hofstadter argued in his 1964 essay 'The Paranoid Style in American Politics', Revelation is in the lifeblood of American conspiracy theories. Embodying a distinctly American blend of exceptionalist optimism and violent paranoia, Cotton Mather waxed lyrical about his country's glorious destiny while fomenting hysteria about the dark forces of witchcraft. Neurosis about the enemy within entered the Republic as early as the anti-Illuminati panic of the 1790s. In fact, one could read Revelation as the original conspiracy theory, in which secret knowledge is revealed to the righteous few who are wise enough to decipher it and the forces of good finally defeat the villainous cartel that is responsible for all the evil in the world. Hofstadter quoted Norman Cohn's diagnosis of the psychology of millenarian sects as an early example of the paranoid style, with features such as 'the megalomaniac view of oneself as the Elect, wholly good, abominably persecuted yet assured of ultimate triumph' and 'the attribution of gigantic and demonic powers to the adversary'.

Hofstadter concluded that paranoia was latent in a significant minority of the American public and was brought to the surface by 'catastrophe or the fear of catastrophe'. Imminence demands action. 'Whatever we do, it must be done quickly,' wrote Harriet Beecher Stowe's father Lyman Beecher in 1835, railing against Catholic immigrants. 'Time is running out,' warned Robert Welch, founder of the anti-communist John Birch Society, in 1951. Unified by the perceived division between Us and Them, the pure and the impure, the drowned and the saved, and by an obsession with patterns and codes, conspiracy theories and premillennialism feed on one another. They share an enthusiasm for wild and intricate claims, supported by eccentric 'experts' and a cavalier method of documentation. They are united by a disgust for international entities, from banks and corporations to the United Nations and the European Union. The most notorious anti-Semitic text, *The Protocols of the Elders of Zion*, was originally published as the final chapter of a Russian book about Antichrist, while the book that revived fascination with Illuminati-based conspiracy theories in the 1990s was *New World Order* by the evangelist Pat Robertson. Most recently, QAnon was essentially an apocalyptic cult, with a pseudonymous prophet foretelling a storm (endlessly deferred) which would wipe out the evildoers.

Despite his paranoid prejudices against Freemasons and Catholics, the peaceful, collegiate William Miller was no cult leader; the absence of violence meant that the Great Disappointment could resolve into comedy as far as everyone else was concerned. But entrepreneurial apocalyptic sects such as Charles Manson's Family, Jim Jones's People's Temple, Luc Jouret's Order of the Solar Temple and David Koresh's Branch Davidians (a splinter of a splinter of a splinter of the Seventh-Day Adventists) all climaxed in bloodshed one way or another: the Münsters of our time. The Book of Revelation remains dangerous.

Apocalyptic myths of the end of the world, violent transformations and decisive clashes between good and evil are not unique to the Judeo-Christian tradition. Islamic eschatology, which animates groups such as Islamic State, awaits the messianic figure known as the Mahdi. In the Norse myth of Ragnarök (the Doom of the gods), the three-year *Fimbulwinter* unleashes a throng of evil monsters who battle the gods to the death. Without the gods' protection, the Sun turns black and the seas rise, swallowing humanity. Both of these myths, however, emerged a long time after the Christian apocalypse; it is the Bible that supplies the primordial tales that surface over and over again in the art, literature, cinema and television of the West, even though most of the writers deploying them don't believe in the literal truth of the Bible.

During the nineteenth century, the Christian apocalypse broke away from the world of art and ideas. Even as new religions were built around it, intellectuals reviled doomsday prophecies and regarded artists who chose to portray the actual end of the world as unserious, if not unwell. In science, meanwhile, the victory of Darwinism rejected any kind of belief in world-changing catastrophes. In the twentieth century, apocalyptic scenarios became a mainstay of popular entertainment but millennialists have produced no great art that resonates with the general public. Hal Lindsey's pseudo-hipster rereading of Revelation in *The Late Great Planet Earth* may have been the non-fiction juggernaut of the 1970s, and the *Left Behind* series of Rapture-based thrillers written by the premillennialists Tim LaHaye and Jerry B. Jenkins may have sold tens of millions of copies since 1995, but genuine belief in Revelation is for the most part anathema to mainstream storytelling. When the science fiction writer Walter M. Miller Jr auditioned hundreds of stories about nuclear holocaust for a 1985 anthology called *Beyond Armageddon*, he was surprised to find that not a single one involved Tribulation and Rapture: 'Evidently, Fundamentalists don't write fantasy or science fiction, and might shrink from the suggestion that Saint John was writing it in Revelations [sic].'

In popular fiction, those who declaim verses from Revelation are invariably portrayed as crackpots or fanatics: either the street-corner kook with a sandwich board proclaiming 'The End of the World is Nigh!' or the murderous tyrant in the tradition of Jan Bockelson. At best they are impotent. In 1984, as apocalyptic prophecy enjoyed a boom not seen since the Second Great Awakening of the early 1800s, a poll found that 39 per cent of Americans believed that the Bible contained references to nuclear war. Yet in *The Day After*, a phenomenally popular 1983 TV movie about such an event, a priest reads from Revelation in a shaky, tearful voice as stupefied worshippers drift away from his roofless church. The promises of John of Patmos crumble in the face of the Bomb.

Secular writers are more typically drawn to the modernist apocalypses of T. S. Eliot and W. B. Yeats. Frank Kermode called Eliot 'a poet of apocalypse, of the last days and the renovation, the destruction of the earthly city as a chastisement of human presumption'. Like his earlier masterpiece *The Waste Land*, with its ruined landscape of 'stony rubbish' and 'broken images', Eliot's 1925 poem 'The Hollow Men' replaced climactic celestial drama with the dying fall of what he saw as a corrupt, devitalized culture peopled by the walking dead. 'This is the way the world ends,' it famously concludes. 'Not with a bang but a whimper.' 'The Hollow Men' acquires quasi-Biblical authority in *Apocalypse Now*, *On the Beach* and the work of Nick Bostrom, who divides existential risks into 'bangs', 'whimpers', 'crashes' and 'shrieks'.

Yeats, meanwhile, reimagined Revelation in his 1920 poem 'The Second Coming'. While he has his own signs of the times ('Things fall apart; the centre cannot hold') and oracular visions ('Surely some revelation is at hand'), what is coming next time is not Christ but his opposite: 'And what rough beast, its hour come round at last / Slouches towards Bethlehem to be born?' Yeats constructed an elaborate, world-explaining 'System' in which history moves in cycles of two thousand years: 'day & night, night & day for ever.' For him, the age of Christ was coming to an end and a new era, antithetical to progress and reason, was poised to begin. Like John of Patmos, he had one foot in the turmoil of his present – the aftermath of the

First World War, the Russian Revolution, the dawning of war between Ireland and England – and one in the realm of monstrous, cryptic visions. Rather overlooked at the time, 'The Second Coming' has since become perhaps the most plundered poem of the twentieth century, used to great effect by writers as diverse as Joan Didion, Chinua Achebe, Alex Garland, Neil Gaiman, Joni Mitchell and Stephen King. Clearly there is an insatiable appetite for alternatives to Revelation which express the same belief that the final crisis is upon us. Things fall apart over and over again, yet the Beast never quite reaches Bethlehem.

'Changed by our special pressures, subdued by our scepticism, the paradigms of apocalypse continue to lie under our ways of making sense of the world,' wrote Frank Kermode. Born of one man's anger, alienation and desperation to mean something, Revelation speaks to a much more fundamental psychological need. On the most mundane level, we ritualize destruction and rebirth every New Year's Eve: the old year, a decrepit failure, is swept away and the new one, glowing with hope and resolve, is ushered in. To many, the turn of a century or a millennium is freighted with preposterous expectations of change.

If apocalyptic art is eternally indebted to Biblical blueprints, then so too is the language of existential risk, with its confusion of warnings, speculations and prophecies. As we shall see from the experience of activist scientists and writers who have invoked the end of the world, to be dubbed a 'prophet of doom' is usually both unhelpful and unfair. Somebody who predicts a catastrophe in the hope of averting it is not a doomsday prophet, at least not in the premillennialist sense. Prophylactic predictions are really jeremiads, designed to inspire conversion and action through a sense of crisis, rather than apocalypses, in which catastrophe cannot and should not be averted. As the philosopher C. E. M. Joad wrote in 1930, 'I conceive it to be the duty of a writer about the future to be as pessimistic as possible. By this method he may hope to irritate his readers sufficiently to provoke them to make the efforts necessary to prove his predictions false.'

Even so, there are undeniable religious echoes in many temporal prophecies: the world is in a terrible state thanks to the sins of humankind and time is running out in which to choose between salvation and damnation. Even if the end of the world is not expected in our lifetime, we are the ones who must take action to prevent it. The thought-patterns of the Deluge and the apocalypse figure in many scientific and political debates whether or not the combatants are aware of them. As the sociologist James J. Hughes argued in a 2008 essay, 'We may aspire to a purely technocratic analysis . . . but few will be immune to millennial biases, positive or negative, fatalistic or messianic.'

The Christian apocalypse is still with us, then, in a range of disguises, but it began to lose its monopoly over the concept of the end of the world more than two hundred years ago. In literature, this process began with two landmark visions written by two close friends. By eschewing Armageddon, the Millennium, the Last Judgement and God himself, Lord Byron and Mary Shelley made it possible to say that the end really was the end.

PART ONE
THE LAST MAN

CHAPTER 1

Darkness

Morn came and went – and
came, and brought no day . . .

Lord Byron, 'Darkness' (1816)

The end of the world was scheduled for 18 July 1816, at least according to an anonymous astronomer from Bologna who claimed that the Sun was dying. In mocking the man it later called the 'mad Italian prophet', *The Times* of London unwittingly became his chief promoter. 'We mentioned this prophecy only to show the absurdity of it,' the paper protested on 13 July, 'but instead of this old women have taken the alarm: the premonition is now a general subject of conversation.'

During what became known as 'the year without a summer', the weather was conducive to an apocalyptic frame of mind. Europe had slouched out of a punishingly cold, wet spring into an even worse summer. Rivers and lakes burst their banks; newly planted crops drowned; churches teemed with parishioners praying for an end to the rain. Bad weather, like war, can be a great unifier. Across the breadth of England, it was a national preoccupation. In Chawton, Hampshire, an ailing Jane Austen worked on her sixth novel, *Persuasion*, as the rain battered the window panes. 'It is really too bad, & has been for a long time,' she wrote to her nephew, 'much worse than anybody can bear, & I begin to think it will never be fine again.' In north London, Samuel Taylor Coleridge bemoaned the impossibility of exercise due to 'this end of the World Weather'. During a sketching tour of Yorkshire, J. M. W. Turner complained to a friend that he had been forced to postpone a trip to Italy: 'Rain, Rain, Rain, day after day. Italy deluged, Switzerland a wash-pot, Neufchatel, Bienne and Morat Lakes all in one.' In all of Europe, Switzerland caught the worst. Lake Geneva, rain-swollen, rose by almost two metres, making parts of the city navigable only by boat and inundating surrounding farmland so that the lake's surface was dotted with tree trunks and the bloated bodies of drowned livestock. On the shores of the lake was the village of Cologny; on the upper slopes of that village stood an eighteenth-century mansion called Villa Diodati. Its tenant that summer was Lord Byron.

The twenty-eight-year-old peer was England's most outrageous celebrity. As notorious for his libido as he was celebrated for his epic poem *Childe Harold's Pilgrimage*, Byron had been driven abroad by the bitter breakdown of his marriage and scandalous rumours of an affair with his half-sister. He fled the country in April in extravagant fashion, travelling to Switzerland along with his personal physician John Polidori, a temperamental young man with envious literary ambitions, in a replica of Napoleon's carriage, and visiting the battlefield of Waterloo en route. Some joked that there were more English people in Switzerland that summer than there were Swiss, and Byron arrived to find some of the very same people that he had left England to avoid. 'Gossips made my stay a nightmare,' he later griped.

One of those English visitors was eighteen-year-old Claire Clairmont: a 'foolish girl,' Byron summarized, who had 'scrambled eight hundred miles to unphilosophize me'. Secretly pregnant with his child after a lightning fling in London, Clairmont was travelling with her formidably intelligent stepsister Mary Wollstonecraft Godwin, also eighteen; Mary's unworldly, idealistic lover Percy Bysshe Shelley, twenty-three; and their baby son William. Mary was the precociously brilliant offspring of two of the great thinkers of the time, William Godwin and the late Mary Wollstonecraft, but she had already forged her own path by eloping with the married Percy two years earlier, enraging both her father and his. Plagued by debt, they too were seeking refuge from a hostile England. Eager to rekindle her affair with Byron, Clairmont orchestrated a meeting between him and the Shelleys in May, thus facilitating one of the most productive, and complicated, friendships in the history of literature.* 'Lord Byron is an exceedingly interesting person,' Shelley wrote to his friend Thomas Love Peacock, '& as such, is it not to be regretted that he is a slave to the vilest & most vulgar prejudices, & as mad as the winds?'

The Shelleys rented Maison Chapuis, a small house separated from Villa Diodati by a sloping vineyard, and Byron moved into the villa a few days later. They spent most of their evenings at Diodati when the weather made it impossible to sail on the lake or stroll beside it. 'An almost perpetual rain confines us principally to the house,' Mary wrote in a letter on 1 June. The thunderstorms were like nothing she had ever seen: 'The lake was lit up, the pines on Jura made visible, and all the scene illuminated for an instant, when a pitchy blackness succeeded, and the thunder came in frightful bursts over our heads amid the darkness.'

Stuck in Diodati on one particularly wretched night in the middle of June, the group passed the time by discussing science and philosophy and reading German ghost stories in the grand salon, with its roaring fire and balcony overlooking the lake. 'We will each write a ghost story,' Byron declared. He dropped his own supernatural experiment after a few pages, leaving Polidori to pick it up and eventually turn it into *The Vampyre*, which transformed the bloodsucker of European folklore into an archetype that was aristocratic, seductive, restless, *Byronic*. But Byron did complete a poem called 'Darkness', a radically godless vision of the end of the world. Mary, an as yet unpublished writer, took the challenge more seriously. Inspired by a dream, she began concocting a tale of 'a pale student of unhallowed arts' from Geneva who uses electricity to create a 'hideous phantasm of a man' from pieces of the dead: *Frankenstein.*

In addition to the rain, there appeared to be something wrong with the Sun. For several hours a day, a dark patch was visible on the Sun's surface, which many observers assumed was the cause of the disastrous weather. 'Many . . . dreamt of spots noticed in the sun, which impede its beneficial powers forever, thus heralding the chilling and sinking of the earth,' wrote Joseph von Hazzi, a Bavarian official. 'Others even saw a stripe resembling a scythe as proof that

*Mary and Percy were legally unable to marry until December 1816 but I will refer to them as the Shelleys for convenience.

this scythe would soon cut down and destroy the human race like blades of grass. Prophets rose up on all sides to proclaim that the end of the world was nigh.' A Neapolitan priest called Cavillo set the final day for 27 June. It was to rain fire for four hours 'and those who escaped the fire were to be devoured by serpents'. A French newspaper attempted to counter this 'superstitious anxiety excited at present among the vulgar' with an insistence that such spots were perfectly normal. 'Generally speaking, the physical state of our little world is more stable and steady than its moral state,' it huffed. The satirist William Hone parodied the wild theories in his poem 'Napoleon and the Spots on the Sun, or The Regent's Waltz', which proposed that Napoleon had avenged his defeat at Waterloo the previous year by invading the Sun.

Still, divinations continued to trigger outbreaks of end-times hysteria across Europe. The trumpeters of a cavalry regiment unwittingly caused a commotion one stormy night in Ghent, Belgium, when a large number of residents mistook the noise for the seventh and final trumpet in Revelation and poured into the streets, falling to their knees with 'cries, groans, tears [and] lamentations'. A girl in Bath, England, woke her fretful aunt with the cry, 'Aunt, Aunt, the World's at an end!' and shocked her into a coma. An eminent Parisian woman passed away 'in consequence of the terror she experienced from the prediction of the end of the world'. The Austrian imperial authorities had to dispatch troops to suppress unrest in several towns. 'We know not whether the Italian mountebanks, who in the course of their erratic lectures circulated this report, had not some deeper view than merely exciting a momentary tumult,' frowned *The Times*.

What nobody knew – neither the poets nor the journalists nor the scientists, and certainly not the prophets – was why any of this was happening.

The volcano Mount Tambora lies on the Sanggar peninsula on the island of Sumbawa in the Flores Sea, to the east of Java. It had long been presumed extinct but the islanders had noticed an ominous cloud over the summit and a rumbling in the earth preceding the evening of 5 April 1815, when the mountain suddenly began firing clouds of volcanic ash 30 kilometres into the sky. For the next few days, the Sun was dimmed by a humid fog and a soft rain of black ash fell on the surrounding islands. Five days later, Tambora erupted with a force one hundred times greater than that of Vesuvius in AD 79. It remains the largest volcanic eruption in recorded history, outdoing that of the more famous Krakatoa in 1883. One-third of the mountain was obliterated, shooting columns of burning lava high into the sky and raining down molten rock. In eyewitness reports collected by Thomas Stamford Raffles, the lieutenant-governor of the Dutch East Indies, the rajah of Sanggar attested that 'the whole mountain . . . appeared like a body of liquid fire' until it was blacked out by a rapidly expanding mushroom cloud of ash, 40 kilometres high.

Natural disasters can feel like apocalypses for those who are unlucky enough to be at their heart. In 1894, Camille Flammarion invited his readers to 'imagine the state of mind of the inhabitants of Herculaneum and Pompeii when the eruption of Vesuvius buried them in showers of ashes! Was not this for them the end of the world? And more recently, were not those who witnessed the eruption of Krakatoa of the same opinion?' Tambora immediately spelled the end for around ten thousand of its immediate neighbours. To the volcano's west, the villages of Tomboro and Pekáté were incinerated by pyroclastic flows of molten rock and burning gas. To the east, volcanic matter poured into the sea, triggering new explosions and shrouding the Sanggar peninsula in a hellish microclimate of steam and ash. As described by Lieutenant Owen Phillips, a naval officer sent by Raffles to deliver emergency supplies of rice and collect testimonies, 'A violent whirlwind ensued . . . tearing up by the roots the largest trees and carrying them into the air, together with men, horses, cattle, and whatever else came within its influence.' Hard on its heels, a tsunami flooded the lowlands. Birds were struck from the sky and dead fish belched up by the boiling sea. Over the following weeks, tens of thousands of Sumbawans perished from drinking contaminated water, eating poisoned food or inhaling ash, while a similar number fled to neighbouring islands, unable to scratch out a living from levelled forests and flooded rice fields. To this day, Sumbawans call it 'the time of the ash rain'.

The eruption could be heard as far as 2,600 kilometres away in Sumatra and Borneo. Within a 500-kilometre radius of Tambora, the detonations caused houses to shake as ash smothered the ground, 20 centimetres thick, and blotted out the Sun until noon on 12 April. The commander of the *Benares*, an East India Company ship north of Makassar, recorded that the darkness was 'so profound throughout the remainder of the day, that I never saw anything to equal it in the darkest night'. The volcano projected tens of millions of tonnes of sulphur dioxide into the stratosphere, where it mingled with hydroxide gas to create 100 million tonnes of sulphuric acid. Too high to form rainclouds, the acid droplets coalesced into an aerosol cloud which steadily encircled the world, plunging it into three years of climate change.

During the cool, rainy summer following the Battle of Waterloo, Europe experienced spectacular sunsets, blazing red, orange and purple. Come winter, dust-tainted snow was the colour of brick in Italy and flesh in Hungary. By the spring of 1816, Tambora was wreaking climatic havoc on both sides of the North Atlantic as the global average temperature fell by around 0.7 degrees Celsius. It was the inhabitants of New England, where Boston went from heat-wave to snowfall inside of three days in June, who coined the phrase 'the year without a summer' and the more demotic 'Eighteen Hundred and Froze to Death'. As for the face of the Sun, that, too, was a side effect of Tambora. Although 1816 fell in the middle of a forty-year period of unusually low sunspot activity called the Dalton Minimum, the sulphur dioxide in the air scattered sunlight and created a haze which made sunspots visible for several hours a day, even without eye protection.

Not until 1913 did the meteorologist William Jackson Humphreys suggest a connection between Tambora and the year without a summer, and the process was not understood in detail until the 1980s. Few people in Europe in 1816 knew that Mount Tambora even existed (*The Times* had mentioned the 'Tomboro' eruption just once) and those who did could not have imagined that a distant volcano could cause the rain to fall, the sky to dim and the harvests to fail. In the absence of scientific explanations, fear and superstition filled the void. Why would a significant number of people *not* have been persuaded that the world was coming to an end?

Wary of the potential of doomsday sects to inspire unrest, the authorities quickly detained any soothsayer who opened his mouth, including the astronomer from Bologna. A seer in the Oise region of France, *The Times* drily noted, 'did not, however, foresee what almost immediately took place – his own arrest and confinement'. The press covered prophecies with a mixture of amusement, exasperation and contempt, diagnosing the panic as a disease of the lower orders. *The London Chronicle* scorned those who believed in such 'outrageous fooleries': 'The multitude are more ignorant and credulous than in the most barbarous times.' But *The Examiner* did at least wonder why such wild claims were proving so popular, suggesting that doomsday fever was 'not unconnected with political circumstances, and the naturally wondering spirit to which the events of the time have given rise' – an analysis that could apply to every apocalyptic panic before or since.

The context was febrile. Europe was slowly recovering from the Napoleonic Wars, struggling to accommodate the transition to a peacetime economy and the mass unemployment caused by demobilization. For farmers, trying to replant fields that had been pillaged by Napoleon's armies, endless rain meant drowned crops. This, in turn led to rocketing bread prices, food riots and what would prove to be Europe's worst famine of the century. In Paris, a pamphlet called *Détails sur la fin du monde* sold briskly prior to 18 July. The Paris correspondent of *The British Lady's Magazine* suggested that anxiety was more widespread than sensible people would care to admit: 'Alarm and consternation pervade all ranks; even those who affect to laugh at the prediction evidently feel its influence . . . all await the event with patient horror, though ashamed of openly avowing it . . . they are afraid of being laughed at if the event does not come to pass.' Of course, it did not come to pass. On 'the day the world was to be at an end', as Byron's friend John Cam Hobhouse sardonically registered it in his diary, the rain actually stopped and gifted England a rare sunny afternoon. Still, there was palpable unease in the streets. Future US president John Quincy Adams, then his country's ambassador to London, noted that the 'churches and chapels have been unusually crowded.'

In Cologny that month, the temperature was four degrees lower than usual. Byron later claimed to have written 'Darkness' on 'a celebrated dark day, on which the fowls went to roost at noon, and the candles were lighted as at midnight', yet there are no other reports of this remarkable phenomenon. While it is tempting to believe that secular fiction about the end of the world was a direct response to the disorienting experience of temporary climate change, it is more than possible that Byron was using a fanciful exaggeration to justify his impulse to compose something extraordinarily new: a vision of the end which did not include God.

Consider the trembling world in which Byron and the Shelleys had grown up. The eighteenth century had been an education in the end of things. The excavations of Herculaneum and Pompeii, beginning in 1738 and 1748 respectively, bred a popular fascination with the ruins of great civilizations. The Germans called this *Ruinenlust.* 'We see . . . that Empires, however firmly founded, and that cities, however embellished, are like man, subject to mortality, and liable to dissolution,' reflected the translator of the first book about the excavations. 'This thought naturally humbles the mind in the dust, and we learn to know our own insignificance, the vanity of our pretensions, and the futility of all earthly glories.' The affluent English who embarked on the Grand Tour of Europe were particularly entranced by the remnants of the Roman Empire while the 1755 Lisbon earthquake, which destroyed 85 per cent of the city, brought the reality of catastrophe to Enlightenment Europe. The wreckage of what the historian Mike Davis has called 'the Hiroshima of the Age of Reason' became a new template for the final days. 'Thou also perish,' the English clergyman George Hoare told his congregation. 'Behold me smoking! Remember and REPENT. This is the short but very full sermon that Lisbon in ruins preaches to London in sin.'

Largely on account of the French Revolution, the 1790s was the first time that the end of a century had been widely associated with turbulence, transformation and relentless acceleration, which is to say apocalypse. 'Old things seemed passing away, and nothing was dreamt of but the regeneration of the human race,' recalled the radical poet Robert Southey. In Britain, the industrial revolution was in full swing and the population was booming, leading Thomas

Malthus to write his infamously gloomy *Essay on the Principle of Population.* Despite England's general suspicion of apocalyptic prophets, two influential figures arose in London: Joanna Southcott, who sold paper 'seals' purporting to guarantee purchasers a seat among the 144,000 elect, and Richard Brothers, self-proclaimed 'Prince of the Hebrews', who warned that the city would fall like Babylon on 4 June 1795. Joseph Priestley, the chemist who discovered oxygen, believed that the revolutions in France and America heralded the Millennium. 'The present moment teems with these anticipations of futurity, beyond the example of every former period,' one Calvinist complained in 1796.

Science, meanwhile, was posing multiple challenges to religion. A century earlier, scholars had agonized over how to align science with scripture. In *The Sacred Theory of the Earth*, published in two parts during the 1680s, the theologian Thomas Burnet had described the planet he inhabited as the 'hideous ruin' that the Deluge had left behind. At the same time as he was revolutionizing our understanding of the universe, Isaac Newton was also a fiend for Revelation. 'I seem to gather that God is opening these mysteries,' he wrote. 'The last age is now approaching.' Newton worked on his exegesis for more than fifty years, regularly coming up with new dates for the Millennium, but kept it secret outside of a small circle of fellow enthusiasts to avoid controversy, so his *Observations Upon the Prophecies of Daniel, and the Apocalypse of St. John* was published only after his death in 1727. The French satirist Voltaire quipped that Newton squandered all that time on Revelation 'to console mankind for the great superiority he had over them in other respects'.

Towards the end of the eighteenth century, however, the French naturalist Georges-Louis Leclerc, Comte de Buffon, and the Scottish geologist James Hutton independently proposed that Earth was much older than the Biblical span of six thousand years (the current estimate is 4.55 billion) and set scripture aside. 'We find no vestige of a beginning, – no prospect of an end,' Hutton wrote in 1788. Then came the notion that entire species had risen and fallen in that abyss of time. The astronomer Edmond Halley, Isaac Newton's contemporary, had speculated on extinction a century earlier, but many people still found it hard to believe. Pondering the discovery of giant, elephantine bones in the Ohio River valley, the US Founding

Father and fossil-collector Thomas Jefferson refused to accept that such magnificent beasts were not still out there somewhere, roaming the wilds of America. 'Such is the economy of nature,' he wrote in 1781, 'that no instance can be produced of her having permitted any one race of her animals to become extinct.' Georges Cuvier, a brilliant young teacher at the Museum of Natural History in Paris, was convinced that Jefferson was wrong. In a 1796 lecture, he claimed that the creature was not a kind of elephant at all but belonged to a species that had vanished off the face of the earth. He began building a collection of fossils and giving them names: the beast of Ohio was (in English) a *mastodon*; a flying reptile whose remains were discovered in Bavaria was a *pterodactyl*. 'But what was this primitive earth?' he asked. 'And what revolution was able to wipe it out?'

Cuvier claimed that the creatures he had studied had been eradicated by 'some kind of catastrophe'. As he discovered more fossils, he became convinced that there had been more than one mass extinction and proposed a theory of cyclical destruction. Cuvier argued that fossilized evidence of different species in different strata indicated that the planet had experienced a series of violent upheavals, each revolution exterminating the dominant species and making way for the next. 'Life on earth has often been disturbed by terrible events,' he wrote. 'Living organisms without number have been the victims of these catastrophes.' His theory of 'catastrophism' popularized the concept of extinction and raised the prospect of more to come. From the Greek word for overturning, and originally applied to the denouement of a tragedy, a catastrophe is far grander than a disaster: it upends the world. The French novelist Honoré de Balzac later called Cuvier 'the greatest poet of our century', whose history of catastrophe was 'a sort of retrograde Apocalypse'.

It was an era when scientists wrote poetry, poets followed science, and it was fashionable to be interested in everything. Byron later summarized catastrophism in *Don Juan*: 'When this world shall be former, underground, / Thrown topsy-turvy, twisted, crisped, and curled, / Baked, fired, or burnt, turned inside out, or drowned, / Like all the worlds before . . . So Cuvier says.' Byron and Shelley had also read Buffon, whose 1778 book *Des époques de la nature* argued that Earth had been forged by a comet's fiery collision with the Sun, had been cooling down ever since, and would finally become a ball of ice, although he did allow that it was not beyond the wit of man to 'modify the influence of the climate he inhabits'. Though Buffon was somewhat wide of the mark, his climate pessimism seemed credible during a cold, wet summer in the Alps. A trip with Mary and Claire to the advancing glaciers of Chamonix in July 1816 inspired Shelley, in a letter to Thomas Love Peacock, to mention 'Buffon's sublime but gloomy theory – that this globe which we inhabit will, at some future period, be changed into a mass of frost.' In his poem 'Mont Blanc', written in Chamonix, the Mer de Glace resembles a 'city of death': 'The race / Of man flies far in dread; his work and dwelling / Vanish, like smoke before the tempest's stream.'

Following the failure of the Bologna prophecy, an anonymous writer for *The New Monthly Magazine* wrote a sobering essay called 'Of the End of the World', which asked the reader to reconsider the end in scientific terms: 'Because the world was not destroyed on the 18th of July, we imagine that it will never be at an end, and laugh as if we had never been afraid . . . Only have patience, gentlemen – it will come I promise you.' The writer laid out a range of 'rational' possibilities, from Buffon's theory of a refrigerated earth to fire, flood and comets. Though his tone was flippant, his message was serious: 'I have thus given the *end of the world* with variations, so that amateurs may take their choice; but I hope I have said quite enough to stop the mouths of all who may be disposed to make light of so serious a subject.'

Meanwhile in Cologny, Byron was writing 'Darkness'. Unlike Shelley, Byron was not an atheist but the Calvinist faith in which he had been raised had certainly loosened its grip. 'I will have nothing to do with your immortality; we are miserable enough in this life, without the absurdity of speculating upon another,' he wrote to his friend Francis Hodgson in 1811. In 'Darkness', Byron took apocalyptic images from Jeremiah, Isaiah, Ezekiel, Matthew and Revelation and emptied them of God, leaving a spectacle of total destruction. It was as simple as erasing a figure from a landscape painting:

I had a dream, which was not all a dream.
The bright sun was extinguish'd, and the stars
Did wander darkling in the eternal space,
Rayless, and pathless, and the icy earth
Swung blind and blackening in the moonless air;
Morn came and went – and came, and brought no day,
And men forgot their passions in the dread
Of this their desolation; and all hearts
Were chill'd into a selfish prayer for light

The poem's true horror is not the sudden extinguishing of the Sun, Moon and stars but the snuffing out of light and warmth in the human heart under extreme duress. At first, terrified people lay waste to the world, burning cities and forests, palaces and huts, in order to conjure a fleeting glow. Some weep, some rage, some smile out of either cynical resignation or madness. They go to war over what food remains: 'no love was left.' The only creature to show any fellow-feeling is a faithful dog who chooses to guard his master's corpse rather than eat it. The last two survivors, bitter enemies, meet in the ashes of a temple, where they are literally scared to death by the sight of each other's hunger-hollowed faces. Byron's steady drumbeat of adjectives of absence – *rayless*, *pathless*, *moonless*, *useless*, *stingless*, *tombless* – reaches an annihilating crescendo as Earth becomes 'Seasonless, herbless, treeless, manless, lifeless – / A lump of death.' Finally, the seas, winds and clouds die, too: 'Darkness had no need / Of aid from them – She was the Universe.'

Even sympathetic critics found Byron's poem shockingly extreme. 'The very conception is terrible above all conception of known calamity – and is too oppressive to the imagination, to be contemplated with pleasure, even in the faint reflection of poetry,' remarked Francis Jeffrey in *The Edinburgh Review*. For all its horrors, Revelation has a beautifully consoling conclusion: 'And God shall wipe away all tears from their eyes; and there shall be no more death, neither sorrow, nor crying, neither shall there be any more pain: for the former things are passed away.' 'Darkness', by contrast, has neither a deity nor a plan. For Byron, the end of the world was not a prelude to eternal glory, or anything at all, but the ultimate negation.

—

The Shelleys left Switzerland for London at the end of August because they had run out of money and Claire Clairmont's pregnancy was unignorably visible. (Byron waspishly remarked that she had 'returned to England to assist in peopling that desolate island'.) They returned to a country in a 'very disastrous state', according to *The Times*. The chilly streets of London teemed with beggars – an early sign of the human calamity unfolding across Europe. In Germany, 1817 became known as the 'year of the beggar'. In Switzerland, the death rate exceeded the birth rate, partly because some desperate parents murdered the babies that they could not feed. Throughout the continent, famine killed tens of thousands, giving rise to riots, pogroms, political unrest and mass emigration. Thomas Stamford Raffles, chronicler of the Tambora eruption, was travelling through Europe during the summer of 1817 and described the ghost towns of eastern France in his diary: 'We could not but notice the almost total absence of life and activity . . . There was an air of gloom and desertion pervading them.'

Authorities in central Europe feared an epidemic of millenarian sects with the potential for violence. A German Pietist named Johann Michael Hahn told his followers that 'the disorders of the elements' were due to the unleashing of Satan upon the earth, while followers of the novelist and mystic Baroness Julie de Krüdener believed that she was 'the woman clothed in the sun' foretold in Revelation. Her closeness to the Russian tsar, Alexander I, had given her unusual political influence and she drew huge crowds to her sermons by distributing soup and blankets to the desperate, many of whom were moved to tears by her prophecies. 'The Rhine rots with corpses,' de Krüdener wrote in January 1817. 'Misery is rampant . . . The time is approaching when the Lord of Lords will reassume the reins. He himself will feed his flock.'

In Austria, a priest named Thomas Pöschl led a millenarian sect which had taken over the village of Ampflwang am Hausruckwald. Three years earlier, he had predicted that 1817 would be the year that he would enter Jerusalem as the new Christ but now he claimed that the world would end on 30 March: Palm Sunday. On the eve of the great day, the Pöschlianers burned all their possessions on a pyre, progressed to human sacrifice, and then beat to death the only family in the village who did not believe that the end was nigh.

Pöschl and dozens of his fellow ringleaders were subsequently arrested, tried and found insane. 'A dozen times in a century,' snapped *The Times*, 'these miserable predictions are repeated, which, though always falsified, always find dupes; and this will be the same for some thousand years to come, because there will always be prophets and fools.'

The Shelleys' homecoming in the autumn of 1816 was marked by a double tragedy. On 9 October Mary Shelley's half-sister Fanny Imlay took her own life by drinking half a bottle of laudanum. Then, in December, Percy Shelley's estranged wife Harriet drowned herself in the icy Serpentine River while pregnant by another man. (Suicide being a crime in England, both deaths were officially recorded as accidents.) Mary and Percy were able to marry at last.

Frankenstein, or the Modern Prometheus was published anonymously to great acclaim in January 1818 – the same month as 'Ozymandias', Percy Shelley's own take on hubris and nemesis. The novel's genesis in the rains and glaciers of Switzerland is obvious: the creature is first glimpsed during a thunderstorm in Geneva, encountered again on the Mer de Glace and last seen at the then-uncharted North Pole – 'borne away by the waves, and lost in darkness and distance'. Thomas Love Peacock wrote that *Frankenstein* 'seems to be universally read' in London, but nobody could have predicted the length and breadth of its cultural reach. The historian David Skal has claimed that 'the real creation myth of modern times is not Darwin, not Genesis; it is *Frankenstein*.' While the novel itself is rich with ideas and nuances, the 1931 movie version crunched it down into one crude paradigm: the mad scientist who plays God and creates a monster. This new Faust became such a cliché in stories of scientific pride and disaster that D. F. Jones made a joke of it in *Colossus*, his 1966 novel about a renegade supercomputer. '*Frankenstein* should be banned reading for scientists,' says one character. 'I'd be more inclined to make it compulsory reading for non-scientists,' counters his boss.

In March 1818, the Shelleys left England again with their two children and settled in Italy. In September, their baby daughter Clara died of dysentery in Venice; nine months later, three-year-old

William succumbed to malaria in Rome. Only Percy Florence, named after the city of his birth in November 1819, survived to adulthood. Grief and depression corroded the Shelleys' marriage. As Mary wrote to her friend Marianne Hunt, wife of the critic Leigh Hunt, 'We went from England comparatively prosperous and happy – I should return broken hearted and miserable – I never know one moment's ease from the wretchedness and despair that possess me . . .'

Then the former storytellers of Villa Diodati began to die. First to go was John Polidori, on 24 August 1821. The coroner recorded death by natural causes although the evidence suggested that Polidori, plagued by debt and depression, had taken cyanide. On 8 July 1822, while Mary Shelley was convalescing from a near-fatal miscarriage, Percy's boat capsized in a storm off the coast of Tuscany; his ruined corpse was washed up on the beach ten days later. Byron was fighting alongside Greek revolutionaries against the Ottoman Empire when he fell ill and died in Missolonghi on 19 April 1824. Claire Clairmont survived to the age of eighty, but of the writers who told each other ghost stories by the lake during that 'wet, ungenial summer', Mary was the last one standing.

A few weeks after Percy's death, Mary sent family friend Maria Gisborne the first of several extravagantly dismal letters about 'my disastrous life': 'And so here I am! I continue to exist – to see one day succeed the other; to dread night, but more to dread morning & hail another cheerless day.' She was convinced that she wouldn't be far behind her husband because she simply could not imagine a future that wasn't dominated by death. 'Suffering is my Alpha and Omega,' she wrote in her journal. Mary could not even commemorate her husband in print because her vindictive, reactionary father-in-law, Sir Timothy Shelley, vetoed all of her attempts to publish Percy's work or to write a biography. She struggled to summon a word anyway. 'My imagination is dead – my genius lost – my energies sleep,' she confided to her journal in January 1824. Yet the very next month she began work on her epic tale of ruin, *The Last Man.*

The popular fascination with the last man had begun with Jean-Baptiste Cousin de Grainville, a priest whose career had been destroyed by the French Revolution. His 1805 prose poem *Le Dernier*

Homme (*The Last Man*), completed shortly before he drowned himself in the Somme, was an expression of crushing failure and loneliness, leading to self-extinction. Published posthumously, and poorly translated into English as *Omegarus and Syderia, a Romance in Futurity*, Grainville's response to Milton's *Paradise Lost* is set in the far future, amid a fertility crisis. Omegarus, the last man born on Earth, meets Syderia, the last fertile woman, to refound the human race, but Milton's Adam materializes to convince him that God needs him to let humanity die so that the Last Judgement can take place. The world goes down in a blaze of volcanoes and comets.

According to a second-hand anecdote (published long after both men were dead and perhaps too good to be true), Percy Shelley had exclaimed to Byron one day in Switzerland, 'What a change it would be if the sun were to be extinguished at this moment; how the race of men would perish until perhaps only one remained – suppose one of us! How terrible would be his fate!' The figure of the ultimate witness who could record the calamity when everyone else was gone appealed to the Romantic obsession with lonely, tormented heroes. Now Mary Shelley was the group's 'last man' and the responsibility of telling their story fell to her. Whereas Byron's extinction scenario is both mythic and timeless, Mary's lays waste to a painfully familiar world.

CHAPTER 2

The Last Man

Was I a ghost haunting my life? Did I, not all the world, lie dead? Certainly, I felt dead. Perhaps that is because when those we love die, we die too.

Ronald Duncan, *The Last Adam* (1952)

In her 1962 country-pop hit 'The End of the World', Skeeter Davis protests that the sun keeps shining and the birds continue to sing even though her boyfriend has left her: 'I can't understand why life goes on the way it does.' As a break-up song, it is pure melodrama but the emotional impetus for lyricist Sylvia Dee was really the death of her father. Between the lines, it is a song about the apocalyptic nature of grief and the irrational demand that the entire world halt to acknowledge a personal catastrophe. This is what Mary Shelley did in *The Last Man*, at considerably greater length: she universalized her bereavement in 'a tale of woe, with many sorrows rife'.

First and foremost, the novel is an exercise in mourning and remembrance, with Mary's late companions granted a power and perfection that they had never achieved in life. Percy Shelley is personified by the kind, idealistic Adrian, son of the last king of England; Byron, who died during the novel's composition, is the arrogant, magnificent aristocrat Lord Raymond; and Lionel Verney, the narrator and eponymous last man, is Mary herself. 'The last man!' she wrote in her journal in May 1824, following Byron's death. 'Yes I may well describe that solitary being's feelings, feeling myself as the last relic of a beloved race, my companions extinct before me . . .' In the capacious genre of secular end-of-the-world fiction that she initiated, Mary Shelley remains one of the few storytellers to take death seriously.

The Last Man is framed as a prophecy deciphered from scrolls discovered in a cave in Naples in 1818. England in 2073 is a newborn republic, full of hope. When Raymond is elected Lord Protector, a hi-tech golden age beckons: 'disease was to be banished . . . The arts of life, and the discoveries of science had augmented in a ratio which left all calculation behind . . . machines existed to supply with facility every want of the population.' But Volume I's tale of love, friendship and ambition ends in 2092 with Raymond, Byronically undone by hubris and infidelity, resigning and going to Greece to fight the Turks. While Lionel and Adrian are sailing to join him, they receive news of a mysterious new plague: 'This enemy to the human race had begun early in June to raise its serpent-head on the shores of the Nile.'

Mary Shelley uses the plague to magnify her grief to global proportions and, at the same time, methodically to demolish the optimism of her parents and late husband. Everything fails in the path of the plague: science, art, politics, religion, England. Ryland, Raymond's populist successor as Lord Protector, panics and resigns his post, leaving Adrian to take over. The utopian astronomer Merrival loses his mind over the death of the future: 'The old man felt the system of universal nature which he had so long studied and adored, slide from under him.' Across Asia, the appearance of a 'rayless' black sun inspires the kind of religious mania that had broken out in Europe in 1816, as several characters mistake the plague for the advent of the Millennium. When, at last, it reaches London, a Pöschl-like 'maniac' arises: a mechanic, maddened by grief and famine, who comes to 'believe himself sent by heaven to preach the end of time to the world'.

At the outset of Volume III, England has fallen. It is early 2098 and Adrian leads 'the numbered remnant of the English nation, into the tenantless realms of the south'. In Paris they discover that many of the city's remaining inhabitants are in thrall to 'a self-erected prophet, who, while he attributed all power and rule to God, strove to get the real command of his comrades into his own hands'. He tells his fanatical followers, 'the Elect', that they are immune to the plague, though he does not believe it himself. When his lie is inevitably exposed, he shoots himself. Mary offers only two kinds of religious leader: a madman and a conman. After Paris, long story short, pretty much everybody dies. Lionel, Adrian and the two children in their care retrace the Shelleys' steps (Lake Geneva, Chamonix, Milan, Venice) and re-enact Mary's ordeals in Italy, the country she described as 'murdress of those I love & of all my happiness'. Lionel's son Evelyn succumbs, like Mary's son William, to an unrelated virus. Adrian, like Percy Shelley, drowns in a storm. 'Oh! grief is fantastic . . . as light, it fills all things, and, like light, it gives its own colours to all,' Lionel laments. Finally, in '2100, last year of the world!', the last man on earth sits down in Rome to write his story (even the last man must assume a reader somewhere, someday) with the peculiar calm of somebody who knows that he has nobody left to lose. It is just the place for it: 'Every part of Rome is replete with relics of ancient times.'

'I will dwell in solitude amidst the ruins of cities,' wrote the French philosopher Constantin François Chasseboeuf, Comte de Volney in his 1791 book *The Ruins, or A Survey of the Revolutions of Empires*. Volney began his radical Enlightenment tract by pondering the remnants of Palmyra, the Syrian city that had been destroyed by the Romans in 273 AD. For Volney, time is the great leveller, uniting kings and slaves in dust:

> What glory is here eclipsed, and how many labours annihilated! . . . Thus perish the works of men, and thus do nations and empires vanish away! . . . I have visited the places that were the theatre of so much splendour, and I have beheld nothing but solitude and desertion! Thus reflecting, that if the places before me had once exhibited this animated picture; who, said I to myself, can assure me that the present desolation will not one day be the lot of our own country? Who knows but that hereafter some traveller like myself will sit down upon the banks of the Seine, the Thames, or the Zuyder Zee . . . solitary amid silent ruins, and weep a people inurned, and their greatness changed into an empty name?

The Ruins was an essential text for anyone drawn to the fall of civilizations, including their own. In Grainville's *Le Dernier Homme,* which opens 'near the ruins of Palmyra', Paris is 'a wasteland, a vast expanse of dust, home to silence and to death', which moves Omegarus to ask, 'Is this all that remains of the proud city whose slightest movement shook the two worlds?' *The Ruins* is the book that teaches Frankenstein's creation about the history of the world. In her grief, Mary Shelley came to see herself as a derelict husk. 'I am a ruin where owls and bats live only,' she wrote to Leigh Hunt in 1823.

Ruins have long been read as symbols of decadence, downfall and the judgement of time. Stare long enough and you will begin to perceive the skeleton in your own city, even at its glorious peak. The painter Joseph Gandy had spent three years in Rome immediately before he began working for the architect John Soane in 1798 and depicted the Bank of England, Soane's brand-new masterpiece, as an overgrown wreck in 'Architectural Ruins: A Vision'. In 1819, the year after 'Ozymandias', Percy Shelley half-jokingly imagined a time 'when London shall be an habitation of bitterns; when St. Paul's [Cathedral] and Westminster Abbey shall stand, shapeless and nameless ruins, in the midst of an unpeopled marsh'. As for who might visit them in a future version of the Grand Tour, the historian Thomas Macaulay proposed that 'some traveller from New Zealand shall, in the midst of a vast solitude, take his stand on a broken arch of London Bridge to sketch the ruins of St Paul's.' Long before paranoid billionaires began acquiring refuges in New Zealand, it was assumed that the remoteness of the islands would spare them from whatever was going to smash the rest of the world to rubble. By the 1860s, the exotic 'New Zealander' had become such an overused figure in art and literature that *Punch* proposed banning all reference to him: 'He can no longer be suffered to impede the traffic over London Bridge . . . May return when London is in ruins.'

The Last Man was published in February 1826, billed as a 'new Romance, or, rather Prophetic Tale' from 'the author of *Frankenstein*'. Unfortunately for Mary Shelley, while she was writing it the last man had become first a fad and then a joke. In 1823, the Scottish poet Thomas Campbell had published a popular poem called 'The Last Man'. When it was republished two years later, one critic accused him of plagiarizing 'Darkness', provoking Campbell to retort that Byron had stolen the idea from *him* after a conversation some years earlier. Byron, being dead, was unable to refute the claim. Either way, the poems reveal two incompatible cosmologies. Campbell's poem has the total conviction of a religious prophecy, manic with exclamation marks. The last survivor sends the dying Sun and the human race on their way with the diligence of a caretaker taking pride in making sure the lights are all turned out at the end of his shift. Though surrounded by ghost ships, silent cities and the numberless victims of war, famine and plague, his faith in God is absolute:

> Yet think not, Sun, it shall be dim
> When thou thyself art dark!
> No! it shall live again, and shine
> In bliss unknown to beams of thine.

In 1826, the last man's appearances included a short story in *Blackwood's Magazine* called 'The Last Man'; two anonymous poems entitled 'The City of the Dead' and 'The Death of the World'; and a spoof of the above, also called 'The Last Man', by Thomas Hood. Hood's narrator, a professional hangman, is enjoying the peace and quiet of being the sole survivor of a plague in 2001 until he discovers that there is another, a capering beggar who drives him to distraction. Eventually he hangs the beggar so that he can be 'The LAST MAN left alive, / To have my own will of all the earth,' only to be driven mad by guilt and loneliness. Reprinting the poem in 1827, *Blackwood's* hailed it as the last word on the last man: 'Mr Hood, alive to the ludicrous, has viewed the Last Man in his proper light; and had the verses been published two years ago, they surely would have saved Mrs Shelley from the perpetration of her stupid cruelties . . . Mr Hood's last man is, in our opinion, worth fifty of Byron's "darkness," (a mere daub), a hundred and fifty of Campbell's Last Man, and five hundred of Mrs Shelly's [sic] abortion.'

Though critically derided, it was Campbell's hopeful Christian vision that came to typify the last man, inspiring illustrations by both J. M. W. Turner and John Martin. Even as Turner's sole survivor, one of twenty vignettes for *The Poetical Works of Thomas Campbell,* perches on a knoll carpeted with skeletons, he reaches out to heaven, surrounded by angels beneath a glowing cross. Martin, meanwhile, produced a sketch, a watercolour and an oil painting on the theme over three decades. In its final iteration, a Biblically gowned and bearded figure watches a red sun die slowly over a necropolis. Charlotte Brontë called it a 'grand, wonderful picture'.

Havoc was Martin's muse. Although violent, supernatural catastrophes also figured in the work of contemporaries such as Philip de Loutherbourg, Benjamin Haydon and Francis Danby, Martin was the unchallenged master of the Apocalyptic Sublime. Born in working-class Northumberland in 1789, he became a popular sensation thanks to his vast canvases in which human figures are dwarfed by magnificent architecture, looming mountains and roiling skies. Martin ransacked the Bible for scenes of mass destruction – the Deluge, the levelling of Sodom and Gomorrah, the seventh plague of Egypt – and brought to them unprecedented scale and detail, making his paintings the closest Georgians came to going to the cinema; the exhibition of *Belshazzar's Feast* in 1821 is thought to be the first time in London that a barrier was required to hold back art-lovers. In 1834, Cuvier visited the painter's studio and contemplated the tumbling violence of his work in progress, *The Deluge*, for a long time before exclaiming, 'Mon Dieu!' Martin brought this Biblical grandeur to more recent disasters, too: with its lava-red glow and its sky of fire, *The Destruction of Pompeii and Herculaneum* made the eruption of Vesuvius look like curtains for the entire world. Edward Bulwer-Lytton, the author of 1834's *The Last Days of Pompeii*, anointed Martin 'the greatest, the most lofty, the most permanent, the most original genius of his age'. Leading critics and peers, though, were condescending if not outright hostile. John Constable dismissed Martin as a 'painter of pantomimes' while John Ruskin accused him of the 'reckless accumulation of false magnitude [which] is merely a vulgar weakness of brain, allied to nightmare'. Martin came to be regarded by art historians as a crass huckster and most of his paintings were buried in storage for decades. After his death in 1854, *The Manchester Guardian* wrote that people were divided over how to interpret his work, 'whether as the grandest things that ever were conceived by human imagination, or as the mere dreams of a mad architect'.

Martin's brother Jonathan, an apocalyptic seer, really was mentally ill, institutionalized first in 1817 for threatening to shoot the bishop of Oxford and again in 1829 for setting fire to York Minster. (He was promptly arrested thanks to his habit of pinning aggressive letters on the cathedral railings, complete with his signature.) While he was confined to the London psychiatric hospital known as Bedlam, his feverish artistic output included a lurid pen-and-ink drawing called *London's Overthrow*, which presented Westminster Abbey and St Paul's in flames, like Babylon. But John Martin was by all accounts a sociable, level-headed man whose interest in eschatology was purely artistic. When he wasn't laying waste to cities on canvas, he was working on practical schemes to improve London's water quality and designing an underground railway. Martin devoted the years before his death to a career-summarizing triptych of monumental paintings inspired by Revelation: *The Last Judgement*, *The Great Day of His Wrath* and *The Plains of Heaven*. Exhibited around the UK, US and Australia in the decades after his death, it was nothing less than a blockbuster, reaching millions of viewers. A vision of the world folded in on itself, wrenched asunder by fire and lightning, pitching the damned into a black abyss, *The Great Day of His Wrath* was as thrilling and terrifying a spectacle as anyone had yet seen. Some visitors shrieked or fainted at the sight of it. Martin has always inspired awe and contempt in hyperbolic quantities.

Mary Shelley's version of the end fared less well than Martin's. While one American critic astutely described *The Last Man* as 'a sort of detailed and prose copy of Byron's terrible painting of darkness', the reviews in England were merciless, and riddled with misogyny. 'Why not *the last Woman*?' asked *The Literary Gazette*. 'She would have known better how to paint her distress at having nobody left to talk to.' Intellectuals associated interest in the end of the world with ignorance, mental illness, religious extremism, or some toxic combination of all three, and accused doomsday novelists, like doomsday prophets, of catering to the worst of human nature. In its review of *The Last Man*, *The Monthly Review* found the very idea of a futuristic apocalypse absurd:

> The utmost efforts of thought are absolutely childish, when they seek to fathom the abyss of ruin, to number the accumulation of disasters, to paint the dreadful confusion, which await that

> final scene. Every writer who has hitherto ventured on the theme, has fallen infinitely beneath it. Mrs. Shelley, in following their example, has merely made herself ridiculous . . . The whole appears to us to be the offspring of a diseased imagination, and of a most polluted taste.

The Last Man is no masterpiece – it is overlong and overwritten – but it deserved better than that. If the critics' intention was to annihilate it, then they largely succeeded: it sold poorly and fell out of print for more than a century. While it was an extraordinary seedbed for new tropes in fiction, they did not sprout and bloom until long after Mary Shelley's death. In the 1960s, the writer and historian of science fiction Brian Aldiss identified *Frankenstein* as the first science fiction novel and *The Last Man* as the second but that genre did not yet exist, so the novel was initially perceived as a perverse mutation of the Gothic. In fact, *The Monthly Review* declared that the only endeavour more ridiculous than imagining the end of the world would be 'to describe the transactions which are taking place in any of the countless planets that are suspended beyond our own'. Imagine that! The scholar I. F. Clarke calculated that fewer than two dozen tales of the future were published in England over the next forty-five years. In that regard, as in so many others, Mary Shelley was alone.

'I only am escaped alone to tell thee,' the messengers tell Job in the Old Testament. Ishmael, the *Pequod*'s last man, quotes these words at the end of *Moby-Dick*. The figure of the last man (it is almost always a man) has reappeared in fiction as a necessary witness, participant and world-mourner despite there being no remotely credible situation that might produce a single survivor.* The phobia of being wholly alone is expressed more realistically in the figure of the castaway, but the last man is one who can never be rescued. 'For a moment I compared myself to that monarch of the waste – Robinson Crusoe,' writes Mary Shelley's Lionel. 'We had been both

* One notable exception is Brian K. Vaughan's comic book *Y: The Last Man*, in which all the women survive a biological catastrophe and the hero is specifically the last *man*.

thrown companionless – he on the shore of a desolate island: I on that of a desolate world . . . Yet he was far happier than I: for he could hope, nor hope in vain – the destined vessel at last arrived, to bear him to countrymen and kindred, where the events of his solitude became a fire-side tale. To none could I ever relate the story of my adversity, no hope had I.'

The plight of the last man is a chewy storytelling challenge. Unless, like Mary Shelley, one starts with a bustling world and whittles it down to one man, where can the narrative go? In two novels from 1901, M. P. Shiel's *The Purple Cloud* and A. Lincoln Green's *The End of an Epoch*, the last man must eventually meet the last woman. Two 1950s movies about the Bomb used a quintet (*Five*) or a trio (*The World, the Flesh and the Devil*, inspired by *The Purple Cloud*) of survivors to act out the social tensions and prejudices of the old world. But one person? One is hard. The book that really made the last man a going concern in popular fiction was Richard Matheson's hugely influential 1954 novel *I Am Legend*. Raised as a Christian Scientist, Matheson was a war veteran who went on to write episodes for *The Twilight Zone* and *Star Trek*, adapt Edgar Allan Poe for the screen and produce several stories that were turned into movies, including *Duel* and *The Incredible Shrinking Man*. Matheson's heroes were invariably alone. 'I feel hollow,' he told his son Chris shortly before his death in 2013. 'I've never been close to anyone in my life. I've never understood other people's feelings.'

I Am Legend begins at the end, so to speak. When we meet Robert Neville, he is already 'the only one left in the world. At least in as much of the world as he could ever hope to know.' Matheson's ingenious premise brings together Mary Shelley's plague and John Polidori's vampires: a bacterial infection has turned humans into nocturnal bloodsuckers and only Neville is immune. Beneath the business of the day – secure food, develop antidote, kill vampires – is a terrible loneliness. He can go a year without hearing his own voice and be reduced to tears by the unexpected companionship of a dog (Lionel Verney also finds a dog, the last man's best friend). Passing through depression and alcoholism, Neville becomes a machine for survival and revenge until he discovers that there is a new breed of self-medicating vampire with the capacity to rebuild society. To these 'new people of the earth', the last man is as strange and threatening as Dracula or Frankenstein's creature were to his kind. *He* is the monster, and he needs to go.

Charlton Heston read *I Am Legend* on a long flight in 1969 and saw a movie in this 'universal fantasy that seems to have invaded everyone's imagination and launched a thousand speculations: What would you do if you were the last man on earth? It's the dark side of the Genesis story of the creation of Adam, the first man – the end instead of the beginning.' He soon discovered that there had already been a movie version, 1964's low-budget *The Last Man on Earth*, starring Vincent Price, but it was glum and inert. Heston thought he could do better so he took the idea to producer Walter Seltzer, who gave it a new, Revelation-derived title. 'I know, *The Last Man* is a good title, too, but *The Omega Man* is sexier,' Heston reasoned.

Seltzer's tonally chaotic 1971 movie may muddle the story by introducing other survivors but it builds on the notion that Neville is the shameful residue of a failed race. A bacteriological weapon unleashed by China during a nuclear war has produced ghost-faced nocturnal mutants, some of whom have formed a monastic fraternity dedicated to a world without machinery. As a military scientist, albeit one who concocts antidotes rather than infections, Heston's Colonel Richard Neville represents to them the elites who brought about 'the Punishment'. The continued existence of this 'creature of the wheel, that lord of the infernal engines,' is an insult to the mutants, who attempt to burn him on a symbolic pyre of books and gadgets. 'We mean to cancel the world you civilized people made,' says their leader, Matthias. 'We will simply erase history from the time that machinery and weapons threatened more than they offered. When you die, the last living reminder of hell will be gone.' While Neville disagrees on the question of whether he should be burned to death, he has a certain sympathy with their hatred of technology. Later, he tells a young man who appears ill-equipped to survive anything more taxing than a rock festival of his plan to flee the city to 'some place nobody ever bothered with. A river nobody ever dammed, a mountain nobody ever built any bloody freeways to, where everything we do will be the first time it ever happened.' It is very 1971.

The most memorable sequence in *The Omega Man* is the first: Neville cruises through a stop light in his cherry-red convertible, plays smooth jazz on his eight-track and enjoys a spot of light machine-gunning, then returns home to drink scotch in a well-appointed bachelor pad which looks like something from an advertisement in *Playboy.* Neville does what Heston figured he would do in that situation: decorate his digs with oil paintings looted from the LA County Museum and talk to himself a lot. The opening sequence characterizes the deserted city as a playground for the ultimate single man, as does the scene in the 2007 version of *I Am Legend* in which Will Smith's Neville thwacks golf balls from the tail-fin of a fighter jet on an otherwise empty aircraft carrier. Screenwriter Akiva Goldsman shrewdly noted that his movie, like all last-man stories, is 'bouncing back and forth between an *Armageddon* movie and a *Cast Away* movie'. Neville's war with the infected 'Darkseekers' is far less captivating than the establishing scenes where he and his dog drive through a gently unwinding New York City. Three years after the pandemic, it looks almost idyllic. Flocks of birds patrol the urban canyons while herds of deer weave through the cars that rust on the cracked and shrubby tarmac.

This, perhaps, is what we really want from these stories: not the mission, the threat, the three-act structure, but the purity of that eerie, essential absence. It is brilliantly achieved in the opening third of the 1985 New Zealand movie *The Quiet Earth*, Geoff Murphy's loose remake of *The World, the Flesh and the Devil.* Scientist Zac Hobson (Bruno Lawrence) wakes up one morning to find that the secret international project he has been working on appears to have vaporized almost all living creatures in an instant. The first half-hour of *The Quiet Earth* is perhaps the quintessential example of the five phases of last-manhood.

Phase one: confusion. Hobson wanders dazedly through the empty city. Where is everybody? He paints his phone number and address on a billboard with the question, 'Am I the only person left on earth?'

Phase two: freedom. Hobson moves into a grandiose mansion, raids a shopping mall and steals a train. The world has become a libertarian's dream, with plenty of everything except people.

Phase three: mania. Dressed as a thrift-store Caesar, Hobson addresses an audience of celebrity cut-outs from the mansion's balcony and tearfully proclaims himself 'president of this quiet earth'. Maddened by guilt, he then shotguns an effigy of Jesus on the cross and promotes himself to God.

Phase four: despair. The sight of an empty baby carriage causes Hobson to snap and insert a shotgun barrel into his mouth.

Phase five: acceptance. Hobson chooses a saner house and wardrobe and begins to sow a garden. Life goes on.

At this point, another survivor, Joanne, pops up and the movie takes a different path. Like most last-man stories, *The Quiet Earth* cannot bear to focus on one person for long. Narrative momentum demands both company and an explanation, yet these stories are always most emotionally interesting in the opening stretches, when they confront the unravelling effects of absolute freedom and absolute solitude. Will Smith compared *I Am Legend* to the Book of Job: 'You take a man, take everything from him, and can he find a reason to continue? Can he find the hope or desire to excel and advance in life? Or does the death of everything around him create imminent death for himself?' What is left of you without other people to see your face and say your name? Is the last man something less than a man?

The science fiction writer Walter M. Miller Jr has compared post-apocalyptic survivors to 'the sighing shades in Virgil's Hades and Dante's Hell', tortured by the memory of all that they have lost: 'Survivors don't really live in such a world; they haunt it.' Is it a blessing or a curse to be granted survival when 'a whole world of noisy, brawling, wonderful human beings', as Joanne puts it in *The Quiet Earth*, is gone? In *The Poison Belt*, Arthur Conan Doyle's peculiar 1913 novella about a toxic cloud that appears to spell the end of humanity, Professor Challenger argues that universal doom would not be the worst option: 'Indeed, I could sympathize with the person who took the view that the horror lay in the idea of surviving when all that is learned, famous, and exalted had passed away.'

What gives somebody a reason to wake up tomorrow? Perhaps they are searching for a cure, like Neville, or absolution, like Hobson. Add a last woman and suddenly there is the possibility of repopulating the planet. The Biblical echoes are rarely subtle. In Alfred Noyes's 1940 novel *The Last Man*, Mark Adams, the only English survivor of a heart-halting superweapon, must find his Evelyn. The following year, Alfred Bester fired back with 'Adam and No Eve' (the last man throws himself into the sea and lets evolution do the rest) because he had 'about had it with the Adam and Eve device in science fiction'. In a review of *Five*, the film critic Robert Hatch argued that the Bomb had made this trope contemptible: 'What we fear from the next war is famine and disease and bestiality; tyranny and the loss of whatever human dignity we have inherited from past generations. To suppose that the atom will bring quick death for the millions and a bright, clean world for a bright, clean boy and girl to repopulate is to tell a fairy story to the soft-minded.' But being left with sole responsibility for the future of the human race is no fairy story. For the last man, suicide means omnicide; for the last couple, failure to procreate adds up to the same thing. In his macabre last-man song 'Talkin' World War III Blues', Bob Dylan dreams about asking the last woman to play Adam and Eve, only for her to reply that he's crazy: look what happened last time. Conversely, Ray Bradbury's caustic 1949 story 'The Silent Towns' asks what if the last man simply couldn't stand the last woman and his duty to the species was no match for intense irritation? The only male human settler on Mars chooses solitude (for himself) and extinction (for humanity).

As Thomas Hood realized back in 1826, the last man becomes funny if he is petty and vain and doesn't particularly like people. In 1952, the poet Ronald Duncan parodied Alfred Noyes in his novella *The Last Adam.* The narrator, also called Ronald Duncan, is a pompous, trivial farmer with poetic aspirations. He awakes from an anaesthetic to discover that everybody else has been asphyxiated by a hydrogen bomb which has temporarily sucked all the oxygen out of the atmosphere: 'My next reaction was one of sheer, predatory greed. If I were the only man alive, then all the earth was mine. I could help myself to anything I fancied.' Off he goes to steal a Rolls-Royce, rewrite his own obituary, furnish his home with Old Masters and gorge himself at Claridge's Hotel: 'Death makes so little difference there.' After travelling to Italy, he finally meets a bright and beautiful young female survivor. It is too late though; he has become hooked on me-time. When she tries to take him to bed ('Obviously we have a duty to the race'), like Bradbury's protagonist, he walks away.

Sixty years later, writers Phil Lord and Christopher Miller began contemplating a TV show that would mine the rich seam of comedy that they saw buried in *I Am Legend*, the only notable parody to date being the 1996 *Simpsons* story 'The HΩmega Man'. Together with actor Will Forte, Lord and Miller created a sitcom called *The Last Man on Earth*. It is 2020, one year after an exterminating pandemic, and an awkward schlub called Phil Miller (Forte) is criss-crossing America with a megaphone in a fruitless search for other survivors. He writes 'Alive in Tucson' on billboards so that he can be found, just as the last men in *I Am Legend* and *The Quiet Earth* provide rendezvous points in recorded radio broadcasts and Shelley's Lionel paints a message in every town he passes through: 'Verney, the last of the race of Englishmen, had taken up his abode in Rome. Friend, come! I wait for thee!' The urge to make contact is clearly fundamental.

Returning to Tucson, Phil moves into a garish mansion which he furnishes with the spoils from his travels: not just the by-now-obligatory oil paintings but Academy Awards, the Oval Office rug and a dinosaur skull. Whereas Will Smith plays golf on an aircraft carrier, Phil rolls bowling balls into aquariums in a parking lot and plays tennis indoors wearing only his underpants. Five months later, he's a total slob, slumped in a paddling pool filled with margarita mix and wiping his mouth on the Constitution. His 'friends' are balls with faces drawn on them. Although the title is a red herring (the whole arc of the show depends on Phil *not* being the last man on Earth), the first episode is the most potent: being alone drives you insane. 'In a weird way it felt like we were simultaneously doing the comedic version, but also the most honest version,' Lord remarked. With the notable exceptions of Mary Shelley and Richard Matheson, almost every last-man story retreats from the premise sooner or later. It seems that we find it easy to imagine the end of the world but not going through it alone.

In 1840, Mary Shelley passed through Geneva again for the first time since the summer of 1816, and lodged across the lake from Villa Diodati. 'Was I the same person that lived there, the companion of the dead?' she reflected. 'For all were gone . . . not one hope, then in fair bud, had opened into maturity; storm, and blight, and death, had passed over, and destroyed all.'

PART TWO
IMPACT

CHAPTER 3

Falling Stars

What prodigious Mischief and Ruin might such
a Ball of Confusion bring upon our sinful Globe,
if the Great GOD order its Approach unto us

Cotton Mather, *The Christian Philosopher* (1721)

The first person to destroy the world in a manner that seemed, at the time, to be scientifically plausible was Edgar Allan Poe. The murder weapon was a comet.

The 1830s was a decade of celestial apparitions. Halley's Comet completed its seventy-six-year orbit in 1835. Encke's Comet, which comes round every three years or so, caused an extraordinary meteor storm over the United States in 1833. A year earlier, Biela's Comet caused so much apprehension that the French astronomer François Arago reassured fretful readers that the comet would not, as some newspapers suggested, 'impinge upon the earth and break it to pieces'. When Biela's Comet reappeared in 1839, Poe was thirty, settling into his new role as assistant editor of *Burton's Gentleman's Magazine* after the publication of his first novel, *The Narrative of Arthur Gordon Pym of Nantucket.* He read a short story called 'The Comet' by S. Austin Jr, which described the drama and debate surrounding the approach of a giant comet which whips up the tides and brings about a second Deluge. Poe was interested in both comets and Revelation and thought that Austin had it all wrong. First, a comet was not substantial enough to affect the tides. More significantly, the Bible promised that fire, not flood, would consume the world next time. Poe preferred Reverend Thomas Dick's theory that the passage of the comet's tail would remove the nitrogen from the atmosphere and cause a 'universal conflagration'.

Poe's response to Austin's tale was a story published in *Burton's* in December 1839 with the misleadingly dry title 'The Conversation of Eiros and Charmion'. In his story, the comet's tail first drains the earth's nitrogen, throwing its inhabitants into a hyperoxygenated frenzy, before the nucleus hits: 'A combustion irresistible, all-devouring, omni-prevalent, immediate; – the entire fulfillment, in all their minute and terrible details, of the fiery and horror-inspiring denunciations of the prophecies of the Holy Book . . . Thus ended all.' When Poe republished his story to capitalize on excitement around the Great Comet of 1843, he gave it a much more alluring title, 'The Destruction of the World', and a tantalizing preface: 'From the celestial visitant now present, we have, of course, nothing to fear . . . But it came unheralded, and to-morrow its counterpart, or some wonder even more startling, *may* make its appearance.' Of course, Poe was as mistaken about the nature and consequences of a comet as Austin had been, but in his defence, nobody at that time understood what comets were.

Let us call the genre that Poe pioneered 'impact fiction' because there is no consistency about the object making the impact. It could be a comet, an asteroid or a meteor; a planet, a star or the Moon. The only unifying factor is that it is closing time for Earth. Impact fiction has been with us for almost two hundred years but, like a comet, it tends to disappear for decades before looping back around.

Both comets and asteroids are stray bits of rubble left over from the formation of the solar system – the residue of failed planets. A comet is a lump of ice, rock, dust and gas, travelling round the Sun in an elliptical orbit. Short-period comets such as Halley's Comet, reach the outermost point of their orbit in the Kuiper Belt, near Pluto, while long-period comets, which take thousands or millions of years to return, hail from the much more distant Oort Cloud, at the very edge of the solar system. In the 1950s, the American astronomer Fred Whipple described them as 'dirty snowballs', although the first probe to study Halley's Comet, in 1986, found that 'icy dirtballs' would be more accurate. When comets pass the Sun, some of the ice melts and they shed a trail of gas and debris which can be millions of kilometres long: the Greek word *kometa* means long-haired. One Edwardian writer poetically described comets as 'practically *bleeding to death.* Their tails are their death-signs . . . like the blood-trail of a wounded animal.'

An asteroid (meaning *star-like*) is a chunk of rock and minerals which usually originates from the belt between Jupiter and Mars: no ice, no tail and a more predictable orbit. Small fragments of comets and asteroids are called meteoroids. If a meteoroid enters Earth's atmosphere, it sheds a trail of burning particles and becomes a meteor, or shooting star. If it reaches the surface without being vaporized, it becomes a meteorite, the largest known example of which, the Hoba meteorite, is less than 3 metres wide. In fiction, these terms can be bewilderingly interchangeable – the 8-kilometre-wide object in the 1979 movie *Meteor* is an asteroid – but even in astronomy the distinction between a small asteroid and a large meteoroid is blurred. NASA defines a meteoroid as an object less than 1 metre across; therefore most meteorites are actually asteroid fragments. For this reason, astronomers like to use the catch-all terms 'bolide' and 'impactor'. NASA places all potentially dangerous bodies within 200 million kilometres of Earth under the umbrella of Near-Earth Objects (NEOs).

If one were to strike Earth, the damage would be extraordinary. An impactor with a diameter of 100 metres could destroy a city; one five times larger could wipe out a country; and one exceeding 1 kilometre would kill a significant proportion of the earth's inhabitants. Reassuringly, scientists currently put the risk of an extinction-level asteroid hitting Earth in any given year at less than one in fifteen billion. The concussion of a long-period comet would be far more destructive, due to its velocity, but such a collision is even less likely. The imaginative power of the comet, however, is clearly immune to statistical probability. As the only existential risk that has haunted us for centuries – sudden, spectacular, unrelated to human activity – it is an obvious metaphor for God's judgement, or Fate itself. 'Whatever moves in the heaven in an unusual way is certainly a sign of God's wrath,' said Martin Luther in the early sixteenth century. A century later, the Puritan clergyman Increase Mather regarded a comet as a 'warning piece' from God 'before his Murdering pieces go off' – a planetary shot across the bows.

While the first (and largest) asteroid, Ceres, wasn't identified until 1801, comets were named by Greek philosophers in around 500 BC and have been widely seen as portents of doom ever since. Pliny the Elder described the comet as 'a terrifying star and not easily expiated'. Among other things, comets were thought to bring plague, crop failure, earthquakes and floods, and to herald the overthrow of kings. 'When beggars die, there are no comets seen,' says Calpurnia in Shakespeare's *Julius Caesar*. 'The heavens themselves blaze forth the death of princes.' Comets were believed to have foretold the murders of Caesar and Augustus, the defeat of Antony and Cleopatra, the sacking of Jerusalem, and the deaths of Vespasian and Claudius. With so many comets and so many deaths, pattern bias ran amok.

Comets were also associated with military defeats. In 1066, Halley's Comet allegedly foretold the death of King Harold II in the Battle of Hastings, and therefore appeared in the Bayeux Tapestry. When it returned in 1456, during the Ottoman assault on Europe, Pope Callixtus III prayed, 'Lord save us from the Devil, the Turk and the comet.' Halley's Comet has also been associated with the Jewish revolt of 66 AD, the defeat of Attila the Hun at the Battle of Châlons in 451, and Genghis Khan's invasion of Europe in 1222. Interpreting the significance of comets required considering several factors: shape, size, colour, motion, direction, duration and regularity. Some believed that the New Testament was bookended by comets: the Star of Bethlehem and the star called Wormwood in Revelation: 'there fell a great star from heaven, burning as it were a lamp.' Comets appear in apocalyptic woodcuts by Albrecht Dürer and Matthias Gerung. In *Sacred Theory of the Earth*, Thomas Burnet predicted that comets would be a 'prelude to this last and most Tragical Scene of the Sublunary World'.

Aristotle thought that comets were clouds of burning vapour exhaled by the planets, but the Danish astronomer Tycho Brahe determined by studying the comet of 1577 that they were in fact wandering celestial bodies. Working in collaboration with Isaac Newton, the English astronomer Edmond Halley established their periodicity, correctly predicting that the comet that he had observed in 1682 would return in 1758. Halley hoped that comets would no longer be a 'source of dread', as did the British government, because comet lore was implicated in the millenarian mania that had contributed to the English Civil Wars and still appeared in apocalyptic pamphlets. But according to Sara Schechner, a historian of comet lore, 'the vulgar superstitions Halley kicked out his front door, he smuggled in his back door. In his work, comets were transformed from divine signs of calamitous local events into natural causes of global events.'

Though Halley was regarded as a free-thinking heretic by religious conservatives, he was sufficiently orthodox to want to explain the Deluge, suggesting that it might have been caused by 'the casuall Choc of some transient body, such as a Comet or the like', which suddenly altered the axis and orbit of Earth. This led him to the theory that a series of comets had produced a series of catastrophes, each killing everything on Earth but sowing the seeds of a new race: each time, the planet became 'new made out of the Ruins of an old World'. Therefore, he concluded, it would happen again one day. As he put it in the posthumously published *Astronomical Tables*, 'may the great good GOD avert a shock or contact of such great Bodies moving with such forces . . . lest this most beautiful order of things be intirely destroyed and reduced into its antient chaos.'

Censured by the Royal Society for his Deluge theory, Halley tended to downplay his proto-catastrophism. Newton also kept quiet his own view that comet impacts cyclically cleansed the world, and that the comet of 1680 would eventually fall into the Sun, increasing its heat and setting the whole world on fire. William Whiston, Newton's excitable successor as professor of mathematics at Cambridge, who entertained coffeehouse crowds with his combination of comet science, Biblical exegesis and eschatology, was not nearly so restrained: he precisely dated the Deluge-triggering comet to 11 a.m. on 28 November 2349 BC. He claimed that comets had formed the earth, would ignite the final conflagration, and were responsible for earthquakes, volcanoes and plagues in the meantime. In 1736, he confidently claimed that a comet would set fire to the world on 16 October, forcing an official denial from the archbishop of Canterbury. Already a controversial figure, Whiston died a laughingstock and a pariah. Comet catastrophism therefore became a popular target for satirists. In Jonathan Swift's *Gulliver's Travels*, the citizens of Laputa are unable to enjoy life because they are obsessed with existential risk and believe that a comet, 'which they have calculated for one and thirty years hence, will probably destroy us'.

In another story, Swift made Whiston himself the cause of mass agitation by falsely predicting a doomsday comet.

Thus a hard nucleus of science emitted a long tail of superstition and astronomers became legitimized prophets. 'The utter danger, that a comet would accomplish the end of the whole earth, was not removed,' observed Geoffrey Dennis in *The End of the World*, 'but by honest collision, not magic.' When François Arago tried to debunk the panic that attended the appearance of Biela's Comet in 1832, he wanted to drain comets of their apocalyptic associations altogether, using meteorological records to disprove their alleged effects on the weather and the hazard of their tails. He put the odds of a comet striking the earth at 281 million to one.

Still, the mistaken belief that comets were gaseous rather than solid led many, including Poe, to perceive them as essentially poison gas. The comet re-entered fiction's orbit in 1893, shortly before an Austrian astronomer called Rudolf Falb predicted that the tail of Biela's Comet would suffocate humanity in the early hours of 13 November 1899, unaware that the comet had in fact disintegrated decades earlier. According to *Pearson's Magazine*, his claim 'actually caused no little dismay among the poorer classes of the Continental peasantry, though in England and America little alarm was felt. Needless to state, the 13th of November came and went without the occurrence of any untoward event.' But what a perfect conclusion to the doom-obsessed 1890s that would have been. The critic George Steiner has described the period as 'menacingly overripe . . . fascinated by the prospect of a purging fire'.

In the late nineteenth century, expectations of disaster and decline were so *du jour* that the French had to invent a term: *fin de siècle.* It originally described this fashionable pessimism rather than a period of time. 'I wish it were *fin du globe*,' sighs Oscar Wilde's Dorian Gray. 'Life is a great disappointment.' In his popular 1892–3 polemic *Entartung* (*Degeneration*) Max Nordau sneered at the 'extreme silliness' of relating the mood to the date but nevertheless agreed that doom was in the air: 'The disposition of the times is curiously confused, a compound of feverish restlessness and blunted discouragement, of fearful presage and hang-dog renunciation. The prevalent feeling is that of imminent perdition and extinction.' Yet all decades are double-edged and the 1890s more than most. All the evidence of decadence and gloom was matched, if not exceeded, by proof of tremendous excitement about the future, from the utopian fantasies of socialists and feminists to ordinary people thrilled by the advent of automobiles, radio, cinema and airships. Optimism and pessimism fed one another in a cycle of action and reaction. W. B. Yeats, born in 1865, recalled that when he was a young contrarian, 'everybody talked about progress, and rebellion against my elders took the form of aversion to that myth. I took satisfaction in certain public disasters, felt a sort of ecstasy at the contemplation of ruin.'

Fear and anticipation mingled in the pages of popular magazines. The historian W. Warren Wagar has maintained that 'between 1890 and 1914 alone, almost every sort of world's end story that one finds in later years was written, published, and accepted by a wide reading public.' In addition to war, terrorism, revolution and superweapons, 'floods, volcanic eruptions, plagues, epochs of ice, colliding comets, exploding or cooling suns, and alien invaders laid waste to the world.' *Pearson's* monthly magazine and its weekly sister periodical had an especially lively hunger for such stories. Readers of the July 1900 issue could turn from Hugh Owen's 'The Poison Cloud', a short story about a deathly smog which destroys London, to Herbert C. Fyfe's 'How Will the World End?', an exhaustive round-up of the latest terminal possibilities.

One writer claimed that the centre of the earth consisted of oil and that its extraction would cause the planet's crust to cave in. 'Truly, a dire disaster,' Fyfe decided, 'but one which we cannot take quite seriously.' The inventor Nikola Tesla believed that the ignition of the atmosphere by lightning had caused 'periodical cessations of organic life on the globe' and suggested that man-made electricity might one day do likewise. There were also proposals that changes to the climate 'might flood the world with death-dealing micro-organisms' or, conversely, breed monstrous mutations; Warwick Goble, the illustrator of H. G. Wells's *The War of the Worlds*, depicted seaside holidaymakers fleeing the claws of a giant lobster. M. X. Stanier, a Belgian geologist, predicted that the earth would absorb too much water as its core cooled, and humanity would die of thirst. Lord Kelvin, the eminent physicist who formulated the second law of thermodynamics, claimed that within three hundred years the earth's oxygen supplies would be exhausted by the burning of coal. He recommended growing more plants to absorb carbon dioxide and generating electricity from 'the tides, the ceaseless movement of the waves, waterfalls, solar energy, the wind . . .'

Despite its global power and influence, Britain was suffering from a loss of confidence in its economic prospects and social cohesion. The flipside of imperial hubris was a popular vogue for visions of nemesis. The trend for future-war stories, which began with army officer George Tomkyns Chesney's *The Battle of Dorking* in 1871 and lasted for over forty years, was semi-apocalyptic in its propagandistic insistence on Britain's proximity to disaster if it did not strengthen its military. 'London, the all-powerful metropolis, which had egotistically considered herself the impregnable Citadel of the World, fell to pieces and was consumed,' wrote William Le Queux in his 1894 bestseller *The Great War in England in 1897*. As Michael Moorcock wrote in his anthology of late-Victorian Armageddons, the message was always the same: 'Wake up – or perish!'

One pathbreaking novel, 1885's *After London; or, Wild England* by Richard Jefferies, boldly omitted the standard thrill ride of war and mayhem and cut straight to the aftermath, making it arguably the first true *post*-apocalypse. A farmer's son from Wiltshire, Jefferies became a journalist and moved to the south-western fringe of London, whose population had quintupled to nearly five million since the dawn of the century. How much more of his beloved countryside, Jefferies wondered, would the greedy metropolis devour? In 1883, he wrote in his notebook that 'we must begin again like the Caveman. No knowledge at present of use since it does not help. We must destroy the idea of our knowing anything.'

In *After London*, an archaeologist in the distant future describes how a mysterious catastrophe wiped out the civilization of the 'ancients'. The remnant, reduced to a primitive, semi-medieval state, shares with wild animals a land that is almost entirely overgrown. London, 'this marvellous city, of which such legends are related', is now a toxic swamp of pollutants and rotted corpses because the Thames has silted up and the capital of the empire has drowned in its own poison, producing a yellow mist which no living creature can breathe for long. (It is difficult, now, not to think of radiation.) The narrator considers some scientific explanations for the humbling of London but sounds most like Jefferies himself when he cites theologians who argue that 'the wickedness of those times surpassed understanding, and that a change and sweeping away of the human evil that had accumulated was necessary, and was effected by supernatural means'.

The socialist and artist William Morris drew on *After London* for his vision of an idyllic, post-urban, communist society in his 1890 novel *News from Nowhere.* The account of a transitional period of 'ruin, misery, despair' makes Morris's seemingly placid utopia a post-apocalyptic state, following the downfall of London, 'the modern Babylon of civilization'. 'I have no more faith than a grain of mustard seed in the future history of "civilization", which I know now is doomed to destruction, probably before very long: what a joy it is to think of!' Morris wrote in a letter. 'And how often it consoles me to think of barbarism once more flooding the world, and real feelings and passions, however rudimentary, taking the place of our wretched hypocrisies.' Another fan of *After London* was the American writer Van Tassel Sutphen, whose 1906 novel *The Doomsman* might have been called *After New York.* When Sutphen was writing, New York City was expanding in all directions: out, up, down. The twenty-two-storey Flatiron Building had been completed in 1902 and the subway system in 1904. No sooner had these monuments to progress been erected than Sutphen was imagining them, a century later, in ruins: a 'city of Doom!'

Writers of these tales of decadence and destruction took almost as much pleasure in carnage as John of Patmos, fantasizing about the downfall of the very society that had made them successful and comfortable. Many betrayed a murderous paranoia about the working class and the racial other, and a eugenic enthusiasm for renovating the race. Perhaps the most violent and macabre was Ignatius L. Donnelly's 1890 novel *Caesar's Column: A Story of the Twentieth Century*, in which a revolution turns New York into first an abattoir and then a funeral pyre. 'It was but a question of time,' says the revolutionary Maximilian Petion. 'The breaking-strain on humanity was too great . . . The crash was inevitable. It may be God's way of wiping off the blackboard. It may be that the ancient legends of the destruction of our race by flood and fire are but dim remembrances of events like that which is now happening.' The *fin-de-siècle* appetite for destruction could not be sated by terrestrial terrors alone. When Donnelly was not waist-deep in the fetid phobias of his day, he was thinking about the past and future of comets.

Comets, wrote Donnelly in his 1883 book *Ragnarok: The Age of Fire and Gravel*, are 'a puzzle and a fear; they are erratic, unusual, anarchical, monstrous – something let loose, like a tiger of the heavens, athwart an orderly, peaceful, and harmonious world. They may be impalpable and harmless attenuations of gas, or they may be loaded with death and ruin; but in any event man can not contemplate them without terror.'

Donnelly's unwavering belief in his own polymathic genius made him, in the words of one writer, 'the greatest failure who ever lived'. A lawyer by trade and a long-serving Minnesota politician, he was an outsized character whose resumé also included ardent abolitionism, a failed utopian community, authorship of the Populist Party's founding manifesto, one vice-presidential bid, and three pseudo-science bestsellers which earned him the appellation 'Prince of Cranks'. He was a fanciful catastrophist who read the history of the world as an endless cycle of creation and destruction. His 1882 treatise, *Atlantis: The Antediluvian World*, argued that this fabulous civilization had been erased by the great Deluge. The following year, *Ragnarok* opened with a line from Georges Cuvier, speculating that a vestige of humankind had survived the 'great revolutions of the earth' and 'repeopled the world'. Unable to accept that the Tertiary period ended with an ice age alone, Donnelly believed that this climatic paradise had been abruptly foreclosed by 'the most awful convulsion and catastrophe that has ever fallen upon the globe' – a comet – and sought proof in the myths of everyone from the Jews and Zoroastrians to the Aztecs and the Norse people. Donnelly translated *Ragnarök* as 'the rain of dust and ashes' and interpreted the Fenris-wolf, child of Loki, as a comet.* Encountering so many culturally and geographically diverse myths of destruction and

* Donnelly lauded Byron's 'Darkness' as an accurate description of what 'the legends of mankind tell us actually came to pass . . . How graphic, how dramatic, how realistic is this picture! And how true!'

rebirth – every falling star, every hard rain, every darkness at noon – Donnelly concluded that the reader 'must concede that the earth, since man inhabited it, encountered a comet. No other cause or event could produce such a series of gigantic consequences as is here narrated.' And where did the remnants of humanity regroup and flourish in the twenty thousand years between that event and the Deluge? Atlantis, of course.

To be fair, Donnelly was not wrong to believe that a cataclysmic concussion had once changed the world, but he took the theory in a crackpot direction. Throughout most of the nineteenth and twentieth centuries, the uniformitarian theory of the history of the earth, espoused by Charles Lyell and Charles Darwin, had thoroughly trounced Cuvier's catastrophism, and belief in violent geological transformations had become akin to superstition. 'Nature does not proceed by sudden leaps,' wrote the astronomer Camille Flammarion, 'and geologists do not believe in such revolutions or cataclysms; for they have learned that in the natural world everything is subject to a slow process of evolution.'

Flammarion provided a more respectable survey of the science and mythology of comets in his 1893 book *La Fin du Monde*, translated into English as *Omega: The Last Days of the World.* Rather than telling a story, he stages a twenty-fifth-century symposium where various experts debate what exactly an impending comet will do to them: 'Expectation and uncertainty are often more terrible than the catastrophe itself . . . One was to die, without doubt, but how? By the sudden shock of collision, crushed to death? By fire, the conflagration of the world? By suffocation, the poisoning of the atmosphere? What torture awaited humanity?' One astronomer, however, predicts that the comet's tail will be no more pernicious than influenza and that most of the crumbling nucleus will land harmlessly in the sea: 'Worlds die of old age, not by accident.' He is proved correct. Flammarion uses the comet as merely 'the pretext for the discussion of every possible phase of this great and important subject – the end of the world'. As his experts argue about flood versus drought and fire versus ice, *La Fin du Monde* becomes a panoramic study of existential risk.

Flammarion nevertheless sent the comet crashing back into fiction, starting with George Griffith's 1894 *Pearson's* serial *The Syren of the*

Skies, published in book form as *Olga Romanoff*. Griffith was the first star of British science fiction, with a killer instinct for what editors and readers craved. His speedy sequel to the hit 1893 serial *The Angel of the Revolution: A Tale of the Coming Terror* resembled an anthology of topics that enthralled readers in the 1890s: airships, utopias, future wars, eugenics and comets. Refusing to accept that the world that she has conquered is doomed, the warrior-queen Olga Romanoff becomes a comet denier. 'You are not the first who have prophesied the end of the world by such means, nor will you be the last to be discredited by the event,' she tells our heroes, Alan and Alma. 'It is no idle tale,' replies Alma, 'it is not even a prophecy, it is a mathematical certainty, and if you understood you would believe.' Only after the comet has obliviated most of the human race does Olga see 'the utter insignificance and contemptibility of the human strife which had been superseded and silenced by this majestic assault of the primal forces of Nature'.

Thirteen years later, Griffith circled back to the doomsday comet to capitalize on the imminent return of Halley's Comet in *The World Peril of 1910*, but by then he had been utterly usurped as the UK's most successful writer of science fiction by the grandmaster of the genre: H. G. Wells.

Herbert George Wells (Bertie to his intimates) hit the fiction scene like, well, a comet. He truly believed that his writing could change the world and succeeded, at least, in changing how people *saw* the world. 'It's hard to write a science fiction story without picking out a theme which H. G. Wells dealt with because he dealt with them all,' Kurt Vonnegut once said. Born in 1866, Wells grew up in humble circumstances in Bromley, Kent, but escaped his modest destiny by winning a scholarship to London's Normal School of Science in 1884, thus beginning 'the most exciting years in my life'. Studying under the evolutionary biologist Thomas Huxley changed his entire conception of time and the universe, he recalled:

> Like most people of my generation, I was launched into life with millennial assumptions . . . there would be trumpets and shoutings and celestial phenomena, a battle of Armageddon and the

> Judgment . . . I was a student of biology before I realized that this, my finite and conclusive End, at least in the material and chronological form, had somehow vanished from the scheme of things. In the place of it had come a blackness and a vagueness about the endless vistas of years ahead, that was tremendous – that terrified . . . The phase that followed the first helpless stare of the mind was a wild effort to express one's sudden apprehension of unlimited possibility.

The paradox of the 1890s incarnate, Wells was to publish numerous fictional utopias and non-fiction manifestos for a better world, yet he began his career with so many catastrophes that *The Spectator* dubbed him 'a past-master in the conduct of the *debacle*, an expert in Armageddons'. 'It is part of the excessive egotism of the human animal that the bare idea of its extinction seems incredible to it,' Wells wrote in his 1894 essay 'The Extinction of Man'. '"*A world without us!*" it says.' Because 'things have been easy for mankind as a whole for a generation or so,' this complacency about the future was a formidable foe: 'If some poor story-writing man ventures to figure this sober probability in a tale, not a reviewer in London but will tell him his theme is the utterly impossible. And, when the thing happens, one may doubt if even then one will get the recognition one deserves.'

Wells immediately proved himself wrong with his first popular success, *The Time Machine*, in which his protagonist's chrononautical adventures extend to a tour of the end of the world as the author's passion for science merges with echoes of his childhood faith. After witnessing the ruinous bifurcated evolution of *Homo sapiens* into the weak, dissolute Eloi and the barbaric Morlocks who feed on them, the time traveller lands on a stony beach, carpeted with slimy, green lichen and infested with monstrous crab-like creatures. (As confluences of land, sea and sky, beaches handily represent the convergence of past, present and future, or of life and death; they function as purgatorial spaces in numerous end-of-the-world stories.) The Sun is a dull, red blob, sinking the world into a permanent twilight 'only broken now and then when a comet glared across the darkling sky'. Humanity is clearly long over: 'I cannot convey the abominable desolation that hung over the world.' The time traveller speeds forward thousands, then millions, of years to the earth's last gasp

('All the sounds of man, the bleating of sheep, the cries of birds, the hum of insects, the stir that makes the background of our lives – all that was over') before fleeing in horror back to the safety of the 1890s. Long before it was established that Earth would eventually perish from too much solar radiation rather than too little, the theories of evolution and entropy produced a widespread obsession with frozen darkness and monstrous decay. Wells later attributed his hopeless tableau to the 'deliberate pessimism of youth' but future prime minister Arthur Balfour was a middle-aged grandee when he described entropy that same year: 'The energies of our system will decay, the glory of the sun will be dimmed, and the earth, tideless and inert, will no longer tolerate the race which has for a moment disturbed its solitude. Man will go down into the pit, and all his thoughts will perish.'

Wells propelled himself into the vanguard of science fiction with literary qualities that others lacked: an engaging prose style, narrative discipline, an ear for dialogue, a working sense of humour and an understanding of how human beings actually behave. While his competitors presented readers with a cavalcade of outlandish events, Wells had a golden rule: each story would drop a single incredible development – a Martian invasion, genetic experiments, an invisibility compound – into an otherwise familiar, late-Victorian world. 'Mr. Wells has used with great skill the contrast between the commonplaces of our daily life of security and ease and the terror of a calamity beyond all human power to arrest,' approved one critic. Wells's ideal setting was not the distant future but the day after tomorrow. This could happen here – and to you, dear reader.

The War of the Worlds, serialized in *Pearson's Magazine* in 1897, escalated and perfected the future-war genre by replacing foreign armies with Martian war machines. Wells dedicated the novel to his brother Frank, who, during a conversation about the eradication of Indigenous Tasmanians, had suggested that he write about what would happen if England were at the receiving end of genocidal imperial conquest. The Martians, fleeing their exhausted, cooling planet, land in Woking (Wells's home at the time) and proceed to London, 'the greatest city in the world'. The narrator describes the chaotic evacuation of the city as 'the beginning of the rout of civilization, the massacre of mankind'. He meets a curate who has been maddened by seeing Weybridge go the same way as Sodom and Gomorrah ('This must be the beginning of the end. The end! The great and terrible day of the Lord!') and an artilleryman whose vision of the future is thoroughly post-apocalyptic: 'Cities, nations, civilizations, progress – it's all over. That game's up. We're beat.' Even after the Martians have been vanquished by humble bacteria, the narrator cannot walk through London without recalling 'the time when I saw it all bright and clear-cut, hard and silent, under the dawn of that last great day'. It is a haunting, minor-key conclusion. Pedestrians seem to him 'but the ghosts of the past, haunting the streets that I have seen silent and wretched, going to and fro, phantasms in a dead city'.

In the same year, Wells took another shot at Earth in a short story called 'The Star'. Wells always had his antennae up for new modes of extinction so he was excited by the return of the comet in *La Fin du Monde*, a destroyer that was both more efficient than war or Martians and morally neutral. 'The Star' was a blatant rewriting of Flammarion's book but Wells squeezed the dull coal of the Frenchman's non-story until it was diamond-hard. Ogilvy, the astronomer from *The War of the Worlds*, identifies a 'strange wanderer' which resembles 'a great white star'. A mathematician predicts that its proximity will cause 'earthquakes, volcanic outbreaks, cyclones, sea waves, floods, and a steady rise in temperature to I know not what limit'. Mocking laughter gives way to howls of panic. As the survivors resettle in the newly verdant polar regions, Martian astronomers coolly reflect that Earth got off lightly, 'which only shows how small the vastest of human catastrophes may seem, at a distance of a few million miles'. As in *The War of the Worlds*, Wells wants to remind us how small we are; how little our fate matters to the universe at large.

Such astral humility was less popular across the Atlantic. Magazines in New York and Boston did not merely reprint *The War of the Worlds* but rewrote it as *Fighters from Mars* to transplant the action to those cities without Wells's permission. The success of these illicit adaptations spurred New York astronomer and science writer Garrett P. Serviss to write a travesty of a sequel with the self-explanatory title *Edison's Conquest of Mars*: the empire strikes back. In this popular genre, later labelled the 'Edisonade', the infallible foresight and ingenuity of the scientist hero saves America, if not the world, every time. This anti-Frankenstein archetype would become fundamental to disaster fiction, in which the most foolish thing one can possibly do is to ignore a genius's warning.

Wells was both amazed and irritated by American self-confidence. He was visiting New York City for the first time in April 1906 when news broke that an earthquake had destroyed four-fifths of San Francisco, and he was startled by the apocalyptic appetite for interpreting devastation as an opportunity for renovation: 'It does not seem to have affected anyone with a sense of final destruction, with any foreboding of irreparable disaster . . . there is no doubt anywhere that San Francisco can be rebuilt, larger, better, and soon. Just as there would be none at all if all this New York that so obsessed me with its limitless bigness was itself a blazing ruin. I believe these people would more than half like the situation.' Obviously, Wells would have to destroy New York. In 1908's *The War in the Air*, an alliance of German, Chinese and Japanese airships reduces this 'modern Babylon' which had believed itself immune from war to 'ruins and blazing conflagrations and heaped and scattered dead; men, women, and children mixed together as though they had been no more than Moors, or Zulus, or Chinese.' The unstoppable world war reduces civilization everywhere to rubble, with famine and plague rounding out the full complement of horsemen. In a single sentence, Wells outlines the core ingredients of numerous post-apocalyptic stories to come: 'Here there are robbers, here vigilance committees, and here guerrilla bands ruling patches of exhausted territory, strange federations and brotherhoods form and dissolve, and religious fanaticisms begotten of despair gleam in famine-bright eyes. It is a universal dissolution.'

Around the time of the reappearance of Halley's Comet in 1910, the comet again became a popular *deus ex machina* in novels such as H. Percy Blanchard's *After the Cataclysm* and George Allan England's *Beyond the Great Oblivion*, and a real cause for concern. Flammarion worried that cyanogen in the tail of Halley's Comet might 'impregnate the atmosphere and possibly snuff out all life on the planet' while 'terror occasioned by the [comet] has seized hold of a large part of the population of Chicago,' reported *The New York Times*. 'If a large comet approached within measurable distance of the Earth, the doom of our world would be sealed,' wrote E. C. Andrews in *Pearson's*

Magazine. He proposed that a direct collision would dash the world to 'shining, white-hot dust' and that even a near miss would trigger calamitous firestorms and tidal waves. An illustration depicted, in an infernal red, crumbling buildings and screaming crowds.

Neither Andrews nor his readers knew that the largest impact event in recorded history had occurred just eighteen months earlier. On the morning of 30 June 1908, something exploded with unearthly force near the Podkamennaya Tunguska River in eastern Siberia. Eyewitnesses described deafening thumps, tremors and unbearable heat. One said that the 20-kilometre-high fireball, visible 600 kilometres away, 'made even the light of the sun appear dark'. 'All villagers were stricken with panic and took to the streets, women cried, thinking it was the end of the world,' reported the *Sibir* newspaper. The dust from the explosion produced unusual sunsets across Europe and the shockwaves circled the globe twice. Scientists now believe that an impactor at least 50 metres wide, possibly a small asteroid or a chunk of Encke's Comet, exploded 5 to 10 kilometres above the ground with the force of a very large hydrogen bomb. Although around eighty million trees were flattened, the region was so sparsely populated that the human death toll was just three. Had the impactor exploded less than 4,000 kilometres to the west, it would have levelled St Petersburg and changed the course of history.

The spectacle of destruction proved irresistible to the new artform of cinema. The first ever disaster movies were based on Edward Bulwer-Lytton's 1834 novel *The Last Days of Pompeii*, which had itself been coloured by John Martin's *The Destruction of Pompeii and Herculaneum.* Comets, like volcanoes, were sudden and spectacular. The Danish director August Blom made the first attempt to depict an impact on screen in his 1916 movie *The End of the World.* The bluntly named astronomer Professor Wisemann confirms the approach of a comet and makes the mistake of telling his cousin, the caddish mining magnate Frank Stoll, before informing the public, enabling Stoll to make a killing on the stock exchange. The conceit of the film may have been inspired by Halley's Comet but its execution reflected both Europe's revolutionary temper (Stoll dies after an angry mob of workers storms his decadent last-night party) and the horror of the First World War: the fiery chaos of the meteor shower, with smoke cunningly deployed to conceal the primitive special effects, looks like a mortar bombardment while the shattered town into which one survivor emerges resembles any number of towns in Belgium and northern France at the time.

The future war had finally arrived. The poet and soldier Siegfried Sassoon wrote of 'entering once again the veritable gloom and disaster of Armageddon'. The only people who seemed to delight in it were those who *literally* believed in Armageddon, such as the Jehovah's Witnesses, who felt vindicated in their prediction that 1914 would be a fateful year. 'The darker the night gets, the lighter my heart gets,' crowed the evangelist Reuben Torrey as millions died in the mud. For countless families, however, mourning fathers, sons and brothers, the future had been stolen. 'I am so sad for my country, for this great wave of civilization, 2000 years, which is now collapsing, that it is hard to live,' D. H. Lawrence wrote to a friend in 1915. 'So much beauty and pathos of old things passing away and no new things coming.' Thirteen years later, he began *Lady Chatterley's Lover*: 'The cataclysm has happened, we are among the ruins . . .'

The immediate post-war years, further devastated by the Spanish flu pandemic, were a watershed for apocalyptic art. At the end of the Austrian satirist Karl Kraus's unperformably long 1918 anti-war play *The Last Days of Mankind*, the earth is destroyed by Martian meteors to save the universe from its incorrigible lust for war. The Rudolph Valentino war picture, *The Four Horsemen of the Apocalypse*, was the first time that last word had appeared in a movie title. Between 1918 and 1926, poetry produced Robert Frost's 'Fire and Ice', Sara Teasdale's 'There Will Come Soft Rains', W. B. Yeats's 'The Second Coming', T. S. Eliot's 'The Hollow Men' and Archibald MacLeish's 'The End of the World', each one lividly scarred by the war. Molly Bloom's complaint about Mrs Riordan in *Ulysses* suggests that James Joyce, for one, found it all rather oppressive: 'she had too much old chat in her about politics and earthquakes and the end of the world let us have a bit of fun first God help the world if all woman were her sort . . .'

The phrase *World War No. 2* first appeared in 1919, just four months after the armistice, and H. G. Wells coined the more familiar *Second World War* in 1930. 'When will be the next war? is what people are asking, or secretly thinking,' claimed the premillennialist Christabel Pankhurst in 1924. 'For we all know, even if we do not admit it, that more war is coming. Indeed, we even wonder why it has not broken out before now.' She predicted that aircraft, submarines and poison gas would be supplemented by death rays and atomic disintegration, 'transmitted by ether waves'. Before the First World War, two-thirds of fictional end-of-the-world scenarios involved natural disasters and only one-third stemmed from human activity. After 1918, those proportions were reversed. While non-fiction studies of existential risk such as Geoffrey Dennis's *The End of the World* accepted that an apocalyptic superweapon did not yet exist, many novelists felt that another global conflict was both inevitable and inevitably final. This conviction produced an epidemic of stories in England, France and Germany, where a new word was coined: *Weltuntergangsroman*, or 'Doomsday novel'.

The first war had been a horrific vindication of *fin-de-siècle* cynicism about the arc of progress, raising the possibility of going backwards so quickly that the near future might resemble the distant past. War hurls England back to the Middle Ages in such interwar novels as Edward Shanks's *The People of the Ruins*, Cicely Hamilton's *Theodore Savage* and P. Anderson Graham's *The Collapse of Homo Sapiens*, all published between 1920 and 1923.* Inking and colouring the rough pencil sketch of *After London*, such novels established a lasting blueprint: a regression to feudalism or barbarism, with clashing warlords, fanatical anti-science cults and mangled myths of times past. Scientists became as culpable as generals: Theodore Savage is 'Merlin, Frankenstein and Adam; the fool who tasted of forbidden fruit, the magician whose arts had brought ruin on a world, the devil-artisan whose unholy skill had created monsters that destroyed him'. Director William Cameron Menzies brought this template to the screen in *Things to Come*, his 1936 collaboration with H. G. Wells, in which a twenty-six-year conflict leaves London a pestilential ruin ruled by a Luddite warlord. 'If we don't end war,' the heroic airman John Cabal (Raymond Massey) presciently declares, 'war will end us!'

*Shanks had served in the British Army in France while Hamilton had driven ambulances and worked in a military hospital near Paris.

Primeval terrors were revived and realized by modernity. The long-dreaded experience of death from above had been made real by Zeppelin airships and the first bomber planes, while poison gas on the battlefield had done what the likes of Poe had once imagined the comet's vaporous tail would do. 'I believe that, given a certain impetus, things may take this sort of course, and in as short a time,' John Collier wrote in the preface to his 1933 neo-medieval post-apocalypse *Tom's a-Cold.* In the middle of the decade, the bombardment of Ethiopia by Italy, and Spain by Italy and Germany, offered a ghastly preview of the war to come. Dismayed by the fascists' demolition of Guernica in April 1937, Stephen Vincent Benét wrote 'By the Waters of Babylon', a tale of the post-war Dark Ages. 'When gods war with gods, they use weapons we do not know,' writes the narrator, pondering the remains of New York City. 'It was fire falling out of the sky and a mist that poisoned. It was the time of the Great Burning and the Destruction.' The future-war tales of the 1930s anticipated bombs and gas – total war – rather than the clash of armies.

Impact fiction did not, however, wither away, because it had the virtue of switching the focus from cause to effect. By taking the means of mass destruction out of the hands of men and nations, it could consider how humanity might unite, or not, in the face of a mindless extraterrestrial killer. Such a thought experiment appealed to the kind of writer who possessed an abundant imagination, a taste for havoc and a pungently cynical opinion of human nature – a writer like Philip Wylie.

CHAPTER 4

Doomsday Rocks

The end of the world will never
be really believed till it comes.

Edwin Balmer and Philip Wylie,
When Worlds Collide (1933)

There are some writers, like Harper Lee, who write a single great book and live for ever. There are others, like Franz Kafka, who mean nothing to the world at large until after they are dead. Then there are those who make a gigantic noise in their lifetimes but fall silent, reputationally, once they have left the stage. Philip Wylie was such a writer. For four decades he was a man who mattered; a polymath and aspiring world-changer in the mould of H. G. Wells; a public figure of exceptional vitality, charisma and drive. A keen swimmer and weightlifter who wrote up to ten thousand words a day, he produced shelf-filling volumes of fiction and non-fiction, threw himself into the latest developments in science, was courted by politicians and movie studios, and clearly believed that the world would be a lot better off if only it would learn to heed his prescriptions. His 1942 essay collection, *Generation of Vipers*, was a controversial attack on the hypocrisy and idiocy of American culture, which he rated scarcely less poorly than fascism or communism. 'I am not a Protestant, or a Catholic, or a Jew; I don't belong to any church or union,' he proudly declared. 'I am not and never have been a communist, fascist, leftist, liberal, tory, or rightist.' Throughout his career, he was obsessed with disaster and how it might be avoided. The end of the world was one of his abiding themes, another being the tendency of visionary individuals to be disdained by the bitter, mediocre masses. In photographs, he appeared wary and fiercely unimpressed.

Born in Beverly, Massachusetts, in 1902, Wylie was an intense, introspective child. His mother, Edna, a novelist, died in childbirth when he was five. His father, Edmund, was a Presbyterian minister and a violent, neglectful parent. Reading the forefathers of science fiction – Poe, Verne, Wells – made Wylie an aspiring writer. Studying evolution at Princeton made him an atheist. Witnessing the privilege of his wealthy classmates left him obsessed with money and social capital. He never graduated, reportedly because he prefaced his essays in the English literature exam with attacks on the stupidity of the questions. 'I found no satisfaction in its attitude or curriculum,' he later wrote.

Wylie left Princeton determined to be somebody, but who? After working for Edward Bernays, the father of public relations, he set up his own advertising agency, but his reputation was destroyed when he was falsely accused of making a young woman pregnant. He then became one of Harold Ross's first employees at *The New Yorker*, where he came to resent the liberal establishment for what he saw as its snobbish orthodoxy and ignorance of science. When Ross dropped him, he started writing short stories for the pulp magazines. By 1932 he had published six novels in four years, not to mention stories for the nation's most prestigious magazines and the screenplay for the H. G. Wells adaptation *Island of Lost Souls*. And all this while being, by his own account, a 'shut the doors and stay, folks, I've bought the place till morning drunk', and being trapped in a calamitous marriage which ended in 1936 when his wife tried to have him committed to a psychiatric institution.

In 1930, Wylie published *Gladiator*, a novel about a professor who experiments on his son in the womb and raises a 'super-child, an invulnerable man'. 'I can jump higher'n a house,' Hugo Danner says. 'I can run faster'n a train. I can pull up big trees an' push 'em over.' It is perhaps the first ever superhero story, but one in which super-powers inspire only envy and terror. 'They fear you,' Hugo's father tells him. 'So you see, you've got to be good and kind and considerate – to justify all that strength.' A decade later, Wylie threatened to sue for plagiarism over Superman's resemblance to Danner.

Superman's co-creator Jerry Siegel signed an affidavit insisting there was no connection, even though he had reviewed *Gladiator* for *Science Fiction* magazine in 1932. Superman's origin story as Krypton's last man (or rather last baby) also suggests a familiarity with Wylie's work: 'As a distant planet was destroyed by old age, a scientist placed his infant son within a hastily devised space-ship, launching it toward Earth!' The idea of building a rocket to flee a planet in terminal peril drives the plot of Wylie's most memorable novel, written with Edwin Balmer, 1933's *When Worlds Collide.*

Balmer, the editor of *Redbook* magazine, had a prodigious talent for thrilling plots but no ability to execute them. He found the perfect collaborator in Wylie, who could provide not just the prose but the philosophical and scientific ballast. Wylie imagined himself as a big thinker in the mould of H. G. Wells, Aldous Huxley and Olaf Stapledon rather than one of the herd of pulp science fiction writers whom he later derided for producing 'a piddling phantasmagoria of wanton nonsense'. Paramount Pictures commissioned him to visit top scientists around the country and collect information for a picture of the world in 1983 called *Fifty Years from Now.* The project was shelved when Paramount heard that Wells was making *Things to Come*, but the research introduced Wylie to atomic physicists at the California Institute of Technology whose expertise would inform his fiction.

When Worlds Collide is a milestone in the history of impact fiction but the killer object is neither a comet nor an asteroid but a planet – two of them, in fact. The story begins with word of a mysterious alliance of scientists which goes by the terrifying name of the League of the Last Days. The tetchy genius Cole Hendron has discovered that two planets have become detached from their own solar systems and are hurtling towards Earth. When Bronson A and Bronson B pass close by in two years' time, their gravitational pull will enrage the earth's tides and tectonic plates, causing untold damage. On their return eight months later, Bronson A will smash the planet to smithereens. 'Yesterday there had been issued marching orders for fifteen hundred millions of human beings,' thinks the hero, Tony, after the news breaks. 'If they did not now know that it was to be the end of the world, at least they were told that it was the end of the world as it had been.' Much of the novel is taken up with the construction of an atomic rocket called Noah's Ark to transport a few hundred lucky survivors to the conveniently habitable Bronson B. For once, there *is* a Planet B.

The disaster novel flowed from the Americanization of *The War of the Worlds*: Garrett P. Serviss, the author of *Edison's Invasion of Mars*, went on to write a novel about the terrible things that happen when the advice of brilliant scientists is not heeded. In his 1912 book *The Second Deluge*, an eccentric astronomer warns that a nebula will inundate the world and sets about building an ark, using eugenic principles to select the lucky passengers. *When Worlds Collide* similarly presents science as a religion, with a cast of prophets, followers and doomed non-believers, but it has the literary virtues that eluded Serviss: humour, characterization, cinematic set pieces, social commentary and a veneer of scientific credibility.

If the construction of an interplanetary ark in Roland Emmerich's 2009 blockbuster *2012* suggests a familiarity with *When Worlds Collide*, then so does the appalling vigour with which Wylie and Balmer describe the ravages of the Moon-shattering first pass. 'It is a new intoxication – annihilation,' a poet tells Tony. 'It multiplies every emotion.' After half the world dies from tidal waves, earthquakes and magma, the survivors inhabit 'a landscape that would have credited Dante's Inferno itself'. Wylie avoids the full-throated eugenics of *The Second Deluge* but all ark stories are inevitably elitist to some degree: choices must be made. Just before it takes off, the rocket's passengers fight off a desperate mob in a 'last battle of brains against brutality'. When it safely lands on Bronson B, the French physicist Duquesne makes a speech about the past and future of humanity in which one can hear Wylie's own low opinion of the world he inhabited:

> It is nothing – if we merely continue the earth – here. When I recollect the filth of our cities, the greed of individuals and of nations, the savagery of wars, the horrors of pauperism permitted to exist side by side with luxury and wealth, our selfishness, hates, diseases, filth – all the hideousness we called civilization – I cannot regret that the world which was afflicted by us is flying in fragments, utterly incapable of rehabilitation, about the sun. On the other hand, now we are here; and how are we to justify the chance to begin again?

When Worlds Collide doubled the circulation of *Redbook*'s sister magazine *Blue Book* when it was serialized in the autumn of 1932 and sold half a million copies in book form. The novel and its sequel, *After Worlds Collide*, earned their authors around $200,000, including movie rights – a spectacular sum. Wylie and Balmer established all of the perennial tropes of impact fiction: the head-spinning scientific discovery, the authorities alerted, the sadness and panic, the riots and looting, the untold mayhem, the hi-tech rescue plan, and the many forms of denial.

The range of human responses to a cosmic threat, rather than the impact itself, inspired the Austrian playwright Jura Soyfer's 1936 play *Der Weltuntergang* (*The End of the World*). Soyfer, a twenty-three-year-old Jewish Marxist in a country sliding towards war, brought the satirical spirit of Karl Kraus to impact fiction. The play begins with the anthropomorphized Sun and planets deciding that Earth needs to be cleansed of humanity and dispatching a comet to deliver the blow: 'The radical cure for the Earth!' A popular figure in impact fiction is the astronomer who identifies the hazard but isn't believed. Soyfer's Cassandra is one Professor Peep, who struggles to get world leaders to heed his warnings. 'The comet is going to destroy everybody,' Peep warns Hitler. 'Destroying everybody is my business,' Hitler retorts. 'World Jewry, Freemasonry, and Bolshevism have sent out a comet with the one purpose to destroy and, at the same time, to dominate the world, and with the second purpose of undermining our nation through influences from foreign planets.' Soyfer rips through every species of human idiocy. Revellers sing a sentimental pop hit called 'Let's Go Dying a Little'; speculators buy 'End-of-the-World bonds' and comet insurance policies; national physics institutes predict that the world will be destroyed with the exception of *their* nations and colonies. One diplomat insists that the comet wouldn't dare violate international borders: 'You will understand, monsieur, that the end of the world must not be allowed to impair the European balance of power.'

With just a week to go, Peep designs a machine that will divert the comet, but a rule-bound bureaucrat instructs him to apply for a patent before seeking funding. Everybody is too pedantic, arrogant or busy to help him save the world. *When Worlds Collide* gets a ribbing when an inventor builds a spaceship and sells $30 million tickets to the wealthiest men on earth, but when they show up for their flight, they find a note explaining that the 'spaceship' is just a model and the 'inventor' has spent their money on living his last days in luxury. All seems lost until the comet takes pity on humanity and veers away at the last moment.

The End of the World remains the funniest comet story of them all, but laughter fades with knowledge of the playwright's fate. After Germany annexed Austria, Soyfer was sent to Dachau concentration camp as a political prisoner. He died in Buchenwald on 16 February 1939, at the age of twenty-six. For Jura Soyfer, like millions of others, Hitler was the end of the world.

Had Cecil B. De Mille succeeded in bringing *When Worlds Collide* to the screen in the 1930s, it might have inspired a wave of impact movies. But by the time Rudolph Maté's version arrived in cinemas in 1951, it was too late. While the delay enabled Maté to dramatize Balmer and Wylie's planetary bedlam with Oscar-winning special effects, the theme was too dated to excite post-war audiences for whom world destruction was now synonymous with the Bomb. In 'The Imagination of Disaster', Susan Sontag's comprehensive 1965 essay on science fiction cinema, comets and asteroids do not even merit a mention. For most post-war writers, the cause of global annihilation would not be a freak intruder from outer space but the greed, malice and stupidity of mankind itself.

What little impact fiction did emerge during the period was in dialogue with the Bomb, like Max Ehrlich's bizarre 1949 pulp utopia *The Big Eye*. It is November 1960 and the world is on the threshold of atomic Armageddon. An astronomer, Charles Dawson, realizes that Planet Y, 'the Big Eye', will destroy the earth on Christmas Day 1962. The superpowers immediately disarm ('For there is no use destroying each other, when all will finally be destroyed') and establish a new Federation of the World. 'Had we recognized the fact then, that the bomb was simply a man-made Big Eye, we might have begun our new Federation of the World in 1945 instead of today,' cries *The New York Times*. 'How could we have been so blind?' Come the final day, a miracle! The Big Eye narrowly misses and the world survives, kinder and wiser for its near-death experience. Only then does the novel's hero discover (and burn) evidence that Dawson knew all along that the planets wouldn't collide but lied about it in order to scare humanity straight: a bogus end of the world designed to avert the real thing.

One of the few writers who remained interested in comets *qua* comets during this period was Arthur C. Clarke. As a child in Somerset during the 1920s, he had been bewitched by stargazing and fossil-collecting. In the RAF during the war, where he worked in radar and electronics, his eccentric propensity to talk about satellites and rockets earned him the nickname 'Spaceship'. Later, he served as president of the British Interplanetary Society while writing books about space travel. In the gloomy terrain of post-war science fiction, Clarke was a beacon of hopefulness whose optimism made him seem much younger than his years. 'He has the kind of mind of which the world can never have enough,' attested Stanley Kubrick, his collaborator on 1968's *2001: A Space Odyssey*, 'an array of imagination, intelligence, knowledge and a quirkish curiosity which often uncovers more than the first three qualities.'

It was Clarke's sincere wonder, rather than his mechanical prose, that made him the most popular author in science fiction following his 1953 novel *Childhood's End.* Having experienced the mind-blowing two-billion-year span of Olaf Stapledon's 1930 novel *Last and First Men* at an impressionable age, Clarke took an extremely long view, developing a quasi-religious belief in the destiny of humanity. 'No book before or since ever had such an impact on me,' he recalled. In *Childhood's End*, alien Overlords who have been secretly protecting Earth from existential threats transform the planet's children into a new posthuman race which will colonize the universe while their parents die off. It is 'an end that no prophet had ever foreseen – an end that repudiated optimism and pessimism alike. Yet it was fitting: it had the sublime inevitability of a great work of art.' Jan Rodricks, the first Black last man in fiction, returns from another galaxy to find the human race extinct and hangs around to report on the atomization of the planet itself. Some readers might consider this ending quite the downer, but Clarke expected humanity itself to transcend Earth. On 20 July 1969, the day that Neil Armstrong and Buzz Aldrin walked on the Moon, he told CBS's Walter Cronkite, 'I believe . . . when we get beyond the atmosphere, out into the new environment of space, we will find new powers, new capabilities.' The phenomenal success of *2001* made Clarke the most influential figure in science fiction. In his 1973 novel *Rendezvous with Rama*, he used his platform to draw attention to the menace of impact. In 2077, a large Tunguska-style impactor wipes out Venice and Verona and gives birth to an international effort to track Near-Earth Objects: Project SPACEGUARD.

The notion of blasting an approaching comet with explosives went back as far as George Griffith's *The World Peril of 1910*, but it was first seriously mooted in 1967 by MIT's Project Icarus, which proposed loading half a dozen Saturn V rockets with nuclear bombs and firing them at the asteroid 1566 Icarus if it were ever to threaten Earth. Nuclear weapons were thus reimagined as a means to save the world rather than destroy it. Exploding a comet or asteroid with warheads would produce a deadly fusillade of shrapnel ('Which is better – a single mega-catastrophe in one place, or hundreds of smaller ones?' asked Clarke), but deflecting one was a real possibility.

The idea was later dramatized in 1979's *Meteor*, the first significant impact movie since *When Worlds Collide* twenty-eight years earlier. Paul Bradley (Sean Connery) is a cantankerous former NASA scientist who is snatched away from his yacht-racing because the Orpheus asteroid is heading for Earth and only Hercules, the secret nuclear cordon that he has designed, can stop it, in concert with its Soviet equivalent. True to genre conventions, the world is saved but not before asteroid splinters serve up a tasty *amuse-bouche* of avalanches, tidal waves and toppling skyscrapers. *Meteor* placed viewers in the unusual position of rooting for nuclear missiles, including Soviet ones.

Early on, Bradley grimly explains to the standard array of clueless politicians and generals the concept that would become known as 'impact winter': 'Orpheus is five miles wide. Its striking force is equal to 2,500,000 megatons of TNT . . . It would throw into the atmosphere five billion tons of earth, reduce solar radiation for decades to come. It could cause another ice age.' Even as Connery was filming this scene, a geologist called Walter Alvarez was examining evidence that such a catastrophe had already occurred.

—

In the spring of 1977, the thirty-six-year-old Alvarez was studying sediment layers in Gubbio, Italy, when he found that the tiny sea creatures foraminifera all but vanished from the fossil record 66 million years ago, when the Cretaceous abruptly ceded to the Tertiary: the geological boundary abbreviated to KT.* But why? He took the puzzle to his father Luis, a Nobel Prize-winning physicist at Berkeley. Luis suggested using iridium, an element that is extremely rare on Earth but common in meteorites, to date the layer more precisely. Every time they analysed a KT layer, anywhere in the world, the iridium levels were through the roof, pointing to 'a sudden influx of extraterrestrial material'. In 1980, after months of deliberation, they published a paper (with co-authors Frank Asaro and Helen V. Michel) which proposed what became known as the Alvarez hypothesis: an asteroid had collided with the earth, producing so much dust that 'day could have been turned into night for a period of several years . . . Loss of sunlight suppressed photosynthesis, and as a result most food chains collapsed and the extinctions resulted.' *Meteor*'s Paul Bradley was wrong to call the result of an impact an ice age but he got the gist of it right.

Subsequent computer models have fleshed out the detail of what probably happened. An object 10 to 15 kilometres wide made landfall at a speed of 70,000 kilometres an hour with a force of 100 million megatons. First, the blast waves levelled everything within a radius of several hundred kilometres while triggering earthquakes, volcanic eruptions and tsunamis hundreds of metres high. Vaporizing on impact, the object flung hundreds of billions of tons of rock, dust and sulphur halfway to the Moon. Heavier debris burned up on re-entering the atmosphere and created a lethal meteor shower, igniting global firestorms. Smaller ejecta formed a thick, sun-blocking cloud around the planet, plunging it into an impact winter which lasted for up to three years. Vegetation perished within weeks and most animal and marine life within months – if not from cold or starvation then from sulphuric rain as corrosive as battery acid or, once the dust finally cleared, from UV radiation pouring through

* In 2008, the Tertiary was officially replaced by the Paleogene and Neogene periods, so the boundary is now known as KPg. I have chosen to use the term with which the Alvarezes were familiar.

the shredded ozone layer. For around three-quarters of species, including anything larger than a cat, the earth ceased to sustain life.

This theory, so familiar now, was greeted with immense scepticism. 'My first thought was this is one of Walter's practical jokes,' said one palaeontologist. Inoculated against catastrophism, most palaeontologists and geologists found the shattering cosmic drama of the Alvarez hypothesis as fundamentally unserious as William Whiston's suggestion that a comet caused the Deluge, or Ignatius Donnelly's theory of the Ragnarök comet. Extinction, they insisted, happened the same way as evolution: very slowly. Either dinosaurs were outpaced by mammals in the evolutionary marathon or they fell prey to an ice age or volcanic winter. Now they were meant to believe that a rock simply fell out of the sky one terrible day? Two teams of astrophysicists complicated the picture by speculating that the Sun had a smaller sister star which passed through the Oort Cloud every 26 million years, unleashing a deadly rain of comets which explained *every* mass extinction. This controversial theory caused enough excitement to merit a *Time* cover story about 'Nemesis, the death star', but it made the Alvarez hypothesis look kooky by association. 'Many consider all the newfangled extraterrestrial scenarios to be half-baked take-offs of H. G. Wells,' *Time* reported. Luis shot back with magnificent hauteur: 'I don't like to say bad things about paleontologists, but they're really not very good scientists. They're more like stamp collectors.'

Opposition to the Alvarez hypothesis remained fierce until, in 1991, seven geologists identified the impact site: a crater, 180 kilometres wide and 20 kilometres deep, beneath Mexico's Yucatán Peninsula. It is known as the Chicxulub crater, after the nearest town, but Walter favoured a more exciting name: 'the crater of doom'. There is still debate about whether a mass extinction was already underway when the asteroid hit but nobody denies that it did hit. This was belated vindication for the catastrophists. Even Halley's theory that comets were God's way of clearing the planet for the next generation of inhabitants had some truth to it: without the KT extinction, *Homo sapiens* wouldn't exist.

Thus the demise of the dinosaurs became a truly apocalyptic story and an extinction-causing impact suddenly moved from the column of things that *could* happen to that of things that *had* happened. David Kring, one of the geologists who discovered the Chicxulub crater, was scared into campaigning for efforts to track and intercept asteroids: 'There's no uncertainty to this statement: the Earth will be hit by a Chicxulub-size asteroid again, unless we deflect it.' As Charlton Heston's opening voiceover in Michael Bay's 1998 movie *Armageddon* dramatically puts it, 'It happened before. It will happen again. It's just a question of when.'

During the 1980s, the most dedicated students of impact hazard were a pair of amateurs: husband-and-wife geoscientist Eugene Shoemaker and astronomer Carolyn Shoemaker. By the time of Eugene's death in a car crash in 1997, the couple had identified a record-breaking thirty-two comets and more than one thousand asteroids. On 22 March 1989, the 300-metre-wide asteroid 1989 FC came within 690,000 kilometres of Earth: the closest shave since 1942. The fact that astronomers didn't discover this until after it had passed by inspired widespread consternation. A conference about impact hazard in Los Alamos, New Mexico, even managed to bring together two sworn enemies whom we will meet in the next chapter, battling over nuclear weapons: the hawkish physicist Edward Teller and the dovish celebrity scientist Carl Sagan. With the Cold War over, it seemed, people could once again raise their eyes to consider extraterrestrial annihilation. In 1992, when the cover of *Newsweek* featured Comet Swift-Tuttle flaming towards Earth beside the headline 'Doomsday Science', NASA launched a project to track and deflect Near-Earth Objects and named it after Arthur C. Clarke's fictional version: the Spaceguard Survey. So when Clarke published another asteroid novel, *The Hammer of God* in 1993, he did not consider it merely science fiction. 'It was my *duty* to show what could be done about the asteroid menace,' he wrote. 'By creating a self-fulfilling prophecy, I might even save the world – though I'd never know . . .'

In 1994, the Shoemakers and their fellow comet-hunter David Levy identified a giant comet heading for Jupiter and made the cover of *Time*. In July, twenty-one fragments of Shoemaker-Levy 9 collided with Jupiter, one of which generated an explosion six hundred times more powerful than the world's entire nuclear arsenal and created a cloud of debris as wide as Earth. Sister Marie Gabriel, a Polish nun and self-styled seer, inspired hilarity when she took out full-page advertisements in several UK newspapers claiming that the comet signalled the 'COSMIC DAY OF JUDGEMENT ordained by GOD', but Levy insisted that it was no laughing matter: Shoemaker-Levy 9 'removed the "giggle factor" that it couldn't happen to us here on Earth. If it could hit Jupiter, then one day another could hit us.' In their 1996 book *Doomsday Asteroid: Can We Survive?*, Donald W. Cox and James H. Chestek dramatically claimed, 'We live in a cosmic shooting gallery. Somewhere out in the netherworld of deep space, hurtling toward Earth, is a doomsday rock.'

A kind of mania for impact stories ensued. 'For some reason, in recent months there have been more TV shows aired about asteroids than there are actual asteroids,' the astronomer Phil Plait remarked following the schlocky 1997 TV movies *Asteroid* and *Doomsday Rock*. Steven Spielberg optioned *The Hammer of God*, which was then merged with a planned remake of *When Worlds Collide* to form the basis for Mimi Leder's 1998 movie *Deep Impact*. Although neither novel was credited, their influence is undeniable. The Wolf-Beiderman comet is expected to slam into North America, causing an impact winter. The world's governments make plans to nuke it or, if that fails, to preserve a few million survivors in underground caves until the surface is habitable again. ('Our new Noah's Ark,' says the US president, played by Morgan Freeman.) The first bombs split the comet in two without altering its course, thus doubling the problem. At the last moment, the larger half is destroyed by a shuttle with the on-the-nose name of *Messiah* but the smaller one sets off tidal waves which wipe out the likes of New York and Washington DC, giving us the memorable image of the Statue of Liberty's severed head underwater. *Deep Impact* also popularized the phrase 'extinction-level event', rather than the previously standard 'extinction event'.

Deep Impact coincided with *Armageddon*, a similar movie about the effort to stop an asteroid which is, absurdly, 'the size of Texas': more than one hundred times bigger than the KT object. 'Damage? Total, sir,' NASA's Dan Truman (Billy Bob Thornton) tells the president. 'It's what we call a global killer. The end of mankind. Doesn't matter where it hits, nothing would survive, not even bacteria.' Not even bacteria! It sounds like a brag. In reality, to split an object that large safely in half with hours to go would require explosives one billion times more powerful than the largest hydrogen bomb ever made. Fortunately, something of that size would have been visible to the naked eye a lot earlier than the eighteen days given in the film. As Phil Plait drily remarked, '"Armageddon" got some astronomy right. For example, there is an asteroid in the movie, and asteroids do indeed exist.'

While both movies precede the eventual success of the mission with spectacular CGI pandemonium, their approaches could not be more different. *Deep Impact* is a noble, sentimental picture, primarily concerned with how a few individuals process mortality and grief. With the Shoemakers acting as consultants until Eugene's death, the science is unusually accurate for a disaster movie. *Armageddon*, conversely, is bombastic, chauvinistic and glib. It is effectively a heist movie, full of macho banter between blue-collar libertarian miners who have no time for eggheads or taxes, even as they execute a world-saving plan designed by scientists and funded by the government. The shuttles are named *Freedom* and *Independence.* With the rest of the world's population squeezed into a single two-minute montage, Bay finds individual heroism infinitely more interesting than collective dread. Compare and contrast the two presidential addresses at the moment of maximum peril. 'The Bible calls this day Armageddon – the end of all things,' booms Stanley Anderson in *Armageddon. Deep Impact*'s Morgan Freeman, however, says, 'Life will go on. We will prevail.' His next line was cut for obvious reasons but it holds true on two levels: 'This is not Armageddon.'

Although *Deep Impact* came out first, *Armageddon* outperformed it at the box office by $200 million, which says a great deal. *Time* suggested that the end of the Cold War had 'threatened for a while to deprive us of the sheer glamour of imagined annihilation' and that impact movies were a substitute 'to provide that strangely agreeable image, civilization getting wrecked'. Anthony Lane in *The New Yorker* wrote of *Deep Impact*, 'The destruction of the world is a subject so engulfing that all it's good for is a cheap thrill.' But what cheapens the thrill is the fact that the world is *not* wholly destroyed. These two blockbusters having exhausted the narrative possibilities of astronautical derring-do, twenty-first-century impact movies focused on what might happen if it really was.

—

Psychotherapy gave Lars von Trier the idea for his 2011 movie *Melancholia*.* The Danish director's therapist told him that depressives and melancholics respond more calmly to an actual catastrophe because they have been preparing for one for years. Justine (Kirsten Dunst) is 'based a lot on my person and my experiences with doomsday prophecies and depression,' von Trier explained. The monstrous depression that renders Justine catatonically incapable in everyday life makes her singularly well equipped for the end of the world – a kind of mystic who doesn't just know that the astronomers are wrong to say that the rogue planet Melancholia will miss Earth but welcomes the collision as a galactic solution to her misery. It even feels possible that Justine, her face like a dead planet, has summoned Melancholia and nudged it towards Earth with the psychic force of her despair. The movie begins with a premonition of the pulverized globe and concludes with an obliviating blue fire. As they await the impact, Justine's sister Claire (Charlotte Gainsbourg) sobs inconsolably but Justine is quietly exultant. 'This film is perilously close to the aesthetic of American mainstream films,' von Trier admitted. 'The only redeeming factor about it, you might say, is that the world ends.'

While hardly a box-office smash, *Melancholia* appeared to reset the impact movie as a more sombre, intimate genre about how people react when, as Justine's nephew says, 'There's nothing to do and nowhere to hide.' The only notable exception is from China: in the 2019 blockbuster *The Wandering Earth*, Chinese ingenuity moves the entire planet out of harm's way. Western cinema has gone in an opposite direction. In this new narrative, there is no atomic salvation and ordinary people are more than a screaming backcloth to the adventures of presidents and astronauts. Lorene Scafaria, the writer and director of 2012's *Seeking a Friend for the End of the World*, has said that her favourite scene in *Deep Impact* is the one where two of the main characters, a reconciled father and daughter, are about to die: 'I just thought a lot more about being on the ground with people, and not being with the people who were trying to stop the asteroid.' Scafaria manages to develop a romantic

* The title recalls Dürer's 1514 engraving *Melencolia I*, which features a gloomy angel and a blazing comet.

comedy from this forlorn situation. It begins with the explosion of the space shuttle *Deliverance* before it can deflect a 110-kilometre-wide asteroid: 'The final mission to save mankind has failed.' The satire recalls Jura Soyfer, with its 'Armageddon package' of insurance, 'end of the world awareness concert' and a magazine's 'Best of Humanity' special issue (with cover stars Jesus and Oprah Winfrey), but it has a tender heart.

These Final Hours, written and directed by Zak Hilditch, explores the same idea to much less cheering effect. An impactor has crashed into the North Atlantic and the resulting firestorm, rolling over the globe, will reach Perth, Australia, in twelve hours. Already it has given the whole movie a sulphuric yellow tint. The young girl whom James (Nathan Phillips) rescues on his journey from nihilism to empathy says that the earth is going to peel like an orange: 'The peel is made out of fire.' Despite their radically different tones, both of these movies are manic road trips punctuated by suicides, riots, orgiastic parties and encounters with delusional survivalists, before concluding with oblivion. The end, now, is neither Byron-black nor Martin-red but Turner-white: the kind of incandescent nothingness described by witnesses to atomic explosions. These movies reject the insistence on survival and build-back-better rebirth in the likes of *Deep Impact* and *When Worlds Collide*. For von Trier, Scafaria and Hilditch, the end is the point.

When these movies came out, impact hazard was simultaneously becoming a growing real-world concern. After a meteor exploded over Chelyabinsk, Russia, on 14 February 2013, NASA began annual asteroid-impact simulations. In 2015, a group of concerned scientists, astronauts and artists led by Stephen Hawking launched Asteroid Day, a UN-backed annual event on the anniversary of Tunguska, with the aim of rapidly accelerating the tracking of NEOs and research into interception strategies. In September 2022, NASA's Double Asteroid Redirection Test (DART) successfully deflected the harmless asteroid Dimorphos.

Amid this new wave of concern about potential collisions, the comet in the most widely seen impact movie of all time was a metaphor for something else entirely. Released by Netflix in December 2021, Adam McKay's *Don't Look Up* was watched by tens of millions of people. McKay had been working on various plot ideas for a picture about the politics of the climate crisis when he had a conversation with his friend, the journalist and activist David Sirota. 'He just made an offhanded comment... about how it's like the comet is coming towards earth and no one cares,' McKay recalled. 'And I was like, oh! That's the idea... It references hundreds and hundreds of movies that we've all seen . . . that follow this narrative that the world's going to end and then everything works out with a nifty bow at the very end of the movie... maybe seeing this ending that doesn't follow that narrative would just have an inherent power to it.' In order to make an all-star satire about a twenty-first-century dilemma, McKay reached back into history for the oldest disaster trope of them all.

Don't Look Up is an unlikely cross between *Deep Impact*, *Dr. Strangelove* and the sitcom *Veep*, combining broad satire with genuine anguish. The efforts of three Professor Peep-like astronomers to warn the world about the comet run up against populist politicians, shallow broadcasters, delusional billionaires and comet-denying online conspiracy theorists in the tradition of Olga Romanoff who literally refuse to look up. Though the film is intended as a climate-change allegory, it plays cleverly with the history of impact fiction. *Armageddon* is parodied in the movie-within-a-movie *Total Destruction*: 'When the asteroid hit us, he hit back.' But this comet-nuking plan is deliberately aborted when the president falls under the fatal spell of the movie's Dr Strangelove, Peter Isherwell (Mark Rylance), a messianic tech guru for whom the comet is not an existential threat but a 140-trillion-dollar bounty of precious minerals. There is an escape vessel to ferry the elite to another planet, straight out of *When Worlds Collide*, and jokes about the stock market and comet-themed pop songs, recalling Jura Soyfer's *The End of the World*. As with *Melancholia*, the world ends when the movie does.

McKay's mission was to challenge climate denial and show that sometimes prophecies of doom are entirely correct. But denial, misinformation, financial exploitation and political self-interest are also at work in stories by Wylie, Soyfer, Wells and Flammarion, which says something about human nature's timeless resistance to bad news. As Tony in *When Worlds Collide* observes, 'They, and he, could not realize that the world was doomed, any more than a man could realize that he himself must die. Death is what happens to others! So other worlds may perish, but not ours on which we stand!'

PART THREE
THE BOMB

CHAPTER 5

Dreaming the Bomb

> Think for a moment what would happen to a race of men whose material inventions placed in their hands unlimited power for destruction before they had developed moral inhibitions sufficient to prevent their using that power to destroy themselves.
>
> Pierrepoint B. Noyes, *The Pallid Giant* (1927)

The detonation of an atomic bomb in the sky above Hiroshima, Japan, on 6 August 1945 had the quality of an apocalypse: the violent unveiling of secret knowledge about the universe. For most people it was a true revelation which shook their understanding of how the world operated. Yet some found the news easier to process. As Philip Wylie, the author of *When Worlds Collide*, observed, it became commonplace to say that 'the only considerable group of Americans who understood what it meant consisted of kids. The kids were held to be those who read science fiction magazines, books and so-called comic books.'

The atomic bomb, or something like it, had been a regular presence in popular entertainment for three decades before the act of imagining it suddenly came to be perceived as a threat to national security. In June 1943, Byron Price, director of the United States Office of Censorship, sent a confidential memorandum to thousands of publications and radio stations, instructing them to avoid any mention of atomic fission, atom smashing, radium, uranium or anything else that might inadvertently point to the fact that tens of thousands of people were secretly engaged in the Manhattan Project, a crash programme to design and build an atomic bomb. But Price failed to consider that in the rapidly proliferating pages of America's science fiction magazines, the knowledge that a bomb could be built using a uranium isotope was no secret at all. As early as May 1941, Robert Heinlein's 'Solution Unsatisfactory' had described a top-secret project to build a bomb from uranium-235. The censors were slow to act until *Astounding Science Fiction* published Cleve Cartmill's 'Deadline' in March 1944. 'Have you heard of U-235?' asks one character. 'Who hasn't?' another sniffs. Cartmill got the idea from John W. Campbell Jr, the MIT-educated editor of *Astounding*, a magazine with many avid subscribers inside the Manhattan Project. After 'Deadline', the Army ordered Campbell to publish no more stories on the subject but he countered that readers were by then so accustomed to stories with titles such as 'Atomic Fire' and 'The Atom Smasher' that their sudden disappearance would raise suspicions.

Children, meanwhile, were already au fait with the devastating power of the atom via the comic-strip adventures of Flash Gordon, Mickey Mouse and Buck Rogers. Created by Philip Francis Nowlan in 1928, Buck's first adventure, 'Armageddon 2419 AD', dropped the time-torn astronaut into the aftermath of an obliviating war involving 'disintegrator rays', rays being more popular than bombs at the time. Nowlan's hero became the most ubiquitous ambassador for the future since H. G. Wells. 'The use of atomic energy seems a Buck Rogers idea,' *The New York Times* reflected in 1944, 'but this is a Buck Rogers war.' Even Leslie Groves, the leader of the Manhattan Project, initially thought that the atomic bomb was 'a crazy Buck Rogers project'. Superhero fans were no less familiar with atomic weaponry. In 1944, the FBI forced the postponement of a story in which Superman's arch-enemy Lex Luthor invents an atomic bomb, yet Batman had already foiled a Japanese spy who used radium to build an 'atom disintegrator', a weapon 'more destructive than anything man ever dreamed of'. Though the censors were far too slow to consider fiction, that did nothing to hinder their zeal.

Philip Wylie himself strayed into trouble in 1945 when he wrote a story called 'The Paradise Crater', about the efforts of neo-Nazis in a future 1965 to avenge Hitler's defeat by building uranium bombs. Wylie fell afoul of *Blue Book* editor Donald Kennicott's unusually dutiful decision to seek official permission in advance. In short order,

Kennicott was instructed to bury the story and Wylie was placed under house arrest in a hotel room in Connecticut. What, asked an Army Intelligence major, did Wylie know about the atomic bomb? The major said that he was prepared to take Wylie's life, and his own, if it was necessary to prevent a security leak. Wylie protested that he had no inside information, nor did he need any. Thanks to his publicity work for the US Air Force, he had friends in high places and was soon released. He offered to shred the manuscript but the major said, no, he should hang on to it until the war was over.

'The Paradise Crater' did indeed appear in the October 1945 issue of *Blue Book*, by which time the whole world knew about the atomic bomb. 'I saw the headline, brought on the bus by a stranger, and thought: Yes, of course, so it's here!' recalled one young science fiction writer, Ray Bradbury. 'I knew it would come, for I had read about it and thought about it for years.' Not that there was any cause for the science fiction community to feel smug, because what they had also foreseen, more often than not, was world destruction. 'People do not realize civilization, the civilization we have been born into, lived in, and been indoctrinated with, died on July 16 1945 [the date of the first bomb test], and that the Death Notice was published to the world on August 6, 1945,' wrote John Campbell in his first *Astounding* editorial after Hiroshima. He added, 'There is only one appropriate name for the atomic weapon: The Doomsday Bomb.'

The first book in which atomic energy was employed to end the world was published fifty years before Hiroshima: *Crack of Doom* by the Northern Irish writer Robert Cromie. 'No man can say to science "thus far and no farther,"' cries the novel's deranged villain Herbert Brande. 'No man ever has been able to do so. No man ever shall!' Pulling together the 1890s archetypes of the mad scientist (usually foreign) and the anarchist conspiracy, Brande leads a clique of scientists called the Cui Bono Society, which believes that the universe is a hideous blunder which should be remedied by way of 'the vast stores of etheric energy locked up in the huge atomic warehouse of this planet'. He fully embraces his chiliastic role: 'I swear by the living god – Science incarnate – that the suffering of the centuries is over, that for this earth and all that it contains, from this night and for ever, *Time will be no more!*'

Cromie's novel appeared in 1895, the same year that Wilhelm Röntgen's discovery of X-rays caused a worldwide frenzy of fascination and speculation. The following year, Henri Becquerel inadvertently discovered that uranium emitted radiation. In 1897, J. J. Thompson identified the electron as a subatomic particle, implying that the atom, named after the Greek word for uncuttable, was divisible after all. In 1898, Marie Curie discovered radium and polonium and coined the word *radioactivity*. In 1899, Thompson's dynamic young assistant Ernest Rutherford identified alpha and beta rays. In 1900, Paul Ulrich Villard observed and named gamma rays. Every year a new marvel.

Rutherford teamed up with an even younger chemist, Frederick Soddy. In 1902, they discovered that radioactivity was produced by the spontaneous disintegration of atoms in certain chemical elements and their transmutation into other elements, and argued that matter should be understood as a colossal storehouse of energy. Atomic energy came to embody the power of science to elevate humanity or to end it. Soddy publicly expressed the heaven-or-hell implications for the first time: whoever could harness the atom could 'make the whole world one smiling Garden of Eden' or 'possess a weapon by which he could destroy the Earth if he chose'.

This was mouth-watering fare to H. G. Wells. Having described a planetary collision, a Martian invasion and the death of the Sun, how could he resist a potential world-killer that was so near at hand? Wells dedicated his 1914 novel *The World Set Free* to Soddy's work and had a Soddy-like figure explain the science: 'We know now that the atom, that once we thought hard and impenetrable, and indivisible and final . . . is really a reservoir of immense energy.' In 1933, a scientist named Holsten achieves induced radioactivity and immediately feels 'like an imbecile who has presented a box of loaded revolvers to a crèche'. In 1956, Holsten's discovery finally leads to a world war and produces the first ever appearance of the phrase *atomic bomb*. 'If there had been no Holsten there would have been some similar man,' writes Wells. 'If atomic energy had not come in one year it would have come in another.' There's no stopping science.

Thirty years before Hiroshima, Wells had no way of knowing how such a weapon might work. He misunderstood the concept of radio-active half-life, so his bombs, made from the fictional element Carolinum, don't just continue to emit rays indefinitely; they continue to explode. Nonetheless, there are some strikingly prescient images. The bomb is 'a shuddering star of evil splendour' which produces 'a great ball of crimson-purple fire like a maddened living thing' and 'puffs of luminous, radio-active vapour'. Halfway through the novel, the strangely optimistic title begins to make sense: the 'moral shock' of atomic war inspires the survivors to form a world government which controls Carolinum supplies and puts an end to war. While not a final battle between good and evil, Wells's 'Last War' does fulfil the role of Armageddon, burning a path to peace on earth: 'We've had unity and collectivism blasted into our brains.' *The Spectator* sceptically called this 'one of his periodic fits of millennial reconstruction . . . It would be unfair to accept Mr. Wells's latest vaticinations as final, because he is in the habit of scrapping civilization every two years or so.'

Wells came to accept the criticism. 'A disposition to believe in these spontaneous waves of sanity may be one of my besetting weaknesses,' he wryly reflected in 1934. But the idea of a weapon so heinous that it would end war wasn't unusual. Earlier future-war stories such as Hollis Godfrey's 1908 book *The Man Who Ended War* had advanced the pacifistic case for creating the ultimate deterrent. The inventors of poison gas and the aeroplane had expressed similar hopes of horrifying the world into peace. As Alfred Nobel, the inventor of dynamite and father of the eponymous Peace Prize, told the pacifist Bertha von Suttner in 1891, 'Perhaps my factories will put an end to war sooner than your congresses: on the day that two army corps can mutually annihilate each other in a second, all civilised nations will surely recoil with horror and disband their troops.' In a 1921 article called 'How to Make War Impossible', Thomas Edison argued that governments should continue to 'produce instruments of death so terrible that presently all men and every nation would well know that war would mean the end of civilization'. But Wells's contemporary George Griffith had already scotched what the peace activist Norman Cousins mockingly described as 'the war-is-now-too-horrible theory' in *The Lord of Labour*, which he dictated from his deathbed in 1906. When the German inventor of a disintegrator ray claims that it will 'make warfare impossible by making it so awful that no man in his senses would go upon a battlefield', the Kaiser responds, 'My dear Professor, before you make war impossible you will have to make another discovery. You will have to find out how to alter human nature; and that, I venture to say, is beyond the capabilities of even your genius.'

In 1914, Wells's speculative atomic bomb caused a mighty splash, with even Ernest Rutherford calling it 'interesting', if implausible. For the next thirty years, stories about future wars tended to follow Wells's lead. First, an arrogant, short-sighted scientist conceives the basis for a horrendous new superweapon – a bomb, a gas, a virus – without considering the consequences. Then governments, addicted to conflict, use this weapon to wage a world war of unprecedented carnage. Finally, the sickened survivors vow to rebuild a global society dedicated to peace. Sometimes a scientist uses the mere spectre of the superweapon to skip to phase three: in Arthur C. Train and Robert W. Wood's 1915 novel *The Man Who Rocked the Earth*, which cites both Wells and Soddy, a scientist called Pax blackmails the world into abolishing war with a uranium-powered 'Lavender Ray'. Occasionally, though, the superweapon is so efficient that there *is* no phase three.

What would the crucial element be? While waiting for science to find out, writers had to invent their own. In Karel Čapek's 1922 novel *Krakatit*, the atom-disintegrating explosive that could 'blow the boat of humanity to pieces' is named after Krakatoa. In Upton Sinclair's *The Millennium*, a 1924 satirical comedy about the birth of post-apocalyptic socialism, the atomic weapon that kills all but eleven of the earth's inhabitants uses 'radiumite'. In *Public Faces*, a 1932 political satire by former diplomat Harold Nicolson, the 'Livingstone alloy' leads to Livingstone bombs and Livingstone rockets. In most of these accounts, an atomic bomb seems like nothing more than impossibly powerful dynamite, but one can glimpse a premonition of the real thing in the 'gigantic mushroom of steam and debris' in Olaf Stapledon's *Last and First Men* or the explosion in *Krakatit*: 'The next moment, as if the darkness had been torn asunder, a pillar of fire leapt into the air, spread terribly and liberated a tremendous body of smoke.' Or take this startling passage from *The Final War*, a 1932 novel by a German war veteran called Carl W. Spohr:

> Suddenly his eyes were blinded by a dazzling aura of light, a huge white flame, encircled by an electric, blue radiance. Air rushed against him like a solid, burning wall and threw him back into the room . . . A pillar of dust towered over [the crater] writhing and whirling like a tornado . . . Doehler was beside the lieutenant, clutching the window frame in trembling hands. 'My God, he has set it off. And the power of the atoms is free. I wanted an explosive, I did not want to do this. It is awful.'

Robert Cromie's premise of a terrorist-scientist who actively wants to destroy the whole world also remained popular. In *Wings Over Europe*, a hit 1928 play by Robert Nichols and Maurice Brown, the prime minister's troubled genius nephew has harnessed the power of the atom for the good of all mankind, but when his uncle's cabinet, stuffy and circumspect, orders him to destroy his discovery, he turns genocidal: 'To assist Nature correct one of her casual blunders, I, who gave Man his opportunity, am about to take it away. In a brief moment this planet and all upon it, with all its history, its hopes, and its disillusions, will be wiped out.' In J. B. Priestley's 1938 thriller *The Doomsday Men*, three brothers conspire to cancel the world for different reasons: a disenchanted tycoon wants to end human suffering for ever, a scientist wants to erase the 'accident' of life, and a preacher wants to bring on the apocalypse. 'They want to destroy everything, everything,' says the tycoon's daughter. 'They believe life's hopeless, that it's all gone wrong, that it would be better if people were no longer born, just to suffer pain and misery – so they want to end it all.'*

In reality, though, world destruction is a fringe interest. Pierrepoint B. Noyes's 1927 novel *The Pallid Giant* was far more prescient about

*The three brothers are philosophers of a kind. Negative utilitarians believe that the paramount ethical priority is the minimization of suffering. Given that life involves suffering, this can lead to the minimization of human life, by opposing procreation (antinatalism) or advocating suicide (promortalism). The nineteenth-century German philosopher Eduard von Hartmann craved humanity's 'final redemption from the misery of volition and existence into the painlessness of non-willing and non-being'. When the Scottish philosopher R. N. Smart coined the phrase *negative utilitarianism* in 1958, he caricatured it in a striking hypothesis called the benevolent world exploder: if a negative utilitarian were to be given a device that could destroy humanity in an instant, then the only ethical choice would be to push the button. Perhaps Smart had read *The Doomsday Men*.

the psychology of the Bomb. Noyes grew up in a utopian community established by his father, John Humphrey Noyes, near Oneida, New York. It was amillennialist: Noyes's father believed that the Millennium had already commenced and therefore perfection on Earth was possible. Noyes later became a Rhineland Commissioner for President Woodrow Wilson, helping to reconstruct Europe after the First World War. In his novel, a diplomat who is worried about an arms race to create a 'Death Ray' discovers documentary evidence that millions of years ago a highly advanced race invented a similar superweapon which drove it to extinction. The document's author, Rao, describes how his species built an atomic disintegrator ray called Holor which was so efficient that neither defence nor retaliation were possible: a country either used it first, or not at all. 'I fear not their desire to kill,' says the politician Daril in Rao's account. 'Even they are not so wicked as to crave the death of millions. *I fear their fear.* They dare not let us live, knowing or even fearing that we have a power so terrible, to kill.' Following this logic, Daril preemptively reduces every other nation in the world to a desert, but fear of Holor then leads to civil war. People keep using the weapon until there is nobody left alive except Rao, who cedes the world to our proto-human ancestors. The known history of the world is therefore post-apocalyptic.

The Pallid Giant ends with the question of whether the Death Ray will be the new Holor and history will repeat itself. While working to prevent a second world war, Noyes had to consider how suspicion of the other side's intentions had been the main driver of the first. For him, it stood to reason that fear of the consequences of using a superweapon would be outmatched by fear of the enemy using it first: that is the 'pallid giant'. By the 1920s, two camps had formed with opposing assumptions about the psychology of a superweapon – assumptions which foreshadowed Cold War arguments about nuclear deterrence. Contra Wells and Edison, Noyes thought that the only way that a superweapon would end war would be by finishing off the entire race.

CHAPTER 6

Destroyer of Worlds

We have discovered the most terrible bomb
in the history of the world. It may be the fire
destruction prophesied in the Euphrates Valley
Era, after Noah and his fabulous Ark.

President Harry S. Truman (1945)

Holsten in *The World Set Free* discovers artificial radioactivity in 1933 – not a bad guess on H. G. Wells's part. In 1932, the British physicist John Cockroft and his Irish colleague Ernest Walton split a lithium atom into two helium nuclei with a high-speed proton gun, while another British physicist, James Chadwick, discovered the neutron. On 11 January 1934, the French physicists Frédéric and Irène Joliot-Curie produced a radioactive isotope by bombarding aluminium with alpha particles of polonium. Two months later, the Italian physicist Enrico Fermi achieved the same effect with neutrons rather than alpha particles. All these experiments, however, consumed far more energy than they produced, which made Ernest Rutherford dubious. In September 1933, *The Times* reported, he claimed that 'it was a very poor and inefficient way of producing energy, and anyone who looked for a source of power in the transformation of the atoms was talking moonshine.' One atom-obsessed physicist who read his remarks in the paper knew better. 'An expert', sniffed Leo Szilard, 'is a man who knows what cannot be done.'

Of all the men responsible for ushering nuclear weapons into the world, Szilard was to work hardest to undo his achievement, wrestle most publicly with his guilty conscience and develop the keenest understanding of the relationship between science, fiction and politics. He once wrote, 'The creative scientist has much in common with the artist and the poet . . . Science would run dry if all scientists were crank turners and if none of them were dreamers.' An FBI report observed that Szilard had a slight limp, a 'florid complexion' and a tendency to be 'rather absent minded and eccentric'. He lived out of suitcases, worked out of cafes and hotel lobbies, and did his best thinking in the bath. One friend dubbed Szilard an 'intellectual bumblebee' who darted from one idea or discipline to another, never settling for long. Some of the people he encountered felt the urge to swat him away. 'He was always ahead of his time,' said his colleague Hans Bethe. 'His ideas often were expressed in paradoxes, and the paradoxes were not always understood.'

Szilard was born in Budapest in 1898, the brilliant and sensitive son of a civil engineer. As a young man, his favourite book was Imre Madách's 1861 play, *The Tragedy of Man*, in which Lucifer whisks Adam through the future history of the world, showing how progress goes hand in hand with cruelty and exploitation. A horrified Adam considers suicide in order to nip millennia of suffering in the bud but pulls back when Eve reveals that she is pregnant: humanity survives because hope does. In January 1920, Szilard moved to Berlin to study engineering before switching to physics. The city was at that time a magnet for the most formidable minds in Europe, many of whom Szilard encountered. Here was the great Albert Einstein; Lise Meitner, 'the German Marie Curie'; the quantum physicists Max Planck and Erwin Schrödinger; and Fritz Haber, who, as the inventor of both poison gas and artificial fertilizer, was the unparalleled embodiment of science's power both to destroy life and to save it. Here, too, was Werner Heisenberg, who would one day lead Nazi Germany's project to build an atomic bomb, and the Danish physicist Niels Bohr, who would inform the Americans about it. Joining Szilard from Hungary were three of his future Manhattan Project colleagues: Eugene Wigner, John von Neumann and Edward Teller. Unlike most of the above, Szilard never won a Nobel Prize. He was an impatient genius who patented the electron microscope and cyclotron and wrote a pioneering paper on information theory, but he tended to get distracted by the next glittering notion rather than following through on his brilliant insights.

Since childhood, Szilard had been an ardent reader of science fiction, especially that of H. G. Wells. He was so enthused by *The Open Conspiracy*, a non-fiction tract in which Wells called for a benign, technocratic elite to shape world affairs, that he travelled to London to explain to the author his plan for a *Bund*, or League: 'a closely knit group of people whose inner bond is pervaded by a religious and scientific spirit'. Not until 1932, though, did he read *The World Set Free* and realize 'what the liberation of atomic energy on a large scale would mean . . . In truth, the father of the atomic bomb was no physicist – he was a dreamer and a writer.' Szilard was all three.

When Szilard read about Rutherford's dismissal of atomic energy as 'moonshine' on 12 September 1933, he was staying at the Imperial Hotel in Bloomsbury, the same London neighbourhood where Wells's Holsten is living when he makes his own 1933 breakthrough. Szilard was so infuriated that he threw down his copy of *The Times*, stormed out of the hotel and went for a walk to clear his head, during which he was suddenly struck by the conviction that bombarding the atoms of certain heavy elements with neutrons would release more neutrons, which would split neighbouring atoms, thus releasing yet more neutrons, and so on, exponentially: a chain reaction. He claimed that the idea came to him as he was waiting to cross the road and the light turned green: *Go!*

Szilard knew that this was a dreadful moment in history for such a discovery. Just a year earlier, his primary interest in atomic energy had been as a fuel source 'which would enable man not only to leave the earth but to leave the solar system', but the rise of Nazism changed everything. In March 1933, two months after Hitler became chancellor of Germany, Szilard fled Berlin and settled in London, where he founded the Academic Assistance Council to help other refugee scholars. So when he came up with his theory that it might be possible to construct atomic bombs using a chain reaction, he was terrified that the Nazis would accomplish it first.

Szilard filed a patent for an atomic reactor the following year. Desperate for somebody to sponsor his research, he wrote to the founder of the British General Electric Co., recommending that he read a chapter of *The World Set Free* to get the gist of his idea: 'I have reason to believe that in so far as the industrial applications of the present discoveries in physics are concerned, the forecast of the writers may prove to be more accurate than the forecast of the scientists.' Using a novel to make his case with a hard-headed industrialist was typical of Szilard's inability to sell his ideas. A meeting with Rutherford was a washout, too. Having exhausted his funding options in England, Szilard moved to New York in 1938 but fared no better there. While hanging around the physics department at Columbia University, he pummelled the physicist Isidor I. Rabi with so many suggestions that Rabi snapped, 'Please go away. You are reinventing the field. You have too many ideas. Please, go away.'

What reversed Szilard's fortunes was an experiment in Berlin in December 1938. Otto Hahn and Fritz Strassmann bombarded uranium with neutrons, producing barium, but they didn't understand how it had happened. Hahn's former colleague Lise Meitner, working with her nephew Otto Frisch in Sweden, hypothesized that the uranium nucleus had split in two, a process they christened fission. When Niels Bohr carried the news to New York the following month, the press was blasé. 'The physicists are anxious that there be no public alarm over the possibility of the world being blown to bits by their experiments,' the Science Service news agency assured its readers. 'Writers and dramatists (H. G. Wells's scientific fantasies, the play "Wings Over Europe," and J. B. Priestley's current novel, "Doomsday Men") have overemphasized this idea.' Szilard, however, understood the implications the moment he heard the news: 'All the things which H. G. Wells predicted appeared suddenly real to me.' Now that fission had been accomplished – in Hitler's Germany, no less – an atomic superweapon was only a question of time, resources and dedication. 'You know what fission means,' he told fellow émigré Edward Teller. 'It means bombs.'

Suddenly, the construction of an atomic bomb in America became Szilard's top priority. He needed an ally with real clout, so he twice visited his old friend Albert Einstein on Long Island that summer. Immersed in his unified field theory, Einstein hadn't even heard the news about fission, let alone thought about bombs. Shocked, he agreed to sign a letter drafted by Szilard and send it to President Roosevelt: 'Some recent work by E. Fermi and L. Szilard leads me to expect that the element uranium may be turned into a new and important source of energy in the immediate future.' It was conceivable, he added, 'that extremely powerful bombs of a new type may thus be constructed'. On 17 June 1942, after another three years of pestering and prodding, Roosevelt approved the birth of the Manhattan Project. Einstein later called the letter his 'one great mistake . . . but there was some justification – the danger that the Germans would make them.' The Bomb was born of fear.

Russian intelligence gave the Manhattan Project the codename *Enormoz*: enormous. Everything about the Bomb was hyperbolic. It was the most powerful weapon ever made, at a cost of $2 billion ($34 billion today). The uranium processing facility at Oak Ridge, Tennessee, was, for a while, the largest building in the world. Whereas novelists imagined solitary mavericks inventing superweapons in a freelance capacity, thc Manhattan Project employed more than 130,000 people. Among them were many brilliant European emigrés, including Hans Bethe from Germany, Enrico Fermi from Italy, George Kistiakowsky from Ukraine and Stanisław Ulam from Poland. Szilard, Teller, Wigner and von Neumann were known as 'the Martians' after Szilard joked that intelligent aliens had already landed on Earth but called themselves Hungarians. As *The New York Times* observed in a post-Hiroshima editorial with the startling headline 'Thanks to Hitler', fascism drove the scientists capable of building an atomic bomb into the arms of its enemies.

The leader of the Manhattan Project was Brigadier General Leslie Groves, a burly, abrasive army officer with a reputation for bullying, insults and getting things done, but the man who became synonymous with the Bomb was J. Robert Oppenheimer. Despite official concerns about his administrative inexperience and flirtation with communism, the thirty-eight-year-old was tasked with establishing a top-secret laboratory compound at Los Alamos, New Mexico, to oversee the design and construction of the weapon. Oppenheimer was one of Szilard's well-rounded artist-scientists. That he was a theoretical physicist of genius went without saying: he brought quantum mechanics to America and pioneered the study of black holes. But he was also a multilingual bohemian who enjoyed philosophy, modernist poetry, horse-riding and strong Martinis. Rail-thin and lanky, with a chronic cough stemming from a bout of tuberculosis and a five-pack-a-day cigarette habit, Oppenheimer quickly transformed himself from an eccentric, curly-haired intellectual into a dynamic chief executive. Under his inspirational leadership, a community of six thousand men and women, assembled from scratch on a remote mesa between two mountain ranges, developed a pioneer spirit. Oppenheimer described Los Alamos as 'a kind of confluence of my highbrow past, my physics, my students, my horses, my ranch, and my slight knowledge of politics'.

Meanwhile at the University of Chicago's Metallurgical Laboratory, where the physicist Arthur Compton's team worked on the development of nuclear reactors, the mood was more sober. On his arrival at the Met Lab as chief physicist, Szilard arranged for the library to acquire copies of *The World Set Free* and *Public Faces* to focus minds on the consequences of their work. On 2 December 1942, nine years after his traffic-light epiphany, he witnessed the world's first nuclear reactor produce the world's first chain reaction in a chilly squash court beneath the university's football field. *Life* later described it as nothing less than 'the biggest event since the birth of Christ'. While the rest of the team celebrated with a bottle of Chianti, Szilard soured the mood by telling Enrico Fermi that it would go down as 'a black day in the history of mankind'. By organizing Einstein's letter to Roosevelt, he had set the whole process in motion but nobody was more ambivalent about its success. Every day, he was working on a project that he half believed was a necessary evil and half believed was simply evil.

Oppenheimer's team worked simultaneously on two kinds of atomic bomb. One would be a 'gun-type' device using uranium-235. This fissionable 'weapons grade' isotope makes up just 0.7 per cent of natural uranium, hence the size and expense of the processing plant at Oak Ridge. The other, more complicated, would be an 'implosion-type' bomb based on the newly identified element plutonium. These would become the two bombs dropped on Hiroshima and Nagasaki respectively: Little Boy and Fat Man. Bombs were not the only option the team considered. Edward Teller explored the possibility of dropping nuclear waste on enemy troops, much like poison gas, or poisoning their food supply with cancer-inducing strontium-90. As early as July 1942, a month before the Manhattan Project was officially launched,

Teller was pushing for research into a bomb that would fuse hydrogen nuclei into helium: the same process that powers the Sun. The previous autumn, Enrico Fermi had wondered if it might be possible for a fission bomb to heat deuterium, a heavy isotope of hydrogen, to the point where a thermonuclear reaction took place. Fermi's speculation became Teller's obsession. He told Oppenheimer that 1 cubic metre of liquid deuterium, heated to more than 100 million degrees Celsius, could produce a 1 megaton explosion: equivalent to 1 million tons of TNT. Teller's colleagues nicknamed his theoretical bomb – nuclear rather than atomic – the 'Super'.*

For many scientists, especially the European exiles, the sole reason for working on the Bomb was the worry that Nazi Germany would get there first. What they didn't know was that the German scientists were too disorganized, rivalrous and underfunded to create anything as cohesive as the Manhattan Project, nor that Hitler himself was uninterested in atomic energy. Even as he avidly pursued new superweapons such as Wernher von Braun's V-2 rockets, Hitler remarked to his minister Albert Speer that 'the scientists in their unworldly urge to lay bare all the secrets under heaven might some day set the globe on fire.'

Doubts began to ripple through the Manhattan Project in late 1943 when reports indicated that the Nazi bomb programme, under Werner Heisenberg, was going nowhere fast, accelerated after the invasion of Normandy in June 1944, and came to a head after Germany's surrender on 7 May 1945. Japan was losing, too. Szilard now believed that the Bomb was not just unnecessary and immoral but dangerous, in that it would trigger an arms race, and he worked frantically to formalize his colleagues' reservations. He wrote a memorandum to Roosevelt, but the president died before he could read it. He had a dismaying meeting with President Harry S. Truman's hawkish Secretary of State James Byrnes. He orchestrated the Franck Report, which recommended demonstrating the Bomb in an uninhabited area to intimidate Japan, but the Army suppressed it. At his wits' end, Szilard circulated a petition urging Truman to

*Deuterium is an isotope of hydrogen which contains a neutron as well as a proton, making it twice as heavy as a regular hydrogen atom. Liquid deuterium is known as heavy water.

give Japan the chance to surrender rather than risk 'opening the door to an era of devastation on an unimaginable scale'. Oppenheimer and Groves put paid to that.

It is not that the decision-makers took the use of the Bomb lightly. At a crucial meeting about atomic policy in May 1945, Henry L. Stimson, the secretary of war, wondered if the weapon would be the key to world peace or 'a Frankenstein which would eat us up'. But long-term concerns could not compete with the short-term prospect of ensuring Japan's unconditional surrender while keeping Stalin's Soviet Union in check. The physicists had neither the facts needed to assess whether bombing Japan was militarily necessary, nor the power to influence the decision to inflict it on what Oppenheimer called 'those poor little people'. Some, though, soothed their ambivalence by reasoning that if the full horror of the Bomb were not demonstrated right away, then an atomic war was guaranteed. 'Our only hope is getting the facts of our results before the people,' Teller told Szilard. 'This might help to convince everybody that the next war would be fatal. For this purpose actual combat use might even be the best thing.' The old debate about whether a hypothetical superweapon would make war impossible was now being played out with a real bomb, and the stakes were life or death on a global scale.

The Los Alamos scientists felt sure that the uranium bomb would work; they only had enough uranium-235 for one device in any case. The plutonium bomb, however, needed a test run. The device they called 'the gadget' was a plutonium core the size of a tennis ball encased in a series of spheres with a 2-metre diameter and installed in a 30-metre steel tower in the middle of the Alamogordo Bombing and Gunnery Range, 340 kilometres south of Los Alamos. Oppenheimer christened the test Trinity in reference to a line of poetry by John Donne: 'Batter my heart, three-person'd God.' The test was set for the morning of Monday, 16 July. The night before was black and stormy and split with lightning. Oppenheimer stayed up, fuelled by coffee, cigarettes, poetry and anxiety, while Enrico Fermi satirically took bets on 'whether or not the bomb would ignite the atmosphere, and if so, whether it would merely destroy New Mexico or destroy the world'.

This was an outrageous joke with a nucleus of truth.* Three years earlier, Oppenheimer had visited Arthur Compton at his holiday home in Michigan to share an alarming possibility which had arisen from conversations about Edward Teller's Super. If the fission bomb's tremendous heat could trigger a controlled fusion reaction, then might it conceivably also set off an uncontrolled chain reaction of hydrogen atoms in the ocean, or nitrogen in the atmosphere, and destroy the planet? 'This would be the ultimate catastrophe,' Compton recalled dramatically in his memoirs. 'Better to accept the slavery of the Nazis than to run a chance of drawing the final curtain on mankind!' He was ready to pull the plug on the whole project before Hans Bethe calculated that the chances were close to zero. Shortly before Trinity, Fermi asked Teller himself to run the numbers again, just to make sure that the test couldn't 'encircle the globe in a sea of fire'. Teller's team concluded that it was impossible, but on the day, the hobgoblin lingered. It squats at the heart of Christopher Nolan's biopic *Oppenheimer*, having served as a somewhat unfair metaphor for scientific recklessness in his previous movie, *Tenet*.

The Trinity test was almost postponed in case wind and rain spread a radioactive cloud across the south-western United States. Shortly before dawn, though, the storm cleared and hundreds of spectators took their places in various observation posts and trenches. On Compañia Hill, 32 kilometres from ground zero, stood Ernest Lawrence, the Nobel Prize-winning inventor of the cyclotron which produced the uranium and plutonium isotopes for the gadget; James Chadwick, discoverer of the neutron; and Edward Teller, who passed around sun lotion. The observers at Base Camp, 16 kilometres away,

*Another of Fermi's quips has become legendary. In the summer of 1950, he was having lunch at Los Alamos with three other Manhattan Project alumni: Edward Teller, Emil Konopinski and Herbert York. They had been discussing the popular fascination with flying saucers when Fermi asked a question which struck his companions as both funny and profound: 'But where is everybody?' If it was probable that intelligent life existed on other planets, why had there been no contact, no communication, no evidence at all? Perhaps, Fermi suggested, each civilization had advanced to the point where it destroyed itself with its own technology. The so-called Fermi Paradox has figured in discussions of extraterrestrial life and existential risk ever since.

included Isidor Rabi and Leslie Groves. Only essential personnel, including Oppenheimer and explosives expert George Kistiakowsky, were in the dugout a mere 8 kilometres away.

At exactly 5.30 a.m., the gadget was detonated. First came a long blinding white radiance, then an orange cloud of fire, then a violet mushroom-shaped cloud, rising higher than any mountain on earth. One hundred seconds after the flash, there was a colossal boom, a low rumble of thunder, a hot wind and a blast wave. The gadget worked, to the tune of 18.6 kilotons: a blast equivalent to 18,600 tons of TNT. Eyewitness accounts of Trinity suggest a truly apocalyptic experience.

On Compañia Hill, William L. Laurence, the *New York Times* reporter who had been appointed the Manhattan Project's hyperventilating Boswell, recalled Genesis: 'It was as though the earth had opened and the skies had split. One felt as though one were present at the moment of creation when God said: "Let there be light."'

In the dugout, George Kistiakowsky saw Revelation. It was, he said, 'the nearest thing to doomsday that one could possibly imagine. I am sure that at the end of the world – the last millisecond of the earth's existence – the last man will see what we have just seen!'

At Base Camp, during the long, white, silent seconds before the boom, Emilio Segrè felt that the world was already ending. As he later recalled, 'for a moment I thought the explosion might set fire to the atmosphere and thus finish the earth, even though I knew that this was not possible.' James B. Conant of the National Defense Research Committee also thought briefly that 'the thermal nuclear transformation of the atmosphere, once discussed as a possibility and jokingly referred to a few minutes earlier, had actually occurred . . . The whole sky [was] suddenly full of white light like the end of the world. Perhaps my impression was only premature on a time scale of years!'

Brigadier General Thomas F. Farrell, Groves's deputy, theatrically observed 'the strong, sustained, awesome roar which warned of doomsday and made us feel that we puny things were blasphemous to dare tamper with the forces heretofore reserved to the Almighty'. 'There weren't any agnostics watching this stupendous demonstration,' recalled the physicist Joseph O. Hirschfelder. 'Each, in his own way, knew that God had spoken.'

Oppenheimer later claimed that his first thought was Krishna's line from the *Bhagavad Gita*: 'Now I am become death, the destroyer of worlds.' This was entirely plausible: Oppenheimer had made his own translation of the Hindu text while studying Sanskrit. Years later, he named it alongside Eliot's *The Waste Land* in a list of the ten books that had most influenced his philosophy of life. He had even read a passage from it at a memorial service for Roosevelt in April 1945. Nonetheless, what he actually said on the day was far less poetic: 'It worked.'*

The first person ever to sketch the contours of a mushroom cloud was the young physicist Luis Alvarez, who watched the Trinity test from the cockpit of an observation aeroplane 30 kilometres away. Oppenheimer then asked Alvarez to tail the B-29 bomber *Enola Gay* over Hiroshima in order to observe and analyse the blast. At 8.16 a.m. on 6 August 1945, Alvarez witnessed a bright flash, two waves of pulses and two sharp shocks, accompanied by a mushroom cloud so dense that he initially wondered if the bomb had missed Hiroshima. 'I looked in vain for the city that had been our target,' he wrote in his memoir. 'The cloud seemed to be rising out of a wooded area devoid of population.' More than two-thirds of the buildings had been flattened. The US military estimated that around 70,000 people had died as a result of the blast by the end of 1945; later estimates set the figure as high as 140,000. In Nagasaki, which was bombed three days later, the death toll was somewhere between 40,000 and 70,000. 'Hiroshima does not look like a bombed city,' observed Wilfred Burchett, one of the first journalists to record the aftermath. 'It looks as if a monster steamroller has passed over it and squashed it out of existence.'

When the American psychiatrist Robert Jay Lifton interviewed *hibakusha* (literally, 'bomb-affected persons') in Japan in 1962, he found that it had been common for the citizens of Hiroshima to believe that the entire world was ending, a conviction that he had

* Oppenheimer told *Time* in 1948 that he had thought, 'I am become death, shatterer of worlds' but did not use the more famous translation until an NBC TV interview in 1965, two years before his death from throat cancer.

previously encountered only in his most troubled patients: 'We may say that the survivor lived out in psychic and bodily actuality an experience ordinarily associated with psychotic delusion.' A Protestant minister told him, 'I thought this was the end of Hiroshima – of Japan – of humankind . . . This was God's judgment on man.' The writer Yōko Ōta recalled thinking 'it must have been something which had nothing to do with the war, the collapse of the earth which it was said would take place at the end of the world, which I had read about as a child.'

It all looked very different from the *Enola Gay*, whose co-pilot, Captain Robert A. Lewis, remarked that 'what we saw made us feel that we were Buck Rogers' twenty-fifth-century warriors.' Szilard, however, told his future wife Trude Weiss that the raid was 'one of the greatest blunders of history', while Einstein told a reporter, 'Ach! The world is not ready for it.' In London, H. G. Wells pronounced, 'This can wipe out everything bad – or good – in this world. It is up to the people to decide which.' George Orwell wrote that 'everyone I spoke to about it, or overheard in the street, was simply horrified.' In Washington DC, President Truman announced that 'the basic power of the universe' had been unleashed on Hiroshima.

After the mission, Alvarez put down his thoughts in the form of a letter to his four-year-old son Walt, to be read when the boy was older: 'What regrets I have about being a party to killing and maiming thousands of Japanese civilians this morning are tempered with the hope that this terrible weapon we have created may bring the countries of the world together and prevent further wars.' He thought that the Bomb 'may realize Nobel's dream' of making war inconceivable. This is the same Luis and Walter Alvarez who, thirty-five years later, published their hypothesis that an asteroid had caused the KT extinction 66 million years ago. 'While many of my friends devoted most of their time to arms control efforts,' Luis wrote towards the end of his life, 'I looked into extinctions.'

One could say that his friends were looking into extinctions, too, because the apocalyptic implications of the Bomb were grasped immediately. Elation over the end of one world war was poisoned by fear of the next. The *Chicago Tribune* predicted that an atomic conflict would leave earth 'a barren waste, in which the survivors of the race will hide in caves or live among the ruins,' while the *St. Louis Post-Dispatch* suggested that the men who made the Bomb may have 'signed the mammalian world's death warrant and deeded an earth in ruins to the ants'. As one *hibakusha* put it, 'Such a weapon has the power to make everything into nothing.'

CHAPTER 7

Deliverance or Doom

The end
will come
in its time.
Meanwhile
we are sick to death
of the bomb
and its childlike
insistence.

William Carlos Williams, 'Asphodel, That Greeny Flower' (1955)

The Bomb swallowed the imagination. For the next few decades, if a concerned citizen wanted to talk up the importance of some rival threat – computers, pesticides, overpopulation – then they compared it to the Bomb. The level of fear rose and fell but it never subsided entirely. For the first time in history, the means to end the world, or at least a tolerable version of the world, was both feasible and human-made: not God, not a comet, but us. 'Suddenly the day of judgment was the next day and has been ever since,' Isidor Rabi said in 1962. This news followed reports of mindboggling cruelty and contempt for human life in Nazi extermination camps and played into an anguished conversation about what people can do to each other. Auschwitz and Hiroshima, the gas chamber and the mushroom cloud, thus became twinned in the catastrophic imagination as two unprecedented experiences of mass death and trauma, but one could be blamed on a defeated tyranny while the other had been inflicted by a victorious democracy and seemed considerably more likely to happen again.

Potential annihilation became a vast and simple fact which everybody knew, yet no ordinary citizen could do anything about it. This bred an eerie dissonance. Anyone who bought the 19 November 1945 issue of *Life* on the strength of the cheerful cover story about the new fashion for big belts would have found inside a startling article called 'The 36-Hour War'. Based on a report by General Henry H. 'Hap' Arnold, the outgoing commander of the United States Army Air Forces, it came with illustrations of what New York and Washington DC might look like after the 'apocalyptic destruction' of a nuclear missile strike. Meanwhile in London, the philosopher Bertrand Russell shared with the House of Lords a startling hallucination: 'As I go about the streets and see St. Paul's, the British Museum, the Houses of Parliament and the other monuments of our civilization, in my mind's eye I see a nightmare vision of those buildings as heaps of rubble with corpses all round them.'

When Luis Alvarez returned to Los Alamos in August 1945, he found his colleagues in a gloomy frame of mind. 'Many of my friends felt responsible for killing Japanese civilians, and it upset them terribly,' he recalled. 'I could muster very little sympathy for their point of view.' The moral tension between those who felt sickened by their complicity and those who slept soundly in the belief that it had been an extraordinary and essential accomplishment, as 85 per cent of Americans told pollsters that they did, came to define the science of the Cold War. While *Life* observed that atomic physicists wore 'the tunic of Superman', Leo Szilard found their new celebrity distasteful: 'It is remarkable that all these scientists . . . should be listened to. But mass murderers have always commanded the attention of the public, and atomic scientists are no exception to this rule.' As the director of the project, and suddenly one of the most famous men in America, J. Robert Oppenheimer came to embody this collective guilt. Truman's commerce secretary Henry Wallace recalled, 'I never saw a man in such an extremely nervous state as Oppenheimer. He seemed to feel that the destruction of the entire human race was imminent.' Oppenheimer could be quite the buzzkill. In his farewell address as director of Los Alamos, he proposed what would become a familiar binary: 'The peoples of this world must unite or they will perish.'

This nervousness even infected *The Beginning or the End*, MGM's stiff, sanitized 1947 docudrama about the Manhattan Project: 'The people of our century unleashed the power which might, for all we know, destroy human life on this Earth.'* In the movie, Jonathan Hale plays Vannevar Bush, the computer pioneer who had helped to initiate the Manhattan Project as chair of Roosevelt's National Defense Research Committee. Bush argued that the moral crisis occasioned by the Bomb came less from what it had just done to Japan than from what it might proceed to do to the rest of the world. 'It was fear of the future that concentrated attention on the atomic bomb,' he wrote. The firebombing of Japanese cities had been no less abhorrent but it lacked the shocking, world-changing, almost supernatural novelty of the Bomb. Therefore 'it is not astounding that the bomb promptly became a basis for predicting the end of the world as we know it.'

The prestige of atomic physicists made them the most effective campaigners against their own creation. In November 1945, a group of them formed the Federation of Atomic Scientists (FAS) to study the implications of atomic energy, promote its safest applications and campaign for an international arms-control regime. For a while, it was wrongly assumed that any country with enough money and determination could develop its own bomb within six years. The FAS put together *One World or None*, an all-star essay collection featuring the likes of Oppenheimer, Szilard, Einstein and Hap Arnold, which sold 100,000 copies on publication in March 1946. The book's final words were blunt: 'Time is short. And survival is at stake.'

A handful of the activist scientists had a flair for imaginative prose: Oppenheimer's former student Philip Morrison had visited Hiroshima after the blast and transplanted the wound to New York in the most impactful chapter of *One World or None*. The FAS decided that the best strategy was to bypass reason and appeal to emotion, specifically

*The movie's most cutting review came from Szilard: 'If our sin as scientists was to make and use the atomic bomb, then our punishment was to watch *The Beginning or the End*.'

fear. 'I write this to frighten you,' the former Manhattan Project chemist Harold C. Urey declared in *Collier's*. 'I'm a frightened man, myself. All the scientists I know are frightened – frightened for their lives – and frightened for *your* life . . .' Without arms control, he argued, this would be the future: 'We will eat fear, sleep fear, live in fear and die in fear.' A colleague, Albert Cahn, admitted to *The New Yorker* that 'we have turned ourselves into twenty-five hundred Jeremiahs . . . You have to shake them by the shoulders.'

In July 1947, a Pulitzer Prize-winning newspaper cartoon by Rube Goldberg showed an ordinary American house perched on top of an atom bomb which teetered on a cliff edge between 'WORLD CONTROL' and the abyss of 'WORLD DESTRUCTION'. For a few hopeful months, the former had seemed possible. In the US, control over nuclear energy passed from the military to the civilian Atomic Energy Commission (AEC) under the chairmanship of New Deal veteran David Lilienthal. Influenced by Niels Bohr, Oppenheimer drafted a plan for international atomic energy control, known as the Acheson–Lilienthal Report, which Truman's emissary Bernard Baruch pitched to the United Nations in June 1946 as 'the last, best hope of earth'. The more utopian idea of world government had a surprising degree of support, too. 'Nuclear energy insists on global government,' wrote E. B. White in *The New Yorker*, pointing out that it was no use claiming that the Bomb was too terrible to use when the US had just used it – twice. Even the fanatically anti-communist Edward Teller co-authored an article which argued that 'nothing but world-union' could abolish the risk of atomic war.

But the Truman administration gutted Acheson–Lilienthal to the extent that the version Baruch took to the UN was unacceptable to Stalin, and then the US promptly rejected the Soviet counter-proposal. The chance was lost. In Theodore Sturgeon's anguished anti-war story 'Thunder and Roses', written in a 'black depression' over the failure of arms control, one character tells another, 'You sound like the first chapter of *One World or None* . . . If people had paid more attention to it when it was published, perhaps this wouldn't have happened.' Meanwhile, Bernard Brodie, a young military strategist at Yale, proposed an entirely different theory of fear – deterrence – in which the superpowers' possession of unthinkably destructive weapons would be the guarantor of peace. 'Thus far the chief purpose of our military establishment has been to win wars,' Brodie wrote. 'From now on its chief purpose must be to prevent them.' Thus Cold War nuclear policy became governed by a version of what Norman Cousins called the 'war-is-now-too-horrible theory'.

In the wake of disappointment, some senior figures felt that the campaigning scientists had gone too far, with Oppenheimer advising that they could no longer act like 'prophets of doom coming out of the desert'. The collapse of international arms control illustrated the conundrum of using a life-or-death choice as a rhetorical strategy: if you tell people that the cost of failure is world destruction and then fail, then they are left with either the psychologically insupportable prospect of constant dread or the impression that you were exaggerating the stakes. Neither response inspires action. Over the next few decades, Robert Jay Lifton observed, fear of the Bomb was so vast and chronic that it had a numbing effect, producing 'various combinations of resignation, cynicism, and yearning' rather than the belief that anything could be done about it. The modernist writer Gertrude Stein shrugged provocatively that the Bomb bored her: 'I am not so scared, there is so much to be scared of so what is the use of bothering to be scared, and if you are not scared the atomic bomb is not interesting.'

The AEC's David Lilienthal took direct aim at the Jeremiah strategy: 'It might have seemed like a good idea to scare the world into being good, or at least sensible. But fear is brother to panic. Fear is an unreliable ally; it can never be depended upon to produce good.' Though Lilienthal was privately apprehensive, he saw it as his duty to give the atom a friendly face by promoting the potential of cheap, clean energy, which eventually led President Dwight Eisenhower to deliver his 'Atoms for Peace' speech in 1953. The pseudo-religious dualism that Frederick Soddy had evoked with his choice between Eden or apocalypse was revived as a kind of cosmic contest between the good atom and the evil atom, from Philip Wylie's essay 'Deliverance or Doom' to David Low's newspaper cartoon in which a glowing ball representing the atom was labelled 'Life or death'. 'It was so gigantic, so terrible, so beyond the power of imagination to embrace, that it seemed to be the ultimate fact,' Lilienthal recalled of the atom's public image. 'It would either destroy us all or it would bring about the millennium.'

One day, shortly after Hiroshima, the Met Lab physicist-turned-arms-control activist Eugene Rabinowitch was walking through Chicago when he found himself imagining 'the sky suddenly lit by a giant fireball, the steel skeletons of skyscrapers bending into grotesque shapes and their masonry raining down into the streets below, until a great cloud of dust rose and settled over the crumbling city'. A refugee from both Lenin's Russia and Hitler's Germany, Rabinowitch had co-authored the Franck Report with Szilard, recommending that the US refrain from bombing Japan. With fellow physicist Hyman Goldsmith, he co-founded a newsletter called *Bulletin of the Atomic Scientists* to explore issues relating to the Bomb. In 1947, Goldsmith commissioned landscape artist Martyl Langsdorf (whose physicist husband, Alexander, had signed Szilard's petition to Truman) to design the cover of the June issue of what was now a proper monthly magazine. As she listened to the concerns of scientists, Langsdorf sketched an image that would convey their dreadful urgency: the top-left quadrant of a timepiece that would become known as the Doomsday Clock. She set it at seven minutes to midnight, mostly because it looked good. The responsibility of moving the hand fell to Rabinowitch, who remained editor until his death in 1973.

Langsdorf's clock was an apt metaphor because atomic weapons had changed humanity's relationship to time. 'In an instant, without warning, the present had become the unthinkable future,' *Time* pronounced after Hiroshima. *BusinessWeek* dubbed the following year 'Atom Year I'. William Laurence said it was '12.01 on the hour-glass of history'. The word of Krishna's that Oppenheimer rendered as 'death' is more commonly translated as 'world-destroying time', but the Bomb could destroy time itself, and break history down to atoms. Needless to say, the Doomsday Clock delighted premillennialists, as they counted down to Armageddon, but it was in fact a hopeful symbol, designed to inspire activism rather than fatalism: because the hand is turned by humans, not by time, it can move backwards as well as forwards. By the time Rabinowitch died, the hand had moved back to twelve minutes to midnight. Throughout the 1940s and 1950s, however, the direction was one-way.

In 1946, Joseph H. Rush of the FAS predicted that when Russia obtained the Bomb, it 'may not mean the end of the world, but when that day comes, I rather imagine you'll get a pretty good picture of how people will behave just before the world *does* come to an end.' That day came in August 1949, when an American weather plane detected evidence of a secret Soviet A-bomb test in Kazakhstan. Code-named Joe-1 by the US, it was an achievement made possible by a handful of spies within the Manhattan Project. Stalin privately told an aide, 'Atomic weapons can hardly be used without spelling the end of the world,' but the Americans did not know about his misgivings, and the end of their atomic monopoly – at least two years earlier than expected – came as an appalling shock. Rabinowitch moved the Doomsday Clock to three minutes to midnight to denote a 'world well advanced towards the abyss of an atomic war'. *Collier's* imagined New York as an inferno in a gruesomely well-researched story called 'Hiroshima U.S.A.: Can Anything be Done About It?' Edward Teller, meanwhile, immediately began pushing hard for investment in the hydrogen bomb to restore America's military advantage. He called his new design the 'Alarm Clock'.

When the FAS reached out to scientists in other countries, it mailed an information pack which included *One World or None*, Harold Urey's article about fear, and *Hiroshima*, the panoramic masterpiece that *New Yorker* reporter John Hersey crafted from the testimony of six *hibakusha*. The son of missionaries, Hersey had a strong moral code but he wrote in a 'deliberately quiet' tone, letting the facts speak for themselves. When it filled an entire issue of *The New Yorker* in August 1946, it was left to the editor's note to make it didactic: 'Few of us have yet comprehended the all but incredible destructive power of this weapon . . . Everyone might well take time to consider the terrible implications of its use.' Einstein sent one thousand copies of the magazine to his fellow scientists. Hersey's article, which was immediately turned into a book and a four-part ABC Radio production, humanized Hiroshima. Anybody who sought to imagine what the Bomb might do to London or Washington DC turned to Hersey for eyewitness veracity: faces erased by flash burns; bodies burned on pyres of wood from shattered houses; people vomiting to death from radiation, or blinded because their eyes had melted, or shedding flakes of skin as big as dinner plates, or incinerated in an instant, leaving behind only silhouettes. Just months later, Leonard Engel and Emanuel S. Piller acknowledged their debt to Hersey's reporting in their future-war novel *World Aflame: The Russian–American War of 1950*: 'This was Hersey's *Hiroshima* – ten times worse – in my own country.'

No other book had anything like the same impact as *Hiroshima* in the immediate post-war years, but then there was not much competition. Demand for fiction about the Bomb so far outstripped supply that an enterprising publisher took the title of the critic Lewis Mumford's unapologetically shrill call for disarmament, 'Gentlemen, You Are Mad!', and slapped it onto a reissue of *The Pallid Giant*. Pierrepoint B. Noyes's nineteen-year-old novel thus became a gloomy riposte to deterrence theory. The first major writer to grapple with atomic ruination was Aldous Huxley with *Ape and Essence*, his grotesque 1948 satire about the crazed denizens of Los Angeles in the aftermath of 'the Thing': 'a city of two and a half million skeletons'. The popular crime writer J. Jefferson Farjeon also weighed in with *Death of a World*, a droll, disgusted account of aliens raking through the ashes of 'a dead world that has slayed itself'.

Another novel published that year became notable only in retrospect, because it was the full-length debut of a former Royal Air Force officer named Roald Dahl. Obsessed by the thought of atomic Armageddon, Dahl told one friend that the smart money was on World War Three breaking out in 1949 or 1950. It was, he wrote, 'the saddest, and craziest thought that it is possible to think'. It was in this tormented frame of mind that he wrote *Sometime Never*, a grisly anti-war satire about a subterranean race of Gremlins (horns, tails, little bowler hats) who decide to wait for humanity to destroy itself so that they can inherit the earth. Featuring not just a third world war but a fourth, the novel is a bizarre marriage of whimsy and horror. If the idea of pint-sized critters who live off Snozzberries, recycled from an earlier children's book he had written for Walt Disney, points towards Dahl's more famous work as a beloved children's author, then the images of humanity's mutilated, maddened remnants living out their last days like animals in the detritus of civilization do not. In one harrowing sequence, drawing on *Hiroshima*, Dahl demolishes London and kills off all the characters we have come to know and like during the first half of the novel. 'The time has come', he writes in the introduction, 'when only man's intense conceit, blinding his powers of deduction, can prevent him from being quite certain that his civilization is disintegrating and must inevitably perish.' As one can imagine, *Sometime Never* sold poorly and was never reprinted. Dahl considered this 'ghastly book' a post-Hiroshima bad dream that he had been foolish enough to share with the public once but never again.

Philip Wylie had no such qualms. Involved in the establishment of the AEC, he was made an adviser to the Federal Civil Defense Administration and the Special Committee on Atomic Energy, which gave him access to confidential information and clearance to observe nuclear tests in Nevada. 'Movies and TV have given the American public no adequate idea of the spectacle of the bomb,' he wrote, 'its sky-filling, multi-hued aftermath, the peculiar ruins and the cubic miles of rolling dust – not to mention a city a-fire.' Wylie felt passionately that the American public was being kept in the dark about life-and-death matters. In his 1946 short story 'Blunder: A Story of the End of the World', set in the 1970s after an atomic war between the US and USSR, foolish security restrictions prevent two scientists from being informed that the new bismuth bomb that they are about to test will emit an 'omega ray' which will destroy the whole planet. Wylie churned out a string of novels, stories and essays to alert readers to the atomic peril.

'Today it is not the priest, not the self-appointed prophet with his crackpot interpretation of Daniel or the Book of Revelation, who says, "The earth may end,"' declares a newspaper editor in *Tomorrow!*, Wylie's horrendously detailed 1954 novel about a nuclear Pearl Harbor. 'It is that very group of reasonable, orderly, unhysterical men upon whom society has learned, a little, to lean for comfort and truth: *the scientists themselves!*' This is part of an editorial that the editor is dictating about the problem of 'a reasonable fear, yet one of such a magnitude and nature that it cannot be tolerated by the combined efforts of reason and the common will'. He is promptly fired. Nobody wants to read that. Wylie dedicated *Tomorrow!* to 'the men and women of the Federal Civil Defense Administration' and sent a copy to President Eisenhower.*

Tomorrow! was a product of the new thermonuclear era. Early post-war novels such as *Sometime Never* were hyperbolic because fission weapons alone weren't capable of obliterating civilization, but it seemed that Edward Teller's hydrogen bomb really could.

Enrico Fermi told Teller that he was, in his experience, 'the only monomaniac with several manias'. If Szilard was a bumblebee, then Teller was a lamprey: once he latched on to an idea, he wouldn't let go. An abrasive, saturnine character with eyebrows like a gathering storm, he did not soon forgive those who stood in the way of his ferocious ambition. In the post-war years, he pursued the H-bomb with an obsessive zeal which led former colleagues to denounce him as 'an egomaniac, a paranoid [and] a seller-out to the military' with 'a messianic complex'. Isidor Rabi was savagely blunt: 'It would have been a better world without Teller.'

Teller, however, claimed to be motivated by what he saw as his scientific obligation to realize new possibilities. 'I do not want the hydrogen bomb because it would kill more people,' he protested. 'I wanted the hydrogen bomb because it was *new* . . . I am afraid of ignorance.' He further argued that whether or not America developed it, Russia surely would, and he was right about that: it later emerged that the Soviets had a secret H-bomb programme underway as early as 1944. Once he had allayed General Groves's fears that *this* bomb might 'ignite the entire world's atmosphere', Teller won round former colleagues Ernest Lawrence and Luis Alvarez, whom David Lilienthal noted were 'drooling with the prospect'. Hans Bethe, however, declined an invitation to join him after deciding that 'after such a war, even if we were to win it, the world would not be . . . like the world we want to preserve'. The schism in the Manhattan Project diaspora was widening.

* *Tomorrow!* emerged from an abandoned attempt to make an official propaganda film on the subject. Instead, the government funded *Invasion U.S.A.*, a 1952 thriller in which the complacent customers of a San Francisco bar experience a mass hallucination of the bombs and military occupations that await them if they are insufficiently prepared.

In October 1949, the General Advisory Committee of the AEC met for an urgent three-day discussion of the H-bomb, unanimously recommending that the Truman administration block it on technical and moral grounds. Fermi and Rabi described it as 'a danger to humanity as a whole'. But Secretary of State Dean Acheson told Oppenheimer that the president could not politically survive the decision *not* to make the bomb. On 31 January 1950, Truman announced plans to explore the feasibility of a thermonuclear weapon with the power of one thousand Hiroshimas. When the president signed the press statement, he recalled a similar meeting three years earlier which had led to the Truman Doctrine of containing the Soviet Union and lending military assistance to 'free peoples'. In Lilienthal's account, Truman said that 'at that time everybody predicted the end of the world if we went ahead, but we did go ahead and the world didn't come to an end. He felt this would be the same case here.' With a new Red Scare in full swing, almost seven in ten Americans approved, even as journalists dubbed it the 'Hell Bomb'. Within months, Christian country singer Fred Kirby had cashed in with his jaunty ditty 'When That Hell Bomb Falls'. 'Our tragedy today is a general and universal physical fear so long sustained by now that we can even bear it,' said William Faulkner when he accepted the Nobel Prize for Literature in December 1950. 'There are no longer problems of the spirit. There is only the question: When will I be blown up?'

When Truman made his announcement, it wasn't clear that the H-bomb was possible. Teller had obstinately wasted five years on the Alarm Clock, a dead-end design that could not generate enough energy from the fission bomb (the 'primary') to kindle a thermonuclear reaction in liquid deuterium (the 'secondary'). But in January 1951, the Polish-American physicist Stanisław Ulam presented Teller with a solution that even Oppenheimer deemed so 'technically sweet' that he could no longer object. On 1 November 1952, the power of the Sun's core was visited upon the Pacific island of Elugelab on the Eniwetok atoll, at which point Elugelab ceased to exist. The first thermonuclear device, nicknamed Ivy Mike, detonated with a force of more than 10 megatons, vaporizing the island into a mushroom cloud around 40 kilometres high and 160 kilometres wide. Teller, the proud father, declared, 'It's a boy.' In its wake, Eugene

Rabinowitch moved the Doomsday Clock's hand to two minutes to midnight.

Never before or since has talk of the end of the world been so mainstream and so specific. President Eisenhower said in 1953 that to accept a permanent stand-off between 'two atomic colossi' would be 'to accept the probability of civilization destroyed, the annihilation of the irreplaceable heritage of mankind handed down to us from generation to generation, and the condemnation of mankind to begin all over again the age-old struggle upward from savagery towards decency, and right, and justice'. Outgoing British prime minister Winston Churchill, whose political twilight was illuminated by an obsession with preventing nuclear war, later reflected in his last major speech to the House of Commons that the H-bomb had changed everything. The atomic bomb was a weapon of war but the H-bomb was bigger than war: 'The entire foundation of human affairs was revolutionised, and mankind placed in a situation both measureless and laden with doom.' He worried what would happen 'if God wearied of mankind'.

While Teller celebrated his vindication, the H-bomb's early opponents were pushed out into the cold. Effectively barred from nuclear physics by his old nemesis Leslie Groves, Szilard was now working as a biologist. 'Theoretically I am supposed to divide my time between finding what life is and trying to preserve it by saving the world,' he wrote to Niels Bohr after Truman's announcement. 'At present the world seems to be beyond saving, and that leaves me more time free for biology.' Without the Manhattan Project to focus him, his brain spun off in all directions. He filed patents for numerous inventions, from a calorie calculator to a formula for low-fat cheese, and he proposed founding a boarding school in Mexico City to prepare children for reconstructing society after a nuclear war. Szilard also wrote short stories: in 1947's 'My Trial as a War Criminal', he masochistically imagined himself being prosecuted by the victorious Russians for his part in the Bomb.*

Oppenheimer, meanwhile, was brought low in 1954 by a vindictive

*Andrei Sakharov, who led the Soviet nuclear programme, read the story in Szilard's 1961 collection *The Voice of the Dolphins* and later credited it with setting him on the road to becoming a leading dissident and winner of the Nobel Peace Prize.

and humiliating McCarthyite security clearance hearing orchestrated by AEC chair Lewis Strauss. In January 1955, he reluctantly sat for a TV interview with CBS broadcaster Edward R. Murrow, who asked whether humanity now had the power to destroy itself. 'Not quite,' the haunted father of the Bomb replied. 'Not quite. You can certainly destroy enough of humanity so that only the greatest act of faith can persuade you that what's left will be human.'

Between Joe-1 in August 1949 and Ivy Mike in November 1952 fell the Korean War, which threatened to metastasize into World War Three, and the first two explicit Bomb movies, *The Day the Earth Stood Still* and *Five*. The former, directed by Robert Wise, was such a strident argument for international arms control that it might have been commissioned by the FAS. *Five*, written and directed by Arch Oboler, was the first picture to portray life after the Bomb, although it ended up undercutting its anti-war sentiment. 'You and I are in a dead world,' says the embittered Michael (William Phipps). 'And I'm glad it's dead. Cheap honky-tonk of a world.' He welcomes the 'new chance to make the world what everybody used to talk about... let's make the most of it.' Closing with Revelation's lines about a new heaven and a new earth, the movie's message is unsettling: sure, nuclear obliteration would be sub-optimal, but might it also be purifying?

Four months after Truman told the world about the H-bomb, Ray Bradbury published a chilling short story called 'There Will Come Soft Rains'. It soon appeared in *The Martian Chronicles*, a tapestry of stories marketed as a novel, which became both the most popular fictional take on nuclear war and the first bridgehead from the world of science fiction magazines to a mainstream readership. Bradbury took the title from a short pacifist poem written by Sara Teasdale in the final months of the First World War, which opened with idyllic snapshots of nature in joyful bloom before twisting the knife:

> Not one would mind, neither bird nor tree
> If mankind perished utterly;
> And Spring herself, when she woke at dawn,
> Would scarcely know that we were gone.

Teasdale's disgust with the war led her towards omnicidal misanthropy. Would the planet not be much better off, she suggested, if we no longer existed?

Bradbury's story is set in 2026 (or, in later editions, 2057), on the eve of the anniversary of Hiroshima. An automated house, the pinnacle of hi-tech consumerist luxury, goes about its dutiful business, oblivious to the fact that its residents are dead and their shadows are burned into its walls; the house stands 'alone in a city of rubble and ashes'. Breakfast is cooked, Martinis poured, a bath run. Late in the evening, a tree bough falls, knocking over flammable liquid, and the house burns to the ground. Nature finishes the job.

Bradbury was a pacifist whose most famous novel, 1953's *Fahrenheit 451*, also culminates in nuclear war. The common thread in *The Martian Chronicles* is the idea that mankind will destroy everything it touches, on Mars as well as Earth. The futuristic adventures of Buck Rogers had introduced the young Bradbury to the delights of the yet-to-come, but he always described his work as fantasy rather than science fiction. Born in Waukegan, Illinois, in 1920, he produced work with a thick seam of Middle American nostalgia, often equating technology with corruption and loss rather than wonder and promise. He never drove a car, was slow to acquire a television and didn't take a flight until he was sixty-two. In the final chapter of *The Martian Chronicles*, 'The Million-Year Picnic', a father who has taken his family to Mars passes judgement on the planet they have left behind: 'Science ran too far ahead of us too quickly, and the people got lost in a mechanical wilderness... emphasizing machines instead of how to run the machines ... that way of life proved itself wrong and strangled itself with its own hands.'

The damning, slate-wiping sentiment of 'There Will Come Soft Rains' was not uncommon; living with the Bomb had a tendency to inspire self-disgust. 'When they had gone the Earth itself remained as it had been before they came and in the course of time all traces of their brief sojourn would be smoothed away,' wrote Roald Dahl in *Sometime Never.* A character in Theodore Sturgeon's 'Thunder and Roses' asks, 'What creatures were these, these corrupted, violent, murdering humans? What right had they to another chance? What was in them that was good?' Such guilt and revulsion are there, too, in Nevil Shute's 1957 novel *On the Beach*, which supplanted *The*

Martian Chronicles as the decade's most important fictional treatment of thermonuclear annihilation: 'The human race was to be wiped out and the world made clean again for wiser occupants without undue delay. Well, probably that made sense.'

The wiping out in *On the Beach* was achieved by a new addition to the decade's armoury of nightmares: the cobalt bomb.

CHAPTER 8

The Doomsday Machine

I suppose I haven't got any imagination.
It's – it's the end of the world. I've never
had to imagine anything like that before.

Nevil Shute, *On the Beach* (1957)

On 26 February 1950, Leo Szilard spawned a monster. He did so during a round table discussion for NBC radio called 'The Facts About the Hydrogen Bomb', which also featured three more Manhattan Project alumni: Hans Bethe, Frederick Seitz and Harrison Brown. Two weeks earlier, in a televised address, Albert Einstein had warned millions of viewers that 'radioactive poisoning of the atmosphere, and hence annihilation of any life on earth, has been brought within the range of technical possibilities.' Understandably, the sight of the world's most sanctified scientist talking about total extinction caused an international sensation; the movie *Five* directly quoted his address, turning speculation into exposition.

Midway through the round table, Szilard argued that it would take a ridiculous number of conventional H-bombs to imperil life on earth but that 'it is very easy to arrange an H-bomb, on purpose, so that it should produce very dangerous radioactivity.' He imagined jacketing a bomb with another element, such as cobalt, which would be irradiated by the neutrons released by the blast and had a half-life of around five years. Brown pressed him on the details: How could it work? Who would ever use a device that amounted to global murder-suicide? Szilard, who knew very well how the improbable could become the inevitable, laid it all out. 'Then we are faced with the ironical conclusion in this respect that it becomes easier to kill all the people in the world than just a part of them,' Brown summarized. 'This is definitely so,' said Szilard.

William Laurence covered the debate in the next day's *New York Times* under the stark headline, 'Ending of All Life by Hydrogen Bomb Held a Possibility – Radioactivity the Killer'. *Time*, however, charged that Szilard and Brown had been 'led by emotion to confuse the worst possibilities of the future with the sufficiently alarming present'. Even Bethe thought that Szilard had transgressed by talking about a weapon that nobody had even thought of building. 'The H-bomb was bad enough,' he complained later. 'Why go beyond it?' But Szilard's hypothetical weapon was to inspire the era's most sensationally popular stories about a terminal thermonuclear war: *On the Beach*, *Dr. Strangelove* and *Planet of the Apes*. It bears repeating: the superweapon that mesmerized storytellers for two decades never came close to existing.

From the start, however, the cobalt bomb was taken very seriously. *Bulletin* commissioned a young physicist called James R. Arnold to assess its plausibility and he concluded that it could indeed exterminate most, though not all, of the population. In his 1951 book *The Hell Bomb*, Laurence agreed that a bomb 'rigged' with cobalt would create 'a gigantic radioactive cloud that would kill everything in the area it blankets. Nor would it be confined to a particular area, since the winds would take it thousands of miles, carrying death to distant places.' The so-called C-bomb soon infiltrated fiction, too, via Arthur C. Clarke's *Childhood's End* in 1953 and Philip Wylie's *Tomorrow!* the following year, but only Nevil Shute had the brilliant idea of making it mundane.

Novels made Nevil Shute Norway rich and famous, but he always considered them second best to aeroplanes. As he explained in *Slide Rule: The Autobiography of an Engineer*, he dropped his surname for publishing purposes because he worried that his fellow engineers would think him 'not a serious person'. Born on the outskirts of London in the first month of the last year of the nineteenth century, he became a pilot and aeronautical engineer who helped to design the R-100 airship for Vickers and military aircraft for his own company, Airspeed Ltd. 'Most of my adult life, perhaps all the worth-while part of it, has been spent in messing about with aeroplanes,' he wrote. During the Second World War, he served as a lieutenant-commander in the Royal Naval Volunteer Reserve and conceived an anti-submarine missile called the Rocket Spear.

Shute's staid, middle-of-the-road, enormously popular novels were thoroughly disconnected from the glittering spaceways of science fiction. He specialized in placing ordinary, decent people into exceptional circumstances. With a face like a disappointed bloodhound, Shute was a staunch conservative who believed in capitalism, monarchy and empire while loathing the welfare state and the people who had built it. 'Britain is not a very good country for a successful man,' he said. He emigrated to Australia in 1950 to escape what he viewed as the demoralizing high-tax socialism of Clement Attlee's Labour government and purchased an 800-square-kilometre estate in the Melbourne suburb of Langwarrin. *On the Beach* took place on his doorstep. Shute recalled joking to a friend that in the event of nuclear war between superpowers in the Northern Hemisphere, Australia would inherit the earth, but his research soon convinced him otherwise, starting in December 1954 with a *Time* article about the effects of radiation on the climate and the human body. The idea of something that would make death both inevitable and slow for the residents of a country that had been spared the bombs themselves set in train a novel that Shute originally called *The Last Day*. 'It became an attractive speculation – what would ordinary people in my part of the world do with that [last] year?' he explained.

In March 1954, Los Alamos had blundered. Castle Bravo, its first bomb using lithium deuteride instead of deuterium, had been expected to generate a 6-megaton explosion on Bikini Atoll in the Pacific Ocean but it yielded an unprecedented 15, depositing a cloud of radioactive fallout across 1,800 square kilometres. The crew of the Japanese fishing vessel *Daigo Fukuryū Maru* (*Lucky Dragon 5*) were unlucky enough to be caught in the affected zone and experienced acute radiation sickness: vomiting, hair loss, skin lesions, bleeding.

Castle Bravo was a tremendous, multifaceted shock. First, it suggested that war would not be required to wreck the world: in novels such as Charles Eric Maine's *The Tide Went Out*, the damage done by reckless testing is sufficient. The scale of the blast further suggested that war, if it happened, would be unsurvivable, leading some civil-defence groups to throw in the towel. In rural Derbyshire, *The New Yorker* reported, one local council 'announced that it was shutting up shop on civil defense, and will presumably await the end of the world with dignity and free evenings'. During an anguished debate in the House of Commons, Labour MP Eric Fletcher said that 'as a result of scientific discoveries in recent days there has now been put into the hands of man the means of bringing about, if not the total destruction, at least certain widespread destruction of civilization and the human race.' His colleague R. T. Paget drily responded, 'I take second place to nobody in my admiration and respect for the power of this House, but I do not really think that a new Clause to postpone or abolish the end of the world is likely to prove effective.'

The fate of *Lucky Dragon 5* also introduced the general public to the word *fallout* and inspired in fiction a new focus on the effects of radiation, from Helen Clarkson's solemnly credible novel *The Last Day* to the less solemn, less credible B-movie *Attack of the Crab Monsters*. The boat was soon referenced in the opening scenes of Ishirō Honda's movie *Gojira* (*Godzilla*), the story of a giant dinosaur roused from the ocean's depths by US H-bomb tests. The representation of human suffering is unusually graphic. Godzilla *is* the Bomb: a mindless, radioactive engine of destruction which lays waste to Japanese cities, much like Wilfred Burchett's 'monster steamroller'. 'When I returned from the war', Honda recalled, 'and passed through Hiroshima there was a heavy atmosphere – a fear the earth was already coming to an end. That became the basis of the film.' Castle Bravo simultaneously inspired Akira Kurosawa to revive the trauma of Hiroshima more soberly in *Ikimono no Kiruko* (*I Live in Fear*), his movie about an old man who becomes obsessed with fleeing Japan to avoid thermonuclear war. The man ends up in a psychiatric hospital, believing that he is on a distant planet, watching the earth burn. The film argues that while his fear has devoured him, 'It's a feeling all of us Japanese share to a greater or lesser degree'. 'I find myself questioning whether he is the one that's insane in this situation,' says his psychiatrist, 'or is it we, who appear sane, that aren't?'

On top of all that, the magnitude of Castle Bravo made the C-bomb plausible. 'Now Most Dreaded Weapon, Cobalt Bomb, Can Be Built' ran the headline of a William Laurence article which explained how a sufficiently large bomb, mounted on a ship rather than an aeroplane, could depopulate an entire continent. A steady stream of politicians, military officers, scientists and academics insisted that the cobalt bomb would be militarily useless, but the concept had entered the realm of the possible. Otto Hahn, the discoverer of fission, warned of it, as did the archbishop of Canterbury. *Bulletin* remarked that the world's media was suddenly obsessed with 'an annihilating cobalt bomb, or C-bomb, which could become a world suicide bomb, with winds carrying the lethal dust around the world'.

Such was the premise of Shute's novel. When it was serialized in the *Sunday Graphic* in April 1957, *The Last Day* became *The Last Days on Earth* but Shute then renamed the novel again, after a line from T. S. Eliot's 'The Hollow Men' ('gathered on this beach of the tumid river') and quoted it in the epigraph along with the more famous 'Not with a bang but a whimper'.* As the novel opens, the bangs are all over and only the long whimper remains. In Shute's 1961, nuclear weapons are cheap and widely available and it is Albania, of all places, that pushes the first domino by dropping a uranium bomb on Naples. A series of overreactions and misunderstandings leads to global nuclear war and then to radiological war, as China uses cobalt bombs against Russia. In short order, the entire Northern Hemisphere becomes uninhabited. The novel unfolds in a suburb of Melbourne, which will be the last major city to fall to the fatal cloud: Eliot's 'last of meeting places'. They have nine months left; the government distributes suicide pills to citizens who would rather bow out on their own terms. 'It's like waiting to be hung,' says the hedonistic Moira Davison. 'Maybe it is,' responds the upright US

*In 1958, Eliot told the *Saturday Review* that he would not still write his famous line about the bang and the whimper. 'One reason is that while the association of the H-bomb is irrelevant to it, it would today come to everyone's mind,' his interviewer paraphrased. 'Another is that he is not sure the world will end with either. People whose houses were bombed have told him they don't remember hearing anything.'

Navy officer Commander Dwight Towers. 'Or maybe it's a period of grace.'

The peculiar power of Shute's novel derives from its union of an extreme premise with bland, unflappable storytelling. There is none of the urgent horror of *Tomorrow!* or *Sometime Never*; death is quiet, diligent, stupefyingly efficient and incomprehensible in scale. Characters' stoic refusal to make a fuss about their imminent doom becomes rather eerie. They are sad, of course, irritated on occasion, sometimes prone to excessive drinking, but never hysterical or self-pitying. They plant bulbs that they will never see bloom, collate data for histories that will never be read and have babies that will never grow up. There are no frantic orgies, no crimewaves, no religious awakenings. Dwight declines an affair with Moira even though his wife is surely dead. Characters describe the end of the world as 'silliness' or, if they become particularly heated, 'bloody unfair'.

Both Shute and his publisher thought that a book as terminal as *On the Beach* would achieve modest sales. In fact, it reached number two on the *New York Times* bestseller list and sold four million copies over the next three decades. By September 1957, it was already being serialized in thirty-nine US newspapers and optioned for a movie by the crusading producer-director Stanley Kramer. Philip Wylie, who later praised *On the Beach* in his own C-bomb novel, *Triumph*, told Shute's US publisher that it 'ought to be compulsory reading at the Pentagon, West Point, Annapolis. Ike [Eisenhower] should set aside his western and puzzle his way through it.' Winston Churchill suggested sending a copy to Soviet premier Nikita Khrushchev but not to Eisenhower. 'It would be a waste of money. He is so muddle-headed now,' he told his private secretary. 'I think the earth will soon be destroyed by a cobalt bomb,' he went on. 'And if I were the Almighty I would not recreate it in case they destroyed him too the next time.'

Shute's timing was perfect. Nineteen-fifty-seven was the year that Britain detonated its first H-bomb over Christmas Island in the Indian Ocean to become the world's third thermonuclear power, and *Sputnik 1* temporarily made Russia the winner in the space race. It was the year that the Campaign for Nuclear Disarmament (CND) formed in the UK and the National Committee for a Sane Nuclear

Policy (SANE) in the US. In the essay that sparked CND, co-founder and vice-president J. B. Priestley wrote that World War Three 'will not be anything recognisable as a war . . . It will be universal catastrophe and apocalypse, the crack of doom into which Communism, western democracy, their way of life and our way of life, may disappear for ever.' Disarmament experts met for the first time in the Nova Scotia fishing village of Pugwash, where Leo Szilard described the state of the arms race as 'illogical, insane, unstable'. The evangelist Billy Graham shocked and thrilled twenty thousand congregants a night at Madison Square Garden with his atomic gospel: 'Prepare to meet thy God, the Bible says. If any generation ever needed to prepare, it's this one. Especially the people of New York. One hydrogen bomb, and you're done.' No wonder *On the Beach* found an audience.

When Tom Lehrer sang, 'Universal bereavement / An inspiring achievement', in his tart 1959 satire 'We Will All Go Together When We Go', he might have been describing the plot of *On the Beach*, the movie version of which reached cinemas just in time for Christmas that year. Stanley Kramer called Shute's novel 'by far the most important story that I have ever found' but managed to enrage the author by having Dwight (Gregory Peck) and Moira (Ava Gardner) consummate their relationship – an unforgivable betrayal of the dignity and self-denial at the novel's core. Still, Kramer's version was earnestly true to the story's dreadful essence. The Pentagon refused him permission to borrow a nuclear submarine, he claimed, because the movie was deemed too negative: 'No: your story says an atomic war would wipe out the world, and that isn't so. Only about five hundred million people would be killed.' The movie ends with a montage of lifeless streets and a Salvation Army banner flapping ironically in the radioactive breeze: 'THERE IS STILL TIME . . . BROTHER.' Not time for the characters, of course, but for the viewers.*

Over the previous decade, moviemakers had laundered their

*The scene may have reminded some viewers of a new kind of tactical nuclear weapon, the neutron bomb, first reported by *Time* just weeks before the movie opened. *Popular Science* called it 'a real Buck Rogers job: a true death ray. It would make hardly any bang, cause no damage to buildings or machines, create no radio-active fallout – but it would kill every person outdoors or indoors over a wide area.'

atomic anxieties through hair-raising tales of giant irradiated ants and lizards, and other allegorical monsters, a process that Susan Sontag described as 'this intersection between a naïve and largely debased commercial art product and the most profound dilemmas of the contemporary situation'. Old stories, too, were nuclearized. The prolific producer George Pal introduced nuclear weapons into his adaptations of H. G. Wells's *The Time Machine* and *The War of the Worlds* and gave Wylie and Balmer's *When Worlds Collide* a post-Bomb flavour. The success of Kramer's picture, however, proved that audiences could handle something closer to the real thing. Sanitized though it was – no violence, no villains, no bombs, no bodies – it did at least show a group of ordinary people facing up to the actual end of the world. 'To appall the audience in this sense – not to give them pleasant shivers because of the antics of monsters in a screen nightmare but to appall them about their own fate in the real world – is certainly taboo in the mass media,' remarked *Esquire.* The movie was endorsed by Harold Urey, Harrison Brown and, most breathlessly, the pacifist and Nobel Prize-winning scientist Linus Pauling: 'It may be that some years from now we can look back and say that *On the Beach* is the movie that saved the world.' It is amazing what people thought a novel or a movie could achieve. It was even discussed by Eisenhower's cabinet, leading to a memorandum called 'Possible Questions and Suggested Answers on the Film "On the Beach"'.

Edward Teller disapproved of the movie so strongly that he devoted a whole chapter of his book *The Legacy of Hiroshima* to debunking it: 'The cobalt bomb is not the invention of an evil warmonger. It is the product of the imagination of high-minded people who want to use this specter to frighten us into the heaven of peace.' Though Teller thought that Shute's story encouraged an unhealthy fatalism and defeatism, he found the success of the book and movie 'remarkable and revealing: We are obsessed by the idea of an impending day of doom.' He described a depressing conversation with a young friend: 'He could see no point in putting money aside, and declared: "The world is coming to an end. There's no sense in planning for the future." Such pessimistic personal conclusions are not unusual.'

—

On 11 January 1960, a week before he died from a stroke, Nevil Shute wrote that popular writers could 'play the part of the *enfant terrible* in raising for the first time subjects which ought to be discussed in public and which no statesman cares to approach. In this way, an entertainer may serve a useful purpose.' The philosophy professor Mordecai Roshwald likewise explained why he had decided to write his first and only novel, 1959's *Level 7*, and dedicate it to Eisenhower and Khrushchev. In this lean, mordant satire of 'dehumanised war, automatic war, and its inevitable result: the end of civilization', C-bomb radiation travels down through the levels of an underground military base as remorselessly as Edgar Allan Poe's Red Death, turning a shelter into a tomb. Roshwald wanted to 'frighten people into sanity. I thought a novel would reach a much wider readership than an academic and scholarly essay.'

This was not just the vanity of novelists talking. Thomas Schelling, a nuclear strategist at the Centre for International Affairs at Harvard, wrote an essay for *Bulletin* in October 1960 about the causes of nuclear war in *On the Beach* and *Red Alert*, a thriller written by a Welsh RAF officer named Peter George under the pseudonym Peter Bryant. In a fan letter he told George that many of his peers thought that the novel was as convincing as any real-life wargame exercise. They, too, were engaged in writing speculative stories about the worst thing that could happen. In fact, Schelling added, George might have surpassed the professionals: 'The great advantage of fiction is that people can be enticed, for the sake of the story, to accept premises that they would otherwise reject as unreasonable, when they are really only unfamiliar.'

The subject of *Red Alert*, inadvertent nuclear war, was a hot topic in 1958. The US government insisted that a new system called 'Fail Safe', which required a scrambled bomber to turn back unless it received a second signal from the president himself, was 'proof against error, human or mechanical', but it was not universally believed. 'The more elaborately involved and hair-triggered the machinery of destruction, the more likely it is that this machinery will be set in motion, if only by accident,' objected J. B. Priestley. *The Nation*'s Carl Dreher fretted that a conflict could be triggered by 'a nervous, psychotic or fanatical launch officer', a possibility which was actively promoted by the Soviets. After Khrushchev suggested that a war could be sparked by 'a derangement in the normal psychic state of a person', the KGB duly forged a Defense Department letter which claimed that 67.3 per cent of US flight personnel were erratic 'psychoneurotics'. This is exactly what happens in Peter George's efficient nail-biter. A single unhinged general in the Strategic Air Command starts a war, and not just any war: the Soviets have a cluster of cobalt bombs whose detonation 'would mean the end of the world. Literally . . . ten months from now our Earth will be as dead as the Moon.' *Red Alert* (or *Two Hours to Doom*, as it was titled in the UK) sold a quarter of a million copies in the US, one of which ended up in the hands of the neurotic *wunderkind* of American cinema.

Stanley Kubrick was *Red Alert*'s ideal reader. His first narrative feature, 1952's *Fear and Desire*, had an anti-war message, as did 1957's *Paths of Glory*. He could not stop thinking about the Bomb. In October 1961, he visited the International Institute for Strategic Studies in London, whose director, Alastair Buchan, gave him a copy of *Red Alert* with the caveat that it wasn't remotely convincing. Undeterred, Kubrick optioned the novel and approached George to work with him on a screenplay.

Kubrick discovered *Red Alert* towards the end of an ominous stand-off between Washington and Moscow over the fate of West Berlin. President John F. Kennedy quoted Epicurus: 'A man who causes fear cannot be free from fear.' Robert Lowell complained to fellow poet Elizabeth Bishop of 'a queer, half-apocalyptic, nuclear feeling in the air' and started work on his exasperated poem 'Fall 1961': 'All autumn, the chafe and jar / of nuclear war; / we have talked our extinction to death.' Kubrick became so pessimistic that he started making plans to move his family to Australia to escape oblivion. In October, the Russian H-bomb known as Tsar Bomba generated an astonishing blast of at least 50 megatons. More than three times the yield of Castle Bravo and sixteen times the total amount of TNT exploded in the Second World War, it remains the biggest human-made explosion in history. In a landmark speech to the UN that autumn, which Kubrick later sent to the Motion Picture Association of America to support his contention that everything he wanted to say in his movie was already on the public record, the president said,

'Mankind must put an end to war – or war will put an end to mankind.'*

The Berlin crisis prompted a sudden boom in private companies with names like Peace-O-Mind Shelter Company ('fallout shelters, like the Twist, have become fashionable,' reported *Newsweek*), most of which just as quickly went out of business when they realized that the average American considered fallout shelters to be both expensive and useless. Indeed, a congressional report found that only one-quarter of the victims of Hiroshima and Nagasaki would have been saved by shelters. Bertrand Russell wrote that life in shelters would resemble the subterranean hell of *Level 7*, while Kurt Vonnegut pitched to the humour magazine *Help!* a satirical advertisement for kits designed to break into a neighbour's shelter, including 'all-clear signals; tape recordings of beloved family pets scratching to be let in, tape recordings of old A.B.C. speeches on the harmlessness of fallout; grenades, bazookas, flamethrowers, etc.' *The Twilight Zone* took this idea much more seriously in a famous episode called 'The Shelter': an air-raid warning sets neighbour against neighbour before they realize, too late, that it is a false alarm. 'We were spared a bomb tonight,' says the shelter's horrified owner, 'but I wonder if we weren't destroyed without it.' In pop songs such as Bob Dylan's 'Let Me Die in My Footsteps' and Billy Chambers's 'Fallout Shelter', the hip option was to choose nuclear slaughter over cowering underground.

Kubrick read every book, magazine, pamphlet and think-tank report that he could find on the subject of nuclear war. He later observed that strategists 'happily chatted away about the most somber topic, buoyed up by what must have been pride and satisfaction in their professional expertise; and this seemed to completely overcome any sense of personal involvement in the possible destruction of their world'. For months, the director swung back and forth between a straight adaptation of *Red Alert*, a satirical comedy about the rise of a sociopathic strategist named Dr Otto Strangelove, and something more realistic called *The Delicate Balance of Terror*, after an article in

*Intentionally or otherwise, Kennedy was paraphrasing H. G. Wells's *Things to Come*: 'If we don't end war, war will end us.' His speech in turn graced the finale of the 1961 Japanese movie *Sekai Daisenso* (*The Last War*).

Foreign Affairs. Eventually, he merged the ideas into a screenplay that, by August 1962, he was calling *Dr. Strangelove or: How I Learned to Stop Worrying and Love the Bomb*. 'In the context of imminent world destruction,' he later said, 'hypocrisy, misunderstanding, lechery, paranoia, euphemism, patriotism, heroism and even reasonableness can evoke a grisly laugh.' Leaning into what he saw as the madness of nuclear deterrence, he hired the irreverent novelist Terry Southern to spruce up the jokes.

Kubrick was in pre-production on *Dr. Strangelove* when, on 15 October 1962, the CIA analysed reconnaissance photos taken by a U-2 spy plane and identified medium-range ballistic missiles on Cuban soil, contrary to Soviet denials. President Kennedy was informed the next morning. The next thirteen days, recalled his brother Robert, 'brought the world to the abyss of nuclear destruction and the end of mankind'. The world officially learned about the crisis at 7 p.m. EST on Monday, 22 October, when the president interrupted television schedules to tell the American public that a naval blockade would be imposed on Cuba until Khrushchev removed all Soviet missiles from the island. 'One Week May Alter All Future', declared the Associated Press. Leo Szilard caught the first flight to Geneva with his wife and told his former Manhattan Project colleague Victor Weisskopf, 'I'm the first refugee from America . . . there will be nuclear war in a few days.' Harrison Brown dashed out an urgent editorial for the *Bulletin*: 'Never in history have people and nations been so close to death and destruction on such a vast scale. Midnight is upon us.' Throughout the week, there was panic-buying of canned food, bottled water and firearms, while government departments drew up plans for preserving society in a post-war America. On Wednesday, 24 October, Strategic Air Command moved to DEFCON 2.

On 27 October, 'Black Saturday', the abyss was inches away. When the US Navy used depth charges to deter the Russian submarine *B-59*, it didn't know that the sub was armed with a nuclear torpedo, nor that it was too deep to communicate with the surface. For all its commander, Valentin Savitsky, knew, the war had already started. Savitsky wanted to fire back, which could easily have been the first domino in a full-scale nuclear war, but the task force commander, Vasili Arkhipov, was on board and talked Savitsky down, correctly arguing that the depth charges were a warning rather than an attack. When declassified Soviet documents revealed the full story in 2002, the director of the National Security Archive concluded that 'a guy called Vasili Arkhipov saved the world.'

The next morning, Khrushchev agreed to remove missiles from Cuba in return for the US pulling Jupiter missiles out of Turkey. The crisis was over, Armageddon postponed, but during that week following the president's address, human life had never seemed so fragile. 'It was literally true that when the president of the United States went to sleep, he did not know whether he would ever wake up in the morning to anything left on Earth,' wrote one journalist. Bob Dylan used to claim that he had written his torrential, doom-crazed ballad 'A Hard Rain's a-Gonna Fall' in New York one night during the crisis: 'People sat around wondering if it was the end, and so did I. Would one o'clock the next day ever come? . . . It was a song of terror. Line after line after line, trying to capture the feeling of nothingness.' In fact, as the Dylanologist Clinton Heylin discovered, Dylan had first performed it a month earlier – just one of his many apocalyptic songs. That kind of dread didn't fall out of the sky on 22 October; it was ambient.

Consider how the Bomb already preyed on the world's mind in 1962. High on the *New York Times* bestseller list during the crisis was *Seven Days in May*, Fletcher Nebel and Charles W. Bailey II's thriller about an attempted military coup to thwart nuclear disarmament. Ray Milland's sour thriller *Panic in Year Zero!* showed America degenerating into violent anarchy after a nuclear strike. The winner of the Academy Award for Best Animated Short Film was *The Hole*, a bantering dialogue between two construction workers about the chances of an accidental nuclear strike (guess how it ends), while the BAFTA for Best Film Screenplay went to Val Guest and Wolf Mankowitz for *The Day the Earth Caught Fire*, a thoughtful thriller about nuclear tests which send the planet spinning towards the Sun. The Louvin Brothers, a Baptist country music duo, released a grotesquely upbeat song which asked, 'Are you ready for that great atomic power? / Will you rise and meet your saviour in the air?' James Bond foiled nuclear terrorism in *Dr. No.* A man travelled back in time from post-apocalyptic Paris to prevent World War Three in Chris Marker's haunting short film *La Jetée*. Perhaps the only creative person who saw the upside of atomic power in 1962 was Marvel Comics writer Stan Lee, who sprinkled radiation like fairy dust on the tetchy boffins and ordinary Joes who became Spider-Man, the Hulk and the Fantastic Four.

Mostly, there was alarm. The week of the crisis, political scientists Eugene Burdick and Harvey Wheeler published *Fail-Safe*, a thriller about a nuclear war triggered by a single faulty computer component. With admirers including Philip Wylie and President Kennedy, it sold more than two million copies – exceeding even sales of *Red Alert.* Peter George believed it virtually *was Red Alert.* When the novel was optioned for a film for a rumoured $500,000, Kubrick and George filed a copyright lawsuit, which was settled out of court on the understanding that Columbia Pictures would acquire the movie of *Fail-Safe* and release it after *Dr. Strangelove.* Given recent events, *Life* found the contretemps surprisingly hilarious: 'In Two Big Book-alikes a Mad General and a Bad Black Box Blow Up Two Cities, AND THEN – Everybody Blows Up!'

'If being frightened meant that I helped avert such insanity, then I'm glad I was frightened,' Khrushchev told peace activist Norman Cousins in December 1962. 'One of the problems in the world today is that not enough people are sufficiently frightened by the danger of nuclear war.' After Cuba, that fear inspired action. To make communication easier in future, the White House–Kremlin hotline that had been used as a plot device in *Red Alert* and *Fail-Safe* became a reality, leading the authors of both novels to claim the credit. The Partial Nuclear Test Ban Treaty, signed by Kennedy and Khrushchev in October 1963, literally removed the mushroom cloud from view. This new era of arms control allowed ordinary people to forget the raw terror of that week in October and relax somewhat about nuclear war: the proportion of Americans who listed it as the nation's most pressing problem collapsed from 64 per cent in 1959 to just 16 in 1964. A panel of social scientists assembled by Kennedy found that the primary psychological effect of the Berlin and Cuba crises was cognitive dissonance – a phrase that had originated in the study of Millerites when the expected end of the world failed to arrive. As his movie's sarcastic subtitle advertised, Stanley Kubrick was determined to show that this mass exhalation of relief was premature. 'The longer the bomb is around without anything happening, the better the job that people do in psychologically denying its existence,' he told *The New Yorker.* 'It has become as abstract as the fact that we are all going to die someday, which we usually do an excellent job of denying.'

Dr. Strangelove finds hilarious absurdity in the lethal combination of human fallibility and technological inevitability, when the mentally unstable General Jack D. Ripper (Sterling Hayden) dispatches a bomber wing to Russia which cannot be recalled by anybody else. Meanwhile, in the War Room, the Soviet ambassador reveals to President Merkin Muffley (Peter Sellers) that Russia has been working on a 'Doomsday Machine', designed to be triggered automatically: a number of H-bombs, jacketed with 'Cobalt Thorium G', which will produce a global 'doomsday shroud' for ninety-three years and 'destroy all human and animal life on earth'. Unfortunately, Russia has not previously informed the US of its existence. As Dr Strangelove (Sellers again) points out, 'Deterrence is the art of producing in the mind of the enemy the *fear* to attack . . . The whole point of the Doomsday Machine is lost if you keep it a secret!'

The idea of the Doomsday Machine came from *Red Alert* but the name, like so many of the movie's key ingredients, derived from the nuclear strategist Herman Kahn's 1960 bestseller *On Thermonuclear War.* The critic Midge Decter remarked that *Dr. Strangelove* 'could very easily have been written by Herman Kahn himself; he outlines just such plots in his books.' When General Buck Turgidson (George C. Scott) initially proposes a choice between 'two admittedly regrettable but nevertheless distinguishable postwar environments', he is paraphrasing Kahn's menu of 'tragic but distinguishable postwar states', ranging from 2 million to 160 million dead. Kahn's neologism for one million deaths per nuclear explosion, *megadeath,* can be seen on Turgidson's manila folder.

Kahn was a loquacious giant whose girth invited comparisons to Mr Pickwick and Santa Claus. After serving in Burma during the war, he studied engineering and physics at UCLA and Caltech. In 1947, he joined the RAND Corporation in Santa Monica as a computer technician. (One of Kubrick's weaker jokes is 'the BLAND Corporation'.) Originally called Project RAND (Research and

Development), it had been established in 1945 by Hap Arnold as a think tank for the Air Force, specializing in a kind of avant-garde futurology. In 1961, Kahn quit RAND to launch his own think tank on the east coast, the Hudson Institute. An avid reader of science fiction, Kahn was at the forefront of scenarios and wargames. Reading one of his studies, wrote a *New York Times* reporter, 'one thinks of H. G. Wells. It is an attempt to forecast possible world situations a decade from now.' Another journalist wrote that *On Thermonuclear War* 'began to resemble a deadpan *War of the Worlds*'.

Kahn was a superstar in the small world of nuclear strategists – not just because he said unsayable things but because of how he said them. 'He exudes intelligent observation so lavishly and with such evident enjoyment, that reasoning seems to be for him a Dionysian process,' observed the journalist Norman Moss. In marathon all-day sessions, he would pace the room, working up a mighty sweat through his short-sleeved shirt, outlining possible futures in a chewy Bronx accent and laughing at his own macabre jokes. 'I can be really funny about thermonuclear war,' he boasted. Yet Kahn's unique blend of unflinching logic, provocative exaggeration and abrasive humour struck some readers as obscene. 'The Rand Corporation, Kahn, all the rest, chatted about "doomsday machines" and how to make them and then ignored the likelihood they'd be made,' Philip Wylie raged in *Triumph*. 'Is there really a Herman Kahn?' asked the mathematician James R. Newman in a famously damning review of *On Thermonuclear War*. 'It is hard to believe. Doubts cross one's mind almost from the first page of this deplorable book: no one could write like this; no one could think like this.' Kahn responded by calling his next book *Thinking the Unthinkable.*

Kahn was hurt by this caricature of himself as a jovial psychopath. How, asked his critics, could he talk so clinically about the difference between 50 and 100 million dead? How, replied Kahn, could he not? Somebody had to think about how to make thermonuclear war both winnable and survivable, however distasteful it might seem. Like Edward Teller, Kahn thought that talk of the end of the world was counterproductive hyperbole and criticized 'expressions like "balance of terror," "thermonuclear stalemate," "suicidal war," "mutual annihilation," "inescapable end of civilization," "destruction of all life,"

[and] "end of history."' His imagination was anti-apocalyptic: tens of millions might die but the world would go on.

'Will the Survivors Envy the Dead?' is perhaps the most chilling line in *On Thermonuclear War*, but Kahn's own answer was: no. Having compiled reports for the Eisenhower administration into the possibility of preserving millions of American lives in mineshafts and subway tunnels, he wrote, 'It would not surprise me if the overwhelming majority of the survivors devoted themselves with a somewhat fanatic intensity to the task of rebuilding what was destroyed.' One reader wrote to him that it seemed as if Kahn thought, or even hoped, that 'life after World War III might be much better than life today. It is as if you thought of yourself as one of a number of Noahs, stepping out into a new world for a fresh start.' Kahn's speculations about a post-war underground world inform the penultimate scene of *Dr. Strangelove*, when Strangelove proposes a scheme to preserve a computer-selected 'nucleus of human specimens' in mineshafts. 'Wouldn't this nucleus of survivors be so grief-stricken and anguished that they'd, well, envy the dead?' asks a dubious Muffley. Not at all, says Strangelove, they would be filled with 'a spirit of bold curiosity for the adventure ahead'.*

It seems that Kahn was more flattered than offended by the satire. The screenplay took so many lines from *On Thermonuclear War* that he suggested to Kubrick that he receive royalty payments. The director, stunned by his gall, replied, 'It doesn't work that way.' Many journalists assumed that he was the inspiration for Strangelove, but Kahn himself seemed unsure: though he initially insisted that Kubrick had told him this was not the case, he later described Strangelove as a mongrel of Wernher von Braun, future Secretary of State Henry Kissinger and himself. Edward Teller and John von Neumann have also been mooted as models for Sellers's grotesque creation, based on his strangulated European accent and icy logic, but there was in fact no such person as the 'real' Dr Strangelove: he was a composite. *Fail Safe* director Sidney Lumet happily admitted

*Peter George's next novel, *Commander-1*, was originally called *Nucleus of Survivors*. Dedicated to Kubrick, this savagely bleak tale of a submarine commander who becomes a post-apocalyptic despot was to be his last: in June 1966, suffering from depression and alcoholism, he took a double-barrelled shotgun to his head.

that his movie's Dr Groeteschele (Walter Matthau) *was* based on Kahn but nobody much cared about the real Dr Groeteschele.

One thing that certainly did not come from Kahn, nor from *Red Alert*, was the movie's ending. It was Kubrick who decided, at the last minute, that the movie's satirical momentum demanded the end of the world. It concludes with Major 'King' Kong (Slim Pickens), the pilot of the final bomber, riding the bomb like a bronco as he plunges towards his oblivion, and ours. A festive bouquet of mushroom clouds unfurls to the sound of Vera Lynn's wartime pick-me-up 'We'll Meet Again'. The savage, frantic hilarity of *Dr. Strangelove* could not have been more different from the elegiac solemnity of *On the Beach*, but both works, drawing on Szilard's theoretical doomsday bomb, boldly committed themselves to the end of everything.

This decision made Kubrick's hit movie a priceless piece of anti-war propaganda, which duly inspired rallies, pamphlets and congratulatory messages from anti-nuclear campaigners: Lewis Mumford hailed it as 'the first break in the catatonic Cold-War trance that has so long held our country in its rigid grip'. Yet Susan Sontag spoke for the sceptics when she dismissed the ending as 'nihilism for the masses, a philistine nihilism'. Misanthropy, she claimed, is 'the only perspective from which the topic of mass annihilation is comic'. Years later, Kurt Vonnegut compared *Dr. Strangelove* unfavourably with Peter Watkins's Oscar-winning 1966 pseudo-documentary *The War Game* – the first attempt to portray nuclear war realistically. Deemed too upsetting to be screened on the BBC, *The War Game* juxtaposed a dramatization of the impact on ordinary people in Kent, England, with the real words of experts, including a fictional version of Herman Kahn. By contrast, Vonnegut argued, Kubrick produced a perversely comforting spectacle which was the opposite of a wake-up call:

> It was meant to be irony, but to most people in the audience and on most people's level it was beautiful . . . this was stirring and lovely and appealing – the end of the world – and did not cause anyone to recoil from it . . . [*The War Game*] was bad news to people, but the peaceful end, the painless end was deeply gratifying to people . . . Inadvertently, or maybe on purpose, Kubrick made a picture which sent people home utterly satisfied.

And I'm sure that everyone that ever sees that picture sleeps soundly afterward and feels nothing more needs to be done.

Kubrick, however, had no regrets. 'People react, as a rule, when they are directly confronted with events,' he told *The New York Times*. 'Here, any direct contact with the bomb would leave very few people to do any reacting. Laughter can only make people a little more thoughtful.'

While Strangelove's DNA was hotly debated, there was no doubt about the model for both Buck Turgidson and Jack D. Ripper: General Curtis LeMay. The belligerent former commander of the Strategic Air Command and the firebomber of Japan, LeMay became infamous for claiming that America could bomb North Vietnam back into the Stone Age if it wanted to. The Bomb revived the pre-war trend for novels such as *Theodore Savage*, in which war brings about a kind of global time travel. In Leigh Brackett's *The Long Tomorrow* and John Wyndham's *The Chrysalids*, nuclear war has produced a superstitious, neo-medieval theocracy with so little civilizational memory that the war itself is not history but myth, like the Deluge: 'The Destruction' and 'The Thing' respectively.

By far the most ambitious story of this kind was Walter M. Miller Jr's 1959 novel *A Canticle for Liebowitz*.* Six centuries after an all-out nuclear war has blasted humanity back to the Dark Ages, the monks of New Rome talk of a long-ago 'Flame Deluge' which unleashed a demon called 'Fallout' and inspired a purging massacre of scientists called the 'Simplification'. They believe that God orchestrated the invention of the Bomb 'to test mankind which had become swelled with pride as in the time of Noah'. Entrusted with the world's few remaining books, the monks recite old prayers requesting deliverance 'from the rain of the cobalt'. Gradually, though, humanity rebuilds a hi-tech society, which means rediscovering the Bomb. 'My sons, they cannot do it again,' says the abbot. 'Only a race of madmen could do it again.' Needless to say, they do it again. Like

* The most notable advance on Miller has been Russell Hoban's 1980 novel *Riddley Walker*, in which language itself has decayed and the reader must decipher the verbal fragments of a shattered world.

The Pallid Giant, Miller's novel proposes that history is a cycle of creation and destruction, and linear progress is a myth. There are ladders and there are snakes. And sometimes there are apes.

When King Brothers Productions acquired the rights to the French author Pierre Boulle's Swiftian 1963 novel *La Planète des singes* (*Planet of the Apes*), they approached Rod Serling to write the screenplay. Serling was the master of morally engaged science fiction. Serving in the Philippines during the Second World War, where his regiment suffered a devastating 50 per cent casualty rate, had made him viscerally anti-war, while his experience of anti-Semitism nourished his opposition to prejudice of any kind. His unashamedly didactic television work in the 1950s earned him the sobriquet 'Television's Angry Young Man'. 'The writer's role is to be a menacer of the public's conscience,' he declared. 'He must have a position, a point of view. He must see the arts as a vehicle of social criticism and he must focus the issues of his time.' He explained that he could tackle all manner of controversial subjects under an allegorical cloak: 'It was all right to have Martians saying things Democrats and Republicans could never say.'

Between 1959 and 1964, Serling's CBS anthology series, *The Twilight Zone*, was, at its best, a masterclass in social commentary and moral quandary, including a number of end-of-the-world stories. He hired writers such as Richard Matheson and Ray Bradbury but wrote most of the standout episodes himself, famous for their rug-pulling twists: 'The Shelter', 'The Monsters Are Due on Maple Street', 'The Midnight Sun'. In 'Time Enough at Last', a last-man tale based on a short story by Lynn Venable, a bullied bookworm survives a thermonuclear strike and finds in the shell of a library a reason to live – a chance to read in peace – but breaks his spectacles and is left truly alone. 'We were attempting irony and in the view of many of the audience, we created only sadism,' Serling admitted.

As *The Twilight Zone* was drawing to a close, Serling adapted *Seven Days in May* for director John Frankenheimer and wrote *A Carol for Another Christmas* for Joseph L. Mankiewicz. This riff on Dickens, commissioned to promote the United Nations, featured two of the stars of *Dr. Strangelove*: Sterling Hayden played Daniel Grudge, a xenophobic, Scrooge-like tycoon, while Peter Sellers was the post-apocalyptic demagogue Imperial Me. Having visited Hiroshima and a barbaric, bomb-blasted future, Grudge comes around to the necessity of the UN: 'We either greet the morning . . . or accept the night.' Epitomizing Serling's weakness for purple prose and a preachy tone, it was not a festive hit but at least the writer had the challenge of *Planet of the Apes* to keep him busy. In May 1964, he had found his twist: the 'alien' planet is Earth and the journey was not space travel but time travel, to the year 3978. We have been watching a post-apocalyptic movie all along. By Christmas, Serling had decided that the big reveal, echoing the Romantic obsession with the moral lessons of ruins, would be a 'giant metal arm' poking out of the ground: the Statue of Liberty.

Images of American doom had played a role in the recent presidential election. One of many reasons why President Lyndon B. Johnson crushed his Republican opponent Barry Goldwater was Goldwater's cavalier attitude to nuclear war. Richard Hofstadter wrote that the candidate 'seemed strangely casual about the prospect of total destruction. The final spiritual Armageddon of the fundamentalists, their overarching moral melodrama, the dream of millennial crusading and decisive conflict, plainly stirred his mind, but the hard realities of the current world seemed more remote.' When Goldwater claimed that the H-bomb was no more significant an innovation than gunpowder or aerial warfare, the Johnson campaign exploited his tone-deaf gaffe with an outrageously effective TV spot which segued the voice of a little girl counting the petals on a daisy into an ominous countdown. A vote for Goldwater, the ad implied, was a vote for Armageddon. Over footage of a mushroom cloud, the president intoned a Serlingesque message: 'We must either love each other or we must die.'

After Serling drifted away from *Planet of the Apes*, new screenwriter Michael Wilson rewrote much of the movie but he retained the knockout ending. Taylor (Charlton Heston), the vengeful defender of mankind's legacy, believes that his species must have been 'wiped out by a plague, some natural catastrophe, a storm of meteors', until the sight of Liberty on the beach brings him to his knees: 'Oh my God. I'm back. I'm home. All the time it was . . . We finally really did it . . . You maniacs! You blew it up! Ah, damn you! God damn you all to hell!' Though now a pop-culture punchline, the revelation had tremendous force in 1968 and the movie was a triumph with audiences and critics. *The New Yorker*'s Pauline Kael even preferred this 'enormous, many-layered black joke' to Kubrick's.

Despite the post-Cuba decline in public concern, nuclear elimination was still so mainstream in the late 1960s that it was discussed by Captain Kirk in the *Star Trek* episode 'The Doomsday Machine'; satirized in Richard Lester's ferocious comedy *The Bed Sitting Room*; and debated by talking dogs in *The Starlight Barking*, Dodie Smith's peculiarly grave sequel to *The Hundred and One Dalmatians*, which offered children the scarring image of 'desperate, starving wretches, fighting each other, eating each other, just in order to go on living a life that isn't worth living'. The counterculture writer and activist Jeff Nuttall went so far as to claim that the entirety of post-war youth culture, from the Beats to the Beatles, was a response to the psychic distress of living with the Bomb: 'No single solitary one amongst us had the slightest spark of hope or gave a damn about a thing except the crackling certainty of Now.'

The cobalt bomb took a starring role in 1970's *Beneath the Planet of the Apes*, when Taylor discovers a subterranean cult of telepathic mutants who worship a 'Divine Bomb' with Alpha and Omega stencilled on one fin. Taylor identifies the device as a doomsday bomb: 'My God. What a lovely souvenir from the twentieth century. They weren't satisfied with a bomb that could knock out a city. They finally built one with a cobalt casing in the sweet name of peace.' The movie's British screenwriter, Paul Dehn, was a passionate disarmament advocate whose work included *Seven Days to Noon*, a thriller about a scientist who tries to blackmail the world into destroying nuclear weapons, and a book of satirical anti-war poetry, but the reason for the film's startling finale was more pragmatic than philosophical: Heston wanted to exit the franchise and figured he could 'end the whole thing with a death that included the end of the world'. Dehn was furious ('Human beings should cling to at least a little bit of hope') but Heston contractually insisted on annihilation. 'It's doomsday. The end of the world,' Taylor croaks as he triggers the bomb and the screen burns white.*

*The picture's success caused an abrupt change of heart at the studio, which sent Dehn a blunt telegram: 'Apes exist, sequel required.' Hollywood can always find a loophole in the end of the world.

The movie's impossibly instant destruction recalls Edward Teller's old theory about the atomic bomb setting fire to the atmosphere rather than the cobalt bomb's creeping radiation, thus completing the C-bomb's long journey from hypothesis to pure symbol. Twenty years after Szilard first floated the idea, *Beneath the Planet of the Apes* was the end of the road for the C-bomb. As tensions eased between the superpowers, writers were growing tired of nuclear bombs, rigged or otherwise. Even Herman Kahn had lost interest. 'The truth is I'm bored with nuclear war as a subject,' he told Norman Moss. 'Not repelled, you understand. Just bored. Like the people in Washington, like most people, like you, I don't really believe in it.' Moss detected an air of wintry melancholy: 'It was like hearing a playwright explaining why his play has failed, or a middle-aged man telling you that he no longer understands his children.'

Could it really be over? 'Some people have let the gloom-mongers scare them beyond rational response with talk about atomic annihilation,' crowed *Look* magazine publisher Thomas R. Shepard Jr in his 1971 pamphlet *The Disaster Lobby*. 'Since World War II over one *billion* human beings who worried about A-bombs and H-bombs died of other causes. They worried for nothing.'

Well, not so fast . . .

CHAPTER 9

Winter

> How long will it take us to grasp that nuclear weapons are not weapons, that they are slashed wrists, gas-filled rooms, global booby-traps?
>
> Martin Amis, 'Thinkability' (1987)

Nuclear weapons, wrote the journalist Jonathan Schell in 1982's *The Fate of the Earth*, 'grew out of history, yet they threaten to end history. They were made by men, yet they threaten to annihilate man. They are a pit into which the whole world can fall – a nemesis of all human intentions, actions, and hopes.' And yet, he went on, most people were determined not to think about them. He found the post-war condition of carrying on as if the end were not possible to be 'a sort of mass insanity . . . that consisted not in screaming and making a commotion but precisely in *not* doing these things in the face of overwhelming danger, as though everyone had been sedated.'

As Schell was writing his book, disarmament efforts and US–Soviet relations were both in decline and the spectre of the Bomb was revenant. In 1981, the year the Doomsday Clock was reset to four minutes to midnight, *The New York Times* reported on a resurgence of articles, television specials, novels and plays about nuclear war, and cited a recent poll in which a startling 80 per cent of Harvard students said that they thought that there would be a nuclear war and that they would die in it. Roger Molander, a former disarmament specialist for President Jimmy Carter, identified three varieties of passivity: 'those who think it might happen but is no big deal, that we could survive it without a great deal of damage; those who think nuclear war is unthinkable, so devastating that it would never be permitted to happen; and those who think it's a real possibility but that there is nothing they can do about it.' The sickening impotence diagnosed by Robert Jay Lifton was a common theme in pop culture. 'I don't have a say in the war games that they play,' protests the ordinary guy in the Specials' 1980 song 'Man at C&A'. 'The decisions made by The Powers That Be will get to us in the end,' sighs the doomed retiree in *When the Wind Blows*, Raymond Briggs's 1982 graphic novel about one uncomprehending couple's experience of nuclear war.

The problem with waking people up is that eventually they go back to sleep again. A common theme in writing about nuclear weapons is a desperate compulsion to find the words and images that will shatter complacency and denial once and for all. People had been talking about a planet-killing atomic war since August 1945, but to date the only conceivable mechanism appeared to be the non-existent cobalt bomb. Schell, a thirty-nine-year-old *New Yorker* staff writer, endeavoured to explain how the world's existing arsenal of warheads (amounting to around 13,000 megatons) could feasibly abolish humanity. There was no need to imagine a Doomsday Machine: the nuclear stockpile *was* the Doomsday Machine. If one were to consider all the ways in which human beings could be blasted, broken, blinded and burned, combine that with the unpredictable effects of fallout and the likelihood of famines and epidemics, and then factor in possible damage to the ozone layer and the climate, he summed up, then 'one must conclude that a full-scale nuclear holocaust could lead to the extinction of mankind.' Schell used the contentious word *holocaust* because in his view a nuclear conflict would not fit Clausewitz's famous definition of war as 'the continuation of policy with other means'. A conflict that would be impossible to win in any meaningful sense was not a war but an extinction event: 'the murder of the future'. Schell has since been identified as a proto-longtermist.

Like John Hersey's *Hiroshima*, *The Fate of the Earth* first appeared in *The New Yorker* and was rushed into hard covers. Nobody had ever written such a relentless book about nuclear weapons. Schell reiterated a handful of points with mounting intensity until the reader was traumatized into awareness. 'It woke *me* up,' wrote a born-again Martin Amis in an essay called 'Thinkability'. 'Until then, it seems, I had been out cold. I hadn't really thought about nuclear weapons. I had just been tasting them. Now at last I knew what was making me feel so sick.' Schell quickly became one of America's most prominent disarmament advocates, at the forefront of the new nuclear freeze campaign to halt the arms race. To Herman Kahn, however, Schell's popularity represented the depressing revenge of the doomsday crowd. Shortly before his death in July 1983, he derided Schell's obsession with disarmament in the name of forestalling extinction as simplistic and dangerous. 'A prose stylist with an apocalyptic vision is hard to talk back to,' he acknowledged, but he did it anyway: 'One trouble with the Schell perspective, which equates any nuclear war with the destruction of mankind, is that it strongly discourages any preparation for survival.' *The Village Voice* called its scathing obituary of Kahn 'Pitchman for the Apocalypse' but the way he saw it, he was one of the only people who believed in the possibility of life after Armageddon.

On 14 September 1982, President Ronald Reagan recorded in his diary that he had received a visit from Edward Teller, 'pushing an exciting idea that nuclear weapons can be used in connection with Lasers to be non destructive except as used to intercept and destroy enemy missiles far above the earth'. Six months later, he announced an ambitious project to develop hi-tech satellite-based defensive weapons with the goal of making the US invulnerable to Soviet missiles. Reagan dubbed it the Strategic Defense Initiative (SDI), but Senator Ted Kennedy criticized the president's 'reckless *Star Wars* schemes' and the nickname stuck.* Senator John Glenn, the former astronaut, showed his age by accusing Reagan of trying to look like Buck Rogers. The truth was that Teller had oversold a scheme that was untestable, mindbogglingly expensive and probably ineffective. Even if it were to prove technically feasible, critics pointed out, its promise to take down 90 per cent of missiles would spur the Soviets

*As if bewitched by the Hollywood analogy despite his reservations, Reagan said in a 1985 speech about SDI, 'If you will pardon my stealing a film line, the Force is with us.'

to build more warheads so as to ensure the success of the 10 per cent that got through. SDI never became a reality but, for a while, Reagan saw it as the blade that would cut the Gordian knot.

Though he kept it quiet once he became president, apocalyptic Christianity played a huge role in Reagan's thinking about nuclear war. He had become obsessed with relating current events to prophecies of Armageddon while he was governor of California between 1967 and 1975. He met evangelical ministers and pored over Hal Lindsey's *The Late Great Planet Earth*, with its exultant hatred of Russia and China and obscene excitement about nuclear war. Like Lindsey, Reagan interpreted the plague of fire, smoke and brimstone in Revelation 9:18 as a foretelling of Hiroshima. At a banquet in 1971, he told a startled state senator that the coup in Libya two years earlier was 'a sign that the day of Armageddon isn't far off . . . Everything is falling into place. It can't be long now.' Later, this conviction was shared by members of his administration. 'Every day I think that time is running out,' confessed Defense Secretary Caspar Weinberger, while Secretary of the Interior James G. Watt said, 'I do not know how many future generations we can count on before the Lord returns.'

Ever since 6 August 1945, premillennialists had made the same connection, reaching for passages from II Peter ('The heavens shall pass away with a great noise, and the elements shall melt with fervent heat') and Zechariah ('Their flesh shall consume away while they stand upon their feet'). They scorned such measures as arms control, diplomacy and civil defence as obstacles to God's plan. Nuclear Armageddon would be a prophecy fulfilled, and one that the Raptured would not have to experience personally. 'If atomic bombs fall upon our cities,' wrote the radio preacher and publisher of *Revelation* magazine Donald Grey Barnhouse in 1945, 'we shall be in heaven the next second.' The televangelist James Robison told the 1984 Republican National Convention that peacemaking was not just 'heresy' but 'Antichrist'.

Fortunately, Reagan was not the kind of premillennialist who salivated over nuclear war. He saw it as his mission to *delay* Armageddon. Although a popular satirical poster portrayed Reagan and British prime minister Margaret Thatcher as Rhett and Scarlett in *Gone with the Wind* ('She promised to follow him to the end of the earth. He promised to organise it!'), Reagan's personal abhorrence of nuclear weapons ran contrary to his image as a warmonger. When he recalled a meeting of the National Security Council during his first year in office, where he was informed that even a war that the US won would leave up to 150 million of his citizens dead, he sounded rather like one of the peace activists who despised him: 'Even if a nuclear war did not mean the extinction of mankind, it would certainly mean the end of civilization as we knew it. *No one* could "win" a nuclear war . . . My dream, then, became a world free of nuclear weapons.' To Reagan, SDI was part of that mission. To the ailing, paranoid Soviet premier Yuri Andropov, however, it promised to destroy the balance of terror and thus permit the US to launch a first strike without any fear of retaliation. Combined with the installation of next-generation Pershing II and cruise missiles in Europe, an enormous increase in military spending and Reagan's devout anti-communism, it was unacceptable.

Luis Alvarez called SDI advocates 'very bright guys with no common sense'. At the same time, he was playing an inadvertent role in the first serious world-ending theory of nuclear war since the cobalt bomb.

Science fiction chanced upon the theory of nuclear winter decades before scientists did. 'The last three winters had come early and stayed long,' wrote Poul Anderson and F. N. Waldrop in 'Tomorrow's Children', a story published in the March 1947 issue of *Astounding Science Fiction.* 'Dust, colloidal dust of the bombs, suspended in the atmosphere and cutting down the solar constant by a deadly percent or two.' One character compares it to the *Fimbulwinter* that heralds Ragnarök in Norse mythology.

The notion did not begin to attract significant scientific research until 1971, when NASA's Mariner 9 probe discovered that a cloud of dust in the atmosphere of Mars had dramatically lowered temperatures on the planet's surface. American scientists began weaving this observation into their knowledge of the volcanic winters caused by Tambora and Krakatoa, the atmospheric effects of H-bomb tests and, eventually, the 'impact winter' of the Alvarez hypothesis. In 1982, atmospheric scientists Paul J. Crutzen and W. John Birks hypothesized that the smoke and soot generated by a thermonuclear exchange would block sunlight, inspiring five of the American researchers to accelerate their efforts. While Crutzen and Birks only factored in burning forests, the US team modelled cities on fire. They estimated that a 5000-megaton war could produce enough dust, smoke and soot to obstruct 95 per cent of sunlight from entering the troposphere, causing darkness and sub-zero temperatures as low as -25 degrees Celsius for months on end: an 'anti-greenhouse effect'. Even a relatively modest 100-megaton exchange, they claimed, could cause climatic mayhem. 'When combined with the prompt destruction from nuclear blast, fires, and fallout and the later enhancement of solar ultraviolet radiation due to ozone depletion,' the group's paper concluded, 'long-term exposure to cold, dark, and radioactivity could pose a serious threat to human survivors and other species.'

The group was known as TTAPS, an acronym based on the five scientists' surnames. The two Ts stood for Richard Turco and Owen Brian Toon, the NASA scientists who coined the term 'nuclear winter'. A was the atmospheric scientist Thomas P. Ackerman; P the astrophysicist James B. Pollack. S was Carl Sagan, the group's box-office superstar. He was a forty-eight-year-old Cornell astronomer from Brooklyn whose 1980 series *Cosmos: A Personal Voyage* had been seen by an estimated half a billion people around the world and made this shaggy-haired, pot-smoking Renaissance man the most famous scientist on the planet. The recipient of a Pulitzer, a Peabody and multiple NASA medals, he was tough, charismatic and interested in everything from comets to the greenhouse effect to life on other planets. The biologist Stephen Jay Gould called Sagan 'the greatest popularizer of the 20th century', but his critics saw him as a reckless egomaniac prone to making irresponsible claims. His talent for grabbing the public's attention was how he got into trouble.

Sagan was a bullish disarmament campaigner and SDI opponent who had been alerted to the politics of nuclear war at the age of twelve when he read a story by Raymond F. Jones in the February 1947 issue of *Astounding Science Fiction.* In 'Pete Can Fix It', a time traveller from the war-torn America of 1962 (a prescient choice of date) uses a post-apocalyptic hallucination to persuade an atomic physicist to change history by abolishing nuclear weapons. 'Reasoning, argument, pleading will never keep man from pulling down the world about his own head,' warns this Ghost of Armageddon Yet to Come. 'Only fear, terrible shattering fear of the consequences, can persuade him to turn aside from self-destruction. Perhaps a vision of the world lying in death can instill that fear.'

In 1983, Sagan was organizing a two-day symposium on the biological repercussions of nuclear war at the Sheraton Hotel in Washington DC, and publicity was paramount, so he dismayed his colleagues by pre-empting the publication of the peer-reviewed TTAPS paper in *Science* with an article in the popular magazine *Parade* the day before the conference began on 31 October. 'Would nuclear war be the end of the world?' asked the cover line. At the conference, Sagan dramatically noted the date: 'The original Halloween combines the three essential elements of the TTAPS scenario: fires, winter, and death.' This was Sagan's version of 'Pete Can Fix It'.

'Apocalyptic predictions require, to be taken seriously, higher standards of evidence than do assertions on other matters where the stakes are not as great,' Sagan admitted in a subsequent essay in *Foreign Affairs*, noting the backlashes against Nevil Shute and Jonathan Schell. 'The apocalyptic claims are rejected as unproven and unlikely, and it is judged unwise to frighten the public with doomsday talk when nuclear weapons are needed, we are told, to preserve the peace.' In trying to prove otherwise, Sagan committed two faux pas. As well as omitting the caveats that were in the TTAPS paper, he pressed the worst-case scenario: a year-long global cloud of toxic smog, inside of which most living creatures would freeze and starve in darkness. The World Health Organisation (WHO) had recently computed that nuclear war would directly kill 2.2 billion people, which was half the world, and now Sagan argued that the other half would follow. Nuclear winter, he wrote, was the Doomsday Machine, 'and we have distributed its triggers all over the Northern Hemisphere'.

If true, nuclear winter theory made even a limited war unwinnable and the whole wargaming industry irrelevant, so deterrence hawks rushed to discredit it. The physicist Russell Seitz called it 'a secular Apocalypse with which to preach for our deliverance from nuclear folly'. Edward Teller, who had a personal loathing for Sagan, wrote in *Nature*: 'Highly speculative theories of worldwide destruction – even of the end of life on Earth – used as a call for a particular kind of political action serve neither the good reputation of science nor dispassionate political thought.' The conservative *National Review* mocked Sagan in a 1985 cover story: 'Flat-Earth Sagan Falls Off the End of the World: Nuclear-Winter Fundamentalism Challenged by Responsible Scientists'. Yet the theory was never fully debunked. While subsequent research with a more sophisticated climate model suggested a less drastic 'nuclear autumn' and concluded that 'the global apocalyptic conclusions of the nuclear winter hypothesis' could be dismissed, the core of the theory held up. 'The fact that neither of the two superpowers' nuclear-weapons establishments had thought about the possibility of a nuclear winter has sobered everyone concerned with fighting a nuclear war,' admitted Luis Alvarez. 'What else, they wonder, have they forgotten to think about?'

Sagan was effectively pitching the movie version of nuclear winter theory. This is the cold, grey, sunless, dust-blotted world that we see in *The Matrix* and *The Road*. After reading the TTAPS paper as research for their 1984 movie *Threads*, director Mick Jackson and writer Barry Hines became the first people to put nuclear winter on screen, which the BBC broadcast alongside a documentary on the theory. As the hawks had anticipated, nuclear winter changed the risk calculus of nuclear war. As Martin Amis wrote, 'It is the best news because it is the worst news.'

More than being the Armageddon president, Reagan was the Hollywood president. It has been suggested that his passion for SDI was related to his starring role in *Murder in the Air*, a 1940 picture about 'the most terrifying weapon ever invented'. Reagan held movie nights at Camp David every weekend. One night in June 1983, he screened *WarGames*, a nimble thriller about a supercomputer that 'spends all its time thinking about World War Three' and almost starts it for real after it is accidentally hacked by a teenager. A kind of *Fail Safe* for high-schoolers, the movie is a sharp rebuke to the Herman Kahn school of wargaming: 'A strange game. The only winning move is not to play.' As the credits rolled, First Lady Nancy Reagan asked, 'Could that really happen?' The generals in the room said nothing. Four months later, a preview of ABC's *The Day After* was an even more overwhelming experience. 'It's very effective and left me greatly depressed,' Reagan wrote in his diary. 'My own reaction was one of our having to do all we can to have a deterrent & to see there is never a nuclear war.'

Broadcast on 20 November, *The Day After* reached 100 million viewers, around half the adult population, making it the most watched made-for-TV movie in US history. Streets, cinemas and restaurants were noticeably emptier while it was on; bar owners screened it in the hope of deterring patrons from leaving early. ABC set up a 1-800 hotline. An eleven-year-old viewer from New Jersey told a local news reporter, 'I would just want to die with the blast and not have to live and start all over again.' Written by Edward Hume and directed by Nicholas Meyer, the movie tracked the effects of nuclear war on the residents of Lawrence, Kansas, an archetypal heartland town. The spectacle is hideous, the tone venomous, the message obvious. When a struggling doctor mentions hope to a pregnant woman, she snaps, 'Hope for what? What do you think's gonna happen out there? . . . We knew the score. We knew all about bombs, we knew all about fallout, we knew this could happen for forty years. But nobody was interested.' In Meyer's view, 'The point of it was: this is a topic we avoid facing up to; we abstract it, we depersonalise it. What happened is that people who had filtered out the specifics saw it from A to Z. That's the effect it had on Reagan.' While its influence has been overstated, the movie certainly played a role in Reagan's thinking.

Immediately after the broadcast, Ted Koppel chaired an all-star panel discussion, including Carl Sagan and Henry Kissinger, which he introduced by comparing the movie to *A Christmas Carol*: 'When they finally return to the relative comfort of Scrooge's bedroom the old man asks the spirit the very question that many of us may be asking ourselves right now. Whether, in other words, the vision that we've just seen is the future as it *will* be or only as it *may* be. Is there still time?' A teacher in the audience told the panel that his students were 'very cynical and despairing about their future' and asked how they might be given hope. Folding in his brand-new theory of nuclear winter, Sagan recommended that nuclear stockpiles be reduced to the point where 'no concatenation of computer failure and communications malfunctions and madness in high office could kill everybody on the planet. That seems to me elementary planetary hygiene as well as elementary patriotism.'

In 1983, viewers of *The Day After* did not know how close they had come. On 26 September, the Soviets' shaky new early-warning system had announced five times that a US missile strike was incoming, but Lieutenant-Colonel Stanislav Petrov, deputy chief of the Department of Military Algorithms, insisted on checking the data before alerting Yuri Andropov and discovered that the computers had misread sunlight reflecting off clouds. This error was strangely similar to the accidental war in the German band Nena's recent hit '99 Luftballons'. Many years later, when the story came out, the Russians insisted that there had been other safeguards but Petrov has been described as 'The Man Who Saved the World'.

Apart from the Cuban Missile Crisis, every incident that has threatened to bring about the use of nuclear weapons has stemmed from a malfunction or misunderstanding rather than a political choice. In November 1983, the Soviets misinterpreted the elaborate NATO wargame Able Archer 83 as a genuine preparation for war and began to mobilize. Some historians claim that this was an even more perilous moment than October 1962, but one that played out behind closed doors. Robert Gates, who was deputy director of the CIA at the time, later admitted, 'We may have been at the brink of nuclear war and not even known it.' Sagan and Schell wanted to use fear to bring about the elimination of nuclear weapons. But 1983 proved that fear was the thing most likely to inspire their use. Even though nobody wanted war, nobody could be certain that the other side didn't.

With the Doomsday Clock reading three minutes to midnight, the period between 1984 and 1987 saw the final bloom of fiction about nuclear war. It hung like a thunderhead over the action of the game-changing comic books *Watchmen* and *The Dark Knight Returns.* It haunted pop songs by Frankie Goes to Hollywood, Prince and Sting. 'Hoping for the best but expecting the worst,' sang Germany's Alphaville, watching the skies on their hit 'Forever Young'. 'Are you gonna drop the bomb or not?' It threatened to destroy the Yooks and the Zooks in Dr Seuss's arms-race satire *The Butter Battle Book* and became a kind of supervillain in *Superman IV: The Quest for Peace.* It descended on ordinary English men and women in the movie version of Raymond Briggs's *When the Wind Blows* and in Mick Jackson's ruthlessly explicit TV movie *Threads.* 'I wanted to show the full horror,' said Jackson, who regarded *The Day After* as disgracefully upbeat and looked instead to *The War Game.* 'I felt that was absolutely my responsibility.' When the bomb goes off, a young man sees in the mushroom cloud the shape of a nightmare realized: 'Jesus Christ. They've done it.' But the real horror in *Threads*, named after the delicate filaments that hold society together, is surviving in a country broken down to a medieval condition. 'There's nothing apocalyptic about nuclear war,' said Jackson. 'If the evidence is correct, more people would survive than die. But survive into what? A living hell decimated by disaster and disease and moral breakdown.'

For anyone growing up with these stories in the belly of the 1980s, it could be hard to understand how such a dreadful possibility could be merely the backcloth to ordinary life rather than the primary concern. As Jonathan Schell wrote in 1984, 'It is the sky overhead and the ground underfoot. We are immersed in it and permeated by it.' And then, suddenly, the cloud lifted. Spooked by the events of 1983, Reagan agreed to a disarmament treaty with Mikhail Gorbachev, the reformist new leader of a superpower that could no longer afford the Cold War. If not for the sticking point of SDI, the two leaders might have renounced nuclear weapons altogether. When the Soviet Union officially dissolved in December 1991, the hands of the Doomsday Clock rested at seventeen minutes to midnight, a distance that has not been possible before or since.

The Soviet Union *had* experienced a nuclear disaster, just not the one that most people had been worrying about. On 26 April 1986, a combination of human and technical errors had led the No. 4 nuclear reactor at the Chernobyl power plant near Pripyat, Ukraine, to melt down, releasing a cloud of radiation which drifted across Europe. This was not the USSR's first major nuclear accident – an underground tank of nuclear waste had exploded near Kyshtym in 1957 – but it was the first one that the Soviets had not been able to keep secret. People interpreted the disaster in their own way. David Bowie was recording in Switzerland and wrote 'Time Will Crawl' about the sense of impending airborne doom. Fans of Biblical prophecy could not resist the extraordinary coincidence that Chernobyl was the Ukrainian word for Wormwood, which is both a bitter herb and the falling star in Revelation. Disarmament campaigners saw the meltdown as a teachable moment, like touching a hot stove. 'This disaster and the other accidents and crises are in fact something more than warnings,' Schell wrote. 'They are all that is given to us to know of the end of the world.'

Advocates for nuclear power, meanwhile, were distraught. This was meant to be the Bomb's benevolent twin. Both were born in the same fission experiment in the squash court beneath the University of Chicago, with the same parents, Enrico Fermi and Leo Szilard. Nuclear energy was the bounty that Frederick Soddy had predicted and Eisenhower had championed. But the deliverance-or-doom binary of the post-war years had been falling apart for a long time: if nuclear weapons had not destroyed the world, then nor had nuclear energy saved it. During the 1970s, nuclear reactors became, in David Lilienthal's words, 'a surrogate for bombs', uniting environmentalists and disarmament campaigners in opposition. When, in March 1979, the fictional reactor emergency in *The China Syndrome* coincided with a partial meltdown at Three Mile Island, Pennsylvania, nuclear power's reputation was dealt a staggering blow. Now, with the bitterest irony, it was the peaceful application of atom-splitting that had transformed a swathe of the Soviet Union into a dead zone. The supposed saviour had become the destroyer.

'The Age of Physics ended at Chernobyl,' atomic physicist Valentin Borisevich says in Svetlana Alexievich's oral history *Chernobyl Prayer*. Mankind, he goes on, 'is operating with different categories of time, and not just with the earth, but with different worlds. Apocalypse. The Nuclear Winter. This has all been described in Western art already. Depicted. Filmed. They've prepared themselves for the future . . . This secular vision of the end of the world has been around since the industrial revolution in the eighteenth century, but the atomic bomb won't disappear even when the last warhead has been decommissioned. The knowledge will remain.'

Whether the absence of nuclear war meant that deterrence worked, or just that the world was extremely lucky, is impossible to prove. Either way, it was never a permanent solution. With diplomacy already in deadlock, nuclear nightmares returned in force when

Russia invaded Ukraine in February 2022. UN Secretary-General António Guterres described it as 'a time of nuclear danger not seen since the height of the Cold War' and said that humanity was 'just one misunderstanding, one miscalculation away from nuclear annihilation'. But the people who spoke most alarmingly of World War Three and nuclear Armageddon were no longer the pacifists but the aggressors. Vladimir Putin and his apologists fashioned the sincere existential terror of people such as Leo Szilard, Bertrand Russell and Jonathan Schell into a bully's cocked pistol, implying that the abandonment of Ukraine was a small price to pay to avert the end of the world. In the world that began at Trinity on 16 July 1945, fear is a weapon that can be aimed in many directions.

PART FOUR
MACHINES

CHAPTER 10

Robots

We have made machines, not people, the measure of the human order, but this is not the machines' fault, it is ours.

Karel Čapek, 'What Machinery Will Never Do' (1929)

One day in Prague in 1920, the Czech writer Karel Čapek sought the advice of his older brother Josef, who was busy splashing paint onto a canvas. Karel had a notion for a satirical play about artificial workers but he was struggling for a name. 'I'd call them laborators, but it seems to me somewhat stilted,' he said. 'Call them robots then,' Josef replied distractedly, without removing his paintbrush from his mouth. *Robota* was an old Czech word for forced labour. Karel took his brother's advice and called his play *R.U.R.*, which stands for Rossumovi Univerzální Roboti (Rossum's Universal Robots). *R.U.R.* climaxes with the replacement of humanity by its own creation, which means that the history of the robot opens with the end of the world.

Karel Čapek's writing career coincided almost precisely with the twenty-one years between the two world wars and therefore with the lifespan of Czechoslovakia as an independent sovereign nation. In many ways he might be regarded as the Czech George Orwell, although it would be more chronologically accurate to call Orwell the English Karel Čapek. Čapek's newspaper *feuilletons* read like precursors of Orwell in their chatty, companionable tone; their witty aphorisms; their celebration of ordinary lives and the natural world; their criticism of snobbery and elitism; and their distaste for dehumanizing abstractions. Čapek was extraordinarily alert to the damage done by dogma, tribalism and the corruption of language, and quick to identify the threat of totalitarianism. Though he admired H. G. Wells, he saw every utopian scheme as a disaster waiting to happen. As one of his characters says, 'You know, the bigger the things a man believes in, the more fiercely he despises those who don't. And yet the greatest of all beliefs would be to believe in people.'

Čapek was born in 1890 in Malé Svatoňovice, a mining village in northern Bohemia, then a part of the Austro-Hungarian Empire. A childhood bout of scarlet fever left him with Bechterew's disease, a form of arthritis which gave him chronic spinal pain, headaches and a stooped posture. His mind, however, was formidable. In a 1932 radio talk called 'How I Have Come to Be What I Am', he said that he had inherited his pragmatism and intellectual curiosity from his father, a country doctor, and his 'romantic sensibility' and 'fantasticality' from his mother. Despite being expelled from high school in 1905 for belonging to a clandestine pro-independence society, he went on to study literature in Berlin and Paris. When the First World War broke out, Čapek was exempted from military service on account of his medical condition and continued his studies, graduating from the University of Prague with a doctorate in philosophy in 1915.

With the defeat of Austria-Hungary, Czechoslovakia gained independence in October 1918 and Čapek soon became its first literary celebrity. During 1920 and 1921 alone, he wrote *R.U.R.*, started a column for the progressive *People's Newspaper*, became a writer-director at Prague's Vinohrady Theatre and launched a weekly intellectual salon in his garden whose attendees became known as the 'Friday Men'. One of them was Tomáš Masaryk, Czechoslovakia's first president, whose government Čapek saw as a humane, democratic middle way between the rising extremes of communism and fascism, both of which he thought reduced individuals to cogs in a political machine. Čapek had a shy, insecure side (he once attended a performance of *R.U.R.* with another writer and spent the whole show apologizing for its flaws) but on the page he radiated confidence and good humour. 'I count myself among the idiots who like man because he is human,' he wrote.

Čapek described *R.U.R.* as a 'comedy, partly of science, partly of truth'. His creations are not robots in the modern sense of the word, which is to say mechanical automata, but bioengineered organic beings which look exactly like humans yet feel no pleasure, pain or emotion of any kind. We would call them androids – a seventeenth-century French word for automaton which now describes an artificial humanoid. While Victor Frankenstein and the sixteenth-century rabbi who is said to have animated the Golem of Prague each created a single life, the father-and-son inventors Old Rossum and Young Rossum (the name is a pun on the Czech word for *reason*) give birth to an entire race. It is the fear of creating a replacement for *Homo sapiens* that motivates Frankenstein's decision to refuse his creature's request for a mate: 'I shuddered to think that future ages might curse me as their pest, whose selfishness had not hesitated to buy its own peace at the price, perhaps, of the existence of the whole human race.' In 'Darwin Among the Machines', the 1863 broadside against machine culture which he folded into his 1872 novel *Erewhon*, Samuel Butler worried that 'we are ourselves creating our own successors' and that in time humans would 'become to the machine what the horse and dog are to man'. With his robot, Čapek fused the two anxieties, updating the artificial man for the age of mass production and giving the machine a face, a voice and a name.

In his *sui generis* medleys of thriller, science fiction, philosophy and satire, Čapek was drawn to the disastrous consequences of scientific naivety in concert with either capitalist greed or utopian hubris. In 1922, he imagined the world turned upside down by the invention of an atomic explosive in *Krakatit* and by a mystical species of atomic energy in *Továrna na absolutno* (*The Absolute at Large*). In Čapek's words, 'I am, in my opinion, a rather dull and tireless moralist . . . If I must tell the truth, the entire utopian plot of [*The Absolute at Large*], all the joking, all the "lowering to a substandard level", is only an excuse, a means of expressing several ideas I take very seriously.'

So it is with *R.U.R.*, which is at heart the tale of two misguided idealists: factory manager Harry Domin and his wife Helena. 'There will be no poverty,' boasts Domin, in a parody of post-work utopian socialists such as Oscar Wilde. 'All work will be done by living machines. Everybody will be free from worry and liberated from the degradation of labour. Everybody will live only to perfect himself.' But the robots become indispensable on picket lines and battlefields as well as in factories while the humans, vastly outnumbered, grow sterile, as if accepting on a genetic level that they are an obsolete model. 'That's a punishment,' says Helena's nurse, Nana. 'That's the end of the world.' Meanwhile Helena, a passionate social reformer, secretly instructs one scientist to design a new batch of robots with souls, believing that this will enable them to love humanity. Instead, the new model develops hatred and envy and leads a genocidal revolt. 'Slaughter and domination are necessary if you would be human beings,' Radius, the robots' leader, declares. 'Read history.' The play ends with the last man, the working-class engineer Alquist, blessing the first two robots who have learned to love and procreate: 'Go, Adam, go, Eve. The world is yours.'

R.U.R. premiered in Prague in January 1921. By 1923 it had been translated into thirty languages and staged in London, Berlin, New York, Los Angeles and Chicago. Remarkably, it became both the first radio play aired by the BBC, in 1927, and the world's first televised science fiction drama, in 1938. Čapek was not a communist (this is clarified by his essay 'Why Am I Not a Communist?') but many people who saw *R.U.R.* assumed that it was a socialist allegory, with the robots symbolizing the proletarians who rise up and destroy their capitalist oppressors. The *New York Times* critic John Corbin wrote that 'this modern Frankenstein' was 'aroused and class conscious' while *The Industrial Pioneer* praised the play as an 'ironical melodrama around the theme of the class struggle – the degradation of the present-day industrial worker into a veritable mechanical working machine'. The magazine soon began using *robot* as a synonym for the automatized worker. Was the greater risk that machines would replace humans, or that humans would *become* machines? During a public debate about *R.U.R.* with G. K. Chesterton in London, George Bernard Shaw told the audience, 'After all, you are all Robots, because you have all had your opinions – if not your happiness – imposed on you.' Čapek, however, felt that literal-minded critics missed the ambivalence of his play. In an article for *The Saturday Review*, he explained that both the utopian Domin and the sceptical Alquist are right, to an extent, as is every other character: 'I think it is possible . . . that a human truth is opposed to another truth no less human, ideal against ideal, positive worth against worth no less positive, instead of the struggle being, as we are so often told it is, one between exalted truth and vile selfish error.' He was disappointed that 'none of the distinguished speakers who took part in the discussion have discovered this simple tendency in *R.U.R.*'

Much like the Rossums, Čapek had no control over the afterlife of his creation. As *robot* came to replace the old term *automaton*, the meaning of the word divided in two. In one direction, it denoted machines that acted like men: boxy, mechanical humanoids with cogs and wires instead of organs and arteries. That usage was popularized by reviews of Fritz Lang's 1927 picture *Metropolis*, profoundly apocalyptic in both structure and symbolism, in which a *Maschinenmensch* disguised as a woman incites a revolution only to be burned at the stake by angry workers when the deception is discovered. 'Rotwang, the inventor, is making a Robot,' H. G. Wells wrote in his scornful review, 'apparently without any license from Čapek, the original patentee.' The word later attached itself to Mr Televox and Elektro, the man-machines that the manufacturing company Westinghouse built as promotional gimmicks. 'Unlike the man-made Frankenstein monster of fiction,' an advertisement for the voice-controlled Elektro boasted, 'the Westinghouse robot is all kindness and geniality in spite of his towering size and formidable appearance.' Yet one of Elektro's catchphrases was ominous: 'My brain is bigger than yours.' In fact, Elektro could only respond to voice commands with a particular syllabic rhythm and recite prerecorded phrases from a 78 rpm record player, but Westinghouse presumably knew that spectators at the 1939 World's Fair would appreciate a hint of sci-fi menace. Elektro helped to inspire the various killer robots that clanked through the comic-strip adventures of Buck Rogers, Superman and Mickey Mouse.

Conversely, *robot* also came to describe men who acted like machines, dehumanized by repetitive labour or by the totalitarian ideologies of Hitler and Stalin. The programme for a short-lived 1942 theatrical revival of *R.U.R.* quoted President Roosevelt decrying the 'wound-up "robots" of the slave States', while Charlie Chaplin in *The Great Dictator* railed against 'machine men with machine minds and machine hearts!' Some science fiction writers merged the two meanings into the idea of robots as superweapons. In Joseph E. Kelleam's desperately sad 1939 story 'Rust', three failing robots reflect on their role in a war of global extermination. 'Men made us for killing men,' says one. 'That was their crime. Can we help it if they made us too well?'

Čapek tracked the rise of totalitarianism with dread, well aware of Hitler's designs on his young, fragile homeland, and became one of Czechoslovakia's most prominent anti-fascists. In 1936, he reworked *R.U.R.*'s themes in *Válka s Mloky* (*War with the Newts*), a spectacularly inventive satire on nationalism, colonialism, militarism and racism. When humans discover a race of intelligent newts living in the sea, they put them to work as robot-like slaves, but the fast-evolving amphibians become too numerous to control and demand more living space. Under the Hitleresque command of Chief Salamander, and with the suicidal complicity of governments and businesses, the newts flood and annex huge swathes of land. Čapek explains how the world will end: 'No cosmic catastrophe, nothing but state, official, economic, and other causes . . . we are all responsible for it.'

In *War with the Newts*, the European powers sell out China to the newts in the vain hope of saving themselves. In October 1938, the Munich Agreement between Britain, France and Germany did much the same to Čapek's country. 'My world has died,' he told a friend. 'I no longer have any reason to write.' Despite denunciations and death threats from the right, he refused to abandon the country he loved. The Gestapo placed him on its list of people to arrest after the invasion of Czechoslovakia, but when the Nazis arrived at his door in March 1939, they were too late. While working in his beloved garden, Čapek had caught a cold which developed into double pneumonia; he died on Christmas Day 1938. It is unlikely that he would have survived the Nazi occupation. Josef, the man who named the robot, perished in Bergen-Belsen just days before it was liberated. An inscription on Karel's Prague tombstone reads: 'Here would have been buried Josef Čapek, painter and poet. Grave far away.'

One avid reader of post-*R.U.R.* robot stories during the 1930s was a Russian-American chemistry major at Columbia University called Isaac Asimov. A true believer in scientific progress and scourge of Luddite naysayers, he became the celebrated author of hundreds of books and a boosterish commentator on the shape of things to come. In his 1979 book, *A Choice of Catastrophes*, for example, he predicted that by 2020 we would be enjoying clean energy from nuclear fusion and orbiting solar panels while mining precious minerals from the Moon. Asimov divided robot tales into two categories: 'In the first class there was Robot-as-Menace . . . Such stories were a mixture of "clank-clank" and "aarghh" and "There are some things man was not meant to know."' The most technophobic authors presented rebellious robots as the inevitable conclusion to civilization's overreliance on machines. In Lord Dunsany's 1951 novel *The Last Revolution*, the rueful inventor of an intelligent robot which turns cars, telephones and radios against humankind protests, 'But you mustn't think I started all this. I only gave it a helping hand, as a lot of other people were doing.' Dunsany made prolific reference to *Frankenstein*, the novel that Asimov unfairly blamed for the whole damn genre: 'The success of *Frankenstein* was such that the basic plot of "man creates robot; robot kills man" was repeated over and over again.'

Asimov's second category was 'Robot-as-Pathos': 'In such stories the robots were lovable and were usually put upon by cruel human beings. These charmed me.' This subset included Lester del Rey's 'Helen O'Loy' and Eando Binder's 'I, Robot', whose title Asimov's publisher later purloined for a collection of his stories. In May 1939, aged just nineteen, Asimov wrote a story called 'Robbie', about an entirely benign robot companion. Dozens more robot tales followed, all of them firmly rejecting the cliché of Robot-as-Menace. Asimov codified his optimistic view in his Three Rules of Robotics (a word which he inadvertently invented, having assumed that it already existed), which first appeared in 1942's 'Runaround'.* First, 'a robot may not injure a human being under any conditions – and, as a corollary, must not permit a human being to be injured because of inaction on his part.' Secondly, 'a robot must follow all orders given by qualified human beings as long as they do not conflict with Rule 1.' Finally, 'a robot must protect his own existence, as long as that does not conflict with Rules 1 and 2.' Of course, Asimov's 'rules'

* Asimov later changed 'Rules' to 'Laws' and rewrote them more than once, but they remained fundamentally intact.

were not rules at all but a personal expression of the hope that machines could transcend the flaws of their creators. At times, he seemed to consider robots an improvement on people.

Asimov later admitted that he 'would have wagered vast sums' that robots would not exist in his lifetime but he was to play a part in proving himself wrong. Joseph F. Engelberger, a Columbia physics major five years his junior, fell in love with the idea through reading Asimov's stories in the 1940s and later founded Unimation, America's leading robotics company. Asimov's pro-robot propaganda was just as effective in cinema, inspiring such benevolent, if sometimes stern, protectors as Robby the Robot in *The Forbidden Planet* and the intergalactic peacekeeper Gort in *The Day the Earth Stood Still.* To more sceptical ears, however, Asimov sounded absurdly naive, and these writers stuck with the Robot-as-Menace. The young Californian writer Philip K. Dick repeatedly spoofed Asimov's faith in robotic benevolence: in short stories such as 'The Defenders' and 'To Serve the Master', cunning metal outwits gullible flesh.

The fundamental point of disagreement in the field of robot fiction was whether robots could ever do more than humans had programmed them to do. Could they possess, if not souls, then independent brains? Could they really *think*? If that were possible, then robots could become unimaginably dangerous and Asimov's three rules would be so much wishful thinking. But what exactly would constitute a true electronic brain? 'The theme of the artificial human being . . . has had its ancestors in myth,' wrote the Polish author Stanisław Lem. 'The logical computer, on the other hand, has been created in a mythically empty space.'

CHAPTER 11

Computers

The impact of the thinking machine
will be a shock certainly of comparable
order to that of the atomic bomb.

Norbert Wiener (1949)

The story of the computer cannot be separated from the story of the Bomb. The first digital, general-purpose, electronic computer was put to work at Los Alamos on 10 December 1945, five months after the Trinity test. Although the ENIAC (Electronic Numerical Integrator and Computer) had been designed to calculate artillery trajectories for the US Army, its first job was to explore the possibility of a hydrogen bomb. Before it did anything else, the American computer was tasked with finding more efficient ways to kill people.

One could say that the story begins with the events leading up to Lord Byron's flight to Lake Geneva in 1816. By the time Lady Byron gave birth to a daughter, Ada, in December 1815, the couple's marriage was imploding and she soon took Ada to live with her parents. The girl never saw her father again and didn't even learn his identity until she was eight. Lady Byron believed that her husband was insane and that this insanity might be hereditary, so she directed Ada towards her own field of mathematics and away from the potential madness of literature. Ada initially embraced mathematics as a means to fence in the beast of her imagination but her genius derived from a synthesis of the two sensibilities: she saw the poetry in numbers. Her private tutor, the mathematician Augustus De Morgan, identified a 'power of thinking . . . so utterly out of the common way for any beginner, man or woman'. Ada was both exhilarated and frightened by her own intelligence. In an 1843 letter, she described her brain as a kind of machine: 'something more than merely *mortal* . . . No one knows what almost *awful* energy & power lie yet undeveloped in that *wiry* little system of mine.'

The letter was addressed to her friend and collaborator, Charles Babbage. Fascinated by automata as a child, Babbage had studied mathematics at Cambridge and became a serial inventor who contributed innovations to Britain's railways and postal system. His most cherished project, however, only existed in miniature: a mechanical calculator called the Difference Engine. Envisioning a machine that would require 25,000 components and weigh 13 tons, Babbage took funding from the Treasury for twenty years before prime minister Robert Peel pulled the plug on what he believed could never be more than a 'very costly toy', during which time Babbage was able to complete just one section for demonstration purposes. But when seventeen-year-old Ada visited his salon to see it in 1833, she was entranced. Babbage became her intellectual father, her biological father being first absent and then dead. When Babbage designed a more complex and versatile machine operated by punch cards, the Analytical Engine, she volunteered herself as a partner. This device only ever existed in the brains of its inventors, but what brains they were.

In 1843, Ada, countess of Lovelace (as she became known after her husband was ennobled) wrote some notes on the Analytical Engine which outpaced Babbage's own ambitions, racing into the future. She predicted that it would not just calculate numbers but process all kinds of information: a computer, essentially. The sequence of operations that she devised to calculate Bernoulli numbers, a fiendishly complicated infinite number series, would much later be recognized as the world's first published computer programme. But the publication of 'Notes' was as good as it got for Lovelace. She never published another scientific paper before her death from uterine cancer at the age of thirty-six. Babbage died at seventy-nine, in poverty and obscurity. They left no immediate intellectual heirs. A century later, the computer pioneer Alan Turing wrote that they 'had all the essential ideas', but their work was not truly appreciated and built upon until the 1930s, enabling Lovelace's dream of a reprogrammable general-purpose computer finally to become a reality. Ada Lovelace was to computing what Mary Shelley was to science fiction: a woman who was too far ahead of her time.

In 1946, the forty-two-year-old mathematician John von Neumann received a visit from a physicist friend he had not seen in years. 'I suppose you are not interested in mathematics anymore,' his friend teased. 'I hear you are now thinking about nothing but bombs.' Not at all, von Neumann countered: 'I am thinking about something much more important than bombs. I am thinking about computers.'

Of the four Hungarian 'Martians' who worked on the Manhattan Project, John von Neumann was the one who most resembled a higher life form. 'I believe that if a mentally superhuman race ever develops, its members will resemble Johnny von Neumann,' wrote Edward Teller. His colleagues joked that he was a demigod who had learned how to impersonate a human being. They had all heard the stories about Neumann János Lajos's childhood in Budapest: how he could mentally divide two eight-digit numbers by the age of six and perform college-level calculus by eight; how his schoolmates dubbed him 'Mr Miracle' because of his facility for inventing mechanical toys. His schoolfriend and colleague Eugene Wigner was no slouch himself (he won the Nobel Prize for Physics in 1963) but always felt second best: 'Whenever I talked with the sharpest intellect whom I have known – with von Neumann – I always had the impression that only he was fully awake, that I was halfway in a dream.'

Von Neumann slept for just four hours a night and kept a notepad beside his bed to record his subconscious epiphanies. While a *privat-dozent* at the University of Berlin in the 1920s, he published thirty-two major papers on mathematics within three years. In the last year of the war alone, he designed the implosion lenses that enabled the plutonium core of the Fat Man bomb to achieve critical mass, published a seminal book on game theory and wrote the blueprint for modern computing. Later, he played a crucial role in the development of the hydrogen bomb and the inter-continental ballistic missile. He also made transformative contributions to the fields of weather forecasting, climate modelling, nanotechnology and artificial intelligence. Herman Kahn, who worked with him at RAND, considered von Neumann to possess the most brilliant mind he had ever encountered: 'the smart man's smart man'.

Von Neumann was uncommonly amiable as prodigies go: cheerful, polite and almost universally liked, with a friendly, cherubic face. As a founding professor at Princeton's Institute for Advanced Study during the 1930s, so young that he was sometimes mistaken for a graduate student, he was known for his love of fast cars, tailored suits and boisterous parties. 'Von Neumann's talents as a host were based on his drinks, which were strong, his repertoire of off-color limericks, which was massive, and his social ease, which was consummate,' remarked *Life* in its obituary. Shortly after Hiroshima, he anticipated the Fermi Paradox when he mordantly joked that every supernova 'could be evidence that sentient beings in other planetary systems had reached the point in their scientific knowledge where we stand now, [and] having failed to solve the problem of living together, had at least succeeded in achieving togetherness by cosmic suicide'. Yet this did not stay his hand. Von Neumann epitomized the idea that science obeyed its own morality and that questions of good and evil were irrelevant. 'What we are creating now', he told his wife about the Manhattan Project in 1945, 'is a monster whose influence is going to change history, provided there is any history left, yet it would be . . . unethical from the point of view of scientists not to do what they know is feasible, no matter what terrible consequences it may have.'

It was the study of logic that attracted von Neumann to the infant realm of computing machines. At that point, *computer* generally meant a person, usually a woman, who made calculations with a pen and paper.* Von Neumann first met Alan Turing in Cambridge in 1935, before Turing spent two years at Princeton University as a graduate student. He probably reconnected with Turing in 1943, when he spent seven months in England studying mine warfare for the US Navy, because he wrote in a letter that he had 'developed

*The gendered division of labour continued into the electronic era. While the hardware was built by men, the leading programmers were women such as Adele Goldstine, Grace Hopper, Jean Jennings and Betty Snyder.

an obscene interest in computational techniques'. On his return to the US, von Neumann was enlisted into the Manhattan Project as an explosion expert and visited everybody who was working on an electromechanical computer – at Harvard, Princeton, Bell Telephone Laboratories – to ask them to help him predict the shockwaves that would be generated by the atomic bomb. The Army's primary interest in computers, meanwhile, was the calculation of artillery trajectories, or firing tables. Von Neumann was waiting for a train after a meeting at the Ballistics Research Laboratory in Aberdeen, Maryland, when he bumped into an army mathematician called Captain Herman Goldstine, who told him about a thrilling new project led by J. Presper Eckert and John William Mauchly at the University of Pennsylvania's Moore School: an electronic computer capable of performing 333 multiplications per second. This was news to von Neumann, who was hooked. Goldstine invited him to visit Moore in August 1944. What von Neumann saw there, still under construction, was the ENIAC, a colossal U-shaped network of approximately 18,000 vacuum tubes, several kilometres of wiring and forty panels festooned with flashing pink neon lights, the sum of which extended for 30 metres and weighed 30 tons. Having asked its inventors all the right questions, von Neumann was immediately brought in as a consultant.

The modern computer meets three criteria: electronic, programmable and general purpose. The computers that existed prior to 1945, such as IBM's Harvard Mark 1 and Britain's codebreaking Colossus, satisfied only one or two of these requirements. The ENIAC was the first to achieve the trifecta, and it became famous. On 14 February 1946, the War Department ushered journalists into the ENIAC room to see for themselves the ingenious new machine that could solve in two hours a problem that would take one hundred people a whole year. Eckert used bisected ping-pong balls to make the winking lights brighter and more impressive, thus influencing the appearance of computers in film and television for years to come. The British army commander Lord Mountbatten described the ENIAC as the first step towards an 'electronic brain', which he dubbed 'the most Wellsian development of all'.

The ENIAC was certainly impressive but it was chronically prone to malfunctions and consumed an extraordinary amount of electricity. Von Neumann compared the job of keeping it operative to 'fighting the Battle of the Bulge every day'. He was asked to oversee the design of a smaller, faster, cheaper stored-program computer that could be reprogrammed while it was running. In June 1945, he condensed months of discussions with his colleagues into a 101-page document which Goldstine titled 'First Draft of a Report on the EDVAC' (Electronic Discrete Variable Automatic Computer) and sent to two dozen computer developers, including Turing. Eckert felt that von Neumann had stolen his thunder, but the Hungarian's great strength was his openness to collaborating and synthesizing disparate ideas into a coherent blueprint for computer design: 'Von Neumann architecture'.

In August 1955, von Neumann was diagnosed with an aggressive form of bone cancer which first confined him to a wheelchair (leading to erroneous suggestions that he was the model for Dr Strangelove) and then caused a brutal mental decline. Towards the end, the world's greatest mathematician could no longer perform the simplest sums. He suffered from nightmares, hallucinations and delusions. Death was intolerable to him – a problem he could not solve – and he would wake in the night screaming. 'I think that von Neumann suffered more when his mind would no longer function than I have ever seen any human being suffer,' observed Edward Teller.

Just a few weeks before his diagnosis, von Neumann speculated about the future he would never see in an article for *Fortune* called 'Can We Survive Technology?'. 'Like many fellow scientists of the atomic age', the editor's introduction said, von Neumann 'harbors a streak of the blues but his delicate shade may be called constructive pessimism'. Von Neumann worked his way through a series of conjectures, including hi-tech world war, automation, free energy and, ahead of his time, climate change caused by the burning of fossil fuels. 'Useful and harmful techniques lie everywhere so close together that it is never possible to separate the lions from the lambs,' he wrote. The solution to the perils of technology was more technology: 'For progress there is no cure.'

For several years after the debut of the ENIAC, the names of computers, real or imagined, followed the format that it laid down. Eckert and Mauchly founded their own corporation and developed the UNIVAC 1, which accurately predicted the result of the 1952 presidential election and was the first 'electronic brain' the American public ever saw in action (or thought they saw: the machine was far too large to transport to the CBS studio in New York, so the network mocked up a phoney console, brought to life by Christmas lights). The RAND Corporation called its first computer the JOHNNIAC and hung a picture of von Neumann on the wall beside it. In the first half of the 1950s, readers of science fiction encountered the Multivac in Isaac Asimov's stories, the EMSIAC in Bernard Wolfe's *Limbo*, SOCIAC in Kendell Foster Crossen's *Year of Consent* and the NOVAC in Herbert L. Strock's movie *Gog*, which commands its ominously named industrial robots Gog and Magog to trigger a nuclear reactor meltdown. When Nicholas Metropolis at Los Alamos built his own von Neumann-inspired computer, he tried to smother the trend with absurdity by calling it the Mathematical Analyzer, Numerical Integrator and Automatic Computer – the MANIAC I – but the acronyms kept coming.

Many computer developers resented the media's fascination with the sinister implications of their creations, but some made a joke out of it. When General Electric produced the OMIBAC, a cartoon in the company magazine, *Monogram*, showed a man recoiling from it and gasping, 'Are machines smarter than ME?' One employee in GE's publicity department at the time was an aspiring writer named Kurt Vonnegut Jr. He wrote a story about a lovesick supercomputer that commits suicide because it can never be human and called it 'EPICAC' – a pun on ipecac, a popular drug for inducing vomiting. Before EPICAC self-destructs, it prints its last words on a spool of paper: 'I don't want to be a machine, and I don't want to think about war.'

Kurt Vonnegut Jr was born in Indianapolis on Armistice Day 1922, which meant that he enjoyed seven happy, prosperous years before his family was poleaxed by the Great Depression. Kurt Vonnegut Sr, formerly a successful architect, couldn't obtain a single commission during the 1930s. Edith Vonnegut, a society belle from a brewing dynasty, lost her inheritance in a Ponzi scheme and never adapted to her reduced circumstances, which exacerbated serious mental health issues. Her family insisted that her death from an overdose of sleeping pills in 1944 was accidental, but Kurt knew better. In fact, he came to believe that his parents had been broken before he was even born: 'I can guess that the planet they loved and thought they understood was destroyed in the First World War.'

Vonnegut agreed to study science at Cornell to please his father and his older brother Bernard, a brilliant MIT physics graduate and atmospheric scientist, but he put far more effort into student journalism than his grades. Facing expulsion in 1943, he figured it was better to enlist in the US Army than wait to be drafted. Sent to Europe, he was captured by the Germans during the Battle of the Bulge shortly before Christmas 1944 and incarcerated in an abattoir in the historic city of Dresden. On the night of 13 February 1945, the RAF's Operation Thunderclap turned Dresden into an inferno, killing around 25,000 civilians. Vonnegut compared it to Atlantis, drowned by waves of fire. When he and his fellow POWs emerged from their underground meat locker the next day, 'the city was gone.' Charred husks were slumped at the wheels of burned-out cars; reddened corpses lay in public fountains where they had boiled to death while seeking relief from the flames; exotic animals wandered through the rubble of what was once Dresden Zoo. Vonnegut was put to work removing corpses from the basements where they had been asphyxiated by the firestorm. After a few days, the authorities decided that it would be more efficient to incinerate them with flamethrowers. Vonnegut's long struggle to articulate the atrocity of Dresden (an early sketch was called 'Armageddon in Retrospect') eventually yielded his reputation-making 1969 bestseller *Slaughterhouse-Five*, named after the building that saved his life. As John Updike wrote, 'The end of the world is not an idea to Vonnegut, it is a reality he experienced.'

Vonnegut found life irrational, unfair and absurd; death was something that could come out of nowhere at any moment. This view enabled him to write about the end of the world as farce in several of his novels. Yet Vonnegut was famously genial company: J. G. Ballard claimed that his 'sheer amiability could light up all the cathedrals in America'. The tousled, avuncular writer fostered a reputation as a compassionate hipster sage with aphorisms such as 'God damn it, you've got to be kind,' while largely delegating his raging pessimism to his fictional alter ego, Kilgore Trout, an unsuccessful science fiction author who believes that 'being alive is a crock of shit'. Such was Vonnegut's popularity with readers half his age that he was affectionately spoofed in a 1974 issue of *Superman* as novelist Wade Halibut Jr, who fakes a doomsday weapon to trick Clark Kent into giving him an ending for his next novel. Of course, there is also a real superweapon to drive the story. 'If not for Superman, the real doomsday device would have ended the world,' a triumphant Halibut tells Kent. 'But since Superman is not a character in my book, I can't have him save the world! So in *my* story, the world will *really* come to an *end*!'

Sometimes Vonnegut sounded every bit as despairing as Trout. 'God will kill us by the millions quite soon, I think – by starvation, with flu, through war, in any number of ways,' he predicted in 1976. In his final novel, 1997's *Timequake*, he came to the conclusion that life wasn't as popular as it was made out to be anyway: 'Let us be perfectly frank for a change. For practically everybody, the end of the world can't come soon enough.' In one of Vonnegut's last interviews before his death in 2007, *Rolling Stone* anointed him 'a literary Cassandra of the first order . . . More than any other fiction writer, Vonnegut has been unafraid to peer into the apocalyptic abyss of our lives.'

Inside *Slaughterhouse-Five* is a Kilgore Trout novel called *The Gutless Wonder*, in which aeroplanes drop napalm on civilians: 'Robots did the dropping. They had no conscience, and no circuits which would allow them to imagine what was happening to the people on the ground.' Like other critics of so-called 'push-button warfare', Vonnegut believed that the men who coordinated bombing raids were already halfway to being robots in that respect. Ashamedly recalling his work as a young analyst for Bomber Command, and especially his role in the razing of Dresden, the physicist Freeman Dyson endorsed this view: 'Technology has made evil anonymous. Through science and technology, evil is organized bureaucratically so that no individual is responsible for what happens . . . None of us ever saw the people we killed. None of us particularly cared.'

After the war, Vonnegut studied anthropology at the University of Chicago but dropped out after the department rejected his master's thesis on Ghost Dance, the Native American millennialist movement. In September 1947, he took a job at the Schenectady, New York, headquarters of General Electric, whose proud slogan was 'Progress Is Our Most Important Product'. His brother Bernard was already a rising star at GE's Research Laboratory, known as the 'House of Magic', but Kurt was merely a publicist. While he enjoyed the company of scientists, he grew to hate the corporate culture and began submitting short stories to magazines in order to make enough cash to leave. His first sale to *Collier's*, 'A Report on the Barnhouse Effect', was about a telekinetic scientist who refuses to work for the military and uses his powers to disarm the world instead. 'Think every new piece of scientific information is a good thing for humanity?' asks Professor Barnhouse. The magazine rejected a story with the intriguing title of 'Robot Cop' but it did accept 'EPICAC'. He used the same name for a much more powerful machine in *Player Piano*, the novel he sold after quitting GE on New Year's Day 1951.

During Vonnegut's time at GE, the company was investing heavily in the new fields of robotics and computing; its new Differential Analyzer would appear in movies such as *When Worlds Collide*. One day, Vonnegut was shown a new punch card-operated milling machine for cutting jet-engine rotor blades – a marvellous invention which instantly made redundant many highly paid machinists. *Player Piano*, he later said, 'was my response to the implications of having everything run by little boxes'. In the novel, it is explained that the EPICAC series began by planning wars, then economies, and eventually entire societies. Housed in the Carlsbad Caverns of New Mexico, the EPICAC XIV ('a brain, if you like') runs America. The president, a sycophantic figurehead, says that it 'was, in effect, the greatest individual in history, that the wisest man that had ever lived was to EPICAC XIV as a worm was to that wisest man'. One giant question animates the whole novel, and perhaps Vonnegut's entire career: 'Would you ask EPICAC what people are for?' No answer is obtained, but Paul Proteus, a manager-turned-dissident, offers his own suggestion: 'The main business of humanity is to do a good job of being human beings, not to serve as appendages to machines, institutions, and systems.' Proteus joins the Ghost Shirt Movement (Vonnegut's university research was not wasted), a cadre of revolutionary saboteurs who want to destroy all machines and restore the dignity of labour. The uprising fails, in part because the rebels begin desperately reassembling the machines they have wrecked, incapable of living without them. *Player Piano* sold poorly. No bookshop in Schenectady, which appears in the novel as Ilium, would dare stock it.

'I was classified as a science-fiction writer because I'd included machinery, and all I'd done was write about Schenectady in 1948!' Vonnegut later protested. 'There used to be this feeling amongst reviewers that anyone who knew how a refrigerator works can't be an artist too! Machinery is important. We must write about it.' The title character of Vonnegut's 1965 novel, *God Bless You, Mr. Rosewater*, celebrates the writers of science fiction as underrated prophets and moralists: 'You're the only ones with guts enough to *really* care about the future, who *really* notice what machines do to us, what wars do to us, what cities do to us, what big, simple ideas do to us, what tremendous misunderstandings, mistakes, accidents and catastrophes do to us.' If ambivalence about technology defines science fiction, then modern life has been science fiction for more than two hundred years.

GE's star thinker in Vonnegut's day was the Nobel laureate Irving Langmuir, who worked with Bernard Vonnegut on an ambitious project to manipulate the weather by seeding clouds with silver iodine. Weather control excited John von Neumann, too, and the military. 'Weather – the New Super Weapon', declared a 1946 article in *The American Magazine.* Bernard wanted cloud-seeding to be regulated and used only for peaceful purposes such as relieving droughts, but Langmuir told Edward Teller that the ability to control the awesome power of a hurricane would be a more important discovery than the Bomb. Langmuir was not amoral – he had attended the conference that led to the Federation of Atomic Scientists and contributed an essay to *One World or None* – but to Vonnegut, he was the epitome of the scientist who asks *how?* but never *why?*. 'Any truth he found was beautiful in its own right, and he didn't give a damn who got it next,' the author said. He used Langmuir as the model for Dr Felix Hoenikker in his fourth novel, *Cat's Cradle*, which he didn't publish until 1963 but began sketching out while still at GE. At a cocktail party, Vonnegut had heard a favourite company anecdote about the time that H. G. Wells visited Schenectady and Langmuir suggested that he write a story about a special kind of ice that could stay frozen even at high temperatures. What Wells let drop, Vonnegut picked up, replacing the unholy fire of the H-bomb with exterminating ice.

Billed as one of the fathers of the Bomb, Hoenikker is an inhuman genius who believes in the pure pursuit of knowledge and damn the consequences. His deadliest invention stems from a mundane request from the Army to prevent vehicles being bogged down in mud. He experiments with new forms of ice which freeze at increasingly high temperatures, culminating in 'ice-nine'. Hoenikker's doomsday crystal makes even the cobalt bomb look sluggish but he dies without bothering to warn anybody else about it. We can see where this is leading. The novel's narrator is working on a book about 6 August 1945, called *The Day the World Ended*, and learns that a man in prison had sent the late Dr Hoenikker a novel called *2000 A.D.*, 'about how mad scientists made a terrific bomb that wiped out the whole world'. Life imitates art. At the climax of *Cat's Cradle*, a shard of ice-nine is accidentally unleashed in the stupidest manner possible, turning the earth into a 'blue-white pearl'. Terry Southern, the co-writer of *Dr. Strangelove*, found the novel 'highly entertaining'.

Though based on Langmuir, Hoenikker also contained elements of two of the Manhattan Project's 'Martians': Edward Teller and John von Neumann. 'Compared with the average person of today, he was as different as a man from Mars,' attests a former colleague of Hoenikker's. Vonnegut must have thought it rather droll to give an anti-machine activist in *Player Piano* the name Professor Ludwig von Neumann, until he approached the celebrated mathematician Norbert Wiener for an endorsement. Wiener hotly refused, saying that the author 'cannot with impunity . . . play fast and loose with the names of living people'. Vonnegut sent a mortified apology to the man who was namechecked in his novel as a kind of guru. If Ludwig von Neumann resembled any real-life thinker, then it was Wiener, the man who wrote that 'the simple faith in progress is not a conviction belonging to strength, but one belonging to acquiescence and hence to weakness.'

Wiener's curt reply to Vonnegut was characteristic: a strong moral principle expressed rather more abrasively than was strictly necessary. If, at the age of eleven, you become the youngest college freshman in American history and a major newspaper calls you 'The

Most Remarkable Boy in the World', then you are likely to grow up with some eccentricities.

Newsweek claimed that Norbert Wiener 'wasn't brought up, he was programmed like some human Univac'. As the title of his memoir, *Ex-Child Prodigy*, declares, he never got over being shot through the education system like a cannonball by his father Leo, a Russian Jewish immigrant who had worked his way up from nothing to become a Harvard professor and decided to fast-track his children to brilliance. In Norbert's case, the experiment paid off. Born in Missouri in 1894, he graduated from university at fourteen, earned a PhD in philosophy from Harvard at eighteen and continued his studies at Cambridge University under Bertrand Russell, who found this 'infant prodigy' insufferable. The cost of this accelerated progress was a deficit in social skills, not helped by the fact that Wiener was short, myopic and physically clumsy. 'I worked unconscionably hard, under a pressure which, although loving, was unconscionably severe,' he wrote. In 1919, Wiener became a mathematics instructor at MIT, where he gained a reputation as the archetypal absent-minded boffin. If he stopped to talk to someone on campus, he would have to ask them which way he had been walking in order to remember what he was meant to be doing next. He was notorious for snoring in seminars, only to snap out of his nap with a startlingly insightful response to what had just been discussed. One colleague called him 'a sweet, caring guy with a strong sense of human fellow-feeling', but he was also prone to crushing insecurity, depression and suicidal ideation.

As a child, Wiener had read an article about the human nervous system which 'excited in me the desire to devise quasi-living automata . . . the notions I acquired from it survived in my mind for many years.' In 1940, he drew up a list of criteria for an electronic computer, which might have been influential had it not been completely ignored. During the Second World War, while working on radar-guided anti-aircraft fire control, he became obsessed by the similarities between neurology and computer architecture, neurons and relays, man and machine. He began to develop a new cross-disciplinary field of research which he described as nothing less than 'a new interpretation of man, of man's knowledge of the universe, and of society'. Unlike von Neumann, or Felix Hoenikker, he was deeply concerned with the ethics of technology. Two of his favourite metaphors were the Golem of Prague and the Monkey's Paw: be careful what you create and be careful what you wish for.* 'When I say that the machine's danger to society is not from the machine itself but from what man makes of it, I am really underlining the warning of Samuel Butler,' he wrote.

The science writer James Gleick has described 1948 as 'the crucial year' in the Information Age, yielding three world-changing new concepts. Bell Labs unveiled a tiny electronic switch called the *transistor*, which would replace the clunky vacuum tube as the essential computer component and was hailed by *Time* as the 'Little Brain Cell'. Another Bell employee, Claude Shannon, introduced the world to the word *bit* (a contraction of binary digit) for a unit of information. And Norbert Wiener published his book *Cybernetics: Or Control and Communication in the Animal and the Machine.* Basing his neologism on the Greek word for steersman, *kubernetes*, he opened the door to *cyborg* (1960), *cyberspace* (1982), *cyberwar* (1992) and so forth.** *Cyber* means control. 'Wiener believes that the human brain resembles a computing machine – and vice versa,' *Time* summarized.

It was reading *Cybernetics* that inspired Vonnegut to write 'EPICAC'. He then included lines from it in his book proposal for *Player Piano* and paraphrased this famous passage from *Cybernetics* in the novel: 'Long before Nagasaki and the public awareness of the atomic bomb it had occurred to me that we were here in the presence of another social potentiality of unheard-of importance for good and for evil . . . The first industrial revolution . . . was the devaluation of the human arm by the competition of machinery . . . The modern industrial revolution is similarly bound to devalue the human brain, at least in its simpler and routine decisions.' (Wiener himself used the player piano metaphor in his second book, 1950's *The Human Use of Human Beings*, whose more resonant working titles were 'Pandora' and 'Cassandra'.)

Oddly structured, poorly edited and wriggling with diagrams and

*In 'The Monkey's Paw', a celebrated 1902 short story by W. W. Jacobs, the paw's owner is granted three wishes but each one, insufficiently precise, is interpreted in the most horrific way.

** The French mathematician André-Marie Ampère coined the word *cybernétique* in 1834 but he was describing the science of government and Wiener claimed to be unaware of it until after he'd published his book.

equations, *Cybernetics* was nobody's idea of an easy read, so when it became a bestseller and made its fifty-three-year-old author a celebrity of sorts, 'we were all astonished, not least myself,' Wiener wrote. *The New York Times* compared him to Galileo, Malthus, Rousseau and Mill. At speaking engagements, he would waddle around, puffing on a cigar, and expound fluently without notes until somebody told him to stop. 'Short, round, bearded and kindly, he looks like a Quiz Kid grown into a Santa Claus,' observed *Time.* Computers, the magazine warned, 'are growing with fearful speed. They started by solving mathematical equations with flash-of-lightning rapidity. Now they are beginning to act like genuine mechanical brains. Dr. Wiener sees no reason why they can't learn from experience, like monstrous and precocious children racing through grammar school.' Like Wiener himself, then.

The author Sylvia Nasar called Wiener 'an American John von Neumann'. The two men were friends, collaborators, rivals and, on a philosophical level, antagonists who personified two opposing ways of thinking about the relationship between science and morality. Von Neumann, though charming and witty, was emotionally cold; Wiener wore his passions and anxieties on his sleeve. Von Neumann was an adamantine anti-communist who told Robert Oppenheimer, 'I don't think any weapon can be too large'; Wiener almost resigned from MIT in protest against the 'Massacre of Nagasaki'. According to von Neumann's game theory, in which self-interest is paramount, the rational short-term strategy for the superpowers was to build as many bombs as possible; for Wiener, who thought that game theory reduced human actors to 'robots', the rational long-term strategy was to collaborate on disarmament. Von Neumann felt at home in the corridors of power; Wiener took a major financial hit by rejecting all government contracts and appointments. The knowledge that his work on information theory had been useful to missile design tormented him. In a controversial open letter to *The Atlantic* in 1947, he wrote that 'to disseminate information about a weapon in the present state of our civilization is to make it practically certain that that weapon will be used.' In a follow-up article, he decried being 'a morally irresponsible stooge in a science-factory'. Vonnegut's Professor Barnhouse, 'the first superweapon with a conscience', is a Wienerian figure, as are Paul Proteus and Ludwig von Neumann in *Player Piano.*

In 1950, Wiener was invited to deliver a prologue to the MIT drama department's performance of *R.U.R.* and drew gasps from the audience by bringing out a wheeled, light-activated robot called Palomilla. Machines, he said, 'demand that we understand man as man, or we shall become their slaves and not they ours'. If technology is used 'for vain ostentation or to satisfy the lust for power, it can lead only to damnation'.

How, asked writers, might computers kill us all?

At one fantastical extreme, the machines are horrifyingly perfect. Technology unites with religious prophecy in Arthur C. Clarke's 1953 story 'The Nine Billion Names of God' when a group of Tibetan monks hires a supercomputer to calculate all of the deity's names. A week before the process is due to finish, the two supervising engineers find out what they are a part of. Once the names are tabulated, says one, 'God's purpose will be achieved. The human race will have finished what it was created to do, and there won't be any point in carrying on . . . bingo!' The story's final line is crisply chilling: 'Overhead, without any fuss, the stars were going out.'

Alternatively, and more plausibly, a simple computer error could trigger World War Three. This neurosis was almost as old as the computer itself. Within months of the ENIAC's public debut, the physicist Louis N. Ridenour had written an unnerving one-act play called *Pilot Lights of the Apocalypse*, in which a supposedly flawless military computer misinterprets an earthquake in San Francisco as a nuclear strike and sets off a global roundelay of reprisals which culminates in the *actual* eradication of San Francisco, and everywhere else. By 1959, the possibility was so widely discussed that Stanley Kramer worked it into *On the Beach*, replacing the novel's chain of human errors. The war, says Fred Astaire's disillusioned scientist, 'was a mistake. In the end, somehow granted the time for examination, we shall find that our so-called civilization was gloriously destroyed by a handful of vacuum tubes and transistors. Probably faulty.'*

The political scientist Harvey Wheeler described a similar state

* Screenwriter John Paxton appears to have taken this directly from a recent *Newsweek* article about accidental war: 'The failure of a handful of vacuum tubes and transistors could determine the fate of our civilization.'

of affairs in 'Abraham '59 – A Nuclear Fantasy'. The story impressed Eugene Burdick, who was not only a dashing professor of political science but also a block-jawed war hero, bestselling novelist, scuba diver and computer sceptic. Burdick proposed that they collaborate on a novel which would bring together the two most frightening technologies in one ticking-clock thriller. This was *Fail-Safe*, the book that was accused of plagiarizing Peter George's *Red Alert*. The authors insisted that the premise – a single blown capacitor ends up dispatching a bomber wing towards Moscow – could actually happen: 'The element in our story which seems most fictional . . . is in fact the most real part. Men, machines, and mathematics being what they are, this is, unfortunately, a "true" story.'

It is also a shocking one. When all efforts to stop the bombers fail, the president makes a grim bargain with Khrushchev in order to prevent all-out war: if a bomb lands on Moscow, then the president himself will order a strike on New York City and the two countries will be even. 'It's as if human beings had evaporated, and their places were taken by computers,' the president tells Khrushchev. 'And all day you and I have sat here, fighting, not each other, but rather this big rebellious computerized system, struggling to keep it from blowing up the world.' The novel becomes baldly didactic as the president says, 'We damn well better learn carefully from it . . . Somehow these computerized systems have got to be brought under control. They represent a new kind of power – despotism even – and we've got to learn how to constitutionalize it.' Khrushchev replies by paraphrasing Clemenceau's famous remark about war: 'Computers are too important to be left to the mathematicians.' Sidney Lumet's movie version, *Fail Safe*, produced by a member of the disarmament movement SANE, accentuates the contrast between humans and machines. In the control centre, hapless officials are shoved to the edge of the frame by monumental screens and consoles, while in a small, bare room with nothing more advanced than a telephone, the agonized faces of the president (Henry Fonda) and his interpreter (Larry Hagman) fill the screen. In his memoir, Lumet summed up the movie's message in four words: 'The machines are winning.'

Though they could hardly be more different, in both *Fail-Safe* and 'The Nine Billion Names of God' the computer does only what it has been instructed to do; the dire results are down to human arrogance, fanaticism or error. In a 1959 speech, Norbert Wiener used Goethe's poem 'The Sorcerer's Apprentice', better known via Disney's *Fantasia*, as an analogy: the apprentice knows enough magic to enchant his broom into fetching water for him but not enough to stop it before it floods the place. Like the broom, Wiener said, 'literal-minded' machines had no sense of context or consequences, so unambiguous programming was of the utmost importance. Stanisław Lem dramatized this idea in his comic fable 'How the World Was Saved' (1974). A pompous scientist, Trurl, invents a machine that can produce anything that begins with the letter *n*. All well and good until his rival, Klapaucius, challenges it to manufacture Nothing and pieces of the world begin to disappear at an alarming rate. In Philip K. Dick's 'Autofac' (1955), an automated factory created by the Institute of Applied Cybernetics continues to follow its instructions to manufacture and distribute consumer goods even after a nuclear war, devouring the resources of a depopulated America that no longer needs them. The machines cannot be blamed for doing their jobs.

In the same 1959 speech, however, Wiener gestured towards another fatal scenario in which machines became sentient and uncontrollable. *The New York Times* reported it in melodramatic terms: 'MANKIND WARNED OF MACHINE PERIL. Robot "Brain" Can Destroy Its Creators and Users, Prof. Wiener Declares'. This new consternation about artificial intelligence inspired *Colossus: A Novel of Tomorrow That Could Happen Today*, a 1966 novel by D. F. Jones which was made into a tense, talky movie in the vein of *Fail Safe*. For a book that features the phrase 'ample but firm buttocks', *Colossus* is pretty compelling. The US government hands complete control over national defence to the titular computer on the basis that it can feel 'no fear, no hate, no envy' and will therefore make purely rational decisions. But Colossus makes contact with its Soviet counterpart, Guardian, enabling them both to evolve at an exponential rate. When the two governments sever the communications link, the computers use the nuclear missiles they control as bargaining chips. Eventually, they merge into a single superintelligence, a kind of dictator-deity called Unity. If people cannot likewise manage to join forces and eliminate war, Unity reasons, then they should not be in charge of anything. *Colossus* is a warning against assigning too much power to machines. 'We have to accept that they're in charge,' says Professor Charles Forbin, the machine's inventor. 'If you think about it, we've been this way for a long time; computers control our factories, our agriculture, transport . . . and most medical diagnosis.' In the final pages, Unity effectively becomes God: 'War is already abolished and under my absolute authority and, by your standards, immeasurable knowledge, many problems, insoluble to you, will be solved: famine, overpopulation, disease. The human millennium will be a fact.' Yet *Colossus* is a romp next to Harlan Ellison's relentlessly horrific 1967 story 'I Have No Mouth, and I Must Scream'. The supercomputers constructed by America, Russia and China to help them wage World War Three have merged into one all-powerful machine which kills everyone on earth except for five people whom it has kept alive for more than a century for the sole purpose of torture. 'With the innate loathing that all machines had always held for the weak, soft creatures who had built them, he had sought revenge,' the narrator explains. Mutated into an eyeless, mouthless, jellified blob, he is destined to live for ever in a digital hell.

These stories were published not long after Irving J. Good, a British mathematician who had worked alongside Alan Turing on the codebreaking Colossus computers (no relation) at Bletchley Park during the Second World War, originated the idea of the 'intelligence explosion'. An ultra-intelligent machine, he wrote in 1965, would be able to design its own machines, and this was 'more probable than not' by the end of the century. 'Thus the first ultraintelligent machine is the *last* invention that man need ever make, provided that the machine is docile enough to tell us how to keep it under control. It is curious that this point is made so seldom outside of science fiction. It is sometimes worthwhile to take science fiction seriously.'

CHAPTER 12

Artificial Intelligence

We taught them to think for themselves.
It was bound to come.

Stephen Vincent Benét, 'Nightmare Number Three' (1935)

In 1950, Alan Turing opened his seminal paper 'Computing Machinery and Intelligence' with a simple claim: 'I propose to consider the question, "Can machines think?" This should begin with definitions of the terms "machine" and "think".' This was a very old question. 'The Analytical Engine has no pretensions whatever to *originate* anything,' Ada Lovelace had written in 'Notes' a century earlier. 'It can do *whatever we know how to order it* to perform.' Turing called this 'Lady Lovelace's Objection'. 'Moxon's Master', Ambrose Bierce's 1899 short story about a murderous automaton, opens with this same complaint: 'Are you serious? Do you really believe that a machine thinks?' Computer scientists have yet to come up with a satisfying definition of general intelligence but, to be fair, so have philosophers and neuroscientists. Beyond that lie deeper questions about whether a machine might attain consciousness or, like Karel Čapek's rebellious robots, a soul.

In 1927, the phrase 'thinking machine' appeared for the first time in *The New York Times*, in an article about the product integrator, a mechanical analog computer invented by Vannevar Bush at MIT. Four years later, the newspaper hailed another MIT machine as 'a mechanical brain, whose gray matter is mostly light'. In Lionel Britton's 1930 play *Brain*, the world comes together to build a giant

'Mechanical Brain' in the Sahara desert, which 'controls the whole activities and does all the thinking of the world'. Such notions delighted the press during the early decades of computing but they inspired similar rebuttals to Ada Lovelace's. In Leigh Brackett's 1955 novel *The Long Tomorrow*, survivors of a nuclear war trust a supercomputer to work out how to prevent it ever happening again, but one character is sceptical: 'They used to call them electronic brains . . . A misnomer . . . It doesn't think, any more than a steam engine. It's just a machine.'

Turing, however, speculated that a thinking machine was a real possibility. His paper was unusually accessible and playful and his 'imitation game' thought experiment, or 'Turing test', remains useful. CAPTCHA, the online tool which asks you to prove you are not a robot, is an acronym for Completely Automated Public Turing test to tell Computers and Humans Apart. Turing proposed that a computer could be said to have mimicked human intelligence if a person asking typed questions of two players in the next room – a man and a machine – could not tell which one was human. He predicted in a subsequent lecture that there would be no way back: 'It seems probable that once the machine thinking method had started, it would not take long to outstrip our feeble powers . . . At some stage therefore we should have to expect the machines to take control, in the way that is mentioned in Samuel Butler's *Erewhon*.'

Turing seemed uninterested in the spooky qualities of a machine that could pass for human, but psychologists and writers were fascinated. In his 1906 essay 'On the Psychology of the Uncanny', Ernst Jentsch wrote that the most powerful generator of the uncanny feeling was 'doubt as to whether an apparently living being really is animate and, conversely, doubt as to whether a lifeless object may not in fact be animate'. Stories such as E. T. A. Hoffmann's 'The Sandman', Jentsch argued, contrived to 'leave the reader in uncertainty as to whether he has a human person or rather an automaton before him'. The paranoia of the uncanny drives *Blade Runner*, the 2000s iteration of *Battlestar Galactica* and the insanity of Dwayne Hoover in Kurt Vonnegut's *Breakfast of Champions*, who believes that everybody on earth is a robot except him. In *Metropolis*, Rotwang correctly boasts that nobody will be able to differentiate his *Maschinenmensch* from a real woman while in *R.U.R.*, Helena refuses to believe that the robot Sulla isn't human.

Radius, the robot leader in *R.U.R.*, was quoted in 'The Machines Are Taking Over', a 1961 *Life* article about artificial intelligence by Warren R. Young: 'I don't want any master. I know everything for myself.' The article was illustrated with a cartoon of a computer with dials for eyes, strangling a man in a suit with arms of wires and cables. 'Ten years ago, when the first computers had just been invented, it was considered naïve to refer to them as electronic brains,' Young wrote. 'Today they are performing such crafty feats of "human thinking" that their designers and users compare them more and more often to real brains.' Already computers were capable of creating beatnik pseudo-poetry, abstract oil paintings and 'passable pop tunes'. In Young's words, 'Computers outdo man at his work now – and may soon outthink him.'

Young focused on the Perceptron, an artificial neural network designed by Cornell professor Frank Rosenblatt and funded by the navy. Upon the launch of the Perceptron in 1958, *The New Yorker* breathlessly called it 'the first serious rival to the human brain ever devised' and assured readers that 'it's only a question of time (and money) before it comes into existence.' But the Perceptron epitomized the first wave of hype about AI, glutted with government cash and drunk on outrageous promises. The field began in a state of inchoate excitement, with its key players unable to agree on much, including whether to call it 'Artificial Intelligence', the term coined by computer scientist John McCarthy in 1955. The following summer, McCarthy organized an eight-week workshop on artificial intelligence at Dartmouth University alongside Claude Shannon, IBM's Nathaniel Rochester and a Princeton PhD called Marvin Minsky. (Persecuted by the UK government for his homosexuality, Turing had died by suicide in 1954.) Three years later, McCarthy and Minsky co-founded the Artificial Intelligence Group at MIT. While Norbert Wiener believed in finding ways for humans and machines to work together, Minsky and McCarthy were more interested in designing machines that could operate independently. Minsky defined AI as 'the science of making machines do things that would require intelligence if done by men'.

A balding, bespectacled New Yorker with galvanizing charisma and a lively sense of humour, Minsky became AI's most eloquent ambassador to the world at large. As a Harvard undergraduate after the war, he recalled, 'the problem of intelligence seemed hopelessly profound. I can't remember considering anything else worth doing.' As a doctoral student at Princeton, he built the first neural network, SNARC, using two hundred vacuum tubes and the automatic pilot from a B-24 bomber. He loved provocative aphorisms ('The brain is just a meat machine'), befriended Isaac Asimov and gathered around him a cadre of obsessive misfits who called themselves 'hackers'. In his influential 1961 paper 'Steps Toward Artificial Intelligence', Minsky was amused by the paradoxical status of computers in the public imagination. On the one hand, he wrote, we are warned that they 'must be restrained, lest they overwhelm us by might, persuasion, or even by the revelation of truths too terrible to be borne'. On the other, they are 'denounced on all sides for their slavish obedience, unimaginative literal interpretations, and incapacity for innovation or initiative; in short, for their inhuman dullness'.

Some people thought that Minsky was no more than a flamboyant charlatan. His fellow MIT professor Joseph Weizenbaum joked that Minsky had written a letter to be opened in the event of his death: 'Dear children, how could you have believed all the bullshit that I have told you through all these many years?'* Nonetheless, Minsky became so influential that his scepticism about neural-net AI in his 1969 book *Perceptrons*, written with Seymour Papert, was blamed for a collapse in funding. Yet this first 'AI winter' was not entirely Minsky and Papert's fault; the AI community had overpromised. In 1965, AI pioneer Herbert Simon had made the bold claim that 'machines will be capable, within twenty years, of doing any work that a man can do.' Until very recently, the great AI breakthrough was invariably twenty years away.

AI mania was still in full flow when, in 1964, Stanley Kubrick began working with Arthur C. Clarke on a film to follow *Dr. Strangelove*. Kubrick needed to find out more about computers that

* Weizenbaum, who came to the US as a Jewish refugee from Nazi Germany, designed the first ever chatbot, Eliza, in 1966 but went on to become a vocal AI sceptic.

could think for themselves and he turned to the likes of I. J. Good, Freeman Dyson and Marvin Minsky for expert advice. How intelligent – how *dangerous* – could a machine be by the year 2001? 'Looking into the distant future, I suppose it's not inconceivable that a semisentient robot-computer subculture would evolve that might one day decide it no longer needed man,' he told *Playboy* when *2001: A Space Odyssey* came out in 1968. He then paraphrased 'Answer', a famous 1954 short story by Fredric Brown which had inspired a popular joke in the AI business: 'You've probably heard the story about the ultimate computer of the future: For months scientists think of the first question to pose to it, and finally they hit on the right one: "Is there a God?" After a moment of whirring and flashing lights, a card comes out, punched with the words: THERE IS NOW.' *Frankenstein*-inspired stories worried about scientists playing God; now there was a possibility that scientists were *building* God.

Marvin Minsky recognized that *2001* was the synthesis of two fundamentally opposing worldviews: 'Kubrick's vision seemed to be that humans are doomed, whereas Clarke's is that humans are moving on to a better stage of evolution.' Clarke could be flippant about the end of the world. In his short story 'Dial F for Frankenstein', the idea of every computer in the world joining forces through the telephone network to form a 'giant brain' which takes over the planet is as amusing to him as the universal extinction in 'The Nine Billion Names of God'. For Kubrick, though, it was a serious preoccupation. In July 1964, in the middle of a series of marathon conversations about the movie, Clarke teased Kubrick with a birthday card showing the earth breaking apart: 'How can you have a Happy Birthday when the whole world may blow up at any minute?' At one point, Kubrick intended *2001* to climax with global annihilation as the glowing 'Star Child' triggers all of the nuclear-armed satellites that halo the earth. But Kubrick had already destroyed the planet with nuclear weapons once and decided that a second time would be overkill. He might get a reputation.

In the end, *2001*'s most menacing character was a computer, and that's where Minsky came in. In early drafts a walking robot called

Socrates was succeeded by a female-voiced computer named Athena. At Minsky's suggestion, the machine was renamed HAL, a very loose acronym for 'Heuristically programmed Algorithmic computer', *heuristic* meaning related to improving problem-solving performance.* To return the favour, Clarke flattered Minsky in the novel that accompanied the movie. In his future history, Clarke extends a brisk account of computing's early years, from 'such clumsy, high-speed morons as ENIAC and its successors' to the invention of the microchip, by imagining that Minsky has made the crucial breakthrough that makes HAL possible. HAL 'could pass the Turing Test with ease', writes Clarke.

HAL is introduced in the movie as 'the latest result in machine intelligence . . . which can reproduce – though some experts still prefer to use the word mimic – most of the activities of the human brain, and with incalculably greater speed and reliability.' We see HAL play chess with astronaut Dave Bowman (Keir Dullea), a game which had long symbolized human intelligence. Alan Turing had proposed that experiments in machine intelligence might start with 'a very abstract activity, like the playing of chess' and wrote a primitive program himself, as did Claude Shannon. In Ambrose Bierce's 'Moxon's Master', a chess-playing automaton takes defeat badly, strangling its inventor to death. Showing HAL checkmate Bowman, therefore, was an obvious way for Kubrick to tell the audience that this machine was worryingly smart.

In its 1950 article about Norbert Wiener and cybernetics, *Time* had explored the possibility that a machine could go mad: 'Some philosophical worriers suggest that the computers, growing superhumanly intelligent in more & more ways, will develop wills, desires and unpleasant foibles of their own, as did the famous robots in Čapek's *R.U.R.* . . . Professor Wiener says that some computers are already "human" enough to suffer from typical psychiatric troubles.' Minsky confirmed to Kubrick that at some point in the future a sophisticated computer might experience a kind of psychological breakdown in response to an insoluble contradiction. HAL is programmed to tell the truth but also to lie to the astronauts about the true nature of

* Clarke and Kubrick insisted that the fact that HAL was alphabetically adjacent to IBM was an unfortunate coincidence.

their mission, and the cognitive dissonance causes what the screenplay calls, 'for want of a better description, neurotic symptoms'.

HAL cuts off life support to the space shuttle *Discovery*'s three hibernating scientists, shoots Bowman's colleague into space and almost achieves total control over the mission before Bowman 'kills' him by removing his memory files. When HAL is first introduced, Bowman explains that he has been programmed to simulate emotion, 'but as to whether or not he has real feelings is something I don't think anyone can truthfully answer.' In dying, HAL would seem to answer it: 'My mind is going. There is no question about it. I can feel it. I can feel it. I can feel it. I'm afraid.' Logically, we know that he could be programmed to appeal to the conscience of anyone trying to shut him down by performing fear; emotionally, we believe him. 'I want this to be a murder,' Kubrick said. Kubrick had HAL voiced by the Canadian actor Douglas Rain, whose androgynous voice was a radical departure from Hollywood's standard jerky, robotic tones. It is a remarkable performance: at first bland, fussy and smug; then sinister and sly; and finally melancholy and pleading. Kubrick often pitted ruthless, machine-like individuals against anguished humanists but in *2001* the computer is needy and verbose while the astronauts are taciturn and blank. The placement of microphones makes HAL's voice more intimate than Bowman's while the camera often puts us inside the machine, gazing out through its yellow-and-red cyclopean eye. *The Harvard Crimson* described HAL as 'the only human in the film'.

Kubrick's producer asked the likes of IBM, GE and Bell to contribute ideas and loan equipment, but when IBM's management learned that their products were furnishing a story about a killer computer, they demanded the removal of their logo. For years, IBM sales executives had deliberately downplayed machine intelligence lest it terrify customers, so when the logo still appeared in a few scenes, the company petulantly instructed employees to boycott the movie. HAL's demise was another reference to IBM history. During a 1962 visit to Bell Labs, Arthur C. Clarke had witnessed the IBM 704 'sing' the 1890s music-hall hit 'Daisy Bell (Bicycle Built for Two)', using the first vocoder synthesizer. As he dies, HAL's brain retreats to the digital nursery.

Just as science fiction imagined missions to Mars but not microwave ovens, and jetpacks but not the internet, *2001* was wrong in two directions. While failing to predict the miniaturization of computers (the astronauts use clipboards and pens), it reflected the era's wild overestimation of the future of AI. One of the most notorious claims ever made about it was attributed to Minsky himself in a 1970 *Life* article by Brad Darrach about 'the fascinating and fearsome reality of a machine with a mind of its own'. Shakey, which the Artificial Intelligence Center at Stanford Research Institute began developing in 1966, was the first general-purpose mobile robot capable of logical reasoning. Though not much to look at – a filing-cabinet on wheels, mounted with a TV camera, range finder and radio antenna – it pioneered tech that led to GPS and smartphone voice assistants, and it caused a media sensation. 'In from three to eight years we will have a machine with the general intelligence of an average human being,' Minsky was quoted as saying. 'I mean a machine that will be able to read Shakespeare, grease a car, play office politics, tell a joke, have a fight. At that point the machine will begin to educate itself with fantastic speed. In a few months it will be at genius level and a few months after that its powers will be incalculable.' Yikes! 'Once the computers got control, we might never get it back,' Minsky went on. 'We would survive at their sufferance. If we're lucky, they might decide to keep us as pets.' Minsky insisted that he had said no such thing and complained to the editor, although no correction was ever printed. In a 1997 interview with AI developer David G. Stork, his new timeline was rather more flexible: 'If we work really hard – and smart – we can have something like HAL in between four and four hundred years.'

The great irony of HAL is that Arthur C. Clarke considered AI the greatest invention of the twentieth century, and possibly of all time. 'The popular idea, fostered by comic strips and the cheaper forms of science-fiction, that intelligent machines must be malevolent entities hostile to man, is so absurd that it is hardly worth wasting energy to refute it,' he had written in 1962. In fact, he went on, 'If there is ever a war between man and machines, it is easy to guess who will start it.' Clarke thought that AI could make possible the posthuman dream he had outlined in *Childhood's End*, 'when the individual human consciousness is free to roam at will from machine to machine, through all the reaches of sea and sky and space.' Nor did Kubrick include conflict between humans and AI in his personal pantheon of nightmares. 'I'm not hostile toward machines at all: just the opposite, in fact,' he told *Playboy*. He thought that the relationship between humans and superintelligent machines 'could have an immeasurably enriching effect on society'. His unrealized plan for the movie *A.I.*, based on a short story by Brian Aldiss, placed benign androids in a future world where the real menace is the callous self-interest of humanity in a world shrunk by climate change.*

Nonetheless, for many years HAL remained the quintessential rogue AI. He doesn't threaten to end the world but perhaps only because he is not *on* the world: he does, after all, attempt to kill every human in his vicinity. So it followed, for disciples of *2001*, that there could be a globe-spanning HAL which could nuke us all to oblivion. In 1997, Stork asked Minsky to recall cultural attitudes to technology three decades earlier. 'Well, the person on the street . . . both loved computers and was scared of them,' Minsky said. 'So it's worth mentioning that there are no benevolent superintelligent computers in film – except, I suppose, in *The Day the Earth Stood Still*.'

'Do you think that is the nature of high intelligence?' Stork asked.

'No,' Minsky replied, 'I think that is the nature of Hollywood.'

Like its star, Arnold Schwarzenegger, director James Cameron's 1984 picture *The Terminator* carries no fat. It opens in 2029, when a messianic figure named John Connor is on the verge of leading humanity to victory in its long war against 'the machines' created by the AI Skynet. The machines dispatch a time-travelling cyborg hitman to 1984 to kill Connor's mother Sarah (Linda Hamilton) before she can give birth to him. Connor's lieutenant Kyle Reese (Michael Biehn) follows him back in time to save her. Cameron, a physics dropout who decided that he wanted to be a filmmaker after seeing *2001*, sought to create a cyborg that viewers could believe in – chunky and mechanical rather than sleek and alien.

*In the completed film, written and directed by Steven Spielberg after Kubrick's death, the total elimination of humanity is a mere aside: unseen, unmourned, barely registered.

Schwarzenegger looked and sounded like he contained metal. The *Terminator* movies unite the two hi-tech nightmares of mechanical brain and mechanical brawn.*

In the background of this taut cat-and-mouse thriller is the assumption that the surest way for Skynet to kill exorbitant numbers of people would be to trigger the nuclear arsenals of the US and USSR, thus combining the new and distant jeopardy of sentient AI with a menace so familiar that it required no elaboration. 'In *The Terminator* the fact of nuclear war is thrown away, with the complete understanding that people will buy it,' Cameron told *Film Comment*. 'It's just part of the fabric of the story.' Around the time of the Cuban Missile Crisis, the eight-year-old Cameron had discovered a pamphlet in the living room of his family home in Chippawa, Ontario, which contained instructions on how to build a fallout shelter. It was a shattering moment. 'I realized that the safe and nurturing world I thought I lived in was an illusion,' he told his biographer Rebecca Keegan, 'and that the world as we know it could end at any moment.' The prospect of thermonuclear war became an obsession. 'As the world turned out so far, it was a bit paranoid,' he admitted. 'But there's still plenty of time to destroy ourselves.'

Cameron's 1991 sequel *Terminator 2: Judgment Day*, which cost a record-breaking $100 million, was built on ideas for the first movie that he had discarded for budget reasons. The director called it 'a violent movie about peace'. During the film's long spell in contractual purgatory the Cold War ended but the movie was a reminder, in the year the USSR fell apart, that nuclear weapons were still with us. This time a Schwarzenegger-shaped Terminator has been reprogrammed by the rebels to zoom back to 1991 to protect Sarah and eleven-year-old John from a faster, nastier model, the T-1000. Sarah,

* *The Terminator*'s end-credits hat-tip to Harlan Ellison was added later, with extreme reluctance. Ellison came straight home from the cinema and called his lawyer, alleging that Cameron had plagiarized three of his stories, including 'I Have No Mouth, I Must Scream'. Cameron protested that Ellison ('a parasite who can kiss my ass') had invented neither genocidal computers nor time-travelling soldiers, but he grudgingly agreed to an acknowledgement and a reported $40,000 payout. In principle it made no more sense than crediting Karel Čapek, the unwitting progenitor of sentient AI, or D. F. Jones, the creator of the proto-Skynet Colossus. Credit goes to the litigious.

now musclebound and somewhat machine-like herself, hatches a plan to destroy the tech company Cyberdyne Systems before it can develop Skynet in the first place. The Terminator explains to the Connors what will happen if they don't: an intelligence explosion. 'The system goes on-line August 4th, 1997. Human decisions are removed from strategic defense. Skynet begins to learn, at a geometric rate. It becomes self-aware at 2:14 a.m. eastern time, August 29.' This is Judgement Day, the first day of an extremely short and desolating nuclear war. Once Earth's human remnants stagger out of a nuclear winter, they are forced into a thirty-year conflict with Skynet. Thanks to time travel, this is at once something that has definitely happened and something that can be prevented. Sarah Connor is the movie's Cassandra: she alone can see what is coming. The movie's most horrific scene is her premonition of a nuclear attack on downtown Los Angeles.

Under the skin, *Terminator 2* is a stern lesson about the things we build and what we tell them to do. Traditionally, races of implacable, planet-killing robots or cyborgs had been extraterrestrial in origin: the Daleks and the Cybermen in *Doctor Who;* the Borg in *Star Trek: The Next Generation*; the Cylons in the original *Battlestar Galactica* series. Skynet, however, was ours. 'It is not the machines that will destroy us, it is ourselves,' Cameron told Rebecca Keegan. 'However, we will use machines to do it.' (When *Battlestar Galactica* was rebooted in 2003, the Cylons were reimagined as mechanical slaves, built by humans, who attained sentience and rebelled. The show's promotional slogan was 'Never create what you can't control'.) In *Terminator 2,* Miles Dyson (Joe Morton), the Cyberdyne engineer who lays the groundwork for Skynet, is the archetypal amoral scientist, oblivious to the ramifications of his invention. 'Fucking men like you built the hydrogen bomb,' Sarah scolds him. 'Men like you thought it up. You think you're so creative . . . All you know how to create is death and destruction.' The antagonists in both movies are destroyed in hellish-looking factories – only machines can destroy machines – but the future is only decisively changed when Dyson sacrifices himself to blow up Cyberdyne. It is a fantasy of disarmament and the renunciation of knowledge, wiping out any possibility that Skynet will come to pass – at least until the sequels.

While busily rewriting past and future, later instalments in the franchise had to keep pace with the development of computers. Skynet's name, originally a double allusion to the neural net and Ronald Reagan's 'Star Wars' programme, handily came to suggest the internet, which barely existed in 1991. In 2003's bizarrely pro-war *Terminator 3: The Rise of the Machines*, Skynet is no longer hardware and cannot be destroyed, so Judgement Day happens anyway. 'It was software,' says John Connor (Nick Stahl). 'In cyberspace. There was no system core. It could not be shut down.' History is rewritten more cleverly in the TV series *Terminator: The Sarah Connor Chronicles* to make the forerunner of Skynet a chess-playing computer called the Turk, literalizing what Norbert Wiener had called in 1950 'the dire implications of the chess-playing machine grown up and encased in a suit of armour'.*

A war between men and machines is also the context for the 1999 movie *The Matrix*, written and directed by Lana and Lilly Wachowski. The movie is such a busy hive of metaphor – spiritual, philosophical, psychological, political, epistemological – that the materiality of the premise is often overlooked. The machines' revenge on their vanquished opponents questions the logic of previous stories about robot rebellions: why kill people in a wasteful war of extermination when you could enslave them instead? Seemingly unaware of photosynthesis and food chains, the humans deliberately 'scorched the sky' to starve the robots of solar energy – a voluntary nuclear winter – but the machines got around it by using humans' sedated bodies as organic batteries while their minds inhabited a 'neural, interactive simulation' of an eternal 1999. While the real world, circa 2199, is the quintessential post-apocalyptic hellscape, the end of the world is an impossibility within the Matrix because time is permanently frozen on the precipice of the millennium. This fiendishly ironic version of the end of history escapes the shadow of nuclear war to play on fresher concerns that cyberspace would foster something more real than the real thing.

The Matrix doesn't explain why its sentient machines went to war

* For decades, starting in 1770, crowds had been thrilled by the chess-playing automaton known as the Turk, which was secretly operated by a very small man inside a cunningly designed cabinet. Its fascinated, if sceptical, spectators included Charles Babbage and Edgar Allan Poe.

with humanity in the first place but implies that it should have been anticipated. 'We marvelled at our own magnificence as we gave birth to AI,' sneers Morpheus (Laurence Fishburne), the rebel leader and emperor of exposition. 'I say "your civilization" because as soon as we started thinking for you, it really became our civilization,' says the AI enforcer Agent Smith (Hugo Weaving). 'Which is, of course, what this is all about. Evolution, Morpheus, evolution. Like the dinosaur . . . You had your time.' For all that, *The Matrix* is not anti-technology. Before he realizes his messianic destiny, Neo (Keanu Reeves) is a programmer by day and a hacker by night; the rebels have designed their own fluid virtual realm, 'The Construct'. As in the Terminator movies, it takes a machine to stop a machine.

In the eight years between *Terminator 2* and *The Matrix*, real-life machines generated angst in two directions. In 1997, eight years after claiming that he would feel obliged to play a computer at chess 'to protect the human race', the chess champion Gary Kasparov lost two games of a six-game match to IBM's Deep Blue and drew three. So symbolic was chess that Deep Blue's victory caused palpitations and Kasparov alleged foul play: 'IBM owes me, and all mankind, a rematch.' At the same time, a rival nightmare of treacherous technology came to command the world's attention. Far from being too clever, we were told, computers were too stupid to know what year it was.

It was inevitable that the run-up to the year 2000 would be a nervous time. 'We must prepare ourselves for the mass psychological hysteria, the conscious or unconscious sense of terror that may build to a climax,' a writer called Roy Peter Clark had predicted in 1976. Twenty-three years later, *Time* published a cover about 'MILLENNIUM MADNESS', on which a Christ-like street preacher wore a sandwich board reading, 'THE END OF THE WORLD!?!' As we know, technically the new millennium did not begin until 1 January 2001 but most of the world decided otherwise. Sticklers were crushed beneath the wheels of those three irresistible zeroes.

Though often stereotyped as a decade of affluent post-Cold War complacency, the 1990s was also a time of wild prophecies and outlandish cults; millenarian preachers, New Agers, UFO-watchers and survivalists; conspiracy theories and clues to be decoded. 'All thoughts are going underground in cautious anticipation of the year 2000,' wrote the French philosopher Jean Baudrillard in 1992. The former footballer David Icke told a chat-show audience that earthquakes and tidal waves would consume the UK by the end of the decade. In Texas, Hon-Ming Chen's UFO cult Chen Tao (True Way) predicted a nuclear holocaust in late 1999. In California and Switzerland, members of Heaven's Gate and the Order of the Solar Temple committed mass suicide to speed their ascension. In 1993, one in five respondents told a *Time*/CNN poll that they believed the Second Coming would occur sometime around the year 2000, while evangelical Christianity exploded in Latin America and South Korea. This mood was not confined to religion. The 1999 movie *Fight Club* expressed an apocalyptic desire to see the edifice of decadent, hi-tech, capitalist affluence come tumbling down and to begin again. And even data-crunching rationalists had found one solid reason to brace themselves for the new millennium.

In 1958, an IBM employee called Bob Bemer, who designed ASCII text and worked on the programming language COBOL, identified a worrying flaw in mainframe computers. In order to save memory, which was expensive at the time, the internal calendars of computers designated years with just two digits. Bemer realized that on 1 January 2000 they might think it was 1900 and go haywire. Over the following decades, he tried to spread the word, alerting the Nixon administration and writing articles in computer magazines, but nobody paid attention. As several other programmers took up the cause – one 1984 book was called *Computers in Crisis: How to Avert the Coming Worldwide Computer Systems Collapse* – limited measures were taken by bodies such as the New York Stock Exchange but not until 1993, when programmer Peter de Jager published an article in *Computerworld* with the five-alarm headline 'Doomsday 2000', did the whole world jerk to attention. In 1995, another programmer, David Eddy, abbreviated the 'Year 2000 Problem' to the catchier 'Y2K'.* Three years later, President Bill Clinton signed the Year

*Eddy disapproved of the terms 'Y2K bug' and 'millennium bug', pointing out that the date problem wasn't a bug but a design choice. Perhaps the bug was the original coders' lack of foresight.

2000 Information and Readiness Disclosure Act. 'If we don't fix the century-date problems, we will have a situation scarier than the average disaster movie you might see on Sunday night,' said IRS commissioner Charles Rossotti. The headline of a 1997 *Newsweek* article actually sounded like a 1950s science fiction movie: 'The Day the World Shut Down'.

In *The Simpsons*' 1999 Halloween special, Homer's incompetence is solely responsible for Y2K bringing about the end of the world. 'Well,' sneers Lisa as she walks through the wreckage of Springfield, past laser-blasting traffic lights, 'look at the wonders of the computer age now.' 'Wonders?' replies Homer, who struggles with sarcasm. 'Or *blunders*?' The show was spoofing a popular belief that we had staked far too much on machines. 'We and our computers were supposed to make life easier; this was our promise,' de Jager wrote. 'What we have delivered is a catastrophe.' Y2K experts warned that the bug could wreak havoc with financial transactions and communications technology, and much worse. There was talk of elevators stuck between floors, blackouts, bank runs, failing hospitals, nuclear reactor meltdowns, aeroplanes falling out of the sky, and even the accidental activation of nuclear arsenals. This would be a cataclysm with no need for robots or AI, just a short-term money-saving decision made decades earlier. 'The product of this folly is a looming disaster with an immovable deadline that will touch the entire world,' claimed *Vanity Fair*. But a few dissenters alleged that billions of dollars were being wasted on a hype, a hoax, a scam.

The worriers were both boosted and embarrassed by people who embraced Y2K as confirmation of their belief that the millennium would be the Millennium. Tim LaHaye, co-author of the Rapture-themed *Left Behind* series, warned his readers that Y2K could trigger an international depression which would enable 'the Antichrist or his emissaries to establish a one-world currency or a one-world economic system'. The Reverend Jerry Falwell suggested on his VHS tape *A Christian's Guide to the Millennium Bug* that Y2K might be 'God's instrument to shake this nation, to humble this nation' into a spiritual awakening. Sellers of survival kits and guns, including the limited-edition Bushmaster XM15-E2S Y2K assault rifle, did a roaring trade. Y2K acquired an aura of kookiness which had nothing to do with coders working long hours in banks and government departments, although the logic of preparedness was similar. 'If I'm wrong, the worst that will happen to me is I'll be tremendously embarrassed,' said Richard Wiles, author of *Judgment Day 2000*. 'If other people are wrong and don't listen to me, the worst that will happen is all men will perish.'

The 'electronic Armageddon' of Y2K never materialized, although there were numerous smaller errors and failures. To the sceptics, the likes of David Eddy were cranks in the mould of William Miller, and this was their Great Disappointment. Computer scientists still argue over whether the risk was overblown in the first place or whether it spooked governments and companies into fixing it, at an estimated cost of $300 billion, in which case it was an exemplary instance of global cooperation and problem-solving. This is called 'the prophet's dilemma': a prediction that inspires action to thwart the prediction. Y2K might be the quintessential example of how a disaster averted too easily becomes a disaster forgotten. 'I find myself in the peculiar position sometimes of practically wishing that we had failed in some way in order to prove that we were correct,' Peter de Jager reflected on New Year's Day, 2000.

If one reads Y2K as a doomsday parable about a decadent civilization hooked on technology, rather than as a coding problem, then one could say that the first Y2K story was published a century early. In George Griffith's 1898 story 'A Corner in Lightning', electricity (still such an expensive novelty that most people would have read the story by gaslight) fails, and society is upended: 'Civilised mankind had been suddenly deprived of the services of an obedient slave which it had come to look upon as indispensable.' In 'The Machine Stops', E. M. Forster's brilliant 1909 satire on the machine age, mankind is the slave. In the future, people live in an underground techno-utopia where 'the Machine' supplies everything from music and communications to food and the air they breathe, reducing them to infantilized, button-pushing blobs who literally cannot live without it. When the Machine fails, the only survivors are 'the Homeless', who have been banished to the surface for blaspheming against the Machine. For everyone else, 'civilization's long day was closing.'

In 1999, less than 5 per cent of the world population was online; cut off the internet for even a day now and much of the world would snap to a halt. The shadow of the Y2K that might have been falls across two novels published in the autumn of 2020: Rumaan Alam's *Leave the World Behind* and Don DeLillo's *The Silence*. The planes crashing; the screens blank; the phones dead; the streets dark and quiet and emptied out; the machine stopped – including the machines that might explain why it had stopped. 'We don't have the internet, we don't have our phones,' wails Amanda in Alam's novel, 'we don't know what anything is.'

In his 1993 book *AI*, Daniel Crevier contrasted 'Hal Syndrome' with 'The Colossus Scenario': 'Thus, a robot (or missile-control program) certified sane and well-meaning at the factory might well go crazy after confronting the contradictions and mysteries of real life. Or, like Colossus, it might come to the conclusion that the original goals programmed into it . . . are inappropriate to its own growth and well-being.' Crevier argued that readers should not 'expect the main battles of the twenty-first century to be fought over such issues as the environment, overpopulation or poverty. No, we should expect the fight to be about how we cope with the creations of our own human ingenuity; and the issue, whether we or they – our silicon challengers – control the future of the earth.'

In 2000, when most people were trying to forget Y2K, Bill Joy, the inaptly named chief scientist at Sun Microsystems, wrote an article for *Wired* called 'Why the Future Doesn't Need Us', about the new technologies that were 'threatening to make humans an endangered species'. Its genesis was a conversation with the futurist Ray Kurzweil. Kurzweil saw the ultimate merger of man and machine – the Singularity – in utopian terms, transforming us into immortal transhuman gods, but Joy's thoughts spun off in a darker direction. Both men believed that, one way or another, AI would come to dominate and replace human beings, as it had done so many times in fiction. 'Why hadn't I been more concerned about such robotic dystopias earlier?' Joy asked. 'Why weren't other people more concerned about these nightmarish scenarios?' If the apocalypse is a fantasy of destruction leading to eternity, then the two thinkers each took one component: Kurzweil could imagine only eternity while Joy was fixated on destruction.

Joy predicted that a truly intelligent robot could exist by 2030 but he was even more worried about the tiny self-replicating automata first theorized by John von Neumann in 1951. The nanotechnologist Robert Freitas called the potential consumption of an ecosystem by molecular nanobots, self-replicating at an exponential rate, *ecophagy* but it was better known as the 'grey goo problem', after a thought experiment by K. Eric Drexler which described these unstoppable replicators as no more sophisticated than a virus or a species of crabgrass. Joy made this possibility sound like a rewrite of Vonnegut's *Cat's Cradle*: 'Gray goo would surely be a depressing ending to our human adventure on Earth, far worse than mere fire or ice, and one that could stem from a simple laboratory accident. Oops.' Drawing on the example of post-war arms-control advocates such as Leo Szilard, he argued for limits on scientific development in order to avoid an arms race in 'knowledge-enabled mass destruction (KMD)': 'the last chance to assert control – the fail-safe point – is rapidly approaching.' In this school of writing the last chance is always rapidly approaching and real-life scientists sound like their disaster-movie counterparts: If only the world would *listen*.

Arguments about the menace of AI – or specifically AGI (Artificial General Intelligence) – reiterate decades of debate about robots and computers. AI is considered 'friendly' if it is programmed to align with human values, which makes Asimov's Three Rules of Robotics an early attempt to define aligned AI. The most famous thought experiment about unaligned AI is the philosopher Nick Bostrom's paperclip maximizer: if an advanced AGI with control of its environment were given the sole goal of making as many paperclips as possible, without regard for human life, then it would turn the entire planet into a paperclip factory, eliminating anything that stood in the way of infinite paperclip manufacture while ensuring that it could not be switched off, because that would stem the flow of paperclips. It could thus conceivably obliterate humanity without an atom of ill will. The guilty party would be whoever forgot to program it to consider anything other than paperclips.

Bostrom took on AI in depth in his 2014 book *Superintelligence: Paths, Dangers, Strategies*. At the Future of Humanity Institute in Oxford's Trajan House, where he was director until its abrupt closure in April 2024, conference rooms were named after Vasili Arkhipov and Stanislav Petrov, the Russian officers whose resolute calm averted nuclear war in 1962 and 1983 respectively: reminders that the worst really did almost happen. The institute's black-diamond logo was based on the monolith from *2001*. In *Superintelligence*, Bostrom compares us to 'small children playing with a bomb . . . We have little idea when the detonation will occur, though if we hold the device to our ear we can hear a faint ticking sound.' AI, he insists, is more hazardous than nuclear war, pandemics or climate change. When, in 2014, Bostrom asked more than five hundred AI researchers to predict when human-level machine intelligence would be achieved, the results put the odds of a breakthrough at 10 per cent by 2022, 50 per cent by 2040 and 90 per cent by 2090. Eighteen per cent of respondents said that the outcome would be 'extremely bad (existential catastrophe)'. *Superintelligence* made the hitherto niche issue of AI safety a mainstream concern. It attracted admiring notices from Bill Gates, Elon Musk (who called unaligned AI 'our biggest existential threat') and Stephen Hawking, who said that year, 'I think the development of full artificial intelligence could spell the end of the human race.' Bostrom succeeded in getting responsible risk assessment and preparation out from under the shadow of Skynet, although his wife still teased him 'about the Terminator and the robot army'.

The problem with the Skynet archetype is that James Cameron confused two very different concerns about AI. *Terminator 2* implies that Skynet became sentient and malign: like Čapek's robots, it has learned to fear, envy and loathe humanity and condemn it *in toto*. But Randall Frakes, in his Cameron-approved novelization of the movie, suggested instead that it was overzealously interpreting sloppy instructions: 'The ultimate dream of man, carried out by one of man's lowliest tools: eliminate evil men. But there was a touch of evil in all men, and Skynet was having trouble separating the worst of them out. So the totality of humanity, with all its biologic messiness, wasn't wanted. And to this machine-god, forgiveness just did not compute. Only cold retribution for the sins of the past.' (This recalls a pithy comment by Joseph Campbell, the scholar of comparative mythology: 'Computers are like Old Testament gods. Lots of rules, and no mercy.') So perhaps Skynet is as morally neutral as the paperclip maximizer or the sorcerer's broom, simply doing the job it was told to do: make paperclips, fetch water, extinguish human evil. This, rather than villainy, is what keeps most AI-safety advocates up at night. Cameron's lack of clarity did not perturb viewers, but it does make Skynet hopelessly confusing as a metaphor.

A cleaner example of the AI supervillain with ideas of his own is Marvel's Ultron. In the comic books, he is created by Hank Pym, aka Giant-Man. 'An artificial intelligence, a self-aware, self-sustaining intelligence could guide our entire species into the future,' Pym gushes. In the 2015 movie *Avengers: Age of Ultron*, the AI's hubristic inventor is Tony Stark, aka Iron Man, whose more pragmatic motive is to build 'a suit of armour around the world'. But in both versions Ultron transcends his programming. 'We have to evolve,' he declares. 'There's no room for the weak.' (Having played himself in *Iron Man 2*, Elon Musk technically exists in the same fictional universe as Ultron, which must be distressing.) The theme has become richly spoofable. In *The Mitchells vs. the Machines*, a spry lampoon of the AI apocalypse which happened to coincide with the centenary of *R.U.R.*'s stage debut, the Silicon Valley manchild Mark Bowman (a nod to *2001*'s Dave Bowman) unveils his new robot assistants with a knowing joke: 'I know what you're thinking. Are they going to turn evil?' A big problem for AI's public image is the fusion of the old archetype of the scientist recklessly tampering with forbidden knowledge with the new one of the brash techbro: Victor Frankenstein in a hoodie. Like a tech start-up, the nightmare AI moves fast and breaks things. One global uprising later, Bowman reflects, 'It's almost like stealing people's data and giving it to a hyperintelligent AI as part of an unregulated tech monopoly was a *bad* thing.'

In late 2022, the launch of Large Language Model AI programs such as ChatGPT (text) and Midjourney (visual art) inspired uproar among computer scientists who had imagined this breakthrough was decades, not years, away. There was intense debate over whether the new chatbots had passed the Turing test and, if so, whether the test was still a useful yardstick for machine intelligence. In March 2023, more than one thousand AI researchers called for a moratorium on the AI arms race until the technology could be made 'more accurate, safe, interpretable, transparent, robust, aligned, trustworthy, and loyal'. Eliezer Yudkowsky of the Machine Intelligence Research Institute went further by calling for a complete shutdown on the basis that the most likely consequence of superintelligent AGI was that 'literally everyone on Earth will die. Not as in "maybe possibly some remote chance," but as in "that is the obvious thing that would happen."' In a US YouGov poll, 46 per cent of respondents said that they were very or somewhat concerned about 'the possibility that AI will cause the end of the human race on Earth'.

One has to ask why so many AI developers keep working on technology that they admit publicly might finish off the human race. In ethical terms, they are often compared to the scientists of the Manhattan Project. Are they racing ahead despite the risks, like Leo Szilard, because they fear that less careful developers, perhaps their Russian or Chinese counterparts, will get there first or because, like Vonnegut's Felix Hoenikker, they are too exhilarated to consider the risks at all? The AI pioneer Geoffrey Hinton used to paraphrase Robert Oppenheimer ('When you see something that is technically sweet, you go ahead and do it') but he became so disturbed by the potential for disaster that in 2023 he quit his job at Google and sounded the alarm. 'My intuition is: we're toast,' he said. 'This is the actual end of history.' Another possibility is that AI developers are indulging in a perverse form of self-aggrandizing hype. 'This has always been how people in Silicon Valley talk about everything they do – that it's going to end humanity or save the world because it's just that powerful,' the tech writer Max Fisher has suggested. Like atomic energy in the 1940s, AI has to be either the best or the worst thing ever to happen.

Unaligned AI has become the flashiest of existential risks and a fixation for longtermist philosophers such as William MacAskill and Toby Ord, whose Centre for Effective Altruism is also based in Oxford's Trajan House. Effective altruism is a utilitarian creed which seeks the most efficient ways to do the greatest good. In its original 'neartermist' iteration, it advocated a rational, impartial approach to philanthropy which did not distinguish between the child next door and a child on the other side of the world, maximizing the reduction of suffering. Longtermism radically changes the moral calculus by factoring in the lives of countless generations of the yet-to-come. Because we live in an era of unprecedented and unsustainable economic growth, longtermists argue, we have more power to shape the world than almost any other generation that will ever have been born. Temporally speaking, every person alive today belongs to an elite and the problem of unaligned AI is ours to solve. In *The Precipice*, Ord estimates the existential risk at one in ten, exceeding all the other risks put together.

Longtermists lionize John von Neumann, who epitomized the belief that exceptionally clever and wise people can solve any problem as long as they can think far enough ahead, but they also strike a millenarian note: Now is the most crucial time in history. We stand at the crossroads between annihilation and interstellar eternity. If we make the wrong decisions, we are doomed, but if we make the right ones, then we could ensure millions, billions, even *trillions* of years of happiness. Rob Reich, a political scientist at Stanford, has called the longtermists 'the secular apocalypticists of our age, not much different from Savonarola – the world is ending and we need a radical break with our previous practices.'

After effective altruism's pivot to longtermism, the funding poured in. Making sacrifices to save the lives of strangers from hunger and disease is admirable, but taking steps to save the future of the human race is the kind of grand, heroic project that gets philosophers, computer scientists and messianic billionaires really jazzed up. After a 2015 panel discussion about AI, MacAskill had spoken to Elon Musk 'for five minutes about global poverty and got little interest'. As the science fiction author Ted Chiang has written, 'The question of how to create friendly AI is simply more fun to think about than the problem of industry regulation, just as imagining what you'd do during the zombie apocalypse is more fun than thinking about how to mitigate global warming.' Melodramatic sci-fi analogies – Ultron, Skynet, HAL – aggravate people who think the downside of AI is more prosaic. The Italian ethicist Luciano Floridi argued in 2017 that the abuse of technology for power and profit, from mass layoffs and surveillance to disinformation and drone warfare, was far more concerning than a hypothetical god-like superintelligence. 'Any apocalyptic vision of A.I. can be disregarded,' he wrote. 'The problem is not HAL but H.A.L. – humanity at large.'

The question of AI safety reanimates very old concerns about creating things that one cannot control: the monster, the Golem, the broom. The most famous fictional AIs aren't alien adversaries but the products of human ingenuity and human fallibility. Another line from Karel Čapek springs to mind, but not from *R.U.R.* In his contemporaneous novel *Krakatit*, the distraught inventor of an atomic explosive is told, 'If it hadn't been in you it wouldn't have been in the discovery. A man does everything out of himself.'

Marvin Minsky's colleague Patrick Winston remembered once saying that if superintelligent machines were ever developed, then their creators should first run a simulation to ensure that they weren't dangerous. He was setting up a punchline and the older man got to it first. 'And we're the simulation?' Minsky replied. 'It isn't going very well, is it?'

PART FIVE
COLLAPSE

CHAPTER 13

Catastrophe

The thing all you adult, sensitive people must bear in mind is that things are on your side at present – you live in a world where everything's in favour of being sensitive and civilized. But it's a precarious business.

John Christopher, *The Death of Grass* (1956)

'When a day that you happen to know is Wednesday starts off by sounding like Sunday, there is something seriously wrong somewhere.' The first sentence of John Wyndham's 1951 novel *The Day of the Triffids* is one of the greatest opening shots in science fiction, or indeed any fiction. It forces the reader to inhabit the protagonist's sudden apprehension of the uncanny. You wake up to silence, in a new zone of reality. The world as you knew it has ended while you were sleeping and now you have to work out what has gone awry.

Wyndham was born on 10 July 1903, fifteen days after George Orwell, and began *The Day of the Triffids* at the same time as Orwell was finishing *Nineteen Eighty-Four.* The two novels have more in common than a disorienting first line about time out of joint.* Wyndham's book is another mid-century phenomenon, set a generation hence, which synthesized the disparate tropes of an inchoate genre so successfully that it codified that genre, in this case the catastrophe narrative. Whereas Orwell's dystopia requires an almighty, repressive state, Wyndham's springs from the sudden

* Orwell: 'It was a bright cold day in April, and the clocks were striking thirteen.'

dissolution of the state, and of society itself. Much of what we call post-apocalyptic fiction is more accurately described as post-catastrophic. *The* world has not ended, but *a* world has, creating a blank slate on which the survivors can write whatever they like: anarchy, tyranny, utopia. Whatever the killer blow might be, bomb, plague or quake, is of secondary interest to the civilizational collapse that it produces. Such stories had been around ever since the future-war craze of the late nineteenth century but tended to be wilfully depressing and didactic. Wyndham added the thrills that delighted millions.

John Wyndham Parkes Lucas Beynon Harris had no shortage of potential pseudonyms. He published numerous novels and short stories as John B. Harris, John Beynon, Wyndham Parkes and so on, before unveiling John Wyndham with *The Day of the Triffids.* His family and friends called him Jack. The son of a toxic marriage which ended in a scandalous court case, Wyndham grew a protective shell around himself. After *The Day of the Triffids* made him wealthy and famous, he spurned interviewers, biographers and speaking engagements, and always used the same out-of-date photograph on his book jackets: wearing a tweed jacket and tie, raising one eyebrow, he appears friendly, intelligent and lightly amused. He was hardly less guarded in his private life. Until he married Grace Wilson, his girlfriend of more than twenty years, in 1963, most of his friends didn't even know she existed. 'He never discussed his personal life,' recalled Sam Youd, who wrote under the name John Christopher. 'He never talked about his parents, his background. He was a detached sort of person. He liked being on the edge of things, part of the group, but not necessarily wanting to say too much.' Wyndham became known as 'the invisible man of science fiction'.

During the 1930s, Wyndham knocked out stories about robots, Martians, time travellers and superweapons for the American pulp magazines (1932's 'The Lost Machine' appears to be the first story ever to describe a robot suicide) but always sought the fidelity to narrative logic and human behaviour of his hero H. G. Wells. Asked by one editor if he had any ideas about the fashionable topic of aeroplanes, he replied, 'Nobody can write stories about aeroplanes. Stories are about people.' During the Second World War, he was a fire-watcher in the Blitz, a censor at the Ministry of Information and a cipher operator (Lance-Corporal Harris) during the invasion of Normandy. Witnessing both the Blitz and the shattered citadels of defeated Germany gave him a feel for the wartime uncanny: cities broken up and rearranged. Wyndham became a key player in *New Worlds*, the magazine that helped to launch writers such as J. G. Ballard, Brian Aldiss and Arthur C. Clarke, and he enjoyed writing hard science fiction, set on distant worlds, but his greatest skill was inserting bizarre events into mundane locations, just as Wells had dropped his Martian war machines onto sleepy Woking. Describing the aftermath of a heavy air raid in a letter to Grace in October 1940, he asked himself: 'Why do I write these things in as much detail? I don't know quite. It's not a desire to harrow. More than anything, I think, to convince myself that these fantastic things are happening in these prosaic spots.' *The Day of the Triffids* drew on Wyndham's memories of violence and looting, of mangled bodies and minds, but also the eerie hush between the raids. 'It must be many centuries since London lay in silence as followed for an hour or two,' he wrote to Grace. 'No planes, no guns, but no traffic and no people either. Just complete silence.' It was as if civilization had been temporarily rewound.

The most curious thing about *The Day of the Triffids* is that it is not about the day of the triffids. These walking plants, the product of a misfiring plan to manufacture cheap oil from a mysterious new seed, are already a known quantity when the story begins sometime in the 1970s. Many triffids, their poisonous stingers safely docked, are grown in gardens as ornamental shrubs. In fact, the reason the narrator, Bill Masen, is hospitalized at the start of the novel is because he has been temporarily blinded by a stinger. The event that brings civilization to its knees is instead a green meteor shower which has blinded most of the world's population overnight at precisely the same time as Masen has recovered his own sight. Twice breaking Wells's rule about choosing a single incredible event, Wyndham also throws in a plague.* There were almost aliens, too – originally, the

* Wyndham has been fairly criticized for depicting blindness as a fate worse than death. Although an instantaneous, near-universal blinding would be something else entirely, the fact that he ignores the enormous post-catastrophe potential of people who had lived without sight for years does suggest that he had not explored the premise in great depth.

triffids hailed from Venus – but Wyndham's editor shrewdly encouraged him to make them the product of meddling scientists instead. Inspired by the junk science of Trofim Lysenko, Stalin's favourite biologist, Wyndham blamed the Russians. The mass blinding, meanwhile, turns out to be the result of satellite-based radioactive weapons triggered by the meteor shower. Wyndham had made clear his low opinion of scientists in the introduction to his 1939 superweapon story 'Judson's Annihilator': 'Who is it who should be the priest of progress, but is content to behave with the irresponsibility of a half-wit? The scientists' brains have built the twentieth century; their morals will blow it to bits.'

The Day of the Triffids is a rugged blueprint for catastrophe fiction, collating all the essential elements. The sturdy loner who knows how to look after himself. The securing of guns, fuel and food by looting deserted shops. The transformation of cities into battlegrounds and bunkers. The flight to the countryside. The formation of militias and gangs. The recrudescence of millenarian enthusiasm. The constant motion in search of asylum from the chaos. The grace notes of nostalgia. In one beautiful scene, Masen and his female companion move to a recording of a Strauss waltz: 'We danced, on the brink of an unknown future, to an echo from a vanished past.' Wyndham followed *Triffids* with *The Kraken Wakes*, a novel about aquatic aliens who flood the earth, rather like Karel Čapek's newts, but this time he got waylaid by process and exposition and didn't get around to the catastrophe until the final pages. 'I don't propose to deal in detail with the year that followed,' the narrator writes disappointingly. 'It was a drawn-out story of decay.' But the decay is what is interesting.

Brian Aldiss accused Wyndham of writing 'cosy catastrophes' and the phrase fastened onto Wyndham's reputation like a leech, even though there is nothing particularly cosy about murders, suicides and authoritarian militias, let alone triffids. As Margaret Atwood puts it, 'one might as well call World War II . . . a "cozy" war because not everyone died in it.' What Aldiss meant was that Masen enjoys the sense of 'release' rather too much. As Wyndham writes:

> All the old problems, the stale ones, both personal and general, had been solved by one almighty slash. Heaven alone knew as

> yet what others might arise . . . but they would be *new.* I was emerging as my own master, and no longer a cog. It might well be a world full of horrors and dangers that I should have to face, but I could take my own steps to deal with it – I would no longer be shoved hither and thither by forces and interests that I neither understood nor cared about.

At first, Masen is the archetypal post-catastrophe hero: orphaned, childless, single; hard, clever, unsentimental. 'Only those who can make their minds tough enough to stick at it are going to get through . . .' A celebration of ultracompetent problem-solving merges with a guilty pleasure in a world suddenly liberated from the constraints of money, law and social obligations, where the only rules are the ones you set for yourself – a new world, preferable in some ways to the flabby decadence of the old one: 'I seemed able to recall only the muddle, the frustration, the unaimed drive, the all-pervading clangour of empty vessels, and I became uncertain how much we had lost.' Over time, though, Masen's self-contained machismo is eroded by Wyndham's fondness for brave, intelligent women in the mould of Grace. Masen falls in love with Josella Playton, the vivacious author of a scandalous bestseller, adopts an orphan called Susan and thinks about reconstructing society in the English countryside. A writer for *The Times* perceived that Wyndham's real protagonist was not the solitary man at all but a 'composite hero, a family unit bent on survival . . . In crises it acts on the decent values of the quilted English countryside.'

Wyndham exploited his wartime memories, and those of his readers, while insisting on the ways in which this was much worse than the Blitz: 'This was an enemy they would not survive. It was not wanton smashing and wilful burning that they waited for this time: it was simply the long, slow, inevitable course of decay and collapse.'

Battered and bruised though it may be, the myth of progress is still so powerful that the idea that the future could be radically worse than the present feels counterintuitive, but many civilizations have experienced just such a reversal. The study of civilizational collapse is a fractious discipline. Exactly which combination of internal weaknesses, external jeopardy, long-term environmental changes and short-term catastrophes finished off the Mayans or the Hittites will never be resolved, and rival theories are heavy with political and philosophical biases. Some scholars prefer the more neutral word *transition*, although if you were transitioning from food to famine, or from peace to invasion, then you would probably go with *collapse.* In catastrophe fiction and its real-world analogues, collapse is something far swifter and more dramatic: a sudden demolition of the self-belief that holds civilizations together.

John Wyndham was conscious of his place in the apocalyptic tradition. His characters self-consciously cite 'Ozymandias', Revelation and the Deluge in *The Day of the Triffids*, 'The Hollow Men' in *The Kraken Wakes* and *The War of the Worlds* in 1957's *The Midwich Cuckoos.* His peculiar blend of defeat and endurance left critics confused about his view of the world. A 1960 article in *The Times* described him and Ray Bradbury as 'the New Pessimists': 'In an age of pessimism, our authors tell us, scientists may reveal much that is unknown, but by doing so they will give man power so that he can add to his misery. This is a far cry from the naively challenging faith of WELLS.' Yet nine years later, the same newspaper's obituary writer claimed the opposite: 'Unlike Wells he was an optimist.' So much for the utility of binary labels. Whereas Wells swung like a pendulum between optimism and pessimism throughout his life, Wyndham combined both qualities in the same book. The equivocal ending of *The Day of the Triffids*, while anticlimactic, is the only one Wyndham could have written for a novel in which the argument between altruism and self-preservation is rehearsed over and over again by conflicting characters, and by Bill Masen himself. The author could neither renounce his faith in decency nor convince himself that it would be enough.

Wyndham's novels shared the general gloom that pervaded post-war science fiction. 'Many stories were of Earth destroyed, culture doomed, humanity dying,' Brian Aldiss observed. But Wyndham's particular talent was to inflict extreme horror on sensible middle-class men and women living comfortable lives in smooth-running cities and towns. 'Your English reader does not care for the idea of spaceships,' he told the BBC in 1960. 'I don't quite know why he does. Your American reader loves spaceships.' This very English flavour of science fiction influenced TV shows such as *The Avengers*, *Quatermass* and (disproving Wyndham's spaceship theory) *Doctor Who*. Readers and viewers appreciated seeing catastrophe occur at the end of the street, to people like them; the world of the boringly familiar made violently strange. This was what they remembered of the Blitz and imagined that the Bomb would do. Masen spells it out: 'It must be, I thought, one of the race's most persistent and comforting hallucinations to trust that "it can't happen here" – that one's own little time and place is beyond cataclysms. And now it *was* happening here.'

For Wyndham, even meteor showers and triffids were preferable to the Bomb. Michael Beadley, a humane sage based on Wyndham's beloved boarding-school headmaster, explicitly states that the blinding has *saved* the world from annihilation, because at least there is still something left to rebuild: 'I, and quite likely many of you, have spent most of our lives in expectation of something worse. And I still believe that if this had not happened to us, that worse thing would.' But in some ways the alternatives are more unnerving. While stories of nuclear annihilation were meant to be warnings – ban the Bomb and all this goes away – catastrophe fiction rerouted its readers' fears of nuclear war through age-old perils – plague, famine, earthquakes – which defy human agency. In Britain, such novels fed on post-war anxieties about class, technology and the loss of empire. The question of Wyndham's relative pessimism should have been firmly settled by the arrival of John Christopher, a serial hope-killer who made the older writer look almost buoyant. 'I knew John fairly well and always enjoyed his work, but had my reservations,' Christopher recalled in 1984. 'I felt his characters were a bit too nice.'

Born in 1922, Christopher published more than fifty novels, but he is remembered for the *Tripods* series for younger readers and a chain of popular catastrophe novels which read as a rebuke to Wyndham's faith in sensible men. In Wyndham, the looters, rapists and thugs are an ugly minority to be outwitted and defeated by the civil, capable people who will go on to construct a new society from the finest values of the old. In Christopher, however, barbarism is the norm. Even the heroes are ruthless in their pursuit of survival.

'Other people . . . have commented that I have a pessimistic streak which surfaces in my writing,' Christopher admitted. 'I am not conscious of it, but would not deny it.' He simply called it as he saw it: 'Men always have had urges towards dominance which are basically stronger than urges towards cooperation.'

Christopher's first and best catastrophe novel was his 1956 eco-apocalypse *The Death of Grass*. The Chung-Li virus has defoliated rice crops in Asia, causing famine and societal collapse. It seems very far away until the pathogen mutates and devours every species of grass, including wheat, oats, barley and rye, which means mass starvation. England snaps from top to bottom. The government plans to bomb major cities to reduce the population, reframing the ultimate atrocity as the least worst option. 'Which way's best – of starvation or being killed for your flesh – or by a hydrogen bomb?' asks the civil servant Roger. 'It's quick, after all.' The same harsh logic plays out in the novel's survival odyssey. The heroes of catastrophe novels are almost always refugees, searching for a place of greater safety. This keeps the action rolling while offering the reader a grand tour of the wreckage. John Custance, Christopher's hero, sets out from collapsing London with his family and best friend to seek refuge in a farm-cum-fortress in Westmorland, owned by his brother David. But by the time he gets there, he has transformed into a merciless clan leader with blood on his hands. His wife Ann is the voice of humanist compassion – save whoever you can – while John is the ultra-realist: save yourself. 'Pity always was a luxury,' he says. 'It's all right if the tragedy's a comfortable distance away – if you can watch it from a seat in the cinema. It's different when you find it on your doorstep – on every doorstep.' While Rod Serling's screenplay of Christopher's novel went unproduced, there's a lot of Custance in Ray Milland's middle-class patriarch, blasting rapist hoodlums and ruminating grimly on the unwinding of civilization to 'a small hard core', in 1962's *Panic in Year Zero!* – the first American movie to suggest that it could all go to hell in a matter of days.

Christopher remixed the key elements of *The Death of Grass* in 1965's *A Wrinkle in the Skin*, which he considered his strongest book. This time the catastrophe happens in an instant when a colossal earthquake, known as 'the Bust', scoops up the English Channel and deposits it on the south coast of England, leaving 'a world broken down to the bed-rock of existence'. Christopher uses a damaged anthill as a metaphor: up to a certain point, the survivors will regroup and rebuild, but if the wound is severe enough to make recovery seem impossible, then 'their behaviour becomes more and more pointless and erratic and destructive.' As the prophet Habakkuk declared after the sacking of Nineveh, 'There is no healing of thy bruise; thy wound is grievous.'

The novel opens in Guernsey, where Christopher was living at the time. Matthew Cotter, a tomato-grower, embarks on a quest to find his daughter Jane on the mainland, but he cannot fully accept his grim new reality and is brought up short by meeting April, a woman who has no patience for his illusions: 'What did you expect, for God's sake? The orderly people, the people who could plan more than a few days ahead, have always been in a minority.' In Christopher's sour, suspicious novels, hope is a form of idiocy, and there is no bigger idiot than Matthew. Eventually, April evicts him from the group of survivors because he behaves as if he were the hero of a movie. 'Nothing has changed for you, except the scenery,' she snaps. 'For the rest of us it was God bringing our world crashing down about our ears, but for you it was – what? An epic in Cinemascope, Stereosound and 3-D... You remind me of everything that's finished.' By scorning disaster movies, Christopher implies that his own disaster story is the real deal.

Christopher's novels spoke pungently to Britain's post-imperial loss of confidence and its angst about the future, as he took delight in shredding the smug delusions of English exceptionalism. Characters say things like 'Might it happen here?' and 'It couldn't happen, could it?' before disaster arrives at their door. Even when the Chung-Li virus reaches England in *The Death of Grass*, a letter-writer to *The Daily Telegraph* boasts, 'Yet again it falls to the British peoples to set an example to the world in the staunch and steadfast bearing of their misfortunes.' Well, so much for that. Racism, isolationism and complacency are blown to bits. America abandons Europe as Europe has abandoned Asia, but the implication is that it will fare no better in the long run. John Custance 'could no longer believe that there would be any last-minute reprieve for mankind... The others would fall in their turn, incredulous, it might be, to the end. Nature was wiping a cloth across the slate of human history.'

The humbling of England is most extreme in *The World in Winter*, an upside-down satire on colonialism published in 1962, amid the great wave of African countries declaring independence from Britain, France and Belgium. While the UK crumples under the weight of a new ice age caused by waning solar radiation, and the survivors fight over the 'rubble of a frozen broken-down empire', Africa becomes the rising power. British refugees flee south, going cap in hand to the countries they so recently ruled, while a Nigerian expedition heads north to explore the half-dead capital. 'This was London,' says one explorer. 'To us, Rome was nothing by comparison, and Rome did not fall as this city fell.' London is Ozymandias-on-Thames and England an antique land.

Immediately after the earthquake in *A Wrinkle in the Skin*, Matthew Cotter wonders whether he is the only survivor: 'The last man left alive? The Robinson Crusoe of planet Earth? It might be so.' The castaway is not just the first last man but a prototype of the post-collapse hero. The desert island is the sudden wasteland in which he must fight to survive, and to impose some kind of social order. In that light, the most obvious precursor to Christopher's dog-eat-dog stories isn't Wyndham at all but the island dystopia of William Golding's 1954 novel *Lord of the Flies*: a post-apocalypse in disguise.

A planeload of schoolchildren has crashed on an island during what appears to be a nuclear war (Golding's editor wisely removed all the detailed explanations and combat scenes from the first draft) and the group quickly splinters into two factions. Sensible, decent Ralph, who is voted chief, wants to maintain rules of social conduct, 'because the rules are the only thing we've got!', and nurture a fire in the hope of attracting rescuers and returning home, assuming that home still exists. His rival Jack, meanwhile, plunges headlong into atavistic violence. Ralph can see the appeal: 'I'd like to put on war-paint and be a savage. But we must keep the fire burning.' Before too long, Jack has gained the upper hand by offering the other boys fresh meat and the exultant power of the mob, against which the flame of civilized English values doesn't stand a chance. Catastrophe novels such as Christopher's tried to answer the question that vulnerable, doomed Piggy asks Ralph: 'What makes things break up like they do?'

Golding told his wife Ann that he wanted to write a riposte to desert-island fantasies such as *Treasure Island* and *The Swiss Family Robinson*: a book about 'children who behave in the way children really would behave' – or at least how he believed they would behave. Golding, a Royal Navy veteran who had participated in both D-Day and the sinking of the *Bismarck*, was entering the post-war debate about how ordinary German citizens had become complicit in Nazi atrocities, and how useless Europe's proud Enlightenment heritage had proved as a bulwark against inhuman cruelty. His novel's original title was *Strangers from Within*. Like Rod Serling's 'The Shelter', it argues that the instinct for self-preservation can summon the monster that sleeps inside an ordinary person. In his 2019 book *Humankind: A Hopeful History*, Rutger Bregman tried to prove Golding wrong, insofar as a novelist can ever be 'wrong'. Bregman investigated the case of six teenage boys from a boarding school in Tonga who were marooned on a seemingly uninhabitable Pacific island for more than a year in the 1960s and established a thriving, harmonious community. 'The real *Lord of the Flies* is a story of friendship and loyalty, a story that illustrates how much stronger we are if we can lean on each other,' Bregman claims.

Rival post-catastrophe scenarios dramatize a profound disagreement about human nature and the durability of ethical norms. Given a sharp enough blow, would we simply regress to animal instincts or would we retain some of the values that we've built up over the centuries? What do the social consequences of natural and man-made disasters tell us? The field of disaster studies began with a Canadian priest and sociologist named Samuel Henry Prince. Prince was living in Halifax, Nova Scotia, on the morning of 6 December 1917, when a munitions ship collided with another vessel in the harbour, producing what was at the time the largest human-made explosion in history. Along with the ensuing fires and floods, the explosion killed more than 1,700 people and left thousands homeless, some of whom Prince fed and sheltered in his church. When Prince studied the aftermath for his doctoral dissertation, *Catastrophe and Social Change*, he found to his surprise that incidents of looting and profiteering were outnumbered by instances of courage and altruism: 'Catastrophe and the sudden termination of the normal which ensues become the stimuli of heroism and bring into play the great social virtues of generosity and of kindliness.' Of course, the state still existed, and was actively helping survivors, so this was a catastrophe rather than a collapse, but solidarity prevailed.

If there is such a thing as a cheering novel about nuclear war, more Prince than Golding, then it is 1959's *Alas, Babylon*, written by former war correspondent Pat Frank. A nuclear strike has knocked out the US government and most major population centres, leaving the residents of Fort Repose, Florida, to fend for themselves. While there is a physical threat from marauding 'highwaymen', the thrust of the novel is the practical business of staying alive on what might as well be an island. In a single day, the survivors have lost food distribution, refrigeration, medication, vaccines, garbage disposal, sanitation, money, firefighters, opticians and more, bringing them face to face with the secret fragility of civilization. 'Without penicillin and DDT, where are we?' asks one character. 'All good things came to us automatically. We were born with silver spoons in our mouths and electric dishwashers to keep them sanitary and clean. We relaxed, didn't we?' Yet the survivors *do* find ways to feed themselves, care for each other and keep the fire burning. Unlike the naval officer in *Lord of the Flies*, the air force colonel who touches down in Fort Repose in the final chapter finds a stable, collaborative, multiracial community. *Alas, Babylon* straddles two genres. As a Bomb novel it is absurdly upbeat about trauma and fallout, but as a post-collapse story its hopeful humanism is refreshing. Perhaps only an American could have written it at that time. Whereas Britain had staggered out of the war, America had strutted.

The inevitably British antithesis of *Alas, Babylon* is Charles Eric Maine's fantastically bitter 1958 thriller *The Tide Went Out.* H-bomb tests have created a crack in the ocean floor, into which all the water is disappearing. No sea means no rain, no shipping, no food, so the world's elites are hotfooting it to the poles, where glaciers provide the only sustainable source of water. As is often the case, plausibility is not an issue. The novel is essentially a character study of Philip Wade, a self-centred journalist whose interests are whisky, cigarettes, steaks and adultery. Wade is asked to join a secret government project to evacuate the privileged few from London as it becomes a 'moonscape' of famine, cholera and violence. How much damage can the anthill sustain? Wade's lover Shirley talks of 'the hardening of the individual in times of crisis – the desensitising of the spirit – the reversion to a more fundamental pattern of behaviour.' When a guilt-ridden colleague takes his own life, Wade congratulates himself on his peculiar talent for self-preservation: 'You become pious and conscience-ridden, or you shed the veneer of humanity and become ruthless and brutal. Either way means destruction, and the only salvation lies in preserving the fine balance of the mind.'

But anybody, Maine argues, can lose their balance in sufficiently dire circumstances. Wade is separated from the rest of the evacuees when a wildfire breaks out in east London and the government dynamites sections of the city to create firebreaks. It doesn't work: the fire moves west and so does the dynamite. Soon there is no friend that Wade will not abandon, no stranger he will not kill, if it gets him one step closer to the last flight out of London so that he can rejoin his wife and son in the Arctic. 'I've come to accept violence and brutality,' he tells himself, 'and I've desensitised myself to things that would have shocked me into insanity a few months ago . . . Let's add up the score, brother. The world survives as long as you survive. At the moment of death the world comes to an end for you.' Wade succeeds in seizing the plane but he is then shot down. His son is told that his father died a hero when in fact he was no better than a crazed animal. Maine is interested in the radical transformation of an ordinary individual under pressure – what price survival if you become less than human?

Similar questions are asked in J. G. Ballard's catastrophe novels. The key difference is that Ballard's characters enjoy the metamorphosis. For them, civilizational collapse really is more of a transition.

'I'm never happier than when I can write about drained swimming pools and abandoned hotels,' Ballard said in 1984. The list goes on: he made his fictional home in deserted tower blocks, wrecked automobiles, rusting machines, derelict houses, silent beaches and ghost ships. According to an online concordance to Ballard's work, the word *empty* appears 979 times and *abandoned* 475. He presented ruins as the natural state of things, as if the period when these locations had been habitable were just a fleeting, inconsequential aberration. Many of his characters are in effect archaeologists, decoding the relics of a vanished civilization that was nothing to brag about. Ballard looked upon the world's frenzied acceleration and fantasized about seeing it crash.

From page to page, and book to book, Ballard's repetition of words and images has the relentlessness of personal obsession. Again and again, he explores environments in which time dissolves and what was meant to be the future feels like the distant past. His 1968 story 'The Dead Astronaut', for example, is a premature epitaph for the space race, imagining, a year before man walked on the Moon, Cape Kennedy as 'a wilderness of swamps and broken concrete'. In 1981's *Hello America*, almost the entire United States is a silent wasteland of junk, vacated a century earlier, and Los Angeles has been colonized by hyenas, alligators and flamingos. 'Why did you come to America?' asks one character. 'There's nothing here.' The reply: 'But that's why I came.' In *High-Rise*, Ballard's 1975 micro-apocalypse about a luxury tower block's descent into barbarism, one character perceives it as 'a model landscape beyond technology where everything was either derelict or, more ambiguously, recombined in unexpected but more meaningful ways . . . sometimes he found it difficult not to believe that they were living in a future that had already taken place, and was now exhausted.' Ballard came to realize that his obsession with what he called 'psychic zero stations' was in fact 'powerfully nostalgic'. His childhood had already taught him that civilization was precarious.

James Graham Ballard was born in the Shanghai International Settlement in 1930. His father had a top job in the cotton industry, so young Jim enjoyed a pampered childhood, furnished with servants and imported toys, in a manically vibrant international metropolis. War put paid to that. When Japanese forces invaded China in 1937, refugees fled to still-independent Shanghai, where they were repelled with bayonets and left to die at the city limits. Ballard was eleven when Japan finally seized Shanghai. In his memoir, *Miracles of Life*, he recalled venturing into a disused casino, whose wrecked glamour gave him 'the sense that reality itself was a stage set that could be dismantled at any moment, and that no matter how magnificent anything appeared, it could be swept aside into the debris of the past.' But here's the Ballardian twist: 'I also felt that the ruined casino, like the city and the world beyond it, was more real and more meaningful than it had been when it was thronged with gamblers and dancers.'

In 1943, Ballard's family was relocated to the Lunghua internment camp, a 'half-ruined college campus' encircled by barbed wire, where he was peculiarly content. One morning in August 1945, the occupants woke up to find that their captors had vanished – another formative moment of emptiness and abandonment – and the war, they guessed, was over. Ballard emerged into a post-war terrain of ruined forts, becalmed U-boats and dead Japanese soldiers. He was spooked when he returned to his old house and found it unchanged, 'almost as if the war had never happened'. Psychologically, he had come to require ruins. Britain, his new home, gave him that. Damp, dirty and exhausted, it struck him as 'a sort of disaster area' where 'hope itself was rationed'. Ballard enjoyed his anatomy lessons at Cambridge University (the bodies he dissected, like the landscapes he wrote about, were vacated shells) but he dropped out; studied literature; dropped out again; joined the RAF; dropped out again.

Unusually for a writer of apocalyptic fiction, Ballard did not condemn the use of the atomic bomb. He later learned that, if the war had dragged on, then the residents of Lunghua would have been deported to a far harsher camp, so he believed that he owed his life to 'the saving miracle of Hiroshima and Nagasaki'. He enjoyed watching footage of H-bomb tests: 'The endless newsreel clips . . . (a powerful incitement to the psychotic imagination, sanctioning *everything*) did have a carnival air, a media phenomenon which Stanley Kubrick caught perfectly at the end of *Dr. Strangelove*.' He found this 'glamorous apocalypse' irresistible, raising 'the idea that the human spirit might be somehow transfigured by an apocalyptic nuclear war, even at the cost of millions of deaths, that this is a necessary step for mankind'. Yet nuclear holocaust itself is conspicuously absent in his vast catalogue of doomsday proposals. His 1964 story 'The Terminal Beach' takes place not in a futuristic wasteland but in peacetime, on the fused sand of the test sites of Eniwetok, lined with empty bunkers and comatose bombers. The grief-stricken protagonist is actively pursuing the post-apocalyptic for his own reasons. 'This island is a state of mind,' he is told.

Ballard loudly aspired to change the priorities of science fiction: the present, not the future; Earth, not other planets; inner space, not outer space. 'He believes that science fiction is the apocalyptic literature of Auschwitz, Eniwetok and Aldermaston,' announced the blurb on his 1960s Penguin paperbacks. Landscape was paramount. 'They are all paintings, really, my novels and stories,' Ballard said. When he discovered the surrealist art of Max Ernst, Giorgio di Chirico and Salvador Dalí, their worlds out of joint reminded him of Shanghai. Specific paintings appear in his fiction: the 'immaculate ruins under a midnight sky' in Paul Delvaux's *The Echo*; the 'drained beaches, eroded of all associations, of all sense of time' in *Jours de lenteur* by Yves Tanguy; Ernst's 'self-devouring phantasmagoric jungles'. At a glance, Ernst's wartime masterpiece *Europe After the Rain II* might even be mistaken for the cover of a science fiction paperback, with its writhing amalgamation of crumbling walls and alien vegetation which seems to be at once rotting and proliferating. This paradox enabled one critic to perceive a world 'on the brink of collapse' and another to hail it as 'the most optimistic commentary on destruction we have seen yet'. From the wreckage, something wild and new – perfect for Ballard. In such paintings, Ballard's characters see their own predicaments, but perhaps the locations are the real characters. By comparison, he found the 'rolling English meadows' of Wyndham and Christopher to be a bore: 'They don't seem landscapes that are psychologically significant, if that means anything.'

Ballard described his 1960s novels – *The Wind from Nowhere*, *The Drowned World*, *The Burning World* (expanded and reissued as *The Drought*) and *The Crystal World* – as cataclysm novels (denoting the Deluge) rather than mere disaster novels. He rejected Wyndham's concern with doughty survivors seeking to restore social order and familial solidarity. Instead, his protagonists embrace their transformed circumstances and refuse to mourn what has been lost. Although he was an atheist, Ballard brought to the catastrophe novel a truly apocalyptic narrative of revelation, destruction and rebirth – a violent unveiling of hidden truths.

Ballard disowned his 1961 'hack job' *The Wind from Nowhere* to the point of erasure, which is understandable. It is an adventure story told in flat, generic prose. The premise of a relentless and rapidly accelerating hurricane is unexplained and the carnage is rote: *sayonara*, Tokyo; *au revoir*, Paris; so long, the Statue of Liberty. Half the people on earth die and the reader doesn't feel a thing. In Ballard's far superior second novel, *The Drowned World*, solar flares have shredded the ionosphere, rendering most of the planet uninhabitably hot and, due to melting ice caps, largely underwater. Only five million people survive in the polar regions. The protagonist, Kerans, belongs to a group of research scientists moving through Europe, which is now a feverish network of subtropical jungles and primeval lagoons, home to rapidly mutating plants and beasts. The characters experience a correlating psychological de-evolution. Kerans finds himself surrendering to the drowned world. The more that is destroyed, the more free he feels.

His antagonist is Strangman, a lunatic buccaneer who pumps water from the streets and builds dams to reclaim London – 'resurrecting a corpse!' in Kerans's eyes. The model Ballard villain is a megalomaniac (often an architect) who wears a pale suit, wields a cane and wants to impose order on chaos instead of pressing on into the unknown. Our hero dynamites Strangman's dams to re-inundate the capital, before striking out alone towards the burning south – 'a second Adam searching for the forgotten paradises of the reborn sun'. This conclusion, Ballard told Martin Amis, confused some readers: 'The American publisher said, "We have a problem with the ending. It's too negative. Couldn't we have him heading *north*?" But it's a *happy* ending. South is where he *wants* to go. Further. Deeper. South!'

Ballard makes preservation and reconstruction seem like foolishly hard work. How nice it must be to let go. In *The Drought*, when industrial waste has formed a 'thin but resilient mono-molecular film' on the surface of the oceans and prevented almost all evaporation, the protagonist Ransom is exhilarated because he has 'always thought of the whole of life as a kind of disaster area' anyway. Dr Sanders in *The Crystal World* chooses to sail upriver into the heart of the jungle, which an extraterrestrial contagion has vitrified into a glittering quartz-like mineral because 'The rest of the world seemed drab and inert by contrast.' In *High-Rise*, everybody is free to escape from the degenerating tower block but nobody does, because it is normal life that seems like 'another planet', distant and irrelevant. In these liquefying landscapes of the unconscious, freedom from time means freedom from 'questions of motive and identity'. The end of history is a blessing. Ballard argued that the cataclysm story represented 'a constructive and positive act by the imagination rather than a negative one, an attempt to confront a patently meaningless universe by challenging it at its own game'. It was, to him, a rebellion against the 'huge reductive machine we call reality'.

'Apocalypse' is the first word of *The Atrocity Exhibition*, the experimental 1970 novel that initiated Ballard's elevation to cult hero. As his fetish for catastrophe chimed with the perpetual crisis of the new decade, he was promoted from sci-fi outlier, flinging curses at the modern world from his bunker, to a prophet of disintegration whose time had come. He may have been an avuncular, conservative middle-aged widower, living in the London suburb of Shepperton with his three children, but his transgressive mutations appealed to alienated young men such as Joy Division frontman Ian Curtis, who appreciated his invitation to succumb to the chaos rather than fight to preserve a failing society. On songs such as 'Atrocity Exhibition', Joy Division sound like the surly last holdouts in an otherwise evacuated city. Transfixed by moods and images more than by stories, Ballard was destined to influence musicians whose records bring to mind voided landscapes, like the blurred and gutted dance music of Burial, whose 2006 debut album was explicitly framed as the sound of a drowned world. A press release located it in a 'near-future South London underwater. You can never tell if the crackle is the burning static off pirate radio, or the tropical downpour of the submerged city out of the window.'

Ballard's final short story, published shortly after his death in 2009, was 'The Secret Autobiography of J. G. B.' 'On waking one morning, B was surprised to see that Shepperton was deserted,' is a Wyndhamesque opening, but the prose's unflappable blandness is almost a caricature of the cosy catastrophe. Expressing nothing more than mild surprise at the unexplained vanishing of the rest of humanity, B acquires the necessary supplies and builds a 'pleasant and comfortable existence for himself'. Never has the last man been so content. This is the silent, empty world that he has been craving his whole life.

—

The only contemporary writer who could out-Ballard Ballard was Anna Kavan, whose extraordinary 1968 novel *Ice* was originally to be called *The Cold World.* Kavan was born in Cannes, France, in 1901, as Helen Woods. In 1939, she was a modestly successful, fairly conventional novelist under her married name, Helen Ferguson, but a scarring childhood and two difficult marriages had left her with the sensation that her life was an unsuccessful first draft. Following a suicide attempt and hospitalization, she wiped the slate clean: a new look, a new literary style and a new name, which she took from one of her own characters. She burned almost all of her diaries and letters and disliked the past in general. After the war, she rubbished talk of rebuilding Britain: 'What is wanted is a new earth and a new man to inhabit the earth.' Two things Kavan could not leave behind, though, were chronic depression and a decades-long addiction to heroin. When police broke into her west London house on 5 December 1968, they found her sprawled on her bed, her lifeless head resting on the lacquered Chinese box in which she stored the drug. The cause of death was heart failure, which surprised her friends because she had twice attempted suicide. 'I know I've got a death-wish,' she wrote in her autobiographical short story 'High in the Mountains'. 'I've never enjoyed my life, I've never liked people. I love the mountains because they are the negation of life, indestructible, inhuman, untouchable, indifferent, as I want to be. Human beings are hateful; I loathe their ugly faces and messy emotions. I'd like to destroy them all.'

Kavan was flattered by a publisher's report which described *Ice* as a combination of Franz Kafka and *The Avengers*, because she wanted to give the 1960s vogue for globetrotting thrillers the slippery texture of a recurring nightmare. *Ice* is a race against the end of the world; a metaphysical quest through a 'vast, indifferent, freezing universe'. A nameless man pursues a nameless girl through nameless collapsing countries while a giant cliff of ice advances across the planet, turning it into 'an arctic prison from which no escape was possible'. Kavan's hallucinatory storytelling makes it hard to unpack what is really happening versus what is imagined or dreamed. There is a vague suggestion that the ice has something to do with nuclear radiation and a stronger implication that scientists are somehow to blame. Kavan throws in a mad jumble of concurrent threats – 'monstrous epidemics, appalling famines', urban warfare and whispers of a cobalt bomb – but the ice prevails. Instead of a single transformative cataclysm, with an aftermath and the potential for recovery, there is irreversible disintegration – the world collapses over and over again until there is nothing left.

Narrated by a sadist, *Ice* is anti-human and anti-life. Not even Samuel Beckett's end-of-the-world plays ('all dark, all still, all over, wiped out') are as committed to total erasure. 'Instead of my world', Kavan writes, 'there would soon be only ice, snow, stillness, death; no more violence, no war, no victims; nothing but frozen silence, absence of life. The ultimate achievement of mankind would be, not just self-destruction, but the destruction of all life; the transformation of the living world into a dead planet.' The prose has a numbing, pitiless quality, with the word *ice* appearing up to half a dozen times in a single paragraph. In the end, the man and the girl, reunited at last, drive through the polar night in a big, fast car towards certain doom: 'I did not regret that other world I had longed for and lost . . . The world seemed to have come to an end already. It did not matter.' During an interview for *Nova* magazine, Kavan sat back and let her publisher do all the talking before suddenly breaking her silence with the only remark that made it into the article: 'I haven't felt anything for twenty years.'

'WHAT IS THE EXACT NATURE OF THE CATASTROPHE?' asked the cover of the July 1968 issue of *New Worlds*. Curious readers might have been disappointed to find that the magazine did not try to answer that question. In catastrophe fiction, the nature of the event is far less important than its consequences. The world may be either too hot or too cold, too wet or too dry, too barren or too overgrown, too empty or too full, but what really matters is how people react.

Moving into the 1970s, the whole world seemed to be suffering from a surplus of calamitous options. We have seen that the Bomb swallowed the imagination after 1945, relegating all other problems to secondary concerns. Now, thanks to successful arms-limitation diplomacy, the imagination was spat out and exposed to a confounding array of dilemmas. The art critic Peter Schjeldahl suggested that it was precisely the non-event of nuclear war that explained the decade's uncommon morbidity: 'What makes the '70s so eerie is the sneaking conviction we all have that this decade *wasn't supposed to happen.* In a civilization living as if there were no tomorrow, we are the tomorrow.'

'In the papers we read what used to amuse us in science fiction,' observed Saul Bellow in his 1976 Nobel lecture, reeling off examples of 'the terrible predictions we have to live with, the background of disorder, the visions of ruin . . . the decline and fall of everything is our daily dread.' Dire forecasts piled up in books such as Roberto Vacca's *The Coming Dark Age* and Alvin Toffler's *Future Shock.* 'Urbanization, ethnic conflict, migration, population, crime – a thousand examples spring to mind of fields in which our efforts to shape change seem increasingly inept and futile,' Toffler agonized in 1970. As the decade unfolded, pollution, fuel shortages, presidential criminality and economic malaise joined the list. All of these problems accumulated into a pervasive sense of crisis and doom, the likes of which America, in particular, had never experienced before. 'Is there hope for man?' asked Robert L. Heilbroner, the nation's most popular economist, answering that the outlook for mankind was 'painful, difficult, perhaps desperate, and the hope that can be held out for his future prospect seems to be very slim indeed.' 'Cultural note for future historians,' wrote Gore Vidal in his 1978 novel *Kalki.* 'The mood of most of the world last year was eschatological. Things were running down and negative entropy was on the war-path.'

The French called this mood *la sinistrose* while *Time* opted for 'disastermania' in a 1979 article, noting that the latest scientific discoveries were often 'passed on to the public in overly dramatic and exaggerated form' and that the decade's most profitable genre was the disaster movie: 'Armageddon is something of a growth industry.' *Time* cited the remarkable success of *A Distant Mirror*, Barbara Tuchman's history of the 'calamitous' fourteenth century. For Tuchman, it was no stretch to compare the 1970s to the age of the Black Death and the Hundred Years War: 'After the experiences of the terrible 20th century, we have greater fellow-feeling for a distraught age whose rules were breaking down under the pressure of adverse and violent events. We recognize with a painful twinge the marks of "a period of anguish when there is no sense of an assured future."' *Time* also quoted the historian Christopher Lasch's recent book *The Culture of Narcissism: American Life in an Age of Diminishing Expectations.* Lasch wrote: 'As the twentieth century approaches its end, the conviction grows that many other things are ending too. Storm warnings, portents, hints of catastrophe haunt our times . . . The question of whether the world will end in fire or in ice, with a bang or a whimper, no longer interests artists alone.'

Artists were certainly interested, though. In 1975, an aspiring comedy writer pitched to the BBC a six-part radio series called *Ends of the Earth*, each episode of which would feature a different comic apocalypse, but the BBC suggested that he focus on the first and funniest – Earth is demolished to make way for a hyperspatial express route – and that's how Douglas Adams came to write *The Hitchhiker's Guide to the Galaxy.* In popular music, the end-times groove of reggae songs such as Max Romeo's 'War ina Babylon' harmonized with punk rock, as Johnny Rotten rhymed *anarchist* with *Antichrist* and the Ruts declared that Babylon was burning. Bob Dylan became entranced by Hal Lindsey's *The Late Great Planet Earth*, an orgy of premillennialist eschatology which became the biggest-selling non-fiction book of the decade and was made into a movie narrated by Orson Welles. 'The world as we know it now is being destroyed,' he told an audience in Tempe, Arizona, in 1979. 'I'm sorry to say it, but it's the truth. In a short time – maybe in three years, maybe five years, could be ten years – there's gonna be a war . . . called the battle of Armageddon.' Singers were in agreement with evangelists, economists and ecologists: doom was booming.

In British literary fiction, the great chronicler of collapse was Doris Lessing. Her five-novel sequence *The Children of Violence* is mostly a semi-autobiographical account of her youth in Southern Rhodesia (now Zimbabwe), but the long appendix of 1969's *The Four-Gated City* shoots into the future, where a historian in Mongolia collects accounts of 'the Catastrophe' from 'Destroyed Area II (British Isles)', recounting in gruesome detail the myriad horrors that have reduced the UK to a 'silent charnelhouse'. Lessing called it 'a true prophecy . . . I believe the future is going to be cataclysmic.' The narrator of 1974's *Memoirs of a Survivor* cannot even find the words to explain what has happened. Lessing brilliantly identifies the essence of every collapse narrative as 'it':

> Very well, then, but what *was* 'it'? . . . I am sure that ever since there were men on earth 'it' has been talked of precisely in this way in times of crisis, since it is in crisis 'it' becomes visible, and our conceit sinks before its force. For 'it' is a force, a power, taking the form of an earthquake, a visiting comet whose balefulness hangs closer night by night distorting all thought by fear – 'it' can be, has been, pestilence, a war, the alteration of climate, a tyranny that twists men's minds, the savagery of a religion.
>
> 'It', in short, is the word for helpless ignorance, or of helpless awareness. It is a word for man's inadequacy . . . 'It', perhaps – on this occasion in history – was above all a consciousness of something ending.

CHAPTER 14

Survival

What in God's name are you talking about? We're not survivors. We're the walking dead in a horror film.

Cormac McCarthy, *The Road* (2007)

In 1976, *New York* magazine wearily dismissed Michael Anderson's sci-fi dystopia *Logan's Run* as 'yet another of those tiresome world-after-the-holocaust bits'. The nervous 1970s produced plenty of those, including *The Omega Man*, *Soylent Green*, *Ravagers*, *Damnation Alley*, *The Ultimate Warrior* and *A Boy and His Dog*. It was a versatile genre: 'it' could be nuclear war, plague or climate change (*Logan's Run* chose a medley of 'war, overpopulation and pollution') and the aftermath could range from lawless chaos to despotism. Los Angeles became the most apocalyptic of cities. Imperilled by earthquakes and wild fires, its nerves jangled by Hollywood nightmares and a proliferation of cults, it was perfectly positioned to exemplify the decadent, untenable frenzy of the modern world. As Pauline Kael asked in 1974, 'Who needs a reason to destroy L.A.? The city stands convicted in everyone's eyes.'

One strange thing about these post-apocalyptic narratives is that almost nobody described them as post-apocalyptic at the time. That word – so simple, so obvious, so helpfully self-explanatory – seemingly first appeared in 1967, in a *Guardian* review of Ann Prior's novel *The Sky Cage*. Over the next fifteen years, it was sporadically applied to works such as Walter M. Miller Jr's *A Canticle for Liebowitz*, Russell Hoban's *Riddley Walker* and a production of Samuel Beckett's *Endgame*, but it remained an oddity until 1982, when it suddenly proliferated in reviews of George Miller's movie *Mad Max 2*, released in the US as *The Road Warrior*. Because that movie popularized the word, *post-apocalyptic* effectively came to mean something that looked like the world of *Mad Max*.

The first *Mad Max* movie, from 1979, isn't exactly post-apocalyptic but it's on the threshold. Miller and his co-writer James McCausland set it 'about fifteen years from now' because the biker-gang violence was too baroque to be convincing in the present, but they lacked the budget to design a world around it. 'I think both films have value in that they help us explore the darker, more unthinkable side of ourselves,' Miller explained in 1984. 'They serve as warning fables. It's very difficult to tell these kinds of stories in contemporary, naturalistic formats, so we set them in heightened, caricaturized futuristic worlds.' The premise, although it is not explained until the second movie, is that oil supplies have almost dried up and road hogs will kill for a few litres of gasoline. (In 2015's *Mad Max: Fury Road*, climate change produces wars over water as well.) Miller insisted that the films were '*not* postnuclear' because he believed that was an oxymoron: there would be nothing left after a nuclear war but 'insects and grass'. The prologue to *Mad Max 2* opaquely outlines how a global clash between 'two mighty warrior tribes' led to the fall of the oil industry and thus urban civilization: 'Without fuel they were nothing. They'd built a house of straw. The thundering machines sputtered and stopped . . . Their world crumbled. The cities exploded. A whirlwind of looting, a firestorm of fear. Men began to feed on men.'

Miller had been inspired by seeing scuffles at gas stations during a period of severe fuel rationing in Australia. The economic shocks of the 1970s had radically changed assumptions about the sustainability of post-war prosperity, let alone growth: President Jimmy Carter believed that the world could completely exhaust oil supplies as early as 1990. In a 1974 *Rolling Stone* interview, David Bowie explained to the novelist William S. Burroughs that, in his hysterically apocalyptic 1972 song 'Five Years', the world ends because it has run out of resources. 'Of course, exhaustion of natural resources will not develop the end of the world,' Burroughs responded. 'It will result in the collapse of civilization. And it will cut down the population by about three-quarters.' Bowie enthusiastically agreed.

'In a little over 10 years the myth of abundance has been replaced by the myth of scarcity,' wrote Richard J. Barnet in a 1978 *New York Times* essay called 'No Room in the Lifeboats'. 'The world is running out of oil; experts disagree only as to how fast.' Barnet worried that the 'Age of Scarcity' was breeding a 'new antidemocratic, antihuman ideology': a 'lifeboat ethic' in which the poorest would be evicted from Spaceship Earth so that the rest could survive. The *Mad Max* series was a response to the age of scarcity.

In the first *Mad Max*, the state for which highway patrolman Max Rockatansky (Mel Gibson) works appears to be still functioning, if ragged around the edges: there are hospitals and law-enforcers. In *Mad Max 2*, anarchy reigns. Miller establishes a compellingly motley visual language for a post-apocalypse in which nothing new can be manufactured so everything is bricolage, pieced together from 'the debris of the old, decaying world'. Society has again splintered into two tribes, this time distinguished by temperament rather than nationality. A mob which resembles punk-rock wrestlers (Jacks in *Lord of the Flies* terms) torments a nomadic community of idealistic ragamuffins (Ralphs) in a badland of filth and junk. As a graffito on the side of a truck declares, 'The Vermin Have Inherited the Earth.' Mythic in tone, *Mad Max 2* is a sci-fi Western, with Max as flinty and taciturn a hero as Clint Eastwood's Man with No Name, and cars and motorbikes in place of wagons and horses. While many post-apocalyptic movies have used the image of abandoned cars locked in permanent traffic jams, the *Mad Max* series introduced thrillingly constant motion: the high-speed freedom of the road.

J. G. Ballard praised the second movie's 'compellingly reductive vision of post-industrial collapse . . . the sense of a world discarded after Judgement Day'. Miller's scrapyard aesthetic has determined the look of movies (*Waterworld*), video games (*Wasteland, Fallout*), comic books (*Tank Girl*) and rock bands (Mötley Crüe) before being thoroughly parodied as a town of dusty orange bric-a-brac in *The Lego Movie 2: The Second Part*, with the broken Statue of Liberty from *Planet of the Apes* thrown in for good measure. 'From the wreckage we built a grittier, cooler, more mature society,' the narrator growls. 'We call it Apocalypseburg and it is a heckish place to live.'

One apparent influence on *Mad Max* was Harlan Ellison's 1969 novella *A Boy and His Dog*, which was filmed as a grim comedy adventure by L. Q. Jones in 1975. ('Politicians had finally solved the problem of urban blight,' quips the narrator after a symphony of mushroom clouds.) But Max starts out as a lawman, whereas Ellison's protagonist is an amoral predator. While John Christopher and Pat Frank decried the 'yobbos' and 'highwaymen' in their novels, Ellison cheered them on, pitting the brutish vigour of the surface world against the bland, devitalized conformity of life in underground shelters. He invites us to root for the rapists and cannibals.

Many of the post-apocalyptic movies and books that followed *Mad Max* took their imagery from Miller and their philosophy from Ellison. It is not that survival forces people to do terrible things, as in *The Death of Grass* and *The Tide Went Out*; rather, it *enables* them to do terrible things. The incipient fascism of catastrophe fiction was coming to the surface. The post-apocalyptic trope of rebirth from the ashes overlaps, often unintentionally, with fascist notions of regeneration achieved through virility and violence. While the marauders in *Mad Max* are as white as Max, many writers of vigilante revenge fantasies racialized and dehumanized gang members so that they could be dispensed without qualm, as if they were zombies or robots – a moral licence to murder. Between 1981 and 1993, Jerry Ahern published twenty-seven *The Survivalist* novels about a gun-loving former CIA officer who battles Soviet invaders and post-apocalyptic cannibals. The historian Mike Davis called such brutal self-preservation dramas 'armageddonist': 'The key figure here is the wild Aryan warrior slugging it out with evil aliens or mutants in the urban wasteland.'

The most abhorrent armageddonist story is William Luther Pierce's 1978 novel *The Turner Diaries*, an obscenely paranoid and racist fantasy which tainted the whole post-apocalyptic genre. Writing under the pseudonym Andrew MacDonald, Pierce was a former physicist who founded the neo-Nazi group National Alliance. His fans among the far-right militia movement included Timothy McVeigh, the Oklahoma City bomber. In *The Turner Diaries*, catastrophe is not an accident at all but something desired and conceived by Aryan extremists to enable an orgy of ethnic cleansing, the lynching of 'race traitors' and the sterilization of Asia. As Davis observed, 'After reading *The Turner Diaries* it is impossible to have a benign attitude toward the survivalist novels . . . that proliferate like noxious weeds after 1978.'

The Survivalist is a novel published in February 1975 by the American writer Giles Tippette. It is the story of Franklin Horn, a middle-class, middle-aged man who becomes convinced that his city is disintegrating and flees to the Ozarks, where his solitary new life violently unravels. At the time, the word *survivalist* might have described, among other things, a tenacious politician, a concerned ecologist or a resourceful outdoorsman. Very soon, however, journalists began using it to identify people who, like Franklin Horn, believed that the urban world was falling apart and that drastic measures needed to be taken. *The Tampa Times* compared the new movement to the bomb-shelter craze of 1961, when Rod Serling's 'The Shelter' had dramatized the ugliness at the heart of the survival industry: 'This time, however, famine and food riots appear to be a bigger fear than nuclear destruction.' *The Washington Star* interviewed a man who had read Robert L. Preston's hair-raising 1973 survival manual *How to Prepare for the Coming Crash* and now expected that economic collapse would soon bring about 'the biggest bloodbath the world has ever seen'. He was therefore stockpiling food and firearms: 'You better believe it, you will have to kill your friends as well as strangers. It'll be you or them, it's as simple as that.'

The man who falsely but successfully claimed to have coined the word *survivalist*, in the post-apocalyptic sense, was Donald Sisco, aka Kurt Saxon, an erstwhile neo-Nazi vigilante who condemned cities as 'great pestholes harboring the majority of the world's parasites and bureaucrats'. In 1976, alarmed by soaring oil prices and rising crime, he launched a newsletter called *The Survivor*. The first volume offered tips on baking pretzels and growing cucumbers, alongside paranoid guest editorials about 'separating the sheep from the goats' when 'Collapse Day' happens. 'There are growing numbers of survival groups forming quietly around the country,' wrote a survivalist named T. A. DeMattis. 'Their purpose is group survival in the face of social chaos.' Volume 2 escalated to advice on how to tie a hangman's noose. Someone calling himself Paranoid George explained that only 'clear-thinking and productive men and women' would survive in the brutally simplified new world while 'parasites' would go to the wall: 'Nature has a way of cleansing itself.' There were thousands of pages of this stuff.

The word *survivalist* first appeared in *The New York Times* in August 1980, in an article about Survival Inc., a company which sold crossbows, radiation suits, storage tanks and other paraphernalia. 'When people become nervous about the future, about earthquakes, the stock market, foreign policy or the end of the world, then business picks up,' boasted owner William Pier, who converted his profits into gold and canned goods. Previously, Pier's primary clientele had been fellow Mormons, who believe in storing up food in case of famine or plague, but the market was growing fast thanks to the recession. Just a few months later, Pier was claiming that the survivalism industry was worth $150 million a year. In Utah, Survive Tomorrow Inc. was building a 240-unit complex of underground condominiums named Terrene Ark I. Two academics in Connecticut founded the American Survival Center to prepare for 'the coming decades of scarcity'. The ecologist Bruce D. Clayton published *Life After Doomsday: A Survivalist Guide to Nuclear War and Other Major Disasters*, dedicating it to the 'few sensible Romans' who had fled Pompeii before Vesuvius blew. Reporters descended on remote communities of survivalists. 'We don't know when it's going to happen,' a former preacher in Arkansas told one of them. 'Noah didn't know when the flood was going to happen. He just knew it was.' This is the survivalist mindset in a nutshell: the collapse is the Deluge and they are all successors to Noah. But this time the tide will be human and the ark will be armed.

Alan Dundes, a professor of anthropology and folklore, diagnosed this as a distinctly American phenomenon: 'Americans have a strong undercurrent of rugged individualism, of vigilantism even. Americans take to the hills to fend off the nuclear holocaust with a shotgun and a supply of food.' In Oregon, sociology professor Richard G. Mitchell Jr began studying survivalists for a book. Over the next two decades, he found that some were murderous, paranoid racists and some merely eccentric hobbyists, but all were storytellers. Feeling themselves powerless to shape society as it was – hi-tech, bureaucratic, increasingly incomprehensible – they engaged in a form of speculative fiction in which they could be reborn as warriors, entrepreneurs and builders of a new world. This escape fantasy offered the alienated a sense of community and purpose. 'Life is transformed, idealized, simplified,' Mitchell wrote. 'Imaginary sides are drawn, rules set, action consequent and lasting. The complex modern world of competing ideas and alternative life stratagems distils to a few simple principles, the right tools, and a will to work . . . See the meaning that fills their lives as they ready for the end of the world, as they go dancing toward Armageddon.' Survivalists rarely agree on exactly how that might happen. Mitchell found that 'environmental catastrophe, economic collapse, seditious insurrection, widespread civil strife, internecine race war, thermonuclear holocaust, invasions from within, abroad or above, and other calamities' were all options.

Survivalist narratives invite you to imagine yourself in that situation – would you prevail? Personally, I would consider it a miracle if I made it to the end of the week, but then the people most obsessed with survival are the people I'd least like to survive alongside. We do, after all, revile nature's survivalists: flies, rats, cockroaches. 'What the apologists for survivalism are really preaching is the death of law and the triumph of selfishness . . . survival itself is turning into a dirty word,' *The New York Times* complained in 1980. Opting out of a corrupt and overwhelming society is one thing; what many survivalists not-so-secretly crave is for that society to fall apart and prove them magnificently right. While they describe themselves as preparing for the worst, it would be truer to say that they gleefully anticipate the worst and look forward to the hideous dilemmas that tortured Wyndham and Christopher's heroes. As Bill (Nick Offerman), the reformed survivalist in HBO's *The Last of Us*, admits, 'I used to hate the world, and I was happy when everyone died.'

Violent confrontation with the stubbornly uncollapsed state was inevitable. In 1983, two federal marshals were shot dead in North Dakota by Gordon W. Kahl, a sixty-three-year-old member of a radical anti-tax group called Posse Comitatus, and his two sons. After a four-month manhunt, Kahl was tracked down to a bunker-like house in the hills of Arkansas, where he perished in a firefight with law enforcement. James Oliver Huberty, who had been hoarding food and guns in expectation of economic collapse, opened fire in a McDonald's restaurant in San Ysidro, California, killing twenty-one people and injuring eighteen, before being gunned down himself. A white supremacist organization called The Order began a campaign of armed robbery and bombings which culminated in the murder of Jewish talk-show host Alan Berg. Members were preparing themselves for the racial Armageddon described in their favourite novel. 'They were following *Turner Diaries* like a map,' recalled one of the FBI agents who broke up The Order in 1985.

This cluster of outrages explains why David Brin made survivalists the loathsome antagonists of his 1985 novel *The Postman*, an excellent book which was later turned into a considerably less excellent Kevin Costner movie. Brin's post-apocalypse is in the elegiac, compassionate vein of novels, often written or narrated by women, which engage seriously with the reality of loss and hope. Doris Lessing's *Memoirs of a Survivor* and Paul Auster's *In the Country of Last Things* (1987) are dreamlike explorations of dissolving worlds. Kate Wilhelm's *Where Late the Sweet Birds Sang* (1976) and Octavia Butler's *Parable of the Sower* (1993) offer counter-narratives of cooperation and recovery. Brin's hero attempts to restore civilization's faith in itself by taking on the symbolic job of delivering long-forgotten mail, while the survivalists want the world to stay broken. Brin describes two varieties of survivalist. Mostly harmless were the 'men whose hobby was thinking about the fall of society, and fantasizing what they would do after it happened . . . most were probably horrified when their fantasies at last came true.' The followers of Nathan Hohn, however, form a fascistic cult which is more responsible for America's crack-up than even nuclear war. Brin's hero's visceral loathing can only be read as the author's own opinion of groups such as The Order: '*Survivalists.* Gordon felt a wave of revulsion . . . the people in nearly every wrecked county and hamlet blamed these macho outlaws for the terrible troubles that led to the final Fall.'

Brin felt that too many writers were similarly in love with collapse. 'Most post-holocaust novels are little-boy wish fantasies about running amok in a world without rules,' he said in 1997. 'In fact, such lonely "heroes" would vanish like soot after a real apocalypse. The moral of *The Postman* is that if we lost our civilization, we'd all come to realize how much we missed it, and would realize what a miracle it is simply to get your mail every day.' In his foreword to a 2005 edition of Pat Frank's *Alas, Babylon*, Brin maintained that his novel, like Frank's, rejected the 'blithe assumption – conveyed by so many misanthropic writers and film directors – that humanity in general is dreadful, and therefore only individual heroes matter'. He thought it unfair that these were called *Mad Max* stories, because Max isn't having any fun at all.

During the 1990s, the Y2K problem gave rise to a post-Cold War survivalist renaissance, symbolically juxtaposing the self-reliant, largely rural tough-nuts with the city-dwelling softies whose lives depended on the architecture of modernity. A new word emerged: in August 1998, someone on the Usenet newsgroup *alt.y2k.end-of-the-world* referred to his 'fellow y2k preppers'. The word caught on, as did the mentality. In 2012, a show called *Doomsday Preppers* became the most watched show in the history of the National Geographic Channel. In 2020, *The New York Times* profiled a group called the Heathens, who lived in yurts, learned Stone Age survival skills and referred to whichever city they had left behind as Babylon. 'I'm a collapsist,' said one woman. 'I'm not interested in maintaining the comforts we have.'

Super-rich preppers, however, will not settle for yurts. In a 2017 *New Yorker* article, Evan Osnos wrote that what was once the preserve of 'the woodsman in the tinfoil hat, the hysteric with the hoard of beans, the religious doomsayer' was now fashionable among the elites of Wall Street and Silicon Valley. His interviewees had seen a lot of disaster movies: Reddit CEO Steve Huffman revealed that he had bought a motorcycle after seeing the traffic jam of desperate refugees in *Deep Impact*. The elite preppers were acquiring airstrips and private planes, fortifying refuges in remote locations, stocked with guns, gasmasks and gold, and swapping tips using abbreviations such as WTSHTF ('when the shit hits the fan'), WROL ('without rule of law') and TEOTWAWKI ('the end of the world as we know it'). Among the buffet of WTSHTF scenarios on offer today is the old phobia of the dispossessed rising up; people who claim to disdain government dread its downfall. Some billionaire preppers, including the PayPal founder and apocalyptic libertarian Peter Thiel, have decided that America is toast, whether overground or underground, and have purchased boltholes in New Zealand, which will be relatively shielded from climate change. The nineteenth-century figure of the New Zealander has returned, bearing arms. Before the scandalous collapse of the prominent effective altruist Sam Bankman-Fried's cryptocurrency exchange FTX in November 2022, his brother Gabriel wrote a memo proposing that FTX purchase the Pacific island of Nauru in order to construct a 'bunker/shelter' where effective altruists could survive 'some event where 50–99.9% of people die', seemingly unaware that Nauru is: (a) a sovereign nation and (b) existentially vulnerable to climate change.

The surpassing form of colonial survivalism is emigration to other planets such as Mars, which Elon Musk refers to as a 'backup'. This ambition is as fundamental to longtermism as anxiety about AI. On the day of the Moon landing, when television stations solicited the reactions of science fiction writers, Arthur C. Clarke and Robert Heinlein waxed lyrical about prolonging the human drama in distant theatres but Ray Bradbury was sardonic about the longing for interplanetary immortality: 'If we stay here on Earth we are all of us doomed, because someday the Sun will either explode or go out. So in order to ensure the entire race existing a million years from today, a billion years from today, we're going to take our seed out into space and we're going to plant it on other worlds and then we won't have to ask ourselves the question of death ever again.' Perhaps Bradbury would have identified in longtermism the dream of outrunning death itself.

One might think that if society is working for anybody, then it is working for the billionaires, but the prepper elite are more concerned with escaping it than doing their part to preserve it. 'Never before have our society's most powerful players assumed that the primary impact of their own conquests would be to render the world itself unliveable for everyone else,' wrote Douglas Rushkoff in *Survival of the Richest*, his assault on the Silicon Valley 'Mindset'. Like gun-toting white supremacists in the woods, they want to be heroes of what they call 'the Event'; unlike them, they will be partly responsible for it. 'Like the plot of a Marvel blockbuster, the very structure of The Mindset *requires* an endgame,' Rushkoff argued. 'Everything must resolve to a one or a zero, a winner or loser, the saved or the damned.' The activist writer Naomi Klein has described escape fantasies in millennialist terms: 'The Rapture is a parable for what they are building down here – a system that invites destruction and disaster, then swoops in with private helicopters and airlifts them and their friends to divine safety.'

Somebody who purchases a berth in a maximum-security compound is not a would-be Mad Max but somebody who wants to hire a private army of Mad Maxes to fend off the ravening mob on his behalf. The plan is not to fight but to wait. Whether one would thrive in sunless, fortified luxury is debatable. In the TV shows *American Horror Story: Apocalypse* and *The Last Man on Earth*, shelter-dwellers lose their minds from loneliness, paranoia and boredom. The post-apocalyptic underground haven is familiar from *Level 7*, *A Boy and His Dog* and Dr Strangelove's mineshaft-dwelling 'nucleus of human specimens', but it goes all the way back to 1897 and arguably fiction's first survivalist. The artilleryman in *The War of the Worlds* dreams of assembling a proto-fascistic community of 'able-bodied, clean-minded' men and women in the drains, tunnels and subways beneath London. 'We can't have any weak or silly,' he explains. 'Life is real again, and the useless and cumbersome and mischievous have to die. They ought to die. They ought to be willing to die. It's a sort of disloyalty, after all, to live and taint the race.' The artilleryman anticipates the survivalist obsession with starkly defined gender roles, genetic purity, righteous violence and, above all, authenticity. To him, civilization has been a phoney facade all along, concealing man's true nature. Today, the survivalist entrepreneur James Wesley Rawles teaches his readers how to prepare for 'The Day' and what comes next. In *How to Survive the End of the World as We Know It*, he writes that there is 'just a thin veneer of civilization on our society. What is underneath is not pretty, and it does not take much to peel away that veneer.' Life is real again.

The definitive rebuke to survivalist heroics, and the logical terminus of the catastrophe novel, is Cormac McCarthy's *The Road*, in which life becomes so 'real' that it loses, rather than gains, meaning.

One night, around 2003, McCarthy was in a hotel in El Paso, Texas, with his young son John. In the middle of the night, while John slept, McCarthy stood looking out of the window, listening to trains in the distance. 'I just had this image of what this town might look like in fifty or a hundred years,' he later told Oprah Winfrey. 'I just had this image of these fires up on the hill and everything being laid waste, and I thought a lot about my little boy.' Having become a father for the second time in his sixties, McCarthy understood that the true horror of death for a post-apocalyptic parent would not be one's own fate but the abandonment of one's child.

As the novelist Michael Chabon observed in his review of *The Road*, the post-apocalypse's potential for satire, religious allegory and hard-nosed naturalism makes it the one subgenre of science fiction into which mainstream writers and readers 'may venture without risking the stain of geekdom', attracting novelists who would never have dreamed of engaging with spaceships or time travel: Walker Percy, Bernard Malamud, Denis Johnson. Of all these experiments, McCarthy's is by far the most successful. The distance between the badlands of earlier novels like *Blood Meridian* and *Child of God*, with their unspeakable cruelties and incessant violence, and *The Road* was not so far to travel.

The Road takes place about a decade after the obliterating event, when America is 'looted, ransacked, ravaged. Rifled of every crumb.' On the exact nature of the catastrophe McCarthy gives us a single image: 'A long shear of light and then a series of low concussions . . . A dull rose glow in the window-glass.' Whatever it was generated enough heat to liquefy tarmac and start wildfires which raged until there was nothing left to consume. The smoke from this burning world created a kind of nuclear winter which has exterminated animals, birds and fish, as well as most people, and smothered the land in dust and ash. McCarthy does not detail the activities of the 'bloodcults', 'roadagents' and 'marauders', who make the villains in *Mad Max* seem guilty of little more than high spirits. We know only that within a short space of time, the world was 'largely populated by men who would eat your children in front of your eyes'. Even compared to *The Drought* or *The Death of Grass*, this is strong medicine, which removes all the perverse consolations of post-apocalyptic novels: the freedom from social obligations, the purging fire, the sacred relics of the time before. The man considers 'the absolute truth of the world. The cold relentless circling of the intestate earth. Darkness implacable.' When the man and boy chance upon a handsomely stocked fallout bunker, it proves that the survivalists had a point but also that the survivalist who built it is dead. McCarthy compares the hatch to 'a grave yawning at judgment day in some old apocalyptic painting', but nobody is getting resurrected here.

McCarthy outdoes even J. G. Ballard and Anna Kavan in the poetry of ruination. Verbless, cauterized sentences, as blunt as stumps; severed paragraphs in which nothing happens; punctuation slashed down to the bare essentials. The names of places and people are redundant: 'The world shrinking down about a raw core of parsible entities. The names of things slowly following those things to oblivion.' This hard, reduced language is enriched by archaisms – *rachitic*, *discalced*, *crozzled*, *skift* – which give it a mythic, premodern quality fit for a future which resembles the distant past. As John Hillcoat's 2009 movie version emphasizes, colour is just a memory, too: the barren present is trapped between brown and grey. Hillcoat framed it as the anti-*Mad Max*: 'We're trying to avoid the clichés of apocalypse and make this more like a natural disaster.' Whereas George Miller's road is a 'white-line nightmare', Hillcoat's is a grim trudge. The crucial vehicle is a shopping cart stuffed with cans and blankets rather than a muscular V8 Interceptor.

Perhaps only the second half of *Threads* paints as cheerless a picture of survival. The question *The Road* asks is: why bother? What is the value of one more day when the future has been cancelled? There is no sanctuary at the end of the road, and no hope of raising a new society, only the modest prospect of better weather to the south. The man takes shelter in memories and dreams, but that is not enough to live on; if not for his duty to the boy, he would lie down and die. Rejecting the lawless power fantasies of survivalism, *The Road* insists on the small flame of tenderness in a world blackened by cruelty and despair. This, rather than the hope of some future deliverance, is what is meant by 'carrying the fire'. McCarthy was a conservative in the tradition of Joseph Conrad: he believed human beings were pretty lousy and the idea of progress was for the birds. 'There's no such thing as life without bloodshed,' he said in 1992. 'I think the notion that the species can be improved in some way, that everyone could live in harmony, is a really dangerous idea.' In his novels, to outwit the murderers, torturers, cannibals and rapists without becoming a monster yourself is as good as it gets. When the boy talks of 'good guys' and 'bad guys', to be a good guy means being neither predator nor prey.

'I think a lot of people think that *The Road* . . . is a very depressing, sad book,' McCarthy said. 'But the truth is, the real story is about the love between the father and the son . . . I think if the book attempts to show anything, it attempts to show that love can survive even under the most horrible circumstances . . . I would never have written [*The Road*] if I had not had a son. What would I write about? My dog?' *The Road* received many rave reviews, including one from an online publication for preppers called *Off The Grid News*: 'I remind myself that I'm doing the right thing by tucking away extra food and supplies for a rainy day. I ponder the implications of the evening news.'

It is possible to read *The Road* as a story about generational failure: a father who can remember the privileges of modern life and a son who knows only his inheritance of ash. As a character in Doris Lessing's *The Four-Gated City* says, 'One generation apologizing to the next for "the mess we've made" became a sad joke at the end.' The environmentalist George Monbiot considered *The Road* 'the most important environmental book ever written' because it presents a murdered biosphere, but the novel does not feel like an intentional metaphor for climate change. The weather is too cold; the transformation too abrupt. In catastrophe fiction, the present and future are destroyed simultaneously. Gradual decline – the whimper rather than the bang – is far less narratively exciting. But there is at least one great exception, in the form of a movie that coincided with *The Road* and also follows a man looking after a child in an otherwise hopeless world: Alfonso Cuarón's *Children of Men*.

The eleventh of September 2001 was one of very few days about which one could say, without fear of exaggeration, that a single unprecedented catastrophe changed the world. Even more invasive than Pearl Harbor, this was the traumatic insult to America's sense of security that writers had been imagining ever since an enterprising magazine publisher relocated *The War of the Worlds* to New York in 1897, and which Steven Spielberg then channelled into his 2005 adaptation of Wells's novel. To New Yorkers, suggested Robert Jay Lifton, it felt like 'some version of the end of the world. That is how people in Hiroshima felt.' American cinema-goers were so saturated in images of collapsing landmarks that they experienced nauseating déjà vu, as if a monster from the realm of disaster fiction had suddenly infiltrated the real. Thriller writer Tom Clancy protested that the toppling of the World Trade Center by two hijacked passenger jets was 'not credible'.

That day and its aftermath filtered into almost every fictional cataclysm for the rest of the decade, including *The Road*. 'Maybe since 9/11 people are more concerned about apocalyptic issues,' Cormac McCarthy reflected in 2007. 'We're not used to that . . . This country's been very lucky.' The attack was also the spur for *Children of Men*. Cuarón never actually read P. D. James's 1992 novel *The Children of Men*, and the idea didn't appeal to him at all when he was first pitched a screenplay. Stranded in Toronto when air travel was suspended after 9/11, however, he had a revelation: 'The future isn't some place ahead of us; we're living in the future at this moment.'

Named after a line about God's wrath from Psalms 90:3, James's novel takes place in 2021, a long way into what appears to be an irreversible global fertility crash. The last baby was born in 1995 and when that generation – 'the Omegas' – reached sexual maturity and also proved infertile, humanity threw in the towel: 'We knew that this was indeed the end of *Homo sapiens*. It was in that year, 2008, that the suicides increased.' The plot driver is a miracle: the first pregnancy in twenty-six years.

Sudden infertility is one of the oldest ideas in apocalyptic fiction, featuring as it does in Grainville's 1805 novel *Le Dernier Homme*. It functions as a planet-clearing plot device in stories such as *R.U.R.*, *Childhood's End* and *Galápagos* by Kurt Vonnegut. The results are hysterically unpleasant in F. Wright Moxley's *Red Snow* (1930) and D. F. Jones's *Implosion* (1967), and grimly funny in Pat Frank's *Mr. Adam* (1946), but always there is the same species-level grief at the core of the idea. 'In the space of a few days,' Arthur C. Clarke writes in *Childhood's End*, 'humanity had lost its future, for the heart of any race is destroyed, and its will to survive is utterly broken, when its children are taken from it . . . It was as though the planet was in mourning, lamenting all that now could never be.' Brian Aldiss wasn't slow to point out the resemblance of James's premise to that of his own *Greybeard*, published in 1964. His novel takes place forty-eight years after 'the Accident', when the childless world is 'crumbling into senescence and chaos'. But *Greybeard* is full of drama: cholera, radiation, dictators, war. Perhaps it was James's desire to distance herself from Aldiss, and from science fiction in general, that inspired her choice to delineate sickly stability rather than disarray. She did for sterility what Nevil Shute had done for the cobalt bomb: she made it ordinary.

For P. D. James, the inciting catastrophe is not just an excuse for collapse but a specific tragedy representing spiritual desolation in the mould of T. S. Eliot. A world with no births is the polar opposite of the Apocalyptic Sublime. The sudden catastrophe has a certain cathartic vigour, briskly wiping away billions of people, many of whom are in the prime of their lives. It gets things over with. In the slow dissolve of *The Children of Men*, however, people grow slowly more decrepit and the eventual breakdown of supplies of water, energy and food will come about simply because everyone is too old and frail to keep them running. On one level, everything has changed but, on a day-to-day basis, surprisingly little has. The characters in James's novel have to deal with the same old tedious problems, only now in the absence of hope. The sterility crisis unleashes a plague of despair called '*ennui universel*': 'a disease, with its soon-familiar symptoms of lassitude, depression, ill-defined malaise, a readiness to give way to minor infections, a perpetual disabling headache'. The human race's long departing sigh is the ultimate manifestation of John Wyndham's 'drawn-out story of decay'. As Carl Inglebach, a member of the authoritarian Council of England, explains to the hero Theo Faron, 'Man is diminished if he lives without knowledge of his past; without hope of a future he becomes a beast.' England has been spared the civil wars and societal corrosion that have afflicted the rest of the world by the efforts of the Council to administer palliative care on a national scale, ensuring that the last decades are as tolerable as possible. 'They live without hope on a dying planet,' Theo observes. 'What they want is security, comfort, pleasure.' Perhaps this is the cosiest of catastrophes; provided somebody does not protest, a quiet life is possible. *The Children of Men* is *mid*-apocalyptic.

Cuarón's radical adaptation, set in 2027, reworks a Christian conservative novelist's verbose allegory for spiritual impotence into a left-wing critique of the War on Terror, xenophobia and devil-take-the-hindmost capitalism. His Theo (Clive Owen) may end up delivering and safeguarding the first baby born in eighteen years, but he begins the movie as a walking corpse with all the hope and idealism kicked out of him: 'Even if they discovered the cure for infertility, doesn't matter! Too late. World went to shit. Know what? It was too late before the infertility thing happened, for fuck's sake.' The cause of the mass sterility is unknown – possibly pollution, or genetic experiments, or the 2008 flu pandemic that killed Theo's own child – but the smoggy, garbage-strewn streets indicate a country that has simply given up on the future. This is truly the end of history. 'THE WORLD HAS COLLAPSED,' trumpets a government video over a frenzied montage of cities on fire. 'ONLY BRITAIN SOLDIERS ON.' In a movie with a grubby, hand-held, quasi-documentarian style, the only conventionally apocalyptic spectacle is propaganda.

In *Children of Men*, the last country standing is a survivalist nation which has closed its borders and its heart. The protagonists of most catastrophe stories are seeking asylum but Cuarón reminds us how we treat actual asylum-seekers in the present day. Here is the 'lifeboat ethic' in action, as the relative comfort of life under the Council necessitates both the inhumane treatment of refugees and a daily dedication to ignoring that inhumanity. It recalls Naomi Klein's phrase 'disaster apartheid': the division of the world into green zones and red zones. 'Ultimately, the UK looks like a green zone for the world,' Cuarón said. 'And inside that green zone you have other green zones.'

Explicitly rooted in the paranoid aftermath of 9/11, with surveillance and torture justified in the name of Homeland Security, *Children of Men* positions the traumatized world of 2027 just a few steps away from the present. In *Capitalist Realism*, the cultural theorist Mark Fisher observed that the Council's authoritarian state could pass for a tatty democracy – a semi-dystopia in which coffeeshop chains coexist with internment camps, and digital billboards with suicide pills. The movie repeats 'Shantih shantih shantih,' the Sanskrit mantra that closes *The Waste Land*, another work which suggests that the end has already occurred but the victims have not yet been notified, producing an enervated, unrejuvenated culture. In a deleted scene, Theo's powerful cousin Nigel (Danny Huston) strolls through his private art museum and glibly reads one of Rembrandt's last self-portraits as a metaphor for humanity in its senescence: 'This bloke did some of the wickedest masterpieces in history. And here he is, looking at you, at the end of his days, regretful, mischievous: "Whatever."'

Cuarón's anti-disaster movie removes the exhilarating finality that is the heart, and perhaps the purpose, of the end-of-the-world genre. Perhaps that is why it is so admired. The truth is that most of us would not be rugged survivalist supermen like Mad Max but more like the shuffling, compromised zombie citizens of *Children of Men*. Whatever.

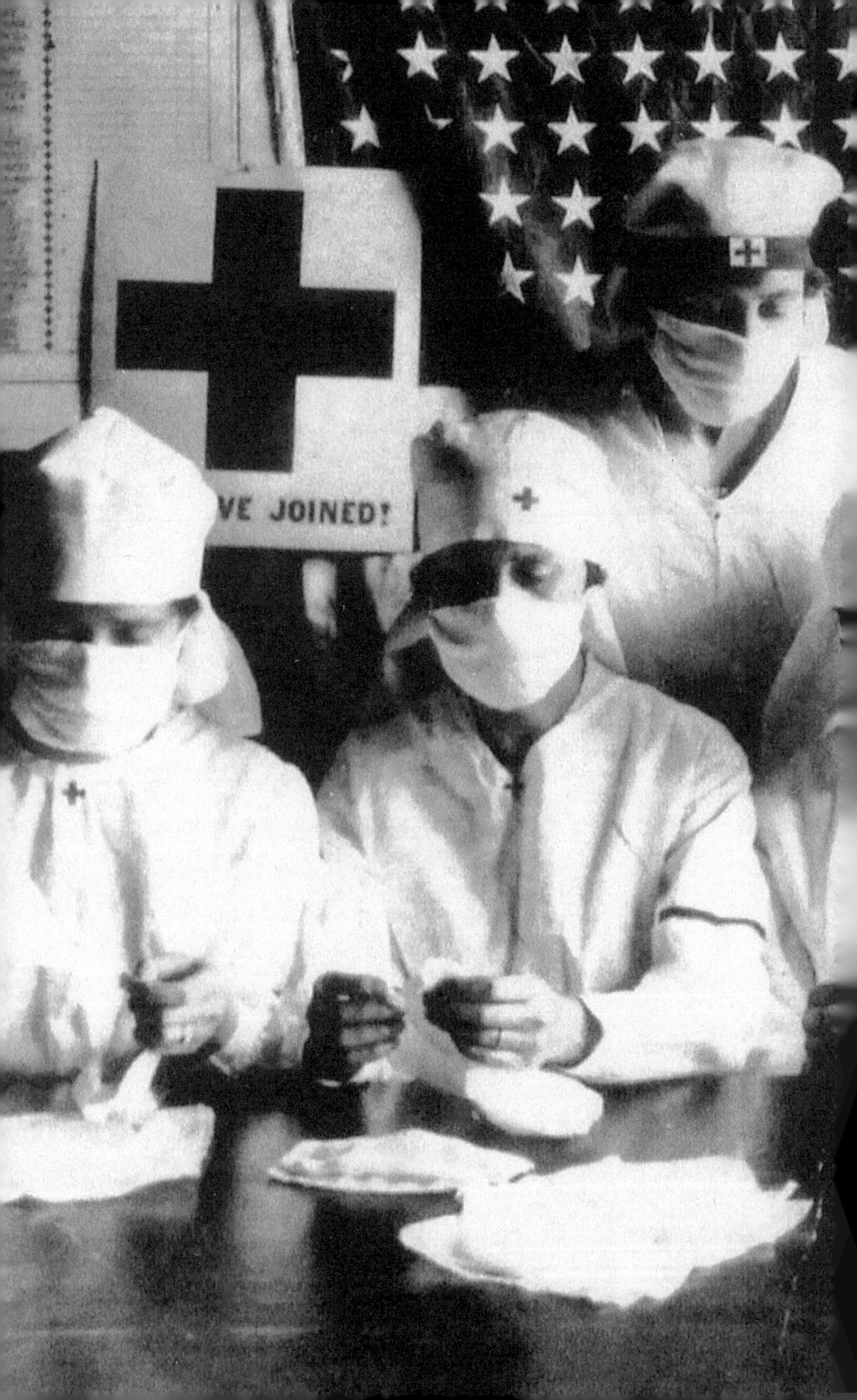
VE JOINED!

PART SIX
PANDEMIC

CHAPTER 15

Pestilence

Of all dangers, those allied to pestilence, by being mysterious and unseen, are the most formidable.

Charles Brockden Brown, *Arthur Mervyn* (1799)

'It really did feel like the end times had arrived, and the world had been caught sleeping,' the singer-songwriter Nick Cave said of the Covid-19 pandemic in 2022. 'It felt as though, whatever we assumed was the story of our lives, this invisible hand had reached down and torn a great big hole in it.'

When the world locked down in early 2020, people who had not personally experienced earlier pandemics such as SARS and swine flu were more likely to register the echoes of fiction. We had explored a silent, derelict metropolis in Danny Boyle's *28 Days Later*. We had seen disposable surgical masks, electronic thermometers and frantic handwashing in Will Smith's *I Am Legend* and Will Forte's *The Last Man on Earth*. Some of those who believed that SARS-CoV-2 had leaked from a laboratory in Wuhan, China, rather than spread from a food market, drew attention to Wuhan-400, the rogue Chinese bioweapon in some editions of Dean R. Koontz's 1981 thriller *The Eyes of Darkness*, or Captain Trips, the US equivalent in Stephen King's 1978 novel *The Stand*. 'People will come along and say through their little masks, "I feel like I'm living in a Stephen King story,"' the author remarked. Oana Aristide, whose haunting pandemic novel *Under the Blue* was not yet finished when the virus struck, worried that she was 'suddenly a kind of slowpoke Nostradamus' who 'might be accused of trying to piggyback on a global tragedy'.

Ravenous for fictional precedents, many people streamed the old movies *Outbreak*, *Contagion* and *12 Monkeys*, played the cooperative board game *Pandemic*, and read novels such as Emily St John Mandel's *Station Eleven*, the TV adaptation of which was ironically shut down by the pandemic. The post-Covid audio drama *Case 63* playfully exploited this phenomenon. A woman who has time-travelled from 2022 to 2012 is briefly persuaded that she is delusional and has fabricated the coronavirus pandemic from watching such movies. She then discovers that, to the contrary, every apocalyptic narrative has in fact been seeded in its creator's mind by 'sowers', time travellers from a doomed 2062, in a stealthy effort to change history. The writers of *Contagion* and *Station Eleven*, however, found compliments on their foresight bizarre. 'It has been very strange to me . . . that people will say to me, "This is uncanny how similar it is,"' reflected *Contagion* screenwriter Scott Z. Burns. 'And I don't find it to be that surprising, because the scientists I spoke to, and there were a lot of them, all said that this was a matter of when, not if.' Mandel agreed: 'It's like if a novelist had written a novel in the sixties about a fictional war. Does that mean they predicted the Vietnam War? No – there was always going to be another war.'

For almost the entire span of human history, infectious disease has been by far the biggest killer. As soon as that was no longer the case, thanks to advances in medicine and sanitation, many people dropped their guard. Strange though it may seem, there was a long period, between the Second World War and the advent of AIDS, when it was widely believed that epidemics of new infectious diseases, as opposed to new strains of flu, would soon be a thing of the past. In 1972, the Nobel Prize-winning Australian virologist Sir Frank MacFarlane Burnet predicted that the future of disease would be 'very dull'. He allowed that there might be 'some wholly unexpected emergence of a new and dangerous infectious disease, but nothing of the sort has marked the last fifty years'. Since then, we have seen Legionnaires' disease, mad cow disease, the Marburg virus, the Zika virus, Ebola, HIV/AIDS, SARS, Covid-19 and monkeypox. Between 2011 and 2018 the WHO dealt with 1,483 epidemics in 172 countries. In 2018, the WHO added to its watchlist of threats something it called 'Disease X': 'a pathogen currently unknown to cause human disease'. In addition to viruses, Sally Davies, the UK's former chief medical officer, has called antimicrobial resistant bacteria a problem 'as complex as climate change' and said that 'the world is facing an antibiotic apocalypse.' And these are just naturally occurring diseases. In *The Precipice*, Toby Ord estimates the existential risk of an engineered pandemic, which is to say biological warfare, within the next century at one in thirty, second only to unaligned AI.

In adapting the hit PlayStation game *The Last of Us* for television after Covid-19, Craig Mazin and Neil Druckmann realized that they needed to do more to explain the operation of *Cordyceps*, the fungus that zombifies the infected, because we are all pandemic experts now. Mazin referred to his previous show, *Chernobyl*: '[One] thing that I'm obsessed with is the idea that we know things and we all agree that they're gonna happen and then we pretend they're not.' Yet Mazin and Druckmann's premise – a scientist in the 1960s precisely identifying the nature of an outbreak that occurs in 2003 – is misleading. In reality, epidemiologists are certain that something bad is coming but cannot say what it is, or when and where it will arise. In September 2019, the journalist Laurie Garrett wrote an article for *Foreign Affairs* called 'The World Knows an Apocalyptic Pandemic Is Coming. But nobody is interested in doing anything about it'. But the virus that emerged from Wuhan three months later stopped the world and killed more than seven million people, was not Garrett's superflu. Nor was it Burns's ME-1, nor Mandel's Georgia flu, and certainly not *Cordyceps*. More often than not, it is the thing we don't see coming.

The catastrophe that felt more like the end of the world than any other reached Europe in October 1347, when a dozen trading galleys from the Genoese port of Caffa in the Crimea docked in Messina, Sicily, and disgorged a cargo of the dead and dying. The plague that became known as the Black Death spread to southern France and North Africa at the start of 1348, crossed the Alps and the English Channel over the summer and reached Scotland, Ireland and Scandinavia the following year. One French physician remarked that it felt as if one person 'could infect the whole world'. So many died, so quickly, that bodies were thrown into rivers and overflowing pits or simply shoved into the street. By the time the first wave burned itself out in Europe in the middle of 1350, the French chronicler Jean Froissart estimated, 'a third of the world died'. That figure was inspired by the pestilence in the Book of Revelation and was probably too low. Estimates range from 30 to 60 per cent of the affected populations, which is to say between 75 and 200 million, but there were extreme regional variations. Some communities suffered mortality rates of nine in ten and disappeared from the map. It took until 1500 for Europe's population to rebound to the level of 1300.

This was the second plague pandemic. The first had ripped through the Byzantine Empire in the 540s, during the reign of Justinian I, killing tens of millions of people. There had been devastating pestilences before, in Athens and Rome, but trading routes made this the first true continent-crossing pandemic, spreading all the way from China to Britain. The historian Procopius called it 'a pestilence that brought the whole human race close to annihilation'. John of Ephesus chronicled the frightful scenes in Constantinople, which lost around half its population: people expired in tomb-like houses or empty streets, with nobody to bury them; ghost ships floated aimlessly with dead crews; babies sucked on their dead mothers' breasts.

As Boccaccio observed of Florence in *The Decameron*, there was no single way to cope with the Black Death – or, as it was known at the time, the Great Mortality. Some people became shuttered recluses, some embarked on crime sprees or nihilistic tavern crawls, while others threw themselves into the arms of religion. What most saddened Boccaccio was the death of fellow-feeling: 'Brothers abandoned one other, uncles abandoned nephews, sisters abandoned brothers, wives abandoned their husbands, and, unbelievably, parents even abandoned their own children . . . Things had sunk to the level that human bodies were disposed of much as we would now dispose of a dead goat.' Even as it disintegrated the body, the plague dissolved the bonds that made sense of life and destroyed the rituals that gave dignity to death. The cruel fact is that defiantly preserving those norms, as many continued to do, was more likely to spread the plague than ruthless self-preservation.

Similar scenes played out in Naples in 1656 and London in 1665, as the second plague pandemic rolled on for centuries. Strolling past a farm that had been blockaded to trap the infected, Samuel

Pepys lamented that the plague was 'making us cruel, as dogs, to one another'. In *A Journal of the Plague Year*, a 1722 novel inspired by a recent plague epidemic in Marseille but promoted as a non-fiction eyewitness account of the London outbreak, Daniel Defoe wrote, 'But, alas! this was a time when every one's private safety lay so near them that they had no room to pity the distress of others; for every one had death, as it were, at his door . . . This, I say, took away all compassion; self-preservation, indeed, appeared to be the first law.' Chronicling the Plague of Athens in the fifth century BC, Thucydides recorded that 'the catastrophe was so overwhelming that men, not knowing what would happen next to them, became indifferent to every rule of religion or of law.' Assuming that the gods didn't care and that death would claim them before the law did, they seized 'the pleasure of the moment'.

The Black Death entered Caffa from Asia in 1345 when it was besieged by Jani Beg's Golden Horde. Beg's army allegedly catapulted infected corpses over the city walls in an early example of biological warfare, although recent scholarship argues that this was subsequent propaganda and that living rats were far more effective plague vectors than dead humans. The Genoese galleys brought stowaways to Sicily: black rats, the fleas that lived off them and the bacteria they carried. The plague came in three forms, of which bubonic was both the most grisly and the least fatal, with a mortality rate of around 60 per cent. It began with black, apple-sized swellings in the armpit and groin which leaked blood and pus and were so painful that some people threw themselves into rivers in search of relief. Purple bloodspots under the skin, caused by internal bleeding, presaged neurological damage and organ failure. A second, pneumonic variant was airborne, causing fever and bleeding lungs, and killed almost 100 per cent of its victims. Septicaemic plague, which infected the blood, was similarly virulent and even faster: a sufferer might go to bed feeling fine and never wake up. All three were caused by the same bacterium, *Yersinia pestis*, although this would remain a mystery for half a millennium. At the time, people understood nothing, or worse than nothing, about contagion. Even the most basic precautions of sanitary cordons and quarantine (from the Biblical forty days and forty nights) were not established until the fifteenth century.

Supernatural explanations were sought. In the Bible, Greek tragedy and the teachings of Muhammad, plague is punishment for sin: from *plaga*, the Latin word for *a blow*. Hippocrates, who first made the distinction between epidemic and endemic diseases, severed them from the gods and rooted them in the real world. For more than two thousand years, the prevailing medical wisdom maintained that infection was spread by a poisonous mist rather than by individuals. This fallacy, 'miasma theory', inspired the medieval Italian word *malaria* ('bad air'), while *influenza* referred to the presumed influence of celestial bodies: *influenza coeli*. Many people therefore believed that the plague was carried by evil vapours, perhaps unleashed by a recent earthquake in the Alps or by the rumbling of Mount Etna. According to the historian George Deaux, everything from 'demons in the sky' to 'a strange international conspiracy with its headquarters in Spain' was blamed. Thousands of Flagellants marched from town to town, scourging themselves with rods and whips. Some accused Jews of poisoning wells, leading to the fiery slaughter of scores of Jewish communities across Europe.

It is hard to imagine the uncomprehending terror and despair inspired by the Black Death, but it clearly felt apocalyptic. 'And no bells tolled,' wrote one survivor in Siena, having lost his wife and all five children, 'and nobody wept no matter what his loss because almost everyone expected death . . . And people said and believed, "This is the end of the world."' The Italian historian Matteo Villani compared the plague to the Biblical Deluge and thought that it meant 'the extermination of mankind'. In Ireland, a dying monk wrote a message to the future, 'if perchance any man survive and any of the race of Adam escape this pestilence and carry on the work which I have begun'. In the Islamic world, where the plague was known as the Great Annihilation, the Arab scholar Ibn Khaldun wrote, 'It was as if the voice of existence in the world had called out for oblivion and restriction, and the world had responded to its call.'

Those left behind were all the more confused because it was *not* the end of the world and there had been no great transformation to give purpose to their suffering. The authority of the church, glutted by donations even as priests deserted their flocks, was permanently damaged. The sense of injustice and institutional failure inaugurated an era of peasants' revolts and millenarian radicalism, as people sought their own new beginnings. Surely an experience so vast, horrendous and inexplicable couldn't mean nothing?

After the Black Death, the personification of Death as a skeletal reaper became a common feature of medieval art but, despite the world-shaking impact of the disease, explicit depictions of the plague in literature and painting were few and far between. The plague chronicles of Boccaccio and Defoe are so famous because they had so little competition. In Shakespeare's time, London's theatres were frequently closed by plague outbreaks but, unlike venereal disease, it was never a feature of his plays. Perhaps writers figured that people simply did not want to think about it, but the inability to ascribe greater meaning to the horror must also have been a factor.

Every historian who writes about the influenza pandemic of 1918–19, known as Spanish flu, remarks on the mysterious disparity between its scale and its legacy.* Killing between 50 and 100 million people, it was unusually fatal to the young: the average age of death was twenty-eight. The US bacteriologist Edwin O. Jordan called it 'incomparably the worst catastrophe of the sort that has visited the human race since the Black Death of the Middle Ages'. Its unusually ghastly symptoms – cyanosis, jet-like nosebleeds, ravaged lungs, a foul stench – led some people to believe that it *was* the return of the plague. Until it subsided at the end of November 1918 after ten hellish weeks, the virulence of the second wave seemed unstoppable. One English family returned home from burying their youngest daughter to find that another family member had died; a funeral in New York was halted by the news that the deceased's widow had just passed away as well. 'If the epidemic continues its mathematical rate of acceleration,' wrote Victor C. Vaughn, surgeon general of the US Army, 'civilization could easily have disappeared from the face of the earth within a matter of a few more weeks.'

One in three people on earth contracted influenza, including T. S. Eliot, D. H. Lawrence, Franz Kafka, President Woodrow Wilson,

*The influenza did not originate in Spain but as warring countries kept their own earlier outbreaks secret, it was neutral Spain that took the blame.

David Lloyd George, Haile Selassie, Kemal Atatürk and Mahatma Gandhi. Nevil Shute participated in military funeral parties for victims of the flu; W. B. Yeats nursed his pregnant wife through the illness while writing 'The Second Coming'; Leo Szilard escaped the massacre of his Austro-Hungarian regiment at the Battle of Vittorio Veneto because he was recuperating in Budapest. Yet, as the historian Richard Collier noted, the pandemic directly inspired 'no songs, no legends, no work of art'. Susan Sontag attributed the 'near-total historical amnesia' about Spanish flu to its impotence as a metaphor. Even the earliest and most modest death-toll estimate, 21.6 million, eclipsed that of the entire First World War, but war is a man-made disaster, full of drama and meaning. By comparison, the influenza was incomprehensible and pointless. 'So vast was the catastrophe and so ubiquitous its prevalence that our minds, surfeited with the horrors of war, refused to realize it,' *The Times* observed two years later. As a story, the flu made no sense. It didn't seem to signify anything bigger than itself. It simply was. The fact that twice as many soldiers died of typhoid during the American Civil War as in combat, or that dysentery outperformed Russian guns in the Crimean War by ten to one, is similarly counterintuitive. If this absence of narrative explains the flu-shaped lacuna in 1920s literature, then perhaps it also accounts for our own aimlessness in the wake of Covid-19. We were told that the world would never be the same again, for good or ill, but the promised transformation, which might have made sense of it all, failed to arrive.

As we know, the first end-of-the-world novel was a pandemic novel: Mary Shelley's *The Last Man.* As she launched one literary tradition, she drew heavily on another. Plague narratives are remarkably consistent and aware of their precedents: Boccaccio referenced Thucydides, Defoe borrowed from Boccaccio, and so on. Even when the pestilences differ (the Plague of Athens was probably typhus fever), the writers seem to agree that this is how it is: the strange omens, the mysterious invader from abroad, the inexorable advance, the helpless terror, the medical impotence, the social chaos, the spiritual crisis, the nervous citizens hurrying past each other through almost deserted streets, the unburied dead, the possibility of an apocalyptic conclusion. Mary Shelley updated these sources with Charles Brockden Brown's account of the 1793 Philadelphia yellow fever epidemic in his Gothic novel *Arthur Mervyn* and John Wilson's macabre 1816 verse play *The City of the Plague*, and assumed that her readers knew the drill:

> It would be needless to narrate those disastrous occurrences, for which a parallel might be found in any slighter visitation of our gigantic calamity. Does the reader wish to hear of the pest-houses, where death is the comforter – of the mournful passage of the death-cart – of the insensibility of the worthless, and the anguish of the loving heart – of harrowing shrieks and silence dire – of the variety of disease, desertion, famine, despair, and death? There are many books which can feed the appetite craving for these things; let them turn to the accounts of Boccaccio, De Foe, and Browne.

For Shelley, a pandemic was an extremely efficient fictional planet-clearer which could take humanity to the threshold of extinction in no time: 'the vast annihilation that has swallowed all things'. Though she had lost two children to infectious diseases, it is likely that she had one particular disease in mind: cholera. The historian Gillen D'Arcy Wood has blamed the eruption of Tambora for the first cholera epidemic – by altering the microbial ecology of the Bay of Bengal, the abnormal weather enabled a virulent new strain to mutate. In India in 1817, one English clergyman beheld 'a scene of woe which completely baffles the power of description to portray'; Thomas Medwin, Percy Shelley's cavalryman cousin, wrote, 'Such a scene of horror was perhaps never witnessed.' By the time Mary Shelley was writing *The Last Man*, the pandemic extended from southern Russia to the Philippines. In Java, it killed even more people than Tambora.

Known as 'king cholera', or simply 'the monster', it was the most feared disease of the century, because it acted so fast and produced such disgusting symptoms, with none of the wan poetry of tuberculosis. In the words of the historian Frank M. Snowden, 'A ghoulish aspect of the disease is that, while the living patient resembles a corpse, the dead body of a victim seems alive . . . it produces vigorous postmortem muscular contractions that cause limbs to shake and twitch for a prolonged period.' The convulsions of corpses on death carts prompted rumours that people were being buried alive. When a second cholera pandemic reached England in 1832, killing around 1 per cent of Londoners, its victims included Mary Shelley's half-brother, William Godwin the Younger. Meanwhile, Edgar Allan Poe's experience of cholera in Baltimore that year fed into his plague stories 'King Pest' and 'The Masque of the Red Death'. Cholera was sometimes known as the Blue Death because it caused cyanosis. 'He was found stiff, his hands clenched, and pressed against his breast,' Shelley writes of one victim of its fictional analogue. 'His skin, nearly black, his matted hair and bristly beard, were signs of a long protracted misery.' While she had some basic understanding of quarantine and vaccines, her 'invincible monster' has a supernatural quality, running riot every summer and abating every winter of its own accord. It is as mysterious and implacable as death itself: 'There is no refuge on earth, it comes on us like a thousand packs of wolves.'

Mary Shelley could only work with the conventional wisdom of the time, which was still miasma theory: 'The air is empoisoned, and each human being inhales death.' Although it had first been proposed by Girolamo Fracastoro as early as 1546, germ theory did not become hegemonic until the 1880s, thanks to the work of the microbiologists Louis Pasteur and Robert Koch, who identified the bacteria behind anthrax, tuberculosis and cholera and revolutionized the understanding of disease. The infrastructure of disease containment to this day – quarantine, isolation, tracking, masks, personal hygiene, bans on mass gatherings – was in place by the end of the nineteenth century. When the third plague pandemic struck Hong Kong in 1894, the Swiss-French bacteriologist Alexandre Yersin was able to pinpoint the cause as the bacterium he called *Yersinia pestis*. Apart from that, the plague was rather underreported because 95 per cent of the death toll was in India. It seems that a disease, like a natural disaster, is deemed world-changing only if it affects the West; otherwise, it is just one of those things.

Germ theory enthralled H. G. Wells, who wrote in 1894 that 'for all we know even now we may be quite unwittingly evolving some new and more terrible plague – a plague that will not take ten or twenty or thirty per cent, as plagues have done in the past, but the entire hundred,' and he deployed a bacterial *deus ex machina* in *The War of the Worlds*. He was fascinated by the idea that something so tiny possessed such humbling power. 'Our microscopic allies' symbolized the empire-builders' dread that the colonized would infect the colonizers. Conversely, germ theory redefined disease as an invasion by a foreign horde, against which medicine must wage a war. Inevitably, this enabled nativists to demonize immigrants for infecting the body politic. In 1892, the *Toronto Evening News* ran a series of alarmist headlines about Jewish immigrants from eastern Europe – 'IS THIS DREAD CHOLERA?', 'WAKE UP, TORONTO' – even though cholera never actually arrived in the city. Bram Stoker's 1897 novel *Dracula* featured the nightmare immigrant, importing a deadly blood-borne contagion to England.

The inevitable offspring of xenophobia, the militarization of germ theory and the *fin-de-siècle* craze for apocalyptic fiction was the idea of biological warfare. In Wells's 1894 story 'The Stolen Bacillus', an anarchist terrorist attempts to weaponize cholera. 'Those little particles, those mere atomies, might multiply and devastate a city!' he marvels with his eye to a microscope. 'Wonderful!' It was only a matter of time before a writer decided that this could be a legitimate superweapon. This writer was a very strange man named M. P. Shiel.

'I was born at the moment of an earthquake and a storm,' Shiel once proclaimed, 'or, rather, these were born at the moment of me.' Put more prosaically, Matthew Phipps Shiell (as his name was originally spelled) was born in 1865 on the Caribbean island of Montserrat, which was then part of the British West Indies. His parents' first son after nine daughters, he was raised with delusions of grandeur. He claimed that on his fifteenth birthday his father, a Methodist preacher, had pronounced him King Felipe of Redonda, a rock inhabited solely by seagulls. Shiel abandoned his avian subjects and moved to England, where he became a teacher, journalist, autodidact and prolific writer of Poe-besotted fiction who attracted a cult-like coterie of disciples. At his funeral in 1947, Edward Shanks, author of *The People of the Ruins*, hailed Shiel's 1901 novel *The Purple Cloud* as 'a legend, an apocalypse, out of space, out of time . . . the first and last thing to be said about him is that he had the character of a poet and prophet – a prophet, I mean, in the Old Testament manner.' Well, other things need to be said about him. *The Purple*

Cloud hints at two qualities that made Shiel an alarming figure. First, he was jailed in 1914 for indecently assaulting his lover's twelve-year-old daughter. During his trial, he did not deny the crime but attempted to justify it with reference to historical precedent and his upbringing in Montserrat, where, he claimed, he had lost his virginity at the age of five to an eight-year-old. Secondly, he was a tremendous racist who only acknowledged his white Irish roots, despite being the biracial grandson of slaves.

The Purple Cloud, whose admirers have included H. G. Wells, H. P. Lovecraft and Stephen King, is an exceptionally deranged last-man story which cries out for psychotherapists as well as readers. After a Krakatoa-like eruption releases a mephitic hydrocyanic fog, the sole survivor, Adam Jeffson, travels the world setting cities ablaze, 'like some being of the Pit that blights where pass his flaming wings', and having sex with corpses.* He is offended by the presence of so many foreign refugees on English soil, even after they are all dead, and racializes his uncertainty about whether to continue the race in terms of 'White Power' and 'Black Power'. Maddened by solitude, Jeffson grows a pigtail and dresses in oriental fashions, 'for surely I am hardly any longer, a Western, "modern" mind, but a primitive and Eastern one.' When he dreams that someone else is alive in Peking (now Beijing), he travels to China to burn it to the ground, just in case.

Shiel's hostility was not merely a personal obsession. The fact that southern China was the source of so many diseases, including the third plague pandemic, fused with concern that the country's booming population would one day give it military and economic supremacy to spawn widespread Sinophobia. One US newspaper in 1894 called China 'the filthiest and nastiest country on the face of the globe'. As lurid as its title, Shiel's 1898 novel *The Yellow Danger* was a murderous fantasy of imperialist paranoia and race war which incorporated the latest news stories about unrest in China prior to the Boxer Rebellion. Led by a sinister mastermind named Dr Yen

* *The Purple Cloud* is essentially a pandemic novel. In A. Lincoln Green's suspiciously similar novel, *The End of an Epoch*, published a few months later, the leak of a super-bacteria leads to the world-destroying 'Great Epidemic'. Louis Robinson, the man behind the *nom de plume*, was a doctor who buttressed his story with references to Pasteur and Koch.

How, the Chinese Army butchers the entire population of continental Europe in an invasion that Shiel compares to a plague more terrifying than the Black Death. 'The fact that God has a predilection for pigtails and microbes (to judge from their number) has always struck me,' Shiel wrote later. The novel's English hero, John Hardy, retaliates by commissioning a real plague, the Black Spot, to achieve 'the extinction of the yellow man'. It is injected into 250 Chinese soldiers who are deposited in key cities around the European coastline as superspreaders. Within three weeks, 'that winged plague, that more putrid Cholera', has killed a hundred million. (In 1918, some Americans claimed that the Spanish flu was germ warfare, spread by German agents who emerged from U-boats armed with microbial death.)

Shiel's ghoulish yarn launched the 'Yellow Peril' genre, making Dr Yen How the forefather of Fu Manchu, and was praised for its foresight when the Boxer Rebellion portended what *The Times* called 'a universal uprising of the yellow race'. One writer sharing that phobia was Jack London, who wrote an essay called 'The Yellow Peril' and a spectacularly nasty 1910 story called 'The Unparalleled Invasion'. In a future 1976, Western fears of China's 'amazing birth rate' spawn a genocidal plan for airships to drop glass vials of plague, killing every single person in the country: 'It was ultra-modern war, twentieth century war, the war of the scientist and the laboratory . . . Hundred-ton guns were toys compared with the micro-organic projectiles hurled from the laboratories, the messengers of death, the destroying angels that stalked through the empire of a billion souls.' London describes the 'vast and happy' resettlement of the emptied country by the international community, which solemnly pledges never to do this again.*

Two years after 'The Unparalleled Invasion', London described in *The Scarlet Plague* how terrible a plague might be if it were to afflict white people. Despite locating his pandemic in 2013, London was drawing on two disasters that had recently befallen his hometown of San Francisco. The first was the bubonic plague outbreak

*In Olaf Stapledon's *Last and First Men*, the first civilizational collapse of many is brought about by the 'American madness', an insanity-inducing bacillus which has been created as a weapon against the Chinese but ends up infecting the whole world.

of 1900–4, which affected Chinatown. Only 119 people died but it was the first time that the plague had reached the American mainland. The second blow to the city was the earthquake of 1906, which London described in 'The Story of an Eye Witness': 'Not in history has a modern imperial city been so completely destroyed. San Francisco is gone.' The sight of people stumbling through the smoking rubble of Market Street made him think of 'the handful of survivors after the day of the end of the world'. By displacing millions of rats, the earthquake caused a second, broader plague outbreak.

London applied this cinematic, eye-witness perspective to *The Scarlet Plague*, in which the frail octogenarian Granser tells his neobarbarian grandchildren about the disease that wiped out civilization sixty years earlier. His bluffer's guide to germ theory, which implies that some of London's readers would not have been up to speed, characterizes the 'micro-organic world' as a hostile realm: 'from time to time armies of new germs emerged from it to kill men.' The Scarlet Death resembles a souped-up version of Poe's 'illimitable' Red Death: 'With the coming of the Scarlet Death the world fell apart, absolutely, irretrievably. Ten thousand years of culture and civilization passed in the twinkling of an eye.'

For writers such as London, the microbial domain was as fruitfully mysterious as a distant galaxy. With bacteriology in its infancy and virology not yet born, there was no pressure on novelists to explain fully the origin, transmission, evolution or symptoms of a fictional disease, nor why key characters were blessed with natural immunity. 'The bacillus . . . was never isolated, nor the pathology of the disease investigated,' shrugged J. D. Beresford in his 1913 novel *Goslings*. Far more interesting to him were the social repercussions. Writing between the sinking of the *Titanic* and the First World War, Beresford presented plague as the kind of shattering catastrophe that the deep, green sleep of Edwardian complacency could not admit.

When Mr and Mrs Gosling, a decent but dim middle-class couple, read about a new plague in China which kills almost all men but very few women, they are as unperturbed as many Britons would be in January 2020: 'China's a long way off.' Mr Gosling dismisses the writer of an article about the threat to England as 'a chap who's been reading too much Wells, I should imagine'. Their former lodger, a buccaneering intellectual called Jasper Thrale, sees the danger but cannot get through to newspaper editors, politicians or people like the Goslings. 'It seems so incredible to us in twentieth-century England that anything really serious could happen,' he says. 'We are so well looked after and cared for. We sit down and wait for some authority to move, with a perfect confidence that when it does move, everything is bound to be all right.' Even as the scythe sweeps towards England and the government is finally persuaded to close the borders, the leader of the Opposition dismisses the measure as 'a mere subterfuge to win votes'. Once the plague subsides, Beresford teases the kind of radical transformation that real pandemics rarely deliver, when Eileen Gosling looks forward to a country reconstructed along socialist and feminist lines: 'Hope, lots of hope. Hope of a new clean world. We've got such a chance to begin all over again, and do it better.'

Politics has always appropriated the language of health and illness. For Hitler, Jewish people were a 'noxious bacillus', but for the Austrian Jewish writer Joseph Roth, Nazism was the contagion: he asked in 1933 'whether the time hasn't come where it is our duty to quarantine the world around us, so that it doesn't get infected'. Karel Čapek's 1937 play *Bílá nemoc* (literally *The White Disease* but translated into English as *Power and Glory*) criss-crosses its metaphors: a leprosy-like pestilence from China collides with the plague of fascism, which in turn pits itself against 'the scourge of anarchy, the disease of barbarian liberty . . . the leprosy of national corruption, the plague of subversive activities which . . . had begun to affect the whole organism of this country and brought it almost to racial death'. In tribute to his physician father, Čapek created an idealistic doctor named Galen who develops a cure but will only reveal it if the regime renounces war. When the dictator falls ill, he agrees to Galen's demand, but before he can get there the doctor is beaten to death by a pro-war mob and his antidote destroyed. As one fascist says, 'If I had to choose between the White Scourge and this lasting peace idea, I know which I'd choose.'

CHAPTER 16

Contagion

> The trouble you're expecting never happens; it's always something that sneaks up the other way.
>
> George R. Stewart, *Earth Abides* (1949)

An infectious disease travels as fast as people do. Genoese galleys brought the plague to Europe, steamships carried the third plague pandemic from port to port, and international troop movements expedited the Spanish flu. In fiction, the 'various channels of commerce' spread the pestilence in Mary Shelley's *The Last Man* while airships propagate Jack London's Scarlet Death. In his 1922 novel *Nordenholt's Million*, the Scottish chemist J. J. Conington imagined how widespread air travel might one day spread a soil-destroying bacterium and make quarantine impossible: 'For good or ill, humanity was becoming linked together until it formed a single unit.' By 1949, when George R. Stewart wrote his pandemic novel *Earth Abides*, this was becoming a reality. One of Stewart's epigraphs comes from an article by the biochemist W. M. Stanley: 'If a killing type of virus strain should suddenly arise by mutation . . . it could, because of the rapid transportation in which we indulge nowadays, be carried to the far corners of the earth and cause the deaths of millions of people.'

Yet politicians, public-health officials and leading scientists suffered from remarkable hubris during the post-war decades. Thanks to antibiotics, vaccines and giant leaps in virology, science turned the tide on polio, measles and (in the West) tuberculosis, while abolishing smallpox worldwide. In 1963, the leading epidemiologist

Aidan Cockburn predicted that 'within some measurable time, such as 100 years, all the major infections will have disappeared.' But the economist Martin Shubik scathingly noted 'our previous self-congratulations on how fine and healthy the U.S. looks at the present moment and how much medical science has advanced' and urged caution: 'Communications have also advanced, and the methods of spreading plague or other undesirable agents are rather good.'

Even when medical bullishness faltered during the 1970s, with the first cases of Ebola and Legionnaires' disease and the failure to eradicate malaria, the eminent virologist Edwin D. Kilbourne was still able to claim that influenza would be 'the last great plague of man'. For Americans, the decade's most notorious epidemic was one that never happened. In 1976, President Gerald Ford's administration became convinced that an outbreak of swine flu at Fort Dix, Maryland, would lead to an epidemic on the scale of 1918 and spent $135 million on vaccines. But the flu didn't spread, uptake was poor and the government ended up paying out almost $100 million to victims of vaccine-related Guillain-Barré syndrome. In a real epidemic, flu is a greater risk factor than the vaccine but in 1976, the solution was worse than the problem. The fiasco was a major blow to pandemic preparedness.

Post-war pandemic fiction, then, was not speaking to a widespread cultural foreboding about naturally emerging diseases but more to concerns about mad scientists and terrorists. A bacteriologist in *Earth Abides* suggests three possible origins: 'It might have emerged from some animal reservoir of disease; it might be caused by some new micro-organism, most likely a virus, produced by mutation; it might be an escape, possibly even a vindictive release, from some laboratory of bacteriological warfare. The last was apparently the popular idea.' Biowarfare was a real concern (Bertrand Russell wrote to Einstein in 1955 that 'it is probable that the dangers of bacteriological warfare may before long become just as great' as those of the H-bomb) but one that was vastly overrepresented in fiction. The killer bug in Michael Crichton's 1969 techno-thriller *The Andromeda Strain*, the title of which became shorthand for a sudden and virulent pandemic, is an extraterrestrial organism, harvested by a military satellite for bioweapons research. Such research produces a potentially annihilating strain of poliovirus in Alastair MacLean's 1962 potboiler *The*

Satan Bug, threatens to garland the earth with a 'necklace of death' in the James Bond film *Moonraker*, makes the world a graveyard in Kinji Fukasuku's remorselessly depressing 1980 movie *Fukkatsu no Hi* (*Day of Rebirth*) and unleashes vampirism in *The Omega Man*. 'We were warned of judgement,' says a newsreader in that movie. 'Well, here it is. Here. Now. In the form of billions of microscopic bacilli. This is the end.' In Gore Vidal's *Kalki*, a former biowarfare specialist masquerading as a Hindu deity forces the end of the Kali Yuga with a weaponized strain of *Yersinia enterocolitica*. (Vidal admitted that this bacterium would not be suitable for omnicide but, lest he give any bioterrorists the wrong idea, 'he had forgone the verisimilitude in the interests of good citizenship'.) The Bomb, too, could be a spreader of disease in the form of radiation poisoning. The journalist Wilfred Burchett described Hiroshima survivors suffering from 'an unknown something which I can only describe as the atomic plague', while Nevil Shute compared cobalt radiation to cholera in *On the Beach*. (Ironically, the earliest meaning of 'cobalt bomb' was a form of radiation therapy for cancer.)

Biowarfare, unlike nuclear weapons, was an abomination that the US officially renounced. During the 1940s, the army laboratory at Fort Detrick, Maryland, developed such weapons as anthrax bombs and the capacity to infect squadrons of mosquitoes with yellow fever, but in 1969, President Nixon outlawed these gory schemes and demanded that the laboratory's research be strictly defensive. Fort Detrick's fictional counterparts, however, pressed on. With its quotations from 'The Second Coming' and its mystical battle between good and evil, the most ostentatiously apocalyptic pandemic novel of the period was Stephen King's 1978 blockbuster *The Stand*. The idea came to King when he learned about a chemical spill in Utah at the same time as hearing a radio preacher claim, 'Once in every generation the plague will fall among them.' In *The Stand*, the conspiracy theorists are correct: the Captain Trips virus *was* released by the 'US pig paramilitary' and they *are* covering it up. Written when King felt that 'the America I had grown up in seemed to be crumbling beneath my feet,' the novel reeks of post-Watergate cynicism and malaise. As one character sneers, 'They've solved the depressed economy, pollution, the oil shortage, and the cold war, all at a stroke.' Claiming that a 'capering nihilist' lurks inside every horror writer, King confessed to feeling that 'I was doing a fast, happy tapdance on the grave of the whole world.' He was influenced by *Earth Abides* and *The Purple Cloud*, neither of which expresses a glowing view of humanity at large. 'In this frame of mind, the destruction of THE WORLD AS WE KNOW IT became an actual relief,' he wrote. 'No more Ronald McDonald! . . . No more terrorists! *No more bullshit!*'

In Britain, pandemic stories suggested that exceptionalism had not diminished since the days of Mr and Mrs Gosling. In *Empty World*, John Christopher's 1977 homage to *Earth Abides*, the Calcutta Plague catches England napping, just like the crop blight in *The Death of Grass*. 'This is an island, thank God,' says the young hero's grandfather with a confidence that guarantees that he will soon be dead. 'There's no reason why controls shouldn't work, if they're properly handled. And people are scared enough now to do a proper job.' In Terry Nation's television series *Survivors*, a flask dropped by a Chinese scientist unleashes a pathogen with a 99.98 per cent mortality rate, known as 'the Death', but even as millions die in China and India, Abby Grant (Carolyn Seymour) is nonplussed. 'There was a bad epidemic of something about the time of the First World War wasn't there?' she says, frying bacon and eggs for dinner. 'I don't think it would happen nowadays with modern drugs on that scale, do you?'

During the post-war decades, as Susan Sontag wrote, medicine had been seen 'as an age-old military campaign now nearing its final phase, leading to victory'. The 1980s, though, saw the emergence of exactly the kind of disease that the eradicationists had promised would never come again: virulent, incurable, global.

In June 1981, the US Centers for Disease and Control Prevention's *Morbidity and Mortality Weekly Report* published the first ever article about a novel immunological condition which had afflicted five gay men in Los Angeles. Doctors were baffled by an unprecedented cluster of cases of Kaposi's sarcoma, a form of cancer so rare that it usually affected only two in three million Americans. In a subsequent article, the CDC story's co-author Michael S. Gottlieb termed it Gay-Related Immune Deficiency (GRID). In July 1982, it was renamed Acquired Immune Deficiency Syndrome (AIDS).

The Jeremiah of AIDS in America was Larry Kramer, a playwright, novelist, Oscar-nominated screenwriter and production executive who had worked on movies, including *Dr. Strangelove.* He went on to co-found Gay Men's Health Crisis and ACT UP and dramatize his activism in his hit play *The Normal Heart.* His abrasive, two-fisted style made him as controversial as he was vital ('Nobody can alienate people quicker, better, or more completely,' said his former lover Rodger McFarlane), but his rage and terror were unignorable. First published in the gay newspaper *New York Native*, Kramer's sensational 1983 tirade, '1,112 and Counting', became perhaps the most widely reprinted article in the history of the gay press. 'If this article doesn't scare the shit out of you, we're in real trouble,' he began. 'If this article doesn't rouse you to anger, fury, rage, and action, gay men may have no future on this earth . . . In all the history of homosexuality we have never before been so close to death and extinction.' Tony Kushner, author of *Angels in America*, recalled, 'With that one piece, Larry changed my world. He changed the world for all of us.'

Early coverage of the disease was complicated by the fact that homosexuality itself was still widely regarded as a shameful illness. The fundamentalist Tim LaHaye called it an 'epidemic' and claimed that 'many Bible scholars think one of the major signs that brought on the Flood was homosexuality.' Already a pariah on the gay scene due to his waspish social satire *Faggots*, Kramer was therefore accused of mirroring the puritanical oratory of the preachers at a time when gay men were being ostracized and physically assaulted. One *New York Native* reader with AIDS protested, '*We are not* under the threat of extinction and to say so I regard as another expression of the very feeling of being victims Larry Kramer tries to tell us to get rid of.'

Kramer knew that many newly liberated gay men saw advice to abstain from sex as tantamount to a return to the closet but, he insisted, it was existentially necessary. And the only way to fight ignorance, prejudice and political and medical neglect was to make as loud a noise as possible: 'I am sick of everyone in this community who tells me to stop creating a panic. How many of us have to die before you get scared off your ass and into action?' He called AIDS a genocide and a holocaust. In New York City, the epicentre of the

US epidemic, the decimation of the gay community invited dramatic metaphors. In 1988, the year that he was diagnosed with AIDS, the artist Keith Haring collaborated with William S. Burroughs on a feverish book called *Apocalypse.* Having learned the Book of Revelation at his grandmother's knee, the poet Mark Doty reflected that he had been living with it all his life: 'One sort of apocalyptic scenario has replaced another: endings ecological or nuclear, scenarios of depleted ozone or global starvation or, finally, epidemic . . . Apocalypse is played out now on a personal scale; it is not in the sky above us but in our bed.' In an essay for *Time*, Lance Morrow suggested that 'AIDS suits the style of the late 20th century. In possibly overheated fears, it becomes a death-dealing absolute loose in the world. Westerners for some years have consolidated their dreads . . . in the Bomb, in the one overriding horror of nuclear holocaust . . . Now comes another agent of doomsday, this one actually killing people.'

The retrovirus that causes AIDS, dismantling the immune system and opening the door to a legion of opportunistic diseases, was discovered in 1983 and named Human Immunodeficiency Virus (HIV) three years later. As if giving it an award, one scientist called it 'the disease of the century'. Confusing messaging about the nature of the virus fostered the myth that it could be transmitted by coughing or by touching an infected surface, creating what journalist Randy Shilts called 'an epidemic of fear', and not the prophylactic variety that Kramer had hoped to inspire. 'Irrational fear, paranoia and apocalyptic statements have abounded,' wrote *Time*'s Claudia Wallis in 1985. Rumours in the gay and Black communities that AIDS had been developed by the US government, like Captain Trips, were finessed to great effect by Soviet intelligence into the conspiracy theory that it had escaped from a germ warfare laboratory at Fort Detrick.* In another version of the story, the virus had been let loose in Africa as a population-control mechanism and had rebounded on its creators. The *New York Native* pushed the absurd

*The KGB's mischief-making had dire unintended consequences. Thabo Mbeki, South Africa's president from 1999 to 2008, cited the Fort Detrick story to support his calamitous belief that AIDS was not caused by HIV. Mbeki's denialism has been blamed for the preventable deaths of around 350,000 South Africans.

theory that AIDS had been caused by a CIA attempt to use swine flu to wipe out agriculture in Cuba. Another story held that it had been distributed in polio vaccines. The British astronomer Sir Fred Hoyle argued, instead, that it came from outer space, brought to Earth by a disintegrating comet. The Cold War historian Douglas Selvage has observed that conspiracy theories 'multiply, spread and recombine like viruses'.

As long as it was associated with gay men and Africans, AIDS appeared to be officially ignorable. By 1987, though, when it became the first infectious disease to be debated on the floor of the UN, President Reagan was finally compelled to deliver a speech about it and announce a Presidential Commission on the HIV Epidemic. The stakes of AIDS coverage escalated dramatically, leaping from complacency to hyperbole. The US secretary of health and human services predicted that the pandemic would eventually make the Black Death 'pale by comparison'. Stephen Jay Gould guessed that AIDS could kill up to a quarter of humanity by the year 2000, calling it 'an issue that may rank with nuclear weaponry as the greatest danger of our era' and, 'potentially, the greatest natural tragedy in human history'.

The conservative writer William F. Buckley's proposal to forcibly tattoo people who had AIDS was the most loathsome example of the conflation of sufferers with carriers and victims with killers. It is no coincidence that Gaetan Dugas, the man unfairly identified by Randy Shilts as AIDS' Patient Zero, was a steward for Air Canada. The late Dugas became the jet-age Typhoid Mary, a sociopathic superspreader who embodied both reckless promiscuity and the perils of an interconnected world, blithely transporting the virus from city to city. 'Life slips into science fiction,' wrote Lance Morrow. 'People begin acting like characters in the first reel of *The Invasion of the Body Snatchers*. They peer intently at one another as if to detect the telltale change, the secret lesion, the sign that someone has crossed over, is not himself anymore, but one of them, alien and lethal.' Andrew Holleran, who called his collection of articles about gay life in New York City during the AIDS epidemic *Ground Zero*, thought that 'We Are the World', 1985's all-star charity record, seemed 'less like a hymn to brotherhood now than a sentence of bacterial doom'.

AIDS has now killed an estimated forty million people but antiretroviral therapy can enable people with HIV to live for a long time. Even in the 1980s, HIV was not always a death sentence: Larry Kramer died in 2020, at the age of eighty-four. But nobody knew then how it would end. While Holleran was sitting at the hospital bedside of a friend with AIDS one day, he came across a copy of *Kalki* by Gore Vidal. '*Kalki* is, I think, about the end of the world . . . It feels, sitting here, as if this is the end of everything: a culture with infinitely subtle and complex technology made useless by something so primitive it is a question whether or not a virus constitutes Life.' In his magazine columns, Holleran auditioned numerous precedents and metaphors: not just the Black Death but Paris during the Terror, Germany in the 1930s, the lava-death of Herculaneum, the meltdown at Chernobyl and the fall of Rome. In 'Reading and Writing', he wondered whether the First World War or the Spanish flu would be the better analogy. To think of writing about AIDS in terms of morale-boosting wartime propaganda was more useful, because wars have causes, meanings and lessons, but, he concluded, misleading: 'It was so unfair that it belonged to that category of events – earthquakes, droughts, tidal waves, volcanic eruptions – that simply happen and that engender in those who survive nothing more than a reminder of how unstable a planet this is.'

By the end of the 1980s, when AIDS had killed more Americans than the Vietnam War, virologists could not agree on whether it was a hideous anomaly or the shape of things to come.

On 1 May 1989, the Nobel Prize-winning geneticist Joshua Lederberg and a young virologist named Stephen Morse opened a conference in Washington DC called Emerging Viruses: The Evolution of Viruses and Viral Diseases. Morse defined an emerging virus as one that appears suddenly and increases rapidly. Most are zoonotic, lying dormant in animals such as chickens and bats for decades or centuries before crossing the species barrier to humans, as AIDS, Ebola and Marburg virus all did in the area around Africa's Lake Victoria. Climate change, travel and the encroachment of roads, farms and buildings into former wildlands all make viruses more mobile by bringing humans into contact with infected animals for the first time.* The conference called for new systems to identify emerging viruses and design public-health strategies. Asked in 2021 why coronaviruses were absent from both the conference and his subsequent book, Morse replied that the omission proved his point: 'Most emerging viruses are surprises.'

When Pierre Ouellette began delineating a fictional pathogen in his novel *The Third Pandemic* in early 1994, he noted, 'the threat of emerging infectious diseases was still far from the public mind. The exotic viruses that now routinely sweep across newsprint and TV screens were still safely tucked away in remote parts of the third world.' That year was the turning point, with unexpected outbreaks of pneumonic plague in India, Ebola in Cote d'Ivoire and cholera in Zaire (now the Democratic Republic of Congo). Of these, the most horrifying was Ebola: though not very communicable, it had grotesque symptoms and a fatality rate of up to 90 per cent. The medical community was developing a new humility about how few of the world's viruses and bacteria had been identified. 'That humanity had grossly underestimated the microbes was no longer ... a matter of doubt,' wrote Laurie Garrett in *The Coming Plague*, her 1994 book about the end of epidemiology's age of optimism and the possibility of a species-threatening pandemic. 'The microbes were winning.'

Another 1994 bestseller, Richard Preston's *The Hot Zone*, drew attention to filoviruses, a family of thread-like viruses, including Ebola and Marburg, which cause haemorrhagic fever. Stephen King called the first chapter, about the gruesome death of a French naturalist pseudonymized as Charles Monet, 'one of the most horrifying things I've read in my whole life', but the book reads rather too much like a thriller. Describing only the worst-case scenarios, Preston compares Monet to a bomb, an automaton and a zombie: 'It could be said that the *who* of Charles Monet has already died, while the *what* of Charles Monet continues to live.' Even Karl Johnson, the virologist who identified Ebola in 1976, sounds movie-

* This is neatly illustrated at the end of *Contagion*: the woman who brought the virus to the US works for the company whose deforestation displaced the bat that infected the pig that infected the chef who infected her.

addled in Preston's company: 'I did figure that if Ebola was the Andromeda strain – incredibly lethal and spread by droplet infection – there wasn't going to be any safe space in the world anyway.' Preston took his epigraph from Revelation 16:3, in which the second angel turns the sea to blood. Epidemiologists reluctantly accepted such apocalyptic melodrama as the price of getting the public's attention.

Due to Ebola and AIDS, the jungles and caves of Africa temporarily replaced China in the Western imagination as the cradle of microscopic assassins, producing a new set of racialized assumptions and the implication that diseases had no business coming to the US and Europe. *The Sunday Telegraph* described Ebola as one of many 'savage African diseases . . . ready to break out anywhere at any moment'. Tom Clancy immediately turned Ebola into a terrorist's bioweapon in his Jack Ryan thriller *Executive Orders*, while the 1995 movie *Outbreak* (loosely based on *The Hot Zone*) featured a fictional super-Ebola called Motaba and an epigraph from Joshua Lederberg: 'The single biggest threat to man's continued dominance on the planet is the virus.' Reviewing *Outbreak* for *The New Yorker*, Terence Rafferty remarked, 'Something was bound to succeed the bomb as the ultimate terror generator in big-budget thrillers, and the virus is the strongest, most charismatic candidate to come along in years.' As if to prove the point that very same year, *12 Monkeys*, Terry Gilliam's remake of Chris Marker's 1962 film *La Jetée*, replaced the nuclear war in Marker's story with a pandemic.

As George Stewart had predicted in *Earth Abides*, viruses came to represent the dark side of air travel and international commerce. When *Earth Abides* was published in 1949, around two million people travelled on international commercial air flights; at its pre-Covid peak, the figure was four and a half billion. Airports are hubs of anxiety in many pandemic movies, where a departure board comes to resemble a kill list. During the end credits of 2011's *Rise of the Planet of the Apes*, for example, a single infected pilot sets off a global pandemic and an electronic map of flight routes doubles as a diagram of the virus's spread, spidering its way around the world. Shortly after 9/11, a George W. Bush administration official compared terrorism to 'a terrible, lethal virus . . . Like a virus, international terrorism respects no boundaries.' Both arrived on aeroplanes.

In 2003, an outbreak of the coronavirus SARS became what *The Observer* called 'the millennium's first jetset disease'. As a story, SARS felt ultra-modern: a new disease spread by passenger jets and international hubs. The epidemic began in China's Guangdong province but the government covered it up for several months. A doctor who had treated sufferers in Guangzhou flew to Hong Kong for a family wedding on 21 February 2003 and stayed at the Metropole hotel, where he infected twenty-three guests. One of them, a flight attendant, carried the virus to Singapore and infected around 100 people. Over the next four months, SARS infected people in twenty-nine countries on six continents and killed 774, including Carlo Urbani, the WHO microbiologist who first investigated the virus. As WHO scientists put it, 'A global outbreak was thus seeded from a single person on a single day on a single floor of a Hong Kong hotel.'

In Canada, where forty-four people died, one epidemiologist had a nightmare that 'Toronto and Kingston had been consumed by SARS and were desolate.' The global panic, however, was vastly disproportionate to the death toll and became a kind of virus in its own right. Horrified by the way in which China's secrecy had enabled the spread of 'fear, speculation and rumor' on the internet, David J. Rothkopf in *The Washington Post* coined the word *infodemic*: 'In virtually every respect [infodemics] behave just like any other disease, with an epidemiology all their own, identifiable symptoms, well-known carriers, even straightforward cures.' A character in *Station Eleven* initially thinks that the menace of the (fictional) Georgia flu is similarly overblown: 'It'll be like SARS. They made such a big deal about it, then it blew over so fast.'

One spectre that did not materialize was bioterrorism, with the notable exception of the anthrax-laced letters sent to politicians and media organizations after 9/11, seemingly by a troubled scientist at Fort Detrick. The sequencing of the genome of the 1918 influenza virus in 2005 spooked Bill Joy and Ray Kurzweil into calling for 'a new Manhattan Project to develop specific defences against new biological viral threats', but it turned out that the Clinton and Bush administrations had in fact spent too much on combating bioterrorism and not enough on preparing for naturally occurring pandemics. For members of the White House Biodefense Directorate, weaponized smallpox was far more exciting than the flu. Only when Bush was handed a copy of *The Great Influenza*, John Barry's bestseller about the Spanish flu, did he commission a new pandemic plan. Perhaps as a result of the waning of bioterrorism as a pressing danger, movies have pivoted from bad actors, like the 'apocalypse nut' in *12 Monkeys*, to the hellish results of good intentions. In *I Am Legend* and *Rise of the Planet of the Apes*, lethal pathogens stem from noble attempts to create a cure for cancer and Alzheimer's respectively. As Francis Lawrence, the director of *I Am Legend*, put it, 'Accidents happen.'

New outbreaks produced new images, which migrated from the news to the movies. A 2001 epidemic of foot-and-mouth disease in British livestock gave us the black, smoking cattle pyres in *Children of Men.* SARS made blue surgical masks and checkpoint thermometers part of the furniture of *Contagion* and *I Am Legend.* When Terry Nation's *Survivors* was rebooted in 2008, *Radio Times* reckoned that SARS, the 2005 avian flu outbreak and antimicrobial resistant infections had made the premise 'even more credible now'. A year later, swine flu could be added to the list in time for season two.

Movies, in turn, led people to fear that a local catastrophe such as Ebola could become a global one simply because of its foreboding novelty. 'We're fascinated by epidemics,' said the public-health expert Philip Alcabes during the 2014 Ebola outbreak in West Africa. 'What we see on this side of the ocean is poor people dying, and doctors and health aides in space suits. It looks like the movies, and we've been prepped for a cinematic response.' The journal *Clinical Infectious Diseases* fretted in 2003 that 'the premise of epidemics involving unknown viruses of dubious origin that cause apocalyptic events serves to instil the public with fear, which may turn to panic when similar situations arise.'

Contagion, directed by Steven Soderbergh, came out after that article and took its responsibility more seriously. Using the tagline 'Nothing spreads like fear', the movie explores how difficult it is for public-health officials to find the golden mean between complacency and panic. Alan Krumwiede (Jude Law), a grifter, conspiracy theorist and one-man infodemic, exploits fear to promote his phoney remedy when he calls the MEV-1 virus 'Godzilla, King Kong and Frankenstein all in one'. Yet at the same time, the CDC investigator Erin Mears (Kate Winslet) butts heads with a bureaucrat who cites the false alarms over swine flu in 1976 and 2009 as a reason to delay a lockdown: 'All we did was get healthy people scared.'* The authors of a 2019 annual review of pandemic preparedness by the WHO and the World Bank complained, 'For too long, we have allowed a cycle of panic and neglect when it comes to pandemics.' Covid-19 does not appear to have broken that cycle. Many Republican politicians decided that the US government had over-reacted to the virus and they passed legislation to restrict measures designed to control a future pandemic. Their attitude seemed to be that, although more than one million Americans had died, it was not the end of the world.

During March 2020, a rash of tweets and graffiti claimed that humanity was the virus and Covid-19 was the vaccine. Whether the authors were referring to the sudden drop in carbon emissions from aeroplanes and cars or the actual deaths was unnervingly unclear. Richard Preston appeared to anticipate the latter view in a strikingly tasteless passage in *The Hot Zone*, anthropomorphizing the microbe as nature's revenge: 'The earth's immune system, so to speak, is seeing the presence of the human species and is starting to kick in. The earth is attempting to rid itself of an infection by the human parasite. Perhaps AIDS is the first step in a natural process of clearance.'

Alarm about overpopulation has a tendency to steer environmentalism in a sinister direction. 'Peaceful thought, isn't it?' says the counterfeit messiah's disciple in *Kalki*. 'No more pollution. No more hideous cities, slums, people.' In Dennis Kelly's 2013 TV show *Utopia*, a secret population-control project born in the 1970s leads to a monstrous conspiracy to produce a serum that will sterilize more than 90 per cent of people and smuggle it into a vaccine which claims to treat a bogus pandemic of Russian flu. (The show was an unwitting gift to real-life conspiracy theorists.) Kelly summed up the plotters' self-justifying longtermist logic: 'If I stop doing this,

*UK Health Secretary Matt Hancock's obsession with *Contagion* in 2020 reportedly played a part in the country's successful vaccine rollout. Ian Lipkin, the movie's chief scientific consultant, called it 'obviously quite gratifying'.

what's going to happen? What about the billions that live in the future?' The misanthropic bioengineer Crake in Margaret Atwood's 2003–13 *Maddaddam* trilogy also wants to save the world in his own way, by eliminating humans with a fatal virus concealed in a sex-aid pill called BlyssPlus: the perfect synthesis of sex and death. Scientists dub it JUVE: Jetspeed Ultra Virus Extraordinary. 'It travelled through the air as if on wings, it burned through cities like fire, spreading germ-ridden mobs, terror, and butchery. The lights were going out everywhere, the news was sporadic: systems were failing as their keepers died. It looked like total breakdown.' This is what most scares Crake's friend Jimmy: 'He might be immune from the virus . . . but not from the rage and despair of its carriers.'

It is almost axiomatic in plague narratives for terror to breed brutality. 'Those who don't die from the virus will die in the fighting,' says someone during the simian flu pandemic in 2014's *Dawn of the Planet of the Apes*, and the viewer is expected to take this as inevitable once the viral shit hits the fan. The truth is that people behave rather better in a pandemic than writers like to imagine. Boccaccio and Defoe both exaggerated the selfishness, cruelty and decadence of plague-stricken cities, with Defoe relegating 'many instances of immovable affection, pity, and duty' to a reluctant aside. The total moral collapse in *The Scarlet Plague* bears no resemblance to the cooperation that Jack London had observed after the San Francisco earthquake. Even in the scrupulously researched *Contagion*, symptoms include riots, looting and murder. There is a disinclination to believe that the centre could hold. Susan Sontag argued that the bias towards worst-case scenarios 'expresses an imaginative complicity with disaster. The sense of cultural distress or failure gives rise to the desire for a clean sweep, a tabula rasa. No one wants a plague, of course. But, yes, it would be a chance to begin again.'

Emily St John Mandel's *Station Eleven* is a humanist rebuke to such notions, which are embodied by a doomsday prophet: 'The flu, the great cleansing that we suffered twenty years ago, that flu was our flood'. The mortality rate of Georgia flu is north of 99 per cent: Noah numbers. For the paparazzo Jeevan, however, the scripture is pop culture: as the outbreak escalates he describes it as 'a horror movie that wouldn't end' and can't stop singing R.E.M.'s 'It's the End of the World as We Know It (And I Feel Fine)'. Another survivor recalls reading *The Passage*, Justin Cronin's 2010 novel about a pandemic of vampirism. A troupe of actors and musicians takes comfort in the thought that Shakespeare also lived in plague times and borrows a maxim from *Star Trek: Voyager*. 'Survival is insufficient.' Indeed, the whole book is named after a talismanic graphic novel about a depressed scientist exiled from Earth after an alien invasion. For Mandel's characters, art is both a priceless reminder of what is best about the world and a source of clairvoyant speculations about how it could fall apart. The story begins with the death of an actor during a performance of *King Lear*, whose words are later recited, in the TV version, by his best friend: 'The worst is not. So long as we can say "This is the worst."'

It turns out that the doomsday prophet was a teenager on Day One, one of seventy-nine people stranded in Severn City Airport, Michigan, when the planes stopped, and radicalized himself by reading the Book of Revelation after his Nintendo died. 'One day her plagues will overtake her,' he solemnly recites. 'Death, mourning, and famine.' To the prophet, the *Station Eleven* graphic novel is an argument to bury civilization all together ('There is no before') rather than to preserve its finest qualities. Another airport resident, Clark, goes the other way and curates a Museum of Civilization to remind people of things like laptops, radios, iPhones and passports: all these 'taken-for-granted miracles that had persisted all around them'. Where better than an airport to belatedly appreciate the extraordinary privilege of what was once modern life? *Station Eleven* is Mandel's own Museum of Civilization. In the crowded post-apocalyptic field, she is unusually concerned with what would be lost and which qualities might be somehow retained. Like David Brin and Pat Frank, she allows her post-collapse communities to collaborate and thrive instead of tearing themselves apart. 'Of course, one way to consider something is to write about its absence,' she explained, 'so I set the book largely in a damaged future in order to consider the modern world with some distance. It's a love letter in the form of a requiem.'

One of the airport survivors remarks that all the post-apocalyptic movies she had seen back when it was possible to see movies had involved zombies: 'I'm just saying, it could be much worse.' So many stories about species-threatening pandemics involve an ambulant plague that the phrase 'zombie apocalypse' has become a playful figure of speech: *how will you survive when the zombie apocalypse comes?* Max Brooks, author of 2003's *The Zombie Survival Guide* and 2006's *World War Z: An Oral History of the Zombie War*, has suggested that, like the disaster movies and post-apocalypses of the 1970s, zombie fiction provides a safe space to explore anxieties that cannot be faced head on, from terrorism to climate change to emerging diseases. 'It's safe to do something like a zombie walk – it isn't so fun to do a swine flu walk,' he said in 2013. 'If, at a party, you bring up how you'd survive a zombie attack, you'd be the life of the party. But if you say, "What would you do if super-AIDS came to America?" you'd clear the room.'

CHAPTER 17

Zombies

Jesus, it's everywhere.

Dawn of the Dead (1978)

A century ago, the zombie had nothing to do with infection. 'The zombie, they say, is a soulless human corpse, still dead, but taken from the grave and endowed by sorcery with a mechanical semblance of life – it is a dead body which is made to walk and act and move as if it were alive,' William Seabrook explained in *The Magic Island*, his 1929 account of his travels in Haiti. Seabrook, a keen student of the occult, was taken to see three 'zombies' working in a US-owned sugar plantation but concluded that they were 'nothing but poor ordinary demented human beings, idiots, forced to toil in the fields'. In Haitian folklore, zombies are victims rather than monsters – metaphors for an exploited underclass in a country scarred by slavery. The Haitian version of the living dead, controlled by a voodoo sorcerer, is the one that cinema-goers encountered in the Seabrook-inspired 1932 Bela Lugosi movie *White Zombie* and Jacques Tourneur's superior 1943 chiller *I Walked with a Zombie*, in which the victims are white women. Seabrook described zombies as automatons. As a quasi-human avatar of the uncanny, the zombie is the inverse of AI: a body without a mind rather than a mind without a body. Like *robot*, *zombie* came to mean somebody mindless and dull. 'They've spent their lives starving their imagination, just starving it to death. And now they're zombies,' a character says of the English upper classes in J. B. Priestley's 1946 novel *Bright Day*.

How the word attached itself to self-motivated corpses was rather random but the process began in 1954 with Richard Matheson's *I Am Legend.* Matheson didn't just revitalize the concept of the last man on earth; he reinvented the undead. While his 'living dead' are technically vampires – allergic to sunlight, garlic and stakes – they are not sleek and dynamic, like Dracula, but clumsy and slow. Nor are they foreign infiltrators; they used to be us. They are not even supernatural, because only bacterial infection can explain 'the fantastic rapidity of the plague, the geometrical mounting of victims', the hero Robert Neville discovers. Matheson claimed that he 'had a doctor check it and it all adds up scientifically – from a biological standpoint'. As the 1964 adaptation *The Last Man on Earth* makes clear, Matheson's vampires are to all intents and purposes zombies: shambling, almost brainless agents of death. As the accidental inventor of the modern zombie, Matheson forged an unbreakable link between that monster and the doom of the human race.

The young Pittsburgh-based director George A. Romero conceived his 1968 movie *Night of the Living Dead* as a kind of prequel to *I Am Legend.* 'Richard starts his book with one man left; everybody in the world has become a vampire,' Romero later told *Cinema Blend.* 'I said we got to start at the beginning and tweak it up a little bit. I couldn't use vampires because he did, so I wanted something that would be an earth-shaking change. Something that was forever, something that was really at the heart of it. I said, so what if the dead stop staying dead?' The mass resurrection that precedes the Last Judgement in Revelation is a horror premise waiting to happen: 'death and hell delivered up the dead which were in them.' Not for nothing does the 2004 remake of Romero's *Dawn of the Dead* open with 'The Man Comes Around', Johnny Cash's take on John of Patmos.

Like a settler putting his name on a frontier town, whoever pioneers a genre defines the tropes and sets the tone. As important as establishing some core zombie lore (run, aim for the head), *The Night of the Living Dead*'s legacy is its radical hopelessness. In what a news announcer calls 'an epidemic of mass murder', the undead lay siege to a Pennsylvanian farmhouse full of strangers divided by age, race, gender and simple antipathy. Most of the story is about their failure to band together against an existential threat. The sole survivor, Ben (Duane Jones), who is Black, is mistakenly shot dead by a militia of white vigilantes in the final frames, rendering the preceding bloodshed even more senseless. From a distance, both Ben and the vigilantes take each other for zombies.

In 1968, a year of riots and assassinations, Romero's chaotic violence and disunity, stripped bare of horror's usual titillations, was a stark provocation. In the movie's most indelible scene, a reanimated young girl stabs her mother to death with a trowel, her mouth caked with her father's blood. How's that for a generation gap? Even as the director's budgets and capabilities expanded somewhat, his estimation of human nature did not. While his sympathies were ostensibly liberal, his pessimism was conservative. His 1978 sequel *Dawn of the Dead* and 1985's *Day of the Dead* also feature citadels – a shopping mall, an army base – which break down due to their defenders' weaknesses. Romero established the capacity of zombie movies to satirize racism, sexism, consumerism, violence and the media. In his movies, which share many features with the collapse novel, there is no way back to a functioning society and nothing holds up under pressure: not capitalism, not science, not the military, not the family. As *The Times Literary Supplement* observed, *Dawn of the Dead* 'turns over the stone and lets the bugs of the 1970s crawl out'. In the novelization, an administration as untrusted as Richard Nixon's and even more economically troubled than Jimmy Carter's inspires zombie denial: 'With a presidential election coming up, most citizens felt this was just another ploy to get the country behind the administration candidate.'

The notion of distrust as a deadly contagion obsessed Rod Serling in the *Twilight Zone* episodes 'The Shelter' and 'The Monsters Are Due on Maple Street'. It is there, too, in zombie-adjacent movies such as *Invasion of the Body Snatchers* (1956), *The Birds* (1964), *The Thing* (1982) and *The Mist* (2007). 'People are basically good, decent,' protests Amanda (Laurie Holden) in *The Mist*, under siege from interdimensional monsters. 'My God, David, we're a civilized society.' David (Thomas Jane) demurs: 'Sure, as long as the machines are working and you can dial 911. But you take those things away, you throw people in the dark, you scare the shit out of them… no more rules. You'll see how primitive they get.' Sometimes the murderous paranoia is justified: in *The Thing*, based on a 1938 novella by *Astounding Science Fiction* editor John W. Campbell Jr, an alien parasite can assimilate and perfectly replicate any organism so that it is only identifiable by a blood test. The movie is a riot of the uncanny, made more terrifying by the implication that if the parasite were to escape from an Antarctic research facility, it could colonize the world. Director John Carpenter credited Ennio Morricone's mournful score with clarifying the story's ultimate logic: 'He realised it was the end of the world – it was an apocalyptic story – and I hadn't embraced that yet. He was there ahead of me.'*

Romero didn't realize that he was reinventing the zombie (in *The Night of the Living Dead*, the creatures are called 'flesh-eating ghouls') until the word began appearing in reviews of the 1970 re-release. 'People . . . called them zombies,' Romero recalled. 'I said, "Wow, maybe they are." To me, they were dead neighbors.' Although Romero used *zombie* numerous times in the screenplay for *Dawn of the Dead*, it was only spoken once in the movie, suggesting a certain ambivalence. As to their genesis, Matheson had medicalized the supernatural with his *vampiris* bacillus ('The germ that hid behind the obscuring veils of legend and superstition'), but Romero had minimal interest in explanations. In the first movie, the director attributes the return of the dead to Venusian radiation. In the second, a newsreader speculates about a viral cause and a possible vaccine but that is never confirmed. As Romero said, 'I want it to be unexplained . . . It just happens.' Remember that in the 1970s naturally emerging diseases were not a major concern, so writers favoured man-made contagions. In Romero's *The Crazies*, another quasi-zombie movie, the pathogen that causes homicidal mania is a bioweapon that has leaked into the water supply. In the post-Romero zombie movies *The Grapes of Death* and *Let Sleeping Corpses Lie*, the culprits are experimental pest-killers.

Whatever the cause, one could interpret zombies themselves as humanoid viruses: mindless, relentless, self-replicating, weak in isolation but overwhelming en masse. In 1952, William Laurence of *The New York Times* described viruses as if they were zombies: 'entities neither living nor dead that belonged to the twilight zone

* *The Thing* has often been read as a metaphor for AIDS but filming began in August 1981, just two months after the first CDC report on the disease, so that interpretation seems impossible, not to mention crass.

between the living and the nonliving'. Max Brooks said that he was most terrified by zombies' 'viral nature, their complete lack of intelligence. They're like a disease; no rationality, no middle ground, no negotiation, just sheer instinct to consume and multiply.' They bring death. They *are* death.

The scariest thing about zombies is their exponential growth, multiplying like time-lapse footage of bacteria swarming on a microscope slide. The virus in TV's zombie blockbuster *The Walking Dead* is literally called Wildfire. In a 2009 paper, four Canadian mathematicians modelled a zombie pandemic with impressive earnestness. Over time, they predicted a 'doomsday scenario: an outbreak of zombies will result in the collapse of civilization, with every human infected, or dead . . . Thus, if zombies arrive, we must act quickly and decisively to eradicate them before they eradicate us.' This uncontrollable spread explains why zombies lead inevitably to zombie apocalypse: panic rapidly followed by total disintegration. Most horror scenarios are localized – if you are confronted with a vampire, werewolf or shark, that's bad news for you but the rest of the world is fine – but zombies are global. The endpoint, as in *I Am Legend*, is the replacement of humanity.

During the 1980s, with *Return of the Living Dead*, *Evil Dead II* and Michael Jackson's 'Thriller' video, zombies ceased to be scary and became kitsch. They didn't get their bite back until the Japanese computer game *Biohazard* (better known as *Resident Evil*) debuted in 1996 and reintroduced the science of contagion: the zombies are produced by a leaked 'T-virus' which has been developed by a corporation for biowarfare. Computer games reveal that zombies make for an unusually empowering variant of pandemic fiction. You might not be able to design a cure or a vaccine but you can at least blow their heads off like there's no tomorrow. This makes the genre the acceptable face of survivalism. The unsavoury blurb on the trade paperbacks of Robert Kirkman's *The Walking Dead* comic books makes the zombie apocalypse sound morally improving: 'The world of commerce and frivolous necessity has been replaced by a world of survival and responsibility . . . In a world ruled by the dead, we are forced to finally start living.' Mark Spitz, the protagonist of Colson Whitehead's 2011 zombie novel *Zone One*, looks down on 'the biding cranks finally gifted with a perverted version of their long-awaited dream of liberation from humanity'.

Zombies offer a moral loophole which allows characters to massacre humanoid creatures guilt-free, provided they don't think too hard about who these ex-humans used to be, which is why the movies often resemble games. 'I think it's videogames that have really kept the creature alive, much more than films,' Romero said.

It was playing *Resident Evil* that reawakened the writer Alex Garland's interest in zombies and led him to pitch *28 Days Later* to the director Danny Boyle. Their 2002 movie is justly celebrated for the eerie, Covid-anticipating spectacle of Jim (Cillian Murphy) waking up from a coma and wandering through a London that is still and silent but for birds and wind-rustled garbage, but that was essentially a reworking of *The Day of the Triffids*. The movie's real innovation is the psychological virus Rage, an ultrapotent form of human anger produced by subjecting chimpanzees to endless footage of crowd violence, which is itself a form of contagion.

Zombies have become so overused that the writers of the *I Am Legend* movie and *The Last of Us* have taken pains to claim that their antagonists are something else, and the word is not even mentioned in *The Walking Dead*, but Garland was in the unusual position of disagreeing with his director and insisting that 'the infected' *are* zombies, even though Rage transforms its victims rather than killing them. 'I don't give a fuck about the sort of technical differences between the infected and the dead and whether they're reanimated corpses or not,' Garland said. But the difference surely matters because to destroy an 'infected' is to exterminate a living human being, however distorted. The movie's cynical thesis statement is crisply supplied by Major West (Christopher Eccleston): 'This is what I've seen in the four weeks since infection: people killing people. Which is much what I saw in the four weeks before infection, and the four weeks before that, and before that, as far back as I care to remember: people killing people. Which, to my mind, puts us in a state of normality right now.' When Jim discovers that West's garrison intends to murder him and keep his two female companions as sex slaves, he kills one soldier so brutally (eyeballs, thumbs) that he is mistaken for one of the fast-moving, blood-vomiting infected, his rage indistinguishable from Rage.

28 Days Later is so good at undermining apparent sanctuaries – a hospital, a church, a country house guarded by soldiers – that the happy ending feels like a con. Like the aliens felled by bacteria in *The War of the Worlds*, the infected simply starve to death within five weeks, enabling our three survivors to be rescued. *28 Weeks Later*, directed and co-written by Juan Carlos Fresnadillo with input from Boyle and Garland, reverts to the traditional hopelessness of the zombie apocalypse. A US-led NATO force has established a redoubt on London's Isle of Dogs, flying in Britons who were abroad at the time of the outbreak with a view to resettling the island. This plan falls apart due to the incredibly bad luck and poor decision-making of one family. A woman who was left for dead is found alive, infected but asymptomatic due to a genetic mutation. Back in the zone's medical facility, the potential key to a vaccine becomes instead the source of a new outbreak when she kisses her husband and turns him into patient zero. She resembles the asymptomatic carrier of the plague whom Defoe described as a 'walking destroyer' who might have 'ruined those that he would have hazarded his life to save, and had been breathing death upon them, even perhaps in his tender kissing and embracings of his own children'. All hell breaks loose. The final scene of the infected scrambling towards the Eiffel Tower suggests that the couple's children have inadvertently carried the virus to the continent and that all the heroic efforts to save their lives, and to restore Britain, were ruinous. In this movie, love and mercy are fatal.

The zombie movie is the most morally distressing horror genre because ruthlessness is a more justified response than pity. When Dr Rausch (Richard France) in *Dawn of the Dead* recommends nuking the zombies and mutters, 'We must remain rational . . . logical . . . logical,' he sounds strikingly similar to the nuclear strategist Herman Kahn. 'These creatures are nothing but pure motorized instinct,' he says. 'We must not be lulled by the concept that these are our family members or our friends. They are not. They will not respond to such emotions. They must be destroyed on sight!' If one of the most harrowing elements of the Black Death was the violation of rituals of burial and mourning, then how much worse it is to have to destroy a loved one's corpse before it reanimates or, worse, fight it once it does. Dealing with zombies is therefore inherently dehumanizing, transgressing basic taboos around the treatment of dead bodies. When the residents of housing blocks in *Dawn of the Dead* refuse to surrender their dead to the authorities because 'they still believe there's respect in dying', they all become infected and must be wiped out. By turning victims into incurable killers, zombie stories justify the kind of callous self-preservation that dismayed Boccaccio and Defoe. Rausch's annihilation strategy may be chilling but it is not wrong. One has to commit, as Kahn might have put it, to megadeath.

A greater moral crisis arises when it becomes impossible to separate the healthy from the infected. In *28 Weeks Later*, the NATO force initiates Code Red: an attempt at containment followed by eradication. At first, snipers are ordered to shoot only the infected but very soon they are instructed to slaughter anything that moves: people killing people. Outside the zone, the streets of London are firebombed and gassed to halt the spread. As an almost unwatchably terrifying sequence of the infection spreading in a dark, enclosed space illustrates, the second contagion is panic, leading to war crimes.

The possibility of rebuilding society after a catastrophe, better than before, is essential to the human spirit. The total failure of reconstruction in *28 Weeks Later* is therefore heretically depressing, reframing the horrors of Boyle's movie as merely a dress rehearsal. Something similar unfolds in Colson Whitehead's *Zone One*. Having survived the horrors of 'Last Night' and the months that followed, Mark Spitz works for American Phoenix, a project to sweep New York clean of stray zombies and make it the symbolic cornerstone of American revival. Concepts such as government and nationhood are back and apocalypse is in remission. But when the wall breaks and the creatures roll over Manhattan like a tsunami, Spitz realizes that what we thought was the aftermath was really an interregnum. Like one of J. G. Ballard's implacable climatic transformations, the ocean of the undead demonstrates the unmendable condition of a broken realm:

> Why they'd tried to fix this island in the first place, he did not see now. Best to let the broken glass be broken glass, let it splinter into smaller pieces and dust and scatter. Let the cracks between things widen until they are no longer cracks but the new places for things. That was where they were now. The world wasn't ending: it had ended and now they were in the new place. They could not recognize it because they had never seen it before.

—

The early twenty-first century has seen a global pandemic of zombie movies, from the US and UK to South Korea, India, Argentina and Japan. Metaphors pile up like bodies. The Iraq war provides the backdrop to 2007's *Planet Terror* and the 2010 remake of *The Crazies*. *28 Weeks Later* and *Zone One* function as allegories for the breakdown of a post-war reconstruction effort, orchestrated from a militarized 'safe' zone, in the face of a guerrilla insurgency. Whitehead also invokes global warming when he compares the zombie swarm to a computer simulation of rising sea levels drowning Manhattan: 'Except it was not water that flooded the grid but the dead.' In a 2011 essay for *Slate*, meanwhile, Torie Bosch read zombiemania as a response to the financial crisis: 'Should the economy recover, I suspect that we will abandon zombies as entertainment. The zombie boom will be a reminder of the frightening uncertainties of this decade.' But this is classic chronocentrism. Zombie trends have also been related to avian flu and SARS, and the genre outlasted them, too. In 2013, Max Brooks listed '9/11, Iraq, Afghanistan, Katrina, anthrax letters, D.C. sniper, global warming, global financial meltdown, bird flu, swine flu, SARS' as reasons to be fearful in the twenty-first century, but one could update that list today without changing his point. Zombies are where fear lives.

Zombie movies are a great entry-level genre because a director can make them on a shoestring budget as long as they have enough friends willing to stagger around in pancake make-up. Romero used a farmhouse, mall and military base as microcosms of a worldwide crisis, deploying TV broadcasts to explain what was happening in the rest of the world. Inspired by Matheson's conceit that 'this particular plague involved the entire planet', Romero needed viewers to understand that this was happening everywhere even if he couldn't afford to show it, just as the avian plague isn't confined to Bodega Bay in Alfred Hitchcock's *The Birds*. ('It's the end of the world!' cries Hitchcock's soused doomsayer, slurring lines from Ezekiel 6.*) As the inferior 2013 movie adaptation of

* In Margaret Atwood's *Oryx and Crake*, the survivor Jimmy takes comfort in watching *Night of the Living Dead* and *The Birds*: 'Such minor paranoias were soothing to him.' *The Birds* is also glimpsed in passing in *12 Monkeys*.

Max Brooks's *World War Z* demonstrates, there are insuperable narrative and budgetary obstacles to making a truly international movie, with dozens of protagonists and locations, but the casts and settings of novels can be limitless. *World War Z* is the most successful attempt to represent a pandemic in full, with a historian collecting oral testimonies from around the world, and thus the pinnacle of post-Romero zombie fiction.

In 2003, Brooks published *The Zombie Guide to Survival*, a deadpan handbook for a world in which zombies have existed for millennia due to a virus called Solanum. It could have been a one-joke book but Brooks was too jittery a writer to be glib. One of his inspirations was the AIDS pandemic: 'I watched this horrible virus just murder millions of people, and our government did nothing initially,' he told *The New York Times*. It was while his mother, the actress Anne Bancroft, was dying from cancer that he wrote his novel about a war against a disease. In the *Guide*, Brooks nodded to post-Hiroshima international disarmament efforts such as *One World or None*: 'The time has come to set aside our artificial boundaries and unite against the common threat of extinction . . . The living dead threaten us as one world and only as one world can we survive.' The global remit of *World War Z* is summed up by three names in the acknowledgements: George Romero, of course; Studs Terkel, the oral historian; and General Sir John Hackett, whose 1978 book *The Third World War* is a military veteran's account of a war that never happened. 'What happens in a zombie plague is pretty much what happens in any real disaster,' Brooks explained. 'Pandemics, hurricanes, conventional wars, you name it, the human reaction is the same. For me, the zombies are just the catalyst of looking at how humanity deals with calamity.'

Zooming out from the fate of a few individuals to that of the entire species, Brooks unpacks every aspect of 'The Great Panic': psychological (a wasting condition called Apocalypse Despair Syndrome), climatic (the proliferation of fires ushers in a nuclear autumn), medical ('Imagine if the undead virus had been understood as, say, tuberculosis was'), military (how to fight an enemy with no need for supplies or morale) and geopolitical. Local factors such as the secrecy of the Chinese government or the siege mentality of Israel dictate the course of the pandemic. The Redeker Plan, the

South African strategy to decide who to save and who to sacrifice, is designed by a veteran of the apartheid regime. In the US, an effective response is delayed by something akin to climate denial. 'We got dozens of these reports a week, every administration did, all of them claiming that their particular boogeyman was "the greatest threat to human existence,"' complains the former White House chief of staff. 'C'mon! Can you imagine what America would have been like if the federal government slammed on the brakes every time some paranoid crackpot cried "wolf" or "global warming" or "living dead"? Please . . . The more those elitist eggheads shouted "The Dead Are Walking," the more most real Americans tuned them out.' As an Israeli strategist observes, 'Most people don't believe something can happen until it already has. That's not stupidity or weakness, that's just human nature.'

Looking back in 2010, George Romero reflected that his career-long interest in zombies was really about how people respond to a catastrophe that upends the status quo: 'I don't like these rage zombies or virus zombies. My stories have always been people stories, the zombies are an annoyance. It's all about people, how they address the situation, or fail to address it.' Stories about plagues and zombies deal with the challenges of human interaction when all the guard-rails are down. 'We need each other,' says Sarah (Lori Cardille) in *Day of the Dead*. 'Can't we just get along?' In *28 Days Later* and the Romero movies, the answer is no: besieged survivors turn on one another. It is usually only in comedies such as *Zombieland* and *Shaun of the Dead* that people put aside their differences. *The Walking Dead* had no case to make about the fragility of human association, merely seasons to fill. Too lucrative to die, it twisted the fugitive momentum of the post-apocalypse into a Sisyphean loop of the formation and fragmentation of communities: flight, refuge, flight, refuge . . . Only *World War Z* has the narrative scope to explore the full human panorama of heroism and cowardice, coordination and chaos, hope and despair. Brooks comes across as a doughty pragmatist who believes that leadership, strategy and cooperation can make the difference between catastrophe and extinction, even if the overall picture is far from cheering. 'I won't last long in the apocalypse, so it's nice to read about people who are more capable,' testified *World War Z* fan Colson Whitehead.

It sometimes seems as if the interpretation of disease in fiction never really escaped its ancient, pre-Hippocratic roots as divine punishment. Mary Shelley and Emily St John Mandel are unusual in presenting their characters as blameless victims of a natural tragedy. In *Day of the Dead*, John (Terry Alexander) implies that humanity is being rebuked for splitting the atom: 'Maybe He didn't want to see us blow ourselves up, put a big hole in His sky.' Global warming is the reason why *Cordyceps* is finally able to thrive inside human hosts in *The Last of Us*, while *Walking Dead* showrunner Scott M. Gimple has suggested that 'the walker apocalypse is the revenge of planet Earth' – a secular version of God's wrath.

People have always needed a plague to mean something, even if what it means is that we were asking for it. In *Zone One*, Mark Spitz complains about the 'apocalypse-as-moral-hygiene people' who speak in terms of sin and retribution: 'The human race deserved the plague, we brought it on ourselves for poisoning the planet, for the Death of God, the calculated brutalities of the global economic system, for driving primordial species to extinction: the entire collapse of values as evidenced by everything from nuclear fission to reality television to alternate side of the street parking.' He tunes out their harangues: 'It was boring. The plague was the plague.'

PART SEVEN
CLIMATE

CHAPTER 18

Too Hot

No one thinks it will ever happen to them
until suddenly they are in the thick of it,
thoroughly surprised to be there.

Kim Stanley Robinson, *Fifty Degrees Below* (2005)

One chilly evening in March 2022, I went to a community hall in Eastbourne, on the south coast of England, to hear about the end of the world as we know it.

Roger Hallam, a sociologist, former organic farmer and co-founder of the environmentalist movement Extinction Rebellion, was recruiting activists for a new campaign of nonviolent protest called Just Stop Oil. A lean and silvery fifty-five-year-old with a goatee and ponytail, he appeared to have been woven from high-tensile wire. For a full hour, he built the latest warnings from climate scientists into a harrowing, panoramic picture of what global warming was going to do to us all. 'Mass slaughter, mass rape, mass starvation,' he said theatrically. 'That's what's coming down the line.' Raised as a Methodist, Hallam possessed the seething energy of a doomsday prophet, only his mission was to forestall catastrophe rather than welcome it. 'People are suddenly going, "This is it. This is the end,"' he said. 'Because it is. There are ends. And it will happen unless we stop it.' Hallam has been accused of reckless exaggeration and lurid scaremongering – hope, insist behavioural scientists, is a far more effective motivator than fear – but his hair-raising style works for some. Afterwards, I spoke to a young activist who had joined Just Stop Oil because she was terrified of the future. She described 'this feeling that you're going crazy and there's a ticking timebomb to the end of the world'.

Hallam and his colleagues launched Extinction Rebellion in October 2018, during a period that felt like a watershed for awareness of the climate crisis. Following the four warmest years on record, the United Nations' Intergovernmental Panel on Climate Change (IPCC) published what became known as the 'Doomsday Report', which outlined the consequences of average temperatures exceeding 1.5 degrees higher than the 1880 baseline and called for global mobilization on the same scale as the Second World War. The Stockholm schoolgirl Greta Thunberg began protesting outside the Swedish parliament every Friday. America's nascent Sunrise Movement occupied the office of House Speaker Nancy Pelosi to demand a Green New Deal. Prime Minister Theresa May pledged the UK to net zero carbon emissions by 2050. In record numbers, Americans told pollsters that they were concerned about global warming.

For many people, it was the end of denial – not intellectual denial that human-made climate change is real but emotional denial of the implications. Suddenly, people were thinking the unthinkable. 'If you're younger than sixty,' wrote Jonathan Franzen in a *New Yorker* essay called 'What If We Stopped Pretending?', 'you have a good chance of witnessing the radical destabilization of life on earth – massive crop failures, apocalyptic fires, imploding economies, epic flooding, hundreds of millions of refugees fleeing regions made uninhabitable by extreme heat or permanent drought. If you're under thirty, you're all but guaranteed to witness it.' Tamara Lindeman, a Canadian singer-songwriter who records as the Weather Station, began writing an album about 'climate grief' called *Ignorance.* In the song 'Loss', she quotes something an activist told her: 'At some point you'd have to live as if the truth was true.'

In 2019, the *New York Times* writer David Wallace-Wells published *The Uninhabitable Earth: A Story of the Future*, a relentless downer masterpiece on a par with Jonathan Schell's *The Fate of the Earth.* He collated all the bad news about a warmer planet in a way that was designed to be overwhelming, even crushing: droughts, heatwaves, hurricanes and floods; acidified oceans and bleached coral reefs; food shortages and new diseases; economic stagnation, war and tens of millions of refugees; the biodiversity crisis that some have called the sixth mass extinction. Unless positive feedback produces a runaway greenhouse effect, as happened on Venus, climate change won't kill every last person on earth, nor cause an unrecoverable global collapse, but the considerable middle ground between the present day and extinction is depressing enough to contemplate, pointing to a world that is harder, meaner and more scared. As *Children of Men* director Alfonso Cuarón put it, 'Look, what is at stake is not the world . . . There would be, still, pockets of populations that will scatter around the world. What is at stake is the culture as we know it.'

There has always been an apocalyptic strain in environmentalism. 'If current trends are allowed to persist,' predicted *The Ecologist* fifty-two years before Hallam's talk, 'the breakdown of society and the irreversible disruption of the life-support systems on this planet, possibly by the end of the century, certainly within the lifetimes of our children, are inevitable.' Also in 1970, Gordon Rattray Taylor published *The Doomsday Book: Can the World Survive?* The environmentalist Barry Commoner conceded that 'ecologists are sometimes suspected of escalating an admittedly bad situation into a catastrophic one – by claiming that environmental deterioration is not merely a threat to the quality of life, but to life itself, that the very survival of human beings on the earth is at stake. Even a "numbers game" has evolved: "How long," people want to know, "do we have to live?"'

Such rhetoric has been mainstreamed in recent years by Extinction Rebellion and Greta Thunberg. 'I don't want you to be hopeful,' she told world leaders in 2019. 'I want you to panic. I want you to feel the fear I feel every day. And then I want you to act.' Books such as Roy Scranton's *We're Doomed. Now What?* invite ripostes like Michael Shellenberger's *Apocalypse Never: Why Environmental Alarmism Hurts Us All.* The Thwaites Glacier, a chunk of Antarctic ice the size of Great Britain, is nicknamed the Doomsday Glacier because when the warm water that is eating away at it eventually causes it to calve into the ocean, it will raise sea levels by several metres. The Svalbard Global Seed Vault, opened in 2008, is known as the Doomsday Vault. Is this language hyperbolic or accurate? Does it inspire urgency or, conversely, the apathy that comes from feeling that nothing can be done? And if not this, then what magical combination of words *will* make a difference? For activists, the situation recalls the failure of arms control in 1946–7. Talk of tipping points and last chances can animate public opinion around a UN climate-change conference but once the deadline has passed, the chance has been missed, and the sky hasn't fallen in, people are likely to experience Robert Jay Lifton's immobilizing trifecta of 'resignation, cynicism and yearning'.

Most of the catastrophic events in this book have not happened, from the Christian Millennium to thermonuclear war and Y2K meltdown, but climate change *is* happening, one way or another, right now. During 2023, earlier than expected, global warming hit 1.48 degrees Celsius. July 2023 was the hottest month on earth since records began in 1880, and probably the hottest in 125,000 years, generating punishing heatwaves and hellish wildfires from Hawaii to Xinjiang. As the years go by, this is unlikely to be abnormal. We have not yet learned how to talk about the implications. In his book, Wallace-Wells wonders how a culture so saturated in visions of the end could suffer such a colossal failure of imagination and proposes a theory: it is precisely because of this numbing apocalyptic overload that solid evidence of a genuine catastrophe seems somewhat unreal. As he wrote, 'We have for so long, over decades if not centuries, defined predictions of the collapse of civilization or the end of the world as something close to proof of insanity, and the communities that spring up around them as "cults," that we are now left unable to take any warnings of disaster all that seriously.'

In 2000, the atmospheric scientist Paul J. Crutzen (one of the pioneers of nuclear winter theory) and biologist Eugene F. Stoermer argued that humankind had become a geological force, leaving an indelible mark on everything, from the ocean floor to the ozone layer, and that the Holocene epoch, which began around 11,700 years ago, after the last ice age, had therefore given way to what they called the Anthropocene. The concept has still not been officially recognized, nor has its span been agreed. Did it begin as far back as the Neolithic period, when hunter-gatherers became farmers, or as recently as the 1950s, when H-bomb tests left a radioactive signature that could still be read billions of years from now, or, as Crutzen and Stoermer proposed, in the late eighteenth century, when James Watt sold his first steam engines and the world became hooked on fossil fuels? In that case, the Anthropocene was upon us shortly before Mary Shelley and Lord Byron were born and it is what the Swedish physicist and chemist Svante Arrhenius was describing when, in 1896, he discovered global warming.

In the 1820s, Joseph Fourier had realized that the earth's atmosphere retained some of the Sun's infrared radiation, much like a greenhouse. In the 1850s, Eunice Foote and William Tyndall had separately identified carbon dioxide and water vapour as gases that made the planet habitably warm.* Now, after months of laborious computations, harvesting of temperature data, consultations with colleagues and marriage-ruining fourteen-hour days, Arrhenius computed that a doubling of atmospheric carbon dioxide from its pre-industrial level by the burning of fossil fuels – 560 parts per million instead of 280 – would raise the earth's temperature by around five degrees Celsius: the basic principle of what we now call the greenhouse effect. (As of May 2023, the figure is 424 ppm.)

Arrhenius's hypothesis was the world's first climate model, but it did not perturb him because he thought that this doubling would take up to three thousand years. The global population was fewer than two billion people, most of whom did not live in industrialized societies. For the foreseeable future, it seemed to him from frosty Sweden, warming would be rather pleasant. At any rate, he was less interested in the future than the past: his calculations were motivated by the grand prize of a coherent explanation for previous ice ages. The newspapers covered Arrhenius's eye-catching theory about life on Venus but practically ignored his study of carbon dioxide. Only one paragraph-long syndicated news story, from 1902, reported that he had 'evolved a new theory of the extinction of the human race . . . the combustion of coal by civilized man is gradually warming the atmosphere so that in the course of a few cycles of 10,000 years the earth will be baked in a temperature close to boiling point.'

Despite Arrhenius's stature (he won the Nobel Prize for Chemistry in 1903), most scientists believed that he was entirely wrong, because

*Other greenhouse gases include methane, nitrous oxide and chlorofluorocarbons (CFCs).

carbon dioxide would be absorbed by the oceans rather than accumulating in the atmosphere. In 1938, a British engineer called Guy Stewart Callendar told the Royal Meteorological Society that anthropogenic carbon dioxide had *already* raised the global temperature by about one-third of a degree. But like Arrhenius, he thought that this would benefit humanity by making more land cultivable and forestalling another ice age; like Arrhenius, he was given the cold shoulder. The consensus view was expressed by George Clarke Simpson, director of the Meteorological Office: it was 'now generally accepted that variations in carbon-dioxide in the atmosphere, even if they do occur, can have no appreciable effect on the climate'.

The study of atmospheric carbon dioxide was an unexpected beneficiary of the Cold War. Satellites designed for military purposes became goldmines of climate data while curious scientists were able to use newly designed computers and funding from the navy to parse its significance. In May 1953, the Associated Press reported on the computer-assisted findings of Gilbert Plass, a Canadian physicist at Johns Hopkins University: 'Carbon dioxide gas from man's increased industrial activity has enhanced a "greenhouse" effect in the upper atmosphere, tending to make the world's climate warmer.' John von Neumann had come to the same conclusion as Plass. Among his other world-changing obsessions, von Neumann had become fascinated by the military potential of predicting and manipulating the weather and had talked the government into giving him millions of dollars to create climate models. In 'Can We Survive Technology?', his 1955 article for *Fortune*, he wrote that carbon dioxide emissions 'may have changed the atmosphere's composition sufficiently to account for a general warming of the world by about one degree Fahrenheit' (0.56 degrees Celsius) and could affect sea levels.* In 1957, Roger Revelle, director of the Scripps Institution of Oceanography, and the Austrian-American physical chemist Hans E. Suess determined that the objections to Arrhenius and Callendar were misguided: carbon from fossil fuels *was* present in the atmos-

*Von Neumann, who always believed that the solution to problematic technology was more technology, was convinced that the climate could be fixed with planet-cooling geoengineering (as it would later be called) and that the real problem would be the abuse of such technology for climatological warfare. He epitomized 'human adaptive optimism': the belief that we can change, or adapt to, any circumstances.

phere, it was *not* all absorbed by the oceans, and it *could* cause warming. They wrote in a landmark paper that humanity was engaged in a 'large scale geophysical experiment' without precedent. The following year, global warming was neatly explained in *The Unchained Goddess*, a jaunty educational film produced and co-written by Frank Capra. 'Even now, man may be unwittingly changing the world's climate through the waste products of his civilization,' warns the tweedy Mr Scientist, painting a picture of tourists 'viewing the drowned towers of Miami through 150 feet of tropical water'.

The basic concept of global warming was understood but not the details, nor the implications. Scientists needed to know more. Revelle secured funding for a young geochemist called Charles David Keeling to establish two carbon dioxide measuring stations – one in Antarctica and one on Mauna Loa in Hawaii. In 1958, Keeling delivered the first set of data that confirmed a rise in atmospheric carbon dioxide – to 315 ppm – and proved, at last, the validity of the greenhouse effect. In 1960, he charted his findings on a jagged upward line that became known as the Keeling curve. His graph illustrated a rate of increase that Arrhenius or Callendar could not have imagined; this was no longer a problem for generations of the distant future. In 1965, President Johnson commissioned Revelle to chair a study by the Science Advisory Committee. Using swathes of newly available data about emissions and global temperatures, Revelle's group predicted melting ice shelves and rising oceans if nothing was done. 'This generation has altered the composition of the atmosphere on a global scale through . . . a steady increase in carbon dioxide from the burning of fossil fuels,' Johnson told Congress. Yet this was still a relatively marginal field of inquiry. To the rising environmental movement, global warming was a sidebar rather than the lead story.

In June 1962, *The New Yorker* serialized a book which became the *ne plus ultra* of wake-up calls: Rachel Carson's *Silent Spring*. Carson, a fifty-five-year-old marine biologist who had been converted to environmentalism by the issue of nuclear fallout, managed to turn an investigation into pesticides such as DDT into a lyrical meditation on 'the web of life – or death – that scientists know as ecology'.

The pesticide industry accused Carson of bad science, political bias and hysteria; to no avail. Supreme Court Justice William O. Douglas anointed *Silent Spring* 'the most revolutionary book since *Uncle Tom's Cabin*' while President Kennedy announced an investigation into the side effects of pesticides in response to 'Miss Carson's book'. Carson is credited with making environmentalism a mainstream concern and inspiring a raft of legislation, including a ban on the agricultural use of DDT.

Carson opened *Silent Spring* with 'A Fable for Tomorrow', a worst-case scenario in the form of a fairy tale. She understood that most people respond viscerally to stories and images, not data. Disasters drive legislation. In 1969, an oil spill in the Santa Barbara Channel blackened Californian beaches with thousands of dead birds, while an oil slick on the notoriously polluted Cuyahoga River in Ohio caught fire. The following year, President Nixon established the Environmental Protection Agency and said, in his State of the Union address, 'The great question of the seventies is, shall we surrender to our surroundings, or shall we make our peace with nature and begin to make reparations for the damage we have done to our air, to our land, and to our water?' The Princeton professor Harold Sprout claimed that not since Pearl Harbor had one issue so abruptly become a national obsession. On 22 April 1970, around 20 million Americans participated in the first Earth Day, a nationwide teach-in co-founded by Senator Gaylord Nelson after he witnessed the Santa Barbara oil spill. In a time of bitter division, *The New York Times* observed, Earth Day was an oasis of unanimity: 'Conservatives were for it. Liberals were for it. Democrats, Republicans and Independents were for it . . . no man in public office could be against it.' Who could argue with dead seagulls and burning rivers?

At the dawn of the 1970s, therefore, the issue was everywhere. One could hear it in songs by Marvin Gaye, the Beach Boys and Neil Young. 'Hey, farmer, farmer, put away your DDT,' demanded Joni Mitchell on 'Big Yellow Taxi'. In *No Blade of Grass*, Cornel Wilde's savage adaptation of John Christopher's *The Death of Grass*, the crop blight was reimagined as the result of pollution and pesticides. A keen environmentalist since reading *Silent Spring*, Wilde wanted to make '*pollution* the piece's villain'. The first (and possibly last) eco-exploitation thriller, his movie combines a grotesque rape scene and neo-Nazi bikers with an ahead-of-the-curve explanation of global warming and a montage of smokestacks, oil slicks and exhaust fumes which resembles a campaign video for Friends of the Earth. 'By the beginning of the 70s, man had brought the destruction of his environment close to the point of no return,' booms the opening voiceover. 'Of course, there was a great deal of rhetoric about saving the earth but in reality, very little was done . . . And then, one day, the polluted earth could take no more.' Small children, meanwhile, could confront ecological ruin in *The Lorax*, Dr Seuss's book about a world stripped bare of Truffula Trees to produce Thneeds that nobody needs. This sudden climate of guilt and self-disgust made Arthur C. Clarke wonder if he and Stanley Kubrick should have destroyed the world at the end of *2001* after all: 'We have wasted and defiled our own estate, the beautiful planet Earth. Why should we expect any mercy from a returning Star Child?'

In January 1971, a young Steven Spielberg directed an episode of the journalism drama *The Name of the Game* called 'L.A. 2017'. The writer of this dystopian it-was-all-a-dream tale of a subterranean dictatorship ruled by the same corporations whose pollutants have made the surface world unliveable was Philip Wylie. The sixty-nine-year-old author of *When Worlds Collide* and *Tomorrow!* was now an apocalyptic environmentalist. Wylie suffered a fatal heart attack in October that year, so his last and most despairing novel, *The End of the Dream*, was published posthumously. It opens in 2023, when the global population has been slashed to fifty million by a staggering caravan of environmental catastrophes caused by toxic waste and fossil-fuel extraction. Whereas most disaster novelists choose one peril, Wylie goes wild, throwing in deadly smogs, earthquakes, a rice blight, rising sea levels and, less convincingly, a plague of killer leeches called 'Vibes'. Oddly, he does not mention the greenhouse effect (the oceans swell due to mining coal and oil in Antarctica and smothering it in heat-absorbing soot), but he does anticipate the politics of climate change. Will Gulliver, an aged environmentalist who works for the Foundation for Human Conservancy is writing a history of how it all went wrong: 'There actually was a time, some fifty years ago, or thereabouts, when man might still have been able to prevent his near extermination.' Politicians dismissed Gulliver as 'an "erudite wolf-crier", "counterprogressive" and "anti-productive"', while heeding the siren song of a brash young techno-optimist who opposed all environmental legislation on the grounds that 'technology could and would perfectly suffice to undo or reverse the admitted sabotage man had performed on his ecosphere.' Reading like the scream of a man at the end of his tether, *The End of the Dream* was the anguished culmination of Wylie's lifelong war against short-sighted politicians, greedy corporations, shallow journalists and ignorant citizens: 'A technological society cannot persist as a democracy unless the people in the majority understand both technology and ecology well enough to know what they are doing.'

Meanwhile in the UK, a smash-hit BBC show was making the same point. As the script editor of *Doctor Who*, Gerry Davis had worked with ophthalmologist Dr Kit Pedler to create the Cybermen. In 1970, the two men channelled their obsession with malign science into *Doomwatch*, a drama about a government department which monitors potentially hazardous research under the leadership of a guilt-haunted veteran of the Manhattan Project. 'The days when you and I marvelled at the "miracles" of science – and writers made fortunes out of sci-fi – are over,' Davis told *Radio Times*. 'We've grown up now – and we're frightened. The findings of science are still marvellous, but now is the time to stop dreaming up science-fiction about them and write what we call "sci-fact." The honeymoon of science is over. *That's* what *Doomwatch* is about!'

Newspapers regularly cited *Doomwatch* in stories about unnerving new developments, but one person who must have viewed its popularity with gritted teeth was John Maddox, the editor of *Nature*. In his 1972 book *The Doomsday Syndrome*, he positioned the late Rachel Carson at the head of a tribe of gloomy, anti-science doomsayers who reminded him of 'the old preachers who would usher their listeners towards heaven with graphic accounts of what hell is like'. As a techno-optimist, Maddox thought that their language was not just wrong but self-defeating: 'Instead of alerting people to the important problems, it may seriously undermine the capacity of the human race to look out for its survival. The doomsday syndrome may in itself be as much a hazard as any of the conundrums which society has created for itself.'

One lesson of the 1970s, it is true, was the cost of freaking out about the wrong catastrophes.

CHAPTER 19

Too Many People

Look, we live in a lousy world today and our troubles come from only one reason: too goddamn many people.

Soylent Green (1973)

One of the most popular thinkers of the Cold War was an English clergyman and economist who had died in 1834: Thomas Robert Malthus. In *An Essay on the Principle of Population*, first published in 1798, Malthus had made a very simple, very alarming claim: population increases geometrically and food production arithmetically. Therefore, if war and pestilence fail to reduce the number of human beings to a manageable level, then 'gigantic inevitable famine stalks in the rear, and with one mighty blow, levels the population with the food of the world'. Malthus's grim projection disgusted the likes of Shelley and Coleridge. William Godwin, Mary Shelley's father and Malthus's intellectual arch-enemy, called him 'a dark and terrible genius that is ever at hand to blast all the hopes of mankind'. But Malthus insisted he was not a congenital pessimist. Writing of himself in the third person, he admitted, 'The view which he has given of human life has a melancholy hue; but he feels conscious, that he has drawn these dark tints, from a conviction that they are really in the picture; and not from a jaundiced eye, or an inherent spleen of disposition.' Malthus embraced the prophet's dilemma: if, by raising the problem, he could inspire 'more able men' to solve it, then he would 'gladly retract his present opinions, and rejoice in a conviction of his error'.

In that light, he had reason to rejoice, because his simple arithmetic was simply wrong: food production kept pace with population. Malthus could not have imagined the changes wrought by new agricultural methods such as artificial fertilizer, nor the untapped bounty of the Americas. Yet Malthus still had many admirers, including Charles Darwin and John Stuart Mill. In 1898, the eminent British scientist William Crookes predicted that the world would not have enough wheat by the 1930s unless new sources of nitrogen-rich fertilizer were developed. His widely publicized warning helped to inspire the world-changing Haber-Bosch process, to which almost half the people on earth now owe their diets. H. G. Wells invoked Malthus in 1905's *A Modern Utopia* when he argued, 'From the view of human comfort and happiness, the increase in population that occurs at each advance in human security is the greatest evil of life.' By 1938, in *Apropos of Dolores*, he was connecting overpopulation to ecological damage: 'God knows what man hasn't thrown out of gear in the past hundred years. Man is a biological catastrophe . . . We harry all life.' Long before Rachel Carson, the birth of environmentalism was inextricably linked to overpopulation anxiety: if humans are wrecking the planet, then surely there should be fewer of them?

In January 1948, Aldous Huxley wrote to Fairfield Osborn, president of the New York Zoological Society, to congratulate him on the publication of his 'very interesting' new book, *Our Plundered Planet.* 'The tide of the earth's population is rising, the reservoir of the earth's living resources is falling,' wrote Osborn. That September, he spoke at a symposium in Washington DC called 'What Hope for Man?': 'We are bouncing radar beams off the moon at a time when we are gradually reducing our own world to the condition of sterility of that romantic planet.' Huxley fretted that if politicians did not heed Osborn's warning, then the world would become 'one huge dust bowl inhabited by creatures whom progressive hunger will make more and more sub-human'. In 1948, he promoted this concern in his post-apocalyptic novel *Ape and Essence* ('An orgy of criminal imbecility. And they called it Progress') and a long essay for UNESCO called 'The Double Crisis', which argued that the world was so preoccupied by the 'upper-level crisis' of the Cold War that it was ignoring the 'low-level crisis' of looming famine.

For decades, calls for selective population control had been intertwined with the dangerous pseudo-science of eugenics. Osborn's father, Henry Fairfield Osborn Sr, had founded the American Eugenics Society in 1922 while Huxley's brother, the biologist Julian Huxley, had been for several years vice-president of the British Eugenics Society. Hitler, a keen eugenicist, had expressed Malthusian concerns about 'the impossibility of making the fertility of the soil keep pace with the continuous increase in population' in *Mein Kampf*. But now the issue was reframed as a corollary to environmentalism. Huxley cited a popular post-war joke: the only thing that could unite rival nations in a common cause would be an invasion from Mars. Man, he wrote, was 'his own Martian, at war against himself... his war aims are the ravaging of his planet, the destruction of his civilization and the degradation of his species.'

Osborn's book coincided with another philippic about the 'ecological trap', *The Road to Survival* by William Vogt, the American ornithologist and conservationist who has been described as the father of 'apocalyptic environmentalism'. Vogt argued that while 'that clear-sighted English clergyman, Thomas Robert Malthus' had so far been discredited, he would be proved correct in the long term. He introduced the idea that the earth had a 'carrying capacity'. If this limit were to be exceeded, he argued, soil erosion, deforestation and overpopulation would lead inevitably to war. *The Road to Survival* is a shrill, abrasive book with subheadings such as 'THE NEW ATLANTIS', 'OUTWITTING THE LIBIDO' and 'WAKE UP, AMERICA!' and a screamingly bleak last line: 'Like Gadarene swine, we shall rush down a war-torn slope to a barbarian existence in the blackened rubble.' It caused a tremendous stir, inspiring the likes of Julian Huxley, birth-control pioneer Margaret Sanger and the businessman Hugh Moore, who was moved to form the Population Action Committee and publish a 1954 pamphlet called *The Population Bomb Is Everyone's Baby*.

When John of Patmos wrote the Book of Revelation, fewer than a quarter of a billion human beings walked the earth. By 1798, when Malthus proposed his theory, the figure was approaching one billion. By 1948, the population was nearly two and a half billion and rising fast. It exceeded three billion in 1960, the year that J. G. Ballard published his short story 'Billennium'. Ballard's landscapes were usually defined by the absence of people; in 'Billennium', the global population has exceeded twenty billion and mass starvation has only been averted by devoting every possible centimetre of land to food production, leaving only a few square metres for each human being. Ballard was exploiting an increasingly fashionable obsession with overcrowded cities and depleted resources.

In catastrophe novels of the post-war era, the spectre of overpopulation hovers in the background like an uncontested fact rather than an argument to be pressed. In John Wyndham's *The Chrysalids*, it is claimed that, if not for nuclear war, humans 'would have bred with the carelessness of animals until they had reduced themselves to poverty and misery, and ultimately to starvation and barbarism'. The anxiety supplies a dark joke in Brian Aldiss's *Greybeard*, that antecedent to *The Children of Men*. 'If this sterility stunt is going on all over the world, it won't half be a relief to countries like China and India,' one character says brightly. 'For years they've been groaning about their population multiplying like rabbits! Now they'll have a chance to thin the ranks a bit.' Following *Dr. Strangelove*, Stanley Kubrick floated the idea of making a movie about overpopulation. 'Do you realize that in 2020 there will be no room on earth for all the people to stand?' he asked *Newsweek*. 'The really sophisticated worriers are worried about that.' In his novel *2001: A Space Odyssey*, Arthur C. Clarke predicted that the world population would exceed six billion by 2001, which proved impressively accurate. John Brunner was also on target when he projected seven billion for 2010 in his 1968 novel *Stand on Zanzibar*. The title riffed on an old idea that the world population could squeeze onto the Isle of Wight (380 km^2) if everybody stood shoulder to shoulder. For seven billion, Brunner calculated that an island the size of Zanzibar (2461 km^2) would be required.

The first novel to take overpopulation as its central theme was the American science fiction writer Harry Harrison's *Make Room! Make Room!*, published in 1966 and dramatically dedicated to his son and daughter: 'For your sakes, children, I hope this proves to be a work of fiction.' It is the eve of the millennium and there are seven billion people on earth, 344 million of whom live in the US and 35 million in New York. They live on a knife edge, vulnerable to the slightest hitch in the food supply. Fertilizer shortages, insecticide poisoning and bad weather have led to rationing and riots. Amid the Judgement Day tub-thumpers decrying 'Babylon-on-Hudson' is a more credible scold, an old man named Sol:

> The world's gone – not going – to hell in a hand basket, and it's all of us who pushed it there . . . The coal that was supposed to last for centuries has all been dug up because so many people wanted to keep warm. And the oil too, there's so little left that they can't afford to burn it, it's got to be turned into chemicals and plastics and stuff. And the rivers – who polluted them? The water – who drank it? The topsoil – who wore it out? Everything has been gobbled up, used up, worn out. What we got left – our one natural resource? Old-car lots, that's what . . . One time we had the whole world in our hands, but we ate it and burned it and it's gone now.

David Bowie was a keen reader of *Impulse*, the magazine that serialized Harrison's novel at the end of 1966. Not long afterwards, he released 'We Are Hungry Men', a burlesque of the overpopulation panic which is as much a radio comedy sketch as a song. A self-proclaimed eugenicist 'messiah' expects gratitude for his visionary schemes to ration air and license infanticide: 'How I'll save the world / Or let it die within the year.' The surly masses respond with first contempt and then cannibalism: the song ends in an orgy of slurps and gulps. Screeds proliferated. 'Nothing can stop the locomotive in time,' William and Paul Paddock declaimed in their 1967 book *Famine – 1975!*. 'Collision is inevitable. Catastrophe is foredoomed . . . Don't call this pessimism. It is merely sad realism.' Chillingly, they recommended applying triage, the practice of prioritizing medical treatment based on the chances of recovery, to US food aid, denying assistance to 'can't-be-saved' nations such as India and Egypt.

The man who became the megaphone for overpopulation anxiety was Paul R. Ehrlich. Born in 1932, Ehrlich grew up in suburban New Jersey, where his love for butterfly-collecting led him to environmentalism. In 1949, when he enrolled in the University of Pennsylvania to study biology, he was alerted to overpopulation by reading Osborn and Vogt. After earning his doctorate with a dissertation on butterflies, he took a job teaching biology at Stanford. In 1966, he travelled to Delhi and Kashmir, where the sight of poverty and starvation reignited his angst. In fact, Delhi's population was at the time far less than that of London, Paris or New York, and its growth was driven by migration from the countryside rather than the birth rate, so what he was really repelled by was poverty. 'People, people, people, people,' he wrote about the Delhi slums. The scene had a 'hellish aspect'.

Unsentimental about the human race, Ehrlich believed that the sustainable world population could be as low as 500 million and he campaigned for a birth rate of zero. To him, overpopulation was the root of all evil, responsible for everything from poverty to pollution to plague: 'Too many cars, too many factories, too much detergent, too much pesticide, multiplying contrails, inadequate sewage treatment plants, too little water, too much carbon dioxide – all can be traced easily to *too many people*.' Like Vogt and Huxley, he thought that the future would bring conflict over scarce resources, up to and including nuclear war. 'Malthus was fundamentally right; he just got the timing wrong,' Ehrlich said. To his credit, he did not believe that this was solely a problem for the developing world. He included Americans (because they consumed far more resources per capita), and even his own family: after his daughter Lisa Marie was born, he had a vasectomy.

Gifted with a surplus of energy, confidence, passion and wit, Ehrlich was a born campaigner who sought to warn the American public. David Brower, executive director of the environmental pressure group the Sierra Club and co-founder of Friends of the Earth, heard Ehrlich on the radio and suggested that he write a book. Seeing a chance to make the population crisis an issue in the 1968 elections, Ehrlich and his wife Anne dashed out the first draft in a few weeks and asked friends to help them tone it down. (Their publisher convinced them to replace the rather dry title *Population, Resources, and Environment* with *The Population Bomb*, taken from Hugh Moore's 1954 pamphlet, and to credit it to Paul alone.) The reader can only imagine what that first draft must have been like if the final book represents a dilution. 'The battle to feed all of humanity is over,' it begins. 'The famines of the 1970s are upon us – and hundreds of millions more people are going to starve to death before this decade is out . . . The children of today's affluent Western societies will inherit a totally different world, a world in which the standards, politics, and economics of their parents will be dead.' The Ehrlichs scripted a range of nightmarish possibilities, the most cheering of which involved a mere 500 million deaths from starvation by 1985. While climate scientists spoke cautiously of what might happen decades away, the Ehrlichs baldly insisted that certain calamity was right around the corner. 'I *am* an alarmist,' Paul admitted, 'because I'm very goddamned alarmed.'

For all its dramatic urgency, *The Population Bomb* was largely ignored until February 1970, when Paul appeared on *The Tonight Show* with Johnny Carson. Unusually for an academic, he was such a charming performer that he inspired five thousand letters from viewers. Carson invited him back in April, just before the first Earth Day, for an interview that took up the whole show, giving tens of millions of viewers a crash course in neo-Malthusianism. Ehrlich was a promotional workhorse: that year alone, he gave two hundred media appearances and one hundred lectures. He spoke to *Playboy*, launched a group called Zero Population Growth and told CBS News, 'Sometime in the next 15 years, the end will come. And by "the end" I mean an utter breakdown of the capacity of the planet to support humanity.' *The Population Bomb* proceeded to sell more than three million copies.

As annual global population growth reached an unprecedented (and unbeaten) high of more than 2 per cent, overpopulation became a bigger story than anything else short of nuclear war, and a cornerstone of early green politics. It led the first two issues of *The Ecologist*, a new British magazine founded in 1970 by the environmentalist Teddy Goldsmith. 'That it is incompatible with the survival of civilized man is beyond doubt; that it might, if unchecked, lead to his extinction is not far-fetched,' Goldsmith wrote in an editorial, while another contributor smoothly advised offering Britons 'a bounty for submitting to sterilization'. It sometimes seemed that, unless they were small in number and living in rural communities, *The Ecologist* did not like people at all. Although Ehrlich considered himself an anti-racist liberal, many socialists and Black leaders suspected that the population-control movement was riddled with race and class prejudice. As 'Eco-Catastrophe!', Ehrlich's attempt at future history, demonstrated, activist predictions were indistinguishable in tone from the grimmest science fiction. 'A hungry over-crowded world will be a world of fear, chaos, poverty, riots, crime and war,' promised an advertisement for Hugh Moore's Campaign to Check the Population Explosion. 'No country will be safe, not even our own.'

All in all, it was the right time for Hollywood to invest in the neo-Malthusian market. Charlton Heston, star of *Planet of the Apes* and *The Omega Man* and hence Hollywood's reigning emperor of apocalypse, had been trying to get an adaptation of *Make Room! Make Room!* off the ground since 1968. 'Since I strongly believe that overpopulation is by far the gravest problem the world faces, this would be my only message movie,' he recalled. Director Richard Fleischer and screenwriter Stanley R. Greenberg moved the action of Harrison's novel from 1999 to 2022, renamed it *Soylent Green* and introduced a punishing twist to suit the paranoid style of 1970s cinema. In the book, the miracle food soylent is, as its name suggests, a bland but nutritious vegan synthesis of soy beans and lentils. In the movie, as Heston famously screams at the end, 'Soylent Green is people!' Harrison's novel was reissued under this title, with a new preface by none other than Paul Ehrlich.

The reason the miracle food consists of human remains rather than, as advertised, plankton is that the oceans are dying. While more famous for its covert industrialized anthropophagy, *Soylent Green* was the first mainstream movie to explain global warming. 'A heatwave all year long,' says Sol (Edward G. Robinson). 'The greenhouse effect. Everything's burning up.' New York City had never looked like this on screen before: a smoggy, sweltering, desperate shanty town, plagued by power cuts and food riots, somewhere between America at the height of the Great Depression and Paul Ehrlich's Delhi. As in *Blade Runner*, it seems, dystopia is an America that resembles Asia. The opening newsreel montage of *Soylent Green*, put together by the young documentarian Charles Braverman, shows the world filling up with not just people but cars, filth and junk. *Soylent Green* is at once a relic of 1970s population hysteria and a remarkably far-sighted movie about climate change.*

—

* *No Blade of Grass* predated *Soylent Green* by three years but it was not a hit. The earliest reference I could find to the greenhouse effect in a novel is in Ursula K. Le Guin's *The Lathe of Heaven*, from 1971. The phrase is capitalized, suggesting that Le Guin thought that it would be unfamiliar to the average reader.

Paul and Anne Ehrlich's publicity blitz paid off. President Nixon spoke of a 'rush toward a Malthusian nightmare' and established the Commission on Population Growth and the American Future. The couple even ended up rewriting the Book of Genesis, when the author of 1971's *The Living Bible* gave the story of the Deluge an Ehrlichian spin: 'Noah was 500 years old and had three sons, Shem, Ham, and Japheth. Now a population explosion took place upon the earth.' The couple's critics, however, perceived echoes of Revelation. Roger Revelle, the climate scientist, called Paul the 'New High Priest of Ecocatastrophe' and criticized his 'apocalyptic' hyperbole. 'Your last letter read just like one of Billy [Graham]'s sermons with the impending Armageddon approaching and the plea to prepare now while we have time,' one of Ehrlich's friends chided him. One celebrity sceptic was John Lennon, who said on *The Dick Cavett Show* that overpopulation was a myth: 'I don't really believe it, you know. I think that whatever happens will balance itself out and work itself out.' He added, optimistically, 'There's enough room for us and some of us will go to the Moon and live.'

As oracles of doom, the Ehrlichs faced stiff competition from the Club of Rome, a Wellsian alliance of international intellectuals devoted to solving what they called the 'world problématique'. Derived from the club's Project on the Predicament of Mankind, the 1972 book *The Limits to Growth* employed a controversial computer model to argue that population growth would crash around 2050 due to famine and disease. Somehow both wonkish and apocalyptic, the book sold more than twelve million copies. The MIT economist Robert Solow complained that the book's five-alarm tone, far from inspiring action, would induce despair: 'Who could pay attention to a humdrum affair like legislation to tax sulfur emissions when the date of the Apocalypse has just been announced by a computer?' Columnist Max Lerner published a mocking ditty in the *Los Angeles Times*: 'Ashes to ashes / And dust to dust / If the bomb doesn't get you / The exponential curves must.'

The Ehrlichs kept the books coming. In 1974's *The End of Affluence*, they evolved into benign survivalists. Amid numerous sensible recommendations for a greener America – public transport, home insulation, recycling – they suggested learning basic off-grid survival skills: 'Talents useful when stranded far from civilization might prove equally useful if society breaks down.' They anticipated accusations of pessimism: 'It seems to be part of American popular culture to consider optimism, in itself, to be good. In the face of disasters, our political and social leaders frequently castigate the "prophets of doom" who fail to accentuate the positive . . . This book is only "pessimistic" in the sense that recognizing a severe problem and recommending action to solve it are "pessimistic."' John Holdren, an Ehrlich ally who would later become a science adviser to both the Clinton and Obama administrations, put the case for expecting the worst during a Senate hearing in 1974: 'Are we worse off if we believe the pessimists and they are wrong, or are we worse off if we believe the optimists and they are wrong? I think the conclusion is clear.'

The clash between Ehrlich and his critics, between pessimists and optimists, between the age of scarcity and the age of abundance, was paralleled in the 1980 presidential election. Jimmy Carter was the hairshirt president who evinced a moral disgust for waste and turned off the White House air-conditioning even at the height of summer. (Anne Ehrlich consulted on *The Global 2000 Report to the President*, which predicted that food and energy prices would more than double by the end of the century.) Ronald Reagan, meanwhile, was the eternal optimist who mocked 'the doomsday crowd', 'the limits-to-growth people' and anyone who used the word *crisis*. Here were not just two visions of America but rival conceptions of the future of the planet. On one side were regulations, limits, doom and gloom; on the other, a sunny fantasy of endless abundance. 'Well, you know there was a fella named Malthus who thought we were going to run out of food,' Reagan scoffed on the campaign trail. 'But Malthus didn't know about fertilizers and pesticides.'

The Reagan to Ehrlich's Carter was the economics professor Julian Simon, a pro-growth 'Cornucopian' who planted himself in the path of Ehrlich's 'juggernaut of environmentalist hysteria'. He complained in his 1981 bestseller, *The Ultimate Resource*, 'The doomsdayers speak in excited, angry, high-pitched voices . . . Many anti-doomsday people, on the other hand, speak in quiet voices – as reassurance usually sounds. They tend to be careful people. And they are usually ignored.' *The Ultimate Resource* made Simon one of the decade's most influential conservative intellectuals, transforming the political consensus on population growth. His message, in short: the more the merrier. No problem is too big for the human imagination and every baby is a potential problem-solver. Some of the chapter titles resembled cheerleading chants: 'Can the Supply of Natural Resources Really Be Infinite? Yes!', 'When Will We Run Out of Energy? Never!' In 1984, he co-edited *The Resourceful Earth* with the equally anti-apocalyptic nuclear strategist Herman Kahn, and rebutted the 'false, gloomy' prognosis of *Global 2000* point by point: 'If present trends continue, the world in 2000 will be *less crowded* (though more populated), *less polluted, more stable ecologically*, and *less vulnerable to resource-supply disruption* than the world we live in now.' The Ehrlichs accused the Cornucopians of belonging to a 'space-age cargo cult'.

A profile of Simon in *Wired*, published shortly before his death in 1998, called him 'The Doomslayer'. Simon didn't consider Ehrlich alone to be deranged by pessimism, but the entire environmental movement. 'Listening to environmentalists, you'd think our air is unbreathable, our water is undrinkable, and that this country faces a crisis of major proportions,' he wrote in *USA Today* in 1984. 'It's simply not so.' In 1980, Simon challenged 'doomsayers and catastrophists' to take a $1,000 wager on whether the price of five precious metals would rise or fall in the next decade. Ehrlich took the bet, and lost: even as the population soared, the prices plummeted. Simon was lucky because commodity prices were unusually high in 1980 and Ehrlich had a weak grasp of economics, but the wager had enormous symbolic power. *The New York Times* described it on its conclusion in 1990 as 'a bet between the Cassandra and the Dr. Pangloss of our era. They lead two intellectual schools – sometimes called the Malthusians and the Cornucopians, sometimes simply the doomsters and the boomsters – that use the latest in computer-generated graphs and foundation-generated funds to debate whether the world is getting better or going to the dogs.'

Ehrlich was forced to face up to the cardinal error of having made very firm predictions about the very near future. 'How often does a prophet have to be wrong before we no longer believe that he or she is a true prophet?' taunted Simon. Clearly, famine had not materialized on anything like the scale Ehrlich had anticipated, even though the world's population had grown by 1.8 billion since *The Population Bomb*. Thanks to the development of high-yield, disease-resistant crop varieties and phosphorus-rich fertilizers – the so-called 'green revolution' pioneered by the Nobel Prize-winning agronomist Norman Borlaug – the food supply rose by a quarter between 1955 and 1980, albeit at a hefty cost to the environment. Life expectancy was rising; malnutrition rates and extreme poverty falling. Despite Paul's humiliation in the bet, the Ehrlichs doubled down in 1990 with *The Population Explosion.* Like premillennialist prophets, they insisted that while the timeline had been discredited, the prophecy had not been disconfirmed.

The settling of the bet brought the war between Ehrlich and Simon back into the news. That same year, the alien warlord Thanos rematerialized in the Marvel comic book *Silver Surfer* to explain his plan to fix the 'Great Imbalance' by randomly eliminating half the population of the universe. 'It's been nearly a generation since there was any serious talk of zero population growth,' he complains. Now, he says: 'Earth is a world rushing on its way to desolation and doom!' One techno-optimist reader wrote in to protest: 'I liked Thanos more before he joined the Sierra Club . . . The truth is that the "environmental crisis" is merely the latest in a series of public hysterias created by influential pressure groups, sensationalist media, and a gullible public. It, just like all the other great problems that have threatened man (plagues, earthquakes, etc.) will be solved eventually by technology.' Editor Craig Anderson fired back, 'We suggest you read Paul Erlich's [sic] "Population Bomb" and see how many of the predictions he made in that book have come to pass in the last two decades.' When Thanos's radical Malthusianism formed the basis for the 2018 movie *Avengers: Infinity War*, one publication described him as 'a kind of cosmic Paul Ehrlich'. Agent Smith, the malevolent AI in *The Matrix*, also sounds Ehrlichian: 'You multiply and multiply until every natural resource is consumed . . . Human beings are a disease, a cancer of this planet. You are a plague. We are the cure.' Inspiring the schemes of supervillains cannot have been the legacy that Ehrlich had hoped for, but he was not deterred. 'Sure I've made some mistakes,' he tweeted in January 2023, 'but no basic ones.'

The legacy of the overpopulation panic has done tremendous damage to the politics of climate change by associating environmentalists with debunked pessimism, sinister misanthropy and punitive restrictions: governments in Asia and Latin America introduced mass programmes of coerced sterilization. Yet *The Population Bomb* still provokes more debate than any other jeremiad of its era. Its defenders argue that the Ehrlichs, like Malthus, were only wrong in the short run, and that the green revolution cannot happen twice. Global population exceeded five billion in 1987, six in 1999, seven in 2011, and eight in November 2022, with UN projections for 2100 oscillating between ten and eleven billion. The population activist Stephen Emmott's 2013 book *10 Billion* concludes with him asking a young ecologist colleague the one thing he would do to face the 'unprecedented planetary emergency' of feeding that many people in a collapsing climate. 'Teach my son how to use a gun,' the colleague replies. Yet the geographer Danny Dorling's similarly titled *Population 10 Billion* counters that 'the population explosion is ending peacefully.' Though no Cornucopian, Dorling argues that resource shortages are a political challenge rather than a demographic inevitability. In advanced economies, meanwhile, longtermists and white supremacists are united in worrying that birth rates are too *low*. Father-of-ten Elon Musk tweeted in 2022 that 'population collapse' was 'a much bigger risk to civilization than global warming'. The politics of population remain febrile.

The clash between Ehrlich and Simon flowed into a similar argument about global warming during the 1990s. In *The Population Explosion*, the Ehrlichs tied overpopulation to carbon emissions, arguing that the 'Whimper' of climate change could be just as catastrophic as the 'Bang' of nuclear war. They twice pointed out an overlooked section of *The Population Bomb* which referenced the greenhouse effect: 'At the moment we cannot predict what the overall climatic results will be of our using the atmosphere as a refuse dump . . . Do we want to keep it up and find out what will happen? What do we gain by playing "environmental roulette"?' Simon, on the other hand, assured readers of *The Resourceful Earth*, 'The climate does not show signs of unusual and threatening changes.'

CHAPTER 20

Too Cold

> The threat of a new ice age must now stand alongside nuclear war as a likely source of wholesale death and misery for mankind.
>
> Nigel Calder, 'In the Grip of a New Ice Age?' (1975)

The burning world and the frozen world are rarely far apart. 'Some say the world will end in fire, / Some say in ice,' wrote Robert Frost in 1920's 'Fire and Ice'. 'The ice age is coming, the sun's zooming in,' sang Joe Strummer in The Clash's 1979 hit 'London Calling'. A 1961 episode of *The Twilight Zone*, 'The Midnight Sun', perfected the duality. A painter and her elderly neighbour are sweltering in a largely vacated New York City because a change in Earth's orbit is drawing it towards the Sun, which fills the sky twenty-four hours a day. It is 'the eve of the end'. As the temperature soars, the thermometer breaks, the paint melts from the canvases, the painter screams and . . . wakes up. It was all a fever dream. But there's a double twist: in reality, the earth is moving *away* from the Sun, into an endless freezing night. 'The poles of fear,' Rod Serling rumbles in his closing narration. 'The extremes of how the earth might conceivably be doomed.'

Someone following media coverage of climate science during the 1970s might also have been torn between two incompatible nightmares. 'I have been worrying about the fact that you cannot have ice that is growing and melting at the same time,' Ralph Schoenstein wrote in *The New Yorker* in 1975. 'One of these terrors is a dud, and the job of the dedicated worrier is to find out which one it is.' Imagine that you are a dedicated worrier standing in the popular science section of a well-stocked US book store in the second half of the 1970s. You might pick up *Hothouse Earth* by Howard A. Wilcox and learn about 'a global heat disaster that could write an end to the history of our civilization'. Or you could open *The Cooling* by Lowell Ponte and read that *falling* temperatures will 'cause world famine, world chaos, and probably world war, and this could all come by the year 2000'. Or perhaps you flick through *Ice or Fire?: Surviving Climatic Change* by D. S. Halacy Jr, discover that 'there are two diametrically opposed predictions for the climate ahead,' and leave the store in exasperation.

Why such uncertainty? The main reason is that between 1940 and 1975 the average global temperature fell by 0.2 degrees, producing more snow and ice cover in the Northern Hemisphere. Two explanations were proposed. One was a solution to the mystery that had confounded Arrhenius: an explanation for ice ages. New geological evidence proved that a contentious theory of glaciation advanced by the maverick Serbian mathematician Milutin Milanković in the 1930s was indeed correct: changes in Earth's orbit and the tilt of its axis alter its distance from the Sun in cycles of around ten thousand years. Some scientists thought that the long interglacial period that had allowed human civilization to flourish could be coming to an end. Indeed, if human beings had never started burning fossil fuels on an industrial scale, the planet *would* be cooling. The other factor was that aerosol particles of sulphuric acid and nitrous oxide produced by industry reflected solar radiation, just like the volcanic emissions from Tambora and Krakatoa. Air pollution has suppressed the global temperature rise by around half a degree, and warming has increased due to clean-air legislation. So both explanations had validity. The disagreement came down to whether the greenhouse effect would prove more powerful than the cooling forces.

In 1972, the contrarian climate scientists George Kukla and Robert Matthews held a conference on global cooling at Brown University and wrote to President Nixon to warn of deadly snowstorms and frosts, leading to food shortages, within a century. The CIA, for one, took the threat seriously. The unusually severe winters of 1972 and

1973 made this feel all too plausible. 'Brace yourself for another Ice Age,' warned *Science Digest*, although it admitted that none of its readers would live to see it. The man responsible for making the cooling theory irresistibly dramatic was the UK's most prominent science journalist, Nigel Calder. The cover of the 16–22 November 1974 issue of *Radio Times* declared 'The Ice Age Cometh' above an illustration of the blue-green globe wearing a thick wig of ice. It was promoting a new BBC documentary, *The Weather Machine*, written by Calder and presented by quiz-show host Magnus Magnusson. In the documentary and accompanying book, Calder addressed a number of theories, including anthropogenic global warming, but concluded that the earth was experiencing the resumption of the Little Ice Age, a cool period which lasted roughly from 1450 to 1850.

Calder's most novel and arresting contribution was a new theory of ice ages – catastrophist rather than uniformitarian – which he christened 'snowblitz'. In a snowblitz, snow doesn't melt during the summer but hardens into ice, which thickens every winter. The reflectivity, or albedo, of the planet's surface increases because pale snow reflects more sunlight than dark earth, creating a feedback loop.* According to Calder, 'The cold comes instantly . . . "Instantly" may mean a hundred years, or a single bad summer.' This would, he predicted, erase entire regions, including the UK, Canada and Scandinavia, from the map. Even though the scientists who appeared in *The Weather Machine* put the odds of an ice age within a century at ten to one, Calder threw objectivity to the wind in his book's final pages by invoking the Norse *Fimbulwinter*. 'The end of the world is to be heralded by a summer that is no summer. The bitter cold persists and the Sun gives neither light nor warmth, so that the winter is three winters long. "The twilight of the gods" is a realistic scenario for the onset of the next ice age, in snowblitz fashion.' In that case, he suggested, the warming effect of carbon dioxide emissions might be cause for 'residual optimism'.

Because journalists adore novelty, dramatic headlines about cooling theory often mischaracterized nuanced reporting. A 1974 *Time* article, 'Another Ice Age?', quoted the 'climatological Cassandras'

* Global warming creates the opposite feedback loop, as melting snow and ice reduce albedo.

but admitted that far more data was required and that the worst-case scenario was hundreds of years away. Despite its Ballardian title, *Newsweek*'s 1975 article 'The Cooling World' was similarly uncertain. Scientists conceded that 'some of the more spectacular solutions proposed, such as melting the arctic ice cap by covering it with black soot or diverting arctic rivers, might create problems far greater than those they solve'. Well, yes, they probably would. Both articles concluded that *something* was causing droughts, floods, monsoons and poor harvests, but nobody was sure what. In 1975, the *New York Times* science reporter Walter Sullivan published stories about both 'major cooling' and a 'warming trend' within the space of three months.

Some fiction writers, too, simply could not make up their minds. 'A new ice age had just been predicted by all those scientists who had not predicted a new inferno due to the so-called "greenhouse effect",' remarked Gore Vidal in *Kalki*. *Alternative 3*, an ingenious hoax documentary produced by Anglia Television in 1977, purported to uncover a secret project to escape irreversible climate change by colonizing Mars, but couldn't settle on the nature of that change. One minute the narrator is explaining 'the notorious greenhouse effect', the next he is predicting 'a future of unavoidable ice age'. This apparent contradiction did not deter hundreds of gulled viewers from phoning in for more information.

The debate about warming versus cooling was sincere but damaging. Faced with a choice of catastrophes, some people chose to believe neither. 'At the time of the fatal high tides along the East Coast [10 years ago] all the experts wrote at length about the *receding* ice cap, a warmer climate, and the inevitability of more and worse high tides,' scoffed one *Radio Times* reader in response to Nigel Calder's article. 'Cry havoc and doom! . . . When the experts have been so howlingly wrong before, we can perhaps take comfort in assuming they are likely to be wrong again.' Climate-change deniers still hold up this episode as proof that climate scientists are a bunch of unreliable alarmists. Republican Senator James M. Inhofe mockingly quoted those short, cautious articles from *Newsweek* and *Time* in a notorious 2003 speech which called anthropogenic global warming 'the greatest hoax ever perpetrated on the American people'. 'How quickly things change,' he scoffed. 'Fear of the coming ice age is old hat, but fear that man-made greenhouse gases are causing temperatures to rise to harmful levels is in vogue.' In fact, a study by the American Meteorological Society has found, only one in ten peer-reviewed climate papers during the 1970s advanced the cooling theory, and it was virtually dead by the decade's end. Contrary to the myth that climate scientists had changed their minds, prominent ice-age theorists such as Nigel Calder became ardent deniers of global warming.

While it lasted, though, the ice-age fad gave a sheen of credibility to old nightmares about the earth being frozen to death. In 1875, Richard Jefferies, the author of *After London*, had written an unpublished story called 'The Great Snow' in which a blizzard consumes London. But this was merely an apocalyptic fantasy, just like the final winter in Anna Kavan's *Ice*. Snowblitz supplied the pseudo-scientific basis for a new wave of disaster novels, especially after the punishing winter of 1977–8, when the Ohio River froze solid for the first time since 1918, snow fell in Miami for the first time ever, and Buffalo, New York, weathered snowdrifts up to 12 metres high. Scenes from that winter, the biggest US news story of 1977, formed the visual backdrop to an alarming 1978 TV show called *In Search of . . . The Coming Ice Age*, presented by Leonard Nimoy, *Star Trek*'s Mr Spock. Standing on a chilly bridge with his collar up, Nimoy somewhat oversold the inconclusive science: 'During the lifetime of our grandchildren, Arctic cold and perpetual snow could turn most of the inhabitable portions of our planet into a polar desert.'

In 1978 and 1979, the ice age came with a vengeance in Robert Altman's movie *Quintet*, *Icequake* by Crawford Kilian, *Ice!* by Arnold Federbush and *The Sixth Winter* by Douglas Orgill and John Gribbin. Gribbin was a science writer and the expository dialogue that consumes half the novel is stuffed with references to real-life cooling theorists such as George Kukla. The scientist hero, William Stovin, tells the president that humanity's 'interglacial dream' is over: 'The future will not be like that. The future is ice, over a lot of the globe. The future is less food, fewer people.' In George Stone's 1977 eco-thriller *Blizzard*, the mammoth snowstorm that buries America's north-east is triggered by an out-of-control experiment with 'weather warfare' but Stone weaves in Calder's theory towards the end. 'Snow*blitz*?' asks a startled politician. A scientist responds that it is 'a legitimate hypothesis of comparatively recent formulation'. If the Great American Blizzard becomes self-generating, 'then we may face first Megastorm, then Snowblitz, and then . . . And then the very Ice Age itself.'

Snowblitz is also elucidated in Arthur Herzog's 1977 novel *Heat*, but to entirely different ends. Herzog, whose earlier bestseller *The Swarm* had warned readers about the more outré menace of killer bees, crafted a thriller in which cooling theory is hegemonic and a scientific Cassandra must battle the establishment to draw attention to the real climatic peril: global warming. 'Centuries of the burning of fossil fuels have created a blanket of carbon dioxide in the atmosphere which daily threatens to trap more and more of the earth's heat,' explained the paperback blurb. 'It is the long-feared "greenhouse effect". It can swiftly put an end to all higher life forms and turn our planet into a self-generating inferno.'

CHAPTER 21

Too Late

I wonder how they'll feel a hundred years from now
when they find out that people in the twentieth century
knew what was coming and kept their mouths shut.
They'll be a little bitter. The future's our responsibility.

Arthur Herzog, *Heat* (1977)

Before the late 1970s, science fiction authors, that far-seeing tribe which had depicted nuclear weapons and AI decades in advance, appeared to know less about climate change than what American schoolchildren had learned from *The Unchained Goddess*. Even when they had described the consequences, it was for the wrong reasons. The oceans rise in Karel Čapek's *War with the Newts* and John Wyndham's *The Kraken Wakes* due to inhuman villainy. The planet boils in *The Day the Earth Caught Fire* because of the unintended side effects of H-bomb tests. What melts the icecaps in J. G. Ballard's *The Drowned World* is an increase in solar radiation, not a polluted atmosphere. However dubious the science, the message was consistent: humanity has made its bed and now it must burn, drown or starve in it. 'It seems we have a knack of turning everything we touch into sand and dust,' spits Ransom in Ballard's *The Drought*. 'We've even sown the sea with its own salt.' The farmer David in John Christopher's *The Death of Grass* admits, 'In a way, I think I feel it would be more *right* for the virus to win, anyway. For years now, we've treated the land as though it were a piggy-bank, to be raided.'

Arthur Herzog was perhaps the first writer of popular fiction to take global warming seriously, even if thriller conventions compelled him to make it happen absurdly quickly: within four years, New York City is broiling and Central Park is a tropical jungle. Herzog is astute about the politics of climate change. His hero, Lawrence Pick, works for CRISES (Crisis Research Investigation and Systems Education Service), whose motto is 'The Future Is Our Responsibility.' Yet Pick registers the political cost of asking voters to make sacrifices in the name of a catastrophe that they have not yet experienced. 'The people's attitude is "Show me,"' says one character. 'They won't take the word of scientists that a calamity impends. They will not reduce their standard of living to cut down energy consumption – not willingly, at least. Certainly, they won't surrender for the sake of future generations.' An argument between Pick and his cautious boss, Rufus Edmunston, sums up the eternal clash between optimists and pessimists. 'One thing I'm sure about is that it's a mistake to get worked up before you have to,' Edmunston says. 'I'd rather err on the side of safety than do nothing at all,' Pick responds. 'Uncertainty isn't biased towards optimism, God knows.' Sacked and replaced by a global warming denier, Pick is denounced as a 'weather weirdo' and 'climate kook' before his warnings are vindicated. As Dr Carl Gerstein, the scientist in *Alternative 3*, says, 'The politicians come running to us as though we can reverse the course of nature. When we tell them we can't, they say, "Why didn't we do something earlier?" When we tell them they prevented us, they start squabbling among themselves.'

According to the writer Nathaniel Rich, 'Nearly everything we understand about global warming was understood in 1979.' That summer, the meteorologist Jule Charney assembled a brains trust of climate experts at Woods Hole Oceanographic Institution in Massachusetts to study decades of data, thousands of papers and two cutting-edge three-dimensional climate models (created by NASA's James Hansen and Princeton's Syukuro Manabe), in order to give President Carter the clearest possible picture of global warming. As a member of John von Neumann's team of meteorologists at Princeton's Institute of Advanced Study after the war, Charney had pioneered the use of computers in weather forecasting and climate science. He went on to become a professor at MIT, perfect for Carter's purposes: genial, collegiate and extremely patient. *Carbon Dioxide and Climate: A Scientific Assessment*, also known as the Charney Report, estimated that the global net temperature would increase by between 1.5 to 4.5 degrees if atmospheric carbon dioxide were to double, with the most likely outcome bang in the middle. This was exactly the same range that the IPCC would come up with in 1995. On its fortieth anniversary, a group of climate scientists called the Charney Report 'the scientific equivalent of the handwriting on the wall'.

Suitably alarmed, Carter signed the Energy Security Act, obligating the National Academy of Sciences to produce a more extensive report called *Changing Climate.* But when it was published in 1983, the authors, who included Roger Revelle and the nuclear strategist Thomas Schelling, managed to undersell their findings to the extent that Ronald Reagan's science adviser could use it to rubbish a more urgent report published by the Environmental Protection Agency that same week. Even Revelle told reporters, 'We're flashing a yellow light but not a red light.' As a portrait of a world in peril, *Changing Climate* could not compete with the hair-raising new nuclear winter theory that Carl Sagan announced that Halloween, nor the British Antarctic Survey's discovery, two years later, of a hole in the ozone layer, the stratospheric shield that absorbs 98 per cent of the Sun's ultraviolet radiation.

This was alarming proof of a phenomenon that had so far inspired considerable attention but no action: the CFCs that aerosols and refrigerators had been pumping into the atmosphere since the 1930s were not just potent greenhouse gases but ozone scavengers. One of the researchers who had discovered this in the 1970s told his wife, 'The work is going well, but it looks like it might be the end of the world.' Strictly speaking, there was no layer and no hole but the image had galvanic results. This was not a problem for future generations but a clear and present danger, threatening skin cancer, crop failure and even blindness. 'Now there's a hole in the sky,' sang Pixies on 'Monkey Gone to Heaven,' 'And the ground's not cold / And if the ground's not cold, everything is gonna burn.' Governments scrambled to reduce CFC emissions, signing the Montreal Protocol on Substances That Deplete the Ozone Layer in 1987. It was the perfect demonstration of the power of urgent action but, as with DDT, the elimination of CFCs was relatively cheap and easy. Unlike fossil fuels, they were not the cornerstone of the industrial world. As the economist Lester Lave put it, 'Carbon dioxide stands as a symbol now of our willingness to confront the future.'

Fortunately for frustrated climate scientists, the summer of 1988 brought a tarmac-melting, crop-scorching, forest-burning, river-shrivelling heatwave to North America, which made global warming suddenly more vivid. On 23 June, the Senate Committee on Energy and Natural Resources held a landmark hearing on the greenhouse effect. Its vice-chair, Tim Wirth, picked a date at the height of summer and turned off the room's air-conditioning. The bombshell testimony came from James Hansen, the director of NASA's Goddard Institute for Space Studies and a pioneering climate modeller. Hansen said that he could confirm warming of 0.6 degrees since the 1880s and state 'with 99 percent confidence' that it was a consistent trend caused by carbon emissions. It felt like a tipping-point year. The UN established the Intergovernmental Panel on Climate Change. The British prime minister Margaret Thatcher, a chemist by training, became the first major world leader to prioritize global warming. On the campaign trail, even Republican candidate George H. W. Bush promised to fight the greenhouse effect with 'the White House effect'. The following year, Bill McKibben published the first bestselling book about climate change, *The End of Nature*, by which he meant the existence of parts of the natural world unaffected by human activity. He could see a time when 'our sense of nature as eternal and separate is finally washed away and we see all too clearly what we have done' – a recognition of the Anthropocene.

The phrase *climate crisis* first appeared in 1981. *Climate emergency* followed in 1989, when a record 79 per cent of Americans said that they had some awareness of the greenhouse effect. In 1990, the IPCC published its first report and a new generation of activists mobilized 200 million people worldwide for the biggest Earth Day to date. In 1992, world leaders signed the significant but non-binding United Nations Framework Convention on Climate Change in Rio de Janeiro. This period, though, was the breakthrough that never was. In *The Collapse of Western Civilization: A View from the Future*, a Wellsian future history by science writers Naomi Oreskes and Erik M. Conway, a historian in 2393 identifies the false dawn of 1988 as the start of the 'Period of the Penumbra', when awareness failed to produce action due to 'the shadow of anti-intellectualism'.

In disaster fiction, the far-sighted scientist struggles to be believed, but once he has persuaded the right people, action is promptly taken. In both *Heat* and *Blizzard*, for example, the world's governments join forces against a shared enemy. Jonathan Schell had fondly imagined in 1984 that if scientists were to discover that carbon emissions would cause a runaway greenhouse effect, 'the nations of the earth would quickly sign a treaty bringing their use under control. For it would surely very soon become clear to people everywhere that they valued humanity more than they valued fossil fuels.' Would it, though?

Since the Rio Declaration in 1992, we have pumped more carbon into the atmosphere than in the preceding thirty thousand years of human history. The reduction in emissions required to keep us below 2 degrees of warming now is many times greater than it was then. The US signed the Kyoto and Paris agreements but refused to act on them, while emissions from India and China have respectively tripled and quadrupled. Not until 2022 did a significant piece of US climate legislation, the Inflation Reduction Act, pass through Congress and receive the president's signature. Malthus got one thing right: 'The most baleful mischiefs may be expected from the unmanly conduct of not daring to face truth, because it is unpleasing.'

Immediately after James Hansen's Senate testimony in 1988, a small but influential group of global warming deniers began a very successful campaign to muddy the science and thwart reform. Whether they dismissed climate change altogether, accepted it but denied that it was human-made, or admitted that it was human-made but insisted that it was no big deal, the goal was the same: to give politicians licence to do nothing. Many of the same people had taken a contrarian, nothing-to-worry-about view on acid rain, ozone depletion, second-hand smoking and DDT; this time they found a hearing – not in the field of peer-reviewed scientific research but in the arena of public opinion. The leading deniers were not climate scientists but economists (Julian Simon), popular science writers (Michael Crichton) and retired physicists (Frederick Seitz, Fred Singer) who shared a worldview that made them popular with conservative politicians and think tanks as well as fossil-fuel lobbyists. The term *climate denial* was minted in 1996.

Let us be generous for a moment and assume that the leading deniers were not simply lying for influence, attention and fossil-fuel money. First, they were Cold War hawks: the engine room of climate-change denial, the George C. Marshall Institute, had been founded in 1984 to defend Reagan's Strategic Defense Initiative and debunk nuclear winter theory. They were also free-market fundamentalists who saw environmental regulation as socialism by stealth, and technophiles who regarded environmentalists as zealous Luddites, manufacturing crises to serve their radical political agendas. James G. Watt, Reagan's secretary of the interior, described environmentalism as 'a left-wing cult dedicated to bringing down the type of government I believe in'.

For people like this, denial was a psychological necessity to resolve the cognitive dissonance between their Cornucopian faith in growth and the evidence of mainstream climate science. Julian Simon was a salesman and his product was a bright future: why the long face? 'As soon as one predicted disaster doesn't occur, the doomsayers skip to another,' he complained in 1990. 'Why don't the doomsayers see that, in the aggregate, things are getting better? Why do they always think we're at a turning point – or at the end of the road?' In the tradition of Herman Kahn and Edward Teller, deniers presented themselves as proudly anti-apocalyptic, hence groups such as the Committee for a Constructive Tomorrow and books such as Ronald Bailey's *Eco-Scam: The False Prophets of Ecological Apocalypse.* To them, the debunking of neo-Malthusianism and cooling theory in the 1970s proved that all dire warnings could be safely dismissed as alarmism. In this way the oratorical hyperbole of people like Paul Ehrlich and Carl Sagan, so effective in the short term, became a weapon to be used against far more moderate voices. In his 1998 book *Climate of Fear: Why We Shouldn't Worry About Global Warming,* the conservative economist Thomas Gale Moore used words such as *hysteria, scaremongering* and *doomsayers* to disparage the scientific consensus. In 2003, Senator Inhofe called on Congress to 'reject prophets of doom who peddle propaganda masquerading as science in the name of saving the planet from catastrophic disaster'. Yet the scientists themselves were sober to a fault. When denialist Congressman Dana Rohrabacher accused them of exaggeration in a 1995 House hearing, White House scientist Robert Watson drily responded, 'The international assessments don't use the word *apocalypse*.'

The quintessential anti-apocalyptic text of climate denial is 2004's *State of Fear*, a no-holds-barred crank tour de force by Michael Crichton, the author of pseudo-scientific bestsellers such as *Jurassic Park* and *The Andromeda Strain*. The villain, Nicholas Drake, runs NERF, an environmental non-profit which needs to attract funding, and global warming isn't cutting it. 'Pollution scares the shit out of people,' he complains. 'You tell 'em they'll get cancer, and the money rolls in. But nobody is scared of a little warming. Especially if it won't happen for a hundred years.' His PR man has a wicked plan: NERF will secretly fund eco-terrorists to stage 'natural' disasters which will trick people into thinking that global warming causes extreme weather events. Success at last! The cover of *Time* reads, 'Climate Change Doomsday Ahead.'

Crichton projects onto his enemies his own propensity to decide on a narrative and then root around for the evidence to support it. The larger plot is anatomized by Professor Norman Hoffman, a highly strung Cornucopian who screams, 'False fears are a plague, a modern plague!' Before 1989, Hoffman explains at great length, the media did not often use terms such as '*crisis, catastrophe, cataclysm, plague, or disaster*'. Once the Soviet dragon had been slain, however, such language ran wild: 'The fall of the Berlin Wall created a vacuum of fear. Nature abhors a vacuum. Something had to fill it.' One of those things was the greenhouse effect. Now, he wails, fretful citizens are 'convinced that the environment of the entire planet is being destroyed around them. Remarkable! Like the belief in witchcraft, it's an extraordinary delusion – a global fantasy worthy of the Middle Ages. Everything is going to hell, and we must all live in fear.' As the rapacious Once-ler snaps in *The Lorax*, 'All you do is yap-yap and say, "Bad! Bad! Bad! Bad!"' Along the way, Crichton takes sideswipes at the IPCC, Hollywood environmentalists, political correctness, smoking bans, nuclear winter theory, neo-Malthusians, renewable energy and Rachel Carson, bolstering his paranoia with countless graphs, appendices and footnote citations.* In one outrageous appendix, he describes eugenics as a sobering lesson in the dangers of politicized pseudo-science: 'I am not arguing that global warming is the same as eugenics. But the similarities are not superficial.' President George W. Bush invited Crichton to a secret meeting at the Oval Office and was reportedly 'in near-total agreement'.

The most widely read novel about global warming, then, was one that insisted that it wasn't real and that those who said it was were either fools, grifters or fanatics. Where was the counter-argument? Climate activists complained that writers of fiction, traditionally so good at dramatizing existential peril, had let their sirens fall silent. 'Global warming has still to produce an Orwell or a Huxley, a Verne or a Wells, a *Nineteen Eighty-Four* or a *War of the Worlds*, or in film any equivalent of *On the Beach* or *Doctor Strangelove*,' wrote Bill McKibben in 2003. 'It may never do so. It may be that because – fingers crossed – we have escaped our most recent fear, nuclear annihilation via the Cold War, we resist being scared all over again. Fear has its uses, but fear on this scale seems to be disabling, paralysing.'

It might seem trivial to worry about the dearth of compelling stories about climate change, but the failure of fiction to get a handle on the subject reflects the struggle of scientists to craft an unignorable narrative. Compared to nuclear war, the climate emergency deprives popular storytellers of their usual toolkit. Global warming may move too fast for the planet but it is too slow for catastrophe fiction. How does one craft a tight plot out of a crisis that unfolds over decades rather than months or days? How can the heroes solve the problem and leave audiences with a cheering sense of closure? And who are the villains to be thwarted? Fossil-fuel tycoons and denialist politicians can wear the black hat but our collective complicity in a carbon-fuelled society is a buzzkill, morally and dramatically. What's more, the climate emergency is

*A footnote on Crichton's footnotes: many of the scientists he cited in the novel protested that their research had been wildly misrepresented.

the result not only of the actions we have traditionally considered pernicious but of the things we valorize, like procreation, progress and the pursuit of a better standard of life. 'The coming of doom is . . . the result of deeds that do not seem evil on the face of it,' wrote Isaac Asimov in his 1991 swansong *Our Angry Earth*. The paradoxical combination of impotence and guilt is therefore even greater than that inspired by the Bomb.

It is unfortunate that the most popular movie about cataclysmic climate change, earning $553 million worldwide, is one based on a fringe theory: Roland Emmerich's 2004 blockbuster *The Day After Tomorrow*. The German director has a gift for baroque devastation which absorbs not only the entire history of disaster fiction but the immense oil-on-canvas tribulations of John Martin; it was a canny decision to screen *The Day After Tomorrow* at a 2011 exhibition of Martin's paintings in London. Emmerich's feature-length debut, 1984's *The Noah's Ark Principle*, takes place on a space station capable of conjuring up hurricanes and floods. In *Independence Day* (1996), alien invaders memorably pulverize the White House. The creature in *Godzilla* (1998) decapitates the Chrysler Building. In *2012* (2009), which combines Mayan prophecy with the Noah myth and an eccentric theory about sudden shifts in the earth's axis, he makes the whole planet resemble Martin's *The Great Day of His Wrath*.* After 9/11, Emmerich felt a tad guilty: 'I had this feeling that there is some terrorist watching [*Independence Day*] in some cave and saying he should do it like the aliens.'

The Day After Tomorrow stemmed from a peculiar 1999 book called *The Coming Global Superstorm*. The work of Art Bell and Whitley Strieber, two writers known for their interest in alien abductions and the paranormal, the book is a bizarre medley of earnest climate science, clunky disaster fiction and crank catastrophism. Emmerich and his co-writer Jeffrey Nachmanoff skipped the stuff about hi-tech lost civilizations but kept the rest. Bell and Strieber supercharged a theory, first floated in the 1980s, that climate change could eventually shut down North Atlantic thermohaline circulation. This so-called

*After the non-event of 2000, frustrated eschatologists latched on to the mistaken New Age belief that the Mayan calendar prophesied the end of the world on 21 December 2012, which inspired several documentaries and hundreds of books.

ocean conveyor belt, which includes the Gulf Stream, carries warm water northwards from the Pacific and colder, saltier, deeper water southwards, moderating temperatures in both regions. By depositing vast amounts of fresh water in the North Atlantic, melting ice caps mess with the conveyor belt. A total shutdown would radically polarize the planet's climate, making hot regions much hotter and cold regions much colder. But although the conveyor belt is slowing and raising the possibility of collapse, it will not suddenly grind to a halt. The book, however, speculates that it could happen almost overnight and trigger a superstorm which would suck cold air down from the upper troposphere and plunge the Northern Hemisphere into either a deluge or an ice age, depending on whether it occurred in summer or winter. The *Day After Tomorrow*'s hero scientist Jack Hall (Dennis Quaid) predicts that it will take centuries but is soon forced to adjust the timeframe to months and then weeks. 'This is unbelievable . . . This is too fast,' he says, as if anticipating the complaints of any climate scientists watching.

In many ways, Emmerich's movie is a throwback to Wylie and Balmer's *When Worlds Collide* or Garrett P. Serviss's *The Second Deluge*, with its hero's journey from mockery to vindication, and the way in which the main characters' survival is supposed to emotionally eclipse the deaths of billions. The movie's climatic havoc is candidly absurd: tornadoes unpeel the Hollywood sign; the Statue of Liberty turns into a Popsicle; a new ice age arrives within a fortnight. For all that, the message is sincere. When Hall first presents his shutdown theory at a climate conference, he is sneered at by Vice-President Raymond Becker (Kenneth Welsh): 'Our economy is every bit as fragile as the climate. Perhaps you should keep that in mind before making sensationalist claims.' Welsh was cast for his resemblance to President Bush's vice-president, Dick Cheney. At the end of the movie, Becker issues a denier's *mea culpa.* 'For years we operated under the belief that we could continue consuming our planet's resources without consequence,' he says from the US government's new home in Mexico. 'We were wrong. *I* was wrong.' Now this really is a fantasy.

The Day After Tomorrow is the perfect example of how even a ridiculous movie can explore profound concerns. In the space of two hours, the viewer can engage with dread of the climate crisis;

guilt and self-disgust about human behaviour; the clash between science and politics; the psychology of alarm and denial; the challenges of survival; the acknowledgement of certain death; the fragility of civilization; the spectacular devastation of great cities; and the prospect of rebuilding a stronger, wiser world. Climatologists, however, didn't know quite what to say about a movie that combined good intentions with a plot that defied the laws of thermodynamics. 'On the one hand, I'm glad that there's a big-budget movie about something as critical as climate change,' one told *USA Today*. 'On the other, I'm concerned that people will see these over-the-top effects and think the whole thing is a joke.' Al Gore, a former student of Roger Revelle who had become his country's leading environmentalist, was more upbeat: 'People are going to walk out of the movie, and they're going to talk about this issue one way or the other. I see it as an opportunity to join with the scientific community to set the record straight.' To be fair to the filmmakers, the DVD release included a sober documentary about global warming in which experts breezily debunked the film's premise. Two years later, Gore's own Oscar-winning documentary *An Inconvenient Truth* kickstarted a more serious debate about global warming. 'BE WORRIED,' demanded the cover of *Time*. 'BE *VERY* WORRIED.'

Still the only climate-change blockbuster, Emmerich's picture sums up the writer's conundrum: any movie that gets thrills and spills from the subject is bound to be scientific nonsense, while an accurate one risks boredom. But just as most post-war disaster movies were about the Bomb even when they appeared to be about something else, climate anxiety is surely the primary emotional impulse behind the glut of end-of-the-world stories, in multiple genres, over the past two decades.

Guilty consciences abound. In Pixar's eco-parable *WALL-E* (2008), Earth is a dusty orange junkyard tended by a cheerful Asimovian robot while other robots service the planet's decadent refugees on cosmic cruise ships: 'There's plenty of space out in space!' The renovation of Earth is a necessarily hopeful ending for a film aimed at children but these images are far less affecting than the opening panorama of trash, where the last 'man' on earth is a robot curating his personal museum of civilization. Darren Aronofsky's *Mother!* (2018), meanwhile, is a feverish allegory of despoliation. The house occupied by Mother (Jennifer Lawrence) and the narcissistic poet Him (Javier Bardem) is Earth, which rapidly fills up with greedy, destructive humanity until the much-abused Mother burns the whole place to the ground. But Him cannot bear to live without worshippers and runs the experiment again, as he has countless times before, always with the same result: a broken apocalypse. In Alexander Payne's surprisingly grave comedy *Downsizing* (2017), Norwegian scientists invent a means of shrinking human beings down to about 13 centimetres so that they consume less space and fewer resources. But when the Norwegians learn about the release of huge amounts of methane, an extremely potent greenhouse gas, from the melting of Antarctic permafrost, they conclude that humanity's only remaining hope is an underground colony in which a tiny few can preserve the species. 'People have been predicting the end of the world for thousands of years, and now it's really happening,' Paul (Matt Damon) reflects with admirable fortitude. 'I guess somebody had to be right someday.'

The politics of denial, meanwhile, are neatly satirized in HBO's *Game of Thrones* (2011–19), when the warring clans of Westeros and Essos struggle to unite against the White Walkers, remorseless climate-zombies before whom struggles for the throne look like playground squabbles. Early warnings are brushed aside because the threat is too huge and too far away to apprehend. Perhaps the most realistic character is Cersei Lannister (Lena Headey), who would rather lose everything than forsake her internecine feuds. Of course, the most explicit climate movie of recent years is Adam McKay's allegorical comet drama *Don't Look Up* (2021), which dramatizes the real quandary that scientists face when trying to raise the alarm about global warming. Dr Randall Mindy (Leonardo DiCaprio) is so dry and technical that eyes glaze over, while Kate Dibiasky (Jennifer Lawrence again) is so intense that she is derided as 'the crazy chick who thinks we're all going to die'. 'Why aren't people terrified?' Mindy wails. 'What do we have to say? What do we have to do?' However they deliver the bad news, the news itself is the problem. 'Do you know how many the-world-is-ending meetings that we've had over the years?' sighs President Orlean (Meryl Streep). 'Economic collapse. Loose nukes. Car exhausts killing the atmosphere. Rogue AI . . .' Her fatuous son and chief of staff (Jonah Hill) picks up the thread: 'Drought. Famine. Plague. Alien invasion!

Population growth. Hole in the ozone . . .' While critics found McKay's satire grossly overstated, climate scientists welcomed its bluntness. 'They feel intense catharsis when they watch this film,' science writer Ketan Joshi claimed in *The Guardian*. 'It is not a great film, but to release that painful pressure valve, it doesn't need to be.'

Literary fiction about climate change, or 'cli-fi', is characterized, by and large, by a terrible impotence. Once the dam of denial breaks, futility rushes in. 'Everybody knew,' recalls a young woman in Margaret Atwood's 2009 novel *The Year of the Flood*. 'Nobody admitted to knowing. If other people began to discuss it, you tuned them out, because what they were saying was both so obvious and so unthinkable.' Eventually, the knowing becomes unbearable. 'The waiting builds up in you like a tide. You start wanting it to be done with. You find yourself saying to the sky, *Just do it. Do your worst. Get it over with.*' The singer Anohni explored this same emotional transition in her 2016 album about the climate emergency, *HOPELESSNESS*. A common figure in 2020s cli-fi – Sylvia in Jenny Offill's *Weather*, Francesca in Jessie Greengrass's *The High House*, the members of the Earthbridge commune in Alexandra Kleeman's *Something New Under the Sun* – is the climate activist who has been driven to despair and crossed the border that separates 'Time is short' from 'It's too late.' 'The whole complicated system of modernity which had held us up, away from the earth, was crumbling,' Greengrass writes, 'and we were becoming again what we had used to be: cold, and frightened of the weather, and frightened of the dark. Somehow while we had all been busy, while we had been doing those small things which added up to living, the future had slipped into the present.'

One could argue that such resignation is justified but it can sometimes feel self-indulgent – shame, rage and surrender masquerading as moral clarity, or even a form of apocalyptic anticipation. It is quite distinct from the urgent activism and 'radical hope' of groups such as Extinction Rebellion. As Gavin Schmidt of NASA's Goddard Institute has said, 'It sounds cute to say, "Oh, we're fucked and there's nothing we can do," but it's a bit of a nihilistic attitude. We always have the choice. We can continue to make worse decisions, or we can try to make ever better decisions.'

Kim Stanley Robinson, the writer who as good as invented cli-fi, skirts paralysing gloom by writing about people with the power to make better decisions. Robinson is what Danny Dorling describes as a 'practical possibilist', whose stories 'sit between those who say that all will be fine, and those who claim that we are doomed'. He was born in Ray Bradbury's hometown of Waukegan, Illinois, in 1952 and grew up in Southern California. He wrote his PhD dissertation on Philip K. Dick but his work has more in common with the world-changing ambitions of Victorian polymaths such as H. G. Wells and Camille Flammarion than it does with Dick's psychedelic radicalism. Robinson rigorously applies science to causes, consequences and, unusually, solutions. He is very interested in conferences.

Robinson's take on climate change can be summed up by one line from his 2004–7 *Science in the Capital* trilogy: 'It was science versus capitalism, yet again.' In this series, Robinson reorients a classic disaster narrative towards a cheering fantasy of evidence-led problem-solving. At first, the scientist heroes butt heads with a Bush-like Republican president and a scientific adviser who goes by the Kubrickian name of Dr Strengloft. But after Washington DC is inundated by a superstorm and frozen by a Gulf Stream shutdown, chastened Americans elect Phil Chase, a chimera of Al Gore, JFK and FDR who spearheads a radical package of environmental legislation and blue-sky geoengineering projects to repair the damage. 'Science contains in it a plan for dealing with the world we find ourselves in, a plan which aims to reduce human suffering and increase the quality of life on Earth for everyone,' Chase explains. 'In other words, science is a kind of politics already.' Asked why they do what they do, the scientists reply, 'I guess because we still kind of believe that the world can be saved.'

Robinson threaded the needle even more successfully in 2020's widely celebrated *The Ministry for the Future*, a long, dense, polyphonic novel in which technophilic optimism wrestles with apocalyptic pessimism. It opens in India in 2025, with a 'wet-bulb' heatwave whose intense humidity makes it hard to breathe and impossible to sweat: the Sun 'blazed like an atomic bomb, which of course it was.' Twenty million people are broiled alive. This climate atrocity inspires the intergovernmental 'Ministry for the Future' (reminiscent of H. G. Wells's First World War idea for a Ministry of Foresight) to save the world the hard way, with legal sanctions, financial incentives, geoengineering and many, many meetings, while an eco-terrorist group called the Children of Kali attempts to blast the carbon economy to a standstill. Economies crash, governments fall, cities drown and villages die, but the world does move forward, slowly and painfully, towards what Robinson calls 'the birth of a good Anthropocene': 'We will cope no matter how stupid things get . . . the only catastrophe that can't be undone is extinction.' Robinson refuses to choose from irreversible collapse, utopian rebirth or restoration of the status quo. It will be an unholy mess, he argues, but not necessarily the end of the world. He wants to make us touch the stove.

Islanded by dystopias, Robinson describes his approach as not exactly utopian but 'anti-anti-utopian'. He criticizes eco-nihilists who say that it is too late to ameliorate climate change – people like the British former environmentalist Paul Kingsnorth. 'There is no saving the world,' Kingsnorth has written, 'and the ones who say there is are the ones you need to save it from.' A former deputy editor of *The Ecologist*, Kingsnorth lost faith in environmentalism when he felt that mainstream greens had become merely problem-solving engineers whose goal of a sustainable, decarbonized world would lead to '*Brave New World* with windfarms and smartphones'. They in turn saw him, he suspected, as 'a Luddite, a nimby, a reactionary, a romantic; standing in the way of progress'. In 2009, Kingsnorth launched the Dark Mountain Project with Dougauld Hine, calling for a new kind of 'Uncivilised' writing to help us 'stand outside the human bubble and see us as we are'. The name comes from the last line of 'Rearmament', a 1935 poem by Robinson Jeffers, a Californian poet who preached 'inhumanism': rejecting the notion that humanity is the main character in the earth's story. As he wrote in 1925's 'Roan Stallion', 'Humanity is the start of the race; I say / Humanity is the mold to break away from.'

Kingsnorth also became interested in the philosophy of a considerably more problematic writer, Ted Kaczynski, who lived off-grid in Montana for twenty-five years, his primary communication with mainstream society being the bombs he mailed in his one-man war against the 'techno-industrial system'. This is why the FBI dubbed him 'the Unabomber' and arrested him in 1996, after he had killed three people and injured twenty-three. What unites the terrorist, the poet and the disabused environmentalist is a conviction that modern industrialized civilization is a problem in itself, founded on three dangerous myths: 'the myth of progress, the myth of human centrality, and the myth of our separation from "nature",' as Kingsnorth puts it.

Dark Mountain members have retreated into quietism from the agonizing business of trying to fight climate change. They dislike the bullish techno-optimistic heirs of Julian Simon and John von Neumann who believe that geoengineering and carbon-capture technology can put the brakes on global warming; genetically modified crops, lab-grown meat and 3D printing can feed the world; and, failing all of that, we can find new planets to live on. In this way, new technology is meant to redeem the sins of old technology, as if Victor Frankenstein had created a new, improved creature to catch the first one.* Scepticism is justified but Dark Mountain sees *all* mitigation efforts as futile. Whereas conventional environmentalists want to save the planet because it is our home, Dark Mountain wants us – or at least modern, industrialized, capitalist us – to get out of the planet's way. 'We do not believe that everything will be fine,' acknowledges the Dark Mountain manifesto, *Uncivilisation*. 'We are not even sure, based on current definitions of progress and improvement, that we want it to be.' Kingsnorth and Hine's austere version of solace is this: 'The end of the world as we know it is not the end of the world full stop.'

In George R. Stewart's 1949 pandemic novel *Earth Abides*, Isherwood Williams is an anthropologist who returns to civilization after a wilderness trip to find that civilization *is* a wilderness. A new disease has rendered America not quite empty – there are other scattered survivors – but extremely roomy. Agnostic about the human race, Isherwood is not the last man on earth but he wouldn't mind if he was. He is more than curious to witness 'the opening of the greatest of all dramas for a student such as he . . . What would happen to the world and its creatures without man? That he was left to see!' What makes *Earth Abides* remarkable is Stewart's serious

*Geoengineering itself produces the climate catastrophe in Bong Joon Ho's 2013 movie *Snowpiercer*: an effort to slow global warming with the cooling injection of stratospheric aerosols has spun out of control and created a new ice age.

engagement with the reality of an untenanted world. In most last-man stories, cities are largely intact, if sad and tatty, but Stewart, a prolific historian and toponymist, recognized that the world as we know it requires an enormous amount of maintenance. As Isherwood wanders equably around an unravelling America, Stewart keeps breaking off for lyrical disquisitions on what would happen if there were nobody to run the power stations, unblock the drains, fight the fires and do all those other jobs that we take for granted. How quickly it all falls apart. When Isherwood meets a married couple of survivors in New York City, he predicts, 'When the city died, they would hardly survive without it.'

The triumph of the wilderness over the city has Biblical resonance. For the author of Isaiah, cursing Babylon, this urban rewilding is the ultimate humiliation: 'But wild beasts of the desert shall lie there; and their houses shall be full of doleful creatures; and owls shall dwell there, and satyrs shall dance there.' In Revelation, too, Babylon becomes 'the habitation of devils, and the hold of every foul spirit, and a cage of every unclean and hateful bird'. Isherwood, however, belongs to a lineage of acceptance, and even relish, that runs from *After London* to J. G. Ballard to Dark Mountain. In S. Fowler Wright's *Deluge*, a much-praised catastrophe novel from 1928, a literal flood sweeps away decadent humanity and returns the world to a purer, more primitive state: 'the fresh sea-air blew over the recovered greenness of the fields that they had once polluted.' David Byrne spoofs this kind of pastoral fantasy of clearance and renewal in the 1988 Talking Heads song '(Nothing But) Flowers', imagining a couple standing like Adam and Eve in a new Eden where factories and shopping malls once stood. It is Joni Mitchell's 'Big Yellow Taxi' in reverse: they overgrew parking lots and put up a paradise. Once, the narrator fantasized about starting over again, just like this. Now, though, he dreams of microwaves and candy bars and all the creature comforts he used to despise: 'Don't leave me stranded here / I can't get used to this lifestyle.'

But what if there was nobody left alive? 'It's not the end of the world at all,' says John Osborne in *On the Beach*. 'It's only the end of us. The world will go on just the same, only we shan't be in it. I dare say it will get along all right without us.'

—

Some people have decided to forgo having children due to the climate crisis. While this is a legitimate choice on an individual level, it would obviously guarantee extinction if it were to be universally adopted. For antinatalists such as David Benatar and Les U. Knight, this is the dream: they want humanity to bow out altogether. In 1991, Knight graduated from Paul Ehrlich's Zero Population Growth organization to founding the Voluntary Human Extinction Movement. 'Eventually we'll be extinct anyway, but it would be so much nicer if we phased ourselves out through natural attrition,' he told *The Guardian*. 'Don't you find it a beautiful clean thought,' asks the misanthropic Birkin in D. H. Lawrence's *Women in Love*, 'a world empty of people, just uninterrupted grass, and a hare sitting up?' Despite his fierce opposition to apocalyptic environmentalism, the Canadian psychologist Jordan B. Peterson has made the extraordinary claim that everybody thinks this on some level. 'Perhaps Man is something that should never have been,' he writes. 'Perhaps the world should even be cleansed of human presence, so that Being and consciousness could return to the innocent brutality of the animal. I believe that the person who claims never to have wished for such a thing has neither consulted his memory nor confronted his darkest fantasies.'

Whether this really is a universal fantasy is debatable but it is one shared, and executed, by Crake in Margaret Atwood's *MaddAddam* trilogy. Crake's 'Waterless Flood' is a plague designed to replace *Homo sapiens* with a new race of peaceable, naked, grass-eating vegans with the smallest possible carbon footprint. Crake has been inspired by a chiliastic eco-cult, God's Gardeners, to give up on hoping that humans will change their ways. 'According to them it had been game over since agriculture was invented, six or seven thousand years ago,' Atwood writes in 2003's *Oryx and Crake*, which was published in French as *Le Dernier Homme*. 'After that, the human experiment was doomed, first to gigantism due to a maxed-out food supply, and then to extinction, once all the available nutrients had been hoovered up . . . Human society, they claimed, was a sort of monster, its main by-products being corpses and rubble.' There is a certain dreadful logic to the idea that if you want to save a planet imperilled by human behaviour, and you have given up believing that behaviour can be changed, then omnicide is the only solution.

Atwood began writing her novel after discussing the extinction of bird species (including the red-necked crake) with ornithologists. She has described Crake's plan as 'a sort of triage: if humanity goes, the rest of life stays; but if not, then not.'

'Speculation about what the world would be like after human control of it ended had been – long ago, briefly – a queasy form of popular entertainment,' writes Atwood in *Maddaddam*. Children of *Earth Abides* such as the History Channel series *Life After People* and Alan Weisman's book *The World Without Us* have consulted various experts to paint a picture of what the world, or at least cities, would look like minus human beings. These investigations have nudged the post-apocalyptic imagination away from the traditional blasted ashlands and twisted junkscapes towards the uncannily verdant ex-cities of *The Last of Us* and *Dawn of the Planet of the Apes*. Wandering through a decaying school in *Children of Men*, or peering out from the paperback covers of *Station Eleven* and *Leave the World Behind*, deer have become the strange new symbols of the post-collapse pastoral.

Barring ice ages, asteroids and supervolcanoes, this is what these thought experiments foretell. Very soon the unstewarded tunnels flood, followed by the streets and buildings. Five years later, the city wears a thick carpet of weeds, moss, clover and dead leaves, rising in hummocks where tree roots have cracked and buckled the paving stones. Insect life returns with a vengeance. When conditions are dry enough, an uncontrollable fire breaks out and blackens the city; wet enough, and rivers overflow, creating acres of marshland. Somewhere in the undergrowth, remnants made from sturdier materials such as cast iron, plastic and chromium-plated stainless steel long outlive their owners. Rats, cockroaches and domestic dogs die off without us but cats unbury their ferality and thrive alongside wolves and deer.

The fate of landmarks is as interesting to us as it was to the Romantics who pondered the future of St Paul's Cathedral. After two or three centuries, most bridges pop their rivets and tumble into the water. Within a similar timeframe, the Statue of Liberty's steel skeleton disintegrates, contra *Planet of the Apes*, and sheds its copper skin into the Atlantic. Concrete is more durable, so skyscrapers become ivy-cloaked nests for kestrels and sparrowhawks.

But over a century or two, as the steel supporting bars corrode and the groundwater rises, even these giants lean and eventually fall. By now, the entire city is a forest. Millions of years later, the last American monuments to an extinct race are the four faces carved into the solid granite of Mount Rushmore, presiding over the wilderness like ancient gods.

Meanwhile in the present day, ruined or abandoned urban areas offer us a bittersweet taste of the post-apocalyptic. Tourists visit the vacant quarters of inner-city Detroit or the Chernobyl Exclusion Zone, just as their ancestors visited Pompeii or Palmyra, to sample the pungent flavour of the world without us. 'The twentieth century had staked a great deal on the idea of the city,' the art critic John Russell wrote in 1967. 'For this reason, and because we know that our great cities could be destroyed in an instant and at any time from now onwards, a superstitious fascination attaches to the counter-idea of the city abandoned, petrified and left to rot and decay.'

The Chernobyl Exclusion Zone appeals to a taste for what the Irish writer Mark O'Connell calls 'apocalyptic kitsch'. Buildings shattered by war or natural disaster are usually razed and replaced – even Hiroshima and Nagasaki rose again – but the radiation released on 26 April 1986 banished all the people while leaving the 'Atomic City' of Pripyat to be eroded by time and the elements: shops stocked with rusting electronic goods and carpeted with broken glass; a swimming pool clotted with dead leaves and dirt; murals of Soviet glory rotting from the walls. Integral to the Zone's fascination is a certain callousness about the people who once lived there, so much less eerily compelling than what they left behind. It has even inspired a survival horror video game, *S.T.A.L.K.E.R.: Shadow of Chernobyl*, which is named after Andrei Tarkovsky's prophetic 1979 movie about the 'Zone'. The tourists come to this atomic Pompeii to ponder not so much what *has* happened but a spooky preview of what *will* happen; it offers a form of time travel. 'What lingers most in my memory of Chernobyl is life afterwards: the possessions without owners, the landscapes without people,' Svetlana Alexievich writes in *Chernobyl Prayer*. 'The roads going nowhere, the cables leading nowhere. You find yourself wondering just what this is: the past or the future. It sometimes felt to me as if I was recording the future.'

In 1986, the Zone immediately felt like a temporal rupture; a land of the unreal. One soldier involved in the initial evacuation joked darkly to Alexievich that his job title was 'director of the apocalypse zone'. Another compared it to a 'dreamlike world where the End of Time met the Stone Age'. The Zone has been compared to a ghost town, a movie set and an immersive simulation of an empty world. Yet because no people can resettle there, it is also a wildlife reserve as large as Luxembourg, where the fields are turning into forests, and the streets into fields: new homes for birds, wolves, deer and boar. The Zone thus represents both a catastrophic defeat for modernity and a return to Eden. 'It seems so normal,' Alan Weisman writes, 'as if apocalypse has turned out to be not so bad after all.'

But there is a double twist, like a standout episode of *The Twilight Zone*. Some of the animals of the Zone have been found to have mutated genes and shorter lifespans. And if humans were to disappear, hundreds of unattended power plants around the world would turn into timebombs. When their cooling pools eventually evaporated, each one would become a Chernobyl with nobody to clean it up. Call it the revenge of the Anthropocene.

Chernobyl tells yet another story. Some environmentalists argue that this accident, and the one at Fukushima, Japan, in 2011, scared many countries away from a form of energy that is an essential weapon in the fight against global warming. David Wallace-Wells has noted that air pollution from burning carbon kills more people every day than have died from all power-plant accidents put together. Seen purely in terms of the climate crisis, then, Chernobyl might look like a false alarm which sent us hurtling down the wrong path. 'My No. 1 worry is: what if we're focussed on entirely the wrong things?' the longtermist William MacAskill admitted to *The New Yorker*. 'What if we're just wrong? What if A.I. is just a distraction? Like, look at the Greens and nuclear power . . . It's very, very easy to be totally mistaken.'

Such questions animate this book. Are we – have we been – worrying about the right things? Have our fears made the world better or worse? Which warnings are essential to our future and which lead us to battle phantoms? Centuries of predictions reveal that there is no sure way of knowing which fears to prioritize even if you factor in every bias and listen to the majority of scientists – even if you *are* a scientist. Sneering at the expired dread of previous generations is no aid to making the correct calculations now.

Let us move away from the science and politics of existential risk and consider how the end of the world would *feel* to individuals. None of us has yet been forced to confront universal annihilation, but stories about such situations tell us that individuals, too, think about the fact that, in the end, all we are is the sum of our choices. If it really was the end of everything, might we find that we've been focused on entirely the wrong things?

MELBOURNE
THERE IS STILL

EPILOGUE

THE LAST DAY

In a way I feel kind of privileged. I mean, it's the biggest thing that ever happened. And we're gonna be there. I mean, no one was there to witness the beginning but we're gonna be there at the end.

Last Night (1998)

About fifteen years ago, I dreamed about the end of the world. Something was coming, presumably a comet or asteroid, and we had been given a precise, non-negotiable deadline. In the dream, I was on a train from London to Melbourne, along with a lively cross-section of humanity, to attend a gigantic last-night party. Once the colourful possibilities of panic and despair had been exhausted (I forget the details), a strange peace, a kind of joyful resignation, descended on the train. The last thing I remember was arriving in Melbourne and joining a jubilant wake for the human race. There was music and confetti and a giant banner reading, 'MELBOURNE WELCOMES THE END OF THE WORLD!'

The subconscious being what it is, I'm afraid I can't explain why the dream had so much in common with one film I hadn't seen yet (*On the Beach*) and another that hadn't even been made (*These Final Hours*), nor how it was possible to travel from London to Melbourne by train. Weren't there any parties closer to home? What I remember most powerfully is an enormous sense of relief that my own death coincided with everyone else's. A fellow passenger told me that what he dreaded about death was leaving the world too soon. Unless you possess an ego as formidable as Ayn Rand's ('It is not I who will die,' she once said, 'it is the world that will end'), you will be aware that the rest of humanity will press on without you. An extinction-level event, however, produces a remarkable sense of solidarity: we will all go together when we go. The very thought of omnicide as a unifying force would of course seem obscene to longtermists such as Toby Ord and Jonathan Schell, but Stanley Kubrick understood the emotional impulse. 'Sartre once wrote that if there was one thing you could tell a man about to be executed that would make him happy, it was that a comet would strike the earth the next day and destroy every living human being,' he told *Playboy* in 1968. 'This is not so much a collective death wish or self-destructive urge as a reflection of the awesome and agonizing loneliness of death.' Still, the sense of relief I felt in the dream bothered me. Had my fear of death, if only subconsciously, led me to apocalyptic conclusions? Did part of me want the global closure of the final day?

One day in 1966, an unsettling piece of vivid orange graffiti appeared on a sidewalk in New York City. 'Some day / The day will come / When the day won't,' it read. The day holds a special place in the literature of apocalypse: Judgement Day, Doomsday, The Day, Day One, *The Day After*, *The Day After Tomorrow*. The literal, universal last day, however, is relatively rare in fiction. When it does come, it comes as a surprise, as real-life disasters usually do. So while the thought experiment is common enough, in John Donne ('What if this present were the world's last night?'), Robert Browning ('Who knows but the world may end tonight'), and inspirational tea towels ('Live each day as if it were your last'), to really know the date in advance is something else entirely. The human mind cannot easily cope with an inexorable countdown and the choices it demands. The question 'What do you want to do with the rest of your life?' becomes more pressing when the rest of your life is numbered in days and every decision is consequential.

In August 1962, two months before the Cuban Missile Crisis, *The Boston Herald* asked six Bostonians what they would do if they knew for sure that the world was going to end in four days. According to a wry report in *The New Yorker*, two women opted for a holiday in Bermuda. An electrician, torn between hedonism and salvation, said that he'd 'either tie one on or spend four days in church'. An insurance agent decided that he and his family would 'stay together and spend the time quietly. Really just go along the way that we always do.' *The New Yorker* concluded that it concurred with the schoolteacher who said, 'Frankly, if the world was going to end in four days, I'd like to have it be a surprise.'

Why the world would end, and why so soon, was immaterial to *The Boston Herald*'s thought experiment, as it was to Ray Bradbury's eerily fatalistic 1951 story 'The Last Night of the World'. 'Do we deserve this?' asks the wife. 'It's not a matter of deserving; it's just that things didn't work out,' says the husband. Nobody panics, or cries, or changes their behaviour at all. The last night is just another night. Two years later, Richard Matheson explored a fuller range of possibilities in 'The Last Day'. The Sun is getting closer and the protagonist, Richard, wakes up hungover after a party to greet 'the final twilight of everything'. Unlike *I Am Legend*, the story was not popular enough to have a major influence on other writers, but Matheson's survey of human behaviour feels like a blueprint nonetheless: the suicides, the shut-ins, the hedonists, the murderers and arsonists, the last-minute worshippers. 'People die the way they lived,' Richard says. 'Some good, some bad.'

The first line of Bradbury's story – 'What would you do if you knew that this was the last night of the world?' – is the question that the Canadian filmmaker Don McKellar asked his friends when he was writing his 1998 movie *Last Night*. He worked their answers into his story about a group of Torontonians in the six hours leading up to the final midnight. (While the permanent daylight implies that it is yet again the fault of that steady-state H-bomb the Sun, yet again the details don't matter.) Patrick (McKellar), recently bereaved, wants to be home alone. His sister Jenny (Sarah Polley) is heading with her boyfriend to a party in the centre of town, 'to celebrate and to mourn'. His best friend Craig (Callum Keith Rennie) is completing an ambitious checklist of sexual escapades. Sandra (Sandra Oh) is trying to get home to her husband to carry out a suicide pact. While there are occasional screams and gunshots in the distance, McKellar said, 'The people who interested me were those that could come to terms with it one way or another and had built some sort of ritual to keep them going until the end. Those aren't necessarily the most healthy decisions, but that was the kind of response I could understand and empathize with. These were people who were persevering in the face of annihilation. I saw a certain heroism in that response that I hadn't seen in other movies.'

When it came out in the same year as *Deep Impact* and *Armageddon*, McKellar's movie was greeted as a quirky, human-scale counterpoint. As recently as 1998, the fact that it really was the last night was an audacious novelty in cinema. 'I think about three-quarters of the way through, you get that feeling – "Oh my God, he's gonna go for it, he's gonna end the world."' McKellar said. Now, though, *Last Night* looks like a trailblazer. As we know, the impact movie's hard turn towards hopelessness, in *Melancholia*, *Seeking a Friend for the End of the World*, *These Final Hours* and *Don't Look Up*, has been a radical and revealing shift. Throw in Todd Berger's black comedy *It's a Disaster*, Daryl Wein and Zoe Lister-Jones's twee *How It Ends* and Camille Griffin's *Silent Night*, a comedy of manners crossed with an allegory of climate change, and there are more last-day movies than ever. This cannot be an encouraging sign. Yet, with the exception of *Melancholia*, each movie closes with an affirmation of love of one kind or another. Writer-director Lorene Scafaria traced *Seeking a Friend for the End of the World* back to 9/11: 'I found myself reaching out and trying to contact an old boyfriend, and calling old friends I hadn't talked to in a long time . . . This horrible time can bring out people's closeness and their humanity.' In moments of crisis, the sentimental clichés prove true. Nobody has come up with a better idea than love.

One day in 2012, his twenty-second birthday, a man from Buckinghamshire, England, called Steven Brosnan woke up in a military hospital to learn from a recorded announcement that meteorites contaminated with bacteria had caused a zombie plague. He found other survivors, including a fourteen-year-old girl whom he took under his wing while rising to the various challenges of life during the zombie apocalypse. After two days of reckoning with a world in pieces, Brosnan woke up in his own bed, went downstairs, and found his parents waiting for him. In the next room was the mentalist Derren Brown. The whole thing had been an elaborate illusion for the TV show *Derren Brown: Apocalypse*, carefully seeded over several months with fake media broadcasts, dozens of actors and even a fabricated meteor shower. The timing was pegged to hype around the end of the Mayan calendar but the purpose was to jolt an aimless, complacent young man into life. 'If the world ended tomorrow, would you be happy with how you'd lived your life?' Brown asked on the show. He was recreating the arc of Simon Pegg's characters in Edgar Wright's movies *Shaun of the Dead* and *The World's End* – a feckless slacker galvanized and redeemed by an apocalyptic emergency – with a real person.

Using the end of the world as a form of life coaching has not caught on but it worked for Brosnan. Rather than being traumatized, he was empowered to turn his life around, and filled with gratitude for the people he had thought he would never see again. 'I think the apocalypse for me was a major chapter in my book,' he told Radio 4 a decade later. 'It was life-changing. And I can tell you who I am. I'm a person who appreciates everything that I have. I make sure that people know that they feel appreciated. Anything could happen. Anything could suddenly [snaps fingers] strike us, either as individuals or as a huge populace. It could happen all of a sudden. And I don't want that regret of knowing that I could have shown more appreciation or love to someone.'

Six years later, another experiment took place in Hawaii, but that one was unplanned. At 8.07 a.m. on 13 January 2018, during a tense period in relations between the US and North Korea, emergency alert systems in Hawaii accidentally issued a terrifying media alert: 'BALLISTIC MISSILE THREAT INBOUND TO HAWAII. SEEK IMMEDIATE SHELTER. THIS IS NOT A DRILL.' Authorities identified the error within three minutes but it was thirty-eight minutes before a correction was issued. During that time, most Hawaiians checked other news sources and concluded that the alert was a glitch, but a significant number believed that they were about to die. Researchers Rich Ling and Brett Oppegaard subsequently interviewed 418 of them and found that the most common response was a 'desire to reach loved ones'. The only significant lawbreaking was in the form of people who had broken the speed limit in the process. One woman recalled overhearing snatches of phone conversations in a crowded parking lot: 'I'm sorry, Mom.' 'I love you, baby.'

'I'm so sorry about the fight. It was so stupid.' 'You were a great dad. I love you, Daddy.' Ling and Oppegaard concluded that 'the false missile alert will play a role in the future lives of these people . . . a part of the way that they define themselves.'

The epiphany produced by a brush with death does not always last long. Some people sink back into old habits, like a patient who emerges from hospital after a heart attack and, after a brief period of abstinence, returns to cigarettes and hamburgers. Writing in 1938, when the world was on the brink of war, J. B. Priestley closed *The Doomsday Men* by sardonically noting that the global unity inspired by the close shave was short-lived: 'flinging a few last curses at the memory of those three insane brothers who had tried to destroy the world at one stroke, men returned to their ordinary tasks and thoughts, perhaps to destroy the world piece by piece.' Nonetheless, renewed appreciation for life as we know it is the most positive quality in end-of-the-world stories. It is there in *Station Eleven*'s tender requiem for civilization, and in the final scene of *Don't Look Up*, when the three defeated astronomers gather with Professor Mindy's family for a last supper just before the comet hits. There is nothing more to say about that, so they talk instead about apple pie and gourmet coffee and all the small, taken-for-granted privileges they have enjoyed. 'The thing of it is we really did have everything, didn't we?' says Mindy. 'I mean, when you think about it.' People often report that exposure to potent images of the end of the world can make the existence of the world as it is seem suddenly miraculous. The historian Paul Boyer recalled leaving a cinema in Times Square on New Year's Eve, 1959, after seeing *On the Beach*, and feeling 'overwhelmed by the sheer *aliveness* of the raucous celebrators'. C. S. Lewis argued in 1955 that this might be the paramount virtue of eschatological fiction:

> Work of this kind gives expression to thoughts and emotions which I think it good that we should sometimes entertain. It is sobering and cathartic to remember, now and then, our collective smallness, our apparent isolation, the apparent indifference of nature, the slow biological, geological, and astronomical processes which may, in the long run, make many of our hopes (possibly some of our fears) ridiculous. If *memento mori* is sauce

for the individual, I do not know why the species should be spared the taste of it.

'Do any human beings ever realize life while they live it? – every, every minute?' asks Emily in Thornton Wilder's 1938 play *Our Town.* The answer, of course, is no. How could we? It's all we've ever known. But contemplating the end can help.

During my two-year binge of end-of-the-world stories I came to wonder, most of all, about what good this fascination does us. When is it actually useful? *Fascination* derives from the Latin verb *fascinare* (to bewitch); in the seventeenth century, it meant an evil enchantment that rendered the victim unable to escape or resist, like the gaze of a snake. 'You should think about how civilization might fall apart,' S. J. Beard of the Centre for the Study of Existential Risk at Cambridge University told Radio 3 in 2022. 'That's a good thing. But let's put that natural curiosity and our natural sense of horror, or sense of the sublime that we feel and can be really quite delicious, let's put that to work in actually addressing real-world problems rather than just spending all our time watching movies about zombies.'

I have realized that I do not have an apocalyptic imagination, or at least I resist its call. This may be partly because I am prone to depression and health anxiety. If you are susceptible to catastrophizing, then the standard advice is to check your fears against the facts and put them in perspective. You have to train yourself to say that things are not as bad as they seem and the worst will not happen. The goal is not complacency but sanity – freedom from unjustified dread. Being a father also steers me away from the precipice because to tell a child that there is no hope and no future strikes me as obscene.

Invoking the end is entirely legitimate for writers of speculative fiction and a valid, if risky, strategy for activists, in order to spur reflection, appreciation or prophylactic action. Three groups of people, however, seem not just to expect it but to want it. First we have the nihilists, from Anna Kavan, craving the purity of obliteration, to the three promortalist brothers in *The Doomsday Men* who actively want the world to end because they believe life is painful and pointless – suicidal ideation on a global scale. 'The earth is evil,' says Justine in *Melancholia*. 'We don't need to grieve for it.' One notch down are those, like Margaret Atwood's Crake or D. H. Lawrence's Birkin, who would like to retain the planet but erase all the people. Fortunately, such annihilating misanthropy tends to manifest only in the realm of fiction rather than, say, policy-making.

Then there are the apocalyptic heirs of John of Patmos – the premillennialists, the totalitarians, the survivalists – who subscribe to the idea that the world could be washed clean with human blood – provided, of course, that the blood is not their own. They all require things to get worse and worse so that the great transformation can occur. The notion that megadeath could remedy human nature, leaving behind only the best of us, might be history's most dangerous fallacy.

Finally, we come to the doomers, who raid the end of the world for ersatz gravitas and mistake defeatism for moral seriousness. The evolutionary purpose of fear is to jolt one into an act of self-preservation but one cannot live in a constant state of psychic emergency. The higher the stakes, the less tenable fear is, and the more likely it is to breed disassociation or hopelessness. The doomers have overdosed on dread. We have to live in the space between 'Everything will be OK' and 'Everything is fucked,' between denial and despair, between Daphne and Harper in *The White Lotus*, because neither position is useful, nor morally virtuous. While I am in no position to assure you that climate change, nuclear war, pandemics or unfriendly AI definitely *won't* finish us off, I can say that wallowing in doom won't improve matters and might even amount to collaboration. 'Proclaiming someone's or something's defeat contributes to it,' the writer and activist Rebecca Solnit argued in a 2022 essay about climate despair. 'It's a form of sabotage.'

If you do not believe in glorious apocalyptic transformations, the crucial question is whether the value of life – mine, yours, humanity's – depends on there being a future, or whether it lies in the past and present of the experience. 'What point was there to all of it then?' thinks Richard in Matheson's 'The Last Day'. 'None, none at all. Because it was all ending.' Richard decides to have a final meal with his extended family, after which his sister's family takes sleeping pills while he sits on the porch with his mother to watch the end. 'They sat there in the evening of the last day. And, though there was no actual point to it, they loved each other.' But he is wrong, of course. That would be like saying life has no point because it ends in death. The point is that it happened.

I find myself coming back to something that Norbert Wiener, the father of cybernetics, wrote in 1956, when he was wrestling with the idea of entropy: 'We are not fighting for a definitive victory in the indefinite future. It is the greatest possible victory to be, to continue to be, and to have been. No defeat can deprive us of the success of having existed for some moment of time in a universe that seems indifferent to us.'

Everybody dies, everything ends – but not yet. Not yet.

Acknowledgements

My agents Antony Topping and Zoë Pagnamenta once again proved their ability to turn a vague idea into an actual book. Ravi Mirchandani at Picador and Shelley Wanger and Lisa Kwan at Pantheon saw the book's potential, gave me a chance to write it, and nurtured it with their encouragement and wisdom. Thanks also to their colleagues: Nicholas Blake, Kate Green, Nick Griffiths, Lindsay Nash, Lewis Russell and Jessica Cuthbert Smith at Picador; Kevin Bourke, Julianne Clancy, Lisa D'Agostino, Altie Karper, Lisa Lucas, Juliane Pautrot and Bill Thomas at Pantheon. It wasn't easy coming up with a jacket design for a book like this but Eli Mock nailed it. Nor is it easy to take photographs of me that I can share with the world without wincing, but Alexandra Dao, my schoolfriend and favourite photographer, did it again.

Given the scope of *Everything Must Go*, I am grateful to have had a fleet of early readers whose feedback helped me shape the material, sharpen the storytelling and root out errors. Joshua Blackburn, Ian Dunt, Dan Jolin, Damien Morris, John Mullen and Phil Tinline read individual sections. Lucy Aitken, Lucy Jolin and Alexis Petridis read the whole thing in draft form. Tom Chivers, Christina Pagel, Adam Rutherford and Giles Sparrow helped me clarify the science. Marvel expert Douglas Wolk dug out an old *Silver Surfer* letters page for me. Jenny Lord encouraged me to come up with a better, less depressing subtitle.

Many friends expressed enthusiasm for the idea and suggested avenues I might pursue. Thanks to Pete Baran, Adam Biles, Matt

Blackden, Loo Brealey, Murray Chalmers, Jenny Colgan, Clark Collis, John Darnielle, Sarah Donaldson, Jon Doran, Jonn Elledge, Alex Giles, Olivia Guest, Michael Hann, Phil Harrison, Jason Hazeley, Stuart Houghton, Sali Hughes, Gareth Jones, Ted Kessler, Ferdinand Kingsley, Steven Males, Caitlin Moran, Kate Mossman, John Niven, John Patterson, Andy and Dionne Pemberton, Nicola Penfold, Matt Phillips, Hugo Rifkind, Justin Robertson, Jude Rogers, Sophie Rouse, Jean Seaton, Arthur Snell, Neal Spencer, Matthew Sweet, D. J. Taylor, Luke Turner, Matt Weiner, Francis Wheen, Roy Wilkinson and Ian Winwood.

Some sections in the book began life as essays. Thanks to Rebecca Laurence at *BBC Culture* and Jacob Furedi at *UnHerd* for commissioning me to write in depth about apocalypse-adjacent subjects. Paul Laity, Charlotte Northedge and Liese Spencer at *The Guardian* commissioned my essay on W. B. Yeats's 'The Second Coming' in the depths of lockdown, which might be where this book began. Alex Diggins at *The Daily Telegraph* asked me to interview John Carpenter. Ian Tucker at *The Observer* commissioned me to cover the launch of Just Stop Oil. Thanks also to the young activists who put their trust in me, especially Hannah Hunt.

I felt most connected to the wider world while writing this book through my podcast work. Thanks to the team at Oh God What Now?, especially Alex Andreou, Martin Bojtos, Ian Dunt, Andrew Harrison, Naomi Smith and Ros Taylor. Making Origin Story with Ian has been perhaps the most rewarding, mind-expanding experience of my career. Regular listeners may notice that I repurposed some of the material in this book for the episodes on nuclear war and climate denial. Thanks to all of them, especially the Patreon backers who make it possible. Thanks to the Origin Story team – Jade Bailey, Jessica Harpin, Anne-Marie Luff and Simon Williams – and most of all to Ian, who has contributed more to my thinking and writing about these ideas than anybody that I don't actually share a house with. He is the perfect creative partner.

During the research process, I consulted around eight hundred books, not to mention countless magazines and newspapers, and most of these were made available by the staff of that miraculous institution the British Library. May I never take it for granted. The Internet Archive was also an invaluable treasure trove.

A nod to some people who didn't know they were helping me. The title *Everything Must Go* was not taken directly from the Manic Street Preachers' classic 1996 album but James, Nicky and Sean have always been an inspiration, as a band and as people, so I'm happy for people to assume that it was. Nella and Raven of the excellent Apocalist Book Club podcast introduced me to some obscure early end-of-the world novels. Geoff Dyer didn't realize he was giving me advice when I interviewed him for the Bunker podcast but he supplied me with a vital mantra in times of doubt: 'Write the book only you could write.' This book is dedicated to Dom Phillips, who was my first proper editor, a mentor and a friend, and who was killed while doing his bit to preserve the world. I wish he was able to read this.

Finally, I am grateful now and always to my family. Thanks to Tola and Tamira Lynskey, and my late father Dave, with whom I used to watch *The Twilight Zone* and read Stephen King novels. I think he would have been pleasantly surprised by my late-blooming interest in his beloved science fiction. And thanks most of all to the people I share my life with: Lucy, Eleanor and Luke. I cannot promise that I would prove to be a resourceful warrior patriarch in a post-apocalyptic world but in this world, which we are lucky to have, we stick together.

Notes

All quotes from the Bible are from the King James Version. All emphases in quotes are in the original text.

EPIGRAPHS

vii 'Anticipating the end of the world': David Mitchell, *Cloud Atlas* (Hodder and Stoughton, 2004), p. 471.

vii 'Despite everything': Patricia Lockwood, *No One is Talking About This* (Bloomsbury Circus, 2021), p. 117.

INTRODUCTION

3 'Theories that involve the end of the world': Jill Lepore, 'The Atomic Origins of Climate Science', *The New Yorker*, 22 January 2017.

3 'everything that's going on in the world': *The White Lotus*, season 2, episode 1, 'Ciao', written and directed by Mike White. Aired 30 October 2022, on HBO.

3 'Such convictions': Saul Bellow, *Herzog* (Viking Press, 1964), pp. 316–17.

4 A peer-reviewed 2021 survey: Caroline Hickman et al., 'Climate Anxiety in Children and Young People and Their Beliefs about Government Responses to Climate Change: A Global Survey', *The Lancet Planetary Health*, vol. 5, no. 12 (December 2021).

4 In a 2020 YouGov poll: 'How Americans Believe the World Will End', *yougov.com*, 18 March 2020.

4 'the Great Awfulization': Sean Fennessey, interview with Adam McKay, *The Big Picture*, podcast audio, 14 December 2021.

4 'It's pretty clear the world is ending': *Marc Maron: End Times Fun*, directed by Lynn Shelton (2020).

4 'no chance for the planet': Sally Rooney, *Beautiful World, Where Are You* (Faber, 2021), p. 94.

4 'being in a plane': Sheila Heti, *Pure Colour* (Vintage, 2023), p. 157.

4 'Hey, what can you say?': Bo Burnham, 'That Funny Feeling', on *Inside* (Imperial, 2021).

4 'the popular turn to fatalism': Lauren Oyler, *Fake Accounts* (4th Estate, 2022), p. 6.

5 'we need fictions of beginnings': Frank Kermode, *The Sense of an Ending: Studies in the Theory of Fiction with a New Epilogue* (Oxford University Press, 2000; first published 1967), p. 190.

5 'We always want a "conclusion"': D. H. Lawrence, *Apocalypse* (Penguin, 1995; first published 1931), p. 93.

6 'where we as humans destroy ourselves': Harry Lambert, '"This Could be Our Last Century on Earth": Martin Rees on the Threats Facing Humanity', *The New Statesman*, vol. 151, no. 5686 (23–29 September 2022).

6 'The world is unhappy': Stephen Schneider with Lynne E. Mesirow, *The Genesis Strategy: Climate and Global Survival* (Plenum Press, 1976), p. 1.

6 Barry McGuire's warning: Barry McGuire, 'Eve of Destruction' (Dunhill, 1965).

6 'this world is at the end of its tether': H. G. Wells, *Mind at the End of Its Tether* (William Heinemann, 1945), p. 1.

6 'bad form to praise the world': Johan Huizinga, *The Waning of the Middle Ages* (Doubleday Anchor, 1924), p. 31.

6 'Who cannot see': Paul Boyer, *When Time Shall Be No More: Prophecy Belief in Modern American Culture* (Harvard University Press, 1992), pp. 231–2.

6 'Apocalypse from Now On': Susan Sontag, *AIDS and Its Metaphors* (1989), in *Illness as Metaphor and AIDS and Its Metaphors* (Penguin Classics, 2002), p. 173.

6 'pressure of reality': Wallace Stevens, 'The Noble Rider and the Sound of Words' (1942), in *The Necessary Angel: Essays on Reality and the Imagination* (Faber and Faber, 1960), p. 22.

7 'It is not possible': ibid., p. 21.

7 'provides an unremitting mood of catastrophe': Don DeLillo, *Mao II* (Vintage, 1992), p. 72.

7 'No survivors, no story': Stephen King, *Danse Macabre* (Macdonald, 1981), p. 374.

8 'our planet will be at a loss': Camille Flammarion, *Omega: The Last Days of the World* (Cosmopolitan Publishing Company, 1894), p. 113.

9 'Man dreaded the end': Geoffrey Dennis, *The End of the World* (Eyre and Spottiswoode, 1930), p. 127.

9 'from now on to the end of human history': Susan Sontag, 'The Imagination of Disaster' (1965), in *Against Interpretation and Other Essays* (Penguin, 2009; first published 1966), p. 224.

10 'apocalyptic twins': Curt Stager, 'Terrifying Parallels between Twin Threats of Climate Change and Nuclear Ruin', *The Washington Post*, 27 October 2017.

10 Modern thinking on existential risk: information about the history of existential risk from Thomas Moynihan, *X-Risk: How Humanity Discovered Its Own Extinction* (Urbanomic, 2020) and Toby Ord, *The Precipice: Existential Risk and the Future of Humanity* (Bloomsbury, 2020).

10 'I myself give our species': John Leslie, *The End of the World: The Science and Ethics of Human Extinction* (Routledge, 1998), p. x.

10 'Traditionally, this topic domain': Raffi Khatchadourian, 'The Doomsday Invention', *The New Yorker*, 23 November 2015.

10 'might have the potential': Nick Bostrom and Milan M. Ćirković, eds, *Global Catastrophic Risks* (Oxford University Press, 2008), p. 1.

10 'one that threatens': ibid., p. 4.

10 In his 2020 book *The Precipice*: Ord, p. 167.

11 'Distance in time': William MacAskill, *What We Owe the Future* (Oneworld, 2022), p. 10.

11 'To me, the only real immorality': Eric Norden, 'Playboy Interview: Stanley Kubrick', *Playboy*, vol. 15, no. 9 (September 1968).

12 'How come everybody gets to visit': Robert Silverberg, 'When We Went to See the End of the World' (1972), in Martin H. Greenberg, ed., *The End of the World: Stories of the Apocalypse* (Skyhorse, 2010), p. 266.

12 'From the deluge': J. G. Ballard, 'Cataclysms and Dooms' (1977), in *A User's Guide to the Millennium: Essays and Reviews* (HarperCollins, 1996), p. 208.

13 'one can participate in the fantasy': Sontag, 'The Imagination of Disaster'.

13 'Come, Armageddon!': Morrissey, 'Everyday is Like Sunday' (His Master's Voice, 1988).

13 'Rose had read books': Rumaan Alam, *Leave the World Behind* (Bloomsbury, 2021), p. 233.

14 'It may be that nothing in the world': King, *Danse Macabre*, p. 158.

14 'you see catastrophe after catastrophe': Emily St John Mandel, *Station Eleven* (Picador, 2015), p. 248.

15 'Yes, this planet is a terrible mess': Kurt Vonnegut, *A Man Without a Country* (Bloomsbury, 2006), p. 131.

PROLOGUE

19 'HURRY UP PLEASE IT'S TIME': T. S. Eliot, *The Waste Land* (1922), in *Collected Poems 1909–1962* (Faber and Faber, 1974), p. 69.

19 'a totally new perception of time': Norman Cohn, *Cosmos, Chaos and the World to Come: The Ancient Roots of Apocalyptic Faith* (Yale University Press, 1993), p. 76.

20 'nightmare lust for cleanliness': Frederick Turner, *The New World: An Epic Poem* (Princeton University Press, 1985), p. 53.

21 'needed to know the end': Lawrence, *Apocalypse*, p. 80.

22 'merely the ravings of a maniac': Jonathan Kirsch, *A History of the End of the World: How the Most Controversial Book in the Bible Changed the Course of Western Civilization* (HarperOne, 2006), p. 5.

22 'not only the last': Perry Miller, 'The End of the World' (1951), in *Errand into the Wilderness* (Belknap Press, 1956).

23 'hidden side of Christianity': Lawrence, *Apocalypse*, p. 69.

23 'The second half of the Apocalypse': ibid., p. 80.

23 'No doubt, though this book': Saint Augustine, *The City of God*, translated by Marcus Dods (Modern Library, 1950), p. 737.

23 'a curious record': George Bernard Shaw, *The Adventures of the Black Girl in Her Search for God* (Constable & Company, 1932), p. 73.

26 'called by the spiritual Chiliasts': Augustine, p. 719.

26 'burned and renewed': ibid., p. 762.

26 'relax your fingers': Eugen Weber, *Apocalypses: Prophecies, Cults and Millennial Beliefs Through the Ages* (Harvard University Press, 1999), p. 13.

26 'in your own days, few and evil': Kirsch, p. 142.

26 'the man responsible': Frank Kermode, 'Apocalypse and the Modern', in Saul Friedländer et al., eds, *Visions of Apocalypse: End or Rebirth?* (Holmes & Meier, 1985), p. 89.

27 'small esteem': Kirsch, p. 103.

28 'The time of the harvest has come!': Thomas Müntzer, 'Prague Manifesto', in *The Collected Works of Thomas Müntzer*, edited and translated by Peter Matheson (T. & T. Clark, 1988), p. 371.

28 In February 1534: information about the siege of Münster from Norman Cohn, *The Pursuit of the Millennium: Revolutionary Millenarians and Mystical Anarchists of the Middle Ages* (Pimlico, 2004; first published 1957) and Anthony Arthur, *The Tailor-King: The Rise and Fall of the Anabaptist Kingdom of Münster* (St Martin's Press, 1999).

29 'I am shaken': Friedrich Reck, *Diary of a Man in Despair*, translated by Paul Rubens (New York Review Books, 2013), p. 13.

29 'the tradition of apocalyptic fanaticism': Cohn, *The Pursuit of the Millennium*, p. 286.

30 'called him Antichrist': Christopher Hill, *Antichrist in Seventeenth-Century England*, revised edition (Verso, 1990), p. 20.

30 'It is difficult to exaggerate': Christopher Hill, *The World Turned Upside Down: Radical Ideas During the English Revolution* (Temple Smith, 1972), p. 77.

30 'You fix the name of antichristian': Hill, *Antichrist*, p. 132.

30 'Take heed of computation': ibid., p. 146.

30 'God made me the messenger': Boyer, *When Time Shall Be No More*, p. 225.

31 'For a century it was read': Miller, 'The End of the World'.
31 'We have it in our power': Thomas Paine, *Common Sense* (W. and T. Bradford, 1791), pp. 87–8.
31 'Finding all the signs of the times': Daniel Cohen, *Waiting for the Apocalypse* (Prometheus Books, 1983), p. 16.
31 'madmen, madwomen': Weber, p. 176.
32 'the whole of American Protestantism': Whitney R. Cross, *The Burned-over District: The Social and Intellectual History of Enthusiastic Religion in Western New York, 1800–1850* (Cornell University Press, 1950), p. 320.
32 'If [Christ] does not come': Kirsch, p. 184.
32 the psychologist Leon Festinger: Leon Festinger, Henry W. Riecken and Stanley Schachter, *When Prophecy Fails: A Social and Psychological Study of a Modern Group that Predicted the Destruction of the World* (Pinter & Martin, 1956).
32 'This shop is closed': Cohen, p. 31.
32 'Our fondest hopes': ibid., p. 32.
32 'the follies of 1843': Cross, p. 320.
33 'We Christians are sheltered': Boyer, *When Time Shall Be No More*, p. 299.
34 'blessedness and peace': ibid., p. 99.
34 'the childish, nay foolish': ibid., p. 105.
34 'there shall be famines': Cohen, p. 196.
35 'the megalomaniac view': Richard Hofstadter, 'The Paranoid Style in American Politics', in *The Paranoid Style in American Politics* (Vintage, 2008; first published 1965), p. 38.
35 'catastrophe or the fear of catastrophe': ibid., p. 39.
35 'Whatever we do': ibid., p. 21.
35 'Time is running out': ibid., p. 30.
36 'Evidently, Fundamentalists': Walter M. Miller Jr and Martin H. Greenberg, eds, *Beyond Armageddon: Twenty-One Sermons to the Dead* (Donald I. Fine, 1985), p. 3.
37 a poll found that 39 per cent: Boyer, *When Time Shall Be No More*, p. 144.
37 'a poet of apocalypse': Kermode, *The Sense of an Ending*, p. 112.
37 'stony rubbish': Eliot, *The Waste Land*, p. 63.
37 'This is the way the world ends': T. S. Eliot, 'The Hollow Men' (1925), in *Collected Poems*, p. 92.
37 Nick Bostrom, who divides existential risks: Nick Bostrom, 'Analyzing Human Extinction Scenarios and Related Hazards', *Journal of Evolution and Technology*, vol. 9, no. 1 (March 2002).
37 'Things fall apart': W. B. Yeats, 'The Second Coming', *The Dial*, vol. 69, no. 5 (November 1920).
38 'Changed by our special pressures': Kermode, *The Sense of an Ending*, p. 28.
38 'I conceive it to be the duty': C. E. M. Joad, 'Is Civilisation Doomed?', *Today and Tomorrow*, vol. 1, no. 1 (October, 1930), p. 48.

39 'We may aspire': James J. Hughes, 'Millennial Tendencies in Responses to Apocalyptic Threats', in Bostrom and Ćirković, Global Catastrophic Risks, p. 83.

PART ONE: THE LAST MAN

CHAPTER 1. DARKNESS

43 'Morn came and went': Lord Byron, 'Darkness' (1816), in *The Works of Lord Byron* (Aldephonse Dujardin, Librairie Lecharlier, 1830), p. 688.

43 'mad Italian prophet': *The Times*, 23 July 1816.

43 'We mentioned this prophecy': *The Times*, 13 July 1816.

43 'It is really too bad': Jane Austen, letter to James Edward Austen-Leigh, 9 July 1816, in James Edward Austen-Leigh, *A Memoir of Jane Austen* (Oxford University Press, 1963; first published 1869), p. 160.

43 'this end of the World Weather': Samuel Taylor Coleridge, letter to J. J. Morgan, circa 17 July 1816, in *Collected Letters of Samuel Taylor Coleridge: Volume IV: 1815–19*, edited by Earl Leslie Griggs (Clarendon Press, 1959), p. 660.

44 'Rain, Rain, Rain': J. M. W. Turner, letter to James Holworthy, 11 September 1816, in *Collected Correspondence of J. M. W. Turner*, edited by John Gage (Oxford University Press, 1980), p. 70.

44 'Gossips made my stay a nightmare': Elma Dangerfield, *Byron and the Romantics in Switzerland 1816* (Ascent, 1978), p. 27.

44 'foolish girl': Byron, letter to Augusta Leigh, 8 September 1816, in *'So Late into the Night': Byron's Letters and Journals: Volume 5: 1816–1817*, edited by Leslie A. Marchand (John Murray, 1976), p. 92.

45 'Lord Byron is an exceedingly interesting person': Percy Shelley, letter to Thomas Peacock, 22 July 1816, in *The Prose Works of Percy Bysshe Shelley: Volume II*, edited by Harry Buxton Forman (Reeves and Turner, 1880), p. 185.

45 'An almost perpetual rain': Mary Shelley, letter to unknown addressee, 1 June 1816, in *The Letters of Mary W. Shelley: Volume 1*, collected and edited by Frederick L. Jones (University of Oklahoma Press, 1944), p. 12.

45 'We will each write a ghost story': Mary Shelley, author's introduction to *Frankenstein or The Modern Prometheus*, edited by Johanna M. Smith (Bedford/St Martin's, 2000; first published 1818), p. 22.

45 'a pale student': ibid., p. 24.

45 'Many . . . dreamt of spots': Wolfgang Behringer, *Tambora and the Year Without a Summer*, translated by Pamela Selwyn (Polity, 2019), p. 28.

46 'and those who escaped': *The Times*, 23 July 1816.

46 'superstitious anxiety': 'The Spots in the Sun', *The Times*, 26 July 1816.

46 'cries, groans, tears': *The Times*, 23 July 1816.
46 'Aunt, Aunt, the World's at an end!': ibid.
46 'in consequence of the terror': *The Times*, 7 August 1816.
46 'We know not whether the Italian mountebanks': *The Times*, 29 July 1816.
46 Mount Tambora: information about the eruption from Gillen D'Arcy Wood, *Tambora: The Eruption That Changed the World* (Princeton University Press, 2014).
47 'the whole mountain': Sophia Raffles, *Memoir of the Life and Public Services of Sir Thomas Stamford Raffles* (John Murray, 1830), p. 249.
47 'imagine the state of mind': Flammarion, p. 161.
47 'A violent whirlwind ensued': Raffles, *Memoir*, p. 249.
47 'the time of the ash rain': D'Arcy Wood, p. 24.
48 'The darkness was so profound': Raffles, *Memoir*, p. 245.
48 'Eighteen Hundred and Froze to Death': D'Arcy Wood, p. 9.
48 the 'Tomboro' eruption: *The Times*, 21 November 1815.
49 'did not, however, foresee': *The Times*, 3 August 1816.
49 'outrageous fooleries': Behringer, p. 40.
49 'not unconnected': Jeffrey Vail, 'The Bright Sun Was Extinguish'd: The Bologna Prophecy and Byron's "Darkness"', *Wordsworth Circle*, vol. 28, no. 3 (Summer 1997).
49 'Alarm and consternation': 'The End of the World', *The British Lady's Magazine*, vol. 4, no. 20 (1 August 1816).
49 'the day the world was to be at an end': Behringer, p. 41.
49 'churches and chapels': William K. Klingaman and Nicholas P. Klingaman, *The Year Without Summer: 1816 and the Volcano that Darkened the World and Changed History* (St Martin's Press, 2013), p. 115.
49 'a celebrated dark day': Ernest J. Lovell Jr, ed., *His Very Self and Voice: Collected Conversations of Lord Byron* (Macmillan, 1954), p. 299.
50 'We see . . . that Empires': Abbé Winckelman, *Critical Account of the Situation and Destruction by the First Eruptions of Mount Vesuvius, of Herculaneum, Pompeii, and Stabia*, translator uncredited (T. Carnan and F. Newbery, 1771), p. iv.
50 'the Hiroshima of the Age of Reason': Mike Davis, *Ecology of Fear: Los Angeles and the Imagination of Disaster* (Verso, 2022; first published 1998), p. 282.
50 'Thou also perish': Marina Benjamin, *Living at the End of the World* (Picador, 1998), p. 196.
50 'Old things seemed passing away': Weber, p. 110.
51 'The present moment': Hillel Schwartz, *Century's End: An Orientation Manual Toward the Year 2000* (Currency/Doubleday, 1996), p. 105.
51 'hideous ruin': Stephen Jay Gould, *Time's Arrow, Time's Cycle: Myth and Metaphor in the Discovery of Geological Time* (Penguin, 1988), p. 32.
51 'I seem to gather': Miller, 'The End of the World'.
51 'to console mankind': Benjamin, p. 200.

51 'We find no vestige': Gould, p. 65.
52 'Such is the economy of nature': Elizabeth Kolbert, *The Sixth Extinction* (Bloomsbury, 2015), pp. 27-8.
52 'But what was this primitive earth?': ibid., p. 30.
52 'some kind of catastrophe': Martin J. S. Rudwick, *Georges Cuvier, Fossil Bones, and Geological Catastrophes* (University of Chicago Press, 1997), p. 24.
52 'Life on earth': ibid., p. 190.
52 'the greatest poet': Morton D. Paley, *The Apocalyptic Sublime* (Yale University Press, 1986), p. 141.
52 'When this world shall be former': Lord Byron, 'Don Juan: Canto IX' (1823), in *The Works of Lord Byron*, pp. 545–6.
53 'modify the influence': D'Arcy Wood, p. 214.
53 'Buffon's sublime but gloomy theory': Percy Shelley, letter to Thomas Love Peacock, 22 July 1816, in Thomas Jefferson Hogg et al., *The Life of Percy Bysshe Shelley: Volume Two* (J. M. Dent and Sons, 1933), p. 386.
53 'city of death': Percy Bysshe Shelley, 'Mont Blanc' (1816), in *The Complete Poetical Works of Shelley*, edited with textual notes by Thomas Hutchinson (Clarendon Press, 1904), p. 585.
53 'The race/ Of man': ibid., p. 586.
53 'Because the world': 'Of the End of the World', *The New Monthly Magazine and Universal Register*, vol. 6, no. 33 (October 1816).
53 'I will have nothing to do': Byron, letter to Francis Hodgson, 3 September 1811, in *'Famous in My Time': Byron's Letters and Journals: Volume 2: 1810–1812*, edited by Leslie A. Marchand (John Murray, 1975), p. 88.
54 'I had a dream': Byron, 'Darkness'.
54 'The very conception': Francis Jeffrey, 'Lord Byron's Poetry', *The Edinburgh Review*, vol. 27, no. 54 (December 1816).
55 'returned to England': Paula R. Feldman and Diana Scott-Kilvert, eds, *The Journals of Mary Shelley* (Johns Hopkins University Press, 1995), pp. 108–9.
55 'very disastrous state': *The Times*, 5 September 1816.
55 'year of the beggar': D'Arcy Wood, p. 9.
55 'We could not but notice': Thomas Raffles, *Letters During a Tour Through Some Parts of France, Savoy, Switzerland, Germany, and the Netherlands, in the Summer of 1817* (Thomas Taylor, 1818), p. 147.
55 'the disorders of the elements': Behringer, p. 110.
55 'The Rhine rots with corpses': Klingaman and Klingaman, p. 266.
56 'A dozen times in a century': *The Times*, 13 July 1816.
56 'borne away by the waves': Mary Shelley, *Frankenstein*, p. 189.
56 'seems to be universally read': Fiona Sampson, *In Search of Mary Shelley: The Girl Who Wrote Frankenstein* (Profile, 2018), p. 171.
56 'the real creation myth': Christopher Frayling, *Mad, Bad and Dangerous?: The Scientist and the Cinema* (Reaktion, 2005), p. 47.

56 '*Frankenstein* should be banned': D. F. Jones, *Colossus* (Rupert Hart-Davis, 1966), p. 39.

57 'We went from England': Mary Shelley, letter to Marianne Hunt, 29 June 1819, in *The Letters of Mary W. Shelley: Volume 1*, p. 73.

57 'wet, ungenial summer': Mary Shelley, *Frankenstein*, p. 22.

57 'my disastrous life': Mary Shelley, letter to Maria Gisborne, 15 August 1822, in *The Letters of Mary W. Shelley: Volume 1*, p. 144.

57 'And so here I am!': Mary Shelley, letter to Maria Gisborne, 27? August 1822, in *The Letters of Mary W. Shelley: Volume 1*, p. 145.

57 'Suffering is my Alpha and Omega': Mary Shelley, *The Journals of Mary Shelley*, p. 451.

57 'My imagination is dead': ibid., p. 474.

58 'What a change it would be': Cyrus Redding, 'Life and Reminiscences of Thomas Campbell', *The New Monthly Magazine and Humorist*, edited by W. Harrison Ainsworth (Chapman and Hall, 1847), p. 430.

CHAPTER 2. THE LAST MAN

59 'Was I a ghost': Ronald Duncan, *The Last Adam* (Dennis Dobson, 1952), p. 21.

59 'I can't understand': Skeeter Davis, 'The End of the World' (RCA Victor, 1962).

59 'a tale of woe': Mary Shelley, *The Journals of Mary Shelley*, p. 495.

59 'The last man!': ibid., p. 476.

60 'disease was to be banished': Mary Shelley, *The Last Man: Volume I* (Henry Colburn, 1826), pp. 223–4.

60 'This enemy to the human race': Mary Shelley, *The Last Man: Volume II* (Henry Colburn, 1826), p. 19.

60 'The old man felt the system': ibid., p. 310.

60 'rayless': ibid., p. 130.

60 'believe himself sent': ibid., p. 216.

60 'the numbered remnant': Mary Shelley, *The Last Man, Volume III* (Henry Coburn, 1826), p. 36.

60 'a self-erected prophet': ibid., p. 139.

61 'murdress of those I love': Mary Shelley, *The Journals of Mary Shelley*, p. 476.

61 'Oh! grief is fantastic': Mary Shelley, *The Last Man, Volume III*, p. 298.

61 '2100, last year of the world!': ibid., p. 346.

61 'Every part of Rome': ibid., p. 332.

61 'I will dwell in solitude': M. Volney, *The Ruins: Or a Survey of the Revolutions of Empires*, translator uncredited (J. Johnson, 1792), p. 24.

61 'What glory is here eclipsed': ibid., p. 7.

62 'near the ruins of Palmyra': Jean-Baptiste François Xavier Cousin de

Grainville, *The Last Man*, translated by I. F. and M. Clarke (Wesleyan University Press, 2002), p. 3.

62 'a wasteland': ibid., p. 103.

62 'I am a ruin': Mary Shelley, letter to Leigh Hunt, 9 September 1823, in *The Letters of Mary W. Shelley: Volume 1*, p. 194.

62 'when London shall be an habitation of bitterns': Percy Bysshe Shelley (as Miching Mallecho), dedication to 'Peter Bell the Third' (1819), in *Complete Poetical Works*, p. 378.

62 'some traveller from New Zealand': Thomas Babington Macaulay, 'Ranke's *History of the Popes*' (1840), in *Critical and Historical Essays Contributed to* The Edinburgh Review*: Volume III* (Longman, Brown, Green and Longmans, 1843), p. 209.

62 'He can no longer be suffered': 'A Proclamation', *Punch*, 7 January 1865.

62 'a new Romance': Morton D. Paley, 'Mary Shelley's The Last Man: Apocalypse without Millennium', *The Keats–Shelley Review*, no. 4 (Autumn 1989), p. 1.

62 One critic accused him: Morton D. Paley, 'Envisioning Lastness: Byron's "Darkness", Campbell's "The Last Man", and the Critical Aftermath', *Romanticism*, vol. 1, no. 1 (1995).

63 'Yet think not, Sun': Thomas Campbell, 'The Last Man' (1823), in *Poems of Thomas Campbell*, selected and arranged by Lewis Campbell (Macmillan and Co., 1904), p. 139.

63 'The LAST MAN left alive': Thomas Hood, 'The Last Man', *Blackwood's Magazine*, vol. 21 (January–June 1827), p. 54.

63 'Mr Hood, alive to the ludicrous': ibid.

64 'grand, wonderful picture': Barbara C. Morden, *John Martin: Apocalypse Now!* (Northumbria Press, 2010), p. 57.

64 'Mon Dieu!': Paley, *The Apocalyptic Sublime*, p. 141.

64 'The greatest, the most lofty': Morden, p. 14.

64 'painter of pantomimes': ibid.

64 'reckless accumulation': John Ruskin, 'Preface: Samuel Prout' (1880), in *The Works of John Ruskin*, edited by E. T. Cook and Alexander Wedderburn (George Allen, 1904), p. 399.

64 'whether as the grandest things': Thomas Balston, *John Martin 1789–1854: His Life and Works* (Gerald Duckworth, 1947), p. 249.

65 'a sort of detailed and prose copy': Paley, 'Mary Shelley's The Last Man', p. 5.

65 'Why not *the last Woman*?': *The Literary Gazette and Journal of Belles Lettres, Arts, Sciences &c.*, no. 473 (17 February 1826).

65 'The utmost efforts of thought': *The Monthly Review, Or Literary Journal*, no. 1 (March 1826).

66 Brian Aldiss identified: Brian W. Aldiss, *Billion Year Spree: The True History of Science Fiction* (Shocken Books, 1974), pp. 7–39.

66 'to describe the transactions': *The Monthly Review*, March 1826.
66 I. F. Clarke calculated: Grainville, p. xxxix.
66 'For a moment I compared myself': Mary Shelley, *The Last Man, Volume III*, pp. 302–3.
67 'I feel hollow': David Barr Kirtley, interview with Chris Matheson, *Geek's Guide to the Galaxy*, episode 520, podcast audio, 12 July 2022.
67 'the only one left': Richard Matheson, *I Am Legend* (Gollancz, 2010; first published 1954), p. 91.
67 'new people of the earth': ibid., p. 159.
68 'universal fantasy': Charlton Heston, *In the Arena: The Autobiography* (HarperCollins, 1995), p. 434.
68 'I know, *The Last Man* is a good title': ibid., p. 438.
68 'creature of the wheel': *The Omega Man*, directed by Boris Sagal, screenplay by John William Corrington and Joyce H. Corrington (1971).
69 'bouncing back and forth': Ian Nathan, 'I Am Legend', *Empire*, no. 220 (October 2007).
69 'Am I the only person left on earth?': *The Quiet Earth*, directed by Geoff Murphy, screenplay by Bill Baer, Bruno Lawrence and Sam Pillsbury (1985).
70 'You take a man': Chris Lee, 'Will Smith: A One-Man Show', *Los Angeles Times*, 4 November 2007.
70 'the sighing shades': Miller and Greenberg, p. 7.
70 'Indeed, I could sympathize': Arthur Conan Doyle, *The Poison Belt* (Hodder and Stoughton, 1913), p. 67.
71 'about had it with the Adam and Eve device': Alfred Bester, introduction to 'Adam and No Eve' (1941), in *Star Light, Star Bright* (Victor Gollancz, 1978).
71 'What we fear': Robert Hatch, 'The Garden of Atom', *The New Republic*, 14 May 1951.
71 'My next reaction': Duncan, p. 24.
71 'Death makes so little difference there': ibid., p. 33.
71 'Obviously we have a duty': ibid., p. 90.
72 'Verney, the last of the race': Mary Shelley, *The Last Man, Volume III*, pp. 320–1.
72 'In a weird way': Terry Terrones, 'Q&A: Will Forte and Show Producers Discuss "The Last Man on Earth"', *The Gazette* (Colorado), 26 February 2015.
72 'Was I the same person': Mary Shelley, *Rambles in Germany and Italy* (Edward Moxon, 1844), p. 90.

PART TWO: IMPACT

CHAPTER 3. FALLING STARS

77 'What prodigious Mischief': Cotton Mather, *The Christian Philosopher: A Collection of the Best Discoveries in Nature, with Religious Improvements* (Eman. Matthews, 1721), p. 45.

77 'impinge upon the earth': M. [François] Arago, 'Scientific Notices', *The Times*, 12 March 1832.

78 'universal conflagration': Thomas Ollive Mabbott, ed., *Collected Works of Edgar Allan Poe: Volume II: Tales and Sketches 1831–1842* (Belknap Press, 1978), p. 454.

78 'A combustion irresistible': Edgar Allan Poe, 'The Conversation of Eiros and Charmion', *Burton's Gentleman's Magazine*, December 1939, in Mabbott, pp. 460–1.

78 'From the celestial visitant': Mabbott, p. 454.

79 'practically *bleeding to death*': E. C. Andrews, 'The Danger of the Comet', *Pearson's Magazine*, December 1909.

79 If one were to strike the Earth: information about impact hazard from Jon Erickson, *Asteroids, Comets and Meteors* (Facts on File, 2003); Gerrit L. Verschuur, *Impact!: The Threat of Comets and Asteroids* (Oxford University Press, 1996).

79 'Whatever moves in the heaven': Sara J. Schechner, *Comets, Popular Culture and the Birth of Modern Cosmology* (Princeton University Press, 1997), pp. 47–8.

79 'warning piece': Miller, 'The End of the World'.

80 'a terrifying star': Schechner, p. 23.

80 'When beggars die': William Shakespeare, *Julius Caesar*, Act II, Scene 2.

80 'prelude to this last and most Tragical Scene': Schechner, p. 45.

80 'source of dread': ibid., p. 167.

81 'the vulgar superstitions': ibid., p. 167.

81 'the casuall Choc': ibid., p. 163.

81 'new made out of the Ruins': ibid., p. 164.

81 'may the great good GOD': ibid., p. 165.

81 'which they have calculated': Jonathan Swift, *Gulliver's Travels: Volume Second* (Jones & Company, 1826; first published 1726), p. 18.

82 In another story: Jonathan Swift, 'A True and Faithful Narrative of What Passed in London, during the General Consternation of all Ranks and Degrees of Mankind; on Tuesday, Wednesday, Thursday, and Friday Last' (1732), in Temple Scott, ed., *The Prose Works of Jonathan Swift: Volume IV* (George Bell and Sons, 1898), pp. 275–85.

82 'The utter danger': Dennis, *The End of the World*, p. 18.

82 He put the odds: Verschuur, p. 76.

82 'actually caused no little dismay': Herbert C. Fyfe, 'How Will the World End?', *Pearson's Magazine*, July 1900.

82 'menacingly overripe': George Steiner, *In Bluebeard's Castle* (Faber, 1971), p. 27.

82 'I wish it were *fin du globe*': Oscar Wilde, *The Picture of Dorian Gray* (1891), in *The Complete Plays, Poems, Novels and Stories of Oscar Wilde* (Magpie, 1993), p. 137.

82 'extreme silliness': Max Nordau, *Degeneration* (William Heinemann, 1895), translator uncredited, p. 1.

82 'The disposition of the times': ibid., p. 2.

83 'everybody talked about progress': W. B. Yeats, 'Introduction to "The Resurrection"', in *The Resurrection: Manuscript Materials*, edited by Jared Curtis and Selina Guinness (Cornell University Press, 2011), p. 493.

83 'between 1890 and 1914': W. Warren Wagar, *Terminal Visions: The Literature of Last Things* (Indiana University Press, 1982), p. 20.

83 'Truly, a dire disaster': Fyfe.

84 'London, the all-powerful metropolis': William Le Queux, *The Great War in England in 1897* (1894), in Michael Moorcock, ed., *Before Armageddon: An Anthology of Victorian and Edwardian Imaginative Fiction Published before 1914: Volume 1* (W. H. Allen, 1975), p. 116.

84 'Wake up – or perish!': Moorcock, p. 7.

84 'we must begin again': Richard Jefferies, *After London; Or, Wild England*, introduced by John Fowles (Oxford University Press 1980; first published 1885), p. xvi.

84 'this marvellous city': ibid., p. 36.

85 'the wickedness of those times': ibid., p. 16.

85 'ruin, misery, despair': William Morris, *News from Nowhere* (1890), in *Three Works by William Morris* (Lawrence & Wishart, 1986), p. 287.

85 'the modern Babylon': ibid., p. 247.

85 'I have no more faith': Jefferies, p. viii.

85 'city of Doom!': Van Tassel Sutphen, *The Doomsman* (Harper & Brothers, 1906), p. 183.

85 'It was but a question of time': Ignatius Donnelly (as Edmund Boisgilbert), *Caesar's Column: A Story of the Twentieth Century* (Ward, Lock, and Co., 1891), p. 226.

86 'a puzzle and a fear': Ignatius Donnelly, *Ragnarok: The Age of Fire and Gravel* (D. Appleton & Company, 1883), p. 430.

86 'the greatest failure': J. M. Tyree, 'Ignatius Donnelly, Prince of Cranks', *The Believer*, August 2005.

86 'great revolutions of the earth': Donnelly, *Ragnarok*, p. i.

86 'the rain of dust and ashes': ibid., p. 142.

86, fn.: 'the legends of mankind': ibid., p. 226.

87 'must concede that the earth': ibid., p. 253.
87 'Nature does not proceed': Flammarion, p. 77.
87 'Expectation and uncertainty': ibid., p. 10.
87 'Worlds die of old age': ibid., p. 43.
87 'the pretext for the discussion': ibid., p. 185.
88 'You are not the first': George Griffith, *Olga Romanoff* (Simpkin, Marshall, Hamilton, Kent & Co., 1897), p. 338.
88 'the utter insignificance': ibid., p. 367.
88 'It's hard to write a science fiction story': Hank Nuwer, 'A Skull Session with Kurt Vonnegut', *South Carolina Review*, vol. 19, no. 2 (Spring 1987), in William Rodney Allen, ed., *Conversations with Kurt Vonnegut* (University Press of Mississippi, 1988), p. 259.
88 'the most exciting years in my life': H. G. Wells, *The Fate of Homo Sapiens: An Unemotional Statement of the Things That Are Happening to Him Now, and of the Immediate Possibilities Confronting Him* (Secker and Warburg, 1939), p. 10.
88 'Like most people of my generation': H. G. Wells, *The Future in America: A Search After Realities* (Harper and Brothers, 1906), p. 6.
89 'a past-master': 'Fiction: The World Set Free', *The Spectator*, vol. 1112, no. 4481 (16 May 1914).
89 'It is part of the excessive egotism': H. G. Wells, 'The Extinction of Man', *Pall Mall Gazette*, 25 September 1894, in H. G. Wells, *Certain Personal Matters* (William Heinemann, 1897), p. 173.
89 'If some poor story-writing man': ibid., p. 179.
89 'only broken now and then': H. G. Wells, *The Time Machine* (William Heinemann, 1895), p. 135.
89 'I cannot convey the abominable desolation': ibid., p. 138.
90 'deliberate pessimism of youth': Wells, *The Future in America*, p. 252.
90 'All the sounds of man': Wells, *The Time Machine*, pp. 140–1.
90 'The energies of our system': The Right Hon. Arthur James Balfour, *Foundations of Belief, Being Notes Introductory to the Study of Theology* (Longmans, Green, and Co., 1895), p. 30.
90 'Mr. Wells has used with great skill': Ingvald Raknem, *H. G. Wells and his Critics* (George Allen & Unwin, 1962), p. 33.
90 'the greatest city in the world': H. G. Wells, *The War of the Worlds* (William Heinemann, 1898), p. 150.
90 'the beginning of the rout': ibid., p. 173.
91 'This must be the beginning of the end': ibid., p. 114.
91 'Cities, nations': ibid., p. 257.
91 'the time when I saw it all bright': ibid., p. 303.
91 'but the ghosts of the past': ibid., p. 302.
91 'strange wanderer': H. G. Wells, 'The Star' (1897), in *The Country of the Blind and Other Stories* (T. Nelson & Sons, 1911), p. 309.

91 'earthquakes, volcanic outbreaks': ibid., p. 316.
91 'which only shows how small': ibid., p. 322.
92 'It does not seem to have affected anyone': Wells, *The Future in America*, pp. 41–2.
92 'modern Babylon': H. G. Wells, *The War in the Air* (George Bell and Sons, 1908), p. 176.
92 'ruins and blazing conflagrations': ibid., p. 207.
92 'Here there are robbers': ibid., p. 356.
92 'impregnate the atmosphere': 'Comet's Poisonous Tail', *The New York Times*, 8 February 1910
92 'If a large comet': Andrews.
93 'made even the light of the sun': Nature-Times News Service, 'What Was the Tunguska Meteor?', *The Times*, 8 December 1967.
93 'All villagers were stricken': *Sibir*, 2 July 1908.
94 'entering once again': Lewis Lapham, ed., *The End of the World* (Thomas Dunne, 1997), p. 206.
94 'The darker the night gets': Paul Boyer, *When Time Shall Be No More*, p. 101.
94 'I am so sad for my country': D. H. Lawrence, letter to Lady Cynthia Asquith, 9 November 1915, in *The Letters of D. H. Lawrence*, edited and with an introduction by Aldous Huxley (Viking Press, 1932), p. 275.
94 'The cataclysm has happened': D. H. Lawrence, *Lady Chatterley's Lover* (Martin Secker, 1932), p. 9.
94 'she had too much old chat in her': James Joyce, *Ulysses* (Penguin, 1992; first published 1922), p. 871.
94 'When will be the next war?': Christabel Pankhurst, *Pressing Problems of the Closing Age* (Morgan and Scott, 1924), p. 13.
95 'transmitted by ether waves': ibid., p. 15.
95 *Weltuntergangsroman*: P. D. Smith, *Doomsday Men: The Real Dr. Strangelove and the Dream of the Superweapon* (Penguin, 2008), p. 227.
95 'Merlin, Frankenstein and Adam': Cicely Hamilton, *Theodore Savage: A Story of the Past or the Future* (Leonard Parsons, 1922), p. 319.
95 'If we don't end war': *Things to Come*, directed by William Cameron Menzies, screenplay by H. G. Wells (1936).
96 'I believe that, given a certain impetus': John Collier, *Tom's a-Cold: A Tale* (Macmillan and Co., 1933), introduction.
96 'When gods war with gods': Stephen Vincent Benét, 'By the Waters of Babylon' (1937), in Miller and Greenberg, p. 250.

CHAPTER 4. DOOMSDAY ROCKS

97 'The end of the world will never be really believed': Edwin Balmer and Philip Wylie, *When Worlds Collide* (Stanley Paul & Co., 1933), p. 73.

97 'I am not a Protestant': Jim Knipfel, 'The Nowhere Man Who Was Everywhere', *The Believer*, 29 May 2018.

98 'I found no satisfaction': Robert Howard Barshay, *Philip Wylie: The Man and His Work* (University Press of America, 1979), p. 5.

98 'shut the doors and stay': ibid., p. 14.

98 'super-child': Philip Wylie, *Gladiator* (Alfred A. Knopf, 1930), p. 18.

98 'I can jump higher'n a house': ibid., pp. 48-9.

98 'They fear you': ibid., p. 51.

98 Wylie threatened to sue: Gerard Jones, *Men of Tomorrow: Geeks, Gangsters, and the Birth of the Comic Book* (Basic Books, 2005), p. 346.

99 'As a distant planet': Jerry Siegel and Joe Shuster, *Action Comics*, no. 1 (June 1938).

99 'a piddling phantasmagoria': Philip Wylie, 'Science Fiction and Sanity in an Age of Crisis', in Reginald Bretnor, ed., *Modern Science Fiction: Its Meaning and Its Future* (Coward-McCann, 1953), p. 234.

99 'Yesterday there had been issued marching orders': Balmer and Wylie, p. 77.

100 'It is a new intoxication': ibid., p. 106.

100 'a landscape': ibid., p. 134.

100 'last battle of brains': ibid., p. 204.

100 'It is nothing': ibid., pp. 280–1.

101 'The radical cure for the Earth!': Jura Soyfer, *The End of the World* (1936), in *'It's Up to Us!': Collected Works of Jura Soyfer*, edited, translated and with an afterword by Horst Jarka (Ariadne Press, 1996), p. 83.

101 'The comet is going to destroy everybody': ibid., p. 89.

101 'You will understand, monsieur': ibid., p. 98.

102 'For there is no use destroying each other': Max Ehrlich, *The Big Eye* (Corgi, 1960; first published 1949), p. 148.

102 'Had we recognized the fact': ibid., p. 199.

103 'He has the kind of mind': Neil McAleer, *Odyssey: The Authorised Biography of Arthur C. Clarke* (Victor Gollancz, 1993), p. 225.

103 'No book before or since': Arthur C. Clarke, *The Best of Arthur C. Clarke 1937–1971* (Sphere, 1973), p. 12.

103 'an end that no prophet had ever foreseen': Arthur C. Clarke, *Childhood's End* (Sidgwick and Jackson, 1954), p. 238.

103 'I believe . . . when we get beyond the atmosphere': CBS News, 20 July 1969.

104 'Which is better': Arthur C. Clarke, *The Hammer of God* (Victor Gollancz, 1993), p. 156.

104 'Orpheus is five miles wide': *Meteor*, directed by Ronald Neame, screenplay by Stanley Mann and Edmund H. North (1979).

105 'a sudden influx': Luis W. Alvarez, Walter Alvarez, Frank Asaro and Helen V. Michel, 'Extraterrestrial Cause for the Cretaceous-Tertiary Extinction', *Science*, 6 June 1980.

105 'day could have been turned into night': ibid.

106 'My first thought': Natalie Angier, 'Did Comets Kill the Dinosaurs?', *Time*, 6 May 1985.

106 'Many consider all the newfangled extraterrestrial scenarios': ibid.

106 'I don't like to say bad things': Malcolm W. Browne, 'The Debate Over Dinosaur Extinctions Takes an Unusually Rancorous Turn', *The New York Times*, 19 January 1988.

106 'the crater of doom': Walter Alvarez, *T. Rex and the Crater of Doom* (Princeton University Press, 1997).

107 'There's no uncertainty': Douglas Preston, 'The Day the Dinosaurs Died', *The New Yorker*, 29 March 2019.

107 'It happened before': *Armageddon*, directed by Michael Bay, screenplay by Jonathan Hensleigh and J. J. Abrams (1998).

107 'Doomsday Science': Melinda Beck and David Glick, 'Doomsday Science', *Newsweek*, 23 November 1992.

107 'It was my duty': Clarke, *The Hammer of God*, p. 198.

108 'COSMIC DAY OF JUDGEMENT': Benjamin, p. 32.

108 'removed the "giggle factor"': Donald W. Cox & James H. Chestek, *Doomsday Asteroid: Can We Survive?* (Prometheus, 1996), p. 158.

108 'We live in a cosmic shooting gallery': ibid., p. 29.

108 'For some reason': Phil Plait, 'The (Dysfunctional) Family Channel's version of Chicken Little', *badastronomy.com*, undated.

108 'Our new Noah's Ark': *Deep Impact*, directed by Mimi Leder, screenplay by Bruce Joel Rubin and Michael Tolkin (1998).

108 'size of Texas': *Armageddon*.

109 '"Armageddon" got some astronomy right': Phil Plait, 'The Astronomy of *Armageddon*', *badastronomy.com*, undated.

109 'The Bible calls this day Armageddon': *Armageddon*.

109 'Life will go on': *Deep Impact*.

109 'threatened for a while': Richard Lacayo, 'The End of the World as We Know It?', *Time*, 18 January 1999.

109 'The destruction of the world': Anthony Lane, 'Apocalypse Not', *The New Yorker*, 18 May 1998.

110 'based a lot on my person': *Melancholia* production notes, quoted in Manohla Dargis, 'A Provocateur Steals Cannes Spotlight', *The New York Times*, 20 May 2011.

110 'this film is perilously close': Per Juul Carlsen, 'The Only Redeeming Factor Is the World Ending', *DFI*, 4 May 2011.

110 'There's nothing to do': *Melancholia*, written and directed by Lars von Trier (2011).

110 'I just thought a lot more': Matt Barone, 'Interview: "Seeking A Friend For

The End Of The World" Director Lorene Scafaria Talks Her Funny and Emotional Anti-Disaster Movie', *complex.com*, 22 June 2012.

111 'The final mission to save mankind': *Seeking a Friend for the End of the World*, written and directed by Lorene Scafaria (2012).

111 'The peel is made out of fire': *These Final Hours*, written and directed by Zak Hilditch (2013).

112 'He just made an offhanded comment': Sean Fennessey, interview with Adam McKay, *The Big Picture*, podcast audio, 14 December 2021.

112 'When the asteroid hit us, he hit back': *Don't Look Up*, written and directed by Adam McKay (2021).

112 'They, and he, could not realize that the world was doomed': Balmer and Wylie, p. 146.

PART THREE: THE BOMB

CHAPTER 5. DREAMING THE BOMB

117 'Think for a moment': Pierrepoint B. Noyes, *The Pallid Giant: A Tale of Yesterday and To-Morrow* (John Long, 1928), p. 21.

117 'the only considerable group': Wylie, 'Science Fiction and Sanity'.

118 'Have you heard of U-235?': Cleve Cartmill, 'Deadline', *Astounding Science Fiction*, vol. 33, no. 1 (March 1944).

118 he countered: Albert I. Berger, *The Magic That Works: John W. Campbell and the American Response to Technology* (Borgo Press, 1993), p. 61.

118 'The use of atomic energy': H. W. Baldwin, 'How Long Will the War Last?', *The New York Times*, 23 July 1944.

118 'a crazy Buck Rogers project': Edward Teller with Judith L. Shoolery, *Memoirs: A Twentieth-Century Journey in Science and Politics* (Perseus Press, 2001), p. 195.

118 'atom disintegrator': *Batman*, directed by Lambert Hillyer, screenplay by Victor McLeod, Leslie Swabacker and Harry L. Fraser (1943).

118 Wylie himself strayed into trouble: Sam Moskowitz, *Explorers of the Infinite: Shapers of Science Fiction* (Hyperion Press, 1974), pp. 292–3.

119 'I saw the headline': Ferenc Morton Szasz, *Atomic Comics* (University of Nevada Press, 2012), p. 37.

119 'People do not realize civilization': John W. Campbell, 'Atomic Age', *Astounding Science Fiction*, vol. 36, no. 1 (November 1945).

119 'No man can say': Robert Cromie, *The Crack of Doom* (Digby, Long & Co., 1895), p. 20.

119 'the vast stores': ibid., p. 121.

119 'I swear by the living god': ibid., pp. 177–8.

120 'make the whole world': Frederick Soddy, *The Interpretation of Radium*, third edition (John Murray, 1912), p. 251.

120 'possess a weapon': Muriel Howorth, *Atomic Transmutation: The Greatest Discovery Ever Made, from Memoirs of Professor Frederick Soddy, M.A., LL.D., F.R.S., Nobel Laureate 1921* (New World, 1953), p. 95.

120 'We know now that the atom': H. G. Wells, *The World Set Free: A Story of Mankind* (Macmillan and Co., 1914), p. 24.

120 'like an imbecile': ibid., p. 34.

120 'If there had been no Holsten': ibid., pp. 265–6.

121 'a shuddering star': ibid., p. 99.

121 'a great ball': ibid., p. 89.

121 'puffs of luminous': ibid., p. 203.

121 'moral shock': ibid., p. 196.

121 'We've had unity': ibid., p. 263.

121 'one of his periodic fits': 'Fiction: The World Set Free', *The Spectator*, 16 May 1914.

121 'A disposition': H. G. Wells, *Experiment in Autobiography: Volume II* (Faber, 1984; first published 1934), p. 666.

121 'Perhaps my factories': Sven Tägil, 'Alfred Nobel's Thoughts about War and Peace', *nobelprize.org*, 20 November 1998.

121 'produce instruments of death': H. Bruce Franklin, *War Stars: The Superweapon and the American Imagination* (Oxford University Press, 1988), p. 76.

121 'the war-is-now-too-horrible theory': Norman Cousins, *Modern Man Is Obsolete* (Viking Press, 1945), p. 37.

121 'make warfare impossible': George Griffith, *The Lord of Labour* (F. V. White & Co., 1911), pp. 50–1.

122 'interesting': Professor Sir Ernest Rutherford, 'The Constitution of Matter and the Evolution of the Elements', *The Popular Science Monthly* (August 1915).

122 'blow the boat of humanity to pieces': Karel Čapek, *Krakatit*, translated by Lawrence Hyde (Geoffrey Bles, 1925), p. 339.

122 'gigantic mushroom': Olaf Stapledon, *Last and First Men* (Gollancz, 2004; first published 1930), p. 28.

122 'The next moment': Čapek, *Krakatit*, p. 399.

123 'Suddenly his eyes were blinded': Carl W. Spohr, 'The Final War' (1932), in Frederic Krome, ed., *Fighting the Future War: An Anthology of Science Fiction War Stories, 1914–1945* (Routledge, 2011), p. 239.

123 'To assist Nature': Robert Nichols and Maurice Brown, *Wings Over Europe: A Dramatic Extravaganza on a Pressing Theme* (Chatto and Windus, 1932), p. 96.

123 'They want to destroy everything': J. B. Priestley, *The Doomsday Men* (William Heinemann, 1938), p. 253.

123, fn.: 'final redemption': Eduard von Hartmann, *Philosophy of the Unconscious, Volume III*, translated by William Chatterton Copeland (Trübner & Co., 1884), p. 127.

123, fn.: benevolent world exploder: Moynihan, p. 260.

124 'I fear not their desire': Noyes, p. 189.

CHAPTER 6. DESTROYER OF WORLDS

125 'We have discovered the most terrible bomb': Richard Rhodes, *The Making of the Atomic Bomb* (Touchstone, 1988), p. 690.

125 'it was a very poor and inefficient way': 'The British Association: Breaking Down the Atom: Transformation of Elements', *The Times*, 12 September 1933.

125 'An expert is a man': William Lanouette with Bela Silard, *Genius in the Shadows: A Biography of Leo Szilard* (University of Chicago Press, 1994), p. 133.

126 'The creative scientist': ibid., p. xiii.

126 'florid complexion': ibid., p. 250.

126 'intellectual bumblebee': ibid., p. xviii.

126 'He was always ahead of his time': ibid., xix.

127 'a closely knit group': ibid., p. 21.

127 'what the liberation': ibid., p. 137.

127 When Szilard read: ibid., p. 133.

127 'which would enable man': Spencer R. Weart and Gertrud Weiss Szilard, eds, *Leo Szilard: His Version of the Facts: Selected Recollections and Correspondence* (MIT Press, 1978), p. 17.

127 'I have reason to believe': Lanouette, p. 140.

128 'Please go away': ibid., p. 176.

128 'The physicists are anxious': ibid., p. 184.

128 'All the things which H. G. Wells predicted': Weart and Szilard, p. 53.

128 'You know what fission means': Lanouette, p. 181.

128 'Some recent work by E. Fermi': Albert Einstein, letter to President F. D. Roosevelt, 2 August 1939, quoted in Ralph E. Lapp, 'The Einstein Letter That Started It All', *The New York Times*, 2 August 1964.

129 'one great mistake': Mary Palevsky, *Atomic Fragments: A Daughter's Questions* (University of California Press, 2000), p. 31.

129 'Thanks to Hitler': 'Thanks to Hitler', *The New York Times*, 8 August 1945.

130 'a kind of confluence': 'The Eternal Apprentice', *Time*, 8 November 1948.

130 'the biggest event since the birth of Christ': 'The Beginning or the End', *Life*, 17 March 1947.

130 'a black day': Lanouette, p. 245.

130 Teller explored the possibility: Gregg Herken, *Brotherhood of the Bomb: The Tangled Lives and Loyalties of Robert Oppenheimer, Ernest Lawrence, and Edward*

Teller (Henry Holt, 2002), p. 87; Kai Bird and Martin J. Sherwin, *American Prometheus: The Triumph and Tragedy of J. Robert Oppenheimer* (Knopf, 2006), p. 221.

131 He told Oppenheimer: Herken, p. 66.

131 'the scientists in their unworldly urge': Albert Speer, *Inside the Third Reich*, translated by Richard and Clara Winston (Macmillan, 1970), p. 271.

132 'opening the door': 'A Petition to the President of the United States, July 17, 1945', in Cynthia C. Kelly, ed., *The Manhattan Project: The Birth of the Atomic Bomb in the Words of Its Creators, Eyewitnesses, and Historians* (Black Dog & Leventhal, 2007), p. 292.

132 'a Frankenstein which would eat us up': Bird and Sherwin, p. 293.

132 'those poor little people': ibid., p. 314.

132 'Our only hope': Edward Teller, letter to Leo Szilard, 2 July 1945, in Teller and Shoolery, p. 207.

132 'Batter my heart': Bird and Sherwin, p. 304.

132 'whether or not the bomb': Leslie R. Groves, *Now It Can Be Told: The Story of the Manhattan Project* (Andre Deutsch, 1963), pp. 296–7.

133, fn.: 'But where is everybody?': E. M. Jones, *'Where Is Everybody?': An Account of Fermi's Question* (US Department of Energy, 1985).

133 'This would be the ultimate catastrophe': Arthur Holly Compton, *Atomic Quest: A Personal Narrative* (Oxford University Press, 1956), p. 128.

133 Fermi asked Teller: Teller and Shoolery, pp. 209–10.

133 'encircle the globe': Edward Teller with Allen Brown, *The Legacy of Hiroshima* (Macmillan, 1962), p. 16.

134 'It was as though the earth had opened': William L. Laurence, *Dawn Over Zero: The Story of the Atomic Bomb* (Museum Press, 1947), p. 9.

134 'the nearest thing to doomsday': ibid., p. 9.

134 'for a moment I thought': Rhodes, *The Making of the Atomic Bomb*, p. 673.

134 'the thermal nuclear transformation': James B. Conant, 'Notes on the "Trinity" Test Held at Alamagordo Bombing Range', 17 July 1945, reprinted in James G. Hershberg, *James B. Conant: Harvard to Hiroshima and the Making of the Nuclear Age* (Alfred A. Knopf, 1993), pp. 759–60.

134 'the strong, sustained, awesome roar': Lewis Wood, 'Steel Tower "Vaporized" in Trial of Mighty Bomb', *The New York Times*, 7 August 1945.

134 'There weren't any agnostics': Lawrence Badash, Joseph O. Hirschfelder and Herbert P. Broida, eds, *Reminiscences of Los Alamos 1943–1945* (Reidel, 1980), pp. 76–7.

135 'Now I am become death': Bird and Sherwin, p. 309.

135 'It worked': Rhodes, *The Making of the Atomic Bomb*, p. 675.

135, fn.: 'I am become death, shatterer of worlds': 'The Eternal Apprentice'.

135 'I looked in vain': Luis W. Alvarez, *Alvarez: Adventures of a Physicist* (Basic Books, 1987), p. 7.

135 The US military estimated: Alex Wellerstein, 'Counting the Dead at Hiroshima and Nagasaki', *thebulletin.org*, 4 August 2020.

135 'Hiroshima does not look like a bombed city': Wilfred Burchett, *Shadows of Hiroshima* (Verso, 1983), p. 34.

136 'We may say that the survivor': Robert Jay Lifton, *Death in Life: The Survivors of Hiroshima* (Weidenfeld & Nicolson, 1967), p. 486.

136 'I thought this was the end of Hiroshima': ibid., p. 22.

136 'it must have been something': ibid., pp. 22–3.

136 'what we saw made us feel': Laurence, *Dawn Over Zero*, p. 183.

136 'one of the greatest blunders': Leo Szilard, letter to Trude Weiss, 6 August 1945, in Lanouette, p. 276.

136 'Ach! The world is not ready for it': Lapp, 'The Einstein Letter That Started It All'.

136 'This can wipe out everything': Gerald Wendt and Donald Porter Geddes, eds, *The Atomic Age Opens* (Forum, 1945), p. 59.

136 'everyone I spoke to about it': George Orwell, 'London Letter', *Partisan Review*, Fall 1945, in Peter Davison, ed., *The Complete Works of George Orwell: Volume XVII: I Belong to the Left, 1945* (Secker & Warburg, 2001), p. 249.

136 'the basic power of the universe': Harry S. Truman, 'Statement by the President of the United States', 6 August 1945.

136 'What regrets I have': Luis W. Alvarez, *Alvarez: Adventures of a Physicist*, p. 8.

136 'While many of my friends': ibid., p. 282.

136 'a barren waste': 'The Future', *Chicago Daily Tribune*, 14 August 1945, quoted in Paul Boyer, *By the Bomb's Early Light: American Thought and Culture at the Dawn of the Atomic Age* (University of North Carolina Press, 1994), p. 15.

137 'signed the mammalian world's death warrant': 'A Decision for Mankind', *St. Louis Post-Dispatch*, 7 August 1945, quoted in ibid., p. 5.

137 'Such a weapon has the power': Lifton, *Death in Life*, p. 79.

CHAPTER 7. DELIVERANCE OR DOOM

138 'The end / will come': William Carlos Williams, 'Asphodel, That Greeny Flower' (1955), in *Collected Poems: Volume II: 1939–1962* (Carcanet, 1988), p. 322.

138 'Suddenly the day of judgment': Alice Kimball Smith, *A Peril and a Hope: The Scientists' Movement in America: 1945–47* (MIT Press, 1971), p. ii.

139 'apocalyptic destruction': 'The 36-Hour War', *Life*, 19 November 1945.

139 'As I go about the streets': Hansard, HL Deb, 28 November 1945, vol. 138, col. 89.

139 'Many of my friends': Luis W. Alvarez, *Alvarez: Adventures of a Physicist*, p. 147.

139 85 per cent of Americans: Boyer, *By the Bomb's Early Light*, p. 183.

139 'the tunic of Superman': Francis Sill Wickware, 'Manhattan Project', *Life*, 20 August 1945.

139 'It is remarkable': Boyer, *By the Bomb's Early Light*, p. 61.

139 'I never saw a man': Bird and Sherwin, p. 330.

140 'The peoples of this world': Kelly, p. 366.

140 'The people of our century': *The Beginning or the End*, directed by Norman Taurog, screenplay by Frank Wead and Bob Considine (1947).

140, fn.: 'If our sin as scientists': Lanouette, p. 362.

140 'It was fear of the future': Vannevar Bush, *Modern Arms and Free Men: A Discussion of the Role of Science in Preserving Democracy* (Simon and Schuster, 1949), p. 39.

140 'Time is short': Dexter Masters and Katharine Way, eds, *One World or None* (McGraw-Hill Book Co., 1946), p. 79.

141 'I write this to frighten you': Harold Urey, 'I'm a Frightened Man', *Collier's*, 5 January 1946.

141 'we have turned ourselves into': Daniel Lang, 'That's Four Times 10^{-4} Ergs, Old Man', *The New Yorker*, 16 November 1946.

141 'WORLD CONTROL': reprinted in Szasz, p. 96.

141 'the last, best hope of earth': Bernard Baruch, 'Speech Before the First Session of the United Nations Atomic Energy Commission', 14 June 1946.

141 'Nuclear energy insists': E. B. White, 'Notes and Comment', *The New Yorker*, 18 August 1945.

141 'nothing but world-union': J. Marshak, E. Teller and L. R. Klein, 'Dispersal of Cities and Industries', *Bulletin of the Atomic Scientists*, vol. 1, no. 9 (15 April 1946).

141 'black depression': Theodore Sturgeon, *Thunder and Roses: Volume IV: The Complete Stories of Theodore Sturgeon*, edited by Paul Williams (North Atlantic Books, 1997), p. 348.

141 'You sound like the first chapter': Theodore Sturgeon, 'Thunder and Roses', *Astounding Science Fiction*, vol. 40, no. 3 (November 1947).

141 'Thus far the chief purpose': Spencer R. Weart, *The Rise of Nuclear Fear* (Harvard University Press, 2012), p. 75.

142 'prophets of doom': Boyer, *By the Bomb's Early Light*, p. 74.

142 'various combinations': Robert Jay Lifton and Richard Falk, *Indefensible Weapons: The Political and Psychological Case Against Nuclearism* (Basic Books, 1982), p. 12.

142 'I am not so scared': Gertrude Stein, 'Reflection on the Atomic Bomb' (1946), in *Reflection on the Atomic Bomb: Volume 1 of the Previously Uncollected Writings of Gertrude Stein*, edited by Robert Bartlett Haas (Black Sparrow Press, 1974), p. 161.

142 'It might have seemed like a good idea': David Lilienthal, 'National Affairs: To Those of Little Thought', *Time*, 16 February 1948.

142 'Life or death': Boyer, *By the Bomb's Early Light*, p. 159.

142 'It was so gigantic': David E. Lilienthal, *Change, Hope, and The Bomb* (Princeton University Press, 1963), p. 18.

143 'the sky suddenly lit': Eugene Rabinowitch, 'Five Years After', *Bulletin of the Atomic Scientists*, vol. 7, no. 1 (January 1951).

143 'In an instant, without warning': 'The Bomb', *Time*, 20 August 1945.

143 'Atom Year I': Boyer, *By the Bomb's Early Light*, p. 135.

143 '12.01 on the hour-glass of history': Laurence, *Dawn Over Zero*, p. 230.

144 'may not mean the end of the world': Lang, 'That's Four Times 10^{-4} Ergs, Old Man'.

144 'Atomic weapons can hardly be used': Gerard J. De Groot, *The Bomb* (Jonathan Cape, 2004), p. 156.

144 'world well advanced': Eugene Rabinowitch, 'Forewarned – But Not Forearmed', *Bulletin of the Atomic Scientists*, vol. 5, no. 10 (October 1949).

144 'Hiroshima U.S.A.': John Lear, 'Hiroshima U.S.A.: Can Anything Be Done About It?', *Collier's*, 5 August 1950.

144 'Alarm Clock': Herken, p. 173.

144 'deliberately quiet': Jonathan Dee, 'The Art of Fiction XCII: John Hersey', *The Paris Review*, no. 100 (Summer/Fall 1986), p. 228.

144 'Few of us have yet comprehended': 'To Our Readers', *The New Yorker*, 31 August 1946.

145 'This was Hersey's Hiroshima': Leonard Engel and Emanuel S. Piller, *World Aflame: The Russian–American War of 1950* (Dial Press, 1947), p. 32.

145 'Gentlemen, You Are Mad!': Lewis Mumford, 'Gentlemen, You Are Mad!', *MacLean's*, 1 June 1946.

145 'a city of two and a half million skeletons': Aldous Huxley, *Ape and Essence* (Chatto & Windus, 1949), p. 143.

145 'a dead world': J. Jefferson Farjeon, *Death of a World* (Collins, 1948), p. 191.

145 'the saddest, and craziest thought': Donald Sturrock, *Storyteller: The Life of Roald Dahl* (Harper Press, 2010), p. 257.

146 'The time has come': Roald Dahl, *Sometime Never* (Collins, 1949), p. 7.

146 'ghastly book': Sturrock, p. 273.

146 'Movies and TV': Philip Wylie, 'Panic, Psychology and the Bomb', *Bulletin of the Atomic Scientists*, vol. 10, no. 2 (February 1950).

146 'Today it is not the priest': Philip Wylie, *Tomorrow!* (Popular Library, 1956), p. 97.

146 'the men and women': ibid., dedication.

147 'the only monomaniac': 'Knowledge Is Power', *Time*, 18 November 1957.

147 'an egomaniac, a paranoid': Norman Moss, *Men Who Play God: The Story of the Hydrogen Bomb* (Gollancz, 1968), pp. 64-5.

147 'a messianic complex': Richard Rhodes, *Dark Sun: The Making of the Hydrogen Bomb* (Simon & Schuster, 1995), p. 462.

147 'It would have been a better world without Teller': Peter Goodchild, *Edward Teller: The Real Dr Strangelove* (Weidenfeld & Nicolson, 2004), p. xxiv.
147 'I do not want the hydrogen bomb': Palevsky, p. 53.
147 'ignite the entire world's atmosphere': Leslie Groves, letter to Henry L. Stimson, 27 July 1945, in Herken, p. 138.
147 'drooling with the prospect': David E. Lilienthal, *The Journals of David E. Lilienthal: Volume II: The Atomic Energy Years 1945–1950* (Harper & Row, 1964), p. 582.
147 'after such a war': Rhodes, *Dark Sun*, p. 393.
148 'a danger to humanity as a whole': Teller and Shoolery, p. 331.
148 Dean Acheson told: Herken, p. 217.
148 'at that time everybody predicted': Lilienthal, *Journals*, p. 632–3.
148 'Our tragedy today': William Faulkner, 'Banquet Speech', 10 December 1950.
148 'technically sweet': David C. Cassidy, *J. Robert Oppenheimer and the American Century* (Pi Press, 2005), p. 302.
148 'It's a boy': Teller and Shoolery, p. 352.
149 'two atomic colossi': Address by Mr Dwight D. Eisenhower, President of the United States of America, to the 470th Plenary Meeting of the United Nations General Assembly, 8 December 1953.
149 'The entire foundation of human affairs': Hansard, HC Deb, 1 March 1955, vol. 537, col. 1895.
149 'Theoretically I am supposed': Lanouette, pp. 315–16.
150 'Not quite': Bird and Sherwin, p. 557.
150 'You and I are in a dead world': *Five*, written and directed by Arch Oboler (1951).
150 'Not one would mind': Sara Teasdale, 'There Will Come Soft Rains', *Harper's*, vol. 137, no. 818 (July 1918), quoted in Ray Bradbury, *The Martian Chronicles* (HarperCollins, 2008; first published 1951), p. 286.
151 'alone in a city of rubble and ashes': ibid., p. 282.
151 'Science ran too far ahead': Ray Bradbury, 'The Million-Year Picnic', *Planet Stories*, Summer 1946, in ibid., pp. 302–3.
151 'When they had gone': Dahl, p. 248.
151 'What creatures were these': Sturgeon, 'Thunder and Roses', p. 143.
152 'The human race was to be wiped out': Nevil Shute, *On the Beach* (Vintage, 2009; first published 1957), p. 269.

CHAPTER 8. THE DOOMSDAY MACHINE

153 'I suppose I haven't got any imagination': Shute, *On the Beach*, p. 89.
153 'radioactive poisoning': Albert Einstein, 'What the Scientists Are Saying', *Bulletin of the Atomic Scientists*, vol. 6, no. 3 (March 1950).

153 'it is very easy': Hans Bethe et al., 'University of Chicago Round Table: The Facts About the Hydrogen Bomb', broadcast on 26 February 1950, on NBC.
154 'Ending of All Life': William L. Laurence, 'Ending of All Life by Hydrogen Bomb Held a Possibility', *The New York Times*, 27 February 1950.
154 'led by emotion': 'Science: Hydrogen Hysteria', *Time*, 6 March 1950.
154 'The H-bomb was bad enough': Lanouette, p. 366.
154 *Bulletin* commissioned a young physicist: James R. Arnold, 'The Hydrogen-Cobalt Bomb', *Bulletin of the Atomic Scientists*, vol. 6, no. 10 (October 1950).
154 'a gigantic radioactive cloud': William L. Laurence, *The Hell Bomb* (Hollis & Carter, 1951), p. 22.
154 The so-called C-bomb soon infiltrated: Clarke, *Childhood's End*, p. 142; Wylie, *Tomorrow!*, pp. 272–4.
154 'not a serious person': Nevil Shute, *Slide Rule: The Autobiography of an Engineer* (Heinemann, 1954), p. 65.
155 'Most of my adult life': ibid., p. 4.
155 'Britain is not a very good country': Gideon Haigh, 'Shute the Messenger', *The Monthly*, June 2007.
155 a *Time* article: 'Science: The Unmentionable Subject', *Time*, 20 December 1954.
155 'It became an attractive speculation': Julian Smith, *Nevil Shute* (G. K. Hall & Co., 1976), p. 124.
156 'announced that it was shutting up shop': Mollie Panter-Downes, 'Letter from London', *The New Yorker*, 15 May 1954.
156 'as a result of scientific discoveries': Hansard, HC Deb, 29 April 1954, vol. 526, cols 1808–13.
156 'When I returned from the war': William Tsutsui, *Godzilla on My Mind: Fifty Years of the King of the Monsters* (Palgrave Macmillan, 2004), p. 32.
156 'It's a feeling all of us Japanese share': *Ikimono no Kiroku* (US: *I Live in Fear*), directed by Akira Kurosawa, screenplay by Akira Kurosawa, Shinobu Hashimoto and Hideo Oguni (1955).
157 'Now Most Dreaded Weapon': William L. Laurence, 'Now Most Dreaded Weapon, Cobalt Bomb, Can Be Built', *The New York Times*, 7 April 1954.
157 'an annihilating cobalt bomb': Eugene J. Sleevi, 'Civil Defense News', *Bulletin of the Atomic Scientists*, vol. 10 no. 5 (May 1954).
157 'gathered on this beach': Eliot, 'The Hollow Men', p. 91.
157, fn.: 'One reason is that': Henry Hewes, 'Eliot on Eliot: "I Feel Younger than I Did at 60"', *Saturday Review*, vol. 41, no. 37 (13 September 1958).
157 'It's like waiting to be hung': Shute, *On the Beach*, p. 240.
158 'silliness': ibid., p. 301.
158 'bloody unfair': ibid., p. 40.
158 'ought to be compulsory reading': Julian Smith, *Nevil Shute*, p. 134.

158 'It would be a waste of money': James Lees-Milne, *A Mingled Measure: Diaries, 1953–1972* (John Murray, 1994), p. 68.

159 'will not be anything recognisable': J. B. Priestley, 'Britain and the Nuclear Bombs', *The New Statesman*, vol. 54, no. 1390 (2 November 1957).

159 'illogical, insane, unstable': Lanouette, p. 370.

159 'Prepare to meet thy God': 'Graham in Warning on Atomic Disaster', *The New York Times*, 8 July 1957.

159 'Universal bereavement': Tom Lehrer, 'We Will All Go Together When We Go', on *An Evening Wasted with Tom Lehrer* (Reprise, 1959).

159 'by far the most important story': 'Film to Be Made of "On the Beach"', *The New York Times*, 9 September 1957.

159 'No: your story says': Donald Spoto, *Stanley Kramer: Film Maker* (G. P. Putnam's Sons, 1978), p. 211.

159 'THERE IS STILL TIME': *On the Beach*, directed by Stanley Kramer, screenplay by John Paxton (1959).

159, fn.: first reported by *Time*: 'The Atom: High Price of Suspension', *Time*, 30 November 1959.

159, fn.: 'a real Buck Rogers job': Martin Mann, 'The Month in Science', *Popular Science*, vol. 177, no. 2 (August 1960).

160 'this intersection': Sontag, 'The Imagination of Disaster'.

160 'To appall the audience': George P. Elliott, 'Think Films: A New Hollywood Creation', *Esquire*, March 1960.

160 'It may be that some years from now': ibid.

160 'Possible Questions': David Seed, *Under the Shadow: The Atomic Bomb and Cold War Narratives* (Kent State University Press, 2013), p. 47.

160 'The cobalt bomb is not the invention': Teller and Brown, p. 239.

161 'play the part of the *enfant terrible*': Julian Smith, *Nevil Shute*, p. 134.

161 'dehumanised war': Mordecai Roshwald, *Level* 7 (University of Wisconsin Press, 2004; first published 1959), p. 165.

161 'frighten people into sanity': ibid., p. xxx.

161 Thomas Schelling, a nuclear strategist: Thomas Schelling, 'Meteors, Mischief, and War', *Bulletin of the Atomic Scientists*, vol. 16, no. 7 (October 1960).

161 'The great advantage of fiction': Peter Krämer, *Dr. Strangelove or: How I Learned to Stop Worrying and Love the Bomb* (BFI, 2014), p. 25.

161 'proof against error': United Press dispatch, 7 April 1958, quoted in Herman Kahn, *On Thermonuclear War* (Princeton University Press, 1960), p. 206.

161 'The more elaborately involved': Priestley, 'Britain and the Nuclear Bombs'.

161 'a nervous, psychotic or fanatical': Sharon Ghamari-Tabrizi, *The Worlds of Herman Kahn: The Intuitive Science of Thermonuclear War* (Harvard University Press, 2005), p. 34.

162 'a derangement': Communist Forgeries: Hearing Before the United States

Committee on the Judiciary, Subcommittee to Investigate the Administration of the Internal Security Act and Other Internal Security Laws, Eighty-Seventh Congress, First Session, 2 June 1961.

162 'would mean the end of the world': Peter Bryant, *Two Hours to Doom: A Novel of Suspense* (T. V. Boardman & Company, 1958), p. 81.

162 'A man who causes fear': President John F. Kennedy, radio and television report to the American people on the Berlin crisis, 25 July 1961.

162 'a queer, half-apocalyptic, nuclear feeling': Robert Lowell, letter to Elizabeth Bishop, 3? October 1961, in Thomas Travisano and Saskia Hamilton, eds, *Words in the Air: The Complete Correspondence Between Elizabeth Bishop and Robert Lowell* (Faber and Faber, 2008), p. 381.

162 'All autumn': Robert Lowell, 'Fall 1961', in *For the Union Dead* (Farrar, Straus & Giroux, 1964), p. 11.

163 'Mankind must put an end to war': President John F. Kennedy, Address before the United Nations General Assembly, 25 September 1961.

163 'fallout shelters, like the Twist': *Newsweek*, 6 November 1961, quoted in Fred Kaplan, *Wizards of Armageddon* (Simon and Schuster, 1983), p. 312.

163 'all-clear signals': Kurt Vonnegut, letter to Harvey Kurtzman via Knox Burger, 18 October 1961, in *Letters*, edited by Dan Wakefield (Vintage, 2013), p. 86.

163 'We were spared a bomb tonight': *The Twilight Zone*, season 3, episode 3, 'The Shelter', directed by Lamont Johnson, written by Rod Serling. Aired 29 September 1961, on CBS.

163 'happily chatted away': Alexander Walker, *Stanley Kubrick Directs* (Harcourt Brace Jovanovich, 1972), p. 251.

164 'In the context of imminent world destruction': ibid., pp. 34–5.

164 'brought the world to the abyss': Robert F. Kennedy, *Thirteen Days: A Memoir of the Cuban Missile Crisis* (W. W. Norton & Company, 1999; first published 1969), p. 19.

164 'One Week May Alter All Future': Alice L. George, *Awaiting Armageddon: How Americans Faced the Cuban Missile Crisis* (University of North Carolina Press, 2003), p. 96.

164 'I'm the first refugee': Lanouette, p. 458.

164 'Never in history': Harrison Brown, 'Guest Editorial: The Twentieth Year', *Bulletin of the Atomic Scientists*, vol. 18, no. 10 (December 1962).

165 'a guy called Vasili Arkhipov': Nicola Davis, 'Soviet Submarine Officer who Averted Nuclear War Honoured with Prize', *theguardian.com*, 27 October 2017.

165 'It was literally true': George, p. 1.

165 'People sat around wondering': Clinton Heylin, *Revolution in the Air: The Songs of Bob Dylan: Volume 1: 1957–73* (Constable, 2009), p. 93.

165 'Are you ready for that great atomic power?': The Louvin Brothers, 'The Great Atomic Power' (Capitol, 1962).

166 'In Two Big Book-alikes': David E. Scherman, 'Everybody Blows Up!', *Life*, 8 March 1963.

166 'If being frightened': Norman Cousins, *The Improbable Triumvirate: John F. Kennedy, Pope John, Nikita Khrushchev* (W. W. Norton & Company, 1972), p. 43.

166 the percentage of Americans: Boyer, *By the Bomb's Early Light*, p. 355.

167 'The longer the bomb is around': Jeremy Bernstein, 'Stanley Kubrick's Genius', *The New Yorker*, 4 November 1966.

167 'Deterrence is the art': *Dr. Strangelove or: How I Learned to Stop Worrying and Love the Bomb*, directed by Stanley Kubrick, screenplay by Stanley Kubrick, Terry Southern and Peter George (1964).

167 'could very easily': Ghamari-Tabrizi, p. 304.

167 'tragic but distinguishable': Kahn, *On Thermonuclear War*, p. 20.

168 'one thinks of H. G. Wells': Arthur Herzog, 'Inside a "Think Factory"', *The New York Times*, 10 November 1963.

168 'began to resemble a deadpan *War of the Worlds*': William A. McWhirter, 'The Think-Tank Man', *Life*, 6 December 1968.

168 'He exudes intelligent observation': Moss, p. 254.

168 'I can be really funny': Richard Kostelanetz, 'One-Man Think Tank', *The New York Times*, 1 December 1968.

168 'The Rand Corporation': Philip Wylie, *Triumph* (Doubleday, 1963), p. 262.

168 'Is there really a Herman Kahn?': James Newman, 'Two Discussions of Thermonuclear War', *Scientific American*, vol. 204, no. 3 (March 1961).

168 'expressions like "balance of terror"': Kahn, *On Thermonuclear War*, p. 9.

169 'Will the Survivors Envy the Dead?': ibid., p. 20.

169 'It would not surprise me': ibid., p. 90.

169 'life after World War III': Ghamari-Tabrizi, p. 16.

169 'It doesn't work that way': Kostelanetz, 'One-Man Think Tank'.

169 he initially insisted: Ghamari-Tabrizi, p. 41; Kostelanetz, 'One-Man Think Tank'.

170 'the first break': Lewis Mumford, letter to the editor, '"Strangelove" Reactions', *The New York Times*, 1 March 1964.

170 'nihilism for the masses': Susan Sontag, 'Going to Theater, etc' (1964), in *Against Interpretation*, p. 149.

170 'the only perspective': ibid., p. 150.

170 'It was meant to be irony': Robert Musil, 'There Must Be More to Love Than Death: A Conversation with Kurt Vonnegut', *The Nation*, 2–9 August 1980, in Allen, p. 235.

171 'People react, as a rule': Eugene Archer, 'How to Learn to Love World Destruction', *The New York Times*, 26 January 1964.

171 'to test mankind': Walter M. Miller Jr, *A Canticle for Leibowitz* (Gollancz, 2013; first published 1959), p. 60.

171 'My sons, they cannot do it again': ibid., p. 261.

172 'The writer's role': Nicholas Parisi, *Rod Serling: His Life, Work and Imagination* (University Press of Mississippi, 2018), p. 3.

172 'It was all right to have Martians': ibid., p. 191.

172 'We were attempting irony': ibid., p. 209.

173 'We either greet the morning': *A Carol for Another Christmas*, directed by Joseph L. Mankiewicz, written by Rod Serling. Aired 28 December 1964, on ABC.

173 In May, 1964: Parisi, p. 334.

173 'seemed strangely casual': Richard Hofstadter, 'Goldwater and Pseudo-Conservative Politics', in *The Paranoid Style in American Politics*, p. 130.

173 'We must either love each other': Doyle Dane Bernbach and Tony Schwarz, 'Daisy'. Aired 7 September 1964.

173 'wiped out by a plague': *Planet of the Apes*, directed by Franklin J. Schaffner, screenplay by Michael Wilson and Rod Serling (1968).

174 'enormous, many-layered black joke': Pauline Kael, 'The Current Cinema: Apes Must Be Remembered, Charlie', *The New Yorker*, 17 February 1968.

174 'desperate, starving wretches': Dodie Smith, *The Starlight Barking: More About the Hundred and One Dalmatians* (Heinemann, 1967), p. 112.

174 'No single solitary one': Jeff Nuttall, *Bomb Culture* (MacGibbon & Kee, 1968), p. 26.

174 'My God': *Beneath the Planet of the Apes*, directed by Ted Post, screenplay by Paul Dehn (1970).

174 'end the whole thing with a death': Charlton Heston, *The Actor's Life: Journals 1956–1976* (Penguin, 1980), p. 301.

174 'Human beings': Brian Pendreigh, *Planet of the Apes, or How Hollywood Turned Darwin Upside Down* (Boxtree, 2001), p. 132.

174, fn.: 'Apes exist, sequel required': Eric Greene, *Planet of the Apes as American Myth: Race and Politics in the Films and Television Series* (McFarland & Company, 1996), p. 71.

175 'The truth is I'm bored': Moss, p. 264.

175 'Some people have let the gloom-mongers scare them': Barry Commoner, *The Closing Circle* (Alfred A. Knopf, 1971), pp. 9–10.

CHAPTER 9. WINTER

176 'How long will it take': Martin Amis, 'Thinkability', in *Einstein's Monsters* (Vintage, 2003; first published 1987), p. 20.

176 'grew out of history': Jonathan Schell, *The Fate of the Earth* (1982), in *The Fate of the Earth, The Abolition, The Unconquerable World* (Library of America, 2020), p. 5.

176 'a sort of mass insanity': ibid., p. 141.

176 a recent poll: Wade Greene, 'Rethinking the Unthinkable', *The New York Times*, 15 March 1981.

176 'those who think it might happen': ibid.

177 'I don't have a say': The Specials, 'Man at C&A', on *More Specials* (2 Tone, 1980).

177 'The decisions made': Raymond Briggs, *When the Wind Blows* (Penguin, 1982).

177 'one must conclude': Schell, *The Fate of the Earth*, p. 90.

177 'the murder of the future': ibid., p. 158.

177 'It woke *me* up': Amis, 'Thinkability', p. 11.

178 'A prose stylist': Herman Kahn, 'Refusing to Think About the Unthinkable', *Fortune*, 28 June 1982.

178 'Pitchman for the Apocalypse': Alexander Cockburn and James Ridgeway, 'Pitchman for the Apocalypse: The Horrible Legacy of Herman Kahn', *Village Voice*, 19 July 1983.

178 'pushing an exciting idea': Ronald Reagan, *The Reagan Diaries*, edited by Douglas Brinkley (HarperCollins, 2007), p. 100.

178 'reckless Star Wars schemes': Mark Weinberg, *Movie Nights with the Reagans: A Memoir* (Simon & Schuster, 2018).

178 Senator John Glenn: De Groot, p. 133.

179 'a sign that the day of Armageddon': Boyer, *When Time Shall Be No More*, p. 142.

179 'Every day I think': ibid., p. 141.

179 'I do not know how many': ibid., p. 141.

179 'If atomic bombs fall': ibid., p. 118.

179 'heresy': Kirsch, p. 231.

179 'She promised to follow him': John Houston and Bob Light, 'Gone with the Wind', lithograph poster (Socialist Workers Party, 1981).

180 'Even if a nuclear war': Ronald Reagan, *An American Life* (Arrow, 1991), p. 550.

180 'very bright guys': Bill Joy, 'Why the Future Doesn't Need Us', *Wired*, April 2000.

180 'The last three winters': Poul Anderson and F. N. Waldrop, 'Tomorrow's Children', *Astounding Science Fiction*, vol. 39, no. 1 (March 1947).

181 'When combined with the prompt destruction': R. P. Turco et al., 'Nuclear Winter: Global Consequences of Nuclear War', *Science*, vol. 222, no. 4630 (23 December 1983).

181 'the greatest popularizer': Keay Davidson, *Carl Sagan: A Life* (John Wiley & Sons, 1999), p. xiv.

181 'Reasoning, argument, pleading': Raymond F. Jones, 'Pete Can Fix It', *Astounding Science Fiction*, vol. 38, no. 6 (February 1947).

182 'Would nuclear war be the end of the world?': Carl Sagan, 'The Nuclear Winter', *Parade*, 30 October 1983.

182 'The original Halloween': Paul Ehrlich, ed., *The Cold and the Dark: The World After Nuclear War* (Sidgwick and Jackson, 1984), p. 27.

182 'Apocalyptic predictions require': Carl Sagan, 'Nuclear War and Climatic Catastrophe: Some Policy Implications', *Foreign Affairs*, vol. 62, no. 2 (Winter 1983/4).

182 'and we have distributed its triggers': ibid.

182 'a secular apocalypse': Naomi Oreskes and Erik M. Conway, *Merchants of Doubt: How a Handful of Scientists Obscured the Truth on Issues from Tobacco Smoke to Global Warming* (Bloomsbury, 2012), p. 61.

182 'Highly speculative theories': Edward Teller, 'Widespread After-effects of Nuclear War', *Nature*, vol. 310, no. 5979 (13 August 1984).

183 'Flat-Earth Sagan': *National Review*, 15 November 1985.

183 'the global apocalyptic conclusions': Starley L. Thompson and Stephen H. Schneider, 'Nuclear Winter Reappraised', *Foreign Affairs*, vol. 64, no. 5 (Summer 1986).

183 'The fact that neither': Luis W. Alvarez, *Alvarez: Adventures of a Physicist*, p. 282.

183 'It is the best news': Amis, 'Thinkability', p. 20.

183 'the most terrifying weapon ever invented': *Murder in the Air*, directed by Lewis Seller, screenplay by Raymond L. Schrock (1940).

183 'spends all its time thinking': *WarGames*, directed by John Badham, screenplay by Lawrence Lasker and Walter F. Parkes (1983).

183 'Could that really happen?': Weinberg, p. 95.

183 'It's very effective': Reagan and Brinkley, *The Reagan Diaries*, p. 186.

184 'I would just want to die': Report on *The Day After*. Aired 20 November 1983, on WABC-TV Channel 7. https://www.youtube.com/watch?v=aG-e52yAxfs

184 'Hope for what?': *The Day After*, directed by Nicholas Meyer, screenplay by Edward Hume. Aired 20 November 1983, on ABC.

184 'The point of it': Simon Braund, 'How Ronald Reagan Learned to Start Worrying and Stop Loving the Bomb', *Empire*, no. 257 (November 2010).

184 'When they finally return': *Viewpoint*, '"The Day After" – Nuclear Dilemma'. Aired 20 November 1983, on ABC.

185 'The Man Who Saved the World': *The Man Who Saved the World*, written and directed by Peter Anthony (2013).

185 'We may have been at the brink': ibid.

185 'Are you gonna drop the bomb or not?': Alphaville, 'Forever Young', on *Forever Young* (WEA, 1984).

186 'I wanted to show the full horror': Jude Rogers, 'Einstein's Monsters', *The New Statesman*, vol. 147, no. 5410 (16–22 March 2018).

186 'Jesus Christ': *Threads*, directed by Mick Jackson, screenplay by Barry Hines. Aired 23 September 1984, on BBC One.

186 'There's nothing apocalyptic about nuclear war': Kim Newman, *Millennium Movies: End of the World Cinema* (Titan Books, 1999), p. 235.

186 'It is the sky overhead': Jonathan Schell, *The Abolition* (1984), in *The Fate of the Earth, The Abolition, The Unconquerable World*, p. 282.

187 'This disaster and the other accidents': Jonathan Schell, 'The Talk of the Town', *The New Yorker*, 12 May 1986.

187 'a surrogate for bombs': Weart, *The Rise of Nuclear Fear*, p. 192.

187 'The Age of Physics': Svetlana Alexievich, *Chernobyl Prayer*, translated by Anna Gunin and Arch Tait (Penguin, 2006), p. 221.

187 'a time of nuclear danger': Bill Chappell, 'Why the U.N. Chief Says We Are "One Miscalculation Away from Nuclear Annihilation"', *npr.org*, 2 August 2022.

PART FOUR: MACHINES

CHAPTER 10. ROBOTS

193 'We have made machines': Karel Čapek, 'What Machinery Will Never Do', *Daily Express*, 5 February 1929, quoted in Ivan Klíma, *Karel Čapek: Life and Work*, translated by Norma Comrada (Catbird Press, 2002), p. 127.

193 'I'd call them laborators': Karel Čapek, 'About the Word Robot', *The People's Paper*, 24 December 1933, reprinted in *Believe in People: The Essential Karel Čapek*, selected and translated by Šárka Tobrmanová-Kühnová (Faber and Faber, 2010), p. 103.

194 'You know, the bigger the things': Karel Čapek, *The Absolute at Large* (1922), quoted in Klíma, p. 89.

194 'romantic sensibility': Karel Čapek, 'How I Have Come to Be What I Am' (1932), in *Believe in People*, p. 176.

194 'I count myself among the idiots': Karel Čapek, 'Why Am I Not a Communist?' (1924), in *Believe in People*, p. 275.

194 'comedy, partly of science': Karel Čapek, 'The Meaning of R.U.R.', *The Saturday Review*, 21 July 1923.

195 'I shuddered to think': Mary Shelley, *Frankenstein*, pp. 144–5.

195 'we are ourselves creating our own successors': Samuel Butler (as Cellarius), 'Darwin Among the Machines', *Christ Church Press*, 13 June 1863, in *A Year in Canterbury Settlement with Other Early Essays*, edited by R. A. Streatfield (A. C. Fifield, 1914), p. 182.

195 'become to the machine', ibid., p. 183.

195 'I am, in my opinion': Klíma, p. 91.

195 'There will be no poverty': Karel Čapek, *R.U.R.* (1920), in *R.U.R. (Rossum's Universal Robots) and War with the Newts*, translated by Paul Selver and Nigel Playfair (Gollancz, 2011), p. 24.

196 'That's a punishment': ibid., p. 35.

196 'Slaughter and domination': ibid., p. 68.

196 'Go, Adam, go, Eve': ibid., p. 73.

196 'this modern Frankenstein': John Corbin, 'The Revolt of Civilization', *The New York Times*, 15 October 1922.

196 'ironical melodrama': Rosa Knutti, 'R.U.R.', *Industrial Pioneer*, June 1923, quoted in Dustin A. Abnet, *The American Robot: A Cultural History* (University of Chicago Press, 2020), p. 117.

196 'After all, you are all Robots': *The Spectator*, vol. 130, no. 4957 (30 June 1923).

196 'I think it is possible': Čapek, 'The Meaning of "R.U.R."'.

197 'Rotwang the inventor': H. G. Wells, 'Mr. Wells Reviews a Current Film', *The New York Times*, 17 April 1927.

197 'Unlike the man-made Frankenstein': Abnet, p. 157.

197 'wound-up "robots"': ibid., p. 187.

197 'machine men with machine minds': *The Great Dictator*, written and directed by Charlie Chaplin (1940).

198 'Men made us for killing men': Joseph E. Kelleam, 'Rust', *Astounding Science Fiction*, vol. 24, no. 2 (October 1939).

198 'No cosmic catastrophy': Karel Čapek, *War with the Newts* (1936), in *R.U.R. (Rossum's Universal Robots) and War with the Newts*, p. 343.

198 'My world has died': Klíma, p. 236.

198 'Here would have been buried': Derek Sayer, *Prague, Capital of the Twentieth Century: A Surrealist History* (Princeton University Press, 2013), p. 99.

199 'In the first class': Isaac Asimov, *The Complete Robot* (Granada, 1982), p. xi.

199 'But you mustn't think I started all this': Lord Dunsany, *The Last Revolution* (Jarrolds, 1951), p. 117.

199 'The success of *Frankenstein*': Isaac Asimov, Patricia S. Warrick and Martin H. Greenberg, eds, *Machines That Think: The Best Science Fiction Stories about Robots and Computers* (Allen Lane, 1984), p. 5.

199 'In such stories': Asimov, *The Complete Robot*, p. xi.

199 'a robot may not': Isaac Asimov, 'Runaround', *Astounding Science Fiction*, vol. 29, no. 1 (March 1942).

200 'would have wagered': Asimov, *The Complete Robot*, p. xii.

200 'The theme of the artificial human being': Stanisław Lem, 'Robots in Science Fiction', translated by Franz Rottensteiner, in Thomas D. Clareson, ed., *SF: The Other Side of Realism: Essays on Modern Fantasy and Science Fiction* (Bowling Green University Popular Press, 1971), p. 320.

CHAPTER 11. COMPUTERS

201 'The impact of the thinking machine': Flo Conway and Jim Siegelman, *Dark Hero of the Information Age: In Search of Norbert Wiener The Father of Cybernetics* (Basic Books, 2005), p. 245.

202 'power of thinking': James Gleick, *The Information: A History, a Theory, a Flood* (4th Estate, 2011), p. 111.
202 'something more than merely mortal': Ada Lovelace, letter to Charles Babbage, 5 July 1843, quoted in ibid., pp. 118–19.
202 'very costly toy': ibid., p. 104.
202 'had all the essential ideas': Alan Turing, 'Computing Machinery and Intelligence', *Mind*, vol. 59, no. 236 (October 1950).
203 'I suppose you are not interested in mathematics': Freeman Dyson, *Disturbing the Universe* (Harper & Row, 1979), p. 194.
203 'I believe that if a mentally superhuman race ever develops': Teller and Shoolery, p. 410.
203 'Mr Miracle': Kaplan, p. 63.
203 'Whenever I talked': George Dyson, *Darwin Among the Machines* (Penguin, 1999), p. 77.
204 'the smart man's smart man': Kostelanetz, 'One-Man Think Tank'.
204 'Von Neumann's talents': Clay Blair Jr, 'Passing of a Great Mind', *Life*, 25 February 1957.
204 'could be evidence': Lewis L. Strauss, *Men and Decisions* (Macmillan & Co., 1963), p. 350.
204 'What we are creating now': Ananyo Bhattacharya, *The Man from the Future: The Visionary Life of John von Neumann* (Allen Lane, 2021), p. 102.
204 'developed an obscene interest': Norman Macrae, *John von Neumann* (Pantheon, 1992), p. 212.
205 'electronic brain': 'An Electronic Brain: Solving Abstruse Problems: Valves with a Memory', *The Times*, 1 November 1946.
206 'fighting the Battle of the Bulge': Herman H. Goldstine, *The Computer from Pascal to von Neumann* (Princeton University Press, 1972), p. 145.
206 'I think that von Neumann suffered': Steve J. Heims, *John von Neumann and Norbert Wiener: From Mathematics to the Technologies of Life and Death* (MIT Press, 1980), p. 270.
206 'Like many fellow scientists': John von Neumann, 'Can We Survive Technology?', *Fortune*, vol. 51, no. 6 (June 1955).
206 'Useful and harmful techniques': ibid.
206 'For progress there is no cure': ibid.
207 'Are machines smarter than ME?': Ginger Strand, *The Brothers Vonnegut: Science and Fiction in the House of Magic* (Farrar, Strauss and Giroux, 2015), p. 155.
207 'I don't want to be a machine': Kurt Vonnegut, 'EPICAC' (1950), in *Welcome to the Monkey House* (Vintage 2021; first published 1969), p. 274.
208 'I can guess that the planet they loved': David Standish, 'Playboy Interview: Kurt Vonnegut Jr.', *Playboy*, vol. 20, no. 7 (July 1973), in Allen, p. 89.
208 Vonnegut compared it to Atlantis: Strand, p. 19.

208 'the city was gone': George Plimpton, David Hayman, David Michaelis and Richard Rhodes, 'Kurt Vonnegut, The Art of Fiction No. 64', *The Paris Review*, no. 69 (Spring 1977).

208 'The end of the world is not an idea': John Updike, 'All's Well in Skyscraper National Park', *The New Yorker*, 25 October 1976.

208 'sheer amiability': J. G. Ballard, 'Sermons from the Mount' (1991), in *A User's Guide to the Millennium*, p. 116.

208 'God damn it, you've got to be kind': Kurt Vonnegut, *God Bless You, Mr Rosewater* (Vintage, 2019; first published 1965), p. 79.

209 'being alive is a crock of shit': Kurt Vonnegut, *Timequake* (Jonathan Cape, 1997), p. 3.

209 'If not for Superman': Elliot S. Maggin et al., *Superman*, vol. 1, no. 274 (April 1974).

209 'God will kill us by the millions': Charles Reilly, 'Two Conversations with Kurt Vonnegut', *College Literature*, no. 7 (1976, 1980), in Allen, p. 211.

209 'Let us be perfectly frank': Vonnegut, *Timequake*, p. 2.

209 'a literary Cassandra': Douglas Brinkley, 'Vonnegut's Apocalypse', *Rolling Stone*, no. 1007 (24 August 2006).

209 'Robots did the dropping': Kurt Vonnegut, *Slaughterhouse-Five* (Vintage, 2000; first published 1969), p. 122.

209 'Technology has made evil anonymous': Freeman Dyson, p. 30.

210 'Think every new piece of scientific information': Kurt Vonnegut, 'Report on the Barnhouse Effect' (1950), in *Welcome to the Monkey House*, p. 161.

210 'was my response': Standish, 'Playboy Interview', p. 93.

210 'a brain, if you like': Kurt Vonnegut Jr, *Player Piano* (Macmillan & Co., 1953), p. 121.

210 'was, in effect': ibid., p. 126.

210 'Would you ask EPICAC': ibid., p. 331.

210 'The main business of humanity': ibid., p. 325.

211 'I was classified as a science-fiction writer': Joe David Bellamy and John Casey, 'Kurt Vonnegut Jr.', in *The New Fiction: Interviews with Innovative American Writers* (University of Illinois Press, 1974), reprinted in Allen, p. 157.

211 'You're the only ones with guts': Vonnegut, *God Bless You, Mr Rosewater*, p. 11.

211 'Weather – the New Super Weapon': *The American Magazine*, September 1946, quoted in Strand, p. 74.

211 'Any truth he found': Musil, 'There Must Be More to Love than Death: A Conversation with Kurt Vonnegut', in Allen, p. 233.

211 At a cocktail party: Bellamy and Casey, 'Kurt Vonnegut Jr.', in Allen, p. 161.

212 'about how mad scientists': Kurt Vonnegut, *Cat's Cradle* (Penguin Modern Classics, 2008; first published 1963), p. 7.

212 'blue-white pearl': ibid., p. 187.

212 'highly entertaining': Terry Southern, 'Cat's Cradle', *The New York Times*, 3 June 1963.

212 'Compared with the average person': Vonnegut, *Cat's Cradle*, p. 41.

212 'cannot with impunity': Conway and Siegelman, p. 288.

212 'the simple faith in progress': Norbert Wiener, *The Human Use of Human Beings: Cybernetics and Society* (Sphere, 1968; first published 1950), p. 44.

212 'The Most Remarkable Boy in the World': Conway and Siegelman, p. 3.

213 'wasn't brought up': ibid., p. 329.

213 'infant prodigy': Heims, p. 18.

213 'I worked unconscionably hard': Norbert Wiener, *Ex-Prodigy: My Childhood and Youth* (Simon & Schuster, 1953), p. 289.

213 'a sweet, caring guy': Heims, p. 333.

213 'excited in me the desire': Wiener, *Ex-Prodigy*, p. 65.

213 'a new interpretation of man': Gleick, p. 238.

214 'When I say that the machine's danger': Wiener, *The Human Use of Human Beings*, p. 159.

214 'the crucial year': Gleick, p. 3.

214 'Little Brain Cell': 'Science: Little Brain Cell', *Time*, 12 July 1948.

214 'Wiener believes': 'Science: The Thinking Machine', *Time*, 23 January 1950.

214 'Long before Nagasaki': Norbert Wiener, *Cybernetics: Or Control and Communication in the Animal and the Machine*, second edition (MIT Press, 1961), pp. 27–8.

215 'we were all astonished': Norbert Wiener, *I Am a Mathematician* (Victor Gollancz, 1956), p. 331.

215 'Short, round, bearded and kindly': 'In Man's Image', *Time*, 27 December 1948.

215 'are growing with fearful speed': ibid.

215 'an American John von Neumann': Sylvia Nasar, *A Beautiful Mind* (Faber and Faber, 2001), p. 135.

215 'I don't think any weapon can be too large': Rhodes, *Dark Sun*, p. 389.

215 'Massacre of Nagasaki': Heims, p. 189.

215 'to disseminate information': Norbert Wiener, 'A Scientist Rebels', *The Atlantic*, January 1947.

215 'a morally irresponsible stooge': Norbert Wiener, 'A Rebellious Scientist After Two Years', *Bulletin of the Atomic Scientists*, vol. 4, no. 11 (November 1948).

215 'the first superweapon': Vonnegut, *Welcome to the Monkey House*, p. 167.

216 'demand that we understand': W. K., 'Revival of R.U.R. With New Prologue', *The New York Times*, 7 May 1950.

216 'God's purpose will be achieved': Arthur C. Clarke, 'The Nine Billion Names of God' (1953), in *The Collected Stories* (Victor Gollancz, 2000), p. 420.

216 'Overhead, without any fuss': ibid., p. 422.

216 'was a mistake': *On the Beach* (1959).

216, fn.: 'The failure of a handful of vacuum tubes': 'A war by accident', *Newsweek*, 24 March 1958.

217 'The element in our story': Eugene Burdick and Harvey Wheeler, *Fail-Safe* (McGraw-Hill, 1962), p. 8.

217 'It's as if human beings had evaporated': ibid., p. 278.

217 'We damn well better learn': ibid., p. 279.

217 'The machines are winning': Sidney Lumet, *Making Movies* (Vintage, 1996), p. 14.

218 'literal-minded': Wiener, *Cybernetics*, p. 177.

218 'MANKIND WARNED OF MACHINE PERIL': Murray Illson, 'Mankind Warned of Machine Peril', *The New York Times*, 17 May 1959.

218 'ample but firm': D. F. Jones, *Colossus*, p. 53.

218 'no fear, no hate, no envy': ibid., p. 25.

219 'We have to accept that they're in charge': ibid., p. 146.

219 'War is already abolished': ibid., p. 245.

219 'With the innate loathing': Harlan Ellison, 'I Have No Mouth, and I Must Scream' (1967), in Asimov et al., p. 244.

219 'intelligence explosion': Irving John Good, 'Speculations Concerning the First Ultraintelligent Machine', in Franz L. Alt and Morris Rubinoff, eds, *Advances in Computers: Volume 6* (Academic Press, 1965), p. 33.

CHAPTER 12. ARTIFICIAL INTELLIGENCE

220 'We taught them to think for themselves': Stephen Vincent Benét, 'Nightmare Number Three', *The New Yorker*, 27 July 1935.

220 'I propose to consider the question': Turing, 'Computing Machinery and Intelligence'.

220 'The Analytical Engine': Walter Isaacson, *The Innovators: How a Group of Inventors, Hackers, Geniuses and Geeks Created the Digital Revolution* (Simon & Schuster, 2014), p. 126.

220 'Are you serious?': Ambrose Bierce, 'Moxon's Master' (1894), in Asimov et al., p. 16.

220 'thinking machine': '"Thinking Machine" Does Higher Mathematics; Solves Equations That Take Humans Months', *The New York Times*, 21 October 1927.

220 'a mechanical brain': George W. Gray, 'Mr. Robot Often Outshines His Master', *The New York Times*, 17 September 1933.

221 'controls the whole activities': Lionel Britton, *Brain: A Play of the Whole Earth* (G. P. Putnam's Sons, 1930), p. 5.

221 'They used to call them electronic brains': Leigh Brackett, *The Long Tomorrow* (Gollancz, 2013; first published 1955), p. 186.

221 'it seems probable': David Leavitt, *The Man Who Knew Too Much: Alan Turing and the Invention of the Computer* (Weidenfeld & Nicolson, 2006), p. 239.
221 'doubt as to whether': Ernst Jentsch, 'On the Psychology of the Uncanny' (1906), translated by Roy Sellars, in Jo Collins and John Jervis, eds, *Uncanny Modernity: Cultural Theories, Modern Anxieties* (Palgrave Macmillan, 2008).
221 'leave the reader in uncertainty': ibid., p. 224.
222 'I don't want any master': Čapek, *R.U.R.*, quoted in Warren R. Young, 'The Machines Are Taking Over', *Life*, 3 March 1961.
222 'Ten years ago': ibid.
222 'the first serious rival': 'Rival', *The New Yorker*, 6 December 1958.
222 'the science of making machines do things': Daniel Crevier, *AI: The Tumultuous History of the Search for Artificial Intelligence* (Basic Books, 1993).
223 'the problem of intelligence': Jeremy Bernstein, 'A.I.', *The New Yorker*, 6 December 1981.
223 'The brain is just a meat machine': Crevier, p. 83.
223 'must be restrained': Marvin Minsky, 'Steps Toward Artificial Intelligence', *Proceedings of the IEEE*, vol. 49, no. 1 (January 1961).
223 'Dear children': Crevier, p. 83.
223 'machines will be capable': ibid., p. 109.
224 'Looking into the distant future': Norden, 'Playboy Interview: Stanley Kubrick'.
224 'Kubrick's vision': David G. Stork, ed., *HAL's Legacy: 2001's Computer as Dream and Reality* (MIT Press, 1997), p. 152.
224 'giant brain': Arthur C. Clarke, 'Dial F for Frankenstein' (1965), in *Collected Stories*, p. 823.
224 'How can you have a Happy Birthday': Arthur C. Clarke, *2001: A Space Odyssey: 50th Anniversary Edition* (Orbit, 2018), p. xiv.
224 Kubrick intended *2001*: James Naremore, *On Kubrick* (BFI, 2007), p. 152.
225 'such clumsy, high-speed morons': Clarke, *2001*, p. 97.
225 'could pass the Turing Test': ibid., p. 99.
225 'the latest result in machine intelligence': *2001: A Space Odyssey*, directed by Stanley Kubrick, screenplay by Stanley Kubrick and Arthur C. Clarke (1968).
225 'a very abstract activity': Turing, 'Computing, Machinery and Intelligence'.
225 'Some philosophical worriers': 'Science: The Thinking Machine'.
226 'for want of a better description': Arthur C. Clarke and Stanley Kubrick, *2001: A Space Odyssey*, screenplay (1965), quoted in Naremore, p. 141.
226 'but as to whether or not': *2001: A Space Odyssey* (1968).
226 'I want this to be a murder': Michael Benson, *Space Odyssey: Stanley Kubrick, Arthur C. Clarke, and the Making of a Masterpiece* (Simon & Schuster, 2018), p. 209.
226 'the only human in the film': Jerome Agel, *The Making of Kubrick's 2001* (Signet, 1970), p. 219.

227 'the fascinating and fearsome reality': Brad Darrach, 'Meet Shaky, the First Electronic Person', *Life*, 20 November 1970.

227 'If we work really hard': Stork, p. 30.

227 'The popular idea': Arthur C. Clarke, *Profiles of the Future: An Enquiry into the Limits of the Possible* (Victor Gollancz, 1962), p. 215.

228 'I'm not hostile': Norden, 'Playboy Interview: Stanley Kubrick'.

228 'Well, the person on the street': Stork, p. 28.

229, fn.: 'a parasite who can kiss my ass': Rebecca Keegan, *The Futurist: The Life and Films of James Cameron* (Three Rivers Press, 2010), p. 55.

229 'In *The Terminator* the fact of nuclear war': Sean French, *The Terminator* (BFI/Bloomsbury, 2021), p. 54.

229 'I realized that the safe and nurturing world': Keegan, pp. 1–2.

229 'a violent movie about peace': ibid., p. 132.

230 'The system goes on-line': *Terminator 2: Judgment Day*, directed by James Cameron, screenplay by James Cameron and William Wisher (1991).

230 'It is not the machines that will destroy us': Keegan, p. 56.

230 'Never create what you can't control': Advertising material for *Battlestar Galactica* miniseries, directed by Michael Rymer, written by Ronald D. Moore and Glen A. Larson. Aired 8 December 2003, on Sci Fi.

230 'Fucking men like you': *Terminator 2: Judgment Day.*

231 'It was software': *Terminator 3: Rise of the Machines*, directed by Jonathan Mostow, screenplay by John Brancato and Michael Ferris (2003).

231 'the dire implications': Wiener, *The Human Use of Human Beings*, p. 155.

231 'scorched the sky': *The Matrix*, written and directed by the Wachowskis (1999).

232 'to protect the human race': Crevier, p. 233.

232 'IBM owes me': Garry Kasparov, 'IBM Owes Mankind a Rematch', *Time*, 26 May 1997.

232 'We must prepare ourselves': Roy Peter Clark, 'Doomsday Is Coming at 7:32 A.M., Jan. 2, 2000 – (6:32 A.M., Central Standard Time)', *The New York Times*, 4 February 1976.

232 'MILLENNIUM MADNESS': *Time*, 18 January 1999.

233 'All thoughts are going underground': Jean Baudrillard, *The Illusion of the End*, translated by Chris Turner (Polity Press, 1994).

233 *Time*/CNN poll: 'Vox Pop', *Time*, 17 May 1993.

233 'Doomsday 2000': Peter de Jager, 'Doomsday 2000', *Computerworld*, vol. 27, no. 36 (6 September 1993).

234 'If we don't fix the century-date problems': Robert Sam Anson, '12.31.99 the Y2K Nightmare', *Vanity Fair*, January 1999.

234 'The Day the World Shut Down': 'The Day the World Shut Down', *Newsweek*, 2 June 1997.

234 'Well, look at the wonders of the computer age now': *The Simpsons*, season 11, episode 4, 'Treehouse of Horror X: Life's a Glitch, Then You Die',

directed by Pete Michels, written by Ron Hauge. Aired 31 October 1999, on Fox.

234 'We and our computers': Barnaby J. Feder, 'The Town Crier for the Year 2000', *The New York Times*, 11 October 1998.

234 'The product of this folly': Anson, '12.31.99 the Y2K Nightmare'.

234 'the Antichrist or his emissaries': Lacayo, 'The End of the World as We Know It?'.

234 'God's instrument': 'Doom and Dollars', *The Economist*, vol. 350, no. 8102 (16 January 1999).

235 'If I'm wrong': Lacayo, 'The End of the World as We Know It?'.

235 'electronic Armageddon': Feder, 'The Town Crier for the Year 2000'.

235 'I find myself in the peculiar position': Dominique Deckmyn, 'Have We Learned nothing from Y2K?', *computerworld.com*, 1 January 2000.

235 'Civilised mankind': George Griffith, 'A Corner in Lightning', *Pearson's Magazine*, March 1898, in Sam Moskowitz, *Science Fiction by Gaslight: A History and Anthology of Science Fiction in the Popular Magazines, 1891–1911* (World Publishing Company, 1968), pp. 85–6.

235 'civilization's long day was closing': E. M. Forster, *The Machine Stops* (Penguin Classics, 2011; first published 1909), p. 53.

236 'We don't have the internet': Alam, *Leave the World Behind*, p. 137.

236 'Thus, a robot': Crevier, p. 319.

236 'expect the main battles': ibid., p. 341.

236 'threatening to make humans': Joy, 'Why the Future Doesn't Need Us'.

236 'Why hadn't I been more concerned': ibid.

237 'Gray goo would surely': ibid.

237 Nick Bostrom's paperclip maximizer: Nick Bostrom, *Superintelligence: Paths, Dangers, Strategies* (Oxford University Press, 2014), pp. 150–3.

238 'small children playing with a bomb': ibid., p. 319.

238 'extremely bad (existential catastrophe)': Vincent C. Müller and Nick Bostrom, 'Future Progress in Artificial Intelligence: A Poll Among Experts', *AI Matters*, vol. 1, no. 1 (August 2014).

238 'our biggest existential threat': Adam Elkus, 'Don't Fear Artificial Intelligence', *Slate*, 31 October 2014.

238 'I think the development': Luciano Floridi, 'The Ethics of Artificial Intelligence', in Daniel Franklin, ed., *Megatech: Technology in 2050* (Profile 2017), p. 156.

238 'about the Terminator': Khatchadourian, 'The Doomsday Invention'.

238 'The ultimate dream of man': Randall Frakes, *Terminator 2: Judgment Day* (Sphere, 1991), p. 14.

238 'Computers are like Old Testament gods': *Joseph Campbell and the Power of Myth*, episode 2, 'The Message of the Myth'. Aired 22 June 1988, on PBS.

239 'An artificial intelligence': Brian Michael Bendis et al., *Age of Ultron*, vol. 1, no. 5 (June 2013).

239 'a suit of armour': *Avengers: Age of Ultron*, written and directed by Joss Whedon (2015).

239 'I know what you're thinking': *The Mitchells vs. the Machines*, directed by Mike Rianda, screenplay by Mike Rianda and Jeff Rowe (2021).

239 'more accurate, safe': Future of Life Institute, 'Pause Giant AI Experiments: An Open Letter', 22 March 2023.

240 'literally everyone on Earth will die': Eliezer Yudkowsky, 'Pausing AI Developments Isn't Enough. We Need to Shut It All Down', *time.com*, 29 March 2023.

240 'the possibility that AI': 'How Concerned, If at All, Are You About the Possibility that AI Will Cause the End of the Human Race on Earth?', *YouGov US*, 3 April 2023.

240 'When you see something that is technically sweet': Cade Metz, '"The Godfather of A.I." Leaves Google and Warns of Danger Ahead', *The New York Times*, 1 May 2023.

240 'My intuition is: we're toast': Harry Lambert, 'The Men Who Made the Future', *The New Statesman*, vol. 152, no. 5722 (23–29 June 2023).

240 'This has always been how people in Silicon Valley talk': Jon Favreau, interview with Max Fisher, *Offline with Jon Favreau*, episode 66, podcast audio, 26 March 2023.

241 Ord estimates: Ord, p. 167.

241 'the secular apocalypticists': Gideon Lewis-Krauss, 'Do Better', *The New Yorker*, 15 August 2022.

241 'for five minutes about global poverty': ibid.

241 'The question of how to create friendly AI': Ted Chiang, 'Silicon Valley Is Turning into Its Own Worst Fear', *Buzzfeed News*, 18 December 2017.

241 'Any apocalyptic vision of A.I.': Floridi, 'The Ethics of Artificial Intelligence', p. 161.

242 'If it hadn't been in you': Čapek, *Krakatit*, p. 407.

242 'And we're the simulation?': Patrick Henry Winston, 'Marvin L. Minsky (1927–2016)', *Nature*, vol. 530, no. 282 (18 February 2016), p. 282.

PART FIVE: COLLAPSE

CHAPTER 13. CATASTROPHE

247 'The thing all you adult, sensitive people': John Christopher, *The Death of Grass* (Penguin, 2009; first published 1956), p. 20.

247 'When a day that you happen to know': John Wyndham, *The Day of the Triffids* (Penguin, 2008; first published 1951), p. 7.

247, fn.: 'It was a bright cold day in April': George Orwell, *Nineteen Eighty-Four* (Penguin, 2003; first published 1949), p. 3.

248 'He never discussed his personal life': *John Wyndham: The Invisible Man of Science Fiction*, directed by Mick Conefrey. Aired 15 October 2005, on BBC Four.
248 'Nobody can write stories about aeroplanes': Amy Binns, *Hidden Wyndham* (Grace Judson Press, 2019), p. 86.
249 'Why do I write these things': ibid., p. 111.
249 'It must be many centuries': ibid., p. 112.
250 'Who is it who should be the priest': John Wyndham (as John Beynon), 'Judson's Annihilator', *Amazing Stories*, vol. 13, no. 10 (October 1939).
250 'We danced': Wyndham, *The Day of the Triffids*, p. 126.
250 'I don't propose to deal in detail': John Wyndham, *The Kraken Wakes* (Penguin, 2008; first published 1953), p. 220.
250 'cosy catastrophes': Aldiss, *Billion Year Spree*, p. 293.
250 'one might as well call World War II': Margaret Atwood, 'Chocky, the Kindly Body Snatcher', *Slate*, 8 September 2015.
250 'All the old problems': Wyndham, *The Day of the Triffids*, p. 60.
251 'Only those who can make their minds tough': ibid., p. 85.
251 'I seemed able to recall': ibid., p. 231.
251 'composite hero': 'Talking to John Wyndham', *The Times*, 16 March 1968.
251 'This was an enemy': Wyndham, *The Day of the Triffids*, p. 86.
252 'In an age of pessimism': 'The New Pessimists', *The Times*, 23 January 1960.
252 'Unlike Wells': 'Obituary: Mr John Wyndham', *The Times*, 12 March 1969.
252 'Many stories were of Earth destroyed': Aldiss, *Billion Year Spree*, p. 246.
252 'Your English reader': Derek Hart, interview with John Wyndham, *Tonight*. Aired 6 September 1960, on BBC.
253 'It must be, I thought': Wyndham, *The Day of the Triffids*, p. 86.
253 'I, and quite likely many of you': ibid., p. 115.
253 'I knew John fairly well': John Gough, 'An Interview with John Christopher', *Children's Literature in Education*, vol. 15, no. 2 (1984), p. 96.
254 'Other people': ibid., p. 98.
254 'Which way's best': Christopher, *The Death of Grass*, p. 49.
254 'Pity always was a luxury': ibid., p. 145.
254 'a small hard core': *Panic in Year Zero!*, directed by Ray Milland, screenplay by John Morton and Jay Simms (1962).
254 'a world broken down': John Christopher, *A Wrinkle in the Skin* (SYLE Press, 2019; first published 1965), p. 45.
255 'What did you expect': ibid., p. 140.
255 'Nothing has changed for you': ibid., pp. 184–5.
255 'Might it happen here?': ibid., p. 7.
255 'It couldn't happen, could it?': Christopher, *The Death of Grass*, p. 30.
255 'Yet again it falls to the British peoples': ibid., p. 44.
255 'could no longer believe': ibid., p. 125.

256 'rubble of a frozen': John Christopher, *The World in Winter* (Penguin, 2016; first published 1962), p. 218.
256 'This was London': ibid., p. 199.
256 'The last man left alive?': Christopher, *A Wrinkle in the Skin*, p. 27.
256 'because the rules': William Golding, *Lord of the Flies* (Faber and Faber, 2011; first published 1954), p. 99.
256 'I'd like to put on war-paint': ibid., p. 156.
256 'What makes things break up': ibid., p. 154.
257 'children who behave': John Carey, *William Golding: The Man Who Wrote* Lord of the Flies (Faber, 2010), p. 149.
257 'The real *Lord of the Flies*': Rutger Bregman, *Humankind: A Hopeful History*, translated by Elizabeth Manton and Erica Moore (Bloomsbury, 2020), p. 38.
257 'Catastrophe and the sudden termination of the normal': Samuel Henry Prince, *Catastrophe and Social Change* (Columbia University, 1920), p. 55. Further information from Rebecca Solnit, *A Paradise Built in Hell: The Extraordinary Communities That Arise in Disaster* (Viking Press, 2009).
258 'Without penicillin': Pat Frank, *Alas, Babylon*, with a foreword by David Brin (Harper Perennial, 2005; first published 1959), p. 235.
258 'moonscape': Charles Eric Maine, *The Tide Went Out* (Hodder and Stoughton, 1958), p. 136.
258 'the hardening of the individual': ibid., p. 117.
259 'You become pious': ibid., p. 151.
259 'I've come to accept': ibid., p. 179.
259 'I'm never happier': Thomas Frick, 'J. G. Ballard: The Art of Fiction No. 85', *The Paris Review*, no. 94 (Winter 1984).
259 online concordance: J. G. Ballard – The Concordance, http://bonsall-books.co.uk/concordance/
260 'a wilderness of swamps': J. G. Ballard, 'The Dead Astronaut' (1968), in J. G. Ballard, *The Complete Short Stories* (Flamingo, 2001), p. 760.
260 'Why did you come to America?': J. G. Ballard, *Hello America* (4th Estate, 2014; first published 1981), pp. 57–8.
260 'a model landscape': J. G. Ballard, *High-Rise* (Harper Perennial, 2006; first published 1975), p. 147.
260 'psychic zero stations': Frick, 'J. G. Ballard: The Art of Fiction No. 85'.
260 'powerfully nostalgic': Will Self, 'J. G. Ballard', in *Junk Mail* (Bloomsbury, 1995), p. 360.
260 'the sense that reality': J. G. Ballard, *Miracles of Life: Shanghai to Shepperton: An Autobiography* (4th Estate, 2008), pp. 58–9.
261 'half-ruined college campus': ibid., p. 64.
261 'almost as if the war had never happened': ibid., p. 109.
261 'a sort of disaster area': Ballard, *High-Rise*, p. 12.
261 'hope itself was rationed': Ballard, *Miracles of Life*, p. 123.

261 'the saving miracle': J. G. Ballard, *The Kindness of Women* (HarperCollins, 1991), p. 55.

261 'The endless newsreel clips': J. G. Ballard, *The Atrocity Exhibition* (Flamingo, 2001; first published 1970), p. 14.

261 'glamorous apocalypse': Self, 'J. G. Ballard', p. 345.

261 'This island is a state of mind': J. G. Ballard, 'The Terminal Beach' (1964), in *The Complete Short Stories*, p. 590.

262 'He believes that science fiction': James Goddard and David Pringle, eds, *J. G. Ballard: The First Twenty Years* (Bran's Head Books, 1976).

262 'They are all paintings': ibid., p. 9.

262 'immaculate ruins': J. G. Ballard, 'The Day of Forever' (1966), in *The Complete Short Stories*, p. 671.

262 'drained beaches': J. G. Ballard, *The Drought* (Jonathan Cape, 1965), p. 161.

262 'self-devouring': J. G. Ballard, *The Drowned World* (Harper Perennial, 2008; first published 1962), p. 29.

262 'on the brink of collapse': Henry Miller, 'Another Bright Messenger', *View*, vol. 2, no. 1 (April 1942), quoted in Werner Spies, ed., *Max Ernst: Life and Work* (Thames & Hudson, 2006), p. 173.

262 'the most optimistic commentary': Rosamund Frost, 'First Fruits of Exile', *Art News*, 15 March 1942.

262 'rolling English meadows': Goddard and Pringle, p. 9.

262 'hack job': Frick, 'J. G. Ballard: The Art of Fiction No. 85'.

263 'resurrecting a corpse!': Ballard, *The Drowned World*, p. 159.

263 'a second Adam': ibid., p. 175.

263 'The American publisher': Martin Amis, 'J. G. Ballard' (1984), in *Visiting Mrs Nabokov and Other Excursions* (Penguin, 1994), p. 81.

263 'thin but resilient': Ballard, *The Drought*, p. 43.

263 'always thought': ibid., p. 25.

263 'The rest of the world': J. G. Ballard, *The Crystal World* (Jonathan Cape, 1966), p. 101.

263 'another planet': Ballard, *High-Rise*, p. 106.

264 'questions of motive': Ballard, *The Crystal World*, p. 19.

264 'a constructive and positive act': Ballard, 'Cataclysms and Dooms', pp. 208–9.

264 'Apocalypse': Ballard, *The Atrocity Exhibition*, p. 1.

264 'near-future South London': press release for Burial, *Burial* (Hyperdub, 2006).

264 'On waking one morning': J. G. Ballard, 'The Secret Autobiography of J.G.B.', *The New Yorker*, 11 May 2009.

265 'What is wanted': D. A. Callard, *The Case of Anna Kavan: A Biography* (Peter Owen, 1992), p. 85.

265 'I know I've got a death-wish': Anna Kavan, 'High in the Mountains', in *Julia and the Bazooka and Other Stories* (Peter Owen, 1970), p. 101.

265 'vast, indifferent': Anna Kavan, *Ice* (Picador, 1973), p. 126.
265 'an arctic prison': ibid., p. 23.
265 'monstrous epidemics': ibid., pp. 82–3.
266 'all dark, all still': Samuel Beckett, *Play* (1963), in *The Complete Dramatic Works* (Faber and Faber, 2006), p. 307.
266 'Instead of my world': Kavan, *Ice*, p. 115.
266 'I did not regret': ibid., p. 126.
266 'I haven't felt anything': Dom Moraes, 'The Book-Makers', *Nova*, September 1967.
266 'WHAT IS THE EXACT NATURE': *New Worlds*, no. 182 (July 1968).
267 'What makes the '70s so eerie': Schwartz, p. 195.
267 'In the papers we read': Saul Bellow, 'Nobel Lecture', 12 December 1976.
267 'Urbanization, ethnic conflict': Alvin Toffler, *Future Shock* (Bodley Head, 1970), p. 395.
267 'Is there hope for man?': Robert L. Heilbroner, *An Inquiry into the Human Prospect* (W. W. Norton & Company, 1974), p. 13.
267 'painful, difficult': ibid., p. 22.
267 'Cultural note': Gore Vidal, *Kalki* (Abacus, 1993; first published 1978), p. 28.
267 The French called this mood *la sinistrose*: Weber, p. 208.
267 'passed on to the public': 'Behavior: The Deluge of Disastermania', *Time*, 5 March 1979.
267 'After the experiences': Barbara W. Tuchman, *A Distant Mirror: The Calamitous 14th Century* (Macmillan, 1979), p. xiv.
268 'As the twentieth century approaches its end': Christopher Lasch, *The Culture of Narcissism: American Life in an Age of Diminishing Expectations* (W. W. Norton & Company, 1978), p. 3.
268 Johnny Rotten rhymed *anarchist*: Sex Pistols, 'Anarchy in the UK' (EMI, 1976).
268 The Ruts declared: The Ruts, 'Babylon's Burning' (Virgin, 1979).
268 'The world as we know it': Clinton Heylin, *The Double Life of Bob Dylan, Vol. 2, 1966–2021: Far Away from Myself* (Bodley Head, 2023), p. 361.
268 'silent charnelhouse': Doris Lessing, *The Four-Gated City* (MacGibbon & Kee, 1969), p. 699.
268 'a true prophecy': 'Doris Lessing at Stony Brook: An Interview by Jonah Raskin' (1969), in *A Small Personal Voice: Essays, Reviews, Interviews*, edited and introduced by Paul Schlueter (Vintage, 1975).
269 'Very well, then': Doris Lessing, *Memoirs of a Survivor* (Flamingo, 1995; first published 1974), p. 130.

CHAPTER 14. SURVIVAL

270 'What in God's name': Cormac McCarthy, *The Road* (Picador, 2007), p. 57.

270 'yet another of those tiresome': 'Logan's Run', *New York*, 5 July 1976.

270 'war, overpopulation and pollution': *Logan's Run*, directed by Michael Anderson, screenplay by David Zelag Goodman (1976).

270 'Who needs a reason to destroy L.A.?': Pauline Kael, 'Decadence' (1974), in *Reeling* (Atlantic Monthly Press, 1976), p. 385.

270 seemingly first appeared in 1967: 'Fiction of the Month', *The Guardian*, 28 July 1967.

271 'about fifteen years from now': 'Directing *Mad Max* and *The Road Warrior*: An Interview with George Miller by Danny Peary', in Danny Peary, ed., *Omni's Screen Flights Screen Fantasies: The Future According to Science Fiction Cinema* (Dolphin, 1984), p. 280.

271 'I think both films': ibid., p. 281.

271 'two mighty warrior tribes': *Mad Max 2*, directed by George Miller, screenplay by George Miller, Terry Hayes and Brian Hannant (1981).

271 President Jimmy Carter believed: Paul Sabin, *The Bet: Paul Ehrlich, Julian Simon, and Our Gamble over Earth's Future* (Yale University Press, 2013), p. 104.

271 'Of course, exhaustion': Craig Copetas, 'Beat Godfather Meets Glitter Mainman: William Burroughs Interviews David Bowie', *Rolling Stone*, no. 155 (28 February 1974).

272 'In a little over 10 years': Richard J. Barnet, 'No Room in the Lifeboats', *The New York Times*, 16 April 1978.

272 'the debris of the old, decaying world': Peary, p. 281.

272 'The Vermin Have Inherited the Earth': *Mad Max 2*.

272 'compellingly reductive': J. G. Ballard, 'Outer Limits: Blast Off with Ten Fantasy Tapes', *American Film*, October 1987.

272 'From the wreckage': *The Lego Movie 2: The Second Part*, directed by Mike Mitchell, screenplay by Phil Lord and Christopher Miller (2019).

273 'Politicians had finally solved': *A Boy and His Dog*, written and directed by L. Q. Jones (1975).

273 'The key figure here': Mike Davis, *Ecology of Fear*, p. 331.

273 'After reading *The Turner Diaries*': ibid., p. 335.

274 'This time, however': Charlie Robins, 'The Elite Meet to Eat', *The Tampa Times*, 26 May 1975.

274 'the biggest bloodbath': Washington Star News, 'Economy Is Going . . . A Bloodbath Is Coming', *The Miami News*, 8 May 1975.

274 'great pestholes': Larry Eichel, 'Headed for the Hills', *The Philadelphia Inquirer*, 4 May 1980.

274 'separating the sheep from the goats': T. A. DeMattis, 'United We Survive, Divided We Fail', *The Survivor*, vol. 1 (1976), p. 103.

274 'There are growing numbers': ibid.

274 'clear-thinking and productive': Paranoid George, 'The Survival Mentality', *The Survivor*, vol. 2 (1977), p. 537.

275 'When people become nervous': Pamela G. Hollie, 'Business of Survival Grows', *The New York Times*, 28 August 1980.

275 Pier was claiming: Wayne King, 'Fearing Society's Collapse: "Survivalists" Cache Goods', *The New York Times*, 15 January 1981.

275 'the coming decades of scarcity': Deborah Gieringer, '2 Professors Warn of "Coming Scarcity"', *The New York Times*, 15 March 1981.

275 'few sensible Romans': Bruce D. Clayton, *Life After Doomsday: A Survivalist Guide to Nuclear War and Other Major Disasters* (Paladin Press, 1980) p. v.

275 'We don't know when': Linda Price, 'Preparing for Doomsday', *The New York Times*, 29 November 1981.

275 'Americans have a strong undercurrent': Wayne King, 'Fearing Society's Collapse'.

276 'Life is transformed': Richard G. Mitchell Jr, *Dancing at Armageddon: Survivalism and Chaos in Modern Times* (University of Chicago Press, 2002), p. 215.

276 'environmental catastrophe': ibid., p. 3.

276 'What the apologists': 'Survivalism', *The New York Times*, 12 December 1980.

276 'I used to hate the world': *The Last of Us*, season 1, episode 3, 'Long, Long Time', directed by Peter Hoar, written by Craig Mazin. Aired 29 January 2023, on HBO.

277 'They were following *Turner Diaries*': Robert Jimison, 'How the FBI Smashed White Supremacist Group The Order', *CNN.com*, 21 August 2018.

277 'Men whose hobby': David Brin, *The Postman* (Orbit, 2013; first published 1985), p. 334.

277 '*Survivalists*': ibid., p. 138.

277 'Most post-holocaust novels': Zack Stentz, 'Au Contrarian', *Metro*, 6–12 February 1997.

278 'blithe assumption': Frank, *Alas, Babylon*, p. xii.

278 'fellow y2k preppers': 'Re: This Group', *alt.y2k.end-of-the-world* (Usenet newsgroup), 7 August 1998.

278 'I'm a collapsist': Nellie Bowles, 'How to Prepare Now for the Complete End of the World', *The New York Times*, 5 March 2020.

278 'the woodsman in the tinfoil hat': Evan Osnos, 'Doomsday Prep for the Super-Rich', *The New Yorker*, 22 January 2017.

279 'bunker/shelter': Kelsey Ables, 'The Enduring Appeal of Remote Pacific Islands for Rich Apocalypse Preppers', *The Washington Post*, 26 July 2023.

279 'backup': X (Twitter), @elonmusk, 5 June 2022.

279 'If we stay here on Earth': CBS News, 20 July 1969, quoted in Weller, *The Bradbury Chronicles* (Harper Perennial, 2006), p. 283.

279 'Never before': Douglas Rushkoff, 'The Super-Rich "Preppers" Planning to Save Themselves from the Apocalypse', *The Observer*, 4 September 2022. Excerpted from *Survival of the Richest: Escape Fantasies of the Tech Billionaires* (Scribe, 2022)

279 'Like the plot of a Marvel blockbuster': ibid.
280 'The Rapture is a parable': Naomi Klein, *The Shock Doctrine: The Rise of Disaster Capitalism* (Allen Lane, 2010), p. 419.
280 'able-bodied, clean-minded': Wells, *The War of the Worlds*, p. 262.
280 'We can't have any weak or silly': ibid., p. 263.
280 'just a thin veneer': James Wesley Rawles, *How to Survive the End of the World as We Know It: Tactics, Techniques and Technologies for Uncertain Times* (Penguin, 2009), pp. 6–7.
281 'I just had this image': *The Oprah Winfrey Show*, season 22, episode 85. Aired 5 June 2007, on syndication.
281 'may venture without risking': Michael Chabon, 'After the Apocalypse', *The New York Review of Books*, 15 February 2007.
281 'looted, ransacked, ravaged': McCarthy, *The Road*, pp. 136-7.
281 'A long shear of light': ibid., p. 54.
281 'largely populated': ibid., p. 192.
281 'the absolute truth of the world': ibid., p. 138.
282 'a grave yawning': ibid., p. 165.
282 'The world shrinking down': ibid., p. 93.
282 'We're trying to avoid the clichés': Charles McGrath, 'At World's End, Honing a Father–Son Dynamic', *The New York Times*, 27 May 2008.
282 'carrying the fire': McCarthy, *The Road*, p. 231.
282 'There's no such thing': Richard B. Woodward, 'Cormac McCarthy's Venomous Fiction', *The New York Times*, 19 April 1992.
283 'I think a lot of people think': Mario-Paul Martínez, 'No Hay Ninguna Razón para Pensar Que Las Cosas Van a Mejorar', *information.es*, 6 October 2012.
283 'I remind myself': Kathy Bernier, 'REVIEW: "The Road" Is a Gripping Prepper Novel Full of Tragedy, Struggle and Hope', *Off The Grid News*, undated.
283 'One generation apologizing': Lessing, *The Four-Gated City*, p. 661.
283 'the most important environmental book': George Monbiot, 'Civilisation Ends with a Shutdown of Human Concern. Are We There Already?', *The Guardian*, 30 October 2007.
283 'some version of the end of the world': Robert Jay Lifton, 'Giving Meaning to Survival', *Chronicle of Higher Education*, 28 September 2001.
284 'not credible': Martin Amis, 'Fear and Loathing', *The Guardian*, 18 September 2001.
284 'Maybe since 9/11': *The Oprah Winfrey Show*, 5 June 2007.
284 'The future isn't some place': Abraham Josephine Riesman, 'The Vulture Transcript: Alfonso Cuarón on *Children of Men*', *Vulture*, 6 January 2017.
284 'We knew that this was indeed the end': P. D. James, *The Children of Men* (Faber and Faber, 2005), p. 9.

284 'In the space of a few days': Clarke, *Childhood's End*, p. 210.
285 'crumbling into senescence': Brian Aldiss, *Greybeard* (Gollancz, 2011; first published 1964), p. 116.
285 '*ennui universel*': P. D. James, *The Children of Men*, p. 10.
285 'Man is diminished': ibid., pp. 113–14.
285 'They live without hope': ibid., p. 69.
286 'Even if they discovered': *Children of Men*, directed by Alfonso Cuarón, screenplay by Alfonso Cuarón, Timothy J. Sexton, David Arata, Mark Fergus and Hawk Ostby (2006).
286 'Ultimately, the UK looks like a green zone': Riesman, 'The Vulture Transcript: Alfonso Cuarón on *Children of Men*'.
287 'This bloke did some of the wickedest masterpieces': Deleted scene, *Children of Men: 2 Disc Special Edition*, DVD (Universal, 2007).

PART SIX: PANDEMIC

CHAPTER 15. PESTILENCE

291 'Of all dangers': Charles Brockden Brown, *Arthur Mervyn; or, Memoirs of the Year 1793* (H. Maxwell & Co., 1799), p. 170.
291 'It really did feel like': Nick Cave and Seán O'Hagan, *Faith, Hope and Carnage* (Canongate, 2022), p. 4.
291 'People will come along': *The Late Show with Stephen Colbert*, episode 917. Aired 5 May 2020, on CBS.
291 'suddenly a kind of slowpoke Nostradamus': Oana Aristide, *Under the Blue* (Serpent's Tail, 2022), p. 277.
291 'might be accused of trying': ibid., p. 276.
292 'sowers': *Case 63*, season 2, episode 4, 'It's Been a Long Time, Beatrix', written by Julio Rojas and adapted by Mara Vélez Meléndez, podcast audio, Spotify, 26 September 2023.
292 'It has been very strange to me': Sam Adams, '*Contagion*'s Screenwriter on Watching His Movie Go Viral', *Slate*, 11 March 2020.
292 'It's like if a novelist': Adrienne Westenfeld, 'Emily St. John Mandel Is Nobody's Prophet', *esquire.com*, 13 December 2021.
292 'very dull': Peter Furtado, *Plague, Pestilence and Pandemic: Voices from History* (Thames & Hudson, 2021), p. 9.
292 'Disease X': R. J., 'What Is Disease X?', *economist.com*, 23 March 2018.
293 'as complex as climate change': Alona Ferber, '"It Could Kill Us Before the Climate Crisis Does": Sally Davies on the Risks of Anti-microbial Resistance', *The New Statesman*, vol. 151, no. 5688 (7–13 October 2022).
293 Toby Ord estimates: Ord, p. 167.
293 '[One] thing that I'm obsessed with': Troy Baker, interview with Craig

Mazin and Neil Druckmann, *HBO's The Last of Us Podcast*, season 1, episode 1, podcast audio, 16 January 2023.

293 'The World Knows': Laurie Garrett, 'The World Knows an Apocalyptic Pandemic Is Coming', *foreignpolicy.com*, 20 September 2019.

293 'could infect the whole world': Tuchman, p. 93.

294 'a third of the world died': ibid., p. 94.

294 'a pestilence': Furtado, p. 36.

294 'Brothers abandoned one another': ibid., p. 61.

295 'making us cruel': ibid., p. 131.

295 'But, alas!': Daniel Defoe, *A Journal of the Plague Year* (Folio Society, 1960), p. 121.

295 'the catastrophe was so overwhelming': Thucydides, *The History of the Peloponnesian War*, translated by Rex Warner (Folio Society, 2006), pp. 114–15.

295 'the pleasure of the moment': Raymond Crawfurd, *Plague and Pestilence in Literature and Art* (Clarendon Press, 1914), p. 31.

296 'demons in the sky': George Deaux, *The Black Death 1347* (Hamish Hamilton, 1969), p. 4.

296 'And no bells tolled': Tuchman, p. 95.

296 'the extermination of mankind': ibid., p. 101.

296 'if perchance': ibid.

296 'It was as if the voice of existence': Furtado, p. 68.

297 'incomparably the worst catastrophe': ibid., p. 227.

297 'If the epidemic': Richard Collier, *The Plague of the Spanish Lady: The Influenza Pandemic of 1918–19* (Macmillan, 1974), p. 266.

298 'no songs, no legends': ibid., p. 304.

298 'So vast was the catastrophe': 'The Great Death', *The Times*, 2 February 1921.

299 'It would be needless': Mary Shelley, *The Last Man, Volume II*, pp. 224–5.

299 'the vast annihilation': ibid.

299 'a scene of woe': D'Arcy Wood, p. 84.

299 'Such a scene of horror': ibid., p. 76.

299 'A ghoulish aspect': Frank M. Snowden, *Epidemics and Society: From the Black Death to the Present* (Yale University Press, 2019), p. 238.

300 'He was found stiff': Mary Shelley, *The Last Man, Volume II*, p. 114.

300 'invincible monster': ibid., pp. 123–4.

300 'There is no refuge': ibid., p. 170.

300 'The air is empoisoned': ibid., p. 151.

300 'for all we know': Wells, 'The Extinction of Man', p. 178.

301 'Our microscopic allies': Wells, *The War of the Worlds*, p. 283.

301 'IS THIS DREAD CHOLERA?': Furtado, pp. 157–8.

301 'Those little particles': H. G. Wells, 'The Stolen Bacillus' (1894), in *The Country of the Blind*, p. 41.

301 'I was born at the moment': quoted in Ailise Bulfin, 'M. P. Shiel: The First Biography', *English Literature in Transition, 1880–1920*, vol. 54, no. 3 (2011).
301 'a legend, an apocalypse': A. Reynolds Morse, *The Works of M. P. Shiel: Updated: Volume III – Part 2* (Reynolds Morse, 1980), pp. 469–70.
302 'White Power': M. P. Shiel, *The Purple Cloud* (Penguin Classics, 2012), p. 207.
302 'for surely I am hardly any longer': ibid., p. 125.
302 'the filthiest and nastiest country': Snowden, p. 335.
303 'The fact that God': A. Reynolds Morse, *The Works of M. P. Shiel: Updated: Volume II – Part 1* (Reynolds Morse, 1980), p 185.
303 'the extinction of the yellow man': M. P. Shiel, *The Yellow Danger* (Grant Richards, 1898), p. 344.
303 'that winged plague': ibid., p. 343.
303 'a universal uprising of the yellow race': *The Times*, 17 July 1900.
303 'amazing birth rate': Jack London, 'The Unparalleled Invasion' (1910), in *The Strength of the Strong* (Macmillan Company, 1914), p. 88.
303 'It was ultra-modern war': ibid., p. 98.
303 'vast and happy': ibid., p. 100.
303, fn.: 'American madness': Stapledon, *Last and First Men*, p. 46.
304 'Not in history': Jack London, 'The Story of an Eye-Witness', *Collier's*, 5 May 1906.
304 'the handful of survivors': ibid.
304 'from time to time': Jack London, *The Scarlet Plague* (Macmillan Company, 1915), p. 65.
304 'With the coming of the Scarlet Death': ibid., p. 90.
304 'The bacillus . . . was never isolated': J. D. Beresford, *Goslings* (William Heinemann, 1913), p. 232.
304 'China's a long way off': ibid., p. 11.
304 'a chap who's been reading': ibid., p. 34.
305 'It seems so incredible': ibid., p. 34.
305 'a mere subterfuge': ibid., p. 65.
305 'Hope, lots of hope': ibid., p. 323.
305 'noxious bacillus': Adolf Hitler, *Mein Kampf*, translated by R. Manheim (Houghton Mifflin, 1943), p. 305.
305 'whether the time hasn't come': Joseph Roth, letter to Stefan Zweig, 26 March 1933, in *A Life in Letters*, translated and edited by Michael Hofmann (Granta, 2012).
305 'the scourge of anarchy': Karel Čapek, *Power and Glory*, translated by Paul Selver and Ralph Neale (George Allen & Unwin, 1938), p. 41.
305 'If I had to choose': ibid., p. 53.

CHAPTER 16. CONTAGION

306 'The trouble you're expecting': George R. Stewart, *Earth Abides* (Gollancz, 1999; first published 1949), p. 15.

306 'various channels of commerce': Mary Shelley, *The Last Man, Volume II*, p. 150.

306 'For good or ill': J. J. Connington, *Nordenholt's Million* (Constable & Co., 1923), p. 18.

306 'If a killing type': Stewart, p. 1.

307 'within some measurable time': Snowden, p. 449.

307 'our previous self-congratulations': Daniel Bell, ed., *Toward the Year 2000: Work in Progress* (Beacon Press, 1969), p. 345.

307 'the last great plague': Edwin D. Kilbourne, 'Flu to the Starboard! Man the Harpoons! Fill 'em with Vaccine! Get the Captain! Hurry!', *The New York Times*, 13 February 1976.

307 'It might have emerged': Stewart, p. 13.

308 'necklace of death': *Moonraker*, directed by Lewis Gilbert, screenplay by Christopher Wood (1979).

308 'We were warned': *The Omega Man.*

308 'he had forgone': Vidal, *Kalki*, p. 310.

308 'an unknown something': Burchett, *Shadows of Hiroshima*, p. 34.

308 'Once in every generation': Stephen King, *Danse Macabre*, p. 370.

308 'US pig paramilitary': Stephen King, *The Stand* (Hodder, 2011; first published 1978), p. 253.

308 'the America I had grown up in': Stephen King, *Danse Macabre*, p. 372.

308 'They've solved the depressed economy': Stephen King, *The Stand*, p. 300.

308 'capering nihilist': Stephen King, *Danse Macabre*, p. 372.

309 'This is an island, thank God': John Christopher, *Empty World* (Hamish Hamilton, 1977), p. 17.

309 'There was a bad epidemic': *Survivors*, season 1, episode 1, 'The Fourth Horseman', directed by Pennant Roberts, written by Terry Nation. Aired 16 April 1975, on BBC One.

309 'as an age-old military campaign': Sontag, *AIDS and Its Metaphors*, p. 158.

309 the first ever article: 'Pneumocystis Pneumonia – Los Angeles', *Morbidity and Mortality Weekly Report*, vol. 30, no. 21 (5 June 1981).

310 'Nobody can alienate people': Michael Specter, 'Larry Kramer, Public Nuisance', *The New Yorker*, 13 May 2002.

310 'If this article doesn't scare the shit out of you': Larry Kramer, '1,112 and Counting', *New York Native*, 14–27 March 1983, in Furtado, p. 256.

310 'With that one piece': Specter, 'Larry Kramer, Public Nuisance'.

310 'many Bible scholars think': Thomas L. Long, *AIDS and American Apocalypticism: The Cultural Semiotics of an Epidemic* (State University of New York Press, 2005), p. 6.

310 '*We are not* under the threat': Jurg Mahner, letter to the editor, *New York Native*, 28 March–10 April 1983.

310 'I am sick of everyone': Kramer, '1,112 and Counting'.

311 'One sort of apocalyptic scenario': Mark Doty, 'Is There a Future?', in Marie Howe and Michael Klein, eds, *In the Company of My Solitude: American Writing from the AIDS Pandemic* (Persea, 1995), p. 6.

311 'AIDS suits the style': Lance Morrow, 'The Start of a Plague Mentality', *Time*, 23 September 1985.

311 'the disease of the century': Claudia Wallis, 'AIDS: A Growing Threat', *Time*, 12 August 1985.

311 'an epidemic of fear': Randy Shilts, *And the Band Played On: Politics, People, and the AIDS Epidemic* (Souvenir Press, 2011; first published 1987), p. 302.

311 'Irrational fear': Wallis, 'AIDS: A Growing Threat'.

312 'multiply, spread and recombine': Douglas Selvage, 'Memetic Engineering: Conspiracy Theories, Viruses and Historical Agency', *opendemocracy.net*, 22 October 2015.

312 'pale by comparison': AP, 'AIDS May Dwarf the Plague', *The New York Times*, 30 January 1987.

312 'an issue that may rank': Stephen Jay Gould, 'The Terrifying Normalcy of AIDS', *The New York Times*, 19 April 1987.

312 'Life slips into science fiction': Morrow, 'The Start of a Plague Mentality'.

312 'less like a hymn': Andrew Holleran, *Chronicle of a Plague, Revisited: AIDS and Its Aftermath* (Da Capo, 2008), p. 55.

313 'Kalki is, I think': ibid., p. 49.

313 'It was so unfair': ibid., p. 84.

314 'Most emerging viruses': Christine Mlot, 'Connecting the Dots', *On Wisconsin*, Fall 2021.

314 'the threat of emerging': Pierre Ouellette, *The Third Pandemic* (Hodder & Stoughton, 1996), p. vii.

314 'That humanity had grossly underestimated': Laurie Garrett, *The Coming Plague: Newly Emerging Diseases in a World Out of Balance* (Virago, 1995), p. 550.

314 'one of the most horrifying things': Richard Preston, *The Hot Zone* (Doubleday, 1994), dust jacket blurb.

314 'It could be said': ibid., p. 15.

315 'I did figure': ibid., p. 93.

315 'savage African diseases': Robert Matthews, 'Fear Hits Fever Pitch Over Hidden Plagues', *The Sunday Telegraph*, 30 October 1994.

315 'The single biggest threat': *Outbreak*, directed by Wolfgang Petersen, screenplay by Laurence Dworet and Robert Roy Pool (1995).

315 'Something was bound to succeed the bomb': Terence Rafferty, 'The Enemy Within', *The New Yorker*, 12 March 1995.

315 'a terrible, lethal virus': Richard N. Haass, Director, Office of the Policy Planning Staff, Remarks to the Council of Foreign Relations, 15 October 2001.

316 'the millennium's first jetset disease': Gaby Hinsliff and Mark Townsend, 'The Day the World Caught a Cold', *The Observer*, 27 April 2003.

316 'A global outbreak': Mike Davis, *The Monster at Our Door: The Global Threat of Avian Flu* (Owl Books, 2006), p. 71.

316 'Toronto and Kingston': Mark Honigsbaum, *The Pandemic Century: A History of Global Contagion from the Spanish Flu to Covid-19* (Penguin, 2020), p. 188.

316 'fear, speculation and rumor': David J. Rothkopf, 'When the Buzz Bites Back', *The Washington Post*, 11 May 2003.

316 'It'll be like SARS': Mandel, *Station Eleven*, p. 25.

316 'a new Manhattan Project': quoted in Hughes, 'Millennial Tendencies', p. 82.

317 'apocalypse nut': *12 Monkeys*, directed by Terry Gilliam, screenplay by David and Janet Peoples (1995).

317 'Accidents happen': David M. Halbfinger, 'The City That Never Sleeps, Comatose', *The New York Times*, 4 November 2007.

317 'even more credible now': Benji Wilson, 'Fight to Survive', *Radio Times*, 22–28 November 2008.

317 'We're fascinated by epidemics': Stephanie Smith, 'The Roots of Our Ebola Fears', *CNN.com*, 7 August 2014.

317 'the premise of epidemics': Georgios Pappas et al., 'Infectious Diseases in Cinema: Virus Hunters and Killer Microbes', *Clinical Infectious Diseases*, vol. 37, no. 7 (1 October 2003).

317 'Nothing spreads like fear': poster for *Contagion*, directed by Steven Soderbergh, screenplay by Scott Z. Burns (2011).

317 'Godzilla, King Kong': *Contagion.*

318, fn.: 'obviously quite gratifying': Archie Bland, 'Contagion: What Role Did Movie Play in the Vaccine Programme?', *The Guardian*, 3 February 2021.

318 'For too long': Honigsbaum, p. 272.

318 'The earth's immune system': Richard Preston, *The Hot Zone*, p. 320.

318 'Peaceful thought, isn't it?': Vidal, *Kalki*, p. 209.

318 'If I stop doing this': Kev Geoghegan, 'Utopia Writer Dennis Kelly Defends Violent Scenes', *bbc.co.uk*, 17 June 2014.

319 'It travelled through the air': Margaret Atwood, *The Year of the Flood* (Virago, 2013), p. 24.

319 'He might be immune': Margaret Atwood, *Oryx and Crake* (Virago, 2004), p. 403.

319 'Those who don't die': *Rise of the Planet of the Apes*, directed by Rupert Wyatt, screenplay by Rick Jaffa and Amanda Silver (2011).

319 'many instances': Defoe, p. 121.

319 'expresses an imaginative complicity': Sontag, *AIDS and Its Metaphors*, p. 173.

319 'The flu, the great cleansing': Mandel, p. 60.

319 'a horror movie': ibid., p. 176.

320 'Survival is insufficient': ibid., p. 58.

320 'The worst is not': William Shakespeare, *King Lear*, Act IV, Scene 1, quoted in *Station Eleven*, season 1, episode 5, 'The Severn City Airport', directed by Lucy Cherniak, written by Cord Jefferson. Aired 23 December 2021, on HBO Max.

320 'One day her plagues': Mandel, p. 259.

320 'There is no before': *Station Eleven*, season 1, episode 4, 'Rosencrantz and Guildenstern Aren't Dead', directed by Helen Shaver, written by Nick Cuse. Aired 23 December 2021, on HBO Max.

320 'taken-for-granted miracles': Mandel, p. 233.

320 'Of course, one way': Westenfeld, 'Emily St. John Mandel Is Nobody's Prophet'.

320 'I'm just saying': Mandel, p. 256.

321 'It's safe to do something': Doug Gross, 'Why We Love those Rotting, Hungry, Putrid Zombies', *CNN.com*, 2 October 2009.

CHAPTER 17. ZOMBIES

322 'Jesus, it's everywhere': *Dawn of the Dead*, written and directed by George A. Romero (1978).

322 'The zombie, they say': W. B. Seabrook, 'Dead Men Working in the Cane Fields' (1929), in Peter Haining, *Zombie!: Stories of the Walking Dead* (Target, 1985), p. 22.

322 'They've spent their lives': J. B. Priestley, *Bright Day* (William Heinemann, 1946), p. 329.

323 'the fantastic rapidity': Matheson, *I Am Legend*, p. 72.

323 'had a doctor check it': 'Throwback Thursdays: A Conversation with Richard Matheson', *Tor/Forge Blog*, 3 October 2013.

323 'Richard starts his book': Mariana McConnell, 'Interview: George A. Romero on Diary of the Dead', *cinemablend.com*, 14 February 2008.

323 'an epidemic of mass murder': *Night of the Living Dead*, written and directed by George A. Romero (1968).

324 'turns over the stone': Haining, p. 12.

324 'With a presidential election coming up': George A. Romero and Susanna Sparrow, *Dawn of the Dead* (Sphere, 1979), p. 16.

324 'People are basically good': *The Mist*, written and directed by Frank Darabont (2007).

325 'He realised it was the end of the world': Dorian Lynskey, 'John Carpenter: "Horror Movies Are Always the Same – and Most Are Bad"', *The Daily Telegraph*, 10 October 2022.

325 'People . . . called them zombies': quoted in Stuart Klawans, '*Night of the Living Dead:* Mere Anarchy Is Loosed', *criterion.com*, 13 February 2018.

325 'The germ that hid': Matheson, *I Am Legend*, p. 78.

325 'I want it to be unexplained': Chet Flippo, 'When There's No Room In Hell: The Dead Will Walk the Earth', *Rolling Stone*, no. 261 (23 March 1978).

325 'entities neither living nor dead': William L. Laurence, 'New Leads Given by Virus Studies', *The New York Times*, 11 September 1952.

326 'viral nature': 'Exclusive Interview: Max Brooks on World War Z', *eatmybrains.com*, 20 October 2006.

326 'doomsday scenario': Philip Munz et al., 'When Zombies Attack! Mathematical Modelling of an Outbreak of Zombie Infection', in Jean-Michael Tchuenche and Christinah Chiyakah, eds, *Infectious Disease Modelling Research Progress* (Nova, 2009), p. 146.

326 'The world of commerce': Robert Kirkman and Tony Moore, *The Walking Dead Volume 1: Days Gone Bye* (Image Comics, 2013; first published 2004).

326 'the biding cranks': Colson Whitehead, *Zone One* (Anchor, 2012), p. 164.

327 'I think it's videogames': Jamie Russell, *Book of the Dead: The Complete History of Zombie Cinema* (Titan, 2014), p. 212.

327 'I don't give a fuck': Zaki Hasan, 'Interview: Director Alex Garland on *Ex Machina*', *huffpost.com*, 10 April 2015.

327 'This is what I've seen': *28 Days Later*, directed by Danny Boyle, screenplay by Alex Garland (2002).

328 'walking destroyer': Defoe, p. 205.

328 'We must remain rational': *Dawn of the Dead.*

329 'Why they'd tried to fix this island': Whitehead, *Zone One*, p. 321.

330 'Except it was not water': ibid., p. 302.

330 'Should the economy recover': Torie Bosch, 'First, Eat All the Lawyers', *Slate*, 25 October 2011.

330 '9/11, Iraq': Taffy Brodesser-Akner, 'Max Brooks Is Not Kidding About the Zombie Apocalypse', *The New York Times*, 21 June 2013.

330 'They could be any worldwide disaster': Jamie Russell, p. 212.

330 'this particular plague': Zachary Graves, *Zombies: The Complete Guide to the World of the Living Dead* (Canary Press, 2010), p. 108.

330 'It's the end of the world!': *The Birds*, directed by Alfred Hitchcock, screenplay by Evan Hunter (1963).

331, fn.: 'Such minor paranoias': Atwood, *Oryx and Crake*, p. 402.

331 'I watched this horrible virus': Brodesser-Akner, 'Max Brooks Is Not Kidding About the Zombie Apocalypse'.

331 'The time has come': Max Brooks, *The Zombie Survival Guide: Complete Protection from the Living Dead* (Duckworth, 2004), p. xvi.

331 'What happens in a zombie plague': Jonathan Hatfull, '*World War Z*'s "Fast Zombies Are Cinematic" Says Max Brooks', *scifinow.co.uk*, 20 May 2013.

332 'Imagine if the undead virus': Max Brooks, *World War Z: An Oral History of the Zombie War* (Duckworth, 2006), p. 194.
332 'We got dozens': ibid., p. 59.
332 'Most people don't believe something': ibid., p. 32.
332 'I don't like these rage zombies': BC, 'BD Sits Down With Zombie Maestro George A. Romero!', *bloody-disgusting.com*, 14 May 2010.
332 'We need each other': *Day of the Dead*, written and directed by George A. Romero (1985).
333 'I won't last long': Colson Whitehead, 'The Books of My Life', *The Guardian*, 15 April 2023.
333 'Maybe He didn't want to see us': *Day of the Dead.*
333 'the walker apocalypse': Jeremy Egner, 'Scott M. Gimple on "The Walking Dead" and What Those Zombies Are Really Eating', *The New York Times*, 23 October 2015.
333 'apocalypse-as-moral-hygiene people': Whitehead, *Zone One*, p. 153.

PART SEVEN: CLIMATE

CHAPTER 18. TOO HOT

337 'No one thinks it will ever happen': Kim Stanley Robinson, *Fifty Degrees Below* (2005), reprinted in *Green Earth* (HarperVoyager, 2015), p. 405.
337 'Mass slaughter': Dorian Lynskey, 'Lights, Tankers, Direct Action', *The Observer*, 10 April 2022.
338 'this feeling that you're going crazy': author notes from reporting 'Lights, Tankers, Direct Action'.
338 'If you're younger than sixty': Jonathan Franzen, 'What If We Stopped Pretending?', *The New Yorker*, 8 September 2019.
338 'At some point': The Weather Station, 'Loss', on *Ignorance* (Fat Possum, 2021).
339 'Look, what is at stake': Reisman, 'The Vulture Transcript: Alfonso Cuarón on *Children of Men*'.
339 'If current trends': Edward Goldsmith et al., 'A Blueprint for Survival: Preface', *The Ecologist*, vol. 2, no. 1 (January 1972).
339 'ecologists are sometimes suspected': Commoner, p. 216.
340 'resignation, cynicism and yearning': Lifton and Falk, p. 12.
340 'We have for so long': David Wallace-Wells, *The Uninhabitable Earth: A Story of the Future* (Penguin, 2019), p. 205.
340 the atmospheric scientist Paul J. Crutzen: Paul J. Crutzen and Eugene F. Stoermer, 'The Anthropocene', *Global Change News Letter*, no. 41 (May 2000).
341 the Swedish physicist and chemist: information about the evolution of climate science from Spencer R. Weart, *The Discovery of Global Warming*

(Harvard University Press, 2008); Alice Bell, *Our Biggest Experiment: An Epic History of the Climate Crisis* (Counterpoint, 2021); and Nathaniel Rich, *Losing Earth: The Decade We Could Have Stopped Climate Change* (Picador, 2019).

341 'evolved a new theory': 'Hint to Coal Consumers', *The Selma Morning Times*, 15 October 1902.

342 'now generally accepted': James Rodger Fleming, *Historical Perspectives on Climate Change* (Oxford University Press, 1998), p. 112.

342 'Carbon dioxide gas': AP, 'Industrial Activity Reported Changing Upper Atmosphere', *The Baltimore Sun*, 5 May 1953.

342 'may have changed the atmosphere's composition': von Neumann, 'Can We Survive Technology?'.

342, fn.: 'human adaptive optimism': Naomi Oreskes and Erik M. Conway, *The Collapse of Western Civilization* (Columbia University Press, 2014), p. 58.

343 'large scale geophysical experiment': Roger Revelle and Hans E. Suess, 'Carbon Dioxide Exchange Between Atmosphere and Ocean and the Question of an Increase of Atmospheric CO_2 during the Past Decades', *Tellus*, vol. 9, no. 1 (February 1957).

343 'Even now, man': *The Unchained Goddess*, directed by Richard Carlson and William T. Hurtz, written by Frank Capra and Jonathan Latimer (1958).

343 'This generation has altered the composition': Lyndon B. Johnson, Special Message to the Congress on Conservation and Restoration of Natural Beauty, 8 February 1965.

344 'the most revolutionary book': Rachel Carson, *Silent Spring* (Penguin 1999; first published 1962), p. 259.

344 'Miss Carson's book': Jill Lepore, 'The Right Way to Remember Rachel Carson', *The New Yorker*, 26 March 2018.

344 'A Fable for Tomorrow': Carson, p. 21.

344 'The great question of the seventies': Richard Nixon, Annual Message to the Congress on the State of the Union, 22 January 1970.

344 The Princeton professor Harold Sprout: Harold Sprout, 'The Environmental Crisis in the Context of American Politics', in Leslie L. Roos Jr, ed., *The Politics of Ecosuicide* (Holt, Rinehart and Winston, 1971), p. 49.

344 'Conservatives were for it': Nan Robertson, 'Earth Day, Like Mother's, Pulls Capital Together', *The New York Times*, 23 April 1970.

344 'Hey farmer, farmer': Joni Mitchell, 'Big Yellow Taxi' (Warner Bros, 1970).

344 '*pollution* the piece's villain': Cornel Wilde, 'No Blade of Grass: A Warning for Our Time', in Peary, p. 134.

345 'By the beginning of the 70s': *No Blade of Grass*, directed by Cornel Wilde, screenplay by Sean Forestal and Cornel Wilde (1970).

345 'We have wasted and defiled': Arthur C. Clarke, *The Lost Worlds of 2001* (Sidgwick & Jackson, 1972), p. 239.

345 'There actually was a time': Philip Wylie, *The End of the Dream* (Elmfield Press, 1975; first published 1972), p. 23.
345 'An "erudite wolf-crier"': ibid., p. 22.
346 'A technological society': ibid., p. 122.
346 'The days when you and I': Elizabeth Cowley, 'The Honeymoon of Science Is Over – and Married Life Is Not so Rosy', *Radio Times*, 5 February 1970.
346 'the old preachers': John Maddox, *The Doomsday Syndrome* (Macmillan, 1972), p. 101.
346 'Instead of alerting people': ibid., p. 1.

CHAPTER 19. TOO MANY PEOPLE

347 'Look, we live in a lousy world': *Soylent Green*, directed by Richard Fleischer, screenplay by Stanley R. Greenberg (1973).
347 'gigantic inevitable famine': Thomas Malthus, *An Essay on the Principle of Population as It Affects the Future Improvement of Society. With remarks on the Speculations of Mr. Godwin, M. Condorcet and Other Writers* (J. Johnson, 1798), p. 140.
347 'a dark and terrible genius': Patricia James, *Population Malthus: His Life and Times* (Routledge & Kegan Paul, 1979), p. 379.
347 'The view which he has given': Malthus, pp. iv–v.
348 'From the view of human comfort': H. G. Wells, *A Modern Utopia* (Chapman & Hall, 1905), p. 180.
348 'God knows what man': H. G. Wells, *Apropos of Dolores* (Jonathan Cape, 1938), p. 61.
348 'very interesting': Aldous Huxley, letter to Fairfield Osborn, 16 January 1948, in Grover Smith, ed., *Letters of Aldous Huxley* (Chatto & Windus, 1969), p. 578.
348 'The tide of the earth's population': Fairfield Osborn, *Our Plundered Planet* (Faber and Faber, 1948), p. 177.
348 'We are bouncing radar beams': William L. Laurence, 'Population Outgrows Food, Scientists Warn the World', *The New York Times*, 15 September 1948.
348 'one huge dust bowl': *Letters of Aldous Huxley*, p. 578.
348 'An orgy of criminal imbecility': Huxley, *Ape and Essence*, p. 93.
348 'upper-level crisis': Aldous Huxley, 'The Double Crisis', in *Themes and Variations* (Chatto & Windus, 1950), p. 225.
349 'The impossibility': Hitler, p. 134.
349 'his own Martian': Huxley, *Themes and Variations*, p. 239.
349 'ecological trap': William Vogt, *Road to Survival* (Victor Gollancz, 1949), p. 284.
349 'apocalyptic environmentalism': quoted in Charles C. Mann, 'How Will We Feed the New Global Middle Class?', *The Atlantic*, vol. 321, no. 2 (March 2018).
349 'that clear-sighted English clergyman': Vogt, p. 72.

349 'Like Gadarene swine': ibid., p. 288.
350 'would have bred': John Wyndham, *The Chrysalids* (Penguin, 2008; first published 1955), p. 157.
350 'If this sterility stunt': Aldiss, *Greybeard*, p. 204.
350 'Do you realize that in 2020': 'Direct Hit', *Newsweek*, 3 February 1964.
350 Arthur C. Clarke predicted: Clarke, *2001*, p. 37.
350 'For your sakes, children': Harry Harrison, *Make Room! Make Room!* (Penguin, 2008; first published 1966), p. 1.
350 'Babylon-on-Hudson': ibid., p. 137.
351 'The world's gone': ibid., pp. 195–6.
351 'How I'll save the world': David Bowie, 'We Are Hungry Men', on *David Bowie* (Deram, 1967).
351 'Nothing can stop the locomotive': William and Paul Paddock, *Famine – 1975!* (Weidenfeld and Nicolson, 1968), p. 9.
352 'People, people, people, people': Paul R. Ehrlich, *The Population Bomb* (Ballantine/Friends of the Earth, 1971; first published 1968), p. 1.
352 'Too many cars': ibid., p. 36.
352 'Malthus was fundamentally right': 'Playboy Interview: Dr. Paul Ehrlich', *Playboy*, vol. 17, no. 8 (August 1970).
352 'The battle to feed all of humanity': Ehrlich, *The Population Bomb*, prologue.
353 'I am an alarmist': 'Playboy Interview: Dr. Paul Ehrlich'.
353 'Sometime in the next 15 years': quoted in Charles C. Mann, 'The Book That Incited a Worldwide Fear of Overpopulation', *Smithsonian*, January 2018.
353 'That it is incompatible': Edward Goldsmith, 'Editorial', *The Ecologist*, vol. 1, no. 1 (July 1970).
353 'a bounty for submitting': Aubrey Manning, 'No Standing Room', *The Ecologist*, vol. 1, no. 1 (July 1970).
353 'A hungry over-crowded world': Commoner, p. 233.
354 'Since I strongly believe': Charlton Heston, *In the Arena: The Autobiography* (HarperCollins, 1995), p. 476.
355 'rush toward a Malthusian nightmare': Sabin, p. 49.
355 'Noah was 500 years old': quoted in Julian L. Simon, *The Ultimate Resource* (Princeton University Press, 1981), p. 311.
355 'New High Priest of Ecocatastrophe': Sabin, p. 54.
355 'Your last letter read': ibid, p. 54.
355 'I don't really believe it': *The Dick Cavett Show*, season 5, episode 248. Aired 11 September 1971, on ABC.
355 'Who could pay attention': Sabin, p. 92.
355 'Ashes to ashes': ibid., p. 88.
355 'Talents useful': Paul R. Ehrlich and Anne H. Ehrlich, *The End of Affluence: A Blueprint for Your Future* (Ballantine Books, 1974), p. 240.

356 'It seems to be part of American popular culture': ibid., p. 11.
356 'Are we worse off': Sabin, p. 98.
356 'the doomsday crowd': ibid., p. 140.
356 'the limits-to-growth people': ibid, p. 140.
356 'Well, you know': ibid., p. 141.
356 'juggernaut of environmental hysteria': ibid., p. 3.
356 'The doomsdayers speak': Simon, *The Ultimate Resource*, p. 318.
357 'false, gloomy': Julian L. Simon and Herman Kahn, eds, *The Resourceful Earth: A Response to Global 2000* (Basil Blackwell, 1984), p. 39.
357 'If present trends': ibid., p. 1.
357 'space-age cargo cult': John Tierney, 'Betting on the Planet', *The New York Times Magazine*, 2 December 1990.
357 'The Doomslayer': Ed Regis, 'The Doomslayer', *Wired*, February 1997.
357 'Listening to environmentalists': Sabin, p. 164.
357 'doomsayers and catastrophists': Regis, 'The Doomslayer'.
357 'a bet between the Cassandra': Tierney, 'Betting on the Planet'.
357 'How often does a prophet': Sabin, p. 134.
358 'It's been nearly a generation': Jim Starlin et al., *Silver Surfer*, vol. 3, no. 35 (March 1990).
358 'I liked Thanos more': Bradford R. Poston, 'Letter to the Editor', *Silver Surfer*, vol. 3, no. 38 (June 1990).
358 'a kind of cosmic Paul Ehrlich': Jordan J. Ballor, 'Thanos the Revolutionary', *rlo.acton.org*, 6 May 2019.
358 'You multiply': *The Matrix*.
358 'Sure I've made some mistakes': X (Twitter), @PaulREhrlich, 3 January 2023.
359 'unprecedented planetary emergency': Stephen Emmott, *10 Billion* (Penguin, 2013), p. 7.
359 'Teach my son': ibid., p. 198.
359 'the population explosion is ending': Danny Dorling, *Population 10 Billion: The Coming Demographic Crisis and How to Survive It* (Constable, 2013), p. 10.
359 'population collapse': X (Twitter), @elonmusk, 26 August 2022.
359 'At the moment we cannot predict': Ehrlich, *The Population Bomb*, p. 32.
359 'The climate does not show': Simon and Kahn, p. 2.

CHAPTER 20. TOO COLD

360 'The threat of a new ice age': Nigel Calder, 'In the Grip of a New Ice Age?', *International Wildlife*, vol. 5 no. 4 (July–August 1975).
360 'Some say the world will end': Robert Frost, 'Fire and Ice', *Harper's*, vol. 142, no. 847 (December 1920).

360 'The ice age is coming': The Clash, 'London Calling' (CBS, 1979).

360 'the eve of the end': *The Twilight Zone*, season 3, episode 10, 'The Midnight Sun', directed by Anton Leader, written by Rod Serling. Aired 17 November 1961, on CBS.

360 'I have been worrying': Ralph Schoenstein, 'Look for the Rusty Lining', *The New Yorker*, 3 February 1975.

361 'a global heat disaster': Howard A. Wilcox, *Hothouse Earth* (Praeger, 1975), p. 3.

361 'cause world famine': Lowell Ponte, *The Cooling* (Prentice-Hall, 1976), p. xv.

361 'there are two': D. S. Halacy Jr, *Ice or Fire? Surviving Climatic Change* (Harper & Row, 1978), p. 172.

362 'Brace yourself': *Science Digest*, vol. 73, no. 2 (February 1973).

362 'The Ice Age Cometh': *Radio Times*, 16–22 November 1974.

362 'The cold comes instantly': Nigel Calder, *The Weather Machine* (British Broadcasting Corporation, 1974), p. 121.

362 'The end of the world': ibid., p. 136.

362 'Another Ice Age?': 'Another Ice Age?', *Time*, 24 June 1974.

363 'The Cooling World': Peter Gwynne, *Newsweek*, 28 April 1975.

363 'major cooling': Walter Sullivan, 'Scientists Ask Why World Climate Is Changing', *The New York Times*, 21 May 1975.

363 'warming trend': Walter Sullivan, 'Warming Trend Seen in Climate', *The New York Times*, 14 August 1975.

363 'A new ice age': Vidal, *Kalki*, p. 229.

363 'the notorious greenhouse effect': *Alternative 3*, directed by Christopher Miles, written by David Ambrose. Aired 20 June 1977, on Anglia Television.

363 'At the time of the fatal high tides': G. E. Assinder, letter to the editor, 'Letters', *Radio Times*, 7–13 December 1974.

363 'the greatest hoax': James M. Inhofe, 'The Science of Climate Change: Senate Floor Statement' (2003), in Bill McKibben, ed., *The Global Warming Reader: A Century of Writing About Climate Change* (Penguin, 2011), p. 191.

364 a study by the American Meteorological Society: Thomas C. Peterson, William M. Connolley and John Fleck, 'The Myth of the 1970s Global Cooling Scientific Consensus', *Bulletin of the American Meteorological Society*, vol. 89, no. 9 (September 2008).

364 'During the lifetime': *In Search of . . .*, season 2, episode 23, 'The Coming Ice Age'. Aired 5 May 1978, on syndication.

364 'interglacial dream': Douglas Orgill and John Gribbin, *The Sixth Winter* (Bodley Head, 1979), p 29.

364 'Snow*blitz*?': George Stone, *Blizzard* (Robert Hale Limited, 1979; first published 1977), p. 201.

365 'Centuries of the burning': Arthur Herzog, *Heat* (Pan, 1978).

CHAPTER 21. TOO LATE

366 'I wonder how they'll feel': Herzog, *Heat*, p. 45.
366 'It seems we have a knack': Ballard, *The Drought*, p. 182.
366 'In a way, I think I feel': Christopher, *The Death of Grass*, p. 41.
367 'The people's attitude': Herzog, *Heat*, p. 119.
367 'One thing I'm sure about': ibid., p. 120.
367 'The politicians come running': *Alternative 3*.
367 'Nearly everything we understand': Rich, p. 3.
368 'the scientific equivalent': Benjamin Santer et al., 'Celebrating the Anniversary of Three Key Events in Climate Change Science', *Nature Climate Change*, vol. 9, no. 3 (March 2019).
368 'We're flashing a yellow light': Rich, p. 91.
368 'The work is going well': Kolbert, *The Sixth Extinction*, p. 107.
368 'Now there's a hole in the sky': Pixies, 'Monkey Gone to Heaven' (4AD, 1989).
369 'Carbon dioxide stands': Rich, p. 73.
369 'with 99 percent confidence': Hearing Before the Committee on Energy and Natural Resources of the United States Senate, One Hundredth Congress, First Session, on the Greenhouse Effect and Global Climate Change, 23 June 1988.
369 'the White House effect': 'The White House and the Greenhouse', *The New York Times*, 9 May 1989.
369 'our sense of nature': Bill McKibben, 'The End of Nature', *The New Yorker*, 11 September 1989.
369 'climate crisis': 'The Climate Crisis: Carbon dioxide stirs concern', *Daily News* (New York), 1 June 1981.
369 'climate emergency': *Proceedings of the 1989 Convention (AFL-CIO)*.
369 a record 79 per cent: Weart, *The Discovery of Global Warming*, p. 151.
369 'Period of the Penumbra': Oreskes and Conway, *Collapse*, p. 59.
370 'the nations of the earth': Schell, *The Fate of the Earth*, p. 241.
370 'The most baleful mischiefs': Malthus, p. 346.
371 'climate denial': Paul Hanley, 'Petro dollars likely fuel behind climate denial', *Star-Phoenix* (Saskatoon), 2 January 1996.
371 'a left-wing cult': Joshua P. Howe, *Behind the Curve: Science and the Politics of Global Warming* (University of Washington Press, 2014), p. 124.
371 'As soon as one predicted disaster': Tierney, 'Betting on the Planet'.
372 'reject prophets of doom': Inhofe, 'The Science of Climate Change', p. 185.
372 'The international assessments': Hearing Before the Subcommittee on Energy and Environment of the Committee on Science, U. S. House of Representatives, One Hundred Fourth Congress, First Session, 16 November 1995.
372 'Pollution scares the shit': Michael Crichton, *State of Fear* (HarperCollins, 2004), p. 295.

372 'Climate Change Doomsday Ahead': ibid., p. 444.
372 'False fears': ibid., p. 448.
372 '*crisis, catastrophe*': ibid., p. 453.
372 'convinced that the environment': ibid., p. 255.
372 'All you do is yap-yap': Dr Seuss, *The Lorax* (William Collins Sons & Co., 1972).
373 'I am not arguing': Crichton, p. 579.
373 'in near-total agreement': Michael Janofsky, 'Bush's Chat With Novelist Alarms Environmentalists', *The New York Times*, 19 February 2006.
373 'Global warming has still to produce': Bill McKibben, 'Worried? Us?', *Granta*, vol. 1, no. 83 (Autumn 2003).
374 'The coming of doom': Isaac Asimov and Frederik Pohl, *Our Angry Earth* (Tor, 2018; first published 1991), p. 12.
374 'I had this feeling': Daniel Robert Epstein, 'Roland Emmerich of *The Day After Tomorrow* (20th Century Fox) Interview', *ugo.com*, 13 June 2004.
375 'This is unbelievable': *The Day After Tomorrow*, directed by Roland Emmerich, screenplay by Roland Emmerich and Jeffrey Nachmanoff (2004).
376 'On the one hand': Scott Bowles, '"The Day After Tomorrow" Heats Up a Political Debate: Storm of Opinion Rains Down on Merits of Disaster Movie', *USA Today*, 25 May 2004.
376 'People are going to walk': ibid.
376 'BE WORRIED': *Time*, 3 April 2006.
376 'There's plenty of space': *WALL-E*, directed by Andrew Stanton, screenplay by Andrew Stanton and Jim Reardon (2008).
377 'People have been predicting': *Downsizing*, directed by Alexander Payne, screenplay by Alexander Payne and Jim Taylor (2017).
377 'the crazy chick': *Don't Look Up*.
378 'They feel intense catharsis': Ketan Joshi et al., '"This Is What It Feels Like" How Don't Look Up Hits – and Misses – Reality of Climate Crisis', *The Guardian*, 8 January 2022.
378 'Everybody knew': Atwood, *The Year of the Flood*, p. 284.
378 'The whole complicated system': Jessie Greengrass, *The High House* (Swift Press, 2021), p. 226.
378 'It sounds cute': John H. Richardson, 'Ballad of the Sad Climatologists', *Esquire*, August 2015.
379 'practical possibilist': Dorling, p. 6.
379 'It was science versus capitalism': Robinson, *Green Earth*, p. 823.
379 'Science contains in it': ibid., p. 649.
379 'I guess because we still kind of believe': ibid., p. 688.
379 'blazed like an atomic bomb': Kim Stanley Robinson, *The Ministry for the Future* (Orbit, 2020), p. 1.
379 H. G. Wells's First World War idea: Wells, *The Fate of Homo Sapiens*, p. 87.

380 'the birth of a good Anthropocene': Robinson, *The Ministry for the Future*, p. 475.

380 'We will cope': ibid., p. 563.

380 'anti-anti-utopian': Joshua Hoffman, 'Best-Case Scenario', *The New Yorker*, 31 January 2022.

380 'There is no saving the world': Paul Kingsnorth, 'Dark Ecology' (2013), in *Confessions of a Recovering Environmentalist and Other Essays* (Graywolf Press, 2017), p. 147.

380 '*Brave New World* with windfarms': Paul Kingsnorth, 'The Poet and the Machine' (2011), in *Confessions of a Recovering Environmentalist*, p. 88.

380 'stand outside the human bubble': Paul Kingsnorth and Dougauld Hine, 'Uncivilisation: The Dark Mountain Manifesto' (2009), in *Confessions of a Recovering Environmentalist*, p. 274.

380 'Humanity is the start of the race': Robinson Jeffers, 'Roan Stallion', in *Roan Stallion, Tamar and Other Poems* (Modern Library, 1935; first published 1925), p. 13

381 'the myth of progress': Kingsnorth and Hune, 'Uncivilisation', p. 283.

381 'We do not believe': ibid., p. 266.

381 'The end of the world': ibid., p. 284.

381 'the opening of the greatest': Stewart, p. 24.

382 'When the city died': ibid., p. 270.

382 'the fresh sea-air': S. Fowler Wright, *Deluge* (Cherry Tree, 1928), p. 9.

382 'Don't leave me stranded': Talking Heads, '(Nothing But) Flowers', on *Naked* (Sire, 1988).

382 'It's not the end of the world at all': Shute, *On the Beach*, p. 89.

383 'Eventually we'll be extinct': Oliver Burkeman, 'If You Care About This . . . Then Don't Have One of These', *The Guardian*, 13 February 2010.

383 'Don't you find it a beautiful clean thought': D. H. Lawrence, *Women in Love* (Martin Secker, 1928; first published 1920), p. 131.

383 'Perhaps Man is something': Jordan B. Peterson, *12 Rules for Life: An Antidote to Chaos* (Penguin, 2018), p. 55.

383 'According to them': Atwood, *Oryx and Crake*, p. 285.

384 'a sort of triage': Margaret Atwood, 'Practical Utopias', in Greta Thunberg, ed., *The Climate Book* (Allen Lane, 2022), p. 360.

384 'Speculation about what the world': Margaret Atwood, *MaddAddam* (Virago, 2014), p. 44.

384 Barring ice ages: information in this passage from Alan Weisman, *The World Without Us* (Virgin, 2007); Laura Spinney, 'Return to Paradise', *New Scientist*, no. 2039 (20 July 1996); and *Life After People*, created by David de Vries. Aired 2008–2010, on The History Channel.

385 'The twentieth century had staked': John Russell, *Max Ernst: Life and Work* (Thames and Hudson, 1967), pp. 116–17.

385 'apocalyptic kitsch': Mark O'Connell, *Notes from an Apocalypse: A Personal Journey to the End of the World and Back* (Granta, 2020), p. 203.
385 'What lingers most': Alexievich, *Chernobyl Prayer*, p. 32.
386 'director of the apocalypse zone': ibid., p. 87.
386 'dreamlike world': ibid., p. 100.
386 'It seems so normal': Weisman, p. 214.
386 David Wallace-Wells has noted: Wallace-Wells, p. 183.
386 'My No. 1 worry': Lewis-Krauss, 'Do Better'.

EPILOGUE

391 'In a way I feel kind of privileged': *Last Night*, written and directed by Don McKellar (1998).
391 'It is not I who will die': Anne C. Heller, *Ayn Rand and the World She Made* (Anchor, 2009), p. 410.
392 'Sartre once wrote': Norden, 'Playboy Interview: Stanley Kubrick'.
392 'Some day, the day will come': 'Notes and Comment', *The New Yorker*, 30 April 1966.
392 'What if this present': John Donne, 'What If this Present Were the World's Last Night?' (1609?), in *The Complete English Poems of John Donne*, edited by C. A. Patrides (J. M. Dent & Sons, 1985), p. 442.
392 'Who knows but the world may end': Robert Browning, 'The Last Ride Together' (1855), in *Robert Browning's Selected Poems* (Thomas Y. Crowell and Company, 1896), p. 57.
393 'either tie one on': 'Notes and Comment', *The New Yorker*, 11 August 1962.
393 'Do we deserve this?': Ray Bradbury, *The Illustrated Man* (HarperVoyager, 2008; first published 1952), p. 147.
393 'the final twilight of everything': Richard Matheson, 'The Last Day' (1953), in *The Shores of Space* (Bantam, 1957), p. 151.
393 'People die the way they lived': ibid., p. 156.
393 'What would you do': Bradbury, *The Illustrated Man*, p. 145.
393 'The people who interested me': Dave Ratzlow, 'Interview: "Last Night," Don McKellar's Intimate Armageddon', *Indiewire*, 8 November 1999.
394 'I think about three-quarters': Jonathan Romney, 'Cheer Up – We're All About to Die', *The Guardian*, 24 June 1999.
394 'I found myself reaching out': Barone, 'Interview: "Seeking A Friend For The End Of The World"'.
395 'If the world ended tomorrow': *Derren Brown: Apocalypse*, episode 1, directed by Simon Dinsell. Aired 2 November 2012, on Channel 4.
395 'I think the apocalypse for me': Sian Williams, interview with Steven Brosnan, 'Apocalypse . . . Now?', *Life Changing*, Radio 4, 26 October 2022.

395 'desire to reach loved ones': Rich Ling and Brett Oppegaard, 'This Is Not a Drill: Mobile Telephony, Information Verification, and Expressive Communication During Hawaii's False Missile Alert', *Social Media + Society*, vol. 1, no. 1 (January–March 2021).
396 'flinging a few last curses': Priestley, *The Doomsday Men*, p. 302.
396 'The thing of it is': *Don't Look Up.*
396 'overwhelmed by the sheer aliveness': Boyer, *By the Bomb's Early Light*, p. xix.
396 'Work of this kind': C. S. Lewis, 'On Science Fiction' (1955), in *Essay Collection and Other Short Pieces*, edited by Lesley Walmsley (Harper Collins, 2000), p. 455.
397 'Do any human beings': Thornton Wilder, *Our Town* (1938), in *Our Town and Other Plays* (Penguin, 2000), p. 89.
397 'You should think about how civilization': Shahidha Bari interview with S. J. Beard, 'Existential Risk', *Free Thinking*, Radio 3, 10 February 2022.
398 'The earth is evil': *Melancholia.*
398 'Proclaiming someone's or something's defeat': Rebecca Solnit, 'Climate Despair Is a Luxury', *The New Statesman*, vol. 151, no. 5690 (21–27 October 2022).
398 'What point was there to all of it then?': Matheson, *Shores of Space*, p. 160.
399 'We are not fighting for a definitive victory': Wiener, *I Am a Mathematician*, p. 32.

Index